Photoshop
CS6

FOR WINDOWS AND MACINTOSH

ELAINE WEINMANN

PETER LOUREKAS

Peachpit Press

For Alicia

Visual QuickStart Guide
Photoshop CS6
Elaine Weinmann and Peter Lourekas

Peachpit Press
1249 Eighth Street
Berkeley, CA 94710

510/524-2178
510/524-2221 (fax)

Find us on the Web at: www.peachpit.com
To report errors, please send a note to errata@peachpit.com
Peachpit Press is a division of Pearson Education

Copyright © 2012 by Elaine Weinmann and Peter Lourekas

Cover Design: Peachpit Press
Interior Design: Elaine Weinmann
Production: Elaine Weinmann and Peter Lourekas
Illustrations: Elaine Weinmann and Peter Lourekas, except as noted

ISBN-13: 978-0-321-82218-5

ISBN-10: 0-321-82218-8

9 8 7 6 5 4 3 2

Printed and bound in the United States of America

Acknowledgments

Nancy Aldrich-Ruenzel has wholeheartedly supported our books during the 16 years that she has been at the helm of Peachpit Press.

Susan Rimerman, editor at Peachpit Press, was responsive to our every question and request.

Lisa Brazieal, eagle-eyed production editor, did an expert job of spearheading the prepress production before sending the files off to RR Donnelley.

Nancy Davis, editor-in-chief; Gary-Paul Prince, promotions manager; Keasley Jones, associate publisher; Glenn Bisignani, marketing manager; and many other terrific, hard-working people at Peachpit contributed their respective talents.

Victor Gavenda, longtime (and multitalented) editor at Peachpit Press, tech edited Chapters 2, 6, 8, 10, 13, 17–19, 21–23, and 25 in Windows.

Wayne Palmer, of palmermultimedia.com, tech edited Chapters 1, 3–5, 7, 9, 11–12, 14–16, and 20 in Windows and provided the first draft of the section on video editing.

Elaine Soares, photo research manager, and Lee Scher, photo research coordinator, of the Image Resource Center at Pearson Education (the parent company of Peachpit Press) quickly procured the stock photos from Shutterstock.com that we requested.

Rebecca Pepper did a thorough, thoughtful, and meticulous job of copy editing.

Steve Rath produced a comprehensive index, carefully customized to our needs.

Scout Festa did excellent work in the final — and final-final — rounds of proofreading.

Adobe Systems, Inc. produces innovative software that is a pleasure to use and write about. For allowing us to test the prerelease version of Photoshop CS6 and for helping us untangle its mysteries by way of the online forum, we thank Zorana Gee, senior product manager of Photoshop and Photoshop Extended; Bryan O'Neil Hughes, senior product manager of Photoshop; Stephen Nielson, product manager of Photoshop and Photoshop Touch; Aditi Bansal, project lead of prerelease programs; and the many other members of the Adobe Photoshop CS6 prerelease team.

Our friends and relatives are there for us in meaningful ways even when we don't have time to see them (can't wait for some unhurried visits!).

Our daughters, Alicia and Simona, are blossoming into terrific adults — and are our greatest joy.

— Elaine Weinmann and Peter Lourekas

★ New or improved Photoshop features are identified by red stars in this table of contents and throughout this book.

Contents

20: Layer Styles

21: Vector Shapes & Masks

22: Actions

23: Presentation

24: Preferences

25: Print & Export

Index

VISIT OUR BLOG! ★

Go to elaineandpeter.com and you'll find a treasure trove of Photoshop tips, tutorials, and design concepts. Upcoming blog posts will feature guest artists and more. Come visit, drop us a line — and help spread the word!

REGISTER THIS BOOK, THEN DOWNLOAD PHOTOS FOR FREE!

Purchasing this book entitles you to more than just a couple of pounds of paper. If you register the book with Peachpit Press, you will also be entitled to download copies of most of the images that are used throughout the book, which you can use to practice with as you follow our step-by-step tutorials.

To get started, follow this link: www.peachpit.com/photoshopcs6vqs, which takes you to the page for this book at peachpit.com (the Peachpit Press website). Sign in to your account. If you don't already have an account, create one — it takes just a minute. After logging in, on the Register a Product page, enter the ISBN code for this book: 0321822188, then click Submit. You'll be taken to a list of your registered products. Find Photoshop CS6: Visual QuickStart Guide on the list, then click Access Bonus Content to get to the page from which you can download the images.

Note: The downloadable images that we have made available are low-resolution (not suitable for printing), and they are copyrighted by their owners, who have watermarked them to discourage unauthorized reproduction. They are for your personal use only — not for distribution or publication.

Welcome to Photoshop! We know you want to dive into the editing features of Camera Raw or Photoshop right away, but achieving successful results will depend on your establishing proper color management settings first.

In this chapter, you will launch Photoshop and familiarize yourself with the Photoshop color basics. Key color management tasks that you will learn about include calibrating your display, choosing and saving color settings in Photoshop, and downloading and installing the correct printer profiles. (In Chapter 25, color management will come into play once more, when you prepare your final files for output.)

Launching Photoshop

To launch Photoshop in Windows:

Do one of the following:

In a 32-bit version of Windows, click the Start button on the taskbar, choose All Programs, then click Adobe Photoshop CS6.

In a 64-bit version of Windows, click the Start button, choose All Programs, then click Adobe Photoshop CS6 (64-bit).

Double-click a Photoshop file icon (the file will open and Photoshop will launch).

To launch Photoshop in the Mac OS:

Do one of the following:

Click the Photoshop icon **Ps** in the Dock. (If that icon isn't in your dock, open the Adobe Photoshop CS6 folder in the Applications folder, then drag the Adobe Photoshop CS6 application icon into the Dock.)

Open the Adobe Photoshop CS6 folder in the Applications folder, then double-click the Adobe Photoshop CS6 application icon. **Ps**

Double-click a Photoshop file icon (the file will open and Photoshop will launch).

FINDING THE NEW STUFF IN THIS BOOK

This symbol ★ identifies Photoshop features that are new or improved.

COLOR MANAGEMENT

1

IN THIS CHAPTER

WANT TO SEE AN IMAGE ONSCREEN?

If you want to make the screen more "live" as you read through this chapter, open one of the photos that we have made available for our readers to download (see page viii).

Photoshop color

The building blocks of a Photoshop image

Onscreen, your Photoshop image is a bitmap — a geometric arrangement, or mapping, of dots on a rectangular grid. Each dot (pixel) represents a different color or shade. If you drag with a painting tool, such as the Brush tool, across an area of an image, pixels below the pointer are recolored. If you display your document at a high zoom level, you will be able to see the individual pixels (and also edit them individually).**A** Bitmap programs like Photoshop are best suited for editing photographic or painterly images that contain subtle gradations of color, called "continuous tones." The images you work with in Photoshop can originate from a digital camera, from a photo print that was input via a scanner, from a file that was saved in another application, or even from scratch using Photoshop features, such as painting tools and filters.

To enable color images to be viewed onscreen, your computer display projects red, green, and blue (RGB) light. Combined in their purest form, these additive primaries produce white light. If you were to send your Photoshop file to a commercial print shop for four-color process printing, it would be rendered using cyan (C), magenta (M), yellow (Y), and black (K) inks. Because your display uses the RGB model, it can only simulate the CMYK inks used in commercial printing.

The successful translation of a digital image to a printed one is more complex than you might expect. For one, the same document may look surprisingly dissimilar on different displays due to such variables as the temperature of the display, the lighting in the room, and even the paint color of the wall. Second, many colors that you see in the natural world or that can be displayed onscreen can't be printed (have no ink equivalents), and conversely, some colors that can be printed cannot be displayed the same way onscreen. And thirdly, the same image will produce different results depending on the device and paper type. The color management techniques that we outline in this chapter are designed to help smooth out the color discrepancies that can arise when an image is transferred from digital input to display onscreen, then finally to print.

Photoshop channels

Every Photoshop image contains one, three, or four channels, each of which stores the intensity of a particular color component (e.g., red, green, or blue) as one of 256 levels of gray. Because the 256 gray levels are represented by 8 bits (short for "binary digits") of computer data, the bit depth of such an image is said to be 8 bits per channel. Files that have a higher bit depth of 16 or 32 bits per channel contain more color information than those containing 8 bits per channel (to learn about 16-bit images, see page 17).

➤ Open an RGB Color image and display the Channels panel 🌑 (Window > Channels) (**A**, next page). Click Red, Green, or Blue on the panel to display only that channel, then click the topmost channel name on the panel to restore the composite display. Although you can make adjustments to individual channels, normally you will edit all the channels simultaneously while viewing the composite image.

In addition to the core channels (e.g., RGB or CMYK), you can add two other kinds of channels to a Photoshop document. You can save a selection as a mask in a grayscale (alpha) channel, and you can add channels for individual spot colors (colors that are output by a commercial print shop using premixed inks).

A *In this extreme close-up of a photo in Photoshop, you can see the individual pixels that make up the image.*

Photoshop document color modes

In Photoshop, a document can be converted to, displayed in, and edited in any of the following color modes: Bitmap, Grayscale, Duotone, Indexed Color, RGB Color, CMYK Color, Lab Color, or Multi-channel. This conversion is done primarily to take advantage of specific editing or output options. The availability of some Photoshop commands and options will vary depending on the current color mode of your document.

To convert a document to a different mode, make a selection from the Image > **Mode** sub-menu. **B** If a mode is dimmed on the menu and you want to make it available, you need to convert the file to a different mode as an intermediary step first. For example, to convert a file to Duotone mode, you need to put it into Grayscale mode first. The most common mode that Photoshop users work in is RGB Color.

Some mode conversions can cause noticeable color shifts. For example, if you convert a file from RGB Color mode (the mode used by computer displays) to CMYK Color mode (which contains fewer colors than RGB but is necessary for com-mercial printing), printable colors in the image will be substituted for any RGB colors that are outside the printable gamut (range). The fewer times you convert a file, the better, as the color data is altered with each conversion. Some conversions flat-ten layers, such as a conversion to Indexed Color, Multichannel, or Bitmap mode. Other conversions (such as from RGB to CMYK) give you the option to preserve layers via a Don't Flatten button in an alert dialog that pops up.

Digital cameras and medium- to low-end scan-ners produce images in the default color mode of RGB. We recommend keeping your files in that mode for faster editing, and to preserve access to all the Photoshop filters. In fact, most desktop color inkjet printers, especially those that use six or more ink colors, are designed to accept RGB files.

➤ To "soft-proof" your RGB document onscreen (make it look as if it was converted to CMYK Color mode without performing an actual mode change), see page 449.

Continued on the following page

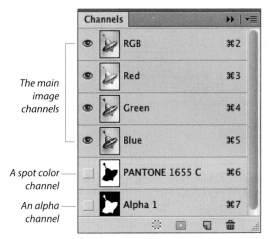

The main image channels

A spot color channel

An alpha channel

A The number of main image channels is determined by the document color mode (alpha and spot color channels are optional additions).

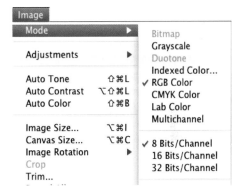

B Use the Mode submenu to change the color mode of your document.

CHANNELS AND THE DOCUMENT COLOR MODE
The number of channels in a document has a major impact on its file size. For instance, if you convert a document from Grayscale mode (one channel) to RGB mode (three channels), it will become three times larger.

DEFAULT NUMBER OF CHANNELS	DOCUMENT COLOR MODE
1	Bitmap, Grayscale, Duotone, Indexed Color
3	RGB, Lab, Multichannel
4	CMYK, Multichannel

The following is a brief summary of the document color modes that are available in Photoshop:

In **Bitmap** mode, pixels are either 100% black or 100% white, and no layers, filters, or adjustment commands are available. To convert a file to this mode, you must convert it to Grayscale mode first.

In **Grayscale** mode, pixels are black, white, or up to 254 shades of gray (a total of 256). If you convert a file from a color mode to Grayscale mode and then save and close it, its luminosity (light and dark) values are preserved, but its color information is deleted permanently. (In Chapter 12, we show you how to change the colors in a layer to grayscale without actually changing the document color mode.)

To produce a **duotone**, a grayscale image is printed using two or more extra plates, which add tonal richness and depth. Producing a duotone requires special preparatory steps in Photoshop, and in the case of commercial printing, expertise on the part of the print shop.

A file in **Indexed Color** mode contains just one channel and a maximum number of 256 colors or shades in an 8-bit color table. When you optimize a file in the GIF format via the Save for Web dialog in Photoshop, the file is converted to this color mode automatically (see pages 465–466).

RGB Color is the most versatile and widely used of all the Photoshop modes. 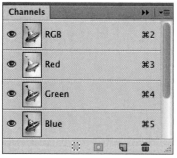 It's the mode in which digital cameras save your photos; the only mode in which all the Photoshop tool options and filters are accessible; and the mode of choice for export to the Web, mobile devices, video, multimedia programs, and most inkjet printers.

In Photoshop, although you can display and edit a document in **CMYK Color** mode,  a better approach is to perform all your image edits in RGB Color mode first, then convert a copy of your file to CMYK Color mode only when required for commercial printing or for export to a page layout application. Images that are saved by high-end scanners in CMYK Color mode are exceptions; you should keep those files in CMYK to preserve their original color data.

Lab Color, a 3-channel mode, was developed for the purpose of achieving consistency among various devices, such as between printers and displays. Lab Color files are device-independent, meaning their color definitions stay the same regardless of how each output device defines color. The channels represent lightness (the image details), the colors green

to red, and the colors blue to yellow. The lightness and color values can be edited independently of one another. Although Photoshop uses Lab Color to produce conversions between RGB and CMYK Color modes internally, Photoshop users like us rarely, if ever, need to convert files to this mode.

Multichannel images contain multiple 256-level grayscale channels. If you convert an image from RGB Color to Multichannel mode, its Red, Green, and Blue channels are converted to Cyan, Magenta, and Yellow (as a result, the image may become lighter and the contrast reduced). Some Photoshop pros assemble individual channels from several images into a single composite image by using this mode.

A *The mode of this document is RGB Color, so it contains three channels.*

B *We converted the document to CMYK Color mode, which upped the number of channels to four.*

THE COLOR MODELS IN PHOTOSHOP

In Photoshop, you can choose colors using the Grayscale, RGB, HSB, CMYK, or Lab Color model, or choose predefined colors from a color matching system, such as PANTONE. See Chapter 11.

Introduction to color management

Problems with color inconsistency can arise due to the fact that hardware devices and software packages read or output color differently. If you were to compare an image onscreen in an assortment of imaging programs and Web browsers, the colors may look completely different in each case, and worse still, may look different from the picture you originally shot with your digital camera. Print the image, and you'll probably find the results are different yet again. In some cases, these differences might be slight and unobjectionable, but in other cases such color shifts can wreak havoc with your design or even turn a project into a disaster!

A color management system can prevent most color discrepancies from arising by acting as a color interpreter. The system knows how each particular device and program interprets color, and if necessary, adjusts the colors accordingly. The result is that the colors in your files will display and output more consistently as you shuttle them among various programs and devices. Applications in the Adobe Creative Suite adhere to standard ICC (International Color Consortium) profiles, which tell your color management system how each specific device defines color.

Each particular device can capture and reproduce only a limited range, or gamut, of colors. In the jargon of color management, this gamut is known as the color space. The mathematical description of the color space of each device, in turn, is known as a color profile. Furthermore, each input device, such as a camera, attaches its own profile to the files it produces. Photoshop uses that profile in order to display and edit the colors in your document; or if a document doesn't contain a profile, Photoshop will use the current working space (a color space that you choose for Photoshop) instead. Color management is important for both print and online output, and when outputting the same document in different media.

On the following pages, we give instructions for choosing color management options, and we strongly recommend that you follow them before editing your images in Photoshop. The steps are centered on using Adobe RGB as the color space for your image-editing work in order to maintain color consistency throughout your workflow. We'll show you how to set the color space of your digital camera to Adobe RGB, give guidelines on calibrating a display, specify Adobe RGB as the color space for Photoshop, acquire the proper profiles for your inkjet printer and paper type, and assign the Adobe RGB profile to files that you have opened in Photoshop.

You'll need to focus on color management later in the production cycle if and when you prepare your file for printing. In Chapter 25, we'll show you how to create a soft-proof setting for your particular inkjet printer and paper using the profiles you have acquired, and then use that setting to soft-proof your document onscreen. The same profile will also be used to output files on a color inkjet printer. Finally, we'll show you how to obtain and install the proper profiles for outputting either to the Web or to a commercial press.

The first step in color management is to establish Adobe RGB as the color space for your camera — before you attend to the settings in Photoshop.

Continued on the following page

Via an onscreen menu, most high-end, advanced amateur digital cameras and digital SLR cameras give you an opportunity to customize how the camera processes your photos. Here a Nikon D700 is used as a representative model for setting a camera to the Adobe RGB color space, but you can follow a similar procedure to set the color space for your camera.

Note: If you shoot photos in the JPEG format, you should choose Adobe RGB as the color space for your camera, regardless of the camera model. If you shoot raw files, the following steps are optional, as you will have an opportunity to assign the Adobe RGB color space to your photos at a later point in Camera Raw (see page 58).

To set a camera's color space to Adobe RGB (Nikon used as an example):

1. On the back of your Nikon camera, press the Menu button to access the menu on the LCD screen, then press the up or down arrow on the multiselector to select the **Shooting Menu** tab.◉

2. From the Shooting Menu, press the down arrow on the multiselector to select the **Color Space** category.A (Note: On a Canon EOS Rebel camera, this category is labeled Parameters). Press the right arrow on the multiselector to move to the submenu.

3. Press the down arrow to select **Adobe RGB**.B–C

4. Press the OK button to set your choice,D then press the Menu button to exit the Menu screen.

NIKON D700

A *From the Nikon Shooting Menu, we selected the Color Space category.*

B *We pressed the right arrow, chose Adobe RGB from the Color Space submenu, then pressed OK.*

CANON EOS REBEL T3

C *Adobe RGB is now the Color Space for our camera.*

D *On a Canon EOS Rebel T3, we clicked the Shooting 2 tab, chose Color Space, chose Adobe RGB, then pressed Set.*

Calibrating your display

Why calibrate a display?

In an LCD (liquid crystal, or flat panel) display, a grid of fixed-sized liquid crystals filters color from a light source in the back. Although the color profile that is provided with a typical LCD display (and that is installed in your system automatically) describes the display characteristics accurately, over time — a period of weeks or months — the colors you view onscreen will gradually become less accurate and will need adjustment.

Although you can adjust the brightness setting on an LCD monitor, it's best to leave that setting alone and give your display a periodic tune-up using an external calibration device instead. This device, or calibrator, will produce a profile containing the proper settings (white point, black point, and gamma) for your particular display. The Adobe color management system, in turn, will interpret the colors in your Photoshop document and display them more accurately based on that profile.

Calibrators range widely in cost, from a $100 to $300 colorimeter to a much more expensive (but more precise) high-end professional gadget, such as a spectrophotometer. Even with a basic colorimeter and its simple step-by-step wizard, you will be able to calibrate your display more precisely than by using subjective "eyeball" judgments.

Among moderately priced calibrators, our informal reading of hardware reviews and other industry publications has yielded the following list of currently popular models: Spyder3Pro and Spyder3Elite by Datacolor; i1 Display Pro by X-Rite; and hueyPro, which was developed jointly by PANTONE and X-Rite.

➤ On our blog at elaineandpeter.com, we show you how to use the Spyder3Elite.

Note: Don't be tempted to use the calibration utility that's built into your computer system — it's not going to give you accurate results. If you want to achieve good output from Photoshop, you owe it to yourself to invest in a hardware calibrator. Even the least expensive external device is superior to the internal controls.

The basic calibration settings

An external calibrator will evaluate and then adjust three basic characteristics of your display: It will set the white (brightest) point to a consistent working standard; it will set the black (darkest) point to the maximum value; and it will establish a gamma (neutral gray) by equalizing the values of R, G, and B.

➤ The **white point** data sets the brightest white for the display to the industry-standard color temperature. Photographers favor using D65/6500K as the temperature setting for the white point; it is the standard white point setting in LCD displays.

➤ The **black point** is the darkest black a display can project. In other words, all the other shades that a monitor displays are lighter than this black. With the black point set correctly, you will be better able to view the shadow details in your photos.

➤ The **gamma** controls the display of midtones (the tones between the black and white points), for improved contrast. A gamma setting of 1.0 reproduces the linear brightness scale that is found in nature. However, a setting of 1.0 would make your photos look washed out because human vision responds to brightness in a nonlinear fashion. Instead, photography experts recommend using a gamma setting of 2.2 for both Windows and Macintosh displays. This higher setting redistributes more of the midtones into the dark range, which our eyes are more sensitive to, and enables your photos to look closer to the way you expect them to.

CALIBRATE, AND STAY CALIBRATED

➤ Computer displays become uncalibrated gradually, and you may not notice the change until the colors are way off. To maintain the color consistency of your display, stick to a regular monthly calibration schedule. (Our calibration software reminds us to recalibrate via a monthly onscreen alert. If yours offers this option, you should take advantage of it.)

➤ Also, be sure to recalibrate your display if you adjust its brightness and contrast settings (intentionally or not), change the temperature or amount of lighting in your office — or repaint your office walls!

Choosing a color space for Photoshop

Next, you will establish the color space for Photoshop (the gamut of colors that Photoshop works with and displays). This is an essential step in color management. If you produce images primarily for print output and you want to get up and running quickly, you can choose a preset, as in these steps.

To choose a color settings preset for Photoshop:

1. Choose Edit > **Color Settings** (Ctrl-Shift-K/ Cmd-Shift-K). The Color Settings dialog opens.

2. Choose Settings: **North America Prepress 2 A** (readers residing outside North America, choose an equivalent for your geographic location). This preset changes the RGB working space to Adobe RGB (1998), and sets all the color management policies to the safe choice of Preserve Embedded Profiles, enabling each file you open in Photoshop to keep its own profile.

3. Click OK.

Here you can delve further into the Color Settings dialog. Be sure to choose options that are suitable for your output requirements.

To choose color settings options for Photoshop:

1. Choose Edit > **Color Settings** (Ctrl-Shift-K/ Cmd-Shift-K). The Color Settings dialog opens.

2. From the **Settings** menu, choose one of the following presets, depending on your output needs:

   Monitor Color sets the RGB working space to your display profile. This preset is a good choice for video output, but not for print output.

   North America General Purpose 2 meets general requirements for screen and print output in North America, but we don't recommend it for print output because it uses the sRGB IEC61966-2.1 color space (see step 3 at right). All profile warnings are shut off.

   North America Newspaper manages color for output on newsprint paper stock.

   North America Prepress 2 manages color to conform to common press conditions in North America using the Adobe RGB (1998) color space. We recommend this preset for print output. When CMYK documents are opened, their values are preserved.

North America Web/Internet is designed for online output. All RGB images are converted to the sRGB IEC61966-2.1 color space.

3. The **Working Spaces** settings govern how colors are treated in documents that lack an embedded profile. You can either leave these menu settings as they are or choose one of these recommended **RGB** color spaces, depending on your output needs (for CMYK settings, see pages 10 and 11):

   Adobe RGB (1998) contains a wide range of colors and is useful when converting RGB images to CMYK. This option is recommended for print output but not for Web output.

   ProPhoto RGB contains a very wide range of colors and is useful for output to high-end inkjet and dye sublimation printers.

   sRGB IEC61966-2.1 is a good choice for Web output, as it reflects the settings of the average computer display. Although this setting isn't a good choice for print output (because it contains fewer colors in the printable CMYK gamut than Adobe RGB), many online Web printing sites accept or require files to be in this color space.

4. Click OK.

➤ Avoid the Working Spaces settings of Apple RGB and ColorMatch RGB, which were designed for displays that are no longer standard. The Monitor RGB [current display profile] is used for sharing files with applications that don't support color management; the display profile on the current user's system is used as the color space. ColorSync RGB matches the Photoshop RGB space to the space that's specified in the Apple ColorSync Utility; the ColorSync space on the current user's system is used as the color space. With both of these settings, color consistency is undermined.

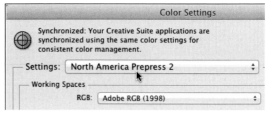

A From the Settings menu in the Color Settings dialog, we chose North America Prepress 2.

Synchronizing color settings among Creative Suite applications

If the color settings differ among the Adobe Creative Suite programs that you have installed on your system (such as between Photoshop and Illustrator or InDesign), an alert will display at the top of the Color Settings dialog.  If you haven't installed one of the full Adobe Creative Suites, you'll have to start up each application and establish its color settings by hand. If you do have one of the suites installed, you can use the Suite Color Settings dialog in Bridge to quickly synchronize the color settings for all of the color-managed Adobe programs in your system.

MATCHING SETTINGS

The presets in the Suite Color Settings dialog match the presets on the Settings menu in the Color Settings dialog (see the previous page).

▶ In the Suite Color Settings dialog, keep the Show Expanded List of Color Settings Files option unchecked to limit the display to just the five basic presets.

Note: Before using Bridge to synchronize the color settings among your Adobe Creative Suite programs, you should establish the correct settings in Photoshop (see the preceding page).

To synchronize the color settings among your Creative Suite applications:

1. Choose File > **Browse in Bridge** (Ctrl-Alt-O/ Cmd-Option-O).

2. In Bridge, choose Edit > **Creative Suite Color Settings** (Ctrl-Shift-K/Cmd-Shift-K). The Suite Color Settings dialog opens.

3. Click the same settings preset that you chose in the Color Settings dialog in Photoshop (e.g., North America Prepress 2), then click **Apply**. Bridge will change (synchronize) the color settings of the other Adobe Creative Suite applications to conform to those in the preset you have selected.

A Use the Suite Color Settings dialog to synchronize the color settings of all the applications in the Adobe Creative Suite that are installed on your system.

Customizing the color policies for Photoshop

Photoshop supports document-specific color, meaning that the profile that is embedded in a document controls how colors in that file are previewed onscreen, edited, and converted upon output. The current color management policies govern whether Photoshop honors or overrides a document's settings if the color profile in the file, when opened or imported, doesn't conform to the current color settings in Photoshop. If you chose the North America Prepress 2 setting in the Color Settings dialog (see page 8), the Ask When Opening policy (the safest option, in our opinion) is already chosen for you, and you can skip these steps.

To customize the color management policies for Photoshop:

1. Choose Edit > **Color Settings** (Ctrl-Shift-K/ Cmd-Shift-K). The Color Settings dialog opens.**A**

2. From each of the **Color Management Policies** menus, choose an option for files that you open or import into Photoshop:

   Off to prevent Photoshop from color-managing the files.

   Preserve Embedded Profiles if you expect to work with both color-managed and non-color-managed files, and you want each document to keep its own profile.

   Convert to Working RGB or **Convert to Working CMYK** to have all files that you open or import into Photoshop adopt the program's current color working space.

3. *Optional:* For Profile Mismatches, check Ask When Opening to have Photoshop display an alert when the color profile in a file you're opening doesn't match the current working space. Via the alert, you will be able to either convert the document colors to the current working space or keep the embedded profile in the document.

   Check Ask When Pasting to have Photoshop display an alert if it encounters a color profile mismatch when you paste or drag and drop imagery into a document. Via the alert, you will be able to accept or override the current color management policy.

4. *Optional:* For Missing Profiles, check Ask When Opening to have Photoshop display an alert when opening a file that lacks a profile, giving you the opportunity to assign one.

5. Click OK.

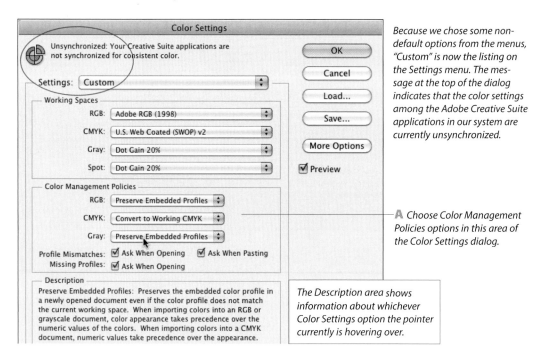

Because we chose some non-default options from the menus, "Custom" is now the listing on the Settings menu. The message at the top of the dialog indicates that the color settings among the Adobe Creative Suite applications in our system are currently unsynchronized.

A *Choose Color Management Policies options in this area of the Color Settings dialog.*

The Description area shows information about whichever Color Settings option the pointer currently is hovering over.

Installing and saving custom color settings

For desktop color printing, we recommended choosing North America Prepress 2 as the color setting for Photoshop (see page 8). For commercial printing, you can let the pros supply the proper color settings: Ask your print shop for a .csf (custom settings) file, which should contain all the correct Working Spaces and Color Management Policies settings for the particular press they will be using for your project. Once you receive the .csf file, all you need to do is install it in the proper location as described below and, when needed, choose it from the Settings menu in the Color Settings dialog.

To install a .csf file in your system:

1. In Windows, put the file in Program Files\Common Files\Adobe\Color\Settings.

   In the Mac OS, put the file in Users/[user name]/Library/Application Support/Adobe/Color/Settings.

2. The .csf is now available as a choice on the Settings menu in the Edit > Color Settings dialog.

If your print shop gives you a list of recommended settings for the Color Settings dialog instead of a .csf file, you can create your own .csf file that contains the recommended settings, as in these steps.

To save custom color settings as a .csf file:

1. Choose Edit > **Color Settings** (Ctrl-Shift-K/ Cmd-Shift-K). The Color Settings dialog opens.

2. Choose and check the settings that your print shop has recommended.

3. Click Save. In the dialog, enter a file name (we suggest including the printer type in the name). Keep the .csf extension (make sure Hide Extension is unchecked) and keep the default location. Click Save.

4. Click OK to exit the Color Settings dialog.

Acquiring printer profiles

Here we summarize how to acquire the proper printer profile(s) so you can incorporate color management into your specific printing scenario.

Most printer manufacturers have a website from which you can download either an ICC profile for a specific printer/paper combination or a printer driver that contains a collection of specific ICC printer/paper profiles. Be sure to choose a profile that conforms to the particular printer/paper combination you are planning to use.

To download the printer profile for your inkjet printer:

1. Do either of the following:

   Download the correct profile from the website for your printer. For Epson, visit epson.com; for Canon, visit canon.com. On both sites (at the time of this writing), you will need to click a "Drivers & Support" type of option first, then choose a printer category (e.g., InkJet) and model. Next, click a link for "Downloads" or "Drivers." On the Epson site, you will need to go one step further and click a link to access profiles for specific paper types.

   ➤ On our blog at elaineandpeter.com, we illustrate the links for accessing the profiles on the Epson and Canon sites.

   Download an ICC profile for a specific printer/paper combo from the website of a paper manufacturer, such as ilford.com or museofineart.com.

2. After visiting the website, install the profile you downloaded by following the instructions that accompany it.

   On pages 448–449, we'll show you how to use the profile you have downloaded to soft-proof your document onscreen.

Changing a document's color profile

When the profile that is embedded in a document doesn't conform to the current working space for Photoshop (which in our case is Adobe RGB), or the document lacks a profile altogether, you can use the Assign Profile command to assign the correct one. You may notice visible color shifts if the color data of the file is reinterpreted to conform to the new profile, but rest assured, the color data in the actual image is preserved. Do keep Preview checked, though, so you can see what you're getting into.

To change or remove a file's color profile:

1. With a file open in Photoshop, choose Edit > **Assign Profile**. If the file contains layers, an alert may appear, warning you that the appearance of the layers may change; click OK.

2. The Assign Profile dialog opens.**A** Check Preview, then click one of the following:

   To remove the color profile, click **Don't Color Manage This Document**.

   To assign the current working space, as established in the Color Settings dialog, click **Working** [the document color mode and the name of your chosen working space]. If you followed our steps on page 8, the menu should already be set to Adobe RGB (1998).

   To assign a different profile, click **Profile**, then choose a profile that differs from your current working space.

3. Click OK. Using the File > Save As dialog, save your file in the Photoshop (.psd) format (see page 20). In that dialog, be sure to check ICC Profile (in Windows) or Embed Color Profile (in the Mac OS) to embed the assigned profile into the file.

The Convert to Profile command lets you preview the conversion of a document to a different output profile and intent, and then it converts the color data to the chosen profile. Use this command to convert a file to sRGB, if that color space is required for online Web printing. Note: This command performs a mode conversion and changes the actual color data in your file, so apply it to a copy of your file (see page 20).

To convert a file's color profile:

1. Choose Edit > **Convert to Profile**. In the Convert to Profile dialog, check Preview.**B**

2. Under Destination Space, from the **Profile** menu, choose the profile to which you want to convert the file (it doesn't necessarily have to be the current working space).

3. Under Conversion Options, choose an **Intent** (for the intents, see the sidebar on page 449).

4. Leave the default Engine as **Adobe (ACE)**, keep the **Use Black Point Compensation** and **Use Dither** options checked and, if available, check Flatten Image to Preserve Appearance to allow Photoshop to merge all layers and adjustment layers into the Background.

5. Click OK.

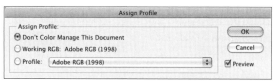

A Use the Assign Profile dialog to either remove a color profile from a file or assign a different one.

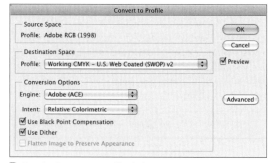

B Use the Convert to Profile dialog to convert your document to a different color profile. Here we switched our file from the Adobe RGB profile to the Working CMYK – U.S. Web Coated (SWOP) v2 profile (for commercial printing).

In Photoshop, you can edit a single photo to your heart's content, create a complex montage of imagery that you gather from multiple files, or paint an image entirely from scratch. Photoshop generously accepts and reads files in a wide assortment of file formats, so your imagery can be gathered from a variety of sources, such as from a digital camera, scanner, or drawing application.

In this chapter, you will learn how to create a new, blank document, create document presets for your favorite settings, learn the characteristics of 16-bits-per-channel files, save and generate new versions of a file, use the Status bar, and close up shop.

Just to give you an idea of where you're headed, in the next chapter, you will learn how to download photos from a camera and use Bridge to open and manage files, and in Chapter 4, you will learn how to correct photos in Camera Raw and then open them into Photoshop.

Calculating the correct file resolution

Resolution and dimensions for Web output

Choosing the correct resolution for Web output is a no-brainer: Set the resolution for your file to 72 ppi.

Choosing the correct dimensions for Web output requires a little more forethought, because you need to calculate how your Photoshop document is going to be used in the Web page layout. The easiest way to create a document with the proper dimensions and resolution for Web output is by choosing a preset, as described in step 3 on page 15.

To determine a maximum custom size for a Photoshop image that is going to be displayed on a Web page, you need to estimate how large the average user's browser window is likely to be, then calculate how much of that window the image is going to fill. On a desktop computer, viewers commonly have their browser window open to a width of approximately 1000 pixels. Subtract the space that is occupied by the menu bar, scroll bars, and other controls in the browser interface, and you're left with an area around 950 pixels wide by 600 pixels high; you can use those dimensions as a guideline. In the more likely event that your Photoshop file is going to be used as a small element within a Web page layout, you can choose smaller dimensions.

Continued on the following page

CREATING FILES

2

Resolution for print output

Most digital cameras provide a choice: You can let the camera capture and save all the pixels as raw files (recommended) or you can let the camera process, compress, and save the data into small, medium, or large JPEG files. We prefer raw files, for reasons that we explain in Chapter 4. When using a scanner to acquire images for Photoshop, you can set the input resolution in the scanner software to control how many pixels the device captures.

Your image files should contain the minimum resolution needed to obtain quality output from your target output device, at the desired output size. High-resolution photos contain more pixels, and therefore finer details, than low-resolution photos, but they also have a larger file size, take longer to render onscreen, require more processing time to edit, and are slower to print. Low-resolution images, however, look coarse and jagged and lack detail, most noticeably when printed. Your goal is to set an appropriate resolution — one that is neither too high nor too low.**A–C**

There are three ways to set the resolution value for a digital file:

➤ If you use Camera Raw to process a raw or JPEG photo, as we recommend, you can specify an image resolution in its Workflow Options dialog (see page 58).

➤ When scanning a photo, you should set the image resolution using the scanning software for that device.

➤ After opening a file into Photoshop, you can change the image resolution via the Image Size dialog (see pages 122–124).

The print resolution for digital images is measured in pixels per inch, or ppi for short. For output to a desktop inkjet printer, an appropriate file resolution is between 240 and 300 ppi. For commercial printing, the first step is to ask your print shop what resolution you should set your document to for their press. If you are told only the halftone screen frequency (lines per inch) setting, you can use that number to quickly calculate the correct resolution for your files. For a grayscale image, set the resolution to approximately one-and-a-half times the lpi setting of the output device (usually a resolution of around 200 ppi); for a color image, set the resolution to approximately twice the lpi (usually a resolution of around 250–350 ppi).

A *72 ppi*

B *150 ppi*

C *300 ppi*

Creating a new, blank document

Although in most cases you are going to open existing photos into Photoshop, you still need to know how to create a new, blank document, as we show you in these steps. To create image content, you can drag and drop or copy and paste imagery into the document from other files, draw or paint imagery by hand using brushes, create shapes with vector tools, or enter type.

To create a new, blank document:

1. Do either of the following:

   Choose File > **New** (Ctrl-N/Cmd-N).

   Right-click the tab of an existing open document and choose **New Document** (now available in both Windows and the Mac OS ★).

2. The New dialog opens. **A** Type a name in the **Name** field.

3. Do either of the following:

   From the **Preset** menu, choose a category: the Default Photoshop Size, commercial printing or photo paper, Web, Mobile & Devices, or Film & Video. Next, from the **Size** menu, choose a specific size for the preset (there are new sizes for Mobile & Devices). ★

   Choose a unit of measure from the menu next to the Width field; the same unit will be chosen automatically for the Height (or to change the

unit for just one dimension, hold down Shift while choosing it). Enter custom **Width** and **Height** values (or use the scrubby sliders).

4. Enter the **Resolution** required for your target output device. For Web output, enter 72; for print output, see the preceding page.

5. Choose a document **Color Mode** (we recommend RGB Color), then from the adjacent menu, choose **8 bit** or **16 bit** as the color depth (see page 17).

6. Note the current **Image Size** on the right side of the dialog. If you need to reduce that size, you can choose smaller dimensions, a lower resolution, or a lower bit depth.

7. From the **Background Contents** menu, choose **White** (the option we recommend if you're a new Photoshop user), or choose **Transparent** if you want the bottommost tier of the document to be a layer (see Chapter 8).

8. Click the Advanced arrowhead, if necessary, to display more options, then choose a **Color Profile** (if you chose RGB Color in step 5, we recommend choosing Adobe RGB here). The list of profiles will vary depending on the document Color Mode. (Note: You can also assign or change the profile at a later time via the Edit > Assign

Continued on the following page

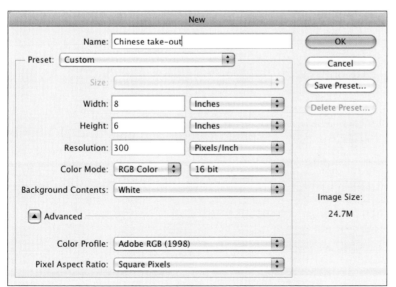

A In the New dialog, enter a file Name; either choose a Preset size or enter custom Width, Height, and Resolution values; choose RGB Color Mode and a Background Contents option; and choose a Color Profile.

Profile dialog. To learn more about color profiles, see pages 10–12.)

For Web or print output, leave the **Pixel Aspect Ratio** on the default setting of Square Pixels. For video output, choose an applicable option (see Photoshop Help).

9. Click OK. A new, blank document window appears onscreen. To save the file, see page 18.

▶ To force the New dialog settings to display the specs of an existing open document, from the bottom of the Preset menu, choose the name of the document that has the desired dimensions.

▶ If the Clipboard contains image data (say, from artwork that you copied from Adobe Photoshop or Illustrator), the New dialog will automatically display the dimensions of that content. Those dimensions will also display if you choose Clipboard from the Preset menu in the New dialog. If you want to prevent the Clipboard dimensions from displaying (and have the dialog show the last-used file dimensions instead), hold down Alt/Option as you choose File > New.

SETTING DEFAULT RESOLUTION VALUES

In Edit/Photoshop > Preferences > Units & Rulers, under New Document Presets Resolutions, you can enter Print Resolution and Screen Resolution values. Thereafter, one or the other of those values will appear in the Resolution field in the File > New dialog when you choose a preset from the Preset menu. The Print Resolution value is used for the Paper and Photo presets (the default value is 300 ppi); the Screen Resolution value is used for the Web and Film & Video presets (the default value is 72 ppi).

Creating document presets

If you tend to choose the same custom document size, color mode, and other settings over and over in the New dialog, here's a way to streamline your workflow and save yourself some startup time. Create a preset for each "group" of settings. Then, as you create a new document, choose one of your presets from the menu in the New dialog.

To create a document preset:

1. Choose File > **New** or press Ctrl-N/Cmd-N. The New dialog opens.

2. Choose settings, including the width, height, resolution, color mode, bit depth, background contents, color profile, and pixel aspect ratio. Ignore any setting that you don't want to include in the preset; you'll exclude it from the preset in step 4.

3. Click **Save Preset**. The New Document Preset dialog opens. **A**

4. Enter a **Preset Name**. Under **Include in Saved Settings**, uncheck any New dialog settings that you don't want to save in the preset. Click OK. Your new preset is now listed on the Preset menu in the New dialog.

▶ To delete a user-created preset, choose it from the Preset menu, click Delete Preset, then click Yes (this cannot be undone).

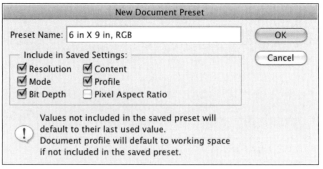

A *Use the New Document Preset dialog to name your new preset and to control which of the current settings in the New dialog it will contain.*

Editing 16-bit files in Photoshop

The 16-bit advantage

To get high-quality output from Photoshop, a wide range of tonal values must be captured by the input device (e.g., your camera or a scanner). The wider the dynamic range of your chosen input device, the finer the subtleties of color and shade in the resulting images.

Most advanced amateur and professional digital SLR cameras capture 12 bits or more of accurate data per channel. Like cameras, scanners range widely in quality: Low-end models capture approximately 10 bits of accurate data per channel, whereas high-end models capture up to 16 bits of accurate data per channel. If your camera can capture 12 to 16 bits per channel, or you work with high-resolution scans, your images will be higher quality, because they will contain an abundance of pixels in all levels of the tonal spectrum. Details (or a lack thereof) will be more noticeable in the shadow areas, because those are the hardest areas for a device to capture well.

The editing and resampling commands in Photoshop (and in particular, tonal adjustment commands such as Levels and Curves), remove pixel data from a photo and alter the distribution of pixels across the tonal spectrum. Signs of pixel loss from these destructive edits are more visible, for example, in a high-end print of an 8-bit image than in that of a 16-bit image. **A–B** Because 16-bit images contain more pixels in all parts of the tonal spectrum at the outset, more tonal values are preserved, even after editing (it's like extra "padding").

Working with 16-bit files

Photoshop can open files that contain 8, 16, or 32 bits per channel. All the Photoshop commands are available for 8-bit files; many of the key Photoshop commands are available for 16-bit files; few Photoshop commands are available for 32 bits-per-channel files (so they're not a practical choice). Downgrade your high-quality 16-bit files only when necessary. For 16-bit files, you have access to the Liquify and Lens Correction filters on the Filter menu and some or all of the filters on the Blur, Noise, Render, Sharpen, Stylize, and Other submenus but not the filters on the other Filter submenus.

If system or storage limitations prevent you from working with 16-bit images in Photoshop, try this two-stage approach: Perform your initial, vital tonal corrections on the 16-bits-per-channel image, then via the Image > Mode menu, convert the file to 8 Bits/Channel for further editing.

If your output service provider requests an 8-bit file instead of 16-bit, but you don't have a problem working with 16-bit files on your computer, do all your editing on the higher-quality file. When you're done editing it, save a copy of it in the lower bit depth for output.

16-bit files can be saved in many formats, such as Photoshop (.psd), Large Document (.psb), Photoshop PDF (.pdf), PNG (.png), TIFF (.tif), and JPEG 2000 (.jpf).

Finally, 16-bit files can be printed as 16-bit from a Mac OS system, provided the printing device supports 16-bit printing.

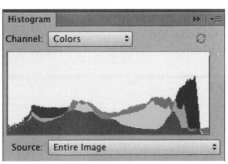

A *A Levels adjustment that we applied to this 8-bit image caused some image data to be discarded, as shown by the spikes and gaps in the histogram.*

B *Here, we applied the same Levels adjustment to a 16-bit version of the same image. Due to the higher bit depth, the smooth tonal transitions were preserved.*

Saving your document

Although Photoshop lets you create, open, edit, and save files in over a dozen different formats, you'll probably encounter or use just a few of them, such as Photoshop (the native Photoshop file format, or PSD for short), Photoshop PDF, JPEG, and TIFF. If you're not sure what format to use, stick with the Photoshop format (we use it for most of our work).

To save an unsaved document:

1. If the document contains any content, you can choose File > **Save** (Ctrl-S/Cmd-S); if it's completely blank, choose File > **Save As** (Ctrl-Shift-S/Cmd-Shift-S). The Save As dialog opens.

2. Type a name in the **File Name** field (Windows) or the **Save As** field (Mac OS).

3. Choose a location for the file.

   In Windows, if you need to navigate to a different folder or drive, use the Save In menu at the top of the dialog.

   In the Mac OS, click a drive or folder in the Sidebar panel on the left side of the window, then click a subfolder in one of the columns, if necessary. To locate a recently used folder, use the menu below the Save As field.

4. From the **Format** menu, choose a file format (**A–B**, next page). Photoshop (PSD), Large Document Format (PSB), Photoshop PDF, and TIFF are the only formats that support layers, which you will be using extensively in Photoshop (learn about flattening layers on page 150).

5. If you're not yet familiar with the features listed in the **Save** area, leave the settings as they are. For the As a Copy option, see step 5 on page 20.

6. If the file contains an embedded color profile and the format you have chosen supports profiles, in the **Color** area, you can check **ICC Profile** [profile name] (in Windows) or **Embed Color Profile** [profile name] (in the Mac OS) to save the profile with the file. (To learn about embedded profiles, see pages 8, 10, and 12.)

7. Click Save.

   ➤ In the Mac OS, to have Photoshop append a three-character extension (e.g., .tif, .psd) to the file name automatically when a file is saved for the first time, in Edit/Photoshop > Preferences > File Handling, choose Append File Extension:

Always. Extensions are required when exporting Macintosh files to the Windows platform and when posting files to a Web server.

➤ Learn about the Maximize PSD and PSB File Compatibility option (in the File Handling panel of the Preferences dialog) on page 438.

Once a file has been saved for the first time, each subsequent use of the Save command overwrites (saves over) the previous version.

To save a previously saved document:

Choose File > **Save** (Ctrl-S/Cmd-S).

➤ An asterisk on a document tab or title bar indicates that the document contains unsaved changes.

➤ To learn about the automatic file recovery feature in Photoshop, see page 437.

The simple Revert command restores your document to the last-saved version.

   Note: We know you can't learn everything at once, but keep in mind for the near future that the History panel, which we have devoted Chapter 10 exclusively to, serves as a full-service multiple undo feature. In fact, each use of the Revert command shows up as a separate state on the History panel, so you can undo any revert by clicking an earlier history state.

To revert a document to the last saved version:

Choose File > **Revert**.

➤ To undo the last edit, choose Edit > Undo (Ctrl-Z/Cmd-Z). Not all edits can be undone by this command.

➤ For more undo and redo commands, see the sidebar on page 99.

FORMATS THAT PRESERVE PHOTOSHOP FEATURES

Photoshop (PSD), Large Document (PSB), TIFF, and Photoshop PDF are the only formats that preserve the following Photoshop features: multiple layers; layer transparency; adjustment, editable type, Smart Object, and shape layers; layer effects; alpha channels; and grids and guides. ICC color management profiles are also preserved by the above-mentioned formats (as well as by the JPEG format).

A This is the Save As dialog in Windows.

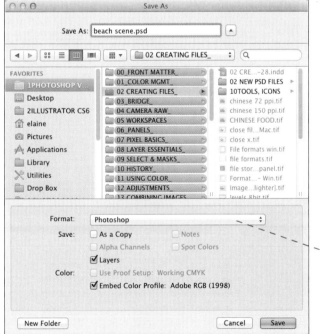

B This is the Save As dialog in the Mac OS.

Using the Save As command, you can save a copy of a file under a new name (say, to create a design or adjustment variation), save it with different options chosen (e.g., with or without alpha channels or layers), or save a flattened copy of it in a different format for export to another application (a necessity when exporting to most non-Adobe applications, which unfortunately can't import Photoshop PSD files or read Photoshop layers).

To save a new version of a file:

1. Choose File > **Save As** (Ctrl-Shift-S/Cmd-Shift-S). The Save As dialog opens.

2. Change the name in the **File Name/Save As** field (if you're planning to change only the file format, this step is unnecessary).

3. Choose a location for the new version of the file from the Save In menu in Windows or by using the Sidebar panel and columns in the Mac OS. (To learn about the Save As to Original Folder preference, see page 437.)

4. *Optional:* From the Format menu, choose a different file format. Only formats that are available for a file's current color mode and bit depth are listed. Note: If you try to save a 16-bit file in the JPEG (.jpg) format, Photoshop will produce a flattened, 8-bit copy of the file automatically.

   Beware! If the format you've chosen doesn't support layers, the Layers option is dimmed automatically, a yellow alert icon displays, and layers in the new version will be flattened.

5. Check any available options in the **Save** area that you deem necessary. For example, you could check **As a Copy** to have the copy of the file remain closed and the original file stay open onscreen, or uncheck this option to have the original file close and the copy stay open.

   In Edit/Photoshop > Preferences > File Handling, under File Saving Options, we choose the setting of Image Previews: Always Save to have Photoshop include file previews automatically. If you choose Ask When Saving as the preference, this preview option will display in the Save As dialog instead; see page 437. For the Append File Extension option (Mac OS only), we also choose the setting of Always.

6. In the **Color** area, check **ICC Profile/Embed Color Profile**: [profile name], if available, to include the current profile, for good color management (see pages 8, 10, and 12).

7. Click Save. Depending on the file format you have chosen, another dialog may appear. For the PDF format, see page 460; for the TIFF format, see page 461; for other formats, see Photoshop Help.

➤ If you fail (or forget) to change the file name or format in the Save As dialog but you do proceed to click Save, an alert will appear.A Click Yes/Replace to replace the original file, or click No/Cancel to return to the Save As dialog, where you should change the file name or format.

➤ For Web output, learn about the GIF and JPEG formats on pages 463–468.

"CHINESE FOOD.psd" already exists. Do you want to replace it?

A file or folder with the same name already exists in the folder 02 CREATING FILES_17–28. Replacing it will overwrite its current contents.

Cancel   Replace

A *If you try to save a file via the Save As command without changing the file name or format, you will get this friendly warning.*

PHOTOSHOP GIGANTIC

In Photoshop, you can create and save a file as large as 300,000 x 300,000 pixels — over 2 gigabytes (GB) — and each Photoshop file can contain up to 56 user-created channels. The Large Document (.psb) format (nicknamed "Photoshop Big") is designed specifically for saving such huge files.

What can you do with PSB files? If you have enough disk space to store and work with them and have access to a wide-format printer that can output super-large images (up to 32,000 x 32,000 pixels), awesome. If not, you will need to drastically lower the resolution in a copy of your PSB file for output to an ordinary printer.

Using the Status bar

Using the Status bar and menu at the bottom of the document window, you can read data pertaining to the currently active document or find out how Photoshop is currently using available memory.

Note: To view more detailed data about a file, use the Metadata panel in Bridge; see page 26.

To use the Status bar:

Open a document, then from the menu adjacent to the Status bar at the bottom of the Application frame, choose the type of data you want Photoshop to display on the bar:

Document Sizes to list the approximate file storage size of a flattened version of the file if it were to be saved in the PSD format (the value on the left) and the storage size of the file including all its current layers and any alpha channels (the value on the right).

➤ For the most accurate file size value, view the file listing in Explorer/Finder.

Document Profile to list the color profile that is embedded in the current file. A If the document doesn't have an embedded profile, the words "Untagged [RGB or CMYK]" will be listed.

Document Dimensions to list the image dimensions (width, height, and resolution).

Scratch Sizes to list the amount of RAM Photoshop is using to process all currently open files (the value on the left) and the amount of RAM that is currently available to Photoshop (the value on the right). If the first value is greater than the second, it means Photoshop is currently utilizing virtual memory on the scratch disk.

Efficiency to list the percentage of program operations that are currently being done in RAM as opposed to the scratch disk (see page 439). A value below 100 indicates the scratch disk is being used.

Current Tool to list the name of the current tool.

32-Bit Exposure to display a slider that you can drag to adjust the preview of a 32-bits-per-channel HDR image.

Save Progress to have a dynamic percentage value display while a file is being saved (e.g., "Saving 88%"). ★

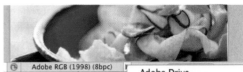

Status bar

Adobe Drive
Document Sizes
✓ Document Profile
Document Dimensions
Measurement Scale
Scratch Sizes
Efficiency
Timing
Current Tool
32–bit Exposure
Save Progress

A *From the menu for the Status bar, choose the type of data you want Photoshop to display on the bar.*

GETTING DOCUMENT INFO FAST

Regardless of which info category is selected on the Status bar menu, at any time you can click and hold on the Status bar to learn the dimensions, number of channels, color mode, bit depth, and resolution of the current document.

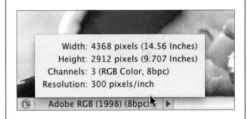

Width: 4368 pixels (14.56 Inches)
Height: 2912 pixels (9.707 Inches)
Channels: 3 (RGB Color, 8bpc)
Resolution: 300 pixels/inch

Adobe RGB (1998) (8bpc)

Ending a work session

To close a document:

1. Do one of the following:

   Click the ✖ in a document tab.**A**

   Choose File > **Close** (Ctrl-W/Cmd-W).

   Click the Close button in the upper-right corner of a floating document window in Windows,**B** or in the upper-left corner of a floating document window in the Mac OS.**C**

2. If you try to close a file that was modified since it was last saved, an alert dialog will appear.**D** Click No (N)/Don't Save (D) to close the file without saving it, or click Yes (Y)/Save (S) to save the file before closing it (or click Cancel or press Esc to dismiss the close command).

➤ To quickly close all (multiple) open documents, press Ctrl-Alt-W/Cmd-Option-W. If an alert dialog appears, you can check Apply to All, if desired, to have just one response apply to all the open documents, then click No/Don't Save or Yes/Save.

➤ In Photoshop, to close a file and launch or go to Bridge, choose File > Close and Go to Bridge or press Ctrl-Shift-W/Cmd-Shift-W.

To exit/quit Photoshop and close all open files:

1. In Windows, choose File > **Exit** (Ctrl-Q) or click the Close button for the application frame.

   In the Mac OS, choose Photoshop > **Quit Photoshop** (Cmd-Q).

2. If any open files contain unsaved changes, an alert dialog will appear for each one. Click No (N)/Don't Save (D) to close the file without saving it, or click Yes (Y)/Save (S) to save it before exiting/quitting Photoshop (or click Cancel or press Esc to dismiss the exit/quit command).

A *To close a document that is docked as a tab, click the X on the tab in the Mac OS or in Windows.*

B *To close a floating document window in Windows, click the Close button.*

C *To close a floating document window in the Mac OS, click the Close (red) button.*

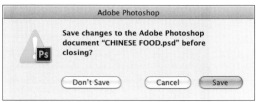

D *If you try to close a file that contains unsaved changes, this alert prompt will appear. A similar prompt will appear if you exit/quit Photoshop and any of your open files contain unsaved changes.*

The Bridge application ships with Photoshop and is aptly named because it serves as a link to the programs in the Adobe Creative Suite. You will initially find that Bridge is useful for viewing both thumbnails and large previews of your images before you open them into Camera Raw or Photoshop. Dig a little deeper, and you will find it offers a wealth of other useful features as well.

In Chapter 1, you used Bridge to synchronize the color settings for your Creative Suite programs. Here we show you how to use Bridge to download photos from a digital camera. Following that, you will learn how to preview, examine, label, rate, sort, and filter image thumbnails in the Bridge window; customize the Bridge workspace; organize thumbnails into collections and collapsible stacks; search for, move, copy, and assign keywords to files; and open files into Photoshop. You will also find instructions for using Mini Bridge, a compact version of Bridge that is accessed as a panel in Photoshop, and for exporting the Bridge cache.

Launching Adobe Bridge

When you launch Adobe Bridge, the Bridge window opens.

To launch Adobe Bridge:

Do one of the following:

In Windows, click the Start button, choose All Programs, then click **Adobe Bridge CS6**.

In the Mac OS, double-click the **Adobe Bridge CS6** application icon **Br** or click the **Bridge** icon **Br** on the Dock.

In Photoshop, press Ctrl-Alt-O/Cmd-Option-O.

➤ If you want to have Bridge launch automatically at startup, but without the Bridge window opening onscreen, go to Edit/Adobe Bridge CS6 > Preferences (Ctrl-K/Cmd-K), Advanced panel, and check Start Bridge at Login. This is called "stealth mode."

IN THIS CHAPTER

Downloading photos from a camera

When you use a digital camera, your photos are stored on a removable memory card — most likely a CompactFlash (CF) or Secure Digital (SD) card. Rather than having to tether your camera directly to a computer, you can remove the memory card and insert it into a card reader device, then download your photos from the card reader to your computer via a USB cable or Firewire cable, depending on which connection your camera supports.

When you start downloading images from a camera, the default application or dialog for acquiring images in your system may launch automatically. Instead of using that application, we recommend using the Photo Downloader application that is included with Bridge, for which instructions are provided here.

To download photos from a card reader via Photo Downloader:

1. Take the card out of your camera and insert it into the appropriate slot in the card reader.

2. Plug the card reader into your computer. If the default system application for acquiring photos launches, exit/quit it.

3. Launch **Bridge**, then click the **Get Photos from Camera** button at the top of the Bridge window. The Photo Downloader dialog opens. **A** If an alert dialog appears and you want to make Photo Downloader the default capture application, click Yes (as we do); if not, click No.

4. From the **Get Photos From** menu in the Source area, select your card reader.

5. In the **Import Settings** area, do the following:

   To change the save location, click **Browse/Choose**, then navigate to the desired folder. Click Select Folder/Open to assign that folder and return to the Photo Downloader dialog.

   To create a new subfolder within the folder you just selected, choose a naming convention from the **Create Subfolder(s)** menu, or choose Custom Name and enter a folder name (or choose None for no new subfolder).

   Optional: To assign recognizable names and shorter sequential numbers to your digital

images in lieu of the long default number, choose a Custom Name option from the Rename Files menu, then enter a name and a starting number. A sample of your entries displays below the field.

Keep **Preserve Current Filename in XMP** unchecked.

Check **Open Adobe Bridge** to have the photos display in Bridge when the downloading process is complete.

Also keep **Convert to DNG** and **Delete Original Files** unchecked.

To send copies of your photos to a designated folder on an external hard disk (as a backup), check **Save Copies To**, click **Browse/Choose**, choose a location, then click Select Folder/Open. This will be your first backup copy.

A *This is the Standard dialog of the Photo Downloader.*

6. If you want to download select photos (instead of the whole batch) from your memory card, click **Advanced Dialog** to display the larger Advanced dialog.**A** Below the thumbnail window, click **UnCheck All**, then check the box below each photo to be downloaded. Or hold down Ctrl/Cmd and click multiple photos, then check the box for one of them; a check mark will appear below each selected photo.

Optional: In the Apply Metadata area, enter Creator and Copyright info to be added to the metadata of all the downloaded photos. (This metadata will display in Bridge.)

➤ To switch back to the smaller Standard dialog at any time, click Standard Dialog.

7. Click Get Media to begin the downloading process. When it's completed, the Photo Downloader dialog is dismissed automatically. If you checked the Open Adobe Bridge option, your photos will display in a new window in Bridge. Don't worry about previewing or opening them just yet. We'll step you through that process later.

8. Unmount your card reader.

9. We recommend that you insert a blank DVD and burn the copies of your photo files to the DVD as your second backup copy. In the Mac OS, you can do this via drag-and-drop in the Finder. If you need to learn how to copy files to a DVD, consult the Help files for your operating system.

Check the box to select a photo for downloading

A *The Advanced dialog of the Photo Downloader contains the same options as the Standard dialog, plus metadata features and an area for selecting photos to be downloaded.*

Features of the Bridge window

We'll identify the main sections of the Bridge window first, starting from the top (**A**, next page). The two rows of buttons and menus running across the top of the window are referred to jointly as the toolbar. The second row of the toolbar is also called the Path bar. If the Path bar is hidden, choose Window > Path Bar.

In the default workspace, Essentials, the main window is divided into three panes: a large pane in the center and a narrower vertical pane on each side. Each pane contains one or more panels, each of which is accessed via its own tab: Favorites, Folders, Filter, Collections, Export, Content, Preview, Metadata, and Keywords. Panels in the side panes let you manage files, preview image thumbnails, filter the display of thumbnails, and display file data; the Content panel in the middle displays file and folder thumbnails. At the bottom of the Bridge window are controls for changing the thumbnail size and display format. (To customize the Bridge window, see pages 28–29 and pages 36–37.)

Next, we'll briefly describe the Bridge panels that you will learn about in this chapter.

The **Favorites** panel displays a list of folders that you've designated as favorites, for quick and easy access. See page 30.

The **Folders** panel contains a scrolling window with a hierarchical listing of all the top-level and nested folders on your hard drive(s). See page 30.

The **Filter** panel lists criteria pertaining to the images in the currently selected folder, such as how many have a specific label, star rating, file type, creation date, or modification date. By clicking various criteria in the Filter panel on or off, you can control which images in the current folder display in the Content panel. To expand or collapse a category, click the arrowhead. See page 41.

The **Collections** panel displays the names and folder icons of collections, which are thumbnail groups. See pages 46–47.

The **Content** panel displays thumbnails for images within the currently selected folder (and optionally, thumbnails for nested folders). In the lower-right corner of the Bridge window, you can click a View Content As button to control whether, and in what

format, metadata pertaining to the current files displays for each thumbnail in the Content panel (see page 37). For any view type, you can change the thumbnail size (see page 36). The Content panel is used and illustrated in tasks throughout this chapter.

The **Preview** panel displays a large preview of the image (or folder) thumbnail that is currently selected in the Content panel. Or if the thumbnail for a video or PDF file is selected, controls for playing the video or for viewing the pages display in this panel. Two or more selected image thumbnails can be previewed in this panel, for comparison, and it has a loupe mechanism that you can use to inspect small details of the preview. See pages 30–32.

The **Metadata** panel has two main sections, both of which display data pertaining to the currently selected thumbnail. The placard at the top contains a quick summary (see the sidebar on page 30), and the main part of the panel lists more detailed data, in collapsible categories. In the File Properties category, for example, you can view the current file name, file size, etc. Via the IPTC Core category, you can attach a copyright notice and other data to a file (see page 39). When the thumbnail for a digital photo is selected, the Camera Data (Exif) category lists the camera settings with which the photo was captured. If the photo was edited in Camera Raw, the panel will also show a Camera Raw category in which the Basic tab settings that are applied to the current photo are listed (to add more Camera Raw specs to this category, go to Edit/Adobe Bridge CS6 > Preferences, Metadata pane, and check boxes under Camera Raw).

Use the **Keywords** panel to assign one or more descriptive subkeywords to your images, such as an event, subject, client, or location, so they can be located quickly using Bridge features (see pages 38–39). You can do a search to find image thumbnails based on keyword criteria, or narrow the display of thumbnails in the Content panel to specific subcategories of images by checking keywords in the Filter panel.

Note: The Export and Inspector panels aren't covered in this book (they are designed for file sharing).

Bridge

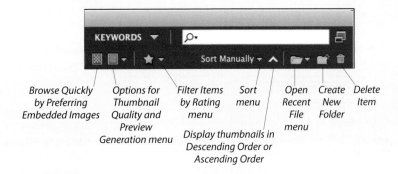

Browse Quickly by Preferring Embedded Images | Options for Thumbnail Quality and Preview Generation menu | Filter Items by Rating menu | Sort menu | Open Recent File menu | Create New Folder | Delete Item

Display thumbnails in Descending Order or Ascending Order

Get Photos from Camera | Open in Camera Raw

Return to last Adobe Creative Suite application | Refine menu (Review Mode, Batch Rename, File Info) | Output menu (Web or PDF) | Rotate selected thumbnails | Name of currently displayed folder | Workspace switcher | Workspace menu | For the navigation controls on the toolbar, see page 30.

Path bar | Compact Mode/ Full Mode

A You'll learn the function of the Bridge features throughout this chapter.

Thumbnail Size slider | Lock Thumbnail Grid | View Content as Thumbnails | View Content as List

View Content as Details

Choosing a workspace for Bridge

To reconfigure the Bridge window quickly, choose one of the predefined workspaces. (To create and save custom workspaces, see pages 36–38.)

To choose a workspace for Bridge:

Do one of the following:

On the upper toolbar, click **Essentials**, **Filmstrip**, **Metadata** (List View for the thumbnails), **Output**, **Keywords**, **Preview**, **Light Table**, **Folders**, or a saved custom workspace.**A** (If there's room on the toolbar and you want to display more workspace names, pull the gripper bar to the left.)

From the **Workspace** menu on the toolbar, choose a workspace **B–C** (and **A–C**, next page).

Press the shortcut for one of the first six workspaces on the switcher (as listed on the Workspace menu): Ctrl-F1/Cmd-F1 through Ctrl-F6/Cmd-F6. The shortcuts are assigned automatically to the first six workspaces on the switcher, according to their current order from left to right. Not working? These shortcuts may already be used by your operating system, in which case they won't work in Bridge.

➤ To change the order of workspaces on the switcher, drag a name to the left or right.

➤ To learn how to resize the thumbnails in the Content panel, see page 36.

➤ To create a second Bridge window, choose File > New Window. By default, the new window will display the same contents as the existing one, but you can display a different workspace and folder in each window.

To reveal more workspace names, drag the gripper bar to the left.

A *To change workspaces, click a workspace name from the workspace switcher…*

B *…or choose a workspace name from the Workspace menu.*

C *The Filmstrip workspace features a large preview of the currently selected thumbnail(s).*

A In the Essentials workspace, all the panels are showing.

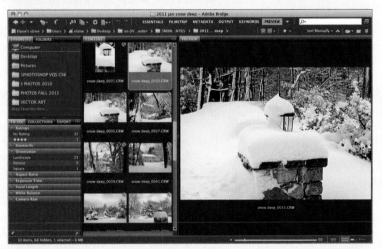

B In the Preview workspace, the thumbnails display in a vertical format (the opposite arrangement from the Filmstrip workspace), and the Metadata and Keywords panels are hidden to make room for a larger preview.

C In the Light Table workspace, the Content panel occupies the entire Bridge window, enabling you to view a large number of thumbnails simultaneously.

Previewing images in Bridge

To add a folder to the Favorites panel:

Do either of the following:

Drag a folder icon from the Content panel or the Explorer/Finder into the Favorites panel (the pointer will be a + symbol).

Right-click a folder in the Folders or Content panel and choose **Add to Favorites**.

➤ Via check boxes in the Favorite Items area of Edit/ Adobe Bridge CS6 > Preferences > General, you can control which system folders are listed in the Favorites panel.

➤ To remove a folder from the list of Favorites, right-click it and choose Remove from Favorites.

To display and select images in Bridge:

1. Do any of the following:

In the **Folders** panel, navigate to a folder. You can use the scroll arrows, and you can expand or collapse any folder by clicking its arrowhead.

Display the contents of a folder by clicking its icon in the **Folders** panel or by double-clicking its thumbnail in the **Content** panel. Note: For folder thumbnails to display in the Content panel, Show Folders must be checked on the View menu.

Click the **Go Back** button ◀ on the toolbar **A** to step back through the last folders viewed, or the **Go Forward** button ▶ to reverse your steps.

Click a folder name in the **Favorites** panel.

From the **Go to Parent or Favorites** menu ▾ on the toolbar, choose a parent or Favorites folder.

Click a folder name on the **Path** bar (Window > Path Bar).

From one of the menus ▶ on the Path bar, choose a folder. If another submenu displays, click yet another folder; repeat until you reach the desired folder.

➤ To display thumbnails for images in all nested subfolders within the current folder, choose Show Items from Subfolders from the folder menu.▶ To restore the normal view, click the Cancel button ⊘ on the Path bar.

2. In the **Content** panel do one of the following:

Click an image thumbnail. A colored border appears around it, and data about the file is listed in the Metadata panel. An enlarged preview of the image also displays in the **Preview** panel, if that panel is showing.

To select multiple, nonconsecutive thumbnails, Ctrl-click/Cmd-click them (**A**, next page).

To select a series of consecutive thumbnails, click the first thumbnail in the series, then Shift-click the last one.

➤ A number in the upper-left corner of an image thumbnail signifies that it's part of a stack (group) of thumbnails. To display or hide the contents of a stack, click the stack number (see page 42).

➤ To cycle through thumbnails in the currently displayed folder, press an arrow key on the keyboard.

➤ To quickly locate and select a particular thumbnail, start typing the file name without clicking anywhere first.

Go Back Go Forward Go to Parent or Favorites Reveal Recent File or Go to Recent Folder

Path bar

A These are the navigation controls in Bridge.

THE METADATA PLACARD

To show the Metadata placard, check Show Metadata Placard on the Metadata panel menu. The left side of the placard lists settings that were used to shoot the currently selected photo (the icons and data vary depending on the camera settings and model). The right side of the placard lists the pixel dimensions, size, resolution, assigned color profile, and color mode of the current file.

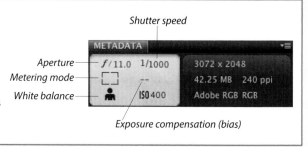

Shutter speed

Aperture
Metering mode
White balance

Exposure compensation (bias)

A *We held down Ctrl/Cmd and clicked to select multiple image thumbnails.*

You can control whether thumbnails and the preview render quickly at low resolution, or more slowly and color-managed at high resolution.

To choose quality options for the Bridge thumbnails and previews:

From the **Options for Thumbnail Quality and Preview Generation** menu ▦ on the Bridge toolbar, choose a preference for the thumbnail quality:

Prefer Embedded (Faster) displays low-resolution thumbnails and is useful for displaying a high volume of images quickly.

High Quality on Demand displays high-resolution, color-managed thumbnails and previews (which are generated from the source files) for selected thumbnails and low-resolution previews for unselected thumbnails. This is a good compromise between the two other options.

Always High Quality, the default setting, displays high-resolution thumbnails and previews, whether the thumbnails are selected or not. Rendering is the slowest with this option.

➤ To quickly access lower-quality, faster previewing, click the Browse Quickly by Preferring Embedded Images button ▦ on the Bridge Path bar; this enables the Prefer Embedded (Faster) option. Click the button again to return to the current setting on the Options for Thumbnail Quality and Preview Generation menu.

➤ The Generate 100% Previews option on the Options for Thumbnail Quality and Preview Generation menu saves actual-size JPEG versions of thumbnails, which in turn enables Bridge to generate higher-quality previews when the loupe is used or when images are displayed at 100% size in Full Screen Preview or Slideshow view. This option utilizes a lot of disk space, so we recommend keeping it unchecked.

To compare two or more image previews:

1. In Bridge, click or choose the Filmstrip or Preview workspace.

2. In the Content panel, Ctrl-click/Cmd-click up to nine thumbnails (the maximum number that can be previewed at a time).**A** Large versions of the thumbnails will display in the Preview panel.

3. *Optional:* Ctrl-click/Cmd-click an unselected thumbnail in the Content panel to add it to the Preview panel, or do the same for a selected thumbnail to remove it from the Preview panel.

To display a full-screen preview of an image thumbnail:

1. Press the Spacebar to display a full-screen preview of the currently selected thumbnail and hide the Bridge window temporarily.

2. To zoom in or out, press + or – or use the scroll wheel on your mouse (you can drag the magnified preview). If desired, press the left or right arrow key to cycle through other thumbnails in the same folder.

3. To redisplay the Bridge window, press the Spacebar or Esc.

To inspect image details via an onscreen loupe:

1. To make the loupe appear, click an image in the Preview panel **B** or click the frontmost image in Review mode (see the next page).

   Note: If the loupe doesn't appear, it's because the Ctrl-Click/Cmd-Click Opens the Loupe When Previewing or Reviewing option is checked in Edit/Adobe Bridge CS6 > Preferences > General. Ctrl-click/Cmd-click the image to make the loupe appear.

2. Click the area to be examined. To zoom in on the loupe display (up to 800%), press + or use the scroll wheel on your mouse; to zoom out, press – .

3. To examine a different area, click that area or drag the loupe to it.

4. *Optional:* If you're previewing two images using two loupes, you can Ctrl-drag/Cmd-drag either loupe to move them simultaneously.

5. To remove the loupe, click inside it.

A *We Ctrl/Cmd-clicked two image thumbnails to display them in the Preview panel, then clicked a preview to display the loupe.*

You can put selected thumbnails into Review mode, in which the thumbnails display as large previews on a black background and the Bridge window is hidden, then cycle through the images as if they're on a carousel. You can also rate thumbnails in this mode.

To preview images in Review mode:

1. Do one of the following:

   Open a folder of images.

   Hold down Alt/Option and click a thumbnail stack (see page 42).

   Select five or more image thumbnails (Ctrl/Cmd or Shift-click them).

2. Press Ctrl-B/Cmd-B, or from the **Refine** menu at the top of the Bridge window, choose Review Mode. The Bridge window is hidden temporarily, and the images display on a black background.

3. To rotate the carousel, do any of the following:

   Drag any image preview to the left or right.

   Click one of the smaller previews to bring it to the forefront.

Click (and keep clicking) the Go Forward or Go Backward button in the lower-left corner, or press the left or right arrow key.

4. To examine the frontmost (enlarged) image with a loupe, click it. Drag the loupe to move it. Click the loupe again to remove it.

5. To rate or label the frontmost thumbnail, right-click it and choose a star rating or a label from the context menu **A** or press Ctrl/Cmd plus a numeral between 1 and 9. (To view a list of shortcuts, press H.)

6. To take the frontmost image out of the carousel, click the down-pointing arrow in the lower-left corner, or drag the image to the bottom of your screen. (This won't delete the actual file.)

   ➤ You can use this method to pare down a selection of images before grouping them as a stack (see pages 42–43) or as a collection (see pages 46–47).

7. To exit Review mode, press Esc or click the in the lower-right corner.

8. Click any image thumbnail to deselect the rest.

A *We held down Ctrl/Cmd and clicked nine image thumbnails, pressed Ctrl-B/Cmd-B to view them in Review mode, then right-clicked the frontmost thumbnail and are choosing a star rating from the context menu.*

Opening files from Bridge into Photoshop

You can open as many files into Photoshop as the currently available RAM and scratch disk space on your computer allow.

Note: To open a raw, JPEG, or TIFF digital photo into Camera Raw (so you can apply corrections to it before opening it into Photoshop), see page 55. To open a file from Mini Bridge into Photoshop, see page 49.

To open files from Bridge into Photoshop:

1. In the Content panel, display the thumbnail for the image(s) to be opened.

2. Do either of the following:

   Double-click an image thumbnail.

   Click an image thumbnail or select multiple thumbnails, then double-click one of them or press Ctrl-O/Cmd-O.

3. Photoshop will launch, if it isn't already running, and the image(s) will appear onscreen. If any alert dialogs appear, see the next page.

➤ If a photo has been opened in Camera Raw and settings were applied to it in that dialog, it will have an icon ⊕ in the top right corner of the thumbnail. If you want to open such a file (or a raw photo) directly into Photoshop (bypassing Camera Raw), Shift-double-click it.

➤ To locate an "actual" file in Explorer/Finder, right-click its thumbnail in Bridge and choose Reveal in Explorer/Reveal in Finder from the context menu. The folder that the file resides in will open in a window in Explorer/Finder and the file icon will be selected.

➤ By default, the Bridge window stays open after you use it to open a file. To minimize the Bridge window as you open a file, hold down Alt/ Option while double-clicking the file thumbnail.

➤ To open an image from Review mode in Bridge into Photoshop, right-click it and choose Open from the context menu.

To reopen a recently opened file:

To reopen a file that was recently opened and then closed, choose the file name in one of these locations:

In Bridge, choose from the **Open Recent File** menu 🖼 on the right side of the Path bar.

In Bridge or Photoshop, choose from the File > **Open Recent** submenu.

In Bridge, from the **Reveal Recent File or Go to Recent Folder** menu, 🖼 choose **Adobe Photoshop** > **Recent Adobe Photoshop Files**. Thumbnails for the recently open files will display in the Content panel. Double-click a thumbnail to open that file. To redisplay the last displayed folder when you return to Bridge, click the Go Back arrow ◀ or a Favorites folder.

In Photoshop, display the Mini Bridge panel (Window > Extensions > Mini Bridge). From the menu in the Navigation pod, choose **Recent Files**, then click Photoshop. Double-click a thumbnail to open that file. See pages 48–49.

GETTING TO PHOTOSHOP QUICKLY

If Photoshop was the last Creative Suite application you were using, you can return to it quickly from Bridge by clicking the Return to Adobe Photoshop (boomerang) button 🔖 on the toolbar. Photoshop will launch, if it isn't already running.

ALAS, THE POOR OPEN COMMAND

➤ With Bridge serving as the best vehicle for opening files, the Open command is relegated to this sidebar. To use the Open command in Photoshop, choose File > Open (Ctrl-O/Cmd-O). In Windows, choose Files of Type: All Formats; in the Mac OS, choose Enable: All Readable Documents. Locate and click the desired file name, then click Open.

To respond to alert dialogs upon opening a file into Photoshop:

➤ If you open a file in Photoshop in which a **missing font** is being used (the font isn't available or installed), an alert dialog will appear. **A** If you click OK to open the file, the Font Missing on System alert icon will display on the offending layer(s) on the Layers panel. If you try to edit the layer, yet another alert dialog will appear, indicating that font substitution will occur if you click OK. **B** You can either click OK to allow the missing font to be replaced or click Cancel, make the required fonts available, then reopen the document.

Note: If you want to replace all missing fonts with different (available) fonts, choose Type > Replace All Missing Fonts.

➤ If the file's color profile doesn't match the current working space for Photoshop, the Embedded Profile Mismatch alert dialog will appear. **C** Click **Use the Embedded Profile (Instead of the Working Space)** if you must keep the document's current profile. Or for consistency with our color management workflow, click **Convert Document's Colors to the Working Space** to convert the profile to the current working space. Click OK. See also pages 8, 10, and 12.

➤ If the Missing Profile alert dialog appears, **D** click **Assign Working RGB: Adobe RGB (1998)** to assign the profile that you chose as the working space for Photoshop (see pages 8 and 12).

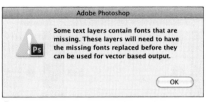

A *This alert dialog appears if fonts that are being used in the file you're opening are missing.*

B *This alert dialog appears if you try to edit an editable type layer that's using a missing font.*

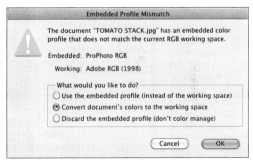

C *If this Embedded Profile Mismatch alert dialog appears, indicate whether you want to continue to use the embedded profile or convert the file to the current working space.*

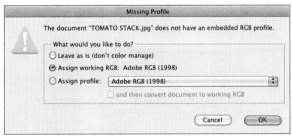

D *If this Missing Profile alert dialog appears, click Assign Working RGB: Adobe RGB (1998) to convert the file to the default working space for Photoshop.*

Customizing the Bridge window

To display or hide individual panels:

On the **Window** menu, check the panels you want to show and uncheck the ones you want to hide.

➤ To quickly hide (and then show) the side panes, press Tab or double-click the dark vertical bar between a side pane and the middle pane.

➤ To display just the Content panel in a compact window, click the Switch to Compact Mode button 🖼 in the upper-right corner of the Bridge window. Click the button again to restore Full Mode (the former window size).

To configure the Bridge panes and panels manually:

Do any of the following:

To make a panel or panel group taller or shorter, drag its horizontal gripper bar upward or downward. **A**

To make a whole pane wider or narrower, drag its vertical gripper bar horizontally; **B** the adjacent pane resizes accordingly.

To minimize a panel or panel group to just a tab (or to restore its former size), double-click its tab.

To move a panel into a different group, drag the panel tab, and release the mouse when the blue drop zone border appears around the desired group.

To display a panel as a separate group, drag its tab upward or downward between two panels, and release the mouse when the horizontal blue drop zone line appears.

To resize the image thumbnails:

At the bottom of the Bridge window, drag the **Thumbnail Size** slider. **C** You could also click the button located to the left or right of the slider to restore the last **Smaller Thumbnail Size** or last **Larger Thumbnail Size**, respectively.

➤ To display only full thumbnails, with grid lines between them, click the Lock Thumbnail Grid button 🎛 at the bottom of the Bridge window. With this option on, no shuffling of thumbnails will occur if you resize the Content panel.

A We're dragging the horizontal bar upward to shorten the Favorites/Folders panel group and lengthen the Filter/Collections/Export panel group.

B Here, we're dragging the vertical bar (for the right pane) to the left to widen the Preview, Metadata, and Keywords panels.

C To resize your image thumbnails, use this slider.

To control how metadata is displayed in the Content panel:

1. In the lower-right corner of the Bridge window, click one of these View Content buttons: A

   View Content as Thumbnails (minimal file data), **View Content as Details** (more file data), B or **View Content as List** (small icons with columns of data).

2. To control which categories of metadata display below or next to the image thumbnails when the View Content as Thumbnails option is chosen, go to Edit/Adobe Bridge CS6 > Preferences > Thumbnails, then select from any or all of the **Details: Show** menus. For example, to display exposure settings, you would choose Exposure.

➤ With View Content as List chosen, you can change the column order by dragging any column header to the left or right. You can also right-click any column header to access options for changing the column data, inserting and closing columns, and changing the column width.

➤ When the View Content as Thumbnails option is chosen for Bridge, you can toggle the display of metadata on and off by pressing Ctrl-T/Cmd-T. When viewing thumbnails in the Light Table workspace, we prefer to keep the metadata hidden.

View Content as   *View Content*   *View Content*
Thumbnails   *as Details*   *as List*

A *These buttons control the display of metadata in the Content panel.*

METADATA IN THE TOOL TIPS

If Show Tooltips is checked in Edit/Adobe Bridge CS6 Preferences > Thumbnails and you rest the pointer on an image thumbnail, the Tool Tip will list the metadata for that image. (Turn this feature off if you find it annoying.)

B *With the View Content as Details button clicked, metadata displays next to the file thumbnails.*

Saving custom workspaces

If you save your customized workspaces, you'll be able to access them again quickly at any time and will avoid having to reconfigure the Bridge window at the beginning of your work sessions.

To save a custom workspace for Bridge:

1. Do all of the following:

   Choose a size and location for the overall Bridge window.

   Arrange the panel sizes and groups as desired.

   Choose a thumbnail size for the Content panel.

   Choose a sorting order for thumbnails from the Sort menu at the top of the Bridge window (see page 41).

   Click a View Content button (see the previous page).

2. From the **Workspace** menu on the workspace switcher, choose **New Workspace**.

3. In the New Workspace dialog, **A** enter a Name for the workspace, check Save Window Location as Part of Workspace and/or Save Sort Order as Part of Workspace (both are optional), then click Save.

   Note: Your new workspace will be listed first on the switcher and will be assigned the first shortcut (Ctrl-F1/Cmd-F1). To change the order of workspaces on the switcher, drag any workspace name horizontally to a different slot. When you do this, the shortcuts will be reassigned based on the new order.

➤ To delete a user-saved workspace, from the Workspace menu, choose Delete Workspace. From the menu in the dialog, choose the workspace to be deleted, then click Delete.

➤ To choose colors for the Bridge interface (including the background shade behind the panels and image previews, and the highlight border around selected thumbnails), see page 444.

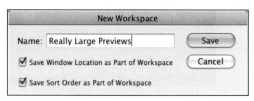

A *Use the New Workspace dialog to name your custom workspace and choose options for it.*

Resetting the Bridge workspaces

If you make a manual change to a saved workspace, the change will stick with the workspace even if you switch to a different one (or exit/quit and relaunch Bridge). For instance, if you were to change the thumbnail size for the Filmstrip workspace, switch to the Essentials workspace, then switch back to Filmstrip, you would see your new thumbnail size again. This is a good thing. On the occasion that you want a fresh start, however, there are commands for restoring the default settings to any individual predefined (standard Adobe) or user-saved workspace, or to all the predefined workspaces at once.

To reset the Bridge workspace:

Do either of the following:

To restore the default settings to one workspace, right-click the workspace name on the switcher and choose **Reset**.

To restore the default settings to all the Adobe predefined workspaces, choose **Reset Standard Workspaces** from the Workspace menu.

Assigning keywords to files

Keywords (words that are assigned to files) are used by operating system search utilities to locate files and by file management programs to organize them. In Bridge, you can create parent keyword categories (for events, places, themes, clients, etc.), and nested subkeywords within those categories, and then assign them to your files. You can locate files by entering keywords as search criteria in the Find dialog, build a Smart Collection based on a search for keywords (see page 46), and display files by checking Keywords criteria in the Filter panel (see page 41).

To create keywords and subkeywords in the Keywords panel:

1. Display the Keywords panel. To create a new parent keyword category, click the **New Keyword** button, type a keyword, then press Enter/Return.

2. To create a nested subkeyword, click a parent keyword, click the **New Sub Keyword** button, type a word, then press Enter/Return (**A**, next page). Each time you want to add a subkeyword, click the parent keyword first. You can also create nested sub-subkeywords.

➤ You can move (drag) any subkeyword from one parent keyword category into another.

To assign keywords to files via the Keywords panel:

1. Select one or more image thumbnails in the Content panel. If keywords are already assigned to any of those files, they will be listed at the top of the Keywords panel (you can assign more).

2. Check the box for one or more subkeywords.**B** You can assign just subkeywords to a file (as we do) or assign parent keywords and subkeywords. To remove a keyword from a file, uncheck the box.

➤ Read about the Keywords Preferences on page 446.

➤ If you select the thumbnail for a file to which keywords were assigned outside of Bridge (e.g., in Photoshop via File > File Info), those keywords will display temporarily in the Keywords panel, under Other Keywords. To convert a keyword to a permanent subkeyword, right-click it and choose Make Persistent from the context menu.

To assign keywords to files via the Metadata panel:

1. Select one or more image thumbnails in the Content panel.

2. Display the Metadata panel, and expand the **IPTC Core** category.

3. Click the **Keywords** listing, then enter keywords, separated by semicolons or commas.**C** Be on the alert for typing errors!

4. Click the **Apply** button ✔ in the lower-right corner of the panel.

➤ You can also use the IPTC Core category in the Metadata panel to assign other data to a file, such as a copyright notice. Use the same method as in the steps above (you can press Tab to proceed from one field to the next).

A We created a new parent keyword entitled "Italian Cuisine," then added some subkeywords to it via the New Sub Keyword button.

B We clicked an image thumbnail, then assigned relevant subkeywords to it by checking boxes.

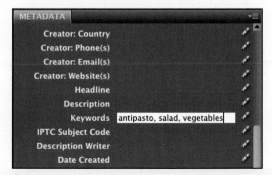

C We're assigning keywords to a file via the Metadata panel.

USING THE KEYWORDS PANEL

Rename a parent keyword or subkeyword	Right-click the word, choose Rename from the context menu, then type a name (this won't alter data that is already embedded).
Delete a parent keyword or subkeyword	Click the word, then click the Delete Keyword button.🗑 If that keyword is assigned to any files, it will now be listed in italics.
Find a keyword or subkeyword on the list	Type the word in the search field at the bottom of the panel. Choose a search parameter from the menu.🔍▾

Rating and labeling thumbnails

If you assign each thumbnail a star rating and/or color label, you'll be able to sort them in the Content panel based on their ranking, control which ones display via the Filter panel, and locate them easily via the Find command. In addition, you can apply a Reject rating to any image thumbnails that you want to hide from the Content panel but aren't ready to delete from your hard drive.

To rate and label thumbnails:

1. Select either View Content as Thumbnails or View Content as Details as the view option for thumbnails (see page 37). Select one or more image thumbnails in the Content panel.

2. Do any of the following:

   From the Label menu, choose a **Rating** (to assign a star ranking) and/or a **Label** (to add a color-coded strip below the thumbnail).

   Click a thumbnail, then click any one of the five dots below it; stars will appear. To remove one star, click the star to its left. To remove all the stars from a thumbnail, click to the left of the first one. (If you don't see the dots or stars, enlarge the thumbnails via the Thumbnail Size slider.)

   Press one of the keyboard shortcuts that are listed on the Label menu, such as Ctrl/Cmd plus a number (e.g., Ctrl-2/Cmd-2 for two stars, or Ctrl-8/Cmd-8 for Approved).

   Right-click a thumbnail in the Content panel, then choose a category from the **Label** submenu from the context menu.

   Right-click in the Preview panel and choose a star rating and/or label from the context menu.

   To label the losers with a red "Reject" label, choose Label > **Reject** or press Alt-Del/Option-Delete. Via the Show Reject Files option on the View menu, you can show or hide all rejected thumbnails.

➤ You can assign custom names to labels in Edit/Adobe Bridge CS6 > Preferences > Labels.

To remove ratings or labels from thumbnails:

1. Select one or more image thumbnails.

2. To remove stars, choose **No Rating** from the Label menu or press Ctrl-0/Cmd-0 (zero). To remove a label, choose **No Label** from the Label menu or press the shortcut for the currently assigned label.

A *This thumbnail has an Approved (green) rating.*

B *We clicked the third dot on this thumbnail to give it a three-star rating…*

C *…but then we changed our minds, so we clicked to the left of the stars to remove them.*

D *We gave this poor fellow a Reject rating (Alt-Del/Option-Delete).*

RATING THUMBNAILS IN REVIEW MODE

To rate or label images in Review mode, right-click the large, frontmost image and choose from the context menu or use one of the assigned shortcuts (as listed on the Label menu.)

Rearranging and sorting thumbnails

To rearrange thumbnails manually:

Drag a thumbnail to a new location; or Ctrl-click/ Cmd-click multiple thumbnails, then drag one of the selected thumbnails. The listing on the Sort menu on the Path bar changes to "Sort Manually."

The current criterion on the Sort menu controls the order in which thumbnails display in the Content panel. After applying ratings to our thumbnails, we choose By Rating from the Sort menu to display them by rating, in ascending order. The sorting order also affects the batch and automate commands in Bridge, because those commands process files based on the current sequence of thumbnails.

To choose a sorting order for thumbnails:

From the **Sort** menu on the Path bar, choose a sorting criterion (such as By Rating).A All thumbnails that are currently displaying in the Content panel will be re-sorted. Note: If you display a different folder, the current sorting order will apply.

➤ To restore the last sequence of thumbnails that was created by dragging them manually, choose Manually from the Sort menu.

➤ To reverse the current order, click the Ascending Order █ or Descending Order █ arrowhead.

Filtering thumbnails

The categories and listings on the Filter panel (e.g., Ratings, Keywords, Date Created) change dynamically depending on the data contained in the currently displayed folder of thumbnails, and also on what categories are checked on the panel menu. When you check the boxes for specific criteria in the panel, only the thumbnails that meet those criteria will display in the Content panel. Note: Filtering doesn't affect thumbnails in stacks.

To filter the display of thumbnails:

Do either of the following:

On the **Filter** panel, click the arrowhead to expand any category, such as Labels, Ratings, or Keywords, then check one or more criteria.**B** For example, to display only files that have an Approved label and a rating of three stars, check Approved under Labels and check the three-star listing under Ratings. To remove a criterion, click the listing again.

From the **Filter Items by Rating** menu █ on the Bridge toolbar,**C** check the desired criteria.

➤ To prevent the current filters (those with check marks) from clearing when you display other folders, activate the Keep Filter When Browsing button on the panel; when activated, the button displays in color.

➤ To remove all check marks from the Filter panel, click the Clear Filter █ button at the bottom of the panel or press Ctrl-Alt-A/Cmd-Option-A.

B *Because we checked the three-star ranking in the Filter panel (Ratings category), only thumbnails that have three stars will display in the Content panel.*

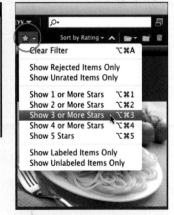

A *From the Sort menu on the Path bar, choose a sorting order for your selected thumbnails.*

C *Via the Filter Items by Rating menu, you can filter thumbnails based on their ratings.*

Using thumbnail stacks

One way to reduce the number of thumbnails that display at a given time is to group them into expandable stacks. You can organize your stacks based on categories, such as landscapes, portraits, or shots taken with a particular camera setting. Unlike collections (see pages 46–47), stacks can't be labeled.

To group thumbnails into a stack:

1. Shift-click or Ctrl-click/Cmd-click to select two or more file thumbnails. **A** The thumbnail that is listed first in your selection will become the "stack thumbnail" (will display on top of the stack).

2. Press Ctrl-G/Cmd-G or right-click one of the selected thumbnails and choose Stack > **Group as Stack**. **B** A stack looks like a couple of playing cards in a pile, with the stack thumbnail on top. The number in the upper-left corner (the "stack number") indicates how many thumbnails the stack contains.

To select the thumbnails in a stack:

To both select and display all the thumbnails in a stack, click the stack number (click it again to collapse the stack). The stack will remain selected.

To select all the thumbnails in a stack while keeping the stack collapsed, click the stack border (the bottom "card") or Alt-click/Option-click the stack thumbnail (the top image in the stack). Note that although the stack is collapsed, because it is selected, all the thumbnails it contains will display in the Preview panel, if that panel is showing.

➤ Provided your thumbnails aren't too small, a slider will display on a bar next to the stack number of a closed stack. You can drag the slider to quickly preview the thumbnails.

To rearrange thumbnails within a stack:

To move a thumbnail to a different position in an expanded stack, click it to deselect the other selected thumbnails, then drag it to a new spot (as shown by the vertical drop zone line).

To move a whole stack to a different position:

1. Collapse the stack, then Alt-click/Option-click the stack thumbnail. The borders of both "cards" in the stack should now be highlighted.

2. Drag the stack thumbnail (not the border).

A We selected several thumbnails for grouping in a stack.

B Next, we chose the Group as Stack command.

➤ If you drag the top thumbnail of an unselected stack, you'll move just that thumbnail, not the whole stack.

To add a thumbnail to a stack:

Drag a thumbnail over a stack thumbnail or into the desired position in an open stack.

To remove a thumbnail from a stack:

1. Click the stack number to expand the stack.
2. Click the thumbnail to be removed, then drag it out of the stack.

To ungroup a stack:

1. If the stack is collapsed, click the stack thumbnail; if the stack is expanded, click the stack number.
2. Press Control-Shift-G/Cmd-Shift-G (Stacks > Ungroup from Stack) or right-click the stack and choose Stack > **Ungroup from Stack**. The stack number and border disappear.

Managing files using Bridge

To create a new folder:

1. Via the Folders panel or the Path bar, navigate to the folder to which you want to add a folder.
2. Click the **New Folder** button 📁 at the right end of the Bridge toolbar. Type a name to replace the highlighted one, then press Enter/Return.

You can move files to a different folder on your hard disk either by dragging the thumbnails manually or via a command.

To move or copy files between folders:

Method 1 (by dragging)
1. Select one or more thumbnails (Content panel).
2. In the Folders panel, navigate to (but don't click) the folder or subfolder into which you want to move the selected files.
3. To move the selected files, drag them over the folder name in the Folders panel (then release), or to copy them, do the same except hold down Ctrl/Option while dragging (a + symbol will appear in the pointer). Note: If you want to move files to another hard disk, hold down Shift/Cmd while dragging.

Method 2 (via the context menu)
1. Select one or more thumbnails in the Content panel.

2. Right-click one of the selected thumbnails, then from the **Move To** or **Copy To** submenu on the context menu, do either of the following:

    Select a folder name under **Recent Folders** or **Favorites**.

    Select **Choose Folder**. Locate a folder in the Open dialog, then click Open.

➤ To copy files via the Clipboard, select one or more thumbnails, press Ctrl-C/Cmd-C to copy them, click the desired folder, then press Ctrl-V/Cmd-V to paste.

To delete a file or folder:

1. Click an image or folder thumbnail or Ctrl-click/Cmd-click multiple thumbnails, or Shift-click a series of them.
2. Do either of the following:

    Press Ctrl-Backspace/Cmd-Delete, then if an alert dialog appears, click OK.

    Press Del/Delete on your extended keyboard, then if an alert dialog appears, click Delete.

➤ Oops! Change your mind? To retrieve a deleted file or folder, choose Edit > Undo immediately. Or to dig it out of the trash, double-click the Recycle Bin/Trash icon for your operating system, then drag the item into the Content panel in Bridge. Phew.

To rename a file or folder:

1. Click a thumbnail, then click the file or folder name. The name becomes highlighted. **A**
2. Type a new name **B** (for an image file, don't try to delete the extension), then either press Enter/Return or click outside the name field.

A To rename a file, click the existing file name…

B …then type a new one.

When you download digital photos from your camera to your computer, they keep the sequential numerical labels (e.g., "CRW_3816") that your camera assigned to them. Via the Batch Rename command in Bridge, you can assign more recognizable names to your photos, to make them easier to identify.

To batch-rename files:

1. Display the contents of the folder that contains the files to be renamed, then select the thumbnails for the files to be renamed.

2. Do either of the following:

   Choose Tools > **Batch Rename** (Ctrl-Shift-R/ Cmd-Shift-R).

   From the Refine menu 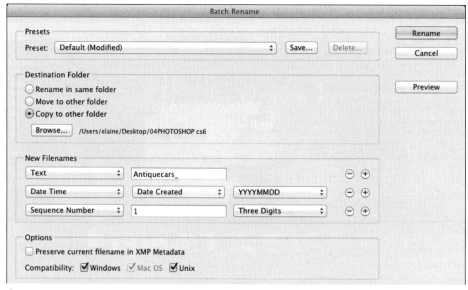 at the top of the Bridge toolbar, choose **Batch Rename**. The Batch Rename dialog opens.**A**

3. From the **Preset** menu, choose **Default**.

4. Under Destination Folder, click one of the following:

   Rename in Same Folder to rename the files and leave them in their current location.

   Move to Other Folder to rename the files and move them to a new location.

   Copy to Other Folder to leave the original files unchanged but rename the copies and move them to a new location (this is a quick way

to duplicate a batch of photos). We recommend using this option, especially if you didn't elect to copy your photos when you downloaded them.

For the Move or Copy option, also click **Browse**, choose or create a new folder, then click Open.

5. In the New Filenames area, specify data to be included in the names: **Text** (enter the desired name); **Date Time** (choose options from both menus); and **Sequence Number** to include an incremental number in the names (enter a starting number and choose a digit option).

   To add another row of criteria fields, click the ⊕ button, or to remove a row of fields, click the ⊖ button.

   Click **Preview** to view a listing of the new file names, then click OK to exit that dialog.

6. Under Options, leave Preserve Current Filename in XMP Metadata unchecked (unless you need to preserve the old names), but for **Compatibility**, check any other operating system in which you want your renamed files to be readable.

7. *Optional:* To save the current New Filenames and Options settings as a preset for future use, click Save, enter a name, then click OK. Your custom preset will appear on the Preset menu.

8. To apply your naming choices to the selected thumbnails, click Rename.

A *Via the Batch Rename dialog, you can quickly rename an entire folder full of photos.*

Searching for files

To find files via Bridge:

1. In Bridge, choose Edit > **Find** (Ctrl-F/Cmd-F). The Find dialog opens. A

2. From the **Look In** menu in the Source area, choose the folder to be searched (by default, the current folder is listed). To select a folder that isn't listed on the menu, choose Look In: Browse, locate the desired folder, then click Open.

3. From the menus in the **Criteria** area, choose search criteria (e.g., Filename, Date Created, Keywords, Label, Rating, or camera settings), choose a parameter from the adjoining menu, and enter data in the field. To add another criterion to the search, click the ⊕ button, or to remove a row of fields, click ⊖.

4. From the **Match** menu, choose "If any criteria are met" to find files based on one or more of the criteria you have specified, or choose "If all criteria are met" to narrow the selection to just the files that meet all your criteria.

5. Check **Include All Subfolders** to include, in the search, any of the subfolders that are inside the folder you chose in step 2.

6. *Optional:* Check Include Non-Indexed Files to search through files that Bridge hasn't yet indexed (any folder Bridge has yet to display). As indicated, this could slow down the search.

7. Click Find. The results of the search will be placed in a temporary folder called Search Results: [name of source folder] and will display in the Content panel. B The folder will be listed on the Path bar and on the Reveal Recent File or Go to Recent Folder menu 📷 on the Bridge toolbar.

8. To create a collection from the results of the search, see the following page.

▶ To discard the current search results and start a new search, click New Search, or to cancel the results, click the Cancel button. ⊠

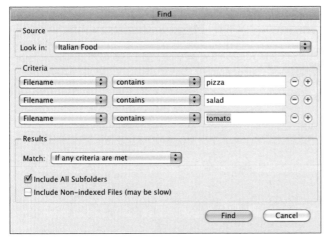

A *We entered three criteria in the Find dialog (then we clicked Find).*

QUICK SEARCH FOR A FILE

In the Favorites panel, click Computer, then double-click the thumbnail for your hard drive; or navigate to a particular folder. In the search field 🔍▾ on the Bridge toolbar, type the name of the file you're looking for or a keyword, then press Enter/Return.

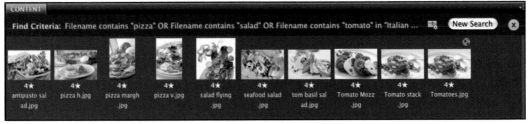

B *The results from our search appeared in the Content panel. The parameters used for the search and the folder that was searched are listed next to "Find Criteria."*

Creating and using collections

Using the collection features in Bridge, you can catalog your file thumbnails without having to relocate
the actual files. There are two kinds of collections: a
Smart Collection that you create from the results of a
Find search, and what we call a "nonsmart" collection,
which is created by dragging thumbnails manually.

To create a Smart Collection:

1. Click the tab for the Collections panel. (If it's
hidden, choose Window > Collections Panel.)

2. Perform a search via the Edit > Find command
(see the preceding page). When the search is
completed, click the **Save as Smart Collection**
button ![icon] at the top of the Content panel. A

3. A new Smart Collection icon ![icon] appears in the
Collections panel. Type a name in the highlighted field, then press Enter/Return. B

➤ To add a collection to the Favorites panel, right-
click the icon and choose Add to Favorites.

➤ To delete a collection, click it, click the Delete
Collection button,![icon] then click Yes if an alert
dialog appears (this won't delete the actual files).

To display the contents of a collection:

In the Collections panel, click the icon or name
of a Smart Collection. ![icon]

If you run a new search for an existing Smart
Collection based on new criteria, the contents of the
collection will update automatically.

To edit a Smart Collection:

1. In the Collections panel, click the icon for an
existing Smart Collection. ![icon]

2. At the top of the Content panel or in the lower-
left corner of the Collections panel, click the **Edit
Smart Collection** button. ![icon] C

3. The Edit Smart Collection dialog opens. It looks
just like the Find dialog, which is shown on the
preceding page. To add another criterion, click
the next ⊕ button, choose and enter data, and
choose "If any criteria are met" from the Match
menu. You can also change the source folder
and/or change or eliminate the original criteria.

4. Click Save. The results of the new search will
display in the Content panel.

Note: If you move a thumbnail from a Smart
Collection (or move the actual file) into a folder
that wasn't used in the search, it will be removed
from the collection, but not from your hard
disk. If you delete a thumbnail from a Smart
Collection, on the other hand — *watch out!* — the
actual file will be deleted from your hard disk!

A *To create a
Smart Collection,
use the Find com-
mand, then click
the Save as Smart
Collection button in
the Content panel.*

B *A new Smart
Collection appears
on the Collections
panel. Type a name
for it in the field.*

C *To edit a Smart
Collection, click its icon
in the Collections panel,
then click the Edit Smart
Collection button.*

You can also create a collection without running a search first. We call this a "nonsmart" collection.

To create a nonsmart collection:

1. Do either of the following:

   On the Content panel, select the image thumbnails to be put into a collection. In the **Collections** panel, click the **New Collection** button, then click Yes in the alert dialog.

   While viewing some thumbnails in **Review mode** (Ctrl-B/Cmd-B), drag any files you don't want to include in the collection out of the carousel, then click the **New Collection** button.

2. Type a name in the highlighted field in the Collection panel.**A** The number of thumbnails the collection contains is listed next to the name.

To add thumbnails to a nonsmart collection:

1. Display the Collections panel.

2. Drag one or more thumbnails from the Content panel over a nonsmart collection icon. **B**

➤ You can copy and paste thumbnails from a Smart Collection into a nonsmart one, or from one nonsmart collection into another. You can't drag thumbnails into a Smart Collection.

To remove thumbnails from a nonsmart collection:

1. On the Collections panel, click the icon for a nonsmart collection to display its contents.

2. Select the thumbnails to be removed, then click **Remove from Collection** at the top of the Content panel.**C**

If you rename a file in Explorer/Finder or move a file from its original location on disk, it may be listed as missing from any nonsmart collections it is a part of, and Bridge will try to relink it to those collections. If Bridge is unsuccessful, do as follows.

To relink a missing file to a nonsmart collection:

1. On the Collections panel, click the collection to which you need to relink one or more files.

2. At the top of the Content panel, click **Fix.D**

3. In the Find Missing Files dialog, click Browse, click the missing file (the name is listed at the top of the dialog), click Open, then click OK.

A To create a nonsmart collection, click the New Collection button, then type a name for it.

B Drag thumbnails to a nonsmart collection listing.

C To remove selected thumbnails from the currently displayed collection, click Remove from Collection.

D To relink a file that's missing from a collection, click Fix.

Using Mini Bridge

Mini Bridge is a compact version of Bridge that you access as a panel in Photoshop. What is called a panel in Bridge is known as a pod in Mini Bridge. The interface has changed significantly from version CS5 (menus were moved, the ability to enlarge one preview in the panel was eliminated for some unfortunate reason, etc.) and takes some getting used to.

To preview files in Mini Bridge: ★

1. Go to Photoshop. If the Mini Bridge panel is hidden, choose either Window > Extensions > **Mini Bridge** or File > **Browse in Mini Bridge** to display it (**A**, next page).

   ➤ If you widen the Mini Bridge panel (drag an edge), the thumbnails will display on the right side; if you narrow it, the thumbnails will display below the Navigation pod.

2. If Bridge isn't running, a "Bridge must be running to browse files" message will display in the Mini Bridge panel; click **Launch Bridge**. Similarly, if you exit/quit Bridge, a "Bridge has disconnected" message will display; click **Reconnect**.

3. If the Navigation pod is hidden, choose **Show Navigation Pod** from the panel menu, and if the toolbar is hidden, choose **Show Tool Bar**.

4. To locate the desired files, from the menu in the Navigation pod, choose **Computer**, the User folder, **Favorites**, **Recent Folders**, **Recent Files**, or **Collections**. Next, click a hard drive, folder, or collection; or if you chose Recent Files, click Photoshop. Click a folder on the list to display its files, or double-click a folder to list its subfolders (if any).

   ➤ To return to a parent folder at any time, either double-click the twin dots at the top of the Navigation pod or click the parent folder name on the Path bar.

   Note: In this new interface, folders don't display as thumbnails in the Content pod.

5. If the Mini Bridge panel is floating (not docked), you can adjust the thumbnail size via the **Thumbnail Size** slider at the bottom of the panel. You can also click the button to the left or right of the slider to restore the last Smaller Thumbnail Size or last Larger Thumbnail Size, respectively.

6. From the **View** menu, ▦▾ Show submenu, choose an option for the display of metadata below the thumbnails, such as Thumbnail Only, File Name, Labels and Ratings, Date Created, or Date Modified. (To identify a thumbnail if metadata is currently hidden, use the Tool Tips.)

7. To sort the image thumbnails, from the **Sort** menu, ⬍▾ choose a criterion, such as By Filename, By Date Created, or By Rating.

8. To filter thumbnails based on ratings that were applied to them in Bridge, check one or more criteria on the **Filter Items by Rating** menu, ▼▾ such as Show 3 or More Stars.

   ➤ Check Keep Filter When Browsing on the same menu to have Mini Bridge filter other folders that you browse using the same criteria.

9. To display a thumbnail as a large preview, do either of the following:

   For a full-screen preview, click the image thumbnail, then press the **Spacebar**. To return to Mini Bridge, press the Spacebar or Esc.

   To preview multiple thumbnails as a slideshow or in Review mode, Ctrl-click/Cmd-click to select them, then from the View menu ▦▾ or the context menu, choose **Slideshow** or **Review Mode** (for the latter, see page 33). To return to Mini Bridge, press Esc.

➤ To add a file to the list of Favorites, right-click the thumbnail and choose Add to Favorites from the context menu. To add the current folder to the list of Favorites, from the bottom of the menu in the Navigation pod, choose Add to Favorites. To remove a folder or file from the list of favorites, right-click it and choose Remove from Favorites.

➤ To rename a file, right-click it and choose Rename. After you alter a thumbnail in some way in Bridge (e.g., rename, duplicate, or move it), if it doesn't update automatically in Mini Bridge, choose Refresh on the View menu ▦▾ in Mini Bridge.

➤ To view a selected image thumbnail in Bridge, either click the Reveal in Bridge button ⬚ at the top of the Mini Bridge panel, or right-click the thumbnail and choose Reveal in Bridge from the context menu.

➤ To display a large preview of the currently selected thumbnail in the Content pod, move the Thumbnail Size slider to the far right (then move it back again). This is a primitive substitute for the defunct Shift-Spacebar shortcut.

Tool | Reveal in | View | Sort | Path bar | Filter Items by | | Show or hide the Navigation
bar | Bridge | menu | menu | | Rating menu | Search | pod and/or toolbar

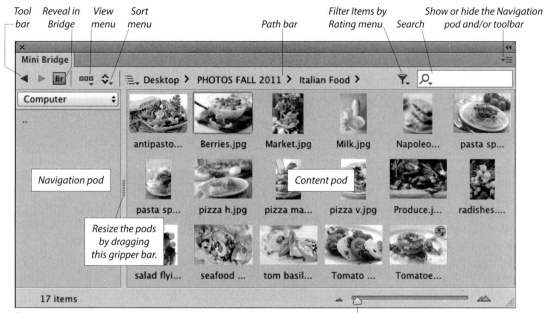

A *The Mini Bridge panel in Photoshop offers many of the same features as Adobe Bridge, except in a more compact, convenient size.*

Thumbnail Size slider

To open files from Mini Bridge into Photoshop:

1. Select one or more image thumbnails.

2. Do one of the following:

   Double-click one of the selected thumbnails. Note: If the file was previously edited in Camera Raw, it will open into Camera Raw (see Chapter 4).

   Drag one of the thumbnails into the Application frame in Photoshop, or onto the dark tab bar at the top of the frame. Depending on a preference setting, the file may arrive as a Smart Object; see page 250.

   Right-click a thumbnail and choose Open With > **Photoshop**.

   Click a **Favorites** file listing in the Navigation pod.

   Note: If any alerts appear, see page 35.

➤ If a file is in a format that can be edited in Camera Raw, you can right-click it and choose Open With > Camera Raw to open it into Camera Raw.

➤ Via the Photoshop submenu on the context menu for any image thumbnail in Mini Bridge, you can access some Photoshop commands, such as Place > In Photoshop (see page 250), Photoshop > Load Files into Photoshop Layers (see page 248), Photoshop > Merge to HDR Pro (see pages 234–237), and Photoshop > Photomerge (see pages 264–265).

FLOATING OR DOCKING THE MINI BRIDGE PANEL

➤ You can float the Mini Bridge panel, dock it in any panel dock, or dock it at the bottom of the Application frame (drag the top bar until the horizontal blue drop zone line appears).

➤ To minimize the panel to a bar, or to expand it to its former size, double-click the panel tab.

SEARCHING FOR FILES VIA MINI BRIDGE

To locate a file in the current folder, start typing the file name without clicking anywhere first; the thumbnail bearing the closest match, if found, will become selected. Or click in the Search field, type a file name, then press Enter/Return; Mini Bridge will search the current folder and any nested subfolders and display the results in a temporary folder. (To return to the last folder, you can click either the Go Back arrow or the parent folder name on the Path bar.)

Exporting the Bridge cache

When the contents of a particular folder are displayed in the Content panel in Bridge for the first time, Bridge creates its own hidden cache files pertaining to those files, and places them in the same folder. Bridge uses the cache to display program features, such as ratings, labels, and high-quality thumbnails. You will notice that the thumbnails in a given folder redisplay more quickly once the cache has been created. Note: These hidden cache files can be read and used only by Bridge.

By setting the following preference, as we recommend, you can ensure that Bridge will include its own cache data with any files that you copy to a removable disc or to a shared folder on a network.

To set a preference to have Bridge export the cache automatically:

1. In Bridge, choose Edit/Adobe Bridge CS6 > Preferences (Ctrl-K/Cmd-K) > Cache.

2. Under Options, check **Automatically Export Cache to Folders When Possible**, then click OK.

If for some reason the cache preference is turned off and you need to export the cache for the files in a specific folder, you may do so via the steps below. The hidden cache files will be placed in the current folder and will also be included if you move or copy the image files.

To export the Bridge cache for the current folder:

1. Display the contents of a folder in Bridge.

2. Choose Tools > Cache > **Build and Export Cache**.

3. In the Build Cache dialog, keep the Build 100% Previews option off but check **Export Cache to Folders**, then click OK.

To display the cache file icons in the current folder:

1. Display a folder in the Content panel.

2. Choose View > **Show Hidden Files**.

If Bridge is having trouble displaying a particular folder of thumbnails, you can usually solve the problem by purging the cache for those thumbnails, which prompts Bridge to rebuild the cache.

To purge cache files from the current folder:

Do either of the following:

To purge all the cache files from the current folder, choose Tools > Cache > **Purge Cache for Folder** "[current folder name]." Multiple new (hidden) cache files will be generated.

To purge the cache files for specific thumbnails, select them, then right-click one of them and choose **Purge Cache for Selection**.

Using the powerful controls in the Adobe Camera Raw plug-in, you can apply corrections to your photos before opening them into Photoshop. In this chapter, you'll learn how to open digital photos into the Camera Raw dialog and then use the controls to correct for defects, such as poor contrast, under- or overexposure, color casts, blurriness, under- and oversaturation, and noise. You will also learn how to enhance your photos with special effects, such as a vignette, grain texture, or tint; merge multiple exposures of the same photo; retouch blemishes; and save your Camera Raw settings as presets.

Notes: The Camera Raw plug-in is included with Photoshop. We refer to the dialog simply as "Camera Raw." Some users also refer to the plug-in as "ACR," short for Adobe Camera Raw.

Why use Camera Raw?

Amateur-level digital cameras store images in the JPEG or TIFF format, whereas advanced amateur and pro models offer the option to save images as raw data files, which offers substantial advantages. The camera applies internal processing to photos that are captured as JPEG or TIFF, such as sharpening, setting the white balance, and automatic color adjustments. With raw files, you get only the original raw information that the lens captured onto the camera's digital sensor, leaving you with full control over subsequent image processing and correction. Each camera manufacturer creates its own variation of a raw file. (For a further discussion of raw files versus JPEG and TIFF files, see page 53.)

The following are some of the advantages to using Camera Raw:

➤ Camera Raw can process raw, TIFF, and JPEG photos from most digital camera models.

➤ Camera Raw offers powerful controls for correcting problems in your photos, such as over- and underexposure and color casts, and for adding enhancements, such as a vignette or a grain texture.

➤ In the case of raw files, Camera Raw edits are saved as instructions in either a separate "sidecar" file or in the Camera Raw database. For TIFF and JPEG files, the instructions are saved in the photo file itself. When you open a photo from Camera Raw into Photoshop, regardless of the file format, the instructions (corrections) are applied to a copy of the file.

CAMERA RAW

4

IN THIS CHAPTER

More reasons to use Camera Raw

In case you're not fully convinced, we'll explore more reasons for using the Camera Raw plug-in instead of opening your digital photos directly into Photoshop.

Ability to preview raw files: The only way to preview a raw photo is through a raw converter, such as Camera Raw. Note: The photo that you view on the LCD screen of your digital camera is merely a JPEG preview of the raw capture, not the "actual" raw capture.

Great correction features: Camera Raw offers many unique and powerful adjustment controls that you simply won't find in Photoshop.

Less-destructive edits: When applying corrections to a photo, the goal is to preserve as much of the image quality as possible. Adjustments that are made to a photo in Camera Raw (and that are applied automatically when the photo is opened in Photoshop) cause less data loss than similar adjustment commands in Photoshop.

16 bits per channel: To preserve more of the original pixel data in a raw photo, Camera Raw keeps the bit depth as 16 bits per channel. Having more original data at the outset helps offset the data loss from subsequent image edits that are made in Photoshop, so the end result is a better-quality photo.

Tonal redistribution: The sensor in a digital camera captures and records the existing range of tonal values in a scene as is, in a linear fashion, without skewing the data toward a particular tonal range. **A** That sounds fine on paper, but the reality is that the human eye is more sensitive to lower light levels than to higher light levels. In other words, we're more likely to notice if shadow areas lack detail and less likely to notice extra details in highlight areas. The result is that digital photos often contain more data than is needed about the highlight values in a scene and insufficient data about the lower midtone and shadow values. In a Camera Raw conversion, data in your photo is shifted more into the midtone and shadow ranges, which not only helps compensate for this peculiarity of human vision, but also helps prepare your photos for subsequent image edits in Photoshop. **B** If you apply tonal adjustments in Photoshop to a photo that contains insufficient shadow data, the result is posterization and a noticeable loss of detail; if you apply the same edits to a photo that has been converted in Camera Raw, the destructive edits will be far less noticeable.

Superior noise reduction and **sharpening**: Not to knock Photoshop, but the noise reduction and sharpening features in Camera Raw are easier to use, cause less data loss, and are more effective than similar features in Photoshop.

Learning about Camera Raw will give you a head start: The Camera Raw controls that you will use to apply tonal and color corrections to your photos are similar to many of the adjustment controls in Photoshop (e.g., Levels, Curves, and Hue/Saturation) that we explore in later chapters. As you proceed through the lessons in this book, you will build on the skills you have mastered in this chapter.

CAPTURING TONAL VALUES: YOUR CAMERA VERSUS THE HUMAN EYE

50% light value

50% light value

A *The digital sensor in a camera captures tonal values in a linear fashion, from light to dark, without altering the incoming data. A light value of 50% is at the midpoint of the tonal range.*

B *Camera Raw redistributes some of the captured tonal values to the shadows and midtones, shifting the 50% light value past the midpoint. As a result, the lower tonal values, in the range the human eye is more sensitive to, contain more data.*

Raw, JPEG, or TIFF?

Unfortunately, Camera Raw can't correct deficiencies in digital JPEG and TIFF photos as fully as it can in raw photos, for several reasons. First, digital JPEG and TIFF photos have been processed down to a bit depth of only 8 bits per channel by the camera, unlike raw photos, in which all of the captured pixels are preserved and are saved at a bit depth of 16 bits per channel.

Secondly, color and tonal processing is applied to JPEGs and TIFFs by the camera ("in camera"). Camera Raw must reinterpret this processed data, with less successful results than when it has access to the raw, unprocessed data.

All of the above notwithstanding, if your camera doesn't shoot raw photos or you acquire JPEG or TIFF photos from other sources, you can still use practically all of the outstanding correction and adjustment features in Camera Raw to process them.

Note: In this chapter, we focus only on processing raw and JPEG files in Camera Raw — not TIFFs. The JPEG format is mentioned only when a particular feature treats JPEGs differently from the way it treats raw files.

➤ Each digital camera model attaches a different extension to the names of its raw files, such as .nef for Nikon and .crw or .cr2 for Canon.

KEEPING CAMERA RAW UP TO DATE

Of the many proprietary raw "formats," some are unique to each manufacturer (such as Nikon or Canon) and some are unique to each camera model. To ensure that the latest interpreters for the raw formats that Camera Raw supports are installed in your system, visit www.adobe.com periodically and download any Camera Raw updates that are posted for your camera.

JPEG ...

JPEG advantages

➤ JPEG files have a smaller storage size than raw files, enabling your digital camera to store more of them.

➤ In sports, nature, and other fast-action photography, speed is a necessity. Photo sequences can be captured more rapidly as JPEG files (due to their smaller storage sizes) than as raw files.

➤ Most software programs can read JPEG files, but only a few programs can read raw files.

JPEG drawbacks

➤ The JPEG format discards some captured pixels due to its lower bit depth of 8 bits per channel.

➤ The JPEG compression methods destroy some image data and can produce defects, such as artifacts, banding, and loss of detail.

➤ The pixel data in JPEG photos is processed internally by the camera. Although Camera Raw can be used to improve your JPEG photos, it won't have access to the original pixel data (nor will you).

... COMPARED TO RAW

Raw advantages

➤ The raw compression methods are nondestructive.

➤ Raw files contain the original, unprocessed pixel data and full range of tonal levels that were captured by the camera. Camera Raw is given all that image data to work with, and the result is higher-quality images — even after adjustments.

➤ Because the white point setting isn't applied to your raw photo (it's merely stored in the metadata of the file), you can adjust that setting at any time in Camera Raw.

➤ Camera Raw does a better job of redistributing tonal values in raw files than in JPEG files, making them better candidates for Photoshop edits.

➤ Raw files have a higher bit depth of 16 bits per channel.

Raw drawbacks

➤ Raw files have larger storage sizes than JPEG files.

➤ Digital cameras create and store raw files more slowly than JPEG files, a potential drawback for fast-action photographers (although as camera technology improves, this may become less of an issue).

The bottom line

Despite the faster speed and smaller storage sizes of JPEG files, raw files offer more advantages.

Opening photos into Camera Raw

To standardize your workflow, we recommend setting a preference so your JPEG or TIFF photos will open directly into Camera Raw instead of into Photoshop.

To set a preference so your raw photos open directly into Camera Raw:

1. In Photoshop, go to Edit/Photoshop > Preferences (Ctrl-K/Cmd-K) > File Handling.

2. Under File Compatibility, check **Prefer Adobe Camera Raw for Supported Raw Files**, then click OK. When you double-click a raw file, it will open into Camera Raw (as opposed to other software that converts raw files).

To set a preference so your JPEG or TIFF photos open directly into Camera Raw:

1. In Bridge, choose Edit/Adobe Bridge CS6 > Camera Raw Preferences.

2. At the bottom of the dialog, from the JPEG menu, choose **Automatically Open JPEGs with Settings**, and from the TIFF menu, choose **Automatically Open TIFFs with Settings**, then click OK (see the Note below).

   Now if you click a JPEG or TIFF photo thumbnail in Bridge, then click the Open in Camera Raw button ⬆ or press Ctrl-R/Cmd-R, the file will open into Camera Raw.

   Note: If you shoot only raw or JPEG photos (not TIFF photos), you can use the approach that we follow to have your raw and JPEG photos open into Camera Raw and your TIFF files open directly into Photoshop: Choose the JPEG setting we recommend in step 2 (in this task), but for the TIFF setting, choose Disable TIFF Support.

➤ If you have chosen both Automatically Open options suggested above, but for some reason you want to open a JPEG or TIFF photo directly into Photoshop instead of into Camera Raw (and if the file hasn't yet been edited in Camera Raw), click the thumbnail, then press Ctrl-O/Cmd-O.

➤ If the Open in Camera Raw button ⬆ is available when you click a thumbnail, you know that the file can be opened into Camera Raw.

You can set a preference to have either Bridge or Photoshop "host" the Camera Raw plug-in when you open a raw or JPEG photo. In the case of Photoshop, the program will launch, if it's not already running.

To choose a host for Camera Raw:

1. In Bridge, choose Edit/Adobe Bridge CS6 > Preferences (Ctrl-K/Cmd-K) > General.

2. Check **Double-Click Edits Camera Raw Settings in Bridge** if you want the Camera Raw dialog to be hosted by Bridge when you double-click the thumbnail in Bridge for a raw photo or for a JPEG that was previously edited in Camera Raw, or uncheck this option to have those files open into Camera Raw, hosted by Photoshop. Click OK.

   Note: When Bridge is the host for Camera Raw, the default button for exiting that dialog is labeled Done, whereas when Photoshop is the host for Camera Raw, the default exit button is Open Image. (If the button is labeled Open Object instead of Open Image, see the tip on page 58.)

UPDATING PHOTOS FROM CAMERA RAW 6.X

When you bring a new, unprocessed photo into Camera Raw 7.x, the dialog uses the most up-to-date profiles for noise reduction, demosaicing, sharpening, color calibration, and other processing. If you want to update a raw photo that was processed in Camera Raw 6 (or earlier) using the new profiles, before applying any custom adjustments, click the ⚠ icon in the bottom right of the preview window; the Process menu in the Camera Calibration tab ⚫ changes to the setting of 2012 (Current). Note: If you want to preserve access to the older rendering of the photo, take a snapshot of it before you update it (see page 81).

RECOGNIZING THE BADGE

In Bridge, the thumbnail for a file that has been opened and edited previously in Camera Raw will display this badge ⬛ in the upper-right corner, and the thumbnail and preview will show the effect of the current settings. Also, if the currently selected file has been edited in Camera Raw, you will see a Camera Raw category in the Metadata panel.

After setting the necessary preferences, familiarize yourself with these generic steps for opening and processing photos in Camera Raw.

To open a raw or JPEG digital photo into Camera Raw:

1. Launch Bridge, display the thumbnail for a raw or JPEG photo, then do either of the following:

   For a raw photo, double-click the thumbnail.

   For a raw or JPEG photo, click the thumbnail, then press Ctrl-R/Cmd-R or click the **Open in Camera Raw** button on the Bridge toolbar ⬆ (or right-click the photo in standard or Review mode and choose Open in Camera Raw).

   ➤ To open a file from the Mini Bridge panel in Photoshop into Camera Raw, right-click the thumbnail and choose Open With > Camera Raw from the context menu.

2. The Camera Raw dialog opens.A An alert symbol ⚠ may display in the upper-right corner of the preview while Camera Raw reads in the image data, and will disappear when it's done.

Information about your photo (taken from the metadata that was embedded into it by the camera) is listed in several locations: the camera model in the title bar at the top of the dialog; the file name below the preview; and the camera settings used to take the photo (aperture, shutter speed, ISO, and focal length) below the histogram.

The adjustment features are found in 10 tabs: Basic, Tone Curve, Detail, HSL/Grayscale, Split Toning, Lens Corrections, Effects, Camera Calibration, Presets, and Snapshots. Switch among the tabs to correct your photo (we cover most of the tabs in depth in this chapter).

3. When you're done correcting the photo, you can either click Open Image to open the photo into Photoshop or click Done to close Camera Raw without opening the photo. In either case, the Camera Raw settings will stick to the photo, and the original data will be preserved.

A *The Camera Raw dialog*   *Toolbox*   *Camera model*   *Toggle Full Screen Mode/previous dialog size (F)*

Zoom controls

Histogram

The original camera settings

Tabs (access to settings)

Camera Raw Settings menu

The Camera Raw tools A

In the upper-left corner of the dialog, click the **Zoom** tool, 🔍 then click the image preview to zoom in or Alt-click/Option-click it to zoom out.

Use the **Hand** tool 🖐 to move a magnified preview image in its window (or if another tool is selected, hold down the Spacebar for a temporary Hand tool).

For the **White Balance** tool, 🖊 see the sidebar on page 60.

Choose the **Color Sampler** tool, 🖊 then click in the image preview to place up to nine samplers. A readout pertaining to the RGB components below each sampler displays below the tool box; the readouts will update as you make color and tonal adjustments. To reposition a sampler, drag it with the Color Sampler tool. To remove all samplers, click Clear Samplers.

For the **Targeted Adjustment** tool 🎯 (or TAT for short), see pages 66–67 and 71.

For the **Crop** 🔲 and **Straighten** 📐 tools, see the facing page.

For the **Spot Removal** 🖊 tool, see page 80.

The **Red-Eye Removal** tool 🔴 works like the Red-Eye tool in Photoshop (for the latter, see page 293).

For the **Adjustment Brush** tool, 🖌 see pages 72–74.

For the **Graduated Filter** tool, ▭ see pages 78–79.

Note: If tool settings are displaying on the right side of the Camera Raw dialog (e.g., if you were using the Adjustment Brush tool) and you want to redisplay the row of tab icons, click one of the first seven tools.

➤ The tools in Camera Raw are "memory-loaded," meaning that you can toggle them. Press a tool shortcut to select a different tool, then press the same key again to return to the original tool.

Other buttons at the top of the dialog:

➤ The **Open Preferences Dialog** button ☰ (or press Ctrl-K/Cmd-K) opens the Camera Raw Preferences dialog.

➤ The **Rotate 90° Counterclockwise** button ↺ and the **Rotate 90° Clockwise** button ↻ rotate the image. The results preview in the dialog.

MORE WAYS TO ZOOM IN THE PREVIEW

➤ Hold down Alt/Option-Spacebar and click to zoom out, or hold down Ctrl/Cmd-Spacebar and click to zoom in.

➤ Press Ctrl –/Cmd – (hyphen) to zoom out or Ctrl-+/Cmd-+ to zoom in.

➤ Use the zoom buttons (– or +) or the Zoom Level menu, located below the image preview.

➤ Double-click the Zoom tool to set the zoom level to 100%.

➤ Double-click the Hand tool to fit the image in the preview window.

Enough options for you?

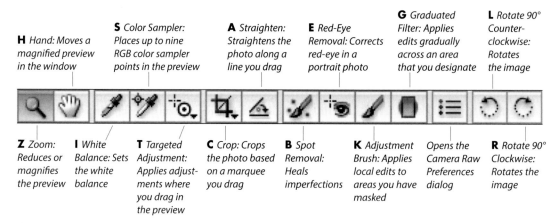

G Graduated	**L** Rotate 90°
	S Color Sampler:	**A** Straighten:	**E** Red-Eye	Filter: Applies	Counter-
H Hand: Moves a	Places up to nine	Straightens the	Removal: Corrects	edits gradually	clockwise:
magnified preview	RGB color sampler	photo along a	red-eye in a	across an area	Rotates
in the window	points in the preview	line you drag	portrait photo	that you designate	the image

Z Zoom: Reduces or magnifies the preview — **I** White Balance: Sets the white balance — **T** Targeted Adjustment: Applies adjustments where you drag in the preview — **C** Crop: Crops the photo based on a marquee you drag — **B** Spot Removal: Heals imperfections — **K** Adjustment Brush: Applies local edits to areas you have masked — Opens the Camera Raw Preferences dialog — **R** Rotate 90° Clockwise: Rotates the image

A The shortcuts for the Camera Raw tools are listed in boldface above.

Cropping and straightening photos

With the Crop and Straighten tools, you can control which portion of a photo opens into Photoshop. You can readjust the crop box at any time without losing any image data, and the outlying areas will remain available even after you click Save, Done, or Open.

To crop a photo:

1. Open a photo into Camera Raw (see step 1 on page 55). Choose the **Crop** tool 🔲 (C).

2. Drag a crop box in the preview image.**A** To move the box, drag inside it; to resize it, drag a handle.

3. To preview the crop results, press Enter/Return or click another tool.

To straighten a crooked photo:

1. Choose the **Straighten** tool 🔺 (A).

2. Drag along an edge in the photo that you want to align to the horizontal or vertical axis.**B** A crop box will display, aligned to the angle you drew.**C**

3. To preview the straighten results, press Enter/ Return or click another tool.**D**

➤ To redisplay the current crop box after using another tool, click the Crop or Straighten tool again. If you want to remove the box, press Esc.

A *With the Crop tool, we drew a crop box in the preview window. Here, we are resizing the box.*

B *With the Straighten tool, we are dragging along an edge that we want to align to the vertical or horizontal axis.*

C *A crop box displays in Camera Raw.*

D *We pressed Enter/Return to preview the results.*

Choosing default workflow settings

Via the Workflow Options dialog, you can change the color space, dimensions, bit depth, and resolution of a photo before opening it into Photoshop — without altering the original digital file. Your choices will become the new default settings.

To choose default workflow settings:

1. Open a photo into Camera Raw, then at the bottom of the dialog, click the underlined link that lists the color space, bit depth, etc. The **Workflow Options** dialog opens.**A**

2. From the **Space** menu, choose a color profile to be used for converting the raw file to RGB: Adobe RGB (1998), ColorMatch RGB, ProPhoto RGB, or sRGB IEC61966-2.1 (or "sRGB," for short). In Chapter 1, you assigned Adobe RGB (1998) as the default color space for color management. To ensure color consistency, you should choose it here, too.

3. From the **Depth** menu, choose a color depth of 8 Bits/Channel or 16 Bits/Channel (see page 17). If you have a large hard disk and a fast system with a lot of RAM, choose 16 Bits/Channel. With the extra pixels, more of the original tonal levels in your photo will be preserved when you edit it in Photoshop.

4. If you need to resize the image, from the **Size** menu, choose a preset size (in megapixels) that matches the proportions of the raw image. (The default size is the one without a minus sign – or plus sign +.) Resampling will occur if you choose a larger size than the original. To help prevent loss of detail, avoid choosing the largest size. (Experts disagree on whether it's better to resample an image in Camera Raw or in Photoshop. Until a consensus is reached, you can decide for yourself.) Note: If the photo has a crop box, the Size menu will be labeled as Crop Size, and it will list the current crop size.

5. Enter a **Resolution**. This value affects only the print output size. (For instance, to output an image that is 2000 x 3000 pixels or larger to an inkjet printer or to a commercial press, you would choose a resolution of 240–300 ppi.)

6. *Optional:* From the Sharpen For menu, choose None, Screen, Glossy Paper, or Matte Paper; predefined output sharpening will be applied to your photo for that medium. From the Amount menu, choose the desired level of sharpening (Standard is usually a good choice).

   Note: The sharpening values that Camera Raw applies via this dialog aren't listed anywhere. If you want to control the sharpening values, choose None from the Sharpen For menu and use the sliders in the Detail tab instead (see page 68).

7. Click OK. The new workflow settings will be listed below the preview, and will be applied to the current photo and to photos that you subsequently open into Camera Raw.

➤ To have future photos open from Camera Raw into Photoshop as a Smart Object when you click Open Object, check Open in Photoshop as Smart Objects in the Workflow Options dialog (see page 249). Turn this feature on only if it suits your usual workflow.

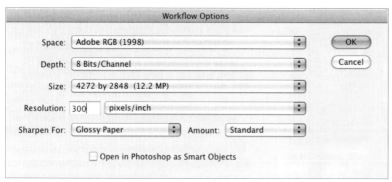

A *Use the Workflow Options dialog to choose color space, bit depth, size (dimensions), and resolution settings for the current — and future — photos.*

Using the Camera Raw tabs

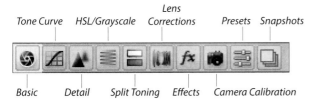

Click a tab icon to access a specialized category of options.

 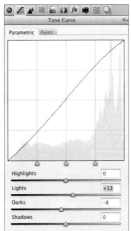  

Basic tab: Adjust the white balance and exposure (see pages 61–65).

Tone Curve tab: Fine-tune the midtones (see pages 66–67).

Detail tab: Apply capture sharpening and reduce noise (see pages 68–69).

HSL/Grayscale tab: Adjust the properties of individual colors (see pages 70–71).

In Camera Raw, we perform most of our correction work in the four tabs shown above.

To restore default settings to sliders in the Camera Raw tabs:

As you work in Camera Raw, you may find a need to undo or reset your slider settings. Use any of the following methods:

➤ Double-click a slider to reset its value to 0 (or, in the Detail tab, to the default value).

➤ Shift-double-click a slider in the Basic tab to reset it to the **Auto** value.

➤ Click **Default** in the Basic or HSL/Grayscale tab to reset all the sliders in just the current tab to 0.

➤ Hold down Alt/Option and click **Reset** (Cancel becomes Reset) to restore the settings, in all tabs, that were in effect when you opened the dialog.

(To learn about related options on the Camera Raw Settings menu, see the next page.)

USING THE SCRUBBIES

To change a value quickly in a Camera Raw tab, instead of dragging a slider, drag to the left or right across the slider name (this is called a scrubby-slider).

TOGGLING THE PREVIEW

Check Preview at the top of the Camera Raw dialog (or press P) to preview changes made in all the tabs; or uncheck Preview to view the result of changes made in all the tabs except the current one, so you can compare the photo with and without the latest changes.

When you open a photo into Camera Raw, by default, it's adjusted according to the built-in profile that was created for your camera model. Also, all the sliders in the Basic tab are set to 0 automatically. To assign a different collection of settings to your file, or to restore the original settings, see the options below.

To restore settings via the Camera Raw Settings menu:

From the Camera Raw Settings menu, ☰ ◢ choose one of these options: A

Image Settings to restore the settings that were attached to the file from either the initial photo shoot or a prior Camera Raw session. When a photo is first opened into Camera Raw, these settings will be the same as the Camera Raw Defaults settings.

Camera Raw Defaults to remove any custom settings and reapply the default settings for your camera model, your specific camera, or the ISO setting that was used to take the photo.

Previous Conversion to apply the settings from the last image that was adjusted in Camera Raw.

Custom Settings to reapply all the custom settings that you chose since opening the Camera Raw dialog.

If a user-saved preset is applied to the current photo, that preset will also be listed as an option on this menu (see page 81).

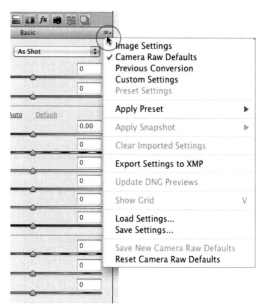

A Use options on the Camera Raw Settings menu to restore the default settings to your photo or to reapply the prior settings.

MAKING LENS CORRECTIONS

A color fringe may appear around the edges of high-contrast shapes if a camera lens doesn't focus all the wavelengths of colored light to precisely the same spot. To remove this fringe, display the nested Profile tab in the Lens Corrections tab, then check Remove Chromatic Aberration. ★ The other controls in the Lens Corrections tab are similar to those found in the Lens Correction filter dialog in Photoshop, which is covered on pages 318–319 and page 407.

DO YOUR BASIC SLIDERS LOOK DIFFERENT?

If you open a photo that was previously processed in Camera Raw 6.x or earlier but don't update the processing to 2012 (Current), the Basic tab will display the same sliders as in Camera Raw 6.x. To update the processing version so the Basic sliders match the ones we describe in this chapter, click the ⚠ icon in the lower-right corner of the preview window.

SETTING THE WHITE BALANCE

The color temperature of the lighting in which a photo is shot, whether natural or artificial, influences the relative amounts of red, green, and blue that are recorded by the camera. A digital camera attempts to balance those three colors to produce an accurate white, which in turn makes other colors in the photo more accurate; this is called the "white balance." In Camera Raw, you can further refine the white balance of your photo.

In the Camera Raw dialog, you could adjust the white balance of your photo with the White Balance tool 🖋 (by clicking the tool on a light gray area that contains some detail, as a sample area), but deciding which area to click can be tricky, so we use the Temperature and Tint sliders in the Basic tab instead, as described on the next page.

Using the Basic tab ★

The Basic tab is rightly named (and displays first, by default) because it contains the most essential correction features of Camera Raw. We have divided the use of this tab into several tasks, beginning with the White Balance sliders on this page, then proceeding through exposure, contrast, and saturation adjustments on pages 62–65.

Using the White Balance controls, you can begin by neutralizing the color temperature of your photo.

To apply white balance adjustments via the Basic tab:

1. With a photo open in Camera Raw, click the **Basic** tab, ⊙ A and double-click the Hand tool ✋ in the toolbox to fit the photo in the preview window.

2. Do either of the following:

    From the **White Balance** menu, choose a preset that best describes the lighting conditions in which the photo was taken. (Note: The presets are available only for raw files.) Choose As Shot at any time to restore the original camera settings.

    Lower the **Temperature** value to add blue and make the image look cooler, B or raise it to add yellow and make the image look warmer. C To fine-tune the temperature correction, move the **Tint** slider slightly to the left to add a bit of green or to the right to add magenta. (The White Balance menu listing changes to Custom, because you chose manual settings.)

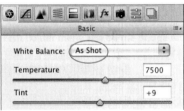

A When a photo is first opened into Camera Raw, the White Balance menu in the Basic tab is set to As Shot. This photo has a high Temperature value and looks too warm (yellowish).

B We lowered the Temperature value too much, so now the photo looks too cool (has a bluish cast).

C For this photo, a Temperature value of 5500 strikes the correct balance between warm and cool.

In the histogram in the Camera Raw dialog, the red, green, and blue areas represent the three color channels in a photo, and the white areas represent the areas where those three colors overlap. Clipping, the shifting of tonal values to absolute black or white in a photo, occurs if the tonal range of a scene is wider than the range that can be captured by the camera. You can tell that pixels are clipped in a photo if the vertical bars are clustered in tall peaks at one or both ends of the histogram (shadow pixels on the left, highlight pixels on the right).

In Camera Raw, your goal is to minimize clipping by bringing the pixels into the range of your chosen RGB color space. As you make slider adjustments, the tonal values in the photo will be redistributed, and the histogram will update accordingly. Note: Remember, we recommended that you choose Adobe RGB as the color space both for your camera (see page 8) and for Camera Raw (see page 58).

To turn on the histogram clipping warnings for the preview:

In the top left corner of the histogram, click the **Shadow Clipping Warning** button (U); **A** shadow clipping displays as blue. In the top right corner, click the **Highlight Clipping Warning** button (O); highlight clipping displays as red. (Note: When the buttons are activated, they have a white border.)

Next, use the middle batch of sliders in the Basic tab to apply tonal corrections to your photo, preferably in the order listed in the dialog (there's a logic to the sequence). At first, all the sliders are set to 0 and the underlined word "Default" is dimmed.

To apply exposure and contrast adjustments via the Basic tab: ★

1. Turn on the Clipping Warning buttons.

2. Use the **Exposure** slider to lighten or darken the entire photo, as needed.

3. Use the **Contrast** slider to increase or reduce the color intensity and tonal contrast (**A–B**, next page).

4. If you increased the contrast, more than likely the highlights and shadows now need to be adjusted:

   To restore details in the highlights, move the **Highlights** slider to the left until only a smidgen remains of the red highlight warning color.

Instructions continue on page 64

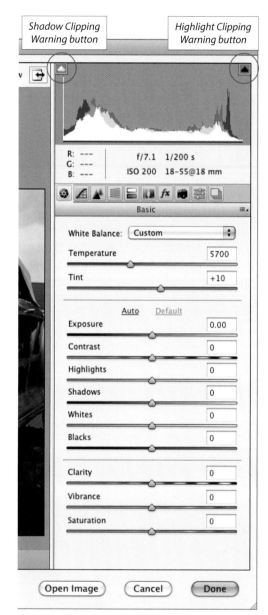

Shadow Clipping Warning button

Highlight Clipping Warning button

A *Use the Clipping Warning buttons to allow Camera Raw to display blue and red highlights on any clipped areas of your photo.*

A *This original photo is underexposed (too dark), so the colors look dull.*

B *The blue warning color in the preview alerts us that shadow details in the photo are clipped. Our goal is to lighten the overall photo and recover details in the midtones and shadows, without washing out the highlights. We increased the Exposure value in the Basic tab first, then increased the Contrast value to intensify the highlights, shadows, and color saturation. We're not concerned that the photo is still too dark, as we can lighten it with further adjustments.*

	Auto	Default
Exposure		+0.60
Contrast		+25
Highlights		0
Shadows		0
Whites		0
Blacks		0
Clarity		0
Vibrance		0
Saturation		0

To restore details in the shadows, move the **Shadows** slider to the right until only a smidgen remains of the blue shadow warning color. A (This slider is similar to the now defunct Fill Light slider.) Or if you need to darken the shadows, move this slider to the left.

5. Now that details have been restored to the mid-tones and highlights, you're ready to adjust the whites and blacks:

Increase the **Whites** value to brighten the white areas in the photo. This slider also has the effect of lightening the upper midtones and brightening the colors.

Use the **Blacks** slider to lighten or darken the black areas (A, next page). This slider may also affect the color brightness.

➤ If the colors are now washed out as a result of your increasing the Whites or Blacks value, one remedy is to try increasing the Contrast value.

➤ To further adjust the tonal values in the midtones, see pages 66–67.

REMOVE CLIPPING IN THRESHOLD PREVIEW

To remove shadow clipping a different way, Alt-drag/Option-drag the Shadows or Blacks slider. A Threshold preview displays (as shown below). Release the mouse when small amounts of color or black display in the white preview.

You can also Alt-drag/Option-drag the Exposure, Highlights, or Whites slider to display a Threshold preview for that adjustment. Release the mouse when only a smidgen of white displays in the dark preview.

	Auto	Default	
Exposure			+0.60
Contrast			+25
Highlights			−100
Shadows			+50
Whites			0
Blacks			0

A *We reduced the Highlights value to recover details in the sky and increased the Shadows value to recover details in the shadows and lower midtones. The colors and detail in the midtones, and the overall balance of lights and darks, are improved. However, reducing the Highlights value had the effect of making the white areas look dull.*

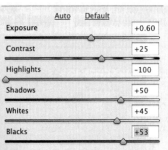

A We increased the Whites value to lighten the upper midtones and brighten the whites, and moved the Blacks slider to recover more details in the shadows. Overall, the brightness, as well as the colors, are much improved.

To apply edge contrast and color saturation adjustments using the Basic tab:

1. To add depth by adjusting the edge contrast in the midtones, increase the **Clarity** value, or reduce this value if you want to deliberately soften the photo (such as in a portrait or landscape).

2. Change the **Vibrance** value to adjust the color saturation.**B**

3. Turn off both clipping warnings by pressing U, then O.

➤ We recommend using the Vibrance slider instead of the Saturation slider to adjust color saturation because the former is less likely to cause oversaturation (and it protects skin tones), whereas the latter is more likely to cause oversaturation and highlight clipping. To view the effect of this, drag the Saturation slider to the far right.

B Finally, we increased the Clarity and Vibrance values slightly to intensify the details and color saturation (e.g., note the change on the car body). Our cumulative adjustments to this photo improved the contrast, clarified the details, and produced richer color. Vroom, vroom!

Using the Tone Curve tab

After using the Basic tab, a next logical step is to make a more refined adjustment of the upper and lower midtones, which we recommend performing individually via the Parametric sliders in the Tone Curve tab. (If you use Adobe Photoshop Lightroom, these Parametric controls will look familiar.)

Note: We avoid manipulating the curve in the nested Point tab, because a misshapen curve can cause a photo to look posterized. The sliders in the Parametric tab don't cause this problem.

To apply tonal adjustments using the Parametric sliders in the Tone Curve tab:

1. With a photo open in Camera Raw, A click the **Tone Curve** tab, ⬛ then the nested **Parametric** tab. Behind the curve you'll see a static display of the current histogram.

2. Do either of the following:

   If you adjusted the Highlights and Shadows sliders in the Basic tab, leave the Highlights or Shadows sliders in this tab alone and tweak the upper and lower midtones using the **Lights** and **Darks** sliders. If you didn't touch the Highlights and Shadows sliders in the Basic tab, you can use the **Highlights, Lights** (upper midtones), **Darks** (lower midtones), or **Shadows** sliders to lighten

or darken each tonal range. As you do this, the corresponding portion of the curve will be raised above or lowered below the diagonal line (**A–B**, next page).

Click the **Targeted Adjustment** tool ⊕ (T). Drag in an area of the photo where the tonal range needs adjustment (**C**, next page). As you do this, the slider and curve that correspond to the tonal range under the pointer will move accordingly.

➤ To boost the contrast in a photo, try moving the Lights slider to the right and the Darks slider to the left.

3. To control the range of tonal values that are affected by the slider adjustments you made in step 2, move any of the region controls (located below the graph). The left region control affects the Shadows slider, the right region control affects the Highlights slider, and the middle region control affects both the Lights and Darks sliders (**D–E**, next page). If moving the control raises the curve, adjacent tonal ranges are lightened; if moving the control lowers the curve, adjacent tonal ranges are darkened.

➤ To quickly select the Targeted Adjustment tool and display the Parametric sliders, press Ctrl-Alt-Shift-T/Cmd-Option-Shift-T.

A *In this photo, the midtones are so dark that few details are visible in those areas.*

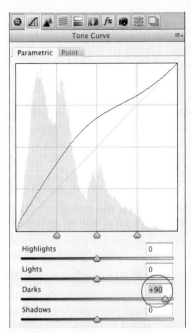

A To lighten the lower midtones, we increased the Darks value, which raised the middle of the curve.

B With the lower midtones now lighter, some details are now visible in the midtones, such as on the sides of the buildings and on the side and surface of the canal. However, the sky area looks a bit dull.

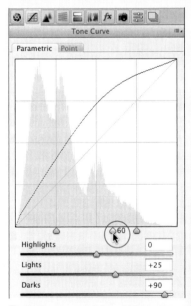

C To lighten the upper midtones (and thereby brighten the clouds, sky, and trees), we dragged upward over a light midtone area with the Targeted Adjustment tool; the Lights value increased automatically.

D Finally, we moved the middle region control slightly to the right, which further lightened the sky. (Both the tool and region control edits raised the upper section of the curve.)

E Now the tonal values in the image look just right.

Using the Detail tab

Via the Sharpening sliders in the Detail tab, you can adjust the sharpness of your photo (this is called "capture" sharpening), and via the Noise Reduction sliders, you can reduce any unwanted color noise.

To sharpen a photo using the Detail tab:

1. Click the **Detail** tab 🔺 **A** and choose a zoom level of 100%.

   ➤ To move a different area of the photo into view, hold down the Spacebar and drag.

   Note: If the words "Sharpening (Preview Only)" display at the top of the Detail tab, click the Open Preferences button ⁝≡ in the toolbox. In the Camera Raw Preferences dialog, choose Apply Sharpening To: All Images, then click OK.

2. Under **Sharpening**, use the **Amount** slider to adjust the degree of edge definition. For subject matter that needs a lot of sharpening, such as hard objects or buildings, set this slider to 100; if less sharpening is needed, try a value of 50–60 (for a JPEG photo, the default value is 0).

   ➤ To evaluate the sharpening effect for a slider using a grayscale preview, Alt-drag/Option-drag the slider, then release.

3. Use the **Radius** slider to control how many pixels surrounding an edge are modified. We recommend keeping this value between 1 and 1.3.

4. Alt-drag/Option-drag the **Detail** slider slightly to the right to sharpen edge details and textures.

5. Alt-drag/Option-drag the **Masking** slider to around 50 to protect low-contrast areas with a black mask, and thereby sharpen only high-contrast areas.

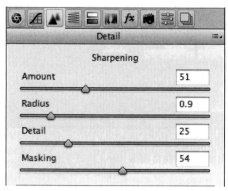

A These are the Sharpening controls in the Detail tab.

All digital cameras produce some luminance (gray-scale) noise and color artifacts (random extraneous pixels). Although budget cameras tend to produce the most noise, it can also be produced by a high-end camera, if used with a high ISO (light sensitivity) setting to capture a poorly lit scene. It's a good idea to remove as much noise from your photos as possible in Camera Raw, because it can become accentuated by image editing in Photoshop.

As you follow these steps, you'll discover that after you shift one slider, another one will need adjusting.

To reduce luminance and color noise using the Detail tab:

1. With a photo open in Camera Raw (**A**, next page), click the **Detail** tab 🔺 and choose a zoom level of 200–300% for the preview.

2. To reduce grayscale noise (graininess), increase the **Luminance** value (**B**, next page). Try a value between 20 and 70.

3. Raising the Luminance value can have the effect of smoothing out the high-contrast edges in a photo. To resharpen those edges, raise the **Luminance Detail** value, but not so much that noise is reintroduced (**C**, next page).

   ➤ To move a different area of the photo into view, hold down the Spacebar and drag.

4. Raise the **Luminance Contrast** value to restore some edge contrast. The effect of this slider is most noticeable in photos that contain a lot of noise.

5. Color artifacts and random speckling tend to be most noticeable in solid-color areas of a photo (e.g., flat surfaces), especially in shadow areas. To reduce these defects, increase the **Color** value from the default value of 25 to around 40–50, depending on the subject matter of the photo (for a JPEG photo, the default value is 0).

6. Raising the Color value may lower the intensity of colors in areas of the photo that were poorly lit. To restore some saturation and intensity to those areas, increase the **Color Detail** value from the default value of 50 to around 75, or until the color saturation looks just right (**D**, next page).

   ➤ To reduce noise in select areas, use the Adjustment Brush tool (see pages 72–74).

   ➤ To judge the overall effect of the settings you have chosen in this tab, lower the zoom level.

A *This is a close-up of a photo of a shop window (viewed at a zoom level of 300%), with the Noise Reduction: Luminance and Color sliders set to 0 (no noise reduction applied). Grayscale noise is evident in the signage, and color artifacts are evident on the poorly lit interior surfaces behind the letters.*

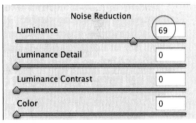

B *To remove noise from the letters, we increased the Luminance value to 69, but this also diminished the edge definition.*

C *To resharpen the edges of the letters, we increased the Luminance Detail value to 65.*

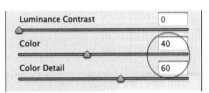

D *To remove color artifacts from the dark areas, we increased the Color value to 40, which also had the effect of desaturating the colors. To revive the colors and produce the final version of the image (shown at left), we increased the Color Detail value to 60.*

Using the HSL/Grayscale tab

Using the powerful sliders in the HSL/Grayscale tab, you can adjust the hue, saturation, and luminance of each hue individually.

To adjust individual colors via the HSL sliders:

1. Click the **HSL/Grayscale** tab,▤ and double-click the Hand tool 🖐 to fit the image in the preview.**A**

2. Click the nested **Hue** tab. Move any slider to shift that color into adjacent hues, as shown in the bar. For example, you could shift the Greens toward yellow to make a landscape look warmer, or toward aqua to make it look cooler.

3. Click the **Saturation** tab. Move any slider to the left to desaturate that color (add gray to it) or to the right to make it more vivid (pure).**B–C** Avoid oversaturating the photo, to ensure that it looks realistic and stays printable.

➤ To make a sky look more vivid, increase the saturation of the Blues and Aquas. To make a sunset look warmer, increase the saturation of the Oranges or Yellows; or to make it look gray and hazy, reduce those values.

A In the original photo, the sky lacks contrast and the reds on the car body are slightly undersaturated.

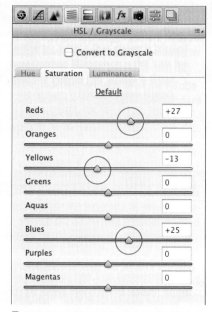

B In the nested Saturation tab of the HSL/Grayscale tab, we reduced the saturation of the Yellows and increased the saturation of the Reds and Blues.

C The Saturation adjustments intensified the reds in the car (particularly in the upper midtones) and intensified the blues in the sky.

4. Click the **Luminance** tab.**A–B** Move a slider to the left to darken that color (add black) or to the right to lighten it (add white). Avoid lightening any of the colors too much, to keep the highlights from being clipped.

➤ For a more accurate rendering of your adjusted pixels, choose a zoom level of 66% or 100% for the Camera Raw preview.

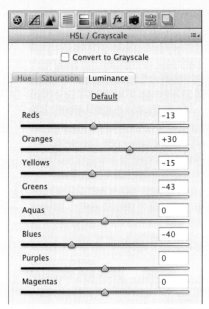

B *It may seem counterintuitive, but decreasing the Blues darkened the colors in the sky, while decreasing the Reds and increasing the Oranges produced a brighter, richer red on the car body. Now the colors are equally intense in the upper and lower areas of the photo.*

A *In the nested Luminance tab, we lightened the Oranges and darkened the Reds, Yellows, Greens, and Blues. (Tip: The effect of reducing the Blues value is like shooting with a polarizing filter on a camera.)*

USING THE TARGETED ADJUSTMENT TOOL

To apply local color adjustments to a photo, hold down Ctrl-Alt-Shift/Cmd-Option-Shift and press H, S, or L; the nested Hue, Saturation, or Luminance tab in the HSL/Grayscale tab displays and the Targeted Adjustment tool (TAT) becomes selected. Drag upward or to the right over a color area to increase the slider values specifically for that area, or downward or to the left to decrease those values. (The sliders corresponding to the color under the pointer will shift automatically.)

Using the Adjustment Brush tool

Unlike corrections made via the Camera Raw tabs, which apply to the overall photo, corrections made with the Adjustment Brush tool are "local" (affect specific areas of the photo). You apply a mask in the preview to define which areas are going to be affected by the adjustment, then you apply the correction via the sliders. Use this tool after you have finished your broad, overall corrections, to fix a few specific areas or to accentuate some details. A Awesome feature!

To apply local edits with the Adjustment Brush tool:

1. After making adjustments in the Basic and Tone Curve tabs, click the **Adjustment Brush** tool 🖌 (K). The sliders for the tool display (some are the same as sliders in the Basic tab). The Temperature, Tint, Highlights, Shadows, Noise Reduction, and Moire Reduction sliders are new. ★

2. Click the + or – button for any slider to "zero out" all the sliders except the one you click.

3. For the brush settings, try a **Feather** value of 60–95 (to allow the edits to fade into surrounding areas), a **Flow** value of 60 (for the amount of adjustment produced by each stroke), and a **Density** value of 60 (for the level of transparency in the stroke).

4. Check **Show Mask** (Y) (scroll down in the settings area if you don't see this option), adjust the brush size by pressing [or], then draw strokes over the areas of the photo that need adjustment. A tint covers the areas where you apply strokes, and a pin appears where you started dragging. B

    ➤ The brush size is represented by the solid circle in the pointer; the feather value is represented by the black-and-white dashed circle.

5. Uncheck Show Mask, then use the sliders to apply adjustments to the masked areas (A, next page).

6. To apply an adjustment to another area of the photo, click New, then repeat steps 2–5 (B–E, next page and A–C, page 74).

➤ To show or hide all the pins, press V or check or uncheck Show Pins. To display the mask for an existing pin temporarily, with the mouse or your stylus, roll over the pin.

➤ To edit an adjustment, click a pin (a black dot appears), then add to the mask and/or move the sliders. To remove areas of a mask, see page 74.

A *We studied this photo and decided on improvements to be made: Smooth the skin, sharpen the eyelashes, darken the eyebrows, and minimize the under-eye circles.*

B *We clicked the Adjustment Brush tool, zeroed out the sliders, checked Show Mask, then drew strokes in the preview on the face (but not on the key facial details).*

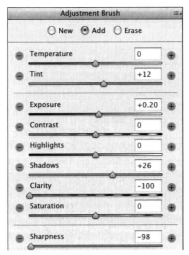

A *We hid the mask, then chose a higher Tint value to add magenta to the skin tones, higher Exposure and Shadows values to lighten the skin tones, and lower Clarity and Sharpness values to smooth the skin texture. The results are shown at right.*

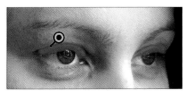

B *To sharpen the eyelashes, we clicked New, checked Show Mask, then masked those areas.*

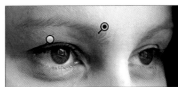

D *To darken the eyebrows, we clicked New, checked Show Mask, then masked those areas.*

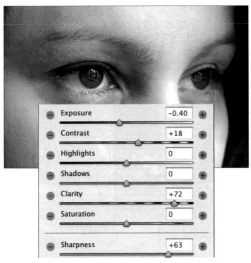

C *We hid the mask, then chose higher Contrast, Clarity, and Sharpness values to accentuate the masked areas, and a lower Exposure value to darken them.*

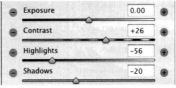

E *We hid the mask, then chose a higher Contrast value to define the hairs more crisply against the skin, and lower Highlights and Shadows values for a darkening effect.*

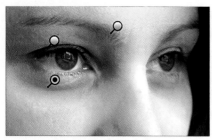

A *To minimize the dark circles under the eyes, we clicked New, checked Show Mask, then applied a mask to those areas.*

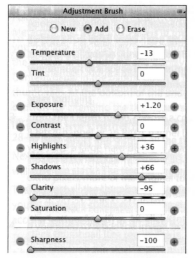

C *This final image shows the cumulative results of all the local corrections that we applied via the Adjustment Brush tool.*

B *We hid the mask, then reduced the Temperature value to cool the redness of the skin tones; increased the Exposure, Highlights, and Shadows values to lighten the skin; and reduced the Clarity and Sharpness values to soften the skin texture.*

To remove Adjustment Brush tool edits:

1. With the **Adjustment Brush** tool 🖌 selected (K), check **Show Mask** (Y) and **Show Pins** (V).

2. Do either or both of the following:

   To remove adjustments locally, click a pin, click the **Erase** button, then apply strokes where you want to erase the mask.

   To remove a pin and its adjustments, click the pin, then press Backspace/Delete.

➤ To remove all Adjustment Brush tool edits and reset the mode to New, click the Clear All button.

USING THE AUTO MASK OPTION WITH THE ADJUSTMENT BRUSH TOOL

To mask an area in an image by color, zoom into that area. Check Auto Mask, position the Adjustment Brush tool over the color, scale the brush tip to cover just the width of the area, and start drawing a stroke. The mask will cover only the areas that match the first color area the brush touches. (You can change the mask overlay color, if needed.)

Using the Split Toning tab

Using the Split Toning controls, you can apply one color tint ("tone") to the highlight areas of a photo and a different tint to the shadow areas. For the best results with this technique (and to mimic its traditional origins), convert the colors in your photo to grayscale first. We've gotten good results on photos of metallic objects, such as the antique car shown here. A

To apply a color tint to a grayscale version of a photo:

1. Click the **HSL/Grayscale** tab, then check **Convert to Grayscale**.
2. Click the **Basic** tab, and adjust the exposure and contrast.
3. Click the **Split Toning** tab.
4. Move both **Saturation** sliders approximately halfway across the bar to make it easier to judge the colors you will apply in the next step.
5. Move the **Highlights Hue** slider to tint the highlights B and the **Shadows Hue** slider to tint the shadows.
6. Readjust the **Saturation** value for each hue.
7. Reduce the **Balance** setting to apply more of the Shadows tint to the entire photo, or increase it to apply more of the Highlights tint to the entire photo. C–D

A This is the original, full-color photo.

B After converting the colors in the photo to grayscale, we used the Split Toning tab to tint the highlights with a brownish yellow hue.

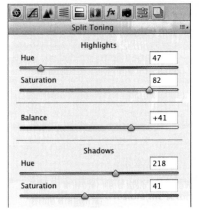
C Next, we tinted the shadows with blue, then moved the Balance slider to the right to favor the highlight color more.

D This is the final result of our Split Toning adjustments. Applying separate tints to the highlights and shadows accentuated the lines and graceful curves of this sleek antique.

Using the Effects tab

In the world of traditional film, the faster the speed, the larger and more apparent the grain. By using the Grain controls in Camera Raw, you can simulate this grainy texture, as a special effect. Choose a photo that won't suffer aesthetically when the details lose definition.

To add a grain texture to a photo:

1. Click the **Effects** tab, *fx* and double-click the Hand tool 🖑 to fit the image in the preview.**A**

2. Under Grain, to control the amount of grain applied, choose an **Amount** value of around 50 to make the grain noticeable.

3. To emulate the fine grain of slow film speed or the coarse grain of fast film speed, do as follows:

   Increase the **Size** value for the size of the grain particles.**B** When this value is greater than 25, a small degree of blurring is also applied, to help blend the grain with the imagery.

   Reduce the **Roughness** value below the default value of 50 for a more uniform grain, or increase it for an uneven, coarse grain.**C** Zoom in to examine the grain, then readjust the Amount value, if needed.

A *This photo is a good candidate for the Grain effect because it contains muted colors and we don't mind if the details are softened.*

B *The first settings we chose were Grain Amount 50 and Size 80 (we left the Roughness control at the default value of 50). The food textures are beginning to blend with the soft background.*

C *We changed the Amount to 75, the Size to 60, and the Roughness to 65. The coarser grain (increased Roughness) further unifies the highlights and background with the food textures. Please pass the Parmesan…*

Using the Post Crop Vignetting controls, you can apply a light or dark vignette to a photo (lighten or darken the outer area). If you crop the photo subsequently in Camera Raw, the vignette will reconform to the new dimensions.

To apply a vignette to a photo:

1. Click the **Effects** tab, *fx* and double-click the Hand tool 🖑 to fit the image in the preview. **A**

2. Under **Post Crop Vignetting**, do all of the following: **B–D**

   Choose Style: **Highlight Priority**.

   Choose a negative **Amount** value for a dark vignette or a positive value for a light vignette.

   Adjust the **Midpoint** value to expand the vignette inward or outward.

   Adjust the **Roundness** value to change the shape of the vignette (make it more oval or more round).

   Adjust the **Feather** setting to control the transition between the vignetted and the nonvignetted areas.

   Adjust the **Highlights** setting to control the brightness of the highlights within the vignette.

A *This is the original image.*

B *In the Effects tab, under Post Crop Vignetting, we chose the values above.*

C *We lowered the Midpoint value and raised the Feather and Highlights values.*

D *When we cropped the image, the vignette readjusted automatically.*

Using the Graduated Filter tool

When shooting landscapes, you may have run into this common predicament: You set the proper exposure for the foreground, and the sky winds up being overexposed. To solve this problem on site, you can reduce the light on the upper part of the lens with a graduated neutral-density filter. To darken a sky in a photo that is shot without such a filter (Plan B!), you can use the Graduated Filter tool in Camera Raw.

To darken part of a photo via the Graduated Filter tool: ★

1. After adjusting your photo via the Basic and Tone Curve tabs, **A** click the **Graduated Filter tool** ▣ (G). The sliders for the tool display.

2. Click the + or – button for any slider to "zero out" all the sliders except the one you click.

3. Shift-drag over an area in the photo to isolate it for editing, starting from where you want the strongest adjustment to be applied.

4. Do either or both of the following:

   Use the sliders to adjust the exposure of the filtered area (**A–C**, next page).

   Use the Temperature and/or Tint slider to make the photo warmer or cooler.

➤ At any time, you can lengthen or shorten the filter overlay by dragging the green or red dot. To reposition the whole overlay, drag the line that connects the two dots.

➤ To apply a separate filter to another area of the photo, click New, then repeat steps 2–4.

➤ To hide the filter overlay, uncheck Show Overlay or press V. To remove the filter overlay, click it, then press Backspace/Delete.

A *Despite our applying Basic and Tone Curve adjustments, the sky in this photo looks overexposed (washed out).*

A *After zeroing out the sliders for the Graduated Filter tool, we Shift-dragged in the photo (as shown by the arrow above), then chose slider settings to darken the exposure in the sky. The overlay defines where the filter edits appear: The adjustment is applied fully at the green dashed edge, gradually diminishing to nil at the red dashed edge.*

B *To add more blue to the upper area of sky, we lowered the Temperature value.*

C *In the final image, the adjustment is strongest in the sky, fading to nil in the upper part of the ground.*

Using the Spot Removal tool

Use the Spot Removal tool to remove small imperfections, such as spots caused by dust on the camera
lens or blemishes in a portrait.

To remove blemishes or spots:

1. Choose the **Spot Removal** tool (B), and zoom
   in on the area to be repaired.

2. Position the pointer at the center of the area that
   is in need of repair, then drag outward to scale
   the target circle so it surrounds the blemish.**A**
   When you release the mouse, the Radius slider
   readjusts, a green and white source circle
   appears (it is linked to the red and white target
   circle), and the area within the target circle is
   repaired.**B**

3. If you need to reposition the target or source
   circle, drag inside it.**C**

4. From the **Type** menu, choose **Heal** to blend
   source pixels into the texture and luminosity
   values of the target pixels or **Clone** to copy the
   source pixels exactly without healing.

5. You can do any of the following optional steps:

   Lower the Opacity value to lessen the retouching
   effect.

   Drag the edge of either circle to resize both
   circles simultaneously.

   Add more circle pairs to correct other blemishes.

6. To hide the circles, press V (Uncheck Overlay) or
   choose a different tool.

➤ The spot removal circles will remain available
   even after you exit Camera Raw. To redisplay
   them, choose the Spot Removal tool. To remove a
   selected pair, press Backspace/Delete; to remove
   all pairs, click Clear All.

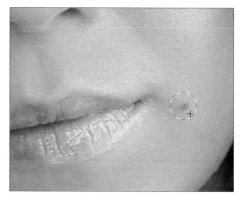

A *With the Spot Removal tool, drag a target circle
around a blemish.*

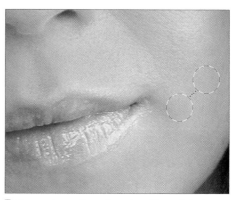

B *Camera Raw will create and position a linked
source circle in a suitably similar area, and will use
pixels from within the source circle to repair the
blemish in the target circle.*

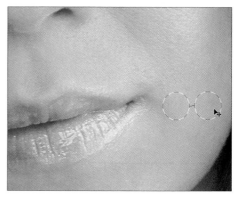

C *To control the area from which source pixels are
sampled, drag the source circle. Pixels within the target
circle will update instantly.*

Saving and applying Camera Raw settings

After carefully choosing custom settings for a photo in Camera Raw, you'll be glad to know that you can save those settings as a preset and then apply the preset to other photos that need the same or similar corrections.

To save Camera Raw settings as a preset:

Method 1 (Camera Raw Settings menu)

1. With your corrected photo open in Camera Raw, choose **Save Settings** from the Camera Raw Settings menu.☰▪

2. The Save Settings dialog opens.**A** Check the categories of settings you want saved in the preset. Or to filter the number of checked boxes, choose a category (tab name) from the Subset menu, then recheck any boxes, if desired.

3. Click Save. Another Save Settings dialog opens (yes, it's confusing that the two dialogs have the same name). Enter a name (preferably one that describes the function of the preset), keep the location as the Settings folder, then click Save.

4. The saved settings preset is now available in the Presets tab ▦ for any open photo.

Method 2 (Presets tab)

1. With your corrected photo open in Camera Raw, click the **Presets** tab,▦ then click the **New Preset** button.▣

2. In the New Preset dialog, enter a name for the preset. Check the settings you want saved in the preset, or choose a category (tab name) from the Subset menu, then recheck any boxes, if desired. Click OK. Your new preset is now available in the tab.

You can apply a user-defined preset (saved collection of settings) to a single photo via Camera Raw (see below), to multiple photos via Bridge (see the following page), or to multiple thumbnails via the synchronize option in Camera Raw (see page 83).

To apply a Camera Raw preset to a photo:

Open a photo into Camera Raw, then do either of the following:

Click the **Presets** tab,▦ then click a preset name.

From the **Apply Preset** submenu on the Camera Raw Settings menu, choose a preset.

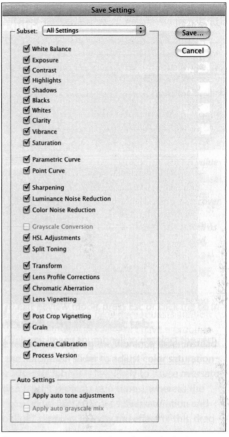

A In the Save Settings dialog, check which of your custom Camera Raw settings are to be saved in a preset.

TAKING SNAPSHOTS OF YOUR EDITS

If you save a snapshot (an editing stage and its settings) of your photo periodically during the course of Camera Raw editing, you will have the option to revert the photo to a snapshot state at any time. Snapshots save with the Camera Raw file in which they're created:

► Click the Snapshots tab,▣ then click the New Snapshot button ▣ at the bottom of the tab. In the New Snapshot dialog, enter a name, then click OK. Resume editing the photo. To restore the photo to a snapshot "state" at any time, click a snapshot name in the Snapshots tab. (If you need to restore your last custom settings, on the other hand, choose Custom Settings from the Settings menu.)

► To update an existing snapshot with the current settings, right-click a snapshot listing and choose Update with Current Settings from the context menu.

The user-created settings presets that are listed in the Presets tab of the Camera Raw dialog can also be applied to multiple photos via the Develop Settings submenu in Bridge. In fact, you could save presets for specific tabs and settings and assign them to multiple photos in sequence (e.g., a preset for the Basic tab first, then a preset for the Tone Curve tab, and so on). Alternatively, you can copy and paste the settings from one photo into one or more other photos.

To apply Camera Raw settings to multiple photos via Bridge:

Method 1 (choose a preset)

1. In Bridge, Ctrl-click/Cmd-click multiple photo thumbnails (or Shift, then Shift-click a consecutive series of photos).

2. To apply settings, from the Edit > **Develop Settings** submenu, choose a preset.A Choose additional presets, if needed.

Method 2 (copy settings from a photo)

1. Click the thumbnail for a photo that has the desired settings, then choose Edit > Develop Settings > **Copy Camera Raw Settings** (Ctrl-Alt-C/ Cmd-Option-C).

2. Click another thumbnail (or Ctrl-click/Cmd-click multiple thumbnails), then choose Edit > Develop Settings > **Paste Camera Raw Settings** (Ctrl-Alt-V/ Cmd-Option-V).

3. The Paste Camera Raw Settings dialog opens. Uncheck the settings you don't want to paste; or choose a tab name from the Subset menu, then remove or add any check marks. Click OK.

➤ To remove all Camera Raw settings from a selected photo thumbnail in Bridge, choose Edit > Develop Settings > Clear Settings.

➤ All of the commands that are mentioned on this page are also available via the context menu that opens if you right-click an image thumbnail.

A *Using the Develop Settings submenu in Bridge, you can apply one or more settings presets to multiple selected thumbnails (or copy and paste the settings from one thumbnail to other thumbnails).*

Synchronizing Camera Raw settings

When you open multiple photos into Camera Raw, they are represented by thumbnails in a filmstrip panel on the left side of the dialog. After adjusting one photo, you can click Synchronize to apply those settings to one or more of the other photos. Because it's unlikely that every single adjustment needed for one photo will be perfectly suited to all the others (even photos from the same shoot), a more practical approach is to adjust subsets of the group. For instance, you could apply a settings preset or some Basic tab adjustments to one photo (say, to correct the white balance and exposure), then apply those settings to most or all of the other photos. Next, you could select incrementally smaller numbers of photos and apply more targeted adjustments.

To synchronize the Camera Raw settings among multiple photos:

1. In Bridge, select two or more photo thumbnails, preferably ones that were shot under the same lighting conditions and that require the same kind of correction (to keep things simple, select all raw files or all JPEG files). Double-click one of the selected thumbnails.

2. In the filmstrip panel on the left side of the Camera Raw dialog, click one of the thumbnails. A

3. Make the needed adjustments to the selected image (including cropping, if you want to crop all the images exactly the same way). You could also apply adjustments by clicking a preset in the Presets tab.

4. Click **Select All** at the top of the filmstrip panel or Ctrl-click/Cmd-click the thumbnails to which you want to apply corrections, then click **Synchronize**. The Synchronize dialog opens (it looks like the Save Settings dialog, which is shown on page 81).

5. Check only the settings to be applied; or choose a category from the Synchronize menu, then remove or add any check marks.

6. To apply the current settings in the categories you checked to all the selected thumbnails, click OK.

➤ To cycle through the photos in the filmstrip panel, click the left or right arrowhead below the preview (in the lower right). If multiple thumbnails are selected, Camera Raw will cycle among only those photos.

A *We opened four photos into Camera Raw. The thumbnails for those images display in the filmstrip panel on the left side of the dialog.*

Converting, opening, and saving Camera Raw files

Still with us? At long last, you get to open your Camera Raw file into Photoshop. (Also see the steps for opening a Camera Raw file as a Smart Object on page 249.)

To open a Camera Raw file into Photoshop:

1. When you're done correcting an image in Camera Raw, click **Open Image**. The current settings will be saved as instructions for converting the photo without altering the original file. (To open multiple images, click Open Images.)

2. Via File > Save in Photoshop, save a copy of the photo in the Photoshop (.psd) format.

➤ Depending on the setting on the "Save Image Settings In" menu in the Camera Raw Preferences dialog (Ctrl-K/Cmd-K), settings for raw photos (but not JPEGs) are saved either in the internal Camera Raw Database on your system or as hidden Sidecar .xmp files in the same folder as the raw files (not to be confused with the user settings files that are created via the Save Settings command).

➤ To close the Camera Raw dialog without opening your file, click Done. Your settings will be saved as instructions and will be available if you reopen the file in Camera Raw (via Bridge or Photoshop).

If you need to open a copy of a Camera Raw file without recording settings into the metadata of the raw file or into the actual JPEG file, do as follows.

To open a copy of a Camera Raw file:

In the Camera Raw dialog, hold down Alt/Option and click **Open Copy** (Open Image becomes Open Copy). The file will be converted using the current settings and will open into Photoshop, but the current settings won't replace any existing instructions in the original raw or JPEG file.

Via the Save Options dialog, you can convert and save a copy of a digital photo in the DNG (Digital Negative), JPEG, TIFF, or Photoshop (PSD) format.

For the DNG format, see the sidebar at right. Camera Raw settings are preserved in DNG files and remain available if you reopen the files in Camera Raw.

When you save a photo in the JPEG, TIFF, or PSD format using the Save Options dialog, your Camera Raw adjustments are applied to it permanently.

Although you can reopen a JPEG or TIFF file into Camera Raw, your custom settings won't be accessible. (If you need to preserve access to your Camera Raw settings for a JPEG, instead of using this dialog, exit Camera Raw by clicking Done.) PSD files can't be opened in Camera Raw.

To save a copy of a file in the DNG, JPEG, TIFF, or PSD format:

1. In the lower-left corner of the Camera Raw dialog, click **Save Image**.

2. The Save Options dialog opens. For the Destination, choose **Save in Same Location** or **Save in New Location**. For the latter, choose a location in the Select Destination Folder dialog, then click Select.

3. In the **File Naming** area, enter a file name; if desired, also choose a naming or numbering convention from the adjacent menu.

4. Choose a **Format** (Digital Negative, JPEG, TIFF, or Photoshop), then choose format-related options. For instance, if you cropped the photo in Camera Raw and chose the Photoshop format, check whether you want to Preserve Cropped Pixels.

5. Click Save.

ARCHIVING PHOTOS AS DNG FILES

Photographs capture unrepeatable moments, and archiving them is both a priority and a concern for photographers. Ideally, there would be one standard file format for digital photos that photographers could depend on with confidence, knowing their photos will be stable and accessible for eternity — or at least for many, many years. At the present time, each camera maker uses a unique, proprietary format for their raw files. Should a manufacturer discontinue its own proprietary format, raw photos from their cameras might become unreadable by Photoshop or other image-editing applications.

Enter DNG (short for Digital Negative), a format developed by Adobe. It preserves all the raw, unprocessed pixel information that is recorded by the camera. The coding for the DNG format is nonproprietary (open standard), meaning that it is accessible to all interested companies. DNG may be the long-term solution that photographers will eventually come to rely on — provided it is adopted as the standard by a majority of camera and software manufacturers.

Now that you know how to create and open documents, you're ready to customize the Photoshop workspace for your needs. In this chapter, you'll learn how to use the main features of the Photoshop interface, such as the Application frame and document tabs. You'll change the zoom level and screen mode, rotate the canvas view, configure the panels, choose a workspace, save custom workspaces, and use the Options bar.

Note: The individual panels (including the Tools panel) are described and illustrated in the next chapter.

ENABLE OPENGL FOR THIS CHAPTER

To use the OpenGL features in Photoshop, such as Animated and Scrubby Zoom (see page 89), flick panning (see page 90), and the Rotate View tool (see page 91), your system must contain a video driver or card that provides OpenGL acceleration. To enable the OpenGL features in Photoshop, in Edit/Photoshop > Preferences > Performance, under Graphics Processor Settings, check Use Graphics Processor, ★ then relaunch Photoshop. See also page 439.

Using the Application frame

In Windows, all the Photoshop features are housed in an Application window. It contains a menu bar and Options bar along the top; panels (including the Tools panel); and documents, which by default are docked as tabs.A

Continued on the following page

WORKSPACES

5

IN THIS CHAPTER

Menu bar   Options bar

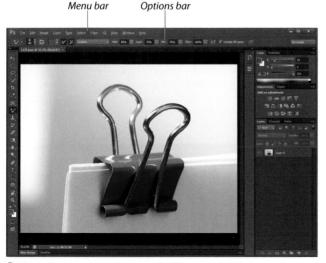

A *This is the onscreen environment for Photoshop in Windows.*

The Application frame in the Mac OS serves the same purpose as the Application window in Windows: It holds the Options bar (see page 98), panels, and open documents (which are docked as tabs). Although the Application frame is an optional feature in the Mac OS, it is showing by default—and for good reason. It keeps all the Photoshop features neatly organized and readily accessible (and hides Desktop clutter!). If the frame is hidden, choose Window > Application Frame. We use and refer to it throughout this book.

Note: For the sake of simplicity, we will also refer to the Windows application window generically as the "Application frame."

➤ To resize the Application frame, drag an edge or the lower-right corner.

➤ To minimize the Application frame in the Mac OS, click the Minimize button in the upper-left corner. To minimize the Application frame in Windows, click the Minimize button in the upper-right corner.

Mac OS X Lion has a new Full-Screen Apps option: In any application that has full-screen capability, you can click the Full Screen button in the upper-right corner of the Application window to have the application fill the entire screen. One more reason to acclimate yourself to the Application frame in Photoshop, if you haven't done so already.

Note: There is no Application bar in Photoshop CS6. If you miss it, let Adobe know.

The document tab lists the file name, file format, current zoom level and layer, color mode, and bit depth. An asterisk indicates that the file contains unsaved changes. To close a document, click the X.

Use the Options bar to choose settings for the current tool.

Store open panels in one or more docks. To save space, you can collapse any dock to icons (see page 94).

A This is the Application frame in the Mac OS.

We recommend docking all open document windows as tabs (the default setting for Photoshop) rather than floating them as separate windows outside the frame (the only option in early versions of Photoshop). With documents docked as tabs, you will be able to keep the documents you're not working on readily accessible but out of view, and take advantage of tiling commands. To display a document that is docked as a tab, simply click the tab.

If documents aren't docking as tabs automatically, we recommend resetting the preference so that they do.

To set a preference to have documents open as tabs:

1. Choose Edit/Photoshop > Preferences, then click Interface on the left to display that pane.

2. Check **Open Documents as Tabs**, then click OK.

If you inadvertently (or out of curiosity) drag a document out of the tab area, and thereby turn a tabbed document into a floating one, follow these instructions to bring it home.

To dock floating document windows as tabs:

Do either of the following:

To dock one floating document window manually, drag its title bar to the tab area (just below the Options bar) of the Application frame, and release when the blue drop zone border appears. **A–B**

To dock all floating documents as tabs, choose Window > Arrange > **Consolidate All to Tabs**; or if at least one document is docked as a tab, right-click a tab and choose **Consolidate All to Here** from the context menu.

➤ To cycle among all currently open documents, press Ctrl-~ (tilde)/Cmd-~. Or if you have small hands, you may be more comfortable pressing Ctrl-Tab/Control-Tab instead.

➤ One of the drawbacks to floating document windows when using the Application frame is that if you click in the frame, your floating documents will be hidden behind it. If you insist on floating your documents, consider at least docking them together by dragging the title bar of one window just below the title bar of another.

A *To dock a floating document window as a tab manually, drag its title bar to the tab area of the Application frame, and release the mouse when the blue drop zone border appears.*

B *The document is now docked within the Application frame.*

Tiling multiple documents

If you need to view or edit multiple documents simultaneously, you can arrange them in a choice of preset layouts, such as two documents side by side or in a vertical format, or four or six documents in a grid.

To tile multiple documents: ★

1. From the Window > **Arrange** submenu, choose a tiling command, such as 2-Up Vertical or 4-Up. 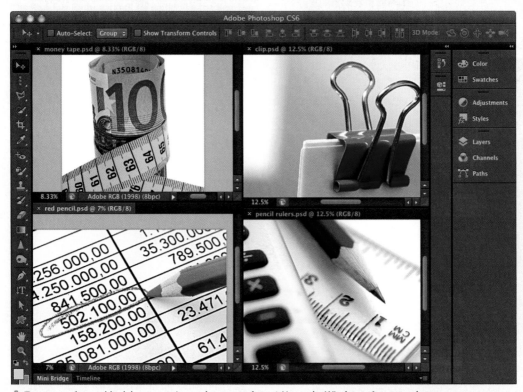A The availability of commands will vary depending on how many documents are open.

   ➤ To resize any window, drag either the bar between two windows or the lower-right corner. To reduce the number of visible windows by one, drag the tab of a document to the tab of another document, and release when the blue drop zone border appears.

2. When you're ready to view just one document at a time, do either of the following:

   Choose Window > Arrange > **Consolidate All to Tabs**.

   Right-click a tab and choose **Consolidate All to Here** from the context menu.

➤ If any open documents are floating when you choose a tiling command, they will be docked as tabs automatically.

ONE IMAGE, TWO WINDOWS

To display the current document in a duplicate (tabbed) window, close any other open documents, then choose Window > Arrange > New Window for [document name]. ★ To show both windows, choose a Tile All or 2-Up option from the Window > Arrange submenu. Some advantages to this setup are that you could choose an option on the View > Proof Colors submenu for one of the documents and not the other, or display the documents at different zoom levels.

A *To arrange these tabbed documents in quadrants, we chose 4-Up on the Window > Arrange submenu.*

Changing the zoom level

You can easily switch between displaying the entire live canvas area of an image in the document window and magnifying just part of the image (to concentrate on a small detail). The current zoom level percentage is listed in three locations: on the document tab, in the lower-left corner of the document window, and on the Navigator panel (if showing).

Note: For smoother and more continuous zooming, in Edit/Photoshop > Preferences > General, check Animated Zoom, and in Preferences > Performance, check Use Graphics Processor. The latter preference must also be checked to use the Scrubby Zoom feature, which is used in the task below. For more Zoom preferences, see page 434.

To change the zoom level with the Zoom tool:

1. Choose the **Zoom** tool, 🔍 or to spring-load the Zoom tool (select it temporarily) while using another tool, hold down Z.

2. Do either of the following:

   Check **Scrubby Zoom** on the Options bar, then in the document window, immediately drag to the right to zoom in **A** or to the left to zoom out. (See also the Note, above right).

   Right-click in the document window and choose a zoom option from the context menu, or click one of these buttons on the Options bar: **Actual Pixels** to set the zoom level to 100%; **Fit Screen** to display the entire image at the largest size that can fit in the window; **Fill Screen** to have the image fill the window (only part of the image may be visible); or **Print Size** to display the image at an approximation of its print size.

Note: The Animated Zoom feature (also called "bird's-eye" zooming) kicks in if you don't drag immediately while scrubby zooming. If you want to prevent this from occurring, uncheck Animated Zoom in Preferences > General. To change the zoom level with the Zoom tool without using scrubby zooming, click or drag to zoom in or Alt-click/Option-click to zoom out.

➤ You can also change the zoom level by entering a percentage in the Zoom Level field in the lower-left corner of the document window.

SHORTCUTS FOR ZOOMING IN AND OUT		
	Windows	Mac OS
Zoom in incrementally	Ctrl-+ (plus)	Cmd-+ (plus)
Zoom out incrementally	Ctrl-– (minus)	Cmd-– (minus)
Zoom in	Ctrl-Spacebar click or drag	Cmd-Spacebar click or drag
Zoom out	Alt-Spacebar click or drag	Option-Spacebar click or drag
Actual pixels (100% view)	Ctrl-Alt-0 (zero)	Cmd-Option-0 (zero)
Fit Screen	Ctrl-0 (zero)	Cmd-0 (zero)

Note: The zoom shortcuts also can be used when some Photoshop dialogs are open.

A With the Zoom tool and Scrubby Zoom checked on the Options bar, drag to the right to zoom in (or to the left to zoom out).

The Navigator panel has two functions. You can use it to change the zoom level of an image, or to reposition the image in the document window (to bring an area you want to edit or examine into view).

To change the zoom level or reposition the image in the window via the Navigator panel:

1. Display the Navigator panel. ❄ A

2. To change the zoom level, do any of the following:

   Ctrl-drag/Cmd-drag across part of the image thumbnail to target that area for magnification.

   Double-click the existing value in the zoom field, type the desired percentage, then press Enter/Return. Or enter a value, then press Shift-Enter/Shift-Return to have the field re-highlight automatically.

   Drag the Zoom slider.

   Click the Zoom Out or Zoom In button.

3. If the image is magnified to the degree that areas are hidden outside the document window, you can reposition it by dragging the view box on the panel.

You can also move a magnified image in the document window by using the Hand tool.

To reposition a magnified image with the Hand tool:

Do one of the following:

Choose the **Hand** tool 🖑 (H) or hold down the Spacebar for a temporary Hand tool, then drag in the document window.

Choose the **Hand** tool 🖑 (H) or hold down the Spacebar for a temporary Hand tool, do a quick little drag in the document, then release. The image will float across the screen (this is called "flick panning"); click again to stop the motion. Note: For this to work, Use Graphics Processor must be checked in Edit/Photoshop > Preferences > Performance upon startup and Enable Flick Panning must be checked in Preferences > General.

To access the Hand tool temporarily if you have another tool selected, hold down the **H**, press the mouse to display a wire-frame view box, drag the view box over the area of the image you want to show, then release the mouse.

➤ If a document is in a tabbed window in the Application frame and is magnified, you can overscroll it — that is, drag it far off to the side (farther than you can drag an image in a floating window).

➤ You can also move a magnified image in the document window by dragging either of the scroll bars.

Zoom   Zoom Out   Zoom   View   Zoom In
field   button   slider   box   button

A *You can use the Navigator panel to change the zoom level of your document and, if the image is magnified, to move it in the document window.*

MATCHING THE ZOOM LEVEL OR LOCATION

If you have multiple documents open in Photoshop, from the Window > Arrange submenu, ★ you can choose Match Zoom to match the zoom level of all open images to that of the currently active image, Match Location to match the relative positions of all open and magnified images within the document window to that of the current one, Match Rotation to match the canvas angle of all open images to that of the current one (the angle is produced by the Rotate View tool; see the next page), or Match All to do all of the above.

If you have multiple documents open (say, in a 2-Up or 3-Up layout), you can save time by scrolling or zooming all of them simultaneously.

To scroll or zoom in multiple document windows:

1. Open two or more documents, then on the Window > Arrange submenu, choose a Tile command or a 2-Up, 3-Up, 4-Up, 5-Up, or 6-Up command. ★

2. Check Scroll All Windows on the Options bar for the Hand tool, or check Zoom All Windows on the Options bar for the Zoom tool. Alternatively, you can leave these options unchecked and enable them temporarily by holding down Shift when using the Hand or Zoom tool.

Rotating the canvas view

Unlike the Image > Image Rotation commands, which rotate an image permanently, the Rotate View tool tilts the canvas temporarily so you can draw, paint, or perform other edits at a more comfortable angle.

Note: To use the Rotate View tool, Use Graphics Processor must be checked in Edit/Photoshop > Preferences > Performance (see page 439).

To rotate the canvas view:

1. Change the zoom level, if necessary, so the entire image is showing in the document window.

2. Choose the **Rotate View** tool 🖐 (R) or hold down R to spring-load the tool, then drag in the image (a compass displays temporarily). **A**

➤ When the Rotate View tool is selected, you can change the Rotation Angle on the Option bar by using the scrubby slider, by entering a value, or by moving the dial.

To reset the canvas view to the default angle:

1. Choose the **Rotate View** tool 🖐 (R) or hold down R to spring-load the tool.

2. On the Options bar, click **Reset View**.

A With the Rotate View tool, drag to tilt the canvas to the desired angle.

Changing the screen mode

The three screen modes control which Photoshop interface features display onscreen.

To change the screen mode:

Press F to cycle through the screen modes or choose a mode from the **Screen Mode** menu 🖳 at the bottom of the Tools panel: **A** ★

Standard Screen Mode (the default mode) to display the full Photoshop interface, including the Application frame, Photoshop menu bar, Options bar, document tabs, and panels — with the Desktop (and other application windows) remaining visible around it.

Full Screen Mode with Menu Bar to display the current document on a full-screen background (default color of medium gray), with all of the above-mentioned interface features showing except the document window tabs and controls.**B**

Full Screen Mode to display only the current document on a full-screen background with the Photoshop interface features hidden and the panels visible only upon rollover (see "To make hidden panel docks reappear" on the next page).

Choosing a workspace

To change your panel setup quickly, choose one of the predefined workspaces, which are designed for different kinds of tasks, or choose a user-defined workspace (see pages 96–97).

To choose a workspace:

From the **Workspace** menu on the right side of the Options bar ★ **C** or from the Window > **Workspace** submenu, choose a predefined workspace, such as Essentials, New in CS6, Painting, Photography, or Typography, or a user-defined workspace.

CUSTOMIZING THE BACKGROUND

➤ To quickly change the background shade around the canvas area for the current screen mode, right-click the background, then on the context menu, choose default, Black, or a shade of gray. Although you also have the option to choose Select Custom Color and then choose a color in the Color Picker, a gray or black background will provide an ideal neutral setting for judging color corrections in your images.

➤ In the Interface panel of the Preferences dialog, in addition to choosing a background color or shade, you can also choose a border style for the canvas area of Line, Drop Shadow, or None (see page 436).

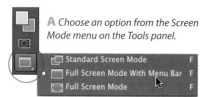

A Choose an option from the Screen Mode menu on the Tools panel.

B When performing color correction work, we choose the screen mode option of Full Screen Mode with Menu Bar.

C We're choosing a workspace on the Workspace menu (Options bar).

Configuring the panels

If you have chosen Standard Screen Mode or Full Screen Mode with Menu Bar for Photoshop and you want to fully maximize your screen space, you can hide all your open panels and make them reappear only when needed.

To hide (or show) the panels:

Do either of the following:

Press Tab to hide (or show) all the currently open panels, including the Tools panel.

Press Shift-Tab to hide (or show) all the currently open panels except the Tools panel.

➤ To open an individual panel when the panels are hidden, choose the panel name from the Window menu.

To make hidden panel docks reappear:

1. Hide the panels as described above or choose Full Screen Mode from the Screen Mode menu 🖵, on the Tools panel. ★

2. If the document is in Standard Screen mode, let the pointer pause on the dark gray vertical bar at the left or right edge of the Application frame; or if your document is in either one of the Full Screen modes, let it pause just inside the edge of your monitor until the dark gray vertical bar appears. **A**

   The panel docks will redisplay temporarily (free-standing panels will remain hidden). **B** Move the pointer away from the panels, and they'll disappear again.

   Note: If this mechanism doesn't appear to be working, right-click any panel tab or icon and check Auto-Show Hidden Panels on the context menu. That should do the trick.

➤ If you prefer to keep your panels visible onscreen but you want to minimize how much space they occupy, shrink them to icons (see the last paragraph on the next page).

A *If the panels are hidden, let the pointer pause just inside the right edge of the monitor or Application frame…*

B *… to make the panel docks appear temporarily. (Move the pointer away from the panels, and away they go.)*

Most of the edits that you make in Photoshop will require the use of at least one of the panels — and more likely several. Fortunately, the panels are easy to hide, collapse, and expand so they don't intrude on your document space when you're not using them.

In the predefined workspaces, panels are arranged in docks on the right side of your screen, except for the Tools panel, which is on the left side. Each dock can hold one or more panels or panel groups, and you can change their configuration to suit the way you normally work.

To reconfigure the panel groups and docks:

Show or hide a panel: Show a panel by choosing its name from the Window menu. The panel will display either in its default group and dock or in its last open location. To bring a panel to the front within its group, click its tab (panel name).

Expand a panel that's collapsed to an icon: Click the icon or panel name. If Auto-Collapse Iconic Panels is checked in Edit/Photoshop > Preferences > Interface and you open a panel from an icon, it collapses to an icon when you click outside it. With this preference off, the panel stays expanded; to collapse it back to an icon, click the Collapse to Icons button on the panel bar (the horizontal gray bar to the right of the panel tab) or click the panel icon in the dock.

➤ To quickly access the Auto-Collapse Iconic Panels option via a context menu, right-click any panel tab, bar, or icon.

Maximize or minimize an expanded panel or group vertically (to toggle the full panel to just a panel tab, or vice versa): Double-click the panel tab or bar.

Use a panel menu: Click the icon to access the menu for the panel that is currently in front in its group.

Close a panel or group: To close a panel, right-click the panel tab and choose Close from the context menu. To close a whole panel group, choose Close Tab Group from the same context menu. To close a floating panel, you can click the close button in the upper-left corner.

Collapse a whole dock to icons, or to icons with names: Click the Collapse to Icons button at the top of the dock; or double-click the topmost bar; **A–B** or right-click a panel tab, bar, or icon and choose Collapse to Icons from the context menu. To expand icons to icons with names, or to reduce icons with names to just icons, drag the vertical edge of the dock horizontally. **C**

A In this workspace, panels in the left dock are collapsed to icons, whereas the panels in the right dock are expanded. The Histogram panel is minimized vertically. We are double-clicking the bar for the rightmost dock …

B … to shrink that dock to icons. Note that the panel groups were preserved.

C Here we're dragging the edge of the rightmost dock to shrink the whole dock to just icons.

Widen or narrow a dock (and panels): Position the pointer over the vertical edge of the dock (✛⋅✛ cursor), then drag horizontally.

Move a panel into a different group: Drag the panel tab over the title bar of the desired group, and release when the blue drop zone border appears.**A**

Move a panel to a different slot in the same group: Drag the panel tab (name) to the left or right.

Move a panel group upward or downward in a dock: Drag the tab bar, then release it when the horizontal blue drop zone bar appears in the desired location.**B**

Create a new dock: Drag a panel tab or bar sideways to the vertical edge of the dock,**C** and release the mouse when the blue vertical drop zone bar appears.

Reconfigure a dock that's collapsed to icons: Use methods like those you would use for an expanded group. Drag the double dotted line ▦▦▦▦ to the edge of a dock to create a new dock, or drag it vertically between groups to restack the group (release when the horizontal drop zone line appears), or drag it into another group to move it to that group (release when the blue drop zone border appears).

Float a docked panel or group: Drag the panel tab, icon, or bar out of the dock. To stack floating panels or groups, drag the bar of one to the bottom of another (release when the horizontal blue drop zone line appears). To resize a floating panel, drag the resize box ▦ inward or outward, or drag the right edge of the panel horizontally; not all panels are resizable.

To redock floating panels into the Application frame: Drag the topmost bar of the panel group to the right edge of the Application frame, and release the mouse when the pointer is over the edge of the frame and a vertical blue drop zone line appears.

➤ To prevent a floating panel from docking as you move it, drag it with Ctrl/Cmd held down.

➤ When using a tool that uses brushes, you can show the Brush panel by clicking the Toggle Brush Panel button ▦ on the Options bar or on the Brush Presets panel. When using a type tool, you can show the Character/Paragraph panel group by clicking this button ▤ on the Options bar.

A *A blue drop zone border appears as we drag a panel into a different group.*

B *A blue horizontal drop zone bar appears as we move our Layers/Channels panel group upward within the same dock.*

C *A blue vertical drop zone bar appears as we create a new dock for the History panel.*

Saving custom workspaces

Now that you have learned how to personalize your workspace for Photoshop, the next step is to save some custom workspaces for different kinds of editing work you do in Photoshop. Your custom workspaces should reflect your normal work habits (and by this we don't mean working late and sleeping late!). For example, to set up a type-related workspace, you could open the Character, Paragraph, Paragraph Styles, and Character Styles panels, hide the panels you don't normally reach for when you work with type, and assign color labels to your favorite commands on the Type menu.

The current panel locations are included automatically when you save a custom workspace. Optionally, you can include custom keyboard shortcuts and/or menu sets (which control the color label and visibility settings for menu commands).

To save a custom workspace:

1. Do any or all of the following:

    Open and position all the desired panels in groups and docks. A

    Collapse the panels you use occasionally to icons and close the ones you rarely use. Or if you prefer to keep all your panels collapsed to icons or icons with names, set them up that way now.

    Resize any of the panels, as well as any of the pickers that open from the Options bar.

    Choose a thumbnail size and other panel display options from the panel menus, and from the menus on the preset pickers that open from the Options bar.

    Choose Edit > Menus (Ctrl-Alt-Shift-M/Cmd-Option-Shift-M) and use that dialog to assign color labels and/or visibility settings to menu commands (for quick identification). Save your changes in a new menu set. (To learn about customizing the Photoshop keyboard shortcuts, see Photoshop Help.)

2. From the Workspace menu on the Options bar, ★ choose New Workspace.

3. In the New Workspace dialog, enter a **Name** for the workspace (include your own name, if desired). B

4. Under Capture, if you customized the Keyboard Shortcuts or the Menus, check those options.

A *This is the panel setup in one of our custom workspaces.*

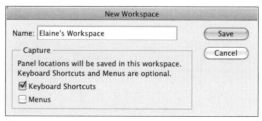

B *In the New Workspace dialog, enter a Name for your workspace and check either or both of the Capture options.*

5. Click Save. Your workspace will appear at the top of the Workspace menu on the Options bar **A** and on the Window > Workspace submenu.

➤ To edit a saved workspace, choose the workspace to be edited, make the desired changes to the Photoshop interface, choose the New Workspace command, retype the same name, click Save, then click Yes in the alert dialog.

➤ If you have dual displays, you can distribute free-standing panel groups or stacks between them and save that arrangement as a new workspace.

➤ All the panels that are open when you exit/quit Photoshop will reappear in the same location upon relaunch.

To delete a saved custom workspace: ★

1. From the Workspace menu on the Options bar, choose any workspace *except* the one you want to delete.

2. From the same menu, choose **Delete Workspace**.

3. In the Delete Workspace dialog, choose the name of the user-defined workspace to be deleted, **B** click Delete, then click Yes in the alert dialog.

Resetting workspaces

Say you chose a workspace and then rearranged some panels manually. If you were to switch to another work-space and then back to your original one, your manual changes would redisplay (in other words, the manual changes are "sticky"). Perform the first task below to restore the original settings to an individual work-space, or the second task to restore the factory-default settings to all the predefined (non-user-defined) workspaces.

To reset the current workspace: ★

From the Workspace menu on the Options bar, choose **Reset** [workspace name].

To reset all predefined (non-user-defined) workspaces:

1. To open the Interface pane of the Preferences dialog, right-click any panel tab, bar, or icon and choose **Interface Options** from the context menu.

2. Under Options, click **Restore Default Workspaces**. If an alert dialog appears, click OK, then click OK to exit the Preferences dialog.

A *Our new workspace (named "Elaine's Workspace") appears on the Workspace menu on the Options bar.*

B *In the Delete Workspace dialog, choose the user-saved workspace you want to get rid of.*

Using the Options bar

If the Options bar is hidden, choose Window > Options. You will use this bar primarily to choose settings for the current tool. For instance, for the Clone Stamp tool, you could choose a brush; a blending mode; flow, opacity, alignment, and sampling settings; and settings for a stylus, if you're using one. For a type tool, you could choose a font and a font family; a point size; anti-aliasing and alignment settings; and a color. Your Options bar settings remain in effect for each individual tool until you change them.

To open a picker, which displays one or more libraries of presets (e.g., brushes or gradients), click the picker icon or arrowhead. A To close a preset picker or other pop-up panel, click outside it, or click the arrowhead on the Options bar.

To cancel a value you have entered on the Options bar and exit the bar, press Esc (this also works for some pickers).

Features on the Options bar change depending on what tool is selected and the way in which it is being used in the document. For instance, if you begin to apply a transformation with the Move tool, Cancel Transform ⊘ and Commit Transform ✔ buttons will appear on the Options bar. If you click either button to exit transformation mode, those buttons will disappear.

The Workspace menu (not shown below) is located on the right side of the Options bar; see page 97. ★

Note that some tool settings can also, or only, be chosen on a related panel. For instance, for the type tools, you will find additional options on the Character and Paragraph panels; for the Brush or Pencil tool, you must choose a Foreground color on the Color or Swatches panel.

Click here to open the Tool Preset picker.

A Click an icon or arrowhead to open a preset picker (the Brush Preset picker is shown here).

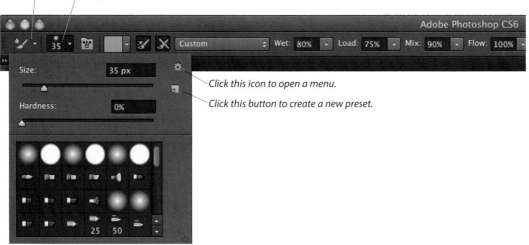

Click this icon to open a menu.

Click this button to create a new preset.

In this screen capture, the Options bar is displaying settings for the Mixer Brush tool.

You will accomplish most of your editing work in Photoshop using the panels, which are the focus of this chapter, as well as the Options bar and various editing tools. To become a Photoshop speed demon, avoid using the menu bar except to choose commands that aren't available elsewhere in the interface. The panels are opened individually via the Window menu.

In the preceding chapter, you learned how to arrange the panels onscreen (see pages 93–95). Here you will learn more about their specific functions. After a quick view of the panel icons and instructions for using the Tools panel, you will find illustrations and a brief summary (in alphabetical order) of all the panels that are used in this book. You can browse through the descriptions with or without glancing at or fiddling with the panels onscreen. Then, as you become more acquainted with Photoshop, you can revisit this chapter and use it as a reference guide. (This chapter is just an introduction to the panels. In other chapters, you will find detailed instructions for specific panels and put them to lots of practical use.)

The final section of this chapter gives steps for managing and saving presets (predefined settings), which are stored and accessed via Photoshop panels and pickers. Some examples of presets are solid colors on the Swatches panel, styles on the Styles panel, and shapes on the Custom Shape picker.

PANELS

6

USING THE UNDO SHORTCUTS

	Windows	Mac OS
Undo the last Photoshop edit (some edits can't be undone)	Ctrl-Z (Edit > Undo)	Cmd-Z (Edit > Undo)
Undo multiple editing steps in reverse order (step backward)	Ctrl-Alt-Z	Cmd-Option-Z
Step forward through your editing steps (reinstate what you have undone)	Ctrl-Shift-Z	Cmd-Shift-Z

The Photoshop panel icons ★

Each panel in Photoshop has a unique icon that displays when the panel is either fully or partially collapsed. Until you learn to identify collapsed panels by their icons, you may want to keep your panel docks only partially collapsed (so the names display) rather than fully collapsed to just icons. A You can identify the panels via Tool Tips (see the sidebar on this page).

A *Eventually, you will be able to quickly identify the panels by their icons.*

USING CONTEXT MENUS

When you right-click in the document window—depending on where you click and which tool is selected—a menu of context-sensitive commands pops up onscreen temporarily. Context menus are also available for features of the Photoshop interface, such as the Layers panel. If a command is available on a context menu (or can be executed quickly via a keyboard shortcut), we let you know in our instructions—to spare you from a trek to the main menu bar.

Note: If your mouse doesn't have a right-click button, hold down Control and click to open the context menu. If you're using a trackpad on a Mac, you can click or tap with two fingers.

This is the context menu for a selection.

USING TOOL TIPS

If you need to identify a panel, button, icon, or menu in the Photoshop interface, you can find the information you need via the Tool Tip: Let the pointer hover over a feature without clicking the mouse button, and the item name pops up onscreen. Not happening? Go to Edit/Photoshop > Preferences > Interface, and check Show Tool Tips.

This Tool Tip is listing a tool name and shortcut.

This Tool Tip is identifying a panel.

The Photoshop panels that are used in this book*

Using the Tools panel

To display the Tools panel if it's hidden, choose Window > **Tools** (the panel is illustrated on the next three pages). To select a tool, do one of the following:

► If the desired tool is visible on the Tools panel, just click it.

► To cycle through related tools in the same slot, hold down Alt/Option and click the visible one.

► To choose a hidden tool, click and hold on the visible tool, then click a tool on the menu.

► To select a tool quickly, press its designated letter shortcut (don't do this if your cursor is inserted in type). The shortcuts are shown on the next three pages, as well as in the Tool Tips. If the Use Shift Key for Tool Switch option is unchecked in Edit/Photoshop > Preferences > General, you can simply press the designated letter to cycle through related tools in the same slot (e.g., press L to cycle through the three lasso tools). If the preference option is checked, you have to press Shift plus the designated letter (e.g., Shift-L).

► To spring-load (access) a tool temporarily while another tool is selected, press and hold down its assigned letter key. See the sidebar on this page.

To see information pertaining to the current tool (called a tool hint), look at the bottom of the Info panel. If you don't see the tool hint, choose Panel Options from the Info panel menu (upper-right corner of the panel), then check Show Tool Hints (see page 110).

Before using a tool that you've selected, you need to choose settings for it on the Options bar. For example, for the Brush tool, you would choose a brush preset, as well as diameter, hardness, blending mode, and opacity settings. If the Options bar is hidden, show it by choosing Window > Options (see page 98).

The current Options bar settings for a specific tool remain in effect until you change them, reset that tool, or reset all tools. To restore the default settings to the current tool, right-click the thumbnail for the Tool Preset picker (located at the left end of the Options bar) and choose Reset Tool from the context

menu.**A** To restore the default settings to all tools, choose Reset All Tools from the same menu, then click OK in the alert dialog.

In Edit/Photoshop > Preferences > Cursors, you can control whether the pointer displays as crosshairs or as the icon of the current tool or, for some tools, as a circle either the size or half the size of the current brush diameter, with or without crosshairs inside it (see page 440).

For editing tools — such as the Brush, Pencil, Clone Stamp, Pattern Stamp, History Brush, Art History Brush, Blur, Sharpen, Smudge, Dodge, and Burn tools — you can choose from hundreds of brush tips, and you can also change many brush characteristics, such as size, hardness, and opacity (see page 272).

A *To access these two commands, right-click the Tool Preset picker thumbnail, which is located at the left end of the Options bar.*

SPRING-LOADING A TOOL

► To quickly access a tool and its current Options bar settings temporarily without having to actually click the tool on the Tools panel, hold down its letter shortcut key. For example, say the Brush tool is selected but you want to move a layer, which requires using the Move tool. You would hold down the V key, drag in the document window, then release the V; the Brush tool will be reselected automatically. To access the Zoom tool temporarily, you would hold down the Z key.

► Spring-loading is slightly less efficient if you need to access a tool that shares a slot with other tools (as most tools do). In this case, the letter shortcut selects whichever tool happens to be visible on the Tools panel. To make this work, you need to plan ahead and select the tools that you want to switch back and forth between before using them.

---

*The 3D tools, and the 3D, Animation, Measurement Log, Notes, and Paths panels aren't covered in this book, so they are not discussed in this chapter.

Tools panel

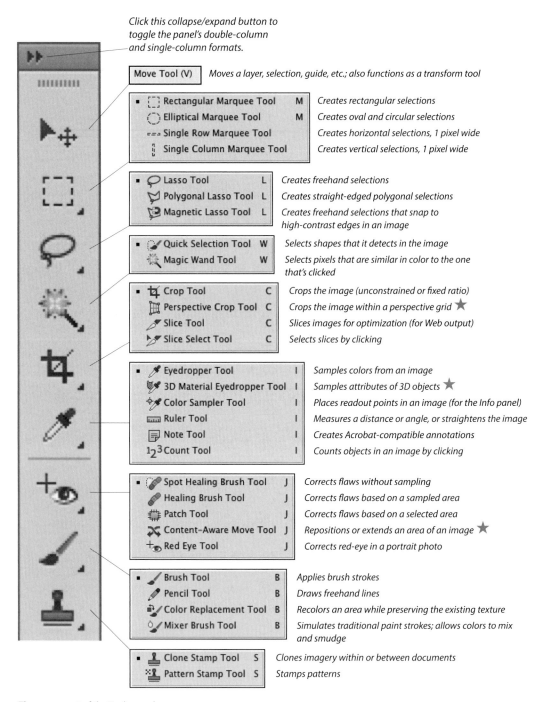

Click this collapse/expand button to toggle the panel's double-column and single-column formats.

Move Tool (V) — Moves a layer, selection, guide, etc.; also functions as a transform tool

Rectangular Marquee Tool	M	Creates rectangular selections
Elliptical Marquee Tool	M	Creates oval and circular selections
Single Row Marquee Tool		Creates horizontal selections, 1 pixel wide
Single Column Marquee Tool		Creates vertical selections, 1 pixel wide

Lasso Tool	L	Creates freehand selections
Polygonal Lasso Tool	L	Creates straight-edged polygonal selections
Magnetic Lasso Tool	L	Creates freehand selections that snap to high-contrast edges in an image

Quick Selection Tool	W	Selects shapes that it detects in the image
Magic Wand Tool	W	Selects pixels that are similar in color to the one that's clicked

Crop Tool	C	Crops the image (unconstrained or fixed ratio)
Perspective Crop Tool	C	Crops the image within a perspective grid ★
Slice Tool	C	Slices images for optimization (for Web output)
Slice Select Tool	C	Selects slices by clicking

Eyedropper Tool	I	Samples colors from an image
3D Material Eyedropper Tool	I	Samples attributes of 3D objects ★
Color Sampler Tool	I	Places readout points in an image (for the Info panel)
Ruler Tool	I	Measures a distance or angle, or straightens the image
Note Tool	I	Creates Acrobat-compatible annotations
Count Tool	I	Counts objects in an image by clicking

Spot Healing Brush Tool	J	Corrects flaws without sampling
Healing Brush Tool	J	Corrects flaws based on a sampled area
Patch Tool	J	Corrects flaws based on a selected area
Content–Aware Move Tool	J	Repositions or extends an area of an image ★
Red Eye Tool	J	Corrects red-eye in a portrait photo

Brush Tool	B	Applies brush strokes
Pencil Tool	B	Draws freehand lines
Color Replacement Tool	B	Recolors an area while preserving the existing texture
Mixer Brush Tool	B	Simulates traditional paint strokes; allows colors to mix and smudge

Clone Stamp Tool	S	Clones imagery within or between documents
Pattern Stamp Tool	S	Stamps patterns

The upper part of the Tools panel

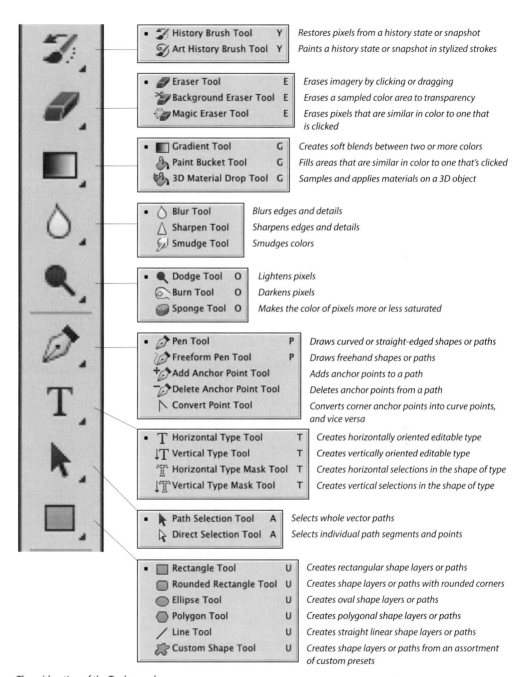

History Brush Tool	Y	Restores pixels from a history state or snapshot
Art History Brush Tool	Y	Paints a history state or snapshot in stylized strokes
Eraser Tool	E	Erases imagery by clicking or dragging
Background Eraser Tool	E	Erases a sampled color area to transparency
Magic Eraser Tool	E	Erases pixels that are similar in color to one that is clicked
Gradient Tool	G	Creates soft blends between two or more colors
Paint Bucket Tool	G	Fills areas that are similar in color to one that's clicked
3D Material Drop Tool	G	Samples and applies materials on a 3D object
Blur Tool		Blurs edges and details
Sharpen Tool		Sharpens edges and details
Smudge Tool		Smudges colors
Dodge Tool	O	Lightens pixels
Burn Tool	O	Darkens pixels
Sponge Tool	O	Makes the color of pixels more or less saturated
Pen Tool	P	Draws curved or straight-edged shapes or paths
Freeform Pen Tool	P	Draws freehand shapes or paths
Add Anchor Point Tool		Adds anchor points to a path
Delete Anchor Point Tool		Deletes anchor points from a path
Convert Point Tool		Converts corner anchor points into curve points, and vice versa
Horizontal Type Tool	T	Creates horizontally oriented editable type
Vertical Type Tool	T	Creates vertically oriented editable type
Horizontal Type Mask Tool	T	Creates horizontal selections in the shape of type
Vertical Type Mask Tool	T	Creates vertical selections in the shape of type
Path Selection Tool	A	Selects whole vector paths
Direct Selection Tool	A	Selects individual path segments and points
Rectangle Tool	U	Creates rectangular shape layers or paths
Rounded Rectangle Tool	U	Creates shape layers or paths with rounded corners
Ellipse Tool	U	Creates oval shape layers or paths
Polygon Tool	U	Creates polygonal shape layers or paths
Line Tool	U	Creates straight linear shape layers or paths
Custom Shape Tool	U	Creates shape layers or paths from an assortment of custom presets

The midsection of the Tools panel

Continued on the following page

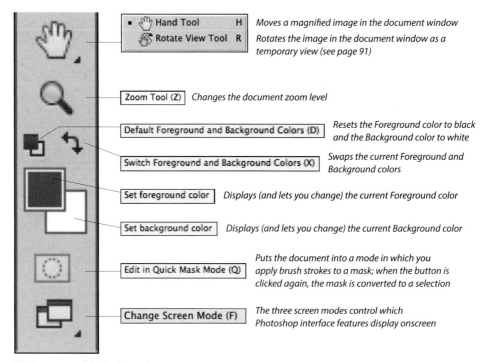

Hand Tool H	Moves a magnified image in the document window
Rotate View Tool R	Rotates the image in the document window as a temporary view (see page 91)

Zoom Tool (Z) Changes the document zoom level

Default Foreground and Background Colors (D) Resets the Foreground color to black and the Background color to white

Switch Foreground and Background Colors (X) Swaps the current Foreground and Background colors

Set foreground color Displays (and lets you change) the current Foreground color

Set background color Displays (and lets you change) the current Background color

Edit in Quick Mask Mode (Q) Puts the document into a mode in which you apply brush strokes to a mask; when the button is clicked again, the mask is converted to a selection

Change Screen Mode (F) The three screen modes control which Photoshop interface features display onscreen

The lower part of the Tools panel

Actions panel

An action is a recorded sequence of commands that can be replayed on one image or on a batch of images. For instance, you could use an action to save a copy of a document (or multiple documents) in a different format or color mode, or to apply filters for a special effect, such as to add a texture or frame. Using the Actions panel, you can record, store, edit, play, delete, save, and load actions. See Chapter 22.

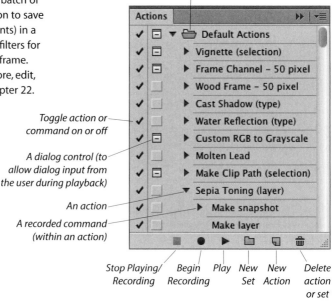

An action set

Toggle action or command on or off

A dialog control (to allow dialog input from the user during playback)

An action

A recorded command (within an action)

Stop Playing/Recording   Begin Recording   Play   New Set   New Action   Delete action or set

Adjustments panel ★

Each button on the Adjustments panel produces a different kind of adjustment layer, which you can use to apply flexible color and tonal edits and corrections to an image (the buttons are identified on page 202). Adjustment layers are listed on the Layers panel, but you choose and edit settings for them on the Properties panel. See Chapter 12.

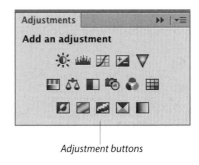

Adjustment buttons

Show the Brush Presets panel

Activate the options set and display its current settings

Brush panel

You will use the Brush panel to choose brush tips and custom brush settings for tools, such as the Art History Brush, Blur, Brush, Burn, Clone Stamp, Dodge, Eraser, History Brush, Mixer Brush, Pattern Stamp, Pencil, Sharpen, or Smudge tool. Using this panel, you can also choose special options for a graphics tablet and stylus.

If you click an options set name on the left side of the panel, the current settings for that set display on the right side. At the bottom of the panel, an example of a brush stroke made with the currently selected tip and settings displays in a preview. See Chapter 14.

Note: You can open this panel in several different ways: by choosing the panel name from the Window menu; by clicking the Toggle Brush Panel button on the Brush Presets panel; or if a tool that uses a brush is selected, by clicking the Toggle Brush Panel button on the Options bar.

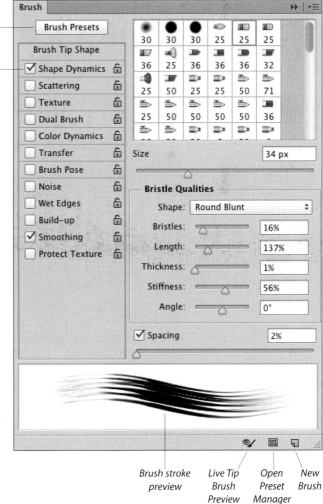

Brush stroke preview   *Live Tip Brush Preview*   *Open Preset Manager*   *New Brush*

Brush Presets panel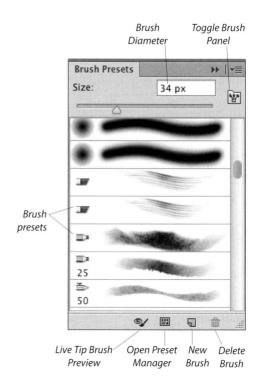

Use the Brush Presets panel to store, display, and choose from an assortment of predefined and user-created brush presets (tips and settings), for use with various editing tools. You can also use this panel to change the size of any brush preset temporarily, and to save a brush that you have customized as a new preset.

Via buttons at the bottom of the panel, you can turn the Live Brush Tip Preview on or off, and also access the Preset Manager dialog. This panel can be opened from the Window menu or by clicking the Brush Presets button on the Brush panel. See page 277.

Brush Diameter *Toggle Brush Panel*

Brush presets

Live Tip Brush Preview *Open Preset Manager* *New Brush* *Delete Brush*

Channels panel

The Channels panel lists and displays the thumbnails for all the color channels in the current document. To show an isolated channel in the document window, click the channel name or press the keystroke that is listed on the panel. To redisplay the composite image (all the channels combined, such as RGB or CMYK), click the topmost channel on the panel or press Ctrl-2/Cmd-2. See pages 2–4.

You can also use this panel to save and load alpha channels, which are saved selections (see page 164). And you can use it to create and store spot color channels, which commercial print shops use to print mixed ink colors (such as those in the PANTONE PLUS family).

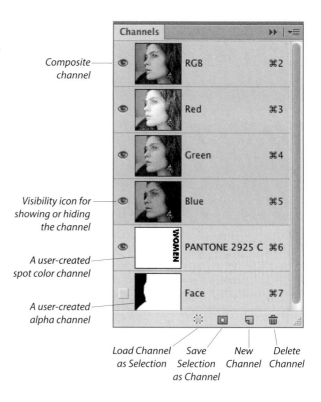

Composite channel

Visibility icon for showing or hiding the channel

A user-created spot color channel

A user-created alpha channel

Load Channel as Selection *Save Selection as Channel* *New Channel* *Delete Channel*

USING SCRUBBY AND POP-UP SLIDERS IN PHOTOSHOP

➤ For a fast way to change numerical values on the Options bar, on some panels (such as the Layers and Character panels), and in some dialogs, use the scrubby slider: Drag slightly to the left or right across the option name or icon.

➤ To access a pop-up slider (e.g., to choose an Opacity percentage on the Layers panel), click the arrowhead. To close a slider, click anywhere outside it or press Enter/Return. Tip: If you click an arrowhead to open a slider, you can press Esc to close it and restore its last setting.

➤ To change a value incrementally, click in a field in a dialog or panel (such as on the Character panel), then press the up or down arrow key on the keyboard.

Character panel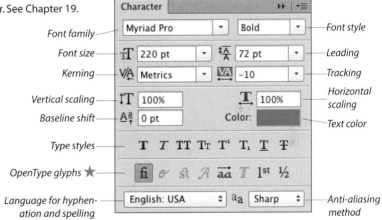

You can choose attributes for the type tools on the Character panel, which is shown here, or on the Options bar (see page 356). Open this panel from the Window menu, or when a type tool is selected, by clicking the Toggle Character and Paragraph Panels button ▤ on the Options bar. See Chapter 19.

Font family — Font style
Font size — Leading
Kerning — Tracking
Vertical scaling — Horizontal scaling
Baseline shift — Text color
Type styles
OpenType glyphs ★
Language for hyphenation and spelling — Anti-aliasing method

Character Styles panel ★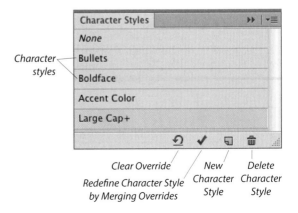

Using type styles, you can format and style your text more efficiently than by choosing individual type attributes, and you also ensure that your type has a consistent look throughout your document and among related documents. When you edit a style, all the text to which the style is linked updates automatically to reflect those changes.

Use character styles to apply unique attributes (e.g., a boldface font style, larger size, or different color) in order to accentuate key characters or phrases. Using the Character Styles panel, you can create and edit character styles and apply them to your text. To style entire paragraphs, use the Paragraph Styles panel. See page 365.

Character styles

Clear Override
Redefine Character Style by Merging Overrides
New Character Style
Delete Character Style

Clone Source panel

The Clone Source panel lets you keep track of up to five different source documents when cloning pixels with the Clone Stamp tool. The sources are represented by a row of buttons at top of the panel. You can also use this panel to hide, show, and control the opacity and mode of the clone overlay, and flip, scale, rotate, invert, or reposition the source pixels before or as you clone them. See pages 262–263.

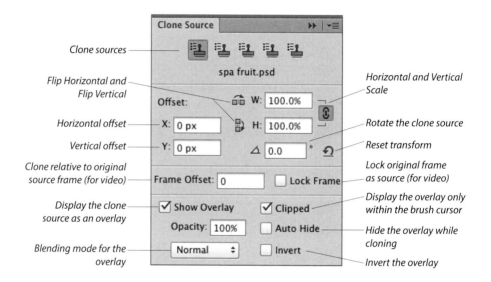

Clone sources

Flip Horizontal and Flip Vertical

Horizontal offset

Vertical offset

Clone relative to original source frame (for video)

Display the clone source as an overlay

Blending mode for the overlay

Horizontal and Vertical Scale

Rotate the clone source

Reset transform

Lock original frame as source (for video)

Display the overlay only within the brush cursor

Hide the overlay while cloning

Invert the overlay

Color panel

There are several ways to choose colors in Photoshop, including via the Color panel. After selecting a color model from the panel menu, you can either mix a color via the sliders or quick-select a color by clicking in the color ramp. See page 188. Colors are applied to an image by various tools (e.g., the Brush tool or Pencil tool) and commands (e.g., Edit > Fill, Image > Canvas Size).

To open the Color Picker (or interchangeably, the Color Libraries dialog), which are other methods for choosing colors, click once on the Foreground Color or Background Color square on the Color panel if it's already selected (has an outer white border), or double-click the square if it's not selected.

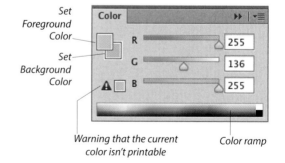

Set Foreground Color

Set Background Color

Warning that the current color isn't printable

Color ramp

Histogram panel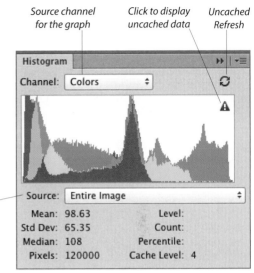

On the Histogram panel, you can view a graph of the distribution of tonal (light and dark) values in the current image, and compare them with modified tonal values as you apply color and tonal adjustments.

Via the Channel menu, you can opt to have the panel display data for the composite channel (all the channels combined, as shown at right) or for just a single channel. You can also expand the panel to display a separate histogram for each channel. See pages 208–209.

Source channel for the graph *Click to display uncached data* *Uncached Refresh*

Source of the pixel data (all layers or just the currently selected layer)

History panel

Each edit that is made to a document during the current work session (e.g., the use of a filter, tool, or command; the creation of a shape, type, or image layer; the application of a layer or layer comp) is listed as a separate state on the History panel, from the "Open" unedited state of the document at the top to the most recent state at the bottom. The most recent (last) edit keeps changing as you continue editing your document. If you click a prior state, the document is restored to that stage of editing. See Chapter 10.

The oldest history states are deleted from the panel as new edits are made — that is, when the maximum number of history states is reached (as specified in the History States field in Edit/ Photoshop > Preferences > Performance). All states are deleted when you close your document.

The New Snapshot command creates states that remain on the panel until you close your document, regardless of the current History States preference setting or the number of edits you apply.

The History Brush tool works in conjunction with the History panel to restore areas within your brush strokes to a state or snapshot that you designate as a source (see pages 283–284).

State of the image when opened

Snapshot (created from a state)

Current source for the History Brush tool

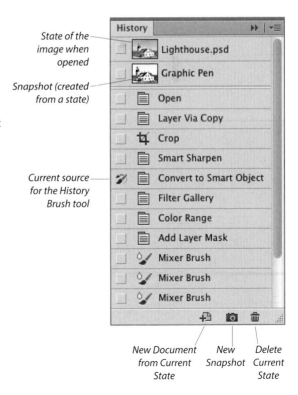

New Document from Current State *New Snapshot* *Delete Current State*

Info panel ℹ️

The Info panel provides up-to-the-minute data about your document. For example, it displays a color breakdown of the pixel under the pointer at its current location. As you apply color corrections, the panel displays the post-edit percentages, too. If you need yet more color data, you can place up to four color samplers in your document, and the Info panel will display readouts for those locations. The panel also lists the current coordinates of the pointer on the x/y axes.

Additional data may display on the Info panel depending on which tool is being used, such as the angle (A) and distance (L) between points as you use the Ruler tool; the dimensions (W and H) of a rectangular or elliptical selection or of a crop box; or the width (W), height (H), angle (A), and horizontal skew (H) or vertical skew (V) values of a layer or selection as you apply a transform edit.

Press a mini arrowhead for a color readout on the panel to choose a color model (it can differ from the current document color mode). If you prefer to do this via a dialog, choose Panel Options from the panel menu, then select a Mode for the First Color Readout and the Second Color Readout (see the dialog below).

In the Info Panel Options dialog, you can also choose Ruler Units for Photoshop (including the rulers in the document window), check which categories of Status Information you want to view in the lower part of the panel, and check Show Tool Hints to have the panel display helpful tips about the current tool. You can also choose a unit of measurement for Photoshop via the menu in the X and Y readout area on the Info panel.

Color breakdown for the pixel currently below the pointer

Menu for choosing a color model (for that readout)

```
Info                                    ▶▶  ▾≡
       R:  116/  74        C:  58/ 72%
  🖋   G:  124/  83    🖋  M:  43/ 56%
       B:  127/  86        Y:  42/ 54%
                           K:   8/ 32%
     8-bit                 8-bit
```

Location of the pointer in the document

```
       X:  3.907          W:  1.640
  +    Y:  3.187     ⌐    H:  2.387
```

Width and height of the current selection

```
Doc: 14.5M/48.4M
Adobe RGB (1998) (8bpc)
8.333 in x 6.773 in (300 ppi)
1 pixel(s) = 1.0000 pixels
Scratch: 675.1M/2.46G
Efficiency: 100%*
1.9s (26%)
Rectangular Marquee
```

Status information

```
Click and drag to move selection outline.
Use Shift, Opt and Cmd for additional
options.
```

Tool hint (tips pertaining to the current tool)

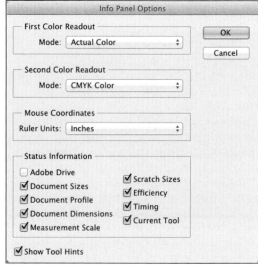

Use the Info Panel Options dialog to control which features are displayed on the panel.

Kuler panel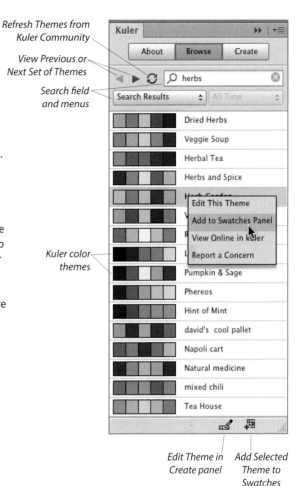

Kuler (pronounced "cooler") is a free, Web-hosted Adobe application that lets users create and upload color groups, called color themes. By using the Kuler panel in Photoshop, you can access and browse those themes. To use this panel, choose Window > Extensions > Kuler, and also make sure Allow Extensions to Connect to the Internet is checked in Edit/Photoshop > Preferences > Plug-Ins.

To use the Kuler panel efficiently, take advantage of its search field and menus. Enter a theme or creator name, or search by choosing ratings criteria from the menus. To add the currently selected theme to the Swatches panel in Photoshop, from the menu on the right side of that theme, choose Add to Swatches Panel. To save your favorite parameters for future searches, choose Custom on the first menu, enter one or more search terms, then click Save; those terms will be listed on the menu. To learn more about Kuler, go to kuler.adobe.com.

Refresh Themes from Kuler Community

View Previous or Next Set of Themes

Search field and menus

Kuler color themes

Edit Theme in Create panel   *Add Selected Theme to Swatches*

Layer Comps panel

When you create a layer comp (short for "composition"), it includes, collectively, any of the following document characteristics: the current layer Visibility settings (which layers are showing and which are not), the Position of imagery on each layer, and Appearance (layer styles, including the layer blending mode and opacity settings, and any layer effects). Via the Layer Comp Options dialog, you can decide which document attributes will be included in a comp, as well as add explanatory comments for the viewer. Layer comps save automatically with the document in which they're created.

Layer comps are useful if you're weighing the pros and cons of multiple versions of a document or if you need to present versions to a client for review. For example, say you've created a few designs for a book cover. You could create a layer comp of each one (e.g., the image with and without type, or with type in two different colors). When presenting your ideas, instead of having to open and close each separate file, you could simply display each version of the same file sequentially by clicking individual Layer Comp icons on and then off. See pages 422–424.

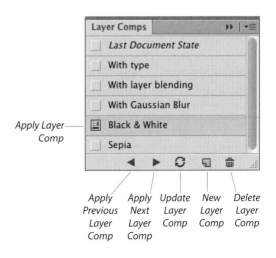

Apply Layer Comp

Apply Previous Layer Comp   *Apply Next Layer Comp*   *Update Layer Comp*   *New Layer Comp*   *Delete Layer Comp*

Layers panel

At minimum, every image contains either a solid-color Background or a transparent layer. Above that, you can add various kinds of layers:

➤ **Image** layers are created when you open a digital photo or paint a picture. See Chapter 8.

➤ **Adjustment** layers apply editable and removable adjustments to underlying layers. See Chapter 12.

➤ **Fill** layers apply an editable color, gradient, or pattern to underlying layers. See pages 193–195.

➤ **Smart Objects** are created when you place an Illustrator or PDF file, another Photoshop file, or a Camera Raw file into a Photoshop document; you can also convert an existing layer to a Smart

Object. To learn about Smart Objects and their unique role in Photoshop, see pages 248-255.

➤ **Editable type** layers are created by the Horizontal Type or Vertical Type tool. See pages 356–357.

➤ **Shape** layers are produced by a shape tool, and contain vector shapes. See Chapter 21. ★

Using the Layers panel, you can create, hide, show, duplicate, restack, group, link, lock, merge, flatten, and delete layers. You can also use this panel to change the blending mode, opacity, or fill opacity of a layer; attach a mask to a layer; and apply layer effects.

You'll be using this panel in every work session!

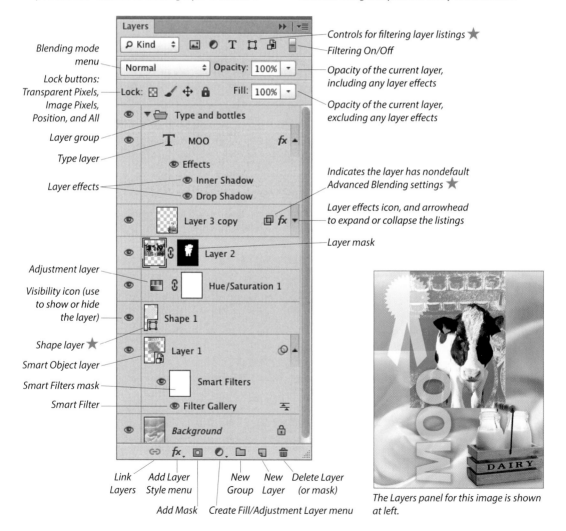

Blending mode menu — Normal

Lock buttons: Transparent Pixels, Image Pixels, Position, and All

Layer group — Type and bottles

Type layer — T MOO

Layer effects — Effects / Inner Shadow / Drop Shadow

Adjustment layer

Visibility icon (use to show or hide the layer)

Shape layer ★

Smart Object layer

Smart Filters mask

Smart Filter

Controls for filtering layer listings ★
Filtering On/Off
Opacity of the current layer, including any layer effects
Opacity of the current layer, excluding any layer effects

Indicates the layer has nondefault Advanced Blending settings ★

Layer effects icon, and arrowhead to expand or collapse the listings

Layer mask

Link Layers / Add Layer Style menu / Add Mask / Create Fill/Adjustment Layer menu / New Group / New Layer / Delete Layer (or mask)

The Layers panel for this image is shown at left.

For the **Mini Bridge panel,** ![Mb] see pages 48–49.

Navigator panel ※

Using the Navigator panel, you can move a magnified image in the document window, change the document zoom level, or target an area for magnification. See page 90. (To zoom or move the image in the window by using tools or keyboard shortcuts instead, see pages 89–91.)

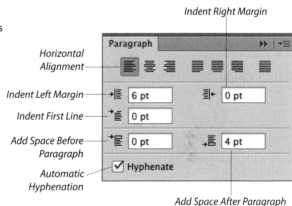

View box (use to magnify or move the document in the window)

52.79%

Zoom field   Zoom Out   Zoom   Zoom In
button   slider   button

Paragraph panel ¶

When creating or editing paragraph type, you can use the Paragraph panel to apply paragraph-level settings, including horizontal alignment, indentation, spacing before, spacing after, and automatic hyphenation. From the panel menu, you can access other type formatting commands (such as hanging punctuation and line-composer options), and open the Justification and Hyphenation dialogs. See page 364.

Indent Right Margin

Horizontal Alignment

Indent Left Margin — 6 pt   0 pt

Indent First Line — 0 pt

Add Space Before Paragraph — 0 pt   4 pt

Automatic Hyphenation — ✔ Hyphenate

Add Space After Paragraph

Paragraph Styles panel ★ 🔲

Using paragraph styles, you can format and style whole paragraphs of text more efficiently than by choosing individual settings, and also ensure that your type looks consistent. When you edit a style, all the text to which the style is linked updates automatically. Using the Paragraph Styles panel, you can create and edit paragraph-level styles and apply them to your text. See page 365.

Paragraph Styles

Basic Paragraph
Buttons
Small Headers+
Body Text
Rollover Text
Large Headers

Clear Override

Redefine Paragraph Style by Merging Overrides

New Paragraph Style

Delete Paragraph Style

Properties panel ★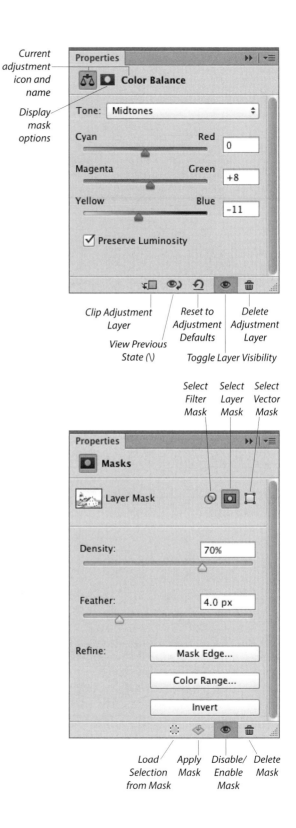

Adjustment layer options on the Properties panel

Tonal and color corrections that you apply directly to a layer via the Image > Adjustments submenu commands are permanent, whereas corrections that you apply to underlying layers via an adjustment layer remain editable and reversible.

To create an adjustment layer, you can use either the Adjustments panel or a menu on the Layers panel. To choose and edit adjustment settings, you use the sliders and fields on the Properties panel (the options are different for each kind of adjustment layer). Via buttons on the Properties panel, you can clip (limit) the adjustment effect to just the underlying layer, view the previous state of the adjustment, restore the default settings, hide and show the current adjustment effect, or delete the current adjustment layer. See Chapter 12.

Mask options on the Properties panel

In Photoshop, you can use a mask to hide areas of a layer. A mask is created for every adjustment layer automatically; you can also add a mask to other kinds of layers, such as image and type layers.

When you click the Select Filter Mask, Select Layer Mask, or Select Vector Mask button on the Properties panel or click a mask thumbnail on the Layers panel, options for editing the mask display on the Properties panel (this replaces the Masks panel from earlier versions of Photoshop).

The nondestructive controls on the Properties panel include a Density slider for adjusting the overall opacity of a layer mask and a Feather slider for softening its edges. The Mask Edge button opens the Refine Mask dialog, which provides the same controls for refining a mask as the Refine Edge dialog does for a selection (see page 175). The Color Range button opens the Color Range dialog, which you can use to redefine the black and white areas in the mask. The Invert button swaps the black and white areas in the mask. Via other buttons on this panel, you can load a mask as a selection, apply a mask to a layer permanently, disable or enable the mask effect, or delete the mask.

For layer masks, see pages 172–176; for filter masks, see pages 344–348; and for vector masks, see pages 392–394.

Styles panel

Each style in Photoshop is a unique collection of layer settings. It may include the settings for layer effects (e.g., Drop Shadow, Outer Glow) and/or the settings for blending options (e.g., layer visibility, opacity, and blending mode). In addition to using the Styles panel to apply a style to a layer, you can also use it create custom styles, which can be used in any document. Via commands on the panel menu, you can save, load, and append style libraries (collections of styles). See pages 382–383.

Swatches panel

The Swatches panel stores predefined and user-defined solid color swatches, which are applied by various tools, filters, and commands. Via commands on the panel menu, you can save, load, and append swatch libraries. See page 189.

Timeline panel

Using the Timeline panel, you can compose a sequence using audio clips and video files (including those from a camera that captures digital video). Imported clips display as tracks on the Timeline. You can alter the duration of a clip, apply a filter or adjustment effect to all or part of a clip, apply preset transition effects, then render a group of tracks into a choice of video file formats. See pages 425–432.

Tool Presets panel

A tool preset is a collection of settings for a particular tool that has been saved to, and can be accessed from, the Tool Presets panel. By using this panel (or the Tool Preset picker, which opens from the Options bar), you can create, save, load, sort, rename, reset, and delete presets for any Photoshop tool. See page 120.

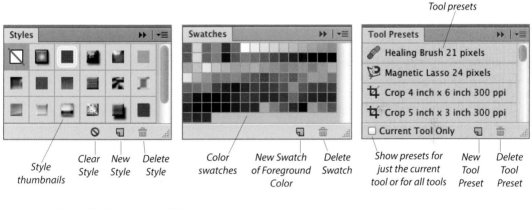

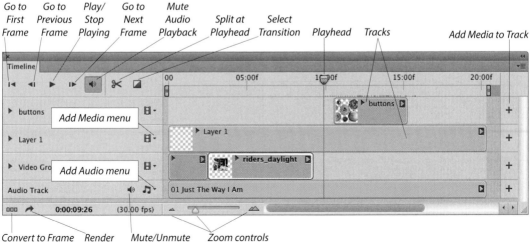

Managing presets via the pickers and panels

Photoshop presets are predefined items that you choose from a picker, such as brushes on the Brush Presets panel or picker or swatches on the Swatches panel. Other presets are found in less obvious locations, such as on the Contour pickers in some panels of the Layer Style dialog and on the Gradient picker in the Gradient Fill dialog. The preset categories include brushes, swatches, gradients, styles, patterns, contours, custom shapes, and tools. A collection of saved presets that can be loaded onto a picker is called a library.

New presets are created in various ways, such as when you define a pattern via the Define Pattern command, add a swatch to the Swatches panel, add a style to the Styles panel, create a gradient in the Gradient Editor dialog, or create a tool preset or brush (see the sidebar on this page).

Unsaved presets are stored in the Adobe Photoshop Preferences file temporarily. They stay on the picker when you relaunch Photoshop, but will be discarded if you replace them with another library or restore the default library to the picker. Thankfully, you can save your custom presets as a library, either via an individual picker (see the steps on the next page) or via the Preset Manager dialog (see page 119). You can load a saved library of presets onto its related picker at any time, and you can share preset libraries with other Photoshop users.

When you use the Preset Manager to create a library, you can pick and choose which presets are included. When you create a library from a panel or a preset picker, all the presets currently on the picker are included — you can't pick and choose. In the latter case, you should delete the presets that you want to exclude from the library first.

Note: When you delete a preset from a picker or panel, no documents are altered and no existing presets are deleted from any libraries.

To delete presets from a panel or picker:

1. Display the picker or panel from which you want to delete presets, such as the Brush Presets panel or picker, the Custom Shape picker, or the Styles, Swatches, or Tool Presets panel.

2. Do either of the following:

   Alt-click/Option-click a preset (scissors pointer). **A**

   Right-click a preset and choose **Delete** [preset name]. If an alert dialog appears, click OK.

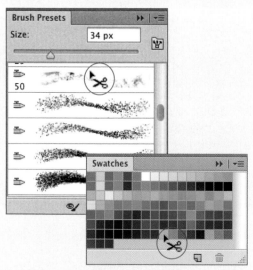

A *Alt-click/Option-click a swatch to delete it.*

HOW ARE PRESETS CREATED?

All of the following methods will produce a preset:

➤ Customize a brush using the Brush panel, then click the New Brush button ⬚ on the Brush or Brush Presets panel, or on the Brush Preset picker, which opens from the Options bar.

➤ Click the New Swatch of Foreground Color button ⬚ on the Swatches panel to add the current Foreground color as a swatch.

➤ Create a tool preset by clicking the New Tool Preset button ⬚ on the Tool Presets panel or the Tool Preset picker (see page 120).

➤ Create a gradient by clicking New in the Gradient Editor, which opens if you select the Gradient tool, then click the Gradient thumbnail on the Options bar, in the Gradient Fill dialog, or in the Layer Style dialog (for a Gradient Overlay effect).

➤ Create a style by clicking the New Style button ⬚ on the Styles panel or by clicking New Style in the Layer Style dialog.

➤ Create a pattern via Edit > Define Pattern.

➤ Create a custom shape by drawing a path or shape then choosing Edit > Define Custom Shape.

To save the presets currently on a picker as a library:

1. Make sure the preset picker or panel contains only the presets to be saved in a library (see the preceding page).

2. Do one of the following:

   From the Brush Presets, Swatches, Styles, or Tool Presets panel menu, ⬛☰ or from the Brush Presets or Custom Shape picker menu, ✿⁃ choose **Save** [preset type].**A**

   For a gradient, in the Gradient Editor, click **Save**; or choose **Save Gradients** from the Gradient picker menu ✿⁃ in the Gradient Fill dialog (for a gradient fill layer) or on the Gradient picker (Options bar, with the Gradient tool chosen).

   For a pattern, choose **Save Patterns** from the Pattern picker menu ✿⁃ in the Layer Style dialog for the Pattern Overlay effect, in the Edit > Fill dialog (Pattern chosen on the Use menu), or in the Pattern Fill dialog (for a fill layer).

3. In the Save dialog, enter a name, keep the default extension and location, then click Save.

4. Relaunch Photoshop to make your new library appear on the panel and/or preset picker menu and on the menu in the Preset Manager.

➤ To replace an existing library, in step 2 above, click the library name in the scroll window, click Save, then click Replace in the alert dialog.

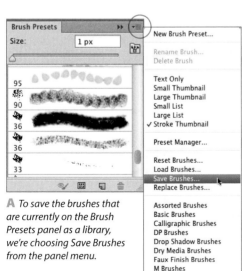

A *To save the brushes that are currently on the Brush Presets panel as a library, we're choosing Save Brushes from the panel menu.*

To load a library of presets onto a panel or picker via an individual panel or picker, follow the steps below; to load presets via the Preset Manager, see page 119.

To load a library of presets:

1. Choose a preset library name in one of these locations:

   The menu on the Brush Presets, Styles, Swatches, or Tool Presets panel. ⬛☰

   The Custom Shape picker menu ✿⁃ on the Options bar (the Custom Shape tool must be selected first); see page 387.

   The Gradient picker menu ✿⁃ in the Gradient Editor dialog (the Gradient tool must be selected first, then the Gradient thumbnail clicked on the Options bar); see pages 196–197.

   The Gradient picker menu ✿⁃ in the Gradient Fill dialog (for a gradient fill layer); see pages 194–195.

   The Custom Pattern picker menu ✿⁃ in the Edit > Fill dialog (choose Pattern from the Use menu); see page 199.

   The Pattern picker menu ✿⁃ in the Pattern Fill dialog (for a pattern fill layer).

   The Styles, Contour, Gradient Overlay, or Pattern Overlay picker menu ✿⁃ in the Layer Style dialog (see pages 371–372 and pages 378–379).

   The Tool Preset picker menu ✿⁃ on the Options bar (see page 120).

2. In the alert dialog, click **Append** to add the chosen library of presets to the currents ones on the panel or picker, or click **OK** to replace the current presets with those in the library.

   Note: If the panel or picker contains unsaved presets, another alert dialog will appear, giving you the option to save the existing presets as a library. Click Don't Save or Save.

➤ If the library you want to load isn't in the default location (and therefore isn't listed on its related panel or picker menu), choose Load [preset name] from the menu, locate the library, then click Open.

You can restore the default library to any panel or picker.

To restore the default presets to a panel or picker:

1. From a panel or picker menu, choose **Reset** [preset name].

2. When the alert dialog appears, click OK to replace the existing presets on the panel or picker with the default ones.

   Note: If you made changes to the current presets, another alert dialog will appear. Click Don't Save; or click Save, then use the Save dialog to save the current presets as a library.

Exporting and importing presets

Using the Export/Import Presets dialog, it's easy to export and import preset libraries and share them among Photoshop users on your network.

To export preset libraries: ★

1. Choose Edit > Presets > **Export/Import Presets**.

2. Click the **Export Presets** tab, click a preset library to be exported, then click the right arrowhead. ➤

Repeat for other libraries. (To remove a selected preset from the list, click the left arrowhead. A To remove or add all the presets on the list, click Remove All or Add All.)

3. Click **Export Presets**.

4. In the Choose a Folder dialog, choose a location, then click Open.

To import preset libraries: ★

1. Choose Edit > Presets > **Export/Import Presets**.

2. Click the **Import Presets** tab, click **Select Import Folder**, locate and click the folder containing the desired preset library or libraries, then click Open.

3. Click a preset library to be imported, then click the right arrowhead. ➤ Repeat for other libraries. (To remove a selected preset from the list, click the left arrowhead. To remove or add all the presets on the list, click Remove All or Add All.)

4. Click **Import Presets**.

➤ To import presets from an earlier version of Photoshop into Photoshop CS6, choose Edit > Presets > Migrate Presets, then click Yes in the alert dialog.

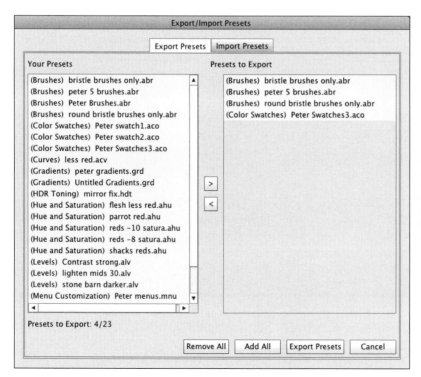

A In the Export/Import Presets dialog, for each selected library we decided to export, we clicked the right arrowhead. (Our next step will be to click Export Presets.)

Using the Preset Manager

Using the all-inclusive Preset Manager dialog, you can save and load Photoshop presets of any variety.

To save presets as a library via the Preset Manager:

1. To open the Preset Manager, do one of the following:

   Choose Edit > Presets > **Preset Manager**. ★

   Choose **Preset Manager** from the menu of any picker or panel (e.g., the Custom Shape picker or the Swatches or Styles panel).

   On the Brush or Brush Presets panel, click the **Open Preset Manager** button. 🖳

2. From the **Preset Type** menu, choose the category of presets for which you want to create a library, or press the shortcut that is listed on the menu.

3. From the menu in the dialog, ✿▾ choose a view option for the scroll window (such as Small Thumbnail or Small List). For Brushes, you can choose Stroke Thumbnail view to display a sample of the brush stroke alongside each thumbnail.

4. Shift-click or Ctrl-click/Cmd-click the presets to be saved in a library, then click **Save Set**. **A**

5. In the Save dialog, enter a name for the new library, keep the default extension and location, then click Save.

6. Click Done to exit the Preset Manager.

7. Relaunch Photoshop.

➤ To rename a preset when the Preset Manager is in a thumbnail view, double-click the thumbnail, then change the name in the dialog. If the Preset Manager is in a text-only or list view, double-click the preset name. You can also select multiple presets and then click Rename, in which case naming dialogs will open in succession.

You can reset any category of presets to the factory defaults, append (add) more presets to the current ones on the picker or panel, or replace the current presets with those in a library. Presets on the pickers and panels remain there when you relaunch Photoshop. Changes made in the Preset Manager appear in the corresponding picker, and vice versa.

To load presets via the Preset Manager:

1. Open the Preset Manager by following step 1 in the instructions at left.

2. From the **Preset Type** menu, choose a category of presets.

3. Any unsaved presets on the chosen picker will be deleted in the next step, unless you select the Append option. To save the current presets as a library before proceeding, follow steps 4–5 at left.

4. From the menu in the dialog, ✿▾ choose a library name; or to reload the default library, choose **Reset** [preset type]. In the alert dialog, click **Append** to add the new library to the current ones on the picker, or click OK to replace the current presets with the new ones.

   If the picker contains any unsaved presets (you didn't follow step 3, above), another alert will appear. Click Don't Save or Save.

5. *Optional:* To delete presets from the picker (not from the library), click a preset to be deleted or Shift-click or Ctrl-click/Cmd-click multiple presets, then click Delete. This can't be undone (but of course you can reload any library).

6. Click Done to exit the Preset Manager.

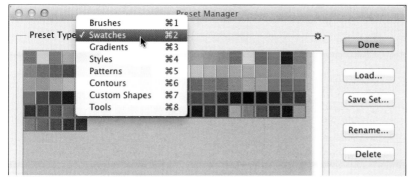

A *In the Preset Manager dialog, choose a category from the Preset Type menu, select all the presets to be saved in a library, then click Save Set.*

Creating tool presets

For any tool, you can choose a preset (such as a brush), Options bar settings, and a Foreground color (if applicable), then save that collection of settings as a tool preset. Thereafter, upon selecting that tool, you can simply choose your preset from the Tool Preset picker on the Options bar or from the Tool Presets panel; it contains all your saved settings. Although tool presets take some time and effort to set up initially, it's time well spent.

To acquaint yourself with the Tool Presets panel, ✂ uncheck Current Tool Only. The tool presets for all tools display. Click a tool preset; the tool with which that preset is used becomes selected automatically. Check Current Tool Only; only presets for the current tool display. Via the panel or picker menu, you can load additional presets (see page 117).

To create a tool preset:

1. Select a tool and choose Options bar settings for it.

   For some tools, such as the brush and shape tools, the current Foreground color can be included in the preset; for the Gradient tool, you can include the currently selected gradient. If you opt to do this, choose that color or gradient now.

2. Do either of the following:

   At the far left end of the Options bar, click the Tool Preset picker thumbnail or arrowhead. **A**

   Show the Tool Presets panel. ✂ **B**

3. Click the **New Tool Preset** button 🔲 on the picker or panel. The New Tool Preset dialog opens.

4. *Optional:* Rename the preset, if desired.

5. *Optional:* Check Include Color or Include Gradient (if listed).

6. Click OK. The new preset appears on the Tool Preset picker and the Tool Presets panel.

7. The presets that are on the Tool Presets panel (for all tools) will still be there when you relaunch Photoshop, ★ but will disappear if you replace them with a library. To preserve your custom presets for future use, see the first task on page 117.

➤ To restore the default tool presets, follow the steps on page 118. Don't confuse the Reset Tools command with the Reset Tool Presets command.

➤ To create a variation of an existing tool preset, click a preset, choose custom settings for it, then follow steps 3–6, above (rename it in step 4).

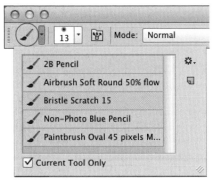

A *To open the Tool Preset picker, click the thumbnail or arrowhead on the Options bar.*

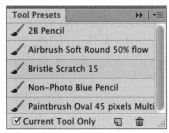

B *You can also create a tool preset via the Tool Presets panel.*

SOME IDEAS FOR TOOL PRESETS

Take note of which tools you use most often, and which settings you normally choose for them. Here are a few ideas for custom presets:

➤ Brush panel settings, Options bar settings, and a Foreground color for the Brush tool or Mixer Brush tool (for the latter tool, remember to choose Wet, Load, and Mix settings)

➤ Custom Options bar settings for the Crop tool

➤ Character panel and Options bar settings for the Horizontal Type or Vertical Type tool, including a color

➤ Frequently used Options bar settings for healing tools, such as the Healing Brush or Spot Healing Brush tool, or for the Clone Stamp or Sharpen tool

➤ Oft-used settings for the selection tools (e.g., Fixed Ratio settings for the Rectangular Marquee tool)

➤ Options bar settings for the Gradient tool, with the "Black, White" gradient preset chosen

Before applying adjustment or image-editing commands to an image in Photoshop, you need to make sure it has the proper resolution and dimensions. At any point, you can also crop or rotate it. In this chapter, you will learn how to change the resolution, dimensions, and canvas size of a file, and how to crop, straighten, flip, and rotate it.

Changing the document resolution and/or dimensions

In this chapter, you will encounter three related terms:

➤ The pixel count (pixel dimensions) of a file is arrived at by multiplying its pixel height and width values (as in 3000 x 2000 pixels).

➤ The resolution (or "res," for short) of a file — the fineness of detail — is measured in pixels per inch, or ppi (as in 250 or 300 ppi).

➤ The process of changing a file's pixel count (adding or deleting pixels) is called "resampling."

Some input devices (e.g., digital cameras that capture 8 megapixels of data or more, and high-end scanners) produce files with a higher pixel count than is needed for most standard printing devices. In Photoshop, you can take advantage of a file's high pixel count to increase its print size or print resolution. You can either keep the pixel count constant as you increase the print size (and thereby lower the resolution) or increase the resolution (and thereby lower the print size). No resampling occurs in either case, so the image quality remains the same.

You will need to resample a file if it contains too few or too many pixels to meet the resolution requirement of your target output device. If you resample a file as you increase its resolution, it will gain pixels and its storage size will increase accordingly. If you resample a file as you decrease its resolution (downsample it), it will lose pixels.

Even more important, resampling can reduce the sharpness of an image. This can be a problem for print output, depending on the output resolution and how drastically the file is resampled — although the blurring can be remedied somewhat by applying a sharpening filter (see pages 322–326). Resampling isn't an issue for Web output.

We'll show you how to resize three common types of files for print output (low res/large dimensions, high res/small dimensions, and medium res/small dimensions), and also how to resize a file for Web output.

PIXEL BASICS

7

PIXELS

Pixels, short for "picture elements," are the building blocks that make up a digital image — the tiny individual dots that a digital camera uses to capture a scene or that a computer uses to display images onscreen. When working in Photoshop and for Web output, you'll need to be aware of the pixel dimensions, or pixel count, of an image. For print output, you'll need to be aware of its resolution.

By default, photographs taken by a digital SLR camera are assigned a low resolution (usually 72 to 180 ppi) and very large width and height dimensions. They contain a sufficient number of pixels for high-quality output (prints as large as 8″ x 12″), provided you increase their resolution to the proper value. You can do this via the Image Size command in Photoshop.

To change the resolution of a digital photo (low res/large dimensions) for print output:

1. With the file open in Photoshop, choose Image > **Image Size** (Ctrl-Alt-I/Cmd-Option-I).

2. The Image Size dialog opens. Because you need to increase the image resolution, uncheck **Resample Image**.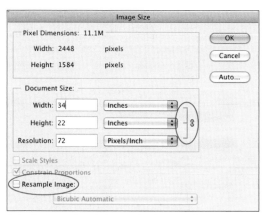

3. In the **Document Size** area, choose a unit of measure from the menu next to the Width field; the same unit will be chosen automatically for the Height.

4. Enter the necessary **Width** or **Height** for the desired print size; the Resolution value increases automatically.

5. If the resolution is now between 240 and 300 pixels per inch, you've achieved your goal, and you can just click OK.**B** The pixel dimensions didn't change, so you don't need to resharpen the image (**A–B**, next page).

   If the resolution is greater than 300 ppi, check **Resample Image**, then enter a **Resolution** of 300. Resampling will cause the Pixel Dimensions value of the image to change. The resampling method (shown on the menu at the bottom of the dialog) controls how Photoshop reassigns color values to any new pixels based on the values of existing pixels. The Bicubic options cause the least reduction in image quality. If you keep the default setting of Bicubic Automatic (our usual choice), Photoshop will use the best method. ★

6. Click OK. Since the image was resampled, you should now resharpen it (see pages 322–326).

➤ To restore the settings that were in effect when you opened the Image Size dialog, hold down Alt/Option and click the Reset button (Cancel becomes Reset).

➤ To specify a default Image Interpolation method for Photoshop features, including the Image Size dialog, see page 434.

A *In the Image Size dialog, uncheck Resample Image to make the Width, Height, and Resolution interdependent (note the link icon).*

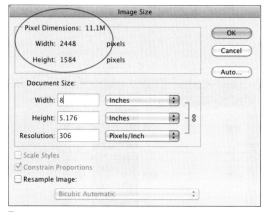

B *When we changed the Width value to 8, the Height value changed automatically and the Resolution value increased to 300, but the Pixel Dimensions remained the same.*

JPEGS PHOTOS IN CAMERA RAW

By default, Camera Raw assigns a resolution of 240 ppi to all photos it opens into Photoshop, including JPEG files. To achieve that resolution, Camera Raw preserves the pixel count but alters the Width and Height (Document Size). To increase the resolution of a JPEG file (say, to 300 ppi) or to reduce its Document Size dimensions, follow the steps on this page.

A *This photo has dimensions of 25 x 35.556 inches (way too large for our printer) and a resolution of 72 ppi.*

B *When we reduced the dimensions of the photo to 6 x 8.533 inches (Image Size dialog), the resolution increased automatically to 300 ppi. Because the pixel count didn't change, the image size and quality were preserved.*

Some scanned images have a high resolution and small dimensions. If you want to produce normal to large-sized printouts from such files, you will need to Increase their dimensions (this is possible because of their high resolution).

To resize an image that has a high resolution and small dimensions, for print output:

1. Choose Image > **Image Size** (Ctrl-Alt-I/Cmd-Option-I). The Image Size dialog opens.

2. Uncheck **Resample Image**.

3. Increase the **Width** or **Height** to the size needed for your printout. The Resolution will decrease.

   If the Resolution falls between 240 and 300 ppi, you're done; click OK. Because no resampling occurred, no sharpening is necessary.

   If the Resolution is still greater than 300 ppi, check **Resample Image,** C then lower the **Resolution** to 300. From the menu at the bottom of the dialog, choose the interpolation method of **Bicubic Automatic** (Photoshop uses the best method). ★ You've just resampled the image, so you should resharpen it after clicking OK (see pages 322–326).

4. Click OK.

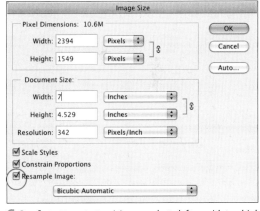

C *Our first attempt at resizing our photo left us with too high a resolution, so here we've checked Resample Image and will lower the Resolution but not the Width and Height.*

PERMITTING STYLES TO SCALE … OR NOT

When Constrain Proportions and Resample Image are checked in the Image Size dialog, you can check or uncheck Scale Styles to control whether any layer styles that were applied to the image will be scaled to fit the new size (to learn about styles, see Chapter 20).

Files with small dimensions and a resolution of only, say, 180 to 200 ppi lack a sufficient number of pixels for print output to be enlarged without resampling, so they must be resampled to achieve the needed dimensions. This is not an ideal scenario, as it reduces the image detail and sharpness.

To resize an image that has a medium resolution and small dimensions, for print output:

1. Choose Image > **Image Size** (Ctrl-Alt-I/Cmd-Option-I). The Image Size dialog opens.

2. Check **Resample Image**, and to preserve the width-to-height ratio of the image (and thereby prevent distortion), check **Constrain Proportions**.

3. Enter the desired **Width** for your printout. The Height value will change proportionally and the pixel dimensions and file storage size will increase.

4. Click OK. Because the image was resampled, you should now use a sharpening filter to resharpen it (see pages 322–326).

Because Web images are viewed on computer displays, which are low-resolution devices, they need to have a lower pixel count and a lower resolution than print images. To set a Web image to the desired output size, you will need to downsample it (discard image pixels).

Note: This is merely the first step in prepping an image for online viewing. On pages 463–468, you will learn how to optimize Photoshop files for the Web.

To change the pixel dimensions of an image for Web output:

1. Use File > Save As to make a copy of your file, then choose Image > **Image Size** (Ctrl-Alt-I/Cmd-Option-I). The Image Size dialog opens.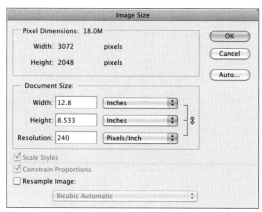

2. Check **Resample Image**, and to preserve the width-to-height ratio of the image (and thereby prevent distortion), check **Constrain Proportions**.

3. From the menu at the bottom of the dialog, choose the interpolation method of **Bicubic Automatic** (Photoshop uses the best method). ★

4. Enter a **Resolution** of 72 ppi.

5. In the **Pixel Dimensions** area, choose pixels from the menu, then enter the exact Width and/or Height dimensions needed.**B**

6. Click OK.

A The initial Image Size values of a typical digital photo are shown above. To prepare this photo for Web output, we will need to lower its pixel count.

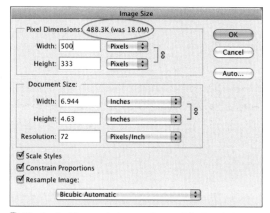

B We checked Resample Image, changed the Resolution to 72, and set the Width (under Pixel Dimensions) to 500. The file size (listed at the top) is now smaller because we lowered the document's pixel count. This image is now the right size for online viewing.

COPYCAT

In some dialogs that have Width and Height fields, if you choose a unit of measure from the menu for the Width, Photoshop sets the Height to the same unit, and vice versa. If you want to prevent this from happening, hold down Shift while choosing a unit; the unit will change just for that dimension.

COMPARING THE DOCUMENT RESOLUTION AND DIMENSIONS

Both the resolution of a document and its current zoom level affect its onscreen size. Figures **A–B** compare the same image at two different resolutions, and figures **C–D** compare the print sizes for those resolutions. The moral of the story is don't judge the output size of an image based on how it looks onscreen.

A *This original image has a resolution of 300 ppi.*

➤ *To set your Status bar to list the current document dimensions and resolution, choose Document Dimensions from the Status bar menu.*

B *This is the same image, same dimensions, except now it has a resolution of 150 ppi — half the resolution of the image shown at left. When viewed at the same zoom level (25%), this lower-resolution image displays at half the size of the original one because it contains fewer pixels (has a lower pixel count).*

C *For this 300 ppi version of the image, we chose View > Print Size, which zoomed the image to an onscreen approximation of the printout size (note the Document Dimensions on the Status bar). The zoom level here is 24%.*

D *We also chose View > Print Size for this low-res (150 ppi) version of the same image; note that the zoom level here is 48%. Although this image and the image at left will print at the same size, the print quality of this one will be lower because of its lower pixel count.*

Changing the canvas size

By using the Canvas Size command, you can enlarge or shrink the live, editable area of a document. Pixels can be added or deleted from one, two, three, or all four sides of the image. This is useful, say, if you want to make room for type, as in the example shown on this page, or to accommodate imagery from other documents in a collage (see Chapter 13).

To change the canvas size of a document:

1. Choose Image > **Canvas Size** (Ctrl-Alt-C/Cmd-Option-C). The Canvas Size dialog opens.

2. *Optional:* Choose a different unit of measure from the Width menu.

3. Do either of the following:

   Enter new **Width** and/or **Height** values. The dimensions are independent of one another; changing one won't affect the other. **A–B**

   Check **Relative**, then increase or reduce the **Width** and/or **Height** values to alter the ratio between those dimensions.

4. *Optional:* The black dot in the center of the Anchor arrows represents the existing image area. Click an arrow to reposition the image relative to the canvas. The arrows point to where the new canvas area will be added.

5. From the **Canvas Extension Color** menu, choose a color for any pixels that are added. Or to choose a custom color, choose Other or click the color square next to the menu, then click a color in the Color Picker (see page 186) or in the document window. Note: If the image doesn't have a Background (take a peek at the Layers panel), this menu won't be available.

6. Click OK. **C** Any added canvas area will automatically be filled with the color you chose in the preceding step, unless the image contains layers but not a Background, in which case the added canvas area will be transparent.

➤ To enlarge the canvas area manually with the Crop tool, see page 132.

A *This is the original image.*

B *To add canvas area to the top of the image, in the Canvas Size dialog, we increased the Height value, then clicked the bottom middle Anchor arrow/square to move the black dot downward.*

C *After adding pixels to the top of the canvas, we created an editable type layer.*

Cropping an image

To crop an image manually: ★

1. Choose the **Crop** tool ⊡ (C or Shift-C). A crop box with handles displays over the image.

2. Using the context menu (right-click in the image) or the **Aspect Ratio** (first) menu on the Options bar, do one of the following:

   To create a crop ratio that differs from the original image, keep the default setting of **Unconstrained**.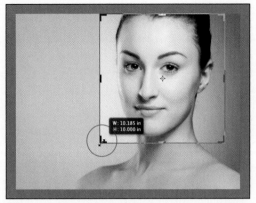

   To preserve the original proportions of the document while cropping it, choose **Original Ratio**.

   Choose a ratio preset (or enter custom ratio values in the fields on the Options bar).

3. To preserve the cropped areas, uncheck **Delete Cropped Pixels** on the Options bar.

4. Drag a handle or an edge of the crop box to define which part of the image you want to keep.**B**

   Optional: To resize the crop box from the center, drag a handle with Alt/Option held down. To preserve the current ratio, Shift-drag a corner handle.

   Optional: To switch the orientation of the crop box, click the Rotate Crop Box button ↻ on the Options bar.**C**

   ➤ To restore the original ratio at any time, choose Original Ratio from the Aspect Ratio menu.

5. Do any of the following (all optional):

   To **reposition** the part of the image that Photoshop will preserve, drag inside the box.

   To **rotate** the image in the crop box, position the cursor just outside the box, then drag in a circular direction. (To change the locus from which the image rotates, drag the reference point away from the center of the box.)

   To **hide** or **show** the cropped areas, press /. For more display options, see the next page.

6. To accept the crop edits, double-click inside the crop box or press Enter/Return. You should resharpen the image, as its pixel count has changed. Note: Because Delete Cropped Pixels was unchecked (in step 3), Photoshop converted the Background to a layer; see the next chapter. You can drag the cropped areas into view with the Move tool.

   ➤ To save a custom ratio for future use, choose Save Preset from the Aspect Ratio menu, enter a name, then click OK; your preset will appear on the menu.

A We chose the Crop tool and the Unconstrained option on the Options bar, and are resizing the crop box.

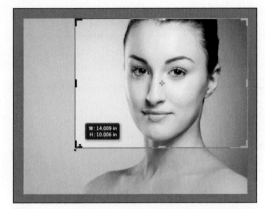

B Here, we chose the 5 x 7 aspect ratio preset on the Options bar, and are dragging a handle on the crop box.

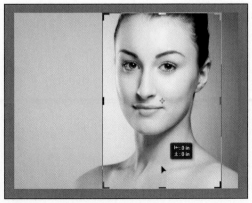

C Next, we clicked the Rotate Crop Box button on the Options bar, and are repositioning the image within the box.

When you reset the crop box, it is restored to the edges of the canvas, the image rotation is reset to the x/y axis, and the Aspect Ratio is reset to Unconstrained.

To reset the crop box: ★

With the Crop tool selected,🔲 click the **Reset** button 🔄 on the Options bar or right-click in the image and choose **Reset Crop**.

To choose preview and shield options for the Crop tool: ★

Select the Crop tool, and from the **Crop Options** menu ⚙. on the Options bar,**A** check any or all of these options:

Auto Center Preview to allow the image to shift in the opposite direction as you drag any of the handles on the crop box.

Show Cropped Area (/) to display the cropped areas in a light opacity around the crop box.

Enable Crop Shield to cover the cropped areas with a tint. From the Color menu, choose Match Canvas (the least obtrusive option); choose an Opacity value; and check Auto Adjust Opacity to let the shield disappear temporarily as you edit the crop box.

➤ To use the new crop features of Photoshop, keep Use Classic Mode unchecked.

➤ If you crop an image nondestructively (Delete Cropped Pixels unchecked), then reselect the Crop tool and click in the image with Show Cropped Area checked, the cropped areas will redisplay.

The overlay options (guide lines) for the Crop tool are based on timeless aesthetic principles.

To choose overlay options for the Crop tool: ★

1. Select the Crop tool and click in an image.

2. On the **View** menu (Options bar), do the following:

   Choose an overlay option (top part of the menu).

   Choose when or if you want the overlay to display: **Auto Show Overlay** (the overlay displays only while the mouse button is pressed), **Always Show Overlay** (the overlay stays visible once you've clicked in the image with the Crop tool), or **Never Show Overlay** (the overlay doesn't display).

3. As you drag a handle of the crop box or reposition the image within it, position a guide line (or sections within the guide lines) over one or more key elements or shapes in your photo **B–C** (and **A–D**, next page).

➤ To cycle through the six guide options, click the Crop tool in the image, then press the letter O. To reverse the orientation of the Triangle or Golden Spiral guide lines, press Shift-O.

A From the Crop Options menu, choose preview and shield options for the Crop tool.

GOLDEN RATIO

B Using the Golden Ratio option, we're positioning the horizontal guide lines at natural divisions in the landscape, with an intersection over the red buildings. (The Rule of Thirds option, a simplified form of Golden Ratio, has equal divisions.)

C This is the result.

TRIANGLE

B *This is the result.*

A *Here, we're using the Triangle view option (Aspect Ratio: Unconstrained). Note how the two most important features of the photo fall within a triangle: The chef's hands and skillet, and the finished plates.*

PRESSING ESC INSTEAD OF RESET

If you press Esc after editing the crop box with the Crop tool, the image will be reset to the *x/y* axis and the box will be reset to the maximum size within the current Aspect Ratio setting (the aspect ratio won't be reset to Unconstrained).

OVERRIDING THE SNAP

Normally, if you resize a crop box near the edge of the canvas area and the View > Snap To > Document Bounds option is on (has a check mark), the box will snap to the edge of the canvas area. If you want to position the crop box slightly inside or outside the edge of the canvas, you will need to override the snap to Document Bounds function temporarily: Start dragging one of the handles of the box, then hold down Ctrl/Control and continue to drag.

GOLDEN SPIRAL

C *Using the Golden Spiral view option, we're positioning the center of the spiral at the key element in the photo.*

D *This is the result.*

Cropping multiple images

Because the current settings stick with the Crop tool until you change them, you can easily apply the same aspect (width-to-height) ratio, size, or resolution values to multiple images. In this first task, we'll show you how to crop documents to the same aspect ratio. The dimensions of the images can vary.

To crop one or more images according to an aspect ratio: ★

1. Open one or more images, then click in one of them. Choose the **Crop** tool 🔲 (C or Shift-C).

2. Do either of the following:

   Right-click in the image and choose **Use Front Image Aspect Ratio**.

   Resize the crop box, then right-click in the image and choose **Use Crop Box Aspect Ratio** from the context menu.

   The width-to-height ratio values of the document will be listed on the Options bar, and will stick with the Crop tool until you change them.

3. Size the crop box, if desired, then double-click inside the box or press Enter/Return to accept it.

4. Click the tab of another open document. Resize the crop box and accept the crop edits; or to accept the crop without resizing it, press Enter/Return twice. Repeat for any other open documents.

Here you will crop multiple documents to an exact resolution value and dimensions. If you like, you can save your settings so they are available as a preset on the Aspect Ratio menu.

To crop multiple images to a specified size and resolution: ★

1. Open two or more images, then click in one of them. Choose the **Crop** tool 🔲 (C or Shift-C).

2. From the **Aspect Ratio** menu on the Options bar, choose **Size & Resolution**.

3. The Crop Image Size & Resolution dialog opens (**A**, next page). Enter the desired Width, Height, and Resolution values. Check Save as Crop Preset, if desired, to have your settings appear as a new preset on the Aspect Ratio menu, then click OK.

4. If you checked Save as Crop Preset, the New Crop Preset dialog opens (**B**, next page). Either keep the default name or change it, then click OK.

5. *Optional:* Resize the crop box (the dimensions and resolution you specified will still apply to the crop box, regardless of its size).

6. To accept the crop edits, either double-click inside the box or press Enter/Return.

7. Click the tab of another open document (**C**, next page). Resize the crop box and accept the crop; or to accept the crop without resizing it, press Enter/Return twice. Repeat for any other open documents.

You can also crop multiple images to the dimensions and resolution of an existing document (this task), or to a crop box and resolution (next task).

To crop multiple images to the size and resolution of a document: ★

1. Open one or more images, including one that has the desired dimensions and resolution.

2. Choose the **Crop** tool 🔲 (C or Shift-C).

3. Right-click in the image that has the desired width, height, and resolution values and choose **Use Front Image Size & Resolution** from the context menu. New width, height, and resolution values display on the Aspect Ratio menu, and will stick with the Crop tool until you change them.

4. Click the tab of another open image. Resize the crop box, if desired, then accept the crop edits; or to accept the crop without editing it, press Enter/Return twice. Repeat for any other documents.

To crop multiple images to a crop box in, and resolution of, a document: ★

1. Open one or more images, including one that has the desired resolution.

2. Choose the **Crop** tool 🔲 (C or Shift-C).

3. In the document that has the desired resolution, resize the crop box to the desired proportions, then right-click in the image and choose **Use Crop Box Size & Resolution** from the context menu.

4. To accept the crop edits, either double-click inside the box or press Enter/Return.

5. Click the tab of another open document. Resize the crop box, if desired, then accept the crop edits; or to accept the crop without editing it, press Enter/Return twice. Repeat for any other documents.

A *We chose the Crop tool, then chose Size & Resolution from the Aspect Ratio menu. In the Crop Image Size & Resolution dialog, we entered values, checked Save as Crop Preset, then clicked OK.*

B *When the New Crop Preset dialog appeared, we clicked OK, then pressed Enter/Return to accept the crop in the current document.*

APPLYING STICKY SETTINGS QUICKLY ★

When you change the settings for the Crop tool, they remain in effect until you change them — even if you exit/quit and relaunch Photoshop. To apply the current (sticky) crop settings to a document, click the Crop tool, press Enter/Return to make the crop box active, then press Enter/Return once more to accept the crop.

USING A SELECTION TO DEFINE A CROP BOX ★

If you create a rectangular selection before choosing the Crop tool, the crop box will match the selection boundary. If you want to force the crop box to ignore the selection, press Esc.

GETTING A NEW PERSPECTIVE

To correct perspective problems in a photo (such as keystoning) that are caused by camera lens distortion, we recommend using the Lens Correction filter (see pages 318–319) instead of the Perspective Crop tool. Why? The filter lets you preview your edits; the tool does not.

C *Our custom size and resolution preset appeared on the Aspect Ratio menu on the Options bar. We clicked another document tab, so as to apply the same preset. If we accept this crop, the document dimensions will shrink from 18½ x 12½ in. (current) to 6 x 4 in., and the resolution will change to 300 ppi.*

if you make the crop box larger than the original image, the canvas size will increase. Unlike the Canvas Size command, this technique gives you manual control over how much canvas area is added and where. Another use for this technique is to include imagery that extends beyond the live canvas area. All layers are affected.

To enlarge the canvas area with the Crop tool: ★

1. To display more of the work canvas (gray area) around the image, enlarge the Application frame or lower the zoom level of your document.

2. Choose the **Crop** tool ▯ (C or Shift-C).

3. From the Aspect Ratio menu on the Options bar, choose **Unconstrained**.

4. Drag a corner or midpoint handle of the box outside the live canvas area. **A**

5. On the Options bar, check **Delete Cropped Pixels** to fill the additional canvas area on the Background with the current Background color; also choose a Background color (see Chapter 11). Or uncheck this option to fill the additional area with transparent pixels and convert the Background to a layer.

6. To accept the crop edits, either press Enter/ Return or double-click inside the box. **B**

The Trim command trims away any excess transparent or solid-color areas from the border of all the layers in an image. Of course, the end result is still a rectangular image.

To trim areas from around an image:

1. If you want to trim transparent areas from a document that contains layers, on the Layers panel, ▼ hide the Background by clicking its visibility icon. ◉

2. Choose Image > **Trim**.

3. In the Trim dialog, click a **Based On** option:

   Transparent Pixels trims transparent pixels from the edges of the image. If Photoshop doesn't detect any such areas in the image, this option isn't available.

   Top Left Pixel Color removes any border areas that match the color of the left uppermost pixel in the image.

   Bottom Right Pixel Color removes any border areas that match the color of the bottommost right pixel in the image.

4. Check which areas of the image you want Photoshop to **Trim Away: Top, Bottom, Left,** and/or **Right**.

5. Click OK.

A We're dragging the right midpoint handle outside the canvas area to add more canvas area to that side of the image (Delete Cropped Pixels was checked).

B When we released the mouse, the added canvas pixels filled automatically with brown, which was our current Background color (we accepted the crop edit).

Straightening a crooked image

When you straighten a crooked image with the Crop tool, all layers in the image are affected.

To straighten a crooked image with the Crop tool: ★

1. Choose the **Crop** tool 🔲 (C or Shift-C). The crop box displays.

2. On the Options bar, click **Straighten** or the Straighten icon 🔲 or hold down Ctrl/Cmd.

3. Drag along a shape in the image to be aligned to the horizontal or vertical axis, then release.**A**

4. *Optional:* To adjust the rotation angle, drag outside the crop box slightly. You can also edit the crop box via the usual controls.

5. Press Enter/Return or double-click inside the box.**B** The image will rotate and the resulting blank areas will be shaved off automatically.

➤ To cancel the straighten and crop edits while the Crop tool is still selected, click the **Reset** button 🔄 on the Options bar.

When you use the Ruler as a straightening tool, only the current layer is affected and pixels outside the live canvas area on that layer are preserved.

To straighten a crooked layer with the Ruler tool: ★

1. Click the Background or a layer.

2. Choose the **Ruler** tool 📏 (I or Shift-I).

3. Drag along a shape in the image to be aligned to the horizontal or vertical axis. The angle will be listed as the **A** value on the Options bar.

4. *Optional:* To change the angle of the line, move either one of its endpoints.

5. On the Options bar, click **Straighten Layer**. If you straightened the Background, it will be converted to a layer.

6. *Optional:* Reposition the layer with the Move tool.

A *This image is slightly askew. We chose the Crop tool, clicked Straighten on the Options bar, then dragged downward along one of the columns.*

B *When we accepted the crop, the image was reoriented along the angle we defined, and the resulting blank areas were trimmed away.*

Flipping or rotating an image

You can flip or rotate all the layers in an image, or just one layer at a time. (To learn about layers, see the next chapter.)

To flip all the layers in an image:

Choose Image > Image Rotation > **Flip Canvas Horizontal A–B** or **Flip Canvas Vertical**.

➤ If you flip a whole image that contains lettering or vector type which is now reading backwards, don't flip out! Just "unflip" that layer using the Flip Horizontal command (see the next task). We've seen photos in magazines and catalogs that were flipped, making it impossible to read, say, the lettering in a stack of books.

To flip one layer:

1. Click a layer on the Layers panel.
2. Choose Edit > Transform > **Flip Horizontal** or **Flip Vertical**. Note: Any layers that are linked to the selected layer or layers will also flip.

To rotate all the layers in an image:

Do either of the following:

Choose Image > Image Rotation > **180°, 90° CW** (clockwise), or **90° CCW** (counterclockwise).

Choose Image > Image Rotation > **Arbitrary**. Enter an **Angle** value, click **°CW** (clockwise) or **°CCW** (counterclockwise), then click OK.

To rotate one layer:

1. On the Layers panel, click a layer.
2. Choose Edit > Transform > **Rotate 180°, Rotate 90° CW**, or **Rotate 90° CCW**.

IT CROPS! IT STRAIGHTENS!

File > Automate > Crop and Straighten Photos locates rectangular areas in a document, rotates and crops those areas to square them off (if necessary), then opens each one as a new document. Note: This action isn't as smart as you are, so it can be fooled. Take into account these suggestions and precautions:

➤ You can use the action to unrotate a Photoshop document that was previously rotated. Apply it to a one-layer document in which the outer part of the image area doesn't contain a lot of white.

➤ You can scan multiple photos at a time and let the action sort them into individual documents. For better results, don't let the photos overlap one another or hang off the side of the scanner.

➤ To control which area is cropped and straightened, select that area, including some extra pixels, before choosing the command. The unselected area will be discarded.

A This is the original image.

B This is the same image after we chose the Flip Canvas Horizontal command.

When you open a photo into Photoshop, the image is listed as the Background on the Layers panel. By adding layers of various kinds on top of the Background, you can build complexity and flexibility into your documents.**A**
For example, above the Background, you could add some editable text on one layer and perhaps a shape or imagery surrounded by transparency on another layer. Layers can be added or deleted as needed, and they can be edited individually.

Unlike the Background, which stays fully opaque and is stacked on the bottom of the Layers panel, a layer can contain partially or fully transparent areas and can be moved upward or downward in the stack. Within the transparent areas in a layer, you can see through to underlying layers. Photoshop uses a checkerboard pattern to represent transparent areas.

Because the Layers panel is so essential to image editing in Photoshop, we have devoted this whole chapter to helping you master its features. By the end of this chapter, you will know how to create, duplicate, select, restack, group, delete, hide, show, move, lock, filter, merge, and flatten layers, as well as change their opacity. Those techniques, along with the selection and masking techniques in the next chapter, will give you the necessary foundation for future tasks in this book.

LAYER ESSENTIALS

8

IN THIS CHAPTER

A *This document contains a type layer and five image layers, all of which are stacked above the Background.*

PRACTICE ON AN IMAGE

You can download the file shown at left (see page xiii). When you open it, click next to a layer name, then hide that layer by clicking the visibility icon. Click again to redisplay the icon and layer.

Creating layers

When you open a digital photo (say, from Camera Raw) into Photoshop, the image appears on the Background. If you create a new, blank document and choose the option of Background Contents: White or Background Color in the File > New dialog, that image will also have a Background. If you were to choose Background Contents: Transparent instead, the document would contain a layer and no Background. In this book, we identify the Background in a Photoshop document with an initial cap "B," to distinguish it from the background (versus foreground) area of an image.

In these steps, you will learn how to create a new, blank image layer. To that layer, you can add pixels by applying brush strokes, cloning imagery, pasting into a selection, or performing other edits. You may add as many layers to a file as you like, but remember that a large image containing many image layers will utilize a fair amount of storage space and system memory.

Note: In later chapters, you will learn how to create adjustment, type, Smart Object, and shape layers.

To add a new, blank layer to a document:

1. Display the Layers panel.
2. Click a layer or the Background. The new layer is going to appear above this selected one.
3. Click the **New Layer** button at the bottom of the panel.**A** The new layer will have the default blending mode of Normal and the default setting for both Opacity and Fill of 100%.**B**

➤ To choose options for a layer as you create it, Alt-click/Option-click the New Layer button or press Ctrl-Shift-N/Cmd-Shift-N. In the New Layer dialog, you can enter a layer Name and choose a nonprinting Color for the area on the Layers panel behind the visibility icon (see "To color-code a layer" on page 145).

➤ To rename a layer right on the panel, see the sidebar on page 138.

A We clicked the Background, then clicked the New Layer button.

B A new blank layer (Layer 1) appeared above the Background.

Another way to create a layer is by copying or cutting imagery from an existing layer or the Background and transferring it to a new layer. This can be done easily via a simple command.

To turn a selection of pixels into a layer:

1. On the Layers panel, click an image layer or the Background, then create a selection in the document (if you're new to Photoshop, see the steps on page 152).**A**

2. To transfer the selected pixels to a new layer, do either of the following:

   To put a copy of the selected pixels onto a new layer while leaving the original layer unchanged, right-click in the document and choose **Layer via Copy** or press Ctrl-J/Cmd-J.**B**

   To put the selected pixels on a new layer and remove them from the original layer, right-click in the document and choose **Layer via Cut** or press Ctrl-Shift-J/Cmd-Shift-J. If you cut pixels from a layer, Photoshop will fill the exposed area on the original layer with transparency; if you cut pixels from the Background, the exposed area will be filled with the current Background color (see pages 185 and 239).

Follow these steps to duplicate a layer or layer group, or to turn a copy of the Background into a layer. (To learn about layer groups, see pages 140–141.)

To duplicate a layer or layer group:

Do one of the following:

Click a layer or a layer group, or Ctrl-click/Cmd-click multiple layers, ★ then press Ctrl-J/Cmd-J.

Drag a layer, layer group, or the Background over the **New Layer** button 🔲 at the bottom of the Layers panel. The duplicate will appear above the one you dragged.

To name the new layer as you create it, right-click one layer, layer group, or the Background and choose **Duplicate Layer(s)** or **Duplicate Group**. In the dialog, change the name in the "As" field (ignore the Destination field), then click OK.

➤ To control whether Photoshop adds the word "copy" to duplicate layer names automatically, choose Panel Options from the Layers panel menu, then check or uncheck the Add "Copy" to Copied Layers and Groups feature.

➤ When you duplicate a layer, any masks and/or effects on that layer are also duplicated.

A We selected an area of the Background in this document.

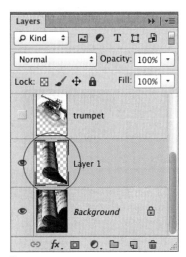

B When we pressed Ctrl-J/Cmd-J, a copy of the selected pixels appeared on a new layer (Layer 1).

There are many things that can be done to a layer that can't be done to the Background. For example, you can't move the Background upward in the layer stack; change its blending mode, Opacity, or Fill setting; attach a mask to it; or embellish it with layer effects. You can, however, convert the Background to a layer, at which time it will adopt all the functions of a normal layer.

To convert the Background to a layer:

On the Layers panel, do either of the following:

Hold down Alt/Option and double-click the Background to turn it into a layer without choosing options.

Double-click the Background **A** to open the New Layer dialog, **B** then do any of the following: Change the Name, choose a Color for the area behind the visibility icon, or change the blending Mode or Opacity percentage. Click OK. **C**

You can also do the reverse of the preceding instructions, which is to convert any layer to the Background. This will come in handy, say, if you use the Crop tool with the Delete Cropped Pixels option off (which converts the Background to a layer), then decide you want to make the bottommost layer into the Background again.

To convert a layer to the Background:

1. Click the layer to be converted.

2. Choose Layer > New > **Background from Layer**. The new Background will appear in its standard stacking position as the bottom listing.

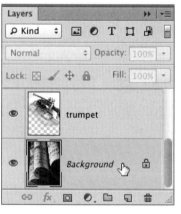

A We double-clicked the Background in this image.

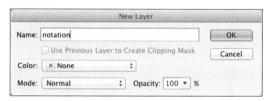

B We typed a name for the layer in the New Layer dialog.

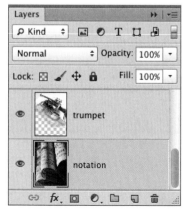

C The former Background is now a full-fledged layer.

RENAMING LAYERS AND LAYER GROUPS

► To rename a layer or layer group, double-click the layer or layer group name, type a new name, then press Enter/Return or click outside the field.

► After double-clicking a layer name, you can press Tab to highlight the name of the next listing below it, or press Shift-Tab to highlight the listing above it (don't include the Background in the cycle). ★

Tip: To identify a layer name (e.g., if the name is too long to display fully), use the Tool Tip. ★

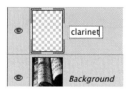

Selecting layers

There are good habits and bad habits. Here's a good one: Before applying a filter, brush stroke, or other image edit to your document, select the layer that you want Photoshop to alter. Easy to do, easy to forget! When a layer or layer group is selected, it has a blue highlight and the layer or group name is listed in the title bar of the document window.

To select layers via the Layers panel:

Do one of the following:

To select a layer or layer group, click either the layer thumbnail or the blank area to the right of the layer or group name.**A**

To select multiple layers, click a layer, then Shift-click the last in a series of consecutively listed layers, or Ctrl-click/Cmd-click individual layers (not their thumbnails). If you need to deselect an individual layer, Ctrl-click/Cmd-click it.

To select all the layers in your document (but not the Background), choose Select > All Layers or press Ctrl-Alt-A/Cmd-Option-A.

To select a layer or layer group by clicking in the document:

1. Choose the **Move** tool or hold down V.

2. Do either of the following:

   To select the topmost layer that contains non-transparent pixels below the pointer, right-click in the document window and choose a layer or layer group name from the context menu.**B** (Adjustment layers may also be listed on the menu; see Chapter 12.)

   Check **Auto-Select** on the Options bar, choose **Group** or **Layer**, then click a visible pixel area in the document. For some reason, the Background can't be selected with this method.

➤ If you're using the Move tool and Show Transform Controls is checked on the Options bar, a bounding box surrounds the nontransparent portion of the currently selected layer. if you find the box to be distracting, uncheck the option. To transform a layer via its bounding box (e.g., scale or skew it), see pages 332–333.

A *To select a layer, just click it.*

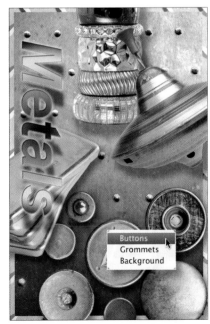

B *From the context menu, choose the name of the layer you want to select.*

Restacking layers

When you restack a layer (move it upward or downward), the layer contents shift forward or backward.

To restack layers:

Drag a layer or group name upward or downward on the Layers panel, and release the mouse when a double horizontal line appears in the desired stacking position.**A–B**

➤ To move the Background upward on the list, you must convert it to a layer first (see page 138). Layers can't be stacked below the Background.

➤ You can also restack a selected layer via commands on the Layer > Arrange submenu (or via the shortcuts that are listed on that submenu).

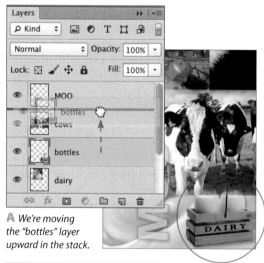

A We're moving the "bottles" layer upward in the stack.

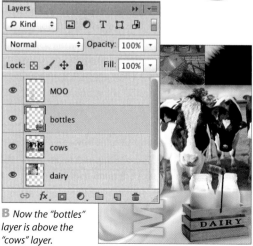

B Now the "bottles" layer is above the "cows" layer.

Creating layer groups

Putting layers in groups is more than just a convenient way to streamline and organize the listings on your Layers panel. You can also move, transform, duplicate, restack, hide, show, lock, or change the blending mode, Opacity, or Fill setting of all the layers in a group simultaneously. When you add a layer mask to a layer group, the mask applies to all the layers in the group (see page 172). You can also nest groups inside other groups.

To create a layer group:

Method 1 (from existing layers)

1. Click a layer, then Shift-click or Ctrl-click/Cmd-click one or more additional layers.**C** The layers can be nonconsecutive or hidden, and they can be of different types.

2. Do either of the following:

   Press Ctrl-G/Cmd-G.

   From the Layers panel menu, choose **New Group from Layers**. In the dialog, type a Name for the group, then click OK.**D**

3. *Optional:* To add more layers to the group, follow step 2 on the next page.

➤ The default blending mode for a group is Pass Through; we recommend keeping that setting.

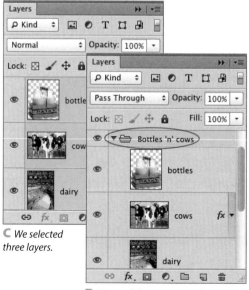

C We selected three layers.

D We used the New Group from Layers command to put those layers in a group.

Method 2 (create a group, then add layers)

1. Do either of the following:

   To create a group without choosing settings for it, click the layer above which you want the group to appear, then click the **New Group** button 📁 at the bottom of the panel.

   To name the group as you create it, Alt-click/ Option-click the New Group button or choose **New Group** from the panel menu. In the dialog, enter a Name, then click OK.

2. Do either of the following:

   Drag layers into the new group listing, releasing the mouse when the dark drop zone border appears around it.

   Click the arrowhead to expand the group list, then drag layers into the group, releasing the mouse when the double lines appear in the desired stacking position.**A**

➤ To expand or collapse a group, including all subgroup, effect, and Smart Filter listings, Alt-click/ Option-click the arrowhead.

MOVING LAYERS OUT OF A GROUP

➤ To move a layer out of a group, drag the layer upward or downward outside it.

➤ To move a layer from one group to another, drag it over the group listing; or if the listing is expanded, you can drag it to the desired stacking position.

A We're moving a layer upward into an existing group.

USING CONTEXT MENUS ON THE LAYERS PANEL

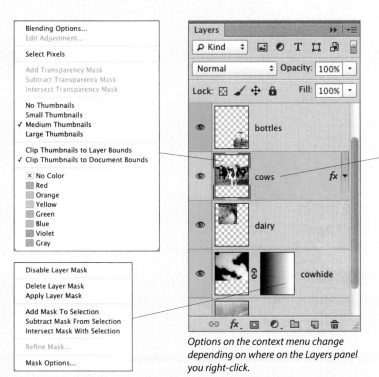

Options on the context menu change depending on where on the Layers panel you right-click.

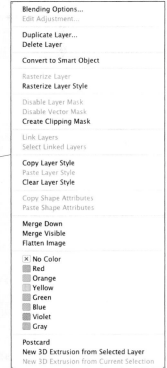

Deleting layers and groups

To delete a layer:

1. If there is an active selection in your document, deselect (press Ctrl-D/Cmd-D).

2. Click the layer to be deleted, then press Backspace/ Delete.

➤ Change your mind? Choose Edit > Undo or click the prior state on the History panel.

➤ To delete a layer another way, click the layer, click the Delete Layer button,🗑 then click Yes in the alert dialog; or to bypass the alert, Alt-click/Option-click the Delete Layer button.

You can delete a layer group and its layers or merely disband the group while preserving the layers.

To delete or ungroup a layer group:

On the Layers panel, do one of the following:

To delete a group and its contents, click the group, then press Backspace/Delete.

Right-click a group and choose **Delete Group** from the context menu (or click a group, then click the Delete Layer button 🗑). In the alert dialog, click **Group Only** or **Group and Contents**.

To ungroup a layer group without deleting its layers, click the group, then press Ctrl-Shift-G/ Cmd-Shift-G. The group icon disappears from the panel and the layer listings are no longer indented.

Hiding and showing layers

You can hide any layer you're not currently working on, either because it's getting in the way of your editing or to eliminate it as a visual distraction. Hidden layers don't print. The instructions below apply both to layers and the Background.

To hide or show layers:

On the Layers panel, do one of the following:

To hide or show one layer or layer group, click in the visibility column.👁 **A–B** The icon disappears.

To hide or show multiple layers, drag upward or downward in the visibility column.

To hide all layers and layer groups except one, Alt-click/Option-click the visibility column for the layer or layer group that you want to keep visible. Repeat to redisplay all the layers (except for layers that were hidden before you used the command).

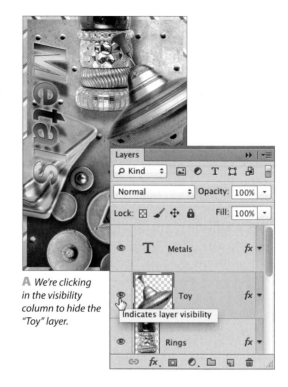

A We're clicking in the visibility column to hide the "Toy" layer.

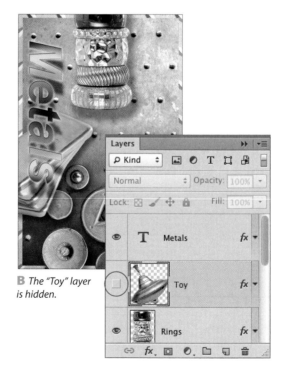

B The "Toy" layer is hidden.

Repositioning layer content

Follow these steps to reposition a selected layer or group of layers in the document.

To reposition layers manually:

Do either of the following:

On the Layers panel, click a layer or layer group, or Shift-click or Ctrl-click/Cmd-click multiple layers, hold down V to spring-load the Move tool, then drag in the document.A–B

Hold down V to spring-load the Move tool. On the Options bar, check Auto-Select, choose Group or Layer from the adjacent menu, then drag a non-transparent area in the document.

➤ If you move part of the layer or layers outside the canvas area, not to worry — those pixels will save with the document and can be moved back into view at any time. See "Working with pixels outside the canvas area" on page 241.

➤ To nudge a selected layer by one pixel at a time, choose the Move tool, then press an arrow key. Or press Shift-arrow to move a layer by 10 screen pixels at a time. (Don't press Alt-arrow/Option-arrow — unless you want to duplicate the layer.)

➤ For a more precise way to reposition layers, use the align buttons on the Options bar. See page 261.

ALIGNING LAYER CONTENT USING SMART GUIDES

You can use Smart Guides to align the edge of a layer you're dragging with the edge or center of the content of other layers. Turn on View > Show > Smart Guides, then with the Move tool, start moving a layer or layer group. Temporary magnetic guide lines will appear onscreen when the edge of the layer imagery you're moving encounters the edge or center of nontransparent pixels, type, or a shape on another layer. To learn more about this feature, see page 268.

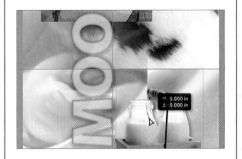

A We're dragging the "Toy" layer with the Move tool.

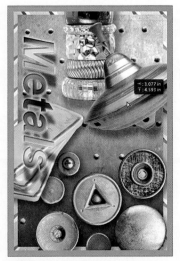

B Now the "Toy" layer is on the right side of the image.

Changing the layer opacity

The Opacity setting on the Layers panel controls whether a layer is semitransparent or opaque.

To change the opacity of a layer or layer group:

1. Select one or more layers or a layer group.

2. Change the **Opacity** percentage on the Layers panel (we like to use the scrubby slider).**A–B**

➤ To learn about the Fill slider, see page 381.

➤ In the Transparency Settings area of Edit/ Photoshop > Preferences > Transparency & Gamut, you can change the size or color of the gray and white checkerboard pattern that Photoshop uses to represent transparent pixels (or to hide the pattern, choose None from the Grid Size menu).

➤ To change the Opacity setting of the currently selected layer via the keyboard (standard or extended), choose a nonediting tool (such as the Move or Eyedropper tool or a selection tool), then press a digit between 0 and 9 (e.g., 2 = 20%) or quickly type a percentage (such as "38" for 38%). Press 0 to set the opacity to 100% or 00 to set it to 0%. ★

Using the lock options

The Lock Transparent Pixels button on the Layers panel prevents or allows the editing of transparent pixels by any command or tool. In these steps, you will use this feature with the Brush tool, just to learn how it works in practice.

To limit edits by locking transparent pixels:

1. Click an image layer (not an editable type layer) that contains some transparent pixels.

2. Choose the **Brush** tool ✍ (B or Shift-B). To change the brush diameter, press [or].

3. Show the Swatches panel, then click a color.

4. On the Layers panel, click the **Lock Transparent Pixels** button, then draw a few brush strokes in the document.**C** Only nontransparent pixels will be recolored.

5. Deactivate the Lock Transparent Pixels button by clicking it again or by pressing /.

6. Apply a few more brush strokes to the layer. Note that both transparent and opaque parts of the layer can be recolored.**D**

A In this image, all the layers have an opacity of 100%.

B We reduced the Opacity of the tomatoes layer to 49%.

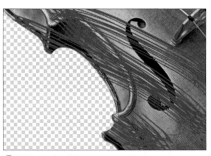

C With the Lock Transparent Pixels option on, our brush strokes can recolor only nontransparent pixels.

D With Lock Transparent Pixels off, our brush strokes can recolor transparent and opaque pixels.

To prevent layer characteristics from being edited, there are three other lock options on the Layers panel, in addition to the Lock Transparent Pixels button.

To lock one or more layers or a layer group:

1. Select one or more layers ★ or a layer group.

2. Click any of the following:

   The **Lock Image Pixels** button 🖌 prevents image layer pixels from being edited, such as by filters or brush strokes. Note: You can still move or restack the layer or change its layer style settings (blending mode, opacity, and effects).

   The **Lock Position** button ✛ locks only the location of the layer. The layer content (e.g., pixels, type characters) can be edited as usual.

   The **Lock All** button 🔒 prevents the layer from being moved and edited (both of the above).**A** Unlike the other lock options, this button is also available for layer groups.

   When a lock button is activated for a layer, a padlock icon displays next to the layer name.

Choosing Layers panel options

To choose thumbnail options for the Layers panel:

Right-click any layer thumbnail and choose any of the following:

   Small Thumbnails, Medium Thumbnails, or **Large Thumbnails.** Note: Turning off thumbnails by choosing No Thumbnails can help boost Photoshop's performance, but frankly, it's pretty darn hard to work productively without them.

   Clip Thumbnails to Layer Bounds to preview, in the panel thumbnails, only the layer content,**B** or **Clip Thumbnails to Document Bounds** to preview the layer content relative to the document.

You can assign a color to the area behind the visibility icons to categorize your layers or make them easier to identify (or just to make the panel look pretty).

To color-code a layer:

   Click a layer (or Ctrl-click/Cmd-click multiple layers), then right-click the layer thumbnail or listing and choose a color label from the context menu.**C** ★

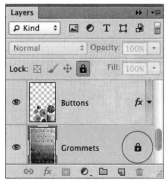

A When the Lock All button option is activated for a layer, the padlock icon is black.

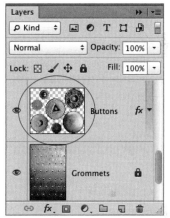

B For Layers panel display options, we chose Large Thumbnails and Clip Thumbnails to Layer Bounds.

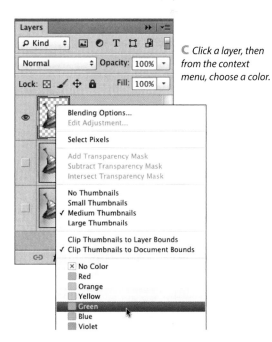

C Click a layer, then from the context menu, choose a color.

Filtering listings on the Layers panel

When you first start working in Photoshop, your Layers panel may look relatively spare, but before you know it, you will be adding image, adjustment, and type layers, Smart Filters, and layer styles, and the number of listings will grow considerably. Finding the layers you need will require you to either scroll in the panel (pain in the butt) or enlarge the panel to display all the listings (takes up too much screen space). A Using the filtering features, you can reduce the listings that display on the panel at a given time to just the categories of layers you need to work on.

To filter the listings on the Layers panel: ★

At the top of the Layers panel, do either of the following:

Set the Filter Type menu to the default option of **Kind**, then click the **Filter for Pixel Layers,** Filter for Adjustment Layers (**A–B**, next page), **Filter for Type Layers,** **Filter for Shape Layers,** or **Filter for Smart Objects** button. Only layers in that chosen category will display. If desired, you can click additional filter buttons to display more layer categories.

From the Filter Type menu, choose **Name, Effect, Mode, Attribute,** or **Color,** then choose a criterion from the adjacent menu (**C–F,** next page) or, in the case of the Name option, start typing a word that appears in one or more layer names. For example, to display only layers that contain a layer mask, choose Attribute from the Filter Type menu and Layer Mask from the second menu; or to display only layers that don't contain layer effects, choose No Layer Effects from the second menu. See also the sidebar on the next page.

To turn off layer filtering:

In the upper-right corner of the Layers panel, click the **Layer Filtering On/Off** button.

➤ If you turn layer filtering back on, the last filtering settings will be reinstated.

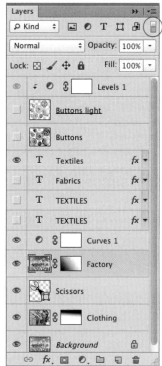

Layer Filtering On/Off button

A *This is the Layers panel for the image shown above, with all the listings showing (unfiltered).*

A *We clicked the Filter for Pixel Layers button: Only image layers are displaying.*

B *We also clicked the Filter for Adjustment Layers button: Now both image and adjustment layers are displaying.*

C *We chose Attribute from the Filter Type menu and Visible from the second menu: Only layers that have a visibility icon display.*

THE LAYER FILTERING CRITERIA

FIRST MENU	BUTTON OR MENUS
Kind	Click the button to display only pixel, adjustment, type, or shape layers, or Smart Objects
Name	Enter a layer name (or partial name) to be searched
Effect	Drop Shadow, Inner Glow, and other effects (from the Layer Style dialog)
Mode	Blending mode (e.g., Normal, Multiply, Screen)
Attribute	Visible, Locked, Empty, Linked, Clipped, Layer Mask, Vector Mask, Layer Effects, Advanced Blending (or the "Not" version of the above)
Color	Red, Orange, Yellow, etc. (the color that is assigned to the visibility column)

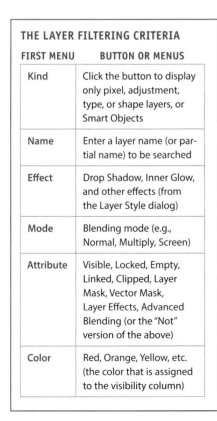

D *We assigned colors to most of the layers.*

E *We chose Color from the Filter Type menu and Yellow from the second menu.*

F *We chose Effect from the Filter Type menu and Drop Shadow from the adjacent menu.*

Merging layers

The merge commands — Merge Down, Merge Layers, and Merge Visible — merge two or more selected layers into the bottommost of the currently selected layers. You can apply any of these commands periodically during the editing process to reduce the file size of your document, or to reduce unnecessary clutter on the Layers panel.

Note: Compare the merge commands with the Flatten Image command (see page 150), which is normally applied to a copy of a file as a final step before output.

To merge select layers:

1. Do one of the following:

   Click the upper layer of two layers to be merged.**A** The bottom one must be an image layer or the Background; it can't be fully locked (the Lock All button must be deactivated) and it can't be a group.

   Ctrl-click/Cmd-click multiple layers. The layers can be solo, within a group, or a combination thereof.

   Click a group. (All the layers in the group will be merged — but just with one another.)

   Note: You can merge an adjustment layer into an image layer, but you can't merge adjustment layers into one another. If you merge a shape layer, an editable type layer, or a Smart Object, it will be rasterized into the underlying image layer.

2. Do either of the following:

   Right-click the selected layer or group, or one of the selected layers, and choose **Merge Down**, **Merge Layers**, or **Merge Group** from the context menu.

   Press Ctrl-E/Cmd-E (use this method for a type layer).**B**

   Notes: If only one layer is selected and you merge it down into an underlying layer that contains a layer mask, an alert dialog will appear. Click Preserve to keep the mask editable, or click Apply to apply the mask effect but discard the mask. If you merge a group, the group icon will disappear from the panel.

➤ To merge an editable type layer into a shape layer, or vice versa, select them both, then choose the Merge Layers command.

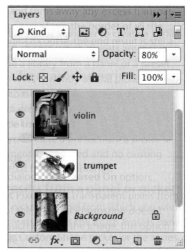

A *We clicked the "violin" layer.*

B *We chose the Merge Down command, which merged the "violin" layer into the "trumpet" layer.*

SMART OBJECT IN LIEU OF MERGE OR FLATTEN

Instead of merging or flattening layers, consider grouping them into a Smart Object (see page 248). You'll achieve the same reduction of layers, plus you'll gain the ability to edit the original layers individually by double-clicking the Smart Object thumbnail (see page 254).

The Merge Visible command merges all the currently visible layers into the bottommost visible layer while preserving any hidden layers. By hiding the layers you don't want to merge before choosing this command, you can control which ones will be merged.

To merge all visible layers:

1. Make sure only the layers you want to merge are visible (have eye icons), and hide any layers (including the Background, if desired) that you don't want to merge.**A**

2. Right-click one of the visible layers (not a type layer) and choose **Merge Visible** (Ctrl-Shift-E/ Cmd-Shift-E).**B**

   Note: This sort of goes without saying, but if you merge down an editable type layer, shape, or adjustment layer, the specific features of that kind of layer (such as the font and other character settings for a type layer, or the settings for an adjustment layer) will no longer be editable.

Both of the commands in this task will copy and merge ("stamp") two or more selected layers into a new layer in one step, while preserving the original, separate layers. This might come in handy, say, if you want to test some edits (such as filters or transformations) on multiple layers simultaneously; use one of these commands first, then apply your edits to the newly merged layer. The Note above also applies to these commands.

To copy and merge layers:

Do either of the following:

Ctrl-click/Cmd-click the layers (not the Background) to be copied or merged into a new layer, then press Ctrl-Alt-E/Cmd-Option-E.

To copy and merge all the currently visible layers into a new layer, including the Background (if visible), click any visible layer, then press Ctrl-Alt-Shift-E/Cmd-Option-Shift-E.

➤ If layers and the Background are selected when you use the first shortcut listed above, content from the selected layers will be stamped into the Background, and no new layer will be created.

➤ For an alternative to the merge commands, see the sidebar on the preceding page.

➤ To create a document from a layer, from the Layers panel menu, choose Duplicate Layer. From the Document menu in the dialog, choose New, enter a document Name, then click OK. Save the new file.

A In this document, we hid the Background because we didn't want our layers to merge into it.

B The Merge Visible command merged all the layers except the Background, which was preserved and stayed hidden.

Flattening layers

When you flatten all the layers in a document, you reduce its file storage size and free up space on your hard disk (see the sidebar at right). Flattening layers may also be a necessary step when preparing a file for output or export. At the present time, multiple layers are preserved only by the Photoshop PDF, Photoshop, Large Document Format, and TIFF formats (provided you keep the Layers option checked in the Save As dialog). If the application into which you're planning to import your file doesn't read or accept layers, you will have to create a flattened copy of it, as in these steps. Any transparency in the bottommost layer will be converted to fully opaque white.

To save a flattened copy of a document:

1. Choose File > **Save As** (Ctrl-Shift-S/Cmd-Shift-S). The Save As dialog opens.

2. Do all of the following:

   Change the file name.

   Choose a location.

   Uncheck Layers (the As a Copy option becomes checked automatically; keep it that way).

   Choose a file format from the Format menu.

   Click Save.

   Note: The layered version will remain open; the flattened version will be saved to disk.

If you're confident that your image is totally complete, *finis,* you can use the Flatten Image command instead of saving a flattened copy. This command merges all currently visible layers (including type, Smart Object, and adjustment layers) into the bottommost visible layer, rasterizes all type and shape layers, and applies all masks and layer styles. Note: This command discards all hidden layers!

To flatten all the layers in a document:

1. Make sure all the layers and layer groups you want to flatten are visible (have eye icons). **A** It doesn't matter which layer is selected.

2. Right-click any layer name (not a type layer) and choose **Flatten Image**.

3. If the file contains any hidden layers, an alert dialog will appear; click OK. Any formerly transparent areas in the bottommost layer are now opaque white. **B**

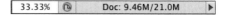

A *In this document, the "Bottles" layer is hidden.*

B *The Flatten Image command flattened all the visible layers into the Background and discarded the hidden layer.*

In this chapter, you will learn how to create and refine selections and layer masks. These techniques are put to practical use in many other chapters, and you will discover that they are essential to your work in Photoshop.

When you select an area of an image layer, only that area can be edited and the rest of the layer is protected. If you apply a filter, for example, only pixels within the selection area on the currently active layer are affected. The function of a layer mask is to hide parts of a layer.

Each mechanism that we cover in this chapter represents the isolation of image areas in a unique way. A selection is displayed as a blinking border, a channel or mask is displayed as black (or gray) and white areas, and a Quick Mask (a temporary mask used for creating or editing a selection) is displayed as red and clear areas.

Creating layer-based selections

To select a whole layer:

On the Layers panel, ☟ click a layer or the Background, then choose Select > **All** or press Ctrl-A/Cmd-A. A border of "marching ants" surrounds the entire layer.

To select just the nontransparent areas of a layer:

On the Layers panel, ☟ Ctrl-click/Cmd-click the layer thumbnail **A–B** or right-click the layer thumbnail and choose **Select Pixels**.

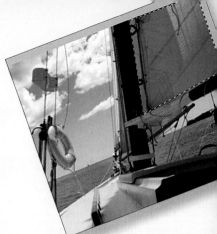

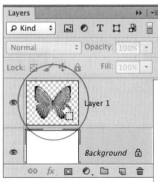

A To select only the nontransparent pixels on a layer, Ctrl-click/Cmd-click the layer thumbnail.

B Just the butterfly is selected.

9

SELECTIONS & MASKS

Using the Rectangular and Elliptical Marquee tools

To create a rectangular or elliptical selection:

1. Click the layer you want to edit.

2. Choose the **Rectangular Marquee** or **Elliptical Marquee** tool (M or Shift-M).

3. *Optional:* For a smoother edge on an elliptical selection, check Anti-alias on the Options bar (see the sidebar on page 159) and set the Feather value to 0 px.

4. Drag diagonally. Hold down Shift while dragging to create a perfect square or circle; hold down Alt/Option while dragging to draw the selection from the center.**A** As you draw a selection, width and height dimensions display in a readout next to the selection ★ (and on the Info panel). When you release the mouse, a selection border appears.

5. *Optional:* To add to the selection, Shift-drag; to subtract from it, Alt-drag/Option-drag.

➤ To move the selection while drawing it, keep the mouse button down, then drag with the Spacebar held down. To move the selection after releasing the mouse, drag inside it with any selection tool.

➤ To create the thinnest possible selection, choose the Single Row Marquee or Single Column Marquee tool, then click in the image.

To create a selection that has a fixed ratio or specific dimensions:

1. Click a layer.

2. Choose the **Rectangular Marquee** or **Elliptical Marquee** tool (M or Shift-M).

3. On the Options bar, set the Feather value to 0, then do either of the following:

   From the Style menu, choose **Fixed Ratio**, enter **Width** and **Height** for the ratio of the selection (e.g., 5 to 7),**B** then drag in the image diagonally to create a selection.**C**

   From the Style menu, choose **Fixed Size**, enter exact **Width** and **Height** values in any unit that can be used in Photoshop (see page 441), then click in the image.**D**

➤ To swap the current Fixed Ratio or Fixed Size values, click the Swap Height and Width button on the Options bar.

A *With the Elliptical Marquee tool, we're holding down Alt/Option while dragging to draw a selection from the center.*

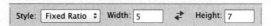

B *For the Rectangular Marquee tool, we chose Fixed Ratio and entered a Width to Height ratio of 5 to 7…*

C *… so any size selection we draw with the tool will have that fixed ratio.*

D *We chose Fixed Size, entered Width and Height values, then clicked in the image to make the border appear (here, we're repositioning it).*

Using two of the lasso tools

We use the Lasso tool to select an area loosely, say, to limit subtle color adjustments to a general area. We also use this tool to clean up selections we make with other tools, such as the Magic Wand or Quick Selection tool.

To create a free-form selection:

1. Click the layer you want to edit.

2. Choose the **Lasso** tool  (L or Shift-L).

3. *Optional:* For a smoother edge on an elliptical selection, check Anti-alias on the Options bar and set the Feather value to 0 px.

4. Drag around an area on the layer.  Your initial selection doesn't have to be perfect, as you will be able to refine it easily in the next step. When you release the mouse, the open ends of the selection will join automatically.

5. To add to the selection, position the pointer inside it, then Shift-drag around the area to be added. **B** To subtract from the selection, position the pointer outside it, then Alt-drag/Option-drag around the area to be removed. **C–D**

➤ To feather an existing selection, see pages 165 and 243.

➤ To create a straight side with the Lasso tool, with the mouse button still down, hold down Alt/Option and click to create corners. To resume creating free-form edges, press the mouse button, release Alt/Option, then drag.

To create a straight-sided selection:

1. Click the layer you want to edit.

2. Choose the **Polygonal Lasso** tool 🎽 (L or Shift-L).

3. Click to create corners. **E** To create a selection edge at a multiple of 45°, hold down Shift while clicking.

4. To **join** the open ends of the selection, do either of the following:

   Click the starting point (a small circle appears next to the pointer).

   Ctrl-click/Cmd-click or double-click anywhere in the document.

➤ To draw a free-form segment while creating a polygonal selection, Alt-drag/Option-drag. Release Alt/Option and click to create more straight sides.

➤ To erase the last corner while using the Polygonal Lasso tool, press Backspace/Delete.

A *With the Lasso tool, we are selecting the left part of the ice cream.*

B *Using Shift, we are adding to the selection, to complete the shape.*

C *To eliminate the pistachio nut from the selection …*

D *… we are holding down Alt/Option and dragging around it with the Lasso tool.*

E *The Polygonal Lasso tool produces straight-edged selections.*

Deselecting and reselecting selections

If you don't like having to retrace your steps (we sure don't), deselect a selection only when you're sure you're done using it. Although selections register as states on the History panel, states disappear when the panel listings reach their maximum number or when you close the document. To preserve a selection for future access and use, save it in an alpha channel (see page 164) or convert it to a layer mask (see page 172).

To deselect a selection:

Do one of the following:

Press Ctrl-D/Cmd-D (Select > Deselect).

Choose the **Lasso,** **Rectangular Marquee,** or **Elliptical Marquee** tool, then click inside or outside the selection. **A**

Choose any selection tool, then right-click anywhere in the document and choose **Deselect**.

To reselect the last selection:

Do one of the following:

Press Ctrl-Shift-D/Cmd-Shift-D (Select > Reselect).

With any selection tool except the Magic Wand, right-click in the document and choose **Reselect**.

On the History panel, click the state labeled with the name of the tool or command that you used to create the selection.

Deleting or filling a selection

When you delete a selection of image pixels from a layer, Photoshop fills that area automatically with transparent pixels. When you delete a selection of pixels from the Background, Photoshop fills the exposed area with a solid color.

To delete or fill a selection:

1. On the Layers panel, click a layer or the Background. For the Background, also choose a Foreground or Background color (see Chapter 11).

2. Do one of the following:

   If a layer is active, press Backspace/Delete. **B–C**

   If the Background is active, press Alt-Backspace/Option-Delete (to fill the selection with the Foreground color) or Ctrl-Backspace/Cmd-Delete (to fill the selection with the Background color). **D**

   To delete the selection and put it on the Clipboard, choose Edit > **Cut** (Ctrl-X/Cmd-X). (To learn about the Clipboard, see pages 239–242.)

   Choose Edit > **Clear**.

B We selected the blue sky on an image layer, then pressed Backspace/Delete.

C Photoshop replaced the deleted area with transparent pixels.

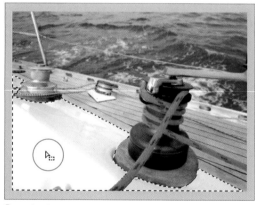

A To deselect this selection, we're clicking inside it with a selection tool.

D Here, with the Background selected, we pressed Ctrl-Backspace/Cmd-Delete, so the selection filled with the current Background color (in this case, the color red).

Moving a selection border

You can move a selection border to a different area of an image without moving its contents.

To move a selection border:

1. Choose any selection tool except the Quick Selection tool or hold down M, L, or W to spring-load a selection tool, and activate the **New Selection** button ☐ on the Options bar.

2. Do either of the following:

   Drag inside an existing selection. **A** To constrain the movement to a multiple of 45°, start dragging, then hold down Shift and continue to drag. The horizontal and vertical distance the selection border is being moved displays in a dynamic readout onscreen.★

   Press any arrow key to nudge the selection border by one pixel at a time, or press Shift-arrow to nudge the border by 10 pixels at a time.

➤ To transform a selection border (but not its contents), choose any selection tool except the Magic Wand. Right-click the image and choose Transform Selection. Use the handles on the transform box to scale, rotate, skew, or distort the selection, as described on pages 332–333.

➤ To copy a selection border between documents, drag it to the tab of another open document with a selection tool, pause to let the second document display, then drag into the active window.

Moving selection contents

In these steps, you will move a selection and its contents.

To move the contents of a selection:

1. Create a selection.

2. *Optional:* For help in positioning the selection precisely at a specific location in the document, display the rulers (Ctrl-R/Cmd-R), drag a guide from the horizontal or vertical ruler, and turn on View > Snap To > Guides.

3. Do either of the following:

   On the Layers panel, click the Background, then choose a Background color (see Chapter 11). The area that is exposed when you move the selection will be filled with this color.

   Click a layer. The area you expose when you move the selection will be filled with transparent pixels.

4. Choose the **Move** tool or hold down V to spring-load the Move tool.

5. Drag from within the selection. **B** You can let the edge of the selection snap to a ruler guide, if you created one. The distance you move the selection displays in a dynamic readout onscreen.★

6. Deselect (Ctrl-D/Cmd-D).

➤ In Chapter 13, Combining Images, you will learn how to copy the contents of a selection, and how to use other alignment aids, such as Smart Guides.

➤ With the Move tool chosen, you can press an arrow key to nudge a selection (and its contents) by one pixel at a time, or press Shift-arrow to nudge it by 10 pixels at a time.

A A selection border is moved with a selection tool.

B Selection contents are moved on a layer with the Move tool.

Using the Quick Selection tool

The Photoshop features we're going to discuss next — the Quick Selection tool, Magic Wand tool, and Color Range command — create selections in a more automatic way than the marquee and lasso tools. With these tools, Photoshop does the work of detecting the color boundaries for you.

If the area you want to select has fairly well-defined borders, try using the Quick Selection tool instead of a lasso tool. Rather than tediously tracing a precise contour, with this tool, you merely drag within a shape and pause to let it detect and select the shape's color boundary. You can push the resulting selection outward to include an adjacent color boundary or inward to make it smaller. This tool is awesome!

To use the Quick Selection tool:

1. Click the layer you want to edit.

2. Choose the **Quick Selection** tool ![icon] (W or Shift-W).

3. On the Options bar, do all of the following:

   Click the **New Selection** button ![icon] to replace any existing selections with the one you're about to create (or press Ctrl-D/Cmd-D to deselect).

   Check **Sample All Layers** to let the tool detect color boundaries on all layers, or uncheck this option to allow it to detect color boundaries on just the current layer.

   Check **Auto-Enhance** for a smoother, more refined selection edge.

4. To choose a brush diameter, Alt-right-click-drag/ Control-Option-drag to the left or right or press] or [, then drag within the area to be selected. A The selection will expand to the first significant color or shade boundary that the tool detects. The selection will preview as you drag, and will become more precise when you release the mouse.

5. Do any of the following optional steps:

   To **enlarge** the selection, click or drag in an adjoining area; the selection will expand to include it. B–C

   To **shrink** the selection, Alt-drag/Option-drag along the edge of the area to be subtracted (the modifier key is equivalent to clicking the Subtract From button) (A–B, next page).

A *We selected the kumquat in the center of this layer by dragging inside it with the Quick Selection tool.*

B *After enlarging the brush diameter, we clicked the kumquat on the right to add it to the selection.*

C *Next, we dragged across the green leaf above the kumquats. The selection spread beyond the edge of the leaf to include some of the background area, which wasn't our intention.*

➤ To block an adjacent area from being included as you enlarge an existing selection, Alt-click/Option-click or drag in that area, release Alt/Option and the mouse, then drag to enlarge the selection area, while avoiding the blocked area. The block will remain in effect until you click the blocked area again with the Quick Selection tool. C–E

You can change the tool diameter between clicks.

➤ To undo the last click or drag of the Quick Selection tool, press Ctrl-Z/Cmd-Z.

➤ To save a selection, see page 164.

➤ To clean up a Quick Selection, you can use another selection tool, such as the Lasso. To refine the selection, see page 165.

A *We Alt-dragged/Option-dragged below the leaf to subtract the background area from the selection…*

B *…and did the same thing to subtract the area below the kumquats.*

C *We zoomed in, reduced the brush diameter, then Alt-clicked/Option-clicked areas around the stems to prevent them from becoming selected.*

D *We dragged along the stems to select them, then held down Alt/Option and clicked the background areas between the stems to remove them from the selection.*

E *Finally, we cleaned up the selection of the stems. (At this point, we could copy the selection to a new layer; it would be surrounded by transparent pixels.)*

Using the Magic Wand tool

With the Magic Wand tool, you simply click a color in the image and the tool selects all adjacent pixels of the same (or a similar) shade or color. Like the Color Range command (see pages 160–161), the Magic Wand lets you control the range of pixels the tool selects, but unlike Color Range, this tool also lets you add nonsimilar colors to the selection.

To use the Magic Wand tool:

1. Click a layer or the Background.

2. Choose the **Magic Wand** tool ⚡ (W or Shift-W).

3. On the Options bar, do all of the following:

    Choose a **Tolerance** value (use the scrubby slider) to control the range of colors the tool selects.

    Check **Anti-alias** to let the tool add semitransparent pixels along the edges of the color areas it detects. This will produce smoother edge transitions for your image edits.

    Check **Contiguous** to limit the selection to areas that are connected to the first pixel you click, or uncheck this option to allow the tool to select similarly colored, noncontiguous (unconnected) areas throughout the image with each click.

    To select occurrences of a similar color on all visible layers, check **Sample All Layers**, or uncheck this option to select colors on just the current layer.

4. Click a color in the image.

5. Do any of the following (optional):

    To **add** to the selection, Shift-click any unselected areas.

    To **subtract** areas from the selection, hold down Alt/Option and click them. Or choose the Quick Selection tool, then with the Alt/Option key held down, drag short strokes across the areas to be subtracted.

    See also the options in "To expand or add to a selection via a command" on the next page.

6. *Optional:* If you selected a background area of the image that you want to remove and you clicked a layer in step 1, press Backspace/Delete;  or if you clicked the Background in step 1, choose a Background color, then press Ctrl-Backspace/Cmd-Delete. Deselect (Ctrl-D/Cmd-D).

➤ To select just one color or shade with the Magic Wand tool, choose a Tolerance value of 0 or 1. You

A *To select the sky in this image layer, we clicked on the right side with the Magic Wand tool (Tolerance 38; Contiguous checked), then Shift-clicked more sky areas to add them to the selection (as shown above).*

B *Some parts of the keys became selected, so we are using the Quick Selection tool with Alt/Option held down to subtract them from the selection.*

C *Finally, we pressed Backspace/Delete to get rid of the selected pixels, to isolate the hand and keys (in this document, the Background is hidden).*

can also lower the Tolerance value incrementally between clicks. For instance, you could click with a Tolerance of 30–40 first, lower the value to 15–20 and click again, then to add unselected areas along the edges of the selection, lower the value to 5–10 and click once more.

The Grow command expands a selection only into contiguous areas, whereas the Similar command can add both contiguous and noncontiguous areas. Both commands use the current Tolerance setting of the Magic Wand tool.

To expand or add to a selection via a command:

Create a selection, click any selection tool, then choose Select > **Grow** or **Similar;** A–B or if the Magic Wand tool is selected, right-click in the image and choose either command from the context menu. You can repeat either command to enlarge the selection further.

➤ To undo the results of the last click made with the Magic Wand tool or the last use of the Grow or Similar command, press Ctrl-Z/Cmd-Z.

Inverting a selection

If one area of an image is easier to select than another, select the easy part first (such as the sky in a landscape photo), then invert the selection.

To invert a selection:

Do either of the following:

With any tool chosen, press Ctrl-Shift-I/Cmd-Shift-I (Select > Inverse). C–D

With any selection tool chosen, right-click in the document and choose **Select Inverse**.

A *We clicked the blue sky area with the Magic Wand tool (Tolerance of 35), Shift-clicked once on the clouds…*

B *…then chose Select > Similar. The Tolerance setting controlled which pixel range was added to the selection.*

C *This is the original selection.*

D *And this is the inverse of the same selection.*

TO ANTI-ALIAS OR NOT?

Before using a selection tool, check Anti-alias (if available) on the Options bar to fade the edge of the selection to transparency, or uncheck this option to produce a crisp, hard-edged selection. The effect of anti-aliasing won't be visible until you copy, move, or edit the selected pixels.

Using the Color Range command

When using the Color Range command, you click a color area in the document window or in the preview area of the dialog, and depending on the parameters you have chosen, all occurrences of just one color or a range of related colors become selected. This command works best on relatively uniform color areas.

To create a selection via the Color Range command:

1. Click a layer. *Optional:* Create a selection to limit where the command may select colors.

2. Choose Select > **Color Range**, or with any selection tool chosen, right-click in the image and choose Color Range.

3. In the Color Range dialog, choose from the **Select** menu to limit the selection to Sampled Colors (shades or colors you'll click with the Color Range eyedropper); to a specific preset color range (e.g.,

Reds or Blues); to a luminosity range (Highlights, Midtones, or Shadows); or to Skin Tones. ★

4. If you chose Sampled Colors in the preceding step, with the Eyedropper tool from the dialog, click to sample a color in either the dialog preview or the image. **A–B** (The command samples colors from all the currently visible layers, regardless of which layer is active.)

5. To **add** colors or shades to the selection, Shift-click in the document or preview window; or to subtract colors or shades from the selection, Alt-click/ Option-click.

To expand or narrow the range of selected colors and to control the number of partially selected pixels, adjust the **Fuzziness** value. **C**

If you chose Skin Tones in step 3, check **Detect Faces**. ★ Note: This option works only for

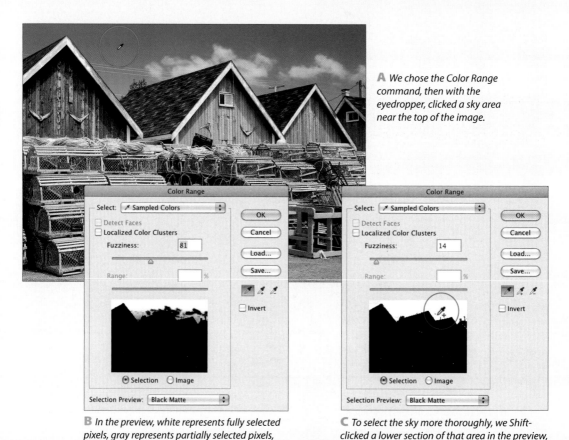

A We chose the Color Range command, then with the eyedropper, clicked a sky area near the top of the image.

B In the preview, white represents fully selected pixels, gray represents partially selected pixels, and black represent unselected pixels.

C To select the sky more thoroughly, we Shift-clicked a lower section of that area in the preview, then lowered the Fuzziness value to 14.

Caucasian skin tones. However, it's useful for limiting the effect of a tonal adjustment, when a precise selection isn't necessary (see the sidebar on this page).

For the Localized Color Clusters option, see the next page.

6. Choose a **Selection Preview** option for the selection in the document: None for no preview, Grayscale to see a larger version of the dialog preview, Black Matte to view the selection against a black background, or White Matte to view the selection against a white background.

   ➤ Press and release Ctrl/Cmd to toggle the Selection and Image previews in the dialog.

7. Click OK.

A *Using the Color Range dialog, we were able to select the entire sky, including noncontiguous areas (e.g., in between the chimney and poles on the right side).*

USING THE SKIN TONES OPTION IN THE COLOR RANGE DIALOG

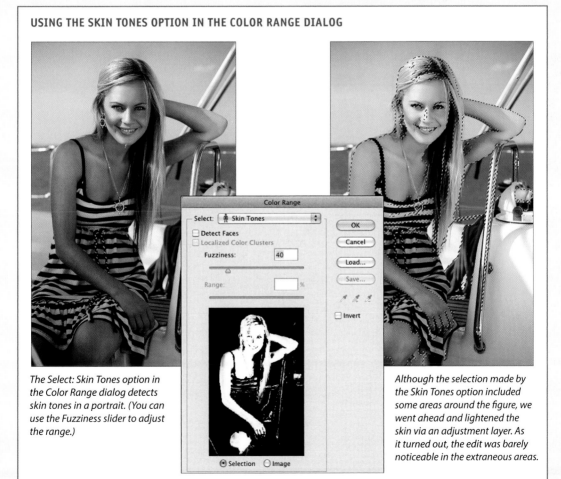

The Select: Skin Tones option in the Color Range dialog detects skin tones in a portrait. (You can use the Fuzziness slider to adjust the range.)

Although the selection made by the Skin Tones option included some areas around the figure, we went ahead and lightened the skin via an adjustment layer. As it turned out, the edit was barely noticeable in the extraneous areas.

USING THE LOCALIZED COLOR CLUSTERS OPTION IN THE COLOR RANGE DIALOG

The Localized Color Clusters option in the Color Range dialog limits the selection to colors that are close to where you click.

Open the Color Range dialog, choose Select: **Sampled Colors**, then with the Eyedropper tool, click in the document to sample a color. **A**

Check **Localized Color Clusters**, then use the **Range** slider to control the distance from the sampled color within which the command may select similar colors. **B**

You can Shift-drag in the preview or document to add more color areas to the selection (within the current range), **C** or Alt-drag/Option-drag to subtract areas. **D**

Remember to click a layer before you apply edits.

A We chose the Color Range command, then with the Eyedropper, clicked the grapefruit in the image.

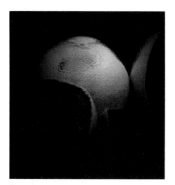

B To limit the selection more closely to the area we clicked, we checked Localized Color Clusters and reduced the Range value to 15 percent.

C Next, we Shift-dragged to select more grapefruit colors (within the current Range).

D Finally, we dragged with Alt/ Option held down to subtract some color areas from the selection.

Hiding and showing the selection border

You can hide the blinking selection border without having to deselect the selection (say, to preview the results of an edit). If you do hide the border, remember that the selection remains in effect!

To hide or show the selection border:

Press Ctrl-H/Cmd-H (Show > Extras).

Note: A one-time alert dialog may appear, offering you the option to assign the Ctrl-H/Cmd-H shortcut to the Extras command in Photoshop (our preference) or to the Hide Photoshop command.

➤ If the Ctrl-H/Cmd-H shortcut doesn't hide the selection border, confirm that Selection Edges is checked on the View > Show submenu. (This shortcut hides or shows all the options that are checked on the View > Show submenu.) Note also that unchecked options in the View > Show > Show Extras Options dialog can be turned on or off only via the Show submenu, not via the shortcut; for this reason, we keep all the options in the dialog checked.

A *We drew an inner selection with the Rectangular Marquee tool on this 300 ppi image, applied a Feather value of 25 px via Refine Edge, then chose Select > Inverse. Next, we used a Levels adjustment to lighten the area within the selection (see pages 210–211).*

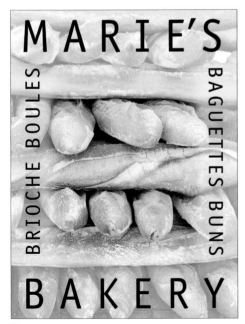

B *Finally, we added four editable type layers. The type is easy to read on the light background.*

Creating a frame-shaped selection

With the Rectangular Marquee or Elliptical Marquee tool, you can create a selection in the shape of a frame, either at the edge of the canvas area or floating within it. Image edits that you apply to the frame-shaped selection (e.g., filters or adjustments) will be visible only in that area.

To create a selection in the shape of a frame:

Method 1 (at the edge of the canvas area)

1. Click a layer.
2. Choose the **Rectangular Marquee** ▣ (M or Shift-M).
3. In the document window, drag a border to define the inner edge of the frame selection.
4. *Optional:* To soften the edges of the selection, click Refine Edge on the Options bar. In the dialog, choose On White (W) from the View menu, set the sliders to 0, then adjust the Feather value to achieve the desired softness level, then click OK.
5. Press Ctrl-Shift-I/Cmd-Shift-I (or right-click in the document and choose Select Inverse).A–B

Method 2 (within the image)

1. Click a layer.
2. Choose the **Rectangular Marquee** or **Elliptical Marquee** tool (M or Shift-M), then drag to define the outer edge of the frame selection.
3. Alt/Option drag inside the first selection to create the inner edge of the "frame."C Before releasing the mouse, you can release Alt/Option then hold down the Spacebar and drag the inner selection. After releasing the mouse, you can drag between the selection borders to reposition the entire "frame."

C *We are holding down Alt/Option and dragging to subtract one rectangular selection from the other.*

Saving and loading selections

Creating a selection can be a laborious process, but fortunately, you can preserve your hard work either as an alpha channel (this page) or as a layer mask (see page 172). Once stored, the channel or mask can be loaded as a selection at any time (see this page and page 176), and you can also add or subtract areas from it.

To save a selection to an alpha channel:

1. Create a selection. A

2. Display the Channels panel,  then click the **Save Selection as Channel** button on the panel. Press Ctrl-D/Cmd-D to deselect. A new alpha channel appears on the panel. B

➤ To reverse the masked and unmasked areas in an alpha channel, click the alpha channel on the Channels panel, then press Ctrl-I/Cmd-I.

➤ To rename an alpha channel, double-click the name, type a new one, then press Enter/Return.

➤ To delete an alpha channel, right-click the listing and choose Delete Channel.

➤ Alpha channels can be saved with files in several formats, such as Photoshop, JPEG 2000, Photoshop PDF, and TIFF. In the File > Save As dialog, be sure to check Alpha Channels.

To edit an alpha channel:

1. On the Channels panel, click an alpha channel.

2. Choose the Brush tool (B or Shift-B), set the Opacity to 100%, then paint with white to expand the selection area or with black to remove areas from it (press X to swap the two colors).

3. Click the topmost channel on the Channels panel.

➤ If you prefer to display and edit an alpha channel as a rubylith (red tint) over the image, click the alpha channel, then click the visibility icon for the topmost channel. To restore the normal display, hide the alpha channel (click its visibility icon).

To load an alpha channel as a selection:

On the Channels panel, do either of the following:

Ctrl-click/Cmd-click the alpha channel thumbnail or listing.

Drag the channel listing to the **Load Channel as Selection** button at the bottom of the panel.

➤ To learn more about options for saving and loading alpha channels, see Photoshop Help.

A *We created a selection …*

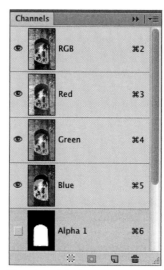

B *… then clicked the Save Selection as Channel button on the Channels panel. The Alpha 1 listing appeared.*

CREATING AND EDITING SELECTIONS WITH VECTOR PATH TOOLS

Advanced Photoshop users who are proficient with the Pen tool can draw a smooth path (e.g., trace an element in an image), then convert the path to a selection.

Refining selection edges

The Refine Edge dialog provides many useful options for refining (e.g., smoothing, feathering, contracting) the edges of a selection, as well as options for outputting the selection (e.g., to a layer or as a layer mask).

To refine the edges of a selection:

1. Create a selection. With your selection tool still chosen, click **Refine Edge** on the Options bar or press Ctrl-Alt-R/Cmd-Option-R. The dialog opens. **A**

2. Set all the sliders to 0, and set the zoom level to enlarge the selection in the document window.

3. To control how the selection previews in the document, choose an option from the **View** menu; or use the letter shortcut, as listed on the menu; or cycle through the options by pressing F. We find these options to be the most useful:

   Overlay (V) to view the selection as a Quick Mask (to view the selection relative to the areas outside it).

   On Black (B) to view the selection on a black background (useful if you're going to copy the selection to a dark background or if the selection edge has a light color).

   On White (W) to view the selection on a white background (useful if you're going to copy the selection to a light background).

   On Layers (L) to view the selection on top of the layer directly below it, if any (to judge how the selection looks on top of that layer).

4. Under Edge Detection, check **Smart Radius** to allow the Radius to adapt to hard and soft edges in the image.

   If you want to enlarge the refinement area to include pixels just outside the selection edge, increase the **Radius** value (use the scrubby slider).

   To view just the current refinement area, check **Show Radius** (J); uncheck it before proceeding.

   ➤ Press P to toggle the original and refined selections.

5. Under Adjust Edge, adjust any of these sliders:

   To smooth out small bumps or jaggedness along the edges, raise the **Smooth** value slightly.

   To feather the edge, increase the **Feather** value.

   To produce a crisp selection edge, increase the **Contrast** value. This option counters the effect of an increased Radius, Smooth, or Feather value.

To contract the selection inward to eliminate background pixels or to expand it outward to include more, adjust the **Shift Edge** value.

6. Under Output:

   If you want to replace a fringe of background pixels along the selection edge with colors from within the selection, check **Decontaminate Colors**, then adjust the **Amount** value.

   Choose **Output To: Selection** to refine the selection without putting the contents on a new layer. Or to copy the selection contents to a new layer, choose **New Layer** (no mask) or **New Layer with Layer Mask** (the selection is converted to white areas in a layer mask). If Decontaminate Colors is checked, only the "New" layer options will be available.

7. *Optional:* Check Remember Settings to have the current settings become the new default values for the dialog (we keep this option off).

8. Click OK. (See also the task on the next four pages.)

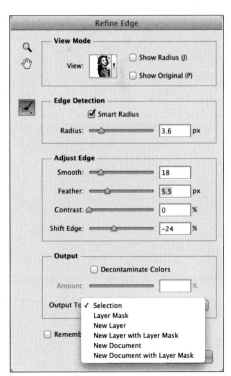

A *The Refine Edge dialog provides many options for refining and outputting a selection.*

Using the Refine Radius tool in the Refine Edge dialog, along with the sliders, you can fine-tune the edge of a selection manually. Here we'll show you how to use these controls to refine a selection of hair (the bane of any Photoshopper's existence!), so you will be able to stack just the figure — surrounded by transparent pixels — above a different background.

To improve a selection of hair via the Refine Edge dialog:

1. Open an RGB portrait in which the figure has flyaway hair, and duplicate the Background.

2. Click the Background, and create a new Solid Color fill layer (see page 193); via the Color Picker, choose a color to appear behind the figure.A Note: You won't see the color in the image until step 5.

3. Click the duplicate image layer, then with the Quick Selection tool,   loosely select the face and hair.B

4. On the Options bar, click **Refine Edge** (Ctrl-Alt-R/ Cmd-Option-R). In the dialog, set all the sliders to 0 and uncheck Decontaminate Colors.

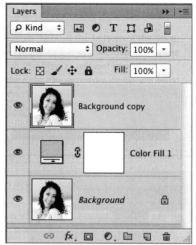

A *We duplicated the Background in this 300 ppi photo, then created a Solid Color fill layer directly above the Background.*

B *With the Quick Selection tool, we made a rough selection of the figure, including just the main part of her hair.*

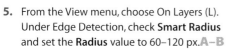

A In the Refine Edge dialog, we checked Smart Radius to allow the Radius to adapt to edges in the image, and increased the Radius value to 120 px.

B In On Layers view, the underlying layer is visible below the unselected areas. Now the selection includes most of her hair, but we will refine it further it to add the fine strands.

5. From the View menu, choose On Layers (L). Under Edge Detection, check **Smart Radius** and set the **Radius** value to 60–120 px.A–B

To display just the refinement area onscreen so you can judge how it is affected by the two radius options, check **Show Radius** or press J.C The higher the Radius value, the wider the area of edge pixels the command analyzes. Smart Radius analyzes the content of the refinement area, narrowing that area where the edges are well defined while keeping it wide where the edges are complex or more finely detailed.

Press J again to turn off the Show Radius option.

Continued on the following page

C We pressed J (Show Radius) to view the refinement area, noting where it was wide versus narrow. Afterward, we pressed J to return to On Layers view.

6. Choose the **Refine Radius** tool 🖌 (E), then press **X** to view the original image layer. Press] or [to set the brush to a medium to large size, then drag over the fine hair strands. Your brush work will display as green strokes.**A–B**

7. Press X to return to On Layers view.

   Optional: To better define the hard edges, reduce the Radius value slightly, but keep the Contrast, Smooth, and Feather values at 0 so they don't impede the effect of the Refine Radius tool.

8. Check **Decontaminate Colors**, then raise the Amount value until all colors from the background are removed. If you need to include yet more fine strands in the selection, increase the Shift Edge value slightly.

9. Choose Output To: **New Layer with Layer Mask**, then click OK (**A–B**, next page).

➤ To make the fine hair strands in dark hair more visible, duplicate the new layer and its layer mask after the last step above (**C**, next page).

A *We clicked the Refine Radius tool, 🖌 pressed X to view the original image, then applied strokes over the fine hair strands to include them in the radius. (We didn't apply strokes to the edge of the sweater because the original selection of that area didn't need more refinement.)*

B *Because we widened the refinement area, Refine Edge added the fine hair strands to the selection.*

A *We checked Decontaminate Colors, set the Amount value to 70%, and increased the Shift Edge value just enough to include more hair strands but none of the original background. From the Output To menu, we chose New Layer with Layer Mask (then clicked OK).*

➤ *If you find that the Decontaminate Colors option produces unwanted colors along the selection edge, narrow the refinement area in those areas with the Erase Refinements tool.*

B *A new layer and layer mask appeared on the Layers panel (Photoshop hid the original duplicate layer automatically).*

C *We duplicated the new layer with its mask (panel not shown) to make the hair strands look darker, then finally to soften the effect, we lowered the Opacity of the new layer to 70%.*

Using Quick Masks

In these steps, you will create a selection, then put your document into Quick Mask mode; the selection will display temporarily as a semitransparent red tint over the image (like a traditional rubylith). You will add or subtract areas from the mask using brush strokes, then put the document back into Standard mode; the mask will be converted back to a (newly reshaped) selection automatically. You can also use this mode to apply a mask to an image (see the next page).

To reshape a selection in Quick Mask mode:

1. Select an area of a layer. **A**

2. Click the **Edit in Quick Mask Mode** button 🔲 on the Tools panel or press Q. A mask should cover the unselected areas of the image. **B** (If it doesn't, for this task, double-click the same button, click Color Indicates: Masked Areas, then click OK.)

3. Choose the **Brush** tool 🖌 (B or Shift-B).

4. On the Options bar, click the Brush Preset picker arrowhead, then click a Hard or Soft Round brush (Soft if you want the selection edge to be slightly feathered); choose Mode: Normal; and set both the Opacity and Flow to 100%.

5. Zoom in on the mask, size the brush cursor by pressing [or], then do either of the following:

   To enlarge the masked (protected) area, press D to reset the default colors, then apply strokes with black.

   To enlarge the unmasked area, press X to swap the Foreground and Background colors (make the Foreground color white), then apply strokes. **C**

   ➤ To create a partial mask, lower the brush opacity via the Options bar (or use the shortcut we describe on page 272) before applying strokes. When you edit pixels within the selection, that area will be only partially affected by your edits.

6. To restore the normal document mode, click the **Edit in Standard Mode** button 🔳 on the Tools panel or press Q. The unmasked areas will turn into a selection.

7. *Optional:* To preserve the selection, store it as an alpha channel (see page 164) or as a layer mask (see page 172). There is no mechanism for saving the Quick Mask while the document is in Quick Mask mode.

A *We selected an area of a layer.*

B *When we put the document into Quick Mask mode, Photoshop covered the unselected area with a red mask.*

C *Here, we're unmasking the helmet by applying strokes with the Brush tool.*

In these steps, you will paint a mask directly in a document without creating a selection first. As with any Quick Mask, when you restore the document to Standard mode, it converts to a selection. One practical use for this technique is to select areas for retouching, such as the eyes or teeth areas in a portrait.

To create a selection via a Quick Mask:

1. Choose the **Brush** tool, and choose tool options as described in step 4 on the preceding page.

2. Double-click the **Edit in Quick Mask Mode** button on the Tools panel.

3. In the Quick Mask Options dialog, 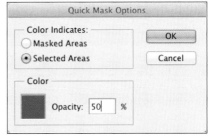 click Color Indicates: **Selected Areas**, then click OK. This option will cause the areas you mask (instead of the unmasked areas) to convert to a selection when you exit Quick Mask mode.

4. Zoom in, size the brush cursor by pressing [or], then with black as the Foreground color, apply strokes to create a mask.**B**

   ➤ You can start by painting with a medium-sized brush, then refine the mask with a smaller one.

   If you need to remove any areas from the mask, press X to switch the Foreground color to white.

5. Press Q to put the document back into Standard mode.**C** The mask converts to a selection.

6. *Optional:* To feather the edges of the selection, use the Feather slider in the Refine Edge dialog (see page 165).

7. *Optional:* To store the selection as a mask on the current layer, see the next page. Or to save it as an alpha channel, see page 164.**D**

A *We clicked Selected Areas in the Quick Mask Options dialog, and also changed the mask color from default red to blue to have it contrast better with the image.*

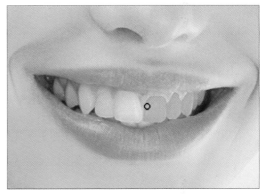

B *We're painting a Quick Mask on teeth.*

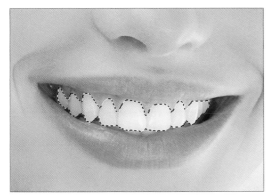

C *When we restored the document to Standard mode, the mask converted to a selection. (To use a selection like this to whiten teeth, see page 292.)*

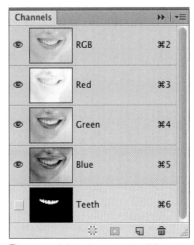

D *We saved the selection as an alpha channel, then renamed the channel.*

Creating layer masks

A layer mask is an editable (and removable) 8-bit grayscale channel that hides all or some of the pixels, type, or vector shapes on a layer. In a layer mask, white areas reveal parts of the layer, black areas hide, and gray areas hide partially. Here's an easy way to memorize this concept: White reveals, black conceals.

When a layer mask thumbnail is selected, you can edit the mask or move or copy it to other layers. At any time, you can disable the mask temporarily, apply it to make its effect permanent, or discard it to undo its effect.

To add a layer mask via the Layers panel:

1. *Optional:* Create a selection, which will become a shape in the mask.

2. On the Layers panel, click an image, type, or shape layer, a layer group, or a Smart Object. **A**

3. Do either of the following:

   To create a white mask that hides none of the layer or that hides only the areas outside an active selection, at the bottom of the Layers panel, click the **Add Layer Mask** button.

   To create a black mask that hides the whole layer or that hides only the areas inside an active selection, Alt-click/Option-click the **Add Layer Mask button** on the Layers panel. **B–C**

   ➤ To create a selection from type, Ctrl-click/Cmd-click an editable type layer thumbnail. You can then hide the type layer by clicking its visibility icon, and use the selection to create a layer mask.

To add a layer mask via the Refine Edge dialog:

1. Create a selection to become a shape in the mask.

2. On the Layers panel, click an image, type, or shape layer, a layer group, or a Smart Object.

3. Click **Refine Edge** on the Options bar, and use the dialog to refine the selection edges (see page 165). From the Output To menu, choose **Layer Mask**, then click OK.

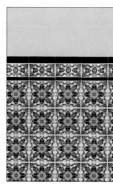

A *The original image contains a photo of tile on a layer above a photo of an archway (Background). We selected the archway, then clicked the tile layer.*

B *To add a black mask to the tile layer, we held down Alt/Option and clicked the Add Layer Mask button on the Layers panel. To blend the tile with the stone wall, we chose Pin Light blending mode and lowered the layer Opacity.*

C *The center of the tile layer is hidden by the arch-shaped layer mask.*

Editing layer masks

In this task, you'll edit a layer mask by applying strokes in the image with the Brush tool. In the steps on the next two pages, you will edit a mask via the Properties panel. Throughout this book, you will have many opportunities to practice these essential skills.

To reshape an existing layer mask:

1. Choose the **Brush** tool (B or Shift-B).

2. On the Options bar, click a brush on the Brush Preset picker; choose Mode: Normal; and choose an Opacity of 100% to mask or unmask areas fully or a lower Opacity to mask or unmask them partially.

3. Do either of the following: ★

   To display the mask as a colored overlay on the image, Alt-Shift-click/Option-Shift-click the layer mask thumbnail on the Layers panel. **A–B**

   To display the mask in black and white with the image hidden, Alt-click/Option-click the layer mask thumbnail on the Layers panel.

4. Size the brush cursor by pressing [or], then do either or both of the following:

   Paint with white as the Foreground color to remove areas of the mask and reveal more of the layer. **C**

   Paint with black as the Foreground color to enlarge the mask and hide more of the layer. **D**

   ➤ To change the brush hardness or opacity, use the shortcut described on page 272. **E**

5. Click the layer (not the mask) thumbnail.

   ➤ In lieu of step 3, you can double-click the layer mask thumbnail, then hold down Alt-Shift/Option-Shift or Alt/Option and click the Layer Mask thumbnail on the Properties panel. ★

   ➤ To change the mask Color or Opacity, right-click any layer mask thumbnail on the Layers panel (the Mask Options dialog opens).

To swap the black and white areas in a layer mask:

Do either of the following:

Double-click a layer mask thumbnail on the Layers panel to display the Properties panel, then click the **Invert** button. ★

Click a layer mask thumbnail on the Layers panel, then press Ctrl-I/Cmd-I.

A We're painting out areas of the mask, which we chose to display as a red overlay.

B This is the result.

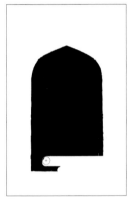
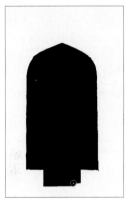

C We're subtracting areas from the mask by painting with white (only the mask is showing in the document).

D We're adding to the mask by painting with black.

E Here we're partially hiding an area of the layer with our brush set to 60% Opacity.

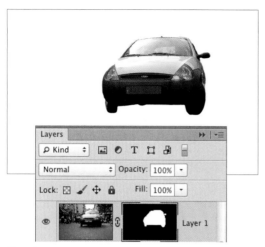

A *In this document, a black, hard-edged mask is hiding everything on the image layer except the car.*

In the Masks pane of the Properties panel, you can use the Density slider to change the opacity of the overall mask and/or the Feather slider to adjust the opacity of the mask edge. The sliders are nondestructive, meaning they don't alter the mask permanently and can be readjusted at any time.

To adjust the density or feather value of a layer mask:

1. Double-click a layer mask thumbnail on the Layers panel **A** to show the Properties panel. ★

2. Do either or both of the following:

    Reduce the **Density** value to lighten the black part of the mask and partially reveal areas of the layer (make the mask more transparent).**B**

    Increase the **Feather** value to soften the edge of the mask, for a more gradual transition between the masked and unmasked areas.**C**

B *To lighten the black part of the mask, we reduced the Density value on the Properties panel.*

C *Next, we increased the Feather value on the Properties panel to soften the edges of the mask. (Note that the layer Opacity is still 100%.) The car is the star of the show, while the faded background plays a supporting role.*

To refine the edges of a layer mask:

1. Double-click a layer mask thumbnail on the Layers panel to show the Properties panel. ★

2. Click **Mask Edge** to open the Refine Mask dialog.

   ➤ If you don't see the Mask Edge button, either scroll downward in the panel or enlarge the panel by dragging the gripper bar downward.

3. Use the Refine Mask controls to adjust the softness or sharpness of the edge of the mask. The controls work like those in the Refine Edge dialog, which is discussed on page 165.

   ➤ We keep the Feather slider in the Refine Mask dialog at 0 because it's destructive, and use the Feather slider on the Properties panel instead because it's nondestructive.

   ➤ If you click Color Range on the Properties panel for a selected mask, you can edit the mask using the same dialog controls that you would use to create a selection via Select > Color Range (see pages 160–161).

   ➤ If you create a mask by applying brush strokes or by converting an imprecise selection, some unwanted image pixels may still be visible along the edge. To expand or contract the mask to include or exclude more pixels, try setting the Radius to around 1 or 2 and fiddling with the Shift Edge slider.

Working with layer masks

By default, every layer mask that you create is linked to its layer thumbnail, and when moved, the two travel together as a unit. If you want to move either component separately, you have to unlink them first.

To reposition layer content or a mask independently:

1. On the Layers panel, click the **Link** icon 🔗 between a layer thumbnail and layer mask thumbnail. The icon disappears.

2. Click either the layer thumbnail or the layer mask thumbnail, depending on which one you want to move.**A–B**

3. Choose the **Move** tool ▸⊕ (or hold down V to spring-load the tool), then drag in the document window.**C**

4. Click between the layer and layer mask thumbnails to restore the Link icon.

A A layer mask is hiding the center of the tile layer and revealing part of the underlying Background photo.

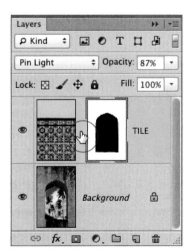

B We clicked the Link icon to disengage the layer image from the mask, then clicked the layer mask thumbnail.

C With the Move tool, we dragged the mask in the document to reveal a different part of the Background. (If you want to move the layer imagery instead, click the layer thumbnail before dragging.)

To move a mask to a different layer:

Drag a layer mask thumbnail to another layer (you can't move it to the Background).

To copy a layer mask to another layer:

Alt-drag/Option-drag a layer mask thumbnail to another layer.

When you load a mask as a selection, it displays in your document as a border of "marching ants."

To load a mask as a selection:

Do either of the following:

On the Layers panel, Ctrl-click/Cmd-click a layer mask thumbnail.

On the Layers panel, double-click a layer mask thumbnail, then on the Properties panel, click the **Load Selection from Mask** button.🔲 ★

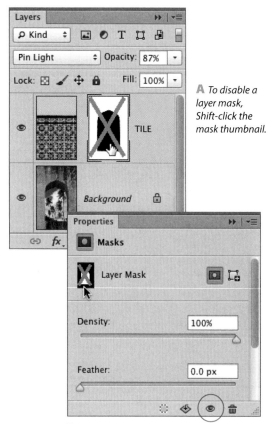

A *To disable a layer mask, Shift-click the mask thumbnail.*

B *Another method is to double-click the mask thumbnail on the Layers panel, then Shift-click the Layer Mask thumbnail on the Properties panel.*

When you disable a layer mask, a red X appears in the thumbnail on both the Layers and Properties panels, and the entire layer becomes visible.

To disable or enable a layer mask: ★

Method 1 (Layers panel)

To disable a layer mask, on the Layers panel,🖤 Shift-click the layer mask thumbnail **A** (this doesn't select the thumbnail). Repeat to reenable the mask.

Method 2 (Properties panel)

To disable a layer mask, on the Layers panel, double-click a layer mask thumbnail, then on the Properties panel, Shift-click the Layer Mask thumbnail.**B** To reenable the mask, click the Layer Mask thumbnail. You can also disable or enable a mask via the Disable/Enable Mask button.👁

You can discard any masks you don't need (this will reduce the file size slightly).

To delete a layer mask:

1. Deleting a mask is a permanent change, so we recommend copying the file first via File > Save As and storing the original for future editing.

2. Do either of the following:

On the Layers panel, right-click a layer mask thumbnail and choose **Delete Layer Mask**.

On the Layers panel, double-click a layer mask thumbnail to display the Properties panel, then click the **Delete Mask** button.🗑 ★

On an image layer (only), you can apply the effect of a mask and delete the hidden pixels permanently. The mask thumbnail disappears from the Layers panel.

To apply a layer mask:

1. Applying a mask is a permanent change, so we recommend copying the file first via File > Save As.

2. Do either of the following:

On the Layers panel, right-click a layer mask thumbnail and choose **Apply Layer Mask**.

On the Layers panel, double-click a layer mask thumbnail to display the Properties panel, then click the **Apply Mask** button.🔳 ★

Using the History panel, you can selectively restore the document to a previous state of the current work session. The panel provides many more options and much more flexibility than the simple Undo command. In this chapter, you will learn how to set options for the History panel; restore the document to a previous history state; delete, purge, and clear history states; preserve states of the current work session via snapshots; and generate a new document from a state or snapshot.

Choosing History panel options

The History panel 🕮 keeps a running list of the states, or edits, that you have made to the currently open document, from the "Open" unedited state of the document at the top of the list to the most recent state at the bottom. (This happens even if you don't have the panel open.)

When you click an earlier state, the document is restored to that stage of the editing process. Recent states may become dimmed and unavailable when you do this, depending on whether the panel is in linear or nonlinear mode.**A** Before using the panel, you need to understand the difference between the two modes.

Continued on the following page

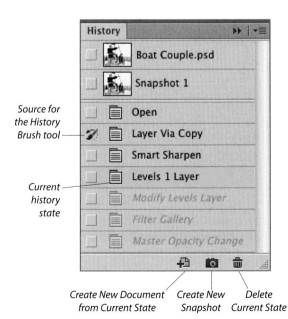

Source for the History Brush tool ⟶

Current history state ⟶

Create New Document from Current State   Create New Snapshot   Delete Current State

A *With our History panel in linear mode, we clicked an earlier state, which caused subsequent states to become dimmed.*

10

HISTORY

A BRUSH WITH HISTORY

In Chapter 14, we provide generic instructions on the use of brushes. On pages 283–284 in that chapter, we provide specific instructions for using the History Brush tool, which you can use to restore a history state within brush strokes.

To choose a mode for the History panel

To choose a mode for the History panel, choose History Options from the panel menu, then in the History Options dialog, check or uncheck **Allow Non-Linear History.A** We recommend keeping the History panel in **linear mode** (unchecking Allow Non-Linear History), particularly if you're a newcomer to Photoshop. With the panel in this mode, if you click an earlier state and either resume image editing from or delete that state, all the subsequent (dimmed) states are discarded. Although this mode offers less flexibility, it enables you to restore your document to an earlier state with a simple, clean break.

In **nonlinear mode**, if you click or delete an earlier state, subsequent states aren't deleted or dimmed.**B** If you resume image editing while an earlier state is selected, your next edit will show up as the latest state on the panel, and all the states in between will be preserved. That is, the latest state will incorporate the earlier stage of the image plus your newest edit. If you change your mind, you can click any intermediate state whenever you like and resume editing from there. Nonlinear is the more flexible of the two modes, but it can also be confusing.

To choose other settings for the History panel

The last option in the History Options dialog, **Make Layer Visibility Changes Undoable**, controls whether the panel creates a "Layer Visibility" state each time you click the visibility icon for a layer on the Layers panel. We keep this option off in order to reserve space on the panel for other states. (For the snapshot options in this dialog, see page 181.)

To specify the number of states that can be listed on the panel at a time, go to Edit/Photoshop > Preferences (Ctrl-K/Cmd-K) > Performance and, under History & Cache, enter a **History States** value (the default value is 20). If the maximum number of history states is exceeded during an editing session, the oldest states are removed to make room for new ones. The maximum number of states may also be limited by other factors, including the image size, the kind of edits made to the image, and currently available system memory. Each open document has its own separate list of states.

Beware! Regardless of the current preference setting, when you close a document, all of its history states and snapshots are deleted from the panel.

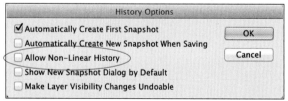

A *In the History Options dialog, uncheck Allow Non-Linear History to put the panel in linear mode, or check it for nonlinear mode.*

B *With our History panel in nonlinear mode, we clicked an earlier state; all the states remained available, including the recent states below the one we clicked.*

Changing history states

Before changing history states, let us remind you of the difference between the two modes for the History panel. If the panel is in linear mode (the Allow Non-Linear History option is off) and you click an earlier state, all the states below the one you click will become dimmed. If you then delete the state you clicked or continue editing the image while that earlier state remains selected, all the dimmed states will be deleted (if you change your mind, you can choose Undo immediately to restore the deleted states).

If the panel is in nonlinear mode and you click an earlier state, then proceed to edit your document, the newest edit will become the latest state, but Photoshop won't delete the prior states.

To change history states:

1. Perform some edits on an image.

2. Do any of the following:

   On the History panel, click a state. **A–B**

   To **Step Forward** one state, press Ctrl-Shift-Z/ Cmd-Shift-Z.

   To **Step Backward** one state, press Ctrl-Alt-Z/ Cmd-Option-Z.

➤ When you choose File > Revert, it is listed as a state on the History panel. You can restore the image to a state prior to or after the Revert state.

➤ Each time you click and change the settings for an existing adjustment layer, the panel lists those edits collectively as one new state (e.g., "Modify Levels Layer" or "Modify Curves Layer").

➤ You can't restack (change the order of) history states on the panel.

A *With our History panel in linear mode, we're clicking a prior state.*

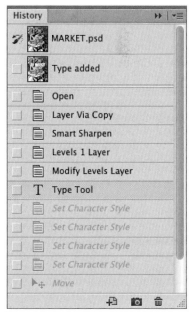

B *All the states listed below the one we clicked became dimmed.*

Deleting, purging, and clearing history states

This task presumes that your History panel is in linear mode (you unchecked the Allow Non-Linear History option). With the panel in this mode, if you delete a state and then resume editing your document, that state and all the subsequent ones will be discarded from the panel.

To delete a history state:

On the History panel, do one of the following:

Right-click a state, choose **Delete** from the context menu, 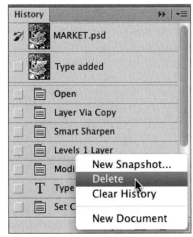 then click Yes in the alert dialog. B

To bypass the alert, drag the state to be deleted to the **Delete Current State** button.

To delete previous states in reverse order without an alert appearing, click a state, then Alt-click/ Option-click the **Delete Current State** button as many times as needed.

Note: The Undo command restores only the last deleted state.

When you purge or clear states from the History panel, the most recent state is left as the only state remaining. All snapshots are preserved.

To purge or clear the History panel:

To clear all states from your History panel for all of the currently open documents in order to free up memory for Photoshop, choose Edit > Purge > **Histories**, then click OK if an alert appears. (To prevent the alert from reappearing, check Don't Show Again ★.) As the alert warns you, this command cannot be undone!

To clear all states from the History panel for just the current document, right-click any state and choose **Clear History**. This command doesn't free up memory for Photoshop, but it can be undone.

A *Right-click a state and choose Delete from the context menu, then click Yes in the alert dialog.*

B *Because our History panel was in linear mode when we deleted a state, Photoshop also deleted all the subsequent states.*

Using snapshots

Photoshop deletes states from the History panel if any of the following occurs: the specified maximum number of history states is exceeded, you clear or purge the panel, or you click an earlier state when the panel is in linear mode and then resume editing the document. Snapshots, which are created from a designated history state, remain on the panel even if any of the above occur. When you click a snapshot, the document is restored to the state from which it was created. Snapshots are represented by thumbnails at the top of the panel, for easy identification. Note that like states, snapshots are deleted when you close your document.

On this page, you will choose default settings for snapshots that apply to all Photoshop files. On the next page, you will create snapshots for a specific document.

A *Because we had the Automatically Create First Snapshot option checked, Photoshop created a snapshot of the opening state of our document. During the course of editing, we added three more snapshots.*

To choose snapshot options:

1. From the History panel menu, choose **History Options**. The History Options dialog opens.**B**

2. Check or uncheck any of the following options, all of which pertain to snapshots:

   Automatically Create First Snapshot to have Photoshop create a snapshot each time a file is opened (this option is checked by default and we keep it that way).

   Automatically Create New Snapshot When Saving to have Photoshop create a snapshot every time a file is saved. Each snapshot is labeled with the time of day it was created.

   Show New Snapshot Dialog by Default to have the New Snapshot dialog appear whenever you click the New Snapshot button, enabling you to choose options.

3. Click OK.

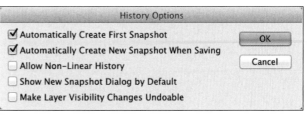

B *The History Options dialog has three snapshot options. We usually keep just the first two checked.*

If the Automatically Create New Snapshot When Saving option is turned off for your History panel, you should get in the habit of creating snapshots periodically as you work and before running any actions on your document. If you follow Method 2 (right), you can choose whether the snapshot is made from all the layers in the document, from all the layers present at a particular state, or from just the current layer.

To create a snapshot of a state:

Method 1 (without choosing options)

1. Edit your document so it contains the changes that you want to capture as a snapshot.

2. If the Show New Snapshot Dialog by Default option is off in the History Options dialog, click the **New Snapshot** button on the History panel; if that option is on, Alt-click/Option-click the New Snapshot button. A new snapshot thumbnail appears below the last one, in the upper section of the panel.

Method 2 (choosing options)

1. Edit your document so it contains the changes that you want to capture as a snapshot.

2. On the History panel, right-click the state to be captured as a snapshot and choose **New Snapshot** from the context menu. **A** The layer that was being edited at that state becomes selected and the New Snapshot dialog opens. **B**

3. Type a name for the snapshot, then choose an option from the **From** menu:

   Full Document to preserve all the layers that were in the document at the designated state.

   Merged Layers to merge all the layers in the document at the designated state into one layer.

   Current Layer to create a snapshot of just the layer that was selected at the designated state.

4. Click OK. **C**

5. If you didn't create the snapshot from the latest state, click the state from which you want to continue editing.

➤ To rename a snapshot, double-click the name.

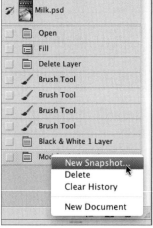

A *After applying some edits to this image, we right-clicked the latest state and are choosing New Snapshot from the context menu.*

B *In the New Snapshot dialog, we entered a name for the snapshot and chose From: Full Document.*

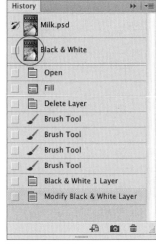

C *A thumbnail for the new snapshot appeared on the History panel.*

Creating snapshots of promising or key document states periodically while editing is a good habit to get into. With their thumbnails, snapshots are easier to identify than states, and unlike states (which Photoshop may delete to make room for new states), snapshots stay on the panel until you close your document. Compare the two different options below, noting the different effect they have on the History panel.

To make a snapshot become the newest state:

After applying some edits to your document and creating one or more snapshots, do either of the following: **A–B**

Click a snapshot name or thumbnail. **C–D** If the History panel is in linear mode, the document will revert to the snapshot stage of editing, and all the states will be dimmed. If you now resume editing, all those dimmed states will be discarded.

Alt-click/Option-click a snapshot name or thumbnail. Earlier states will remain available and the snapshot you clicked will become the most recent state. Use this method if you want to preserve access to prior edits.

➤ To delete a snapshot, drag it to the Delete Current State button 🗑 or right-click the snapshot name and choose Delete from the context menu.

A *This is the original image.*

B *During the course of editing the image (applying some filters), we created a few snapshots of different states.*

C *We clicked a snapshot.*

D *Now the image matches the state of the snapshot.*

Creating documents from history states

By using the New Document command, you can spin off versions of your current document (and the current state of the Layers panel) from any state or snapshot.

To create a new document from a history state or snapshot:

1. On the History panel, do either of the following:

   Right-click a snapshot or a state and choose **New Document** from the context menu. A

   Click a snapshot or a state, then click the **New Document from Current State** button.

2. Save the new document that appears onscreen. B The starting state for the document will be listed as "Duplicate State."

A *We right-clicked a snapshot and are choosing New Document from the context menu.*

B *A new document appeared, bearing the name of the snapshot from which it was created.*

In this chapter, you'll learn ways to choose the colors that are applied by various Photoshop tools and commands. You will also learn how to choose a blending mode for a layer or tool, apply a tint via a Solid Color Fill layer, apply and edit gradients, and create and apply patterns.

Choosing colors in Photoshop
The Foreground and Background colors

The current Foreground color is applied by some tools, such as the Brush, Pencil, and Mixer Brush, and by some commands. The current Background color is applied by other procedures, such as when you enlarge the canvas area with the Crop tool (Delete Cropped Pixels option enabled) or use the Eraser tool on, or cut an area from, the Background. One or both of these colors are also used by some of the Photoshop filters.

The Foreground and Background colors are displayed in color squares on the Tools panel **A** and on the Color panel. **B** Note: In this book, Foreground color and Background color are written with an uppercase "F" and "B" to differentiate them from the foreground and background areas of a picture.

On the following pages, you will learn how to choose Foreground and Background colors via these methods:

➤ Use the controls in the **Color Picker** dialog or via an on-image color picker.

➤ Choose a predefined color from a matching system via the **Color Libraries** dialog.

➤ Use the sliders on the **Color** panel.

➤ Click a solid color swatch on the **Swatches** panel.

➤ Sample a color in an image with the **Eyedropper** tool.

USING COLOR
11

The Default Foreground and Background Colors button (D) makes the Foreground color black and the Background color white.

The Switch Foreground and Background Colors button (X) swaps the two current colors.

The currently selected square has an extra, outer border.

Foreground color square

Background color square

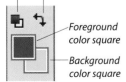

Foreground color square

Background color square

Color ramp

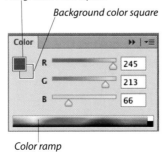

A *These are the color controls on the Tools panel.*

B *The two color squares also appear on the Color panel.*

The color models

Colors in Photoshop can be chosen from four models and a wide assortment of matching systems. When output on a commercial press, your Photoshop image will be printed using different percentages of cyan (C), magenta (M), yellow (Y), and black (K) inks, which together create the impression of smooth, continuous tones. In the printing industry, colors are standardized by number, with each company providing its own system and printed fan guide (similar to the way you might pick house paint colors). Spot colors, which are premixed inks based on set formulas (e.g., PANTONE PLUS), are sometimes used in addition to CMYK inks where color accuracy is critical, such as for a company logo. For commercial printing, the only way to get dependable results is by referring to a printed fan guide. If you pick colors based on whether they look appealing onscreen (even on a well-calibrated display), you may be in for an unpleasant — and potentially costly — surprise when you see them in print.

RGB colors (based on the components of red, green, and blue light in a computer display) are used solely for screen output; for these colors, you don't need to refer to a printed fan guide. For Web output, some designers also use hexadecimal colors. For the HSB color model, see the sidebar on page 188.

Using the Color Picker

To choose a color via the Color Picker:

1. Do either of the following:

   On the Tools panel, click the Foreground or Background color square.

   On the Color panel, click the Foreground or Background color square if it's already selected (has an extra outer border), or double-click the square if it's not selected.

   Note: If the square you click contains a custom color from a matching system (such as PANTONE PLUS), the Color Libraries dialog will open instead of the picker. Click the Picker button to get to the Color Picker dialog.

2. Do one of the following:

   Click a color on the vertical color ramp or drag the slider to choose a hue, then click a brightness and saturation value of that hue in the large square. **A** (You can also click or drag in the image to sample a color while the Color Picker dialog is open.)

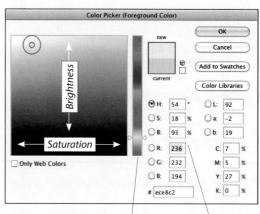

A To pick a color, click a hue on this color ramp or drag the slider, then click a color in the large square.

Alternatively, enter values in the fields for a color model.

USING THE HUD COLOR PICKER

To access Color Picker controls quickly without opening the dialog, choose a tool that uses colors, Alt-Shift-right-click/Cmd-Option-Control-click in the image to display the on-image picker, drag to choose a hue on the hue bar or wheel, then drag to choose a brightness and saturation value in the square. If you want to change the hue without changing the current brightness and saturation values, when the picker displays, release the keys but keep the mouse button down, hold down the Spacebar and drag to the hue bar or wheel, release the Spacebar, then drag to the desired hue (practice, practice).

Note: For this feature to work, Use Graphics Processor must be checked in Edit/Photoshop > Preferences > Performance upon launch. In General preferences, via the HUD Color Picker menu, you can choose a strip or wheel design and size for the HUD Color Picker (including two new small sizes). ★

To choose a process color for print output, enter C, M, Y, and K percentages from a printed formula guide for a process color matching system.

For onscreen output, enter R, G, and B values (0 to 255).

To choose a hexadecimal color (for Web output only), enter the number in the # field.

3. Click OK. The color will appear in the selected color square on the Tools and Color panels. To add the color to the Swatches panel, see page 189.

➤ To change the interface of the Color Picker, in Edit/Photoshop > Preferences > General, from the Color Picker menu, select either Windows/Apple (the picker for your system) or Adobe (the default Photoshop picker).

➤ You don't need to restrict yourself to Web-safe colors for Web graphics, because most computers display millions of colors. Ignore the non-Web-safe icon 🌐 if it appears in the Color Picker, and keep Only Web Colors unchecked. For the out-of-gamut icon,⚠ see the sidebar on the next page.

Choosing colors from a library

Before choosing spot colors for print output, ask your commercial print shop which brand of ink they're going to use, then choose colors from a printed fan guide for that system (each manufacturer makes its own guide). Note: By default, Photoshop color-separates both process and spot colors in a document into C, M, Y, and K process colors. If you need to output a spot color to a separate plate, you must create a separate spot color channel for it (see page 370).

COLOR LIBRARIES FOR PRINT OUTPUT

➤ ANPA colors are used in the newspaper industry.

➤ DIC Color Guide and TOYO Color Finder colors are used in Japan.

➤ FOCOLTONE is a process color system that was developed to help prevent registration problems. It can be used in North America.

➤ HKS process colors and HKS spot colors (without "Process" in the name) are used primarily in Europe.

➤ PANTONE PLUS (+) ★ process and spot colors are widely used in North America.

➤ TRUMATCH is a process color system, organized in a different way from PANTONE. It is used worldwide.

To choose a color from a library:

1. Do either of the following:

   On the Tools panel, click the Foreground or Background color square.

   On the Color panel, 🎨 click the Foreground or Background color square if it's already selected (has an extra outer border), or double-click the square if it's not selected.

2. If the color square you clicked isn't a custom color, the Color Picker dialog will open. Click **Color Libraries** to show the Color Libraries dialog.

3. From the **Book** menu, choose a matching system. For commercial printing, choose the system that your print shop has recommended, and find the desired color in a formula guide.

4. Do either of the following:

   Without clicking anywhere, type the number of the desired color; that swatch will become selected.**A**

   Click a color on the vertical color slider to display a family of hues, then click a swatch on the left side of the dialog.**B**

5. Click OK. To add the chosen color to the Swatches panel, see page 189.

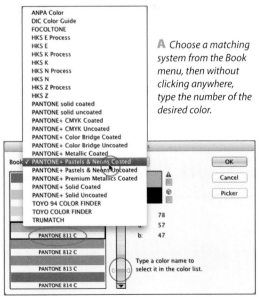

A *Choose a matching system from the Book menu, then without clicking anywhere, type the number of the desired color.*

B *Another option is to click a color on the vertical color ramp (or move the slider), then click a swatch on the scroll list.*

Using the Color panel

Another way to select RGB or HSB colors for Web output, or for output to an inkjet printer, is via the color ramp, sliders, or fields on the Color panel.

To choose an RGB or HSB color using the Color panel:

1. Click the Foreground or Background color square on the Color panel, 🎨 if the desired square isn't already selected. **A**

2. From the top portion of the Color panel menu, choose a color model for the sliders. **B** For output to an inkjet printer, choose RGB Sliders; for Web output, choose RGB Sliders or HSB Sliders (see the sidebar at right).

3. Do any of the following: **C**

   Move any of the sliders.

   Click on or drag in the color ramp.

   Enter values in the fields.

4. *Optional:* To add your new color to the Swatches panel, see the instructions on the next page.

➤ To change the style of the color ramp, right-click the ramp and choose from the context menu.

➤ Alt-click/Option-click the color ramp to choose a color for whichever color square (Foreground or Background) isn't currently selected.

➤ If Dynamic Color Sliders is checked in Preferences (Ctrl-K/Cmd-K) > General, colors in the bars above the sliders will update interactively as you mix or choose a color.

HSB AND RGB DEMYSTIFIED

➤ In the HSB model, the hue (H) is the wavelength of light for which a color is named (such as "red" or "blue"); brightness (B) is the lightness of a color; and saturation (S) is the purity of a color (how much gray it contains, versus pure color).

➤ In the RGB model, which is used by your computer display, white (the presence of all colors) is produced when all the sliders are at the far right (at 255) on the Color panel, black (the absence of all colors) is produced when all the sliders are at the far left (0), and gray is produced when all the sliders are aligned vertically with one another at any other location.

THE OUT-OF-GAMUT ALERT

An out-of-gamut alert icon ⚠ on the Color Picker or Color panel indicates that the current color isn't printable (has no ink equivalent). If you click the icon, Photoshop will substitute the closest print-able color, as shown in the swatch next to or below the icon. Similarly, if the color currently under the pointer is outside the printable gamut, exclamation points will display next to the CMYK color values on the Info panel. The out-of-gamut range is defined by the current CMYK output profile, which is chosen on the Working Spaces: CMYK menu in Edit > Color Settings. When your image is converted to CMYK mode for commercial printing, all the image colors are brought into the printable gamut automatically. You need to pay attention to the alerts only if you want to convert specific colors manually.

A *Click the Foreground or Background color square.*

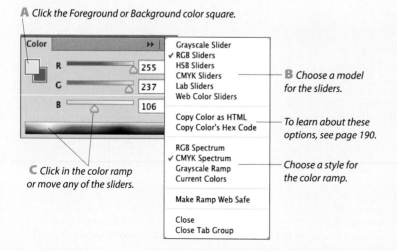

C *Click in the color ramp or move any of the sliders.*

B *Choose a model for the sliders.*

To learn about these options, see page 190.

Choose a style for the color ramp.

Using the Swatches panel

Note: For easy access, detach the Swatches panel from the Color panel group by dragging its tab.

To choose a color via the Swatches panel:

1. Display the Swatches panel.▣

2. Do either of the following:

   To choose a Foreground or Background color for the color square that is currently selected on the Tools and Color panels, click a swatch.

   To choose a Foreground or Background color for the color square that isn't selected on the Tools and Color panels, Ctrl-click/Cmd-click a swatch.

➤ To access other libraries of swatches, see page 117 or 119. To access a wide assortment of process color swatches, use the Kuler panel; see page 111.

Colors that you add to the Swatches panel will remain there until the swatches are deleted, replaced, or reset, and are available for use in all documents. (To save swatches as a permanent library, see "To save the presets currently on a picker as a library" on page 117.)

To add a color to the Swatches panel:

1. Choose a Foreground color via the Color panel or Color Picker, or select a color in the image with the Eyedropper tool (see the next page).

2. On the Swatches panel,▣ do one of the following:

   Click the **New Swatch of Foreground Color** button.▣

   Click the blank area below the swatches.**A**

   Right-click any existing swatch and choose **New Swatch** from the context menu.

3. In the Color Swatch Name dialog, enter a name for the swatch,**B** then click OK. The new swatch will be displayed (or listed) last on the panel.**C**

➤ To create a new swatch without opening the Color Swatch Name dialog, hold down Alt/Option and click the blank area in the Swatches panel.

➤ To rename an existing swatch, double-click it, then change the name in the dialog. To learn a swatch name, either use the Tool Tip or list the swatches by name (choose Small List or Large List from the panel menu).

➤ To restore the default swatches to the Swatches panel, see page 118.

➤ If you want to use the current swatches on the panel in another Adobe Creative Suite application, save them via the Save Swatches for Exchange command from the panel menu.

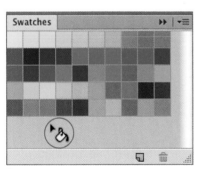

A To add a color to the Swatches panel, we're clicking the blank area below the swatches.

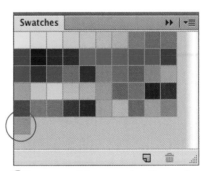

C Our new swatch appeared on the panel.

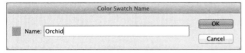

B We entered a name for the swatch.

Using the Eyedropper tool

To sample a color from an image using the Eyedropper:

1. Choose the **Eyedropper** tool 🖋 (or hold down I to spring-load the tool) and click the Foreground or Background color square on the Color panel.

2. On the Options bar, do the following:

   Choose a **Sample Size** (see the sidebar below, right).

   Choose an option from the **Sample** menu to control from which layer(s) the tool samples a color. Notes: If you choose a "Current" option, also click a layer. Choose a "No Adjustments" option to sample color values minus the effect of any adjustment layers. ★

   Optional: Check Show Sampling Ring. Note: To access the sampling ring, Use Graphics Processor must be checked in Edit/Photoshop > Preferences > Performance upon launch.

3. Do either of the following:

   Click a color in any open document. **A**

   Drag in any document, and release the mouse when the pointer is over the desired color.

   If you checked Show Sampling Ring, the sampled color will preview at the top of a ring in the image and the former color will display on the bottom.

   ➤ Alt-click/Option-click or drag in an image with the Eyedropper tool to choose a Background color when the Foreground color square is selected, or vice versa.

A *With Show Sampling Ring checked for the Eyedropper tool on the Options bar, we are clicking a color in the image.*

Copying colors as hexadecimals

For Web output, you can copy a color as hexadecimal values from a document in Photoshop and then paste it into an HTML file or Web page layout program.

To copy a color as a hexadecimal value:

1. To copy a color to the Clipboard as a hexadecimal value, do either of the following:

   Choose the **Eyedropper** tool 🖋 (I or Shift-I) and choose Options bar settings for the tool. Right-click a color in the document window, then choose **Copy Color as HTML** (HTML color tag) or **Copy Color's Hex Code** (HEX number).

   Choose a Foreground color via the Color panel, Color Picker, or Swatches panel. From the Color panel menu, choose **Copy Color as HTML** or **Copy Color's Hex Code**.

2. To paste the color into an HTML file, display the HTML file in your HTML-editing application, then choose Edit > Paste (Ctrl-V/Cmd-V).

SAMPLE SIZE FOR THE EYEDROPPER TOOL

➤ To change the size of the area from which the Eyedropper tool takes a sample, from the Options bar, choose Sample Size: Point Sample (to sample only the exact pixel you click) or one of the Average options to sample an average value from the area (e.g., from a 5 by 5-pixel square area).

➤ You can also right-click in the document with the Eyedropper tool and choose a sample size from the context menu.

➤ The 3 by 3 Average and 5 by 5 Average options are useful for sampling continuous tones, such as skin tones in a portrait photo or the background area in a landscape (we usually use 3 by 3 Average). The 11 by 11 Average through 101 by 101 Average options are better choices for very high-resolution files.

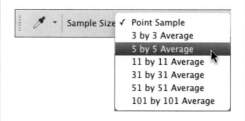

Choosing a blending mode

The blending mode that you choose for a tool or layer affects how that tool or layer interacts with underlying pixels. To produce a blending mode effect, Photoshop compares the colors of two layers on a channel-by-channel basis, or compares each color in a layer to a corresponding color in the underlying layer (the base color), or compares the paint color being applied by a tool to the existing color in the layer.

You can choose from a menu of blending modes in many locations in Photoshop, such as the Options bar (for most painting and editing tools), the Layers panel, A and the Layer Style and Fill dialogs. In order to see the results of a blending mode choice for a layer, the contents of the selected layer must overlap some contents of the underlying layer. B–C

➤ When choosing an Opacity percentage for a tool (via the Options bar), keep in mind that the results will also be affected by the opacity of the layer that you edit. For example, strokes applied with a Brush tool of 50% Opacity on a layer that has an Opacity of 50% will appear lighter than the same strokes if applied to a layer that has an Opacity of 100%.

Blending modes	Description
✓ Normal Dissolve	The Basic blending modes replace the base colors.
Darken Multiply Color Burn Linear Burn Darker Color	The Darken blending modes darken the base colors.
Lighten Screen Color Dodge Linear Dodge (Add) Lighter Color	The Lighten blending modes lighten the base colors.
Overlay Soft Light Hard Light Vivid Light Linear Light Pin Light Hard Mix	The Contrast blending modes change the amount of contrast.
Difference Exclusion Subtract Divide	The Comparative blending modes invert the base colors.
Hue Saturation Color Luminosity	The Component blending modes apply a specific color component.

A *The blending modes are grouped in categories based on their function and effect.*

B *We applied light blue strokes to a blank layer above the image layer. The layer containing the brush strokes has a blending mode of Darker Color.*

C *This is the same image, except we chose the blending mode of Lighter Color for the layer that contains the brush strokes.*

Here you will choose a blending mode for a layer to change how its color values blend with values in the underlying layer. Some blending modes, such as Soft Light, produce subtle changes, whereas others, such as Difference, produce marked color shifts. You can't choose a blending mode for the Background. (To learn about advanced blending controls, see pages 330–331.)

To choose a blending mode for a layer:

1. Click any kind of layer (not the Background), such as a duplicate image layer **A** or a type, adjustment, fill, shape, or Smart Object layer. You can also select multiple layers. ★

2. From the menu in the upper-left corner of the Layers panel, choose a **blending mode.B** (No blending occurs In the default mode of Normal.)

3. *Optional:* Adjust the Opacity setting.**C**

➤ In Photoshop CS6, unlike in former versions of the program, the mode and Opacity settings for a selected, hidden layer are listed on the panel. ★

A *This is the original image.*

B *We duplicated the Background, chose Color Dodge mode for the duplicate layer, and lowered the layer Opacity to 57%.*

CYCLING THROUGH THE BLENDING MODES

To cycle through the blending modes for the current painting or editing tool, or for the currently selected layer when using a nonediting tool (such as the Move tool or a selection tool), press Shift - + (plus) or Shift - – (minus).

C *The final image is a combination of the two layers.*

Creating a Solid Color fill layer

When we need to add a solid background below type or below an image layer that contains some transparent pixels, we use a Solid Color fill layer. The advantages to using this method are that we can quickly preview and change the color of the fill layer, hide or remove it, or edit its mask (to make it partially visible) at any time. In contrast, the results from using the Fill dialog are permanent; and a Color Overlay layer effect, although editable, can't be given its own mask.

To create a Solid Color fill layer:

1. Click the layer above which you want the fill layer to appear. It can be below a type layer, or below an image layer that contains some transparent pixels.

2. *Optional:* To make the solid color visible in only part of the layer, create a selection.

3. From the **Create Fill/Adjustment Layer** menu ⬤. on the Layers panel, choose **Solid Color**.

4. In the Color Picker dialog, choose a color for the tint. Don't sweat over your color choice; you can easily change it later. Click OK. **A–B**

5. *Optional:* Change the Opacity or blending mode of the fill layer (see the preceding page).

➤ To change the color of the fill layer, double-click the layer thumbnail; the Color Picker reopens. **C–D**

➤ Whether you created a selection in step 2 or not, you can edit the mask by applying brush strokes (black to reveal, white to conceal).

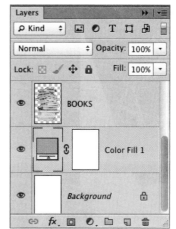

A We clicked the Background in this document, then created a Solid Color fill layer (we chose a tan color).

B The color from the fill layer is visible below the transparent areas in the "BOOKS" layer.

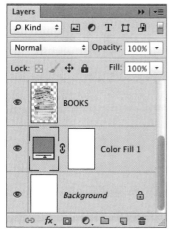

C We double-clicked the Color Fill layer thumbnail on the Layers panel, then, via the Color Picker, changed the tan color to teal.

D This is the image after we changed the color in the fill layer.

Creating a Gradient fill layer

A gradient is a soft blend between two or more opaque or semitransparent colors. A good use of this feature is to enhance the area behind imagery or type. We will show you how to apply a gradient via a Gradient fill layer and the Gradient tool, and how to create and modify a gradient via the Gradient Editor.

A gradient that you apply via a Gradient fill layer appears in its own layer, complete with a layer mask that you can edit to control where the gradient is visible. Like an adjustment layer, this type of gradient is editable, unlike a gradient that is applied directly to a layer, and it does not increase the file storage size.

To apply a gradient via a fill layer:

1. Click a layer on the Layers panel. If you want the gradient fill to display below type or an image layer that contains some transparency, click the layer directly below that image or type layer. **A**

2. *Optional:* To make the gradient visible in only part of the layer, create a selection.

3. From the **Create Fill/Adjustment Layer** menu ⬤, on the Layers panel, choose **Gradient**. The Gradient Fill dialog opens.

4. Click the Gradient picker arrowhead at the top of the dialog, click a gradient preset on the picker, **B** then click back in the dialog and keep it open.

   ➤ To load more gradients, open the preset picker menu, ⚙️ ▾ choose a library name from the assortment at the bottom, then click Append or OK in the alert dialog (see page 117).

5. Choose a gradient **Style** of Linear (a good choice if this is your first try), Radial, Angle, Reflected, or Diamond.

6. Do any of the following optional steps:

   To change the angle of the gradient, move the **Angle** dial or enter a value. **C**

   To scale the gradient relative to the layer, use the **Scale** slider or field. The greater the Scale percentage, the more gradual the transition between colors in the gradient.

   To reposition the gradient, drag in the document window (with the dialog still open).

   To swap the order of colors in the gradient, check **Reverse**.

   To minimize banding (stripes) in the gradient on print output, check **Dither**.

A *The original image consists of an image layer (that contains transparent pixels) above a white Background. We clicked the Background on the Layers panel …*

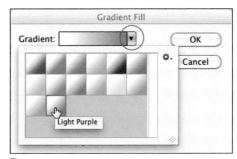

B *… then chose Gradient from the Create Fill/Adjustment Layer menu. In the Gradient Fill dialog, we clicked the Gradient picker arrowhead, then loaded the Simple library via the picker menu. Here, we are clicking a preset in the picker.*

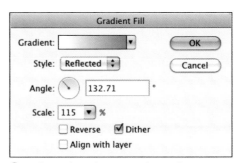

C *Finally, we chose the settings shown above, including changing the Angle to align the gradient with the saucepan in the image.*

If you created a selection in step 2, check **Align with Layer** to fit the complete gradient within the selection area, or uncheck this option to have the gradient stretch across the whole layer (in which case only part of the gradient will display within the selection).

7. Click OK. A

8. If the Gradient fill layer is completely obscuring all the layers below it, do any of the following: Lower the Opacity of the fill layer; B restack it below the layers you want to show; lower the Opacity of some of the color stops (see the next page); or click the fill layer mask thumbnail, then apply black brush strokes (the gradient will be hidden where you apply strokes).

➤ To edit the settings for the Gradient fill layer, double-click the layer thumbnail; the Gradient Fill dialog reopens.

➤ To set a preference so that all new Solid Color, Gradient, and Pattern fill layers are given a mask automatically, open the Panel Options dialog from the Layers panel menu, then check Use Default Mask on Fill Layers. Via the Properties panel, you can adjust the density of any black areas in the mask, or feather the edge.

➤ To apply a gradient to an image based on luminosity values, see pages 228–229.

DESIGNING FOR COLOR-BLIND VIEWERS

At some point in your career, you may be hired to design graphics, such as signage, that are fully accessible to color-blind viewers. In fact, some countries require graphics in public spaces to comply with Color Universal Design (CUD) guidelines. The View > Proof Setup > Color Blindness – Protanopia-Type and Color Blindness – Deuteranopia-Type commands in Photoshop simulate how your document would look to viewers with common forms of color blindness.

In case you're not familiar with those two terms, for protanopes, the brightness of red, orange, and yellow is dimmed, making it hard for them to differentiate red from black or dark gray. Protanopes also have trouble differentiating violet, lavender, and purple from blue because the reddish components of those colors look dimmed. Deuteranopes are unable to distinguish between colors in the green-yellow-red part of the spectrum and experience color blindness similar to that of protanopes, but without the problem of dimming.

A *This is the image with the Gradient fill layer.*

B *As a variation, we created a new, blank layer below the Gradient Fill layer and filled it with a Scripted pattern (Stucco 2 in the Texture Fill 2 library, Script: Spiral), and lowered the Opacity of the Gradient fill layer to 77%.*

Creating and editing a gradient preset

You can create a variation of any existing gradient preset or create new, custom presets. When you edit a preset, Photoshop forces you to work on a copy automatically, so as to preserve the original one in the library. We'll show you how to add and change the colors in a gradient, adjust the color transitions, and make specific colors semi- or fully transparent.

To create or edit a gradient preset:

1. Open the Swatches and/or Color panels, which you will be using to pick colors for the gradient (you can collapse the panels to icons).

2. To open the Gradient Editor, do either of the following:

   Choose the **Gradient** tool ▦ (G or Shift-G), then click the Gradient thumbnail on the Options bar. **A**

   Double-click the thumbnail for an existing **Gradient Fill** layer, then click the gradient thumbnail at the top of the Gradient Fill dialog.

3. In the Gradient Editor, click the preset swatch that you want to create a variation of (when you begin editing the gradient, the Name will change to Custom). Keep the Gradient Type as Solid and the Smoothness setting at 100%.

   If you want to create a gradient that uses whichever Foreground and Background colors are in effect when the gradient is applied, click the Foreground to Background preset.*

4. For any gradient except Foreground to Background, click the starting (left) or ending (right) color stop under the gradient bar (**A**, next page), then do either of the following:

   Click a color on the Swatches panel, or on the color ramp at the bottom of the Color panel, or in any open document window (the pointer becomes a temporary Eyedropper tool).

   Double-click a color stop or click the Color swatch at the bottom of the Gradient Editor. Choose a color in the Color Picker, then click OK.

5. Do any of these optional steps:

   To add an **intermediate** color to the gradient, click below the gradient bar to produce a stop, then choose a color for that stop, as described in the preceding step (**B**, next page).

To add an **opacity** stop, click above the gradient bar, then use the scrubby slider to change the Opacity percentage (**C**, next page). You can also click any existing opacity stop and change its Opacity percentage. In the gradient bar, transparency is represented by a checkerboard pattern.

To change the **location** of a color or opacity stop in the gradient, drag the stop to the left or right.

To control the abruptness of a transition between color or opacity stops, click a stop, then drag the **midpoint diamond** (found on either side of the stop) to the left or right (**D**, next page). The diamond marks the point at which two adjacent colors are evenly mixed.

To **delete** an opacity or color stop, drag it upward or downward off the bar.

➤ Use Ctrl-Z/Cmd-Z if you need to undo the last edit (some edits can't be undone).

6. Don't click OK yet! To create a preset of your custom gradient, type a name in the **Name** field, then click **New**.

   Your custom presets will be deleted from the picker if you allow them to be replaced by another gradient library or if the Photoshop Preferences file is deleted or damaged. To save the presets on the picker as a permanent library, click Save, enter a name, keep the default location, then click Save again. (See page 117 or 119.)

7. Click OK to exit the Gradient Editor, and again if necessary, to exit the Gradient Fill dialog (**E**, next page). Your new gradient preset is the last one on the Gradient picker.

➤ To delete a gradient preset from the picker, Alt-click/Option-click the preset thumbnail.

➤ To rename a gradient preset, double-click the swatch in the Gradient Editor, and edit the name in the Gradient Name dialog.

A We are opening the Gradient Editor by clicking the Gradient thumbnail on the Options bar.

*Foreground to Background is the first preset in the default gradient library. To reload that library, choose Reset Gradients from the Gradient picker menu, then click Append or OK.

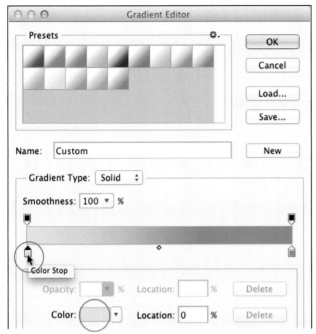

A *In the Gradient Editor dialog, we clicked a preset (in the Simple library), double-clicked one of the original color stops, and changed the Color.*

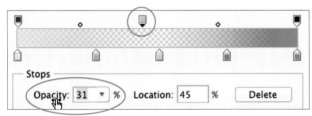

B *We clicked below the gradient bar to add three more color stops, and chose a color for each one.*

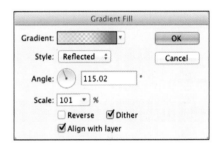

C *We clicked above the bar to add an intermediate Opacity stop, and lowered the Opacity setting for that stop. (We also lowered the Opacity of the leftmost opacity stop to 80%.)*

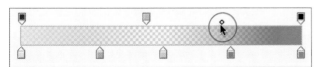

D *We dragged the midpoint diamond for the middle opacity stop. (We named our custom gradient, clicked New, then exited both dialogs.)*

CREATING MORE COMPLEX GRADIENT EFFECTS

By applying gradients that contain some transparency to separate layers, either via Gradient fill layers or by using the Gradient tool, you can achieve complex gradient effects. If you do this, try varying the gradient angle (on the fill layers), or with the Gradient tool, drag in different directions.

E *We applied our custom gradient via a Gradient fill layer (above an image layer). The dialog settings we chose are shown above. Note that we used the Reflected style.*

Using the Gradient tool

With the Gradient tool, you apply a gradient by dragging in the image. Although you can't edit the results in the same way that you would edit a Gradient fill layer, if you use the tool on a separate layer, you will be able to change the layer blending mode or opacity.

To apply a gradient via the Gradient tool:

1. Create a new, blank layer to contain the gradient.

2. *Optional:* To confine the gradient to an area of the layer, create a selection.

3. Choose the **Gradient** tool ■ (G or Shift-G).

4. On the Options bar, do all of the following:

   Click the Gradient picker arrowhead, then click a preset on the picker.

   Click a Style button: Linear, Radial, Angle, Reflected, or Diamond.

   Choose Mode: Normal and Opacity 100%.

5. On the Options bar, check any of the following optional features:

   Reverse to swap the order of colors in the gradient.

   Dither to minimize banding (stripes) in the gradient on print output.

   Transparency to enable any transparency that was edited into the gradient, or turn this feature off to apply a fully opaque gradient.

6. For a Linear gradient, drag from one side or corner of the image or selection to the other. For any other gradient style, drag from a center point outward (Shift-drag to constrain the angle to a multiple of 45°).**A–C** Drag a long distance to produce subtle transitions between colors or a short distance for abrupt transitions; this has the same effect as changing the Scale value in the Gradient Fill dialog.

7. *Optional:* Change the gradient layer mode or Opacity.

➤ To delete the Gradient tool results, click the prior state on the History panel.

➤ You can use a gradient to create a gradual transition in the mask on an image, editable type, adjustment, fill, Smart Filter, or shape layer. See page 259.

A *With the Gradient tool (Diamond style chosen), we dragged diagonally from the middle to the lower right on a new, blank layer.*

B *This is the Layers panel for the image shown below.*

C *This is the final image.*

Creating custom and scripted patterns

To create a custom pattern:

1. Click a layer, or select an area of a layer, that contains the elements to be saved as a pattern.

   Note: For the best results when creating a tile for use with Scripted Patterns, open a small document. Select an area; if desired, feather it via Refine Edge; copy it to a new layer; and hide all other layers.

2. Choose Edit > **Define Pattern.**

3. In the Pattern Name dialog, type a name, then click OK. Your new pattern is now available on the preset picker in the Fill dialog, in the Layer Style dialog for the Pattern Overlay effect (see page 379), as a Texture option for the Bevel & Emboss effect (see pages 374–375), and as a fill layer (choose Pattern from the Create Fill/Adjustment menu on the Layers panel). Via any of the latter three options, you can choose a Scale value for the pattern.

➤ If you create a custom pattern, then discover that the tiles look too large when used as a fill in your document, lower the Image Size of the document from which you created the pattern, then create a new pattern from that smaller document.

Using the Scripted Patterns feature in the Fill dialog, you can choose from an assortment of preset scripts that control how pattern tiles are colored and positioned. You can get some great effects by applying this command to more than one layer. For added richness, experiment with layer blending modes.

To fill an area with a scripted pattern: ★

1. Create a new, blank layer to contain the pattern.

2. *Optional:* To confine the pattern to an area of the layer, create a selection.

3. Choose Edit > **Fill** (Shift-Backspace/Shift-Delete). The Fill dialog opens.

4. From the Contents: Use menu, choose **Pattern.**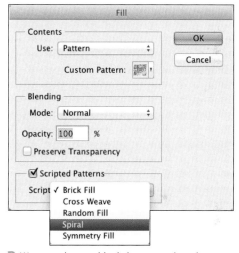 Click the Custom Pattern thumbnail, then click a pattern preset (you can load additional pattern libraries from the lower part of the picker menu).

5. Check **Scripted Patterns**, then choose an option from the **Script** menu. Keep the Opacity setting as 100%, and uncheck Preserve Transparency to permit transparent areas in the layer to be filled.

6. Click OK **C** (and **A–E**, next page). Note: Unfortunately, the dialog doesn't have a preview; your only recourse is to undo your edits via the History panel.

A We selected an area of this image, then chose Edit > Define Pattern.

B We created a new, blank document, then chose these Pattern options in the Fill dialog.

C This is the result. The Spiral script rotates tiles in a spiral pattern, originating from the middle of the layer or selection. It doesn't tint the tiles, as the other scripts do.

SCRIPTED PATTERNS

A *The Brick Fill script (shown in the background of this image) offsets the pattern tiles every other row by half the width of the tile and varies the pattern colors randomly. The Random Fill script (foreground) positions and scales the pattern tiles randomly.*

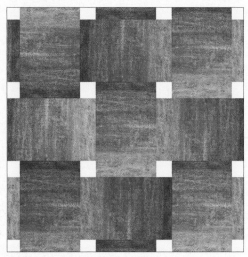

B *The Cross Weave script rotates the pattern tiles by 90°, varies the colors randomly, and, provided the pattern tile isn't square, nudges the tiles slightly to reveal small gaps.*

C *We used the layer shown at far left to create a custom pattern. The Symmetry Fill script tinted the tiles randomly and arranged them in circles.*

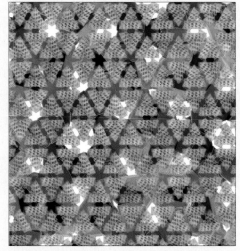

D *We filled a second layer with another pattern.*

E *These patterns were created using various scripts.*

When you open a photo into Photoshop, take a few minutes to study it. Is it over- or under-exposed (too light or too dark)? Could it use a boost in contrast (brighter highlights, richer shadows)? Are the colors too bright or too dull (over- or undersaturated)? Does it have a color cast? Would you like to transform the photo in some way, say, by tinting it with colors from a gradient, or give it a vintage look by converting the colors to grayscale? Enter the digital darkroom!

If you normally capture your photos as raw files or in the JPEG or TIFF format, you can rectify most or all of their tonal and color flaws in Camera Raw. If for some reason you don't use Camera Raw to correct your photos, or if you want to tweak those corrections at any point in the editing cycle, Photoshop offers an impressive array of adjustment commands.

Most tonal and color corrections in Photoshop can be applied as adjustment layers, a method that offers the greatest flexibility in editing. At the beginning of this chapter, you will find generic instructions for creating and editing an adjustment layer and its mask. You will also learn how to read the graph on the Histogram panel to monitor changes in the tonal levels of your document as you apply corrections. From page 210 onward, you will find instructions for a wide-ranging assortment of adjustment features. By the end of this chapter, you will have mastered most of the key Photoshop commands!

ADJUSTMENTS

12

IN THIS CHAPTER

A FEW RECOMMENDATIONS

► Before performing any tonal or color adjustments in Photoshop, make sure your display is calibrated properly (see page 7 in this book and also our blog at elaineandpeter.com).

► Keep your documents in RGB Color mode for your work in Photoshop, including the adjustments in this chapter (remember, digital photos are captured as RGB).

► If you need to make final corrections to an image for CMYK output (such as commercial printing), copy the file, soft-proof the copy onscreen to make sure there are no color problems (see pages 448–449), apply any needed adjustments, then convert the image to CMYK (see page 457).

Creating adjustment layers

The effects of a command that you apply via the Image > Adjustments submenu are permanent, whereas the effects of an adjustment layer become permanent only when you merge it downward into the underlying layer or flatten your document. We recommend using an adjustment layer because its settings will remain editable. You can hide its effect in areas of the image by editing its mask — plus you can restack, hide, or delete it, and even drag-copy it between files. Moreover, adjustment layers increase the file size only slightly.

You create an adjustment layer via either the Adjustments or Layers panel, then choose and edit the settings for it via the Properties panel. Each adjustment type has unique options, and each adjustment layer keeps its own settings. Some controls are easy to get the hang of, whereas others take some effort to master but enable you to apply more targeted corrections. For some adjustment types, you also have a choice of presets. The Properties panel also provides controls for viewing, clipping, and restoring adjustment settings.

To create an adjustment layer: ★

1. On the Layers panel, 🗘 click an image layer or the Background. **A** The adjustment layer is going to appear above the layer you select.

2. *Optional:* Create a selection, to become the white area in the editable adjustment layer mask, and therefore the only area in which the adjustment effect is visible.

3. Do either of the following:

    On the **Adjustments** panel, ⬤ click the button for the desired adjustment type. **B**

    From the **Create Fill/Adjustment Layer** menu ⬤. on the Layers panel, choose an adjustment type (**A**, next page).

4. Controls for the chosen command appear on the Properties panel. Choose settings to correct your document (**B**, next page). For a Levels, Curves, Exposure, Hue/Saturation, Black & White, Channel Mixer, or Selective Color adjustment, another option is to choose a preset from the menu at the top of the panel (you can also customize the settings from the preset).

    A new adjustment layer with a layer mask appears on the Layers panel (**C–D**, next page).

A *The original image lacks contrast.*

B *On the Adjustments panel, we clicked the Levels button.*

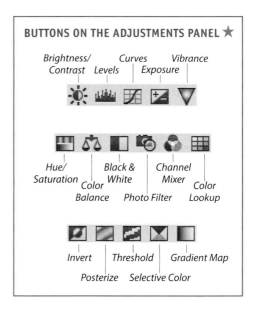

BUTTONS ON THE ADJUSTMENTS PANEL ★

Brightness/   Curves   Vibrance
Contrast   Levels   Exposure

Hue/   Black &   Channel
Saturation   White   Mixer
     Color   Color
     Balance   Photo Filter   Lookup

Invert   Threshold   Gradient Map
   Posterize   Selective Color

A *Alternate route, same result: You can use the Create Fill/Adjustment Layer menu on the Layers panel instead of the Adjustments panel.*

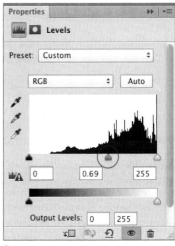

B *To darken the midtones, we dragged the top middle slider to the right.*

C *You can identify each adjustment layer type by its unique icon in the layer thumbnail.*

D *One simple (editable) step corrected the contrast.*

A NOTE REGARDING OUR STEPS

For the sake of brevity, in our steps for creating specific adjustments (from page 210 through the end of this chapter), we instruct you to create an adjustment layer by clicking a button on the Adjustments panel. If you prefer to create your adjustment layers via the Create Fill/Adjustment Layer menu on the Layers panel, by all means do so. Some folks like clicking buttons and are comfortable switching between the Layers and Adjustments panels; others like to stick with the Layers panel.

Editing adjustment layer settings

Note: For the steps in this section, we recommend showing the Properties panel (it can be in a dock). If your Properties panel is closed, you will need to double-click the adjustment layer to display the Properties panel (instead of just a single click, as in our instructions).

To change the settings for an adjustment layer: ★

1. On the Layers panel,❧ click an adjustment layer. The layer becomes selected and the current settings display on the Properties panel.**A**

2. Edit the settings.**B**

➤ To undo the last individual Properties panel edit, press Ctrl-Z/Cmd-Z.

➤ To lessen the overall impact of an adjustment layer, lower its opacity via the Layers panel.

The View Previous State button gives you a temporary view of the image without the current edits you are making to the adjustment layer settings.

To view the image without the newest adjustment layer edits: ★

1. On the Layers panel, click an adjustment layer, then edit the settings on the Properties panel. Keep the layer selected and stay on the panel.

2. To toggle your latest edits off (and then on again), press and hold down the **View Previous State** button 👁↩ or the \ key, then release.

To restore settings to an adjustment layer: ★

1. On the Layers panel, click an adjustment layer.

2. After editing any of the settings on the Properties panel, click the **Reset to Adjustment Defaults** button;↩ the last chosen settings will be restored. To restore the default settings for that adjustment type, click the button again.

To hide the effect of an adjustment layer: ★

To hide the effect of an adjustment layer, click the visibility icon 👁 on the Properties panel or Layers panel (clicking the icon in one location also makes it disappear in the other location). To show the effect, click the icon (or in the icon column) again.

A *We used a Curves adjustment to darken the midtones in this photo.*

B *Later, we double-clicked the Curves layer thumbnail to display the current settings, and tweaked the adjustment by reshaping the curve for the midtones and highlights.*

Normally, an adjustment layer affects all the layers below it, but you can clip (restrict) its effect to just the layer directly below it.

To clip an adjustment layer to the layer directly below it: ★

1. On the Layers panel, click an adjustment layer. A–B Make sure it is stacked directly above the layer that you want to clip it to.

2. Do either of the following:

   On the Properties panel, 🔲 click the **Clip to Layer** button. 🔲 C–D

   On the Layers panel, hold down Alt/Option and click the line between the adjustment layer and the layer below it (🔲 icon).

   The adjustment layer listing is now indented. To "unclip" it at any time, repeat either step.

> **THE AUTO-SELECT PARAMETER OPTION**
>
> The Auto-Select Parameter option causes the first entry field on the Properties panel (if the chosen adjustment type indeed has a field) to become highlighted automatically when you create an adjustment layer or when you click an existing adjustment layer on the Layers panel. Although this option lets you enter or change values more quickly and may be appreciated by some power Photoshop users, it can be an annoyance because it prevents some shortcuts from working (e.g., you can't select a tool via its letter shortcut or delete a layer by pressing Backspace/Delete). To turn this option on or off, choose Auto-Select Parameter from the Properties panel menu.

A This image contains an image layer, a type layer, and a Background image (the texture).

B We applied a Hue/Saturation adjustment to boost the saturation of the Tomatoes layer, but the edit gave the Background texture a pinkish cast.

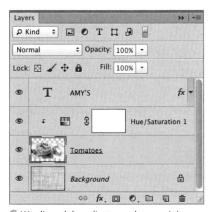

C We clipped the adjustment layer so it is affecting just the Tomatoes layer.

D This is the result of our clipping the adjustment.

Saving adjustment presets

You can save your custom adjustment settings for future use in any document. If you have a group of photos, say, that were shot under the same lighting conditions, have the same color profile, and require the same correction, you can save those settings as a preset, then apply that preset to each of the files.

To save custom adjustment layer settings as a preset: ★

1. Create and choose settings for an adjustment layer. Presets can be saved only for a Levels, Curves, Exposure, Hue/Saturation, Black & White, Channel Mixer, or Selective Color adjustment.

2. From the Properties panel menu, choose **Save** [adjustment type] **Preset**. In the Save dialog, enter a name, keep the default location and extension, then click Save. Your user preset is now available on the menu at the top of the Properties panel when the controls for that adjustment type are displaying.

➤ To delete a user preset, choose that preset, choose Delete Current Preset from the panel menu, then click Yes in the alert dialog.

➤ If you created an adjustment that you want to copy to another document — but it can't be saved as a preset — open the source and destination documents (both RGB) and tile them via the Window > Arrange submenu. Click in the source document, then drag and drop the adjustment layer from the Layers panel into the other document window.

Merging and deleting adjustment layers

When you merge an adjustment layer downward, the adjustments are applied permanently to the underlying image layer. If you change your mind, click the prior state on the History panel.

To merge an adjustment layer:

On the Layers panel, ☰ do either of the following:

Click the adjustment layer to be merged downward (or Shift-click multiple adjustment layers and the layer into which you want to merge them), **A** then press Ctrl-E/Cmd-E. **B**

Right-click on or near the adjustment layer name and choose **Merge Down** from the context menu.

Note: Adjustment layers can't be merged with one another. If you use the Merge Visible command (see page 149) or the Flatten Image command (see page 150), the effect of any adjustment layers in the file will be applied to the resulting merged layer (and will disappear from the Layers panel).

To delete an adjustment layer: ★

Do either of the following:

Click the icon for an adjustment layer on the Layers panel, then click the **Delete Layer** button 🗑 on the same panel or the **Delete Adjustment Layer** button 🗑 on the Properties panel. If an alert dialog, appears, click Yes. (Click Don't Show Again if you want to prevent the alert from reappearing.)

Click the adjustment layer on the Layers panel, then press Backspace/Delete. (See also the sidebar on the previous page.)

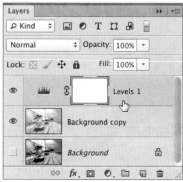

A We clicked the adjustment layer to be merged downward.

B The Merge Down command applied the Levels values from the adjustment layer to the underlying image layer, which in this case was a copy of the Background.

Editing an adjustment layer mask

Photoshop creates a mask for every adjustment layer. If you create a selection before creating an adjustment layer, the selection will appear as the white area in the mask. If you didn't create a selection first, or you want to edit the mask at any time, follow these steps.

To edit the adjustment layer mask:

1. Click the mask thumbnail on an adjustment layer.

2. Press D to choose the default colors, then press X to switch to black as the Foreground color.

3. To hide the adjustment in some areas of the image, do either or both of the following:

   Create a selection with any selection tool (e.g., Rectangular Marquee or Lasso); refine it via the Refine Edge dialog, if desired; choose Edit > **Fill** (Shift-Backspace/Shift-Delete); choose Use: Foreground Color; then click OK. Deselect.

   Choose the **Brush** tool ![brush] (B or Shift-B). On the Options bar, choose a Soft Round brush, Mode: Normal, and an Opacity of 100% (or a lower Opacity to apply a partial mask), press [or] to set the brush diameter, then apply strokes in the image.**A–C**

4. *Optional:* To remove black areas of the mask, press X to swap colors (make the Foreground color white), then apply brush strokes.

➤ To remove all black areas from the mask, deselect, click the adjustment layer mask, choose Edit > Fill, then choose Use: White in the dialog.

➤ To confine the effect of an adjustment layer to a small area, start with a fully black mask (click Invert on the Properties panel ★ or apply Edit > Fill, Use: Black), then apply strokes with white.

➤ To create a gradual mask by applying a gradient, see pages 259–260. To adjust the edge or density of a mask, see pages 174–175.

A *The bottom area of this photo looks too pink.*

B *We corrected the color via Curves, clicked the mask thumbnail on the adjustment layer, then applied brush strokes to hide the adjustment in the top part of the image. The adjustment is visible in only the bottom half of the photo.*

C *Our brush strokes are represented by black areas in the adjustment layer mask thumbnail.*

SHORTCUTS FOR LAYER MASKS

View just the mask in the document window	Alt/Option click the layer mask thumbnail; repeat to restore the normal view
View the mask in the image as a Quick Mask	Alt-Shift/Option-Shift click the layer mask thumbnail; repeat for normal view
Deactivate or activate the mask	Shift-click the layer mask thumbnail (Layers panel) or click the Disable/Enable button 👁 (Properties panel)
Convert the unmasked area into a selection	Ctrl/Cmd click the layer mask thumbnail (Layers panel) or click the Load Selection from Mask button ⬚ (Properties panel)

Using the Histogram panel

The **Histogram** panel 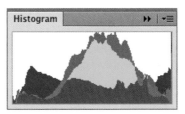 displays a graph of the distribution of tonal (light and dark) values in the current image. The horizontal axis on the graph represents the grayscale or color levels between 0 and 255, the vertical bars represent the number of pixels at specific color or tonal levels, and the contour of the graph shows the overall tonal range. Before you begin editing your document, study the histogram to evaluate the existing distribution of tonal values. Then as you edit your document, note how the graph updates to reflect changes to the tonal values. The panel remains accessible even while the Properties panel is being used or an adjustment dialog is open.

A *This Histogram panel is in Compact View.*

To choose a view for the Histogram panel:

From the Histogram panel menu, choose one of the following: **Compact View** (just the histogram),**A** **Expanded View** (the histogram plus statistics and a menu providing access to individual channels),**B** or **All Channels View** (all the features of Expanded View, plus a separate histogram for each channel). When the panel is in either of the latter two views, you can check Show Statistics on the panel menu to display file data on the panel.

For Expanded or All Channels view, choose an option from the **Channel** menu: RGB (all the channels combined),**C** a specific channel, Luminosity, or Colors. To display the individual channels in color when the panel is in All Channels view, check Show Channels in Color on the panel menu.

While a large file is being edited, Photoshop maintains the redraw speed of the Histogram panel by reading the data from the histogram cache — not from the actual image. When this is occurring, a Cached Data Warning icon **A** displays on the panel. Try to remember to keep updating the panel, as described below (even while editing the settings for an adjustment layer), so it will continue to reflect the current tonal values of the image.

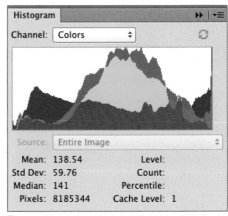

B *Here the panel is in Expanded View. By default, the Channel menu is set to Colors.*

To update the Histogram panel:

Do one of the following:

Double-click anywhere on the histogram.

Click the **Cached Data Warning** icon.**A**

Click the **Uncached Refresh** button.**C**

➤ To specify a Cache Levels value for screen redraw in Photoshop (including this panel), see page 439.

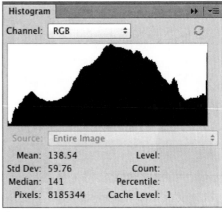

C *With RGB chosen on the Channel menu, the current tonal values in the image are represented by black areas in the graph.*

Interpreting the histogram

If you want to focus on monitoring tonal values when using the Histogram panel, choose Expanded View from the panel menu and choose RGB from the Channel menu. In the graph, pixels are represented by vertical bars: shadows on the left, midtones in the middle, and highlights on the right. For a dark, low-key image, the bars will be clustered primarily on the left side of the graph; for a medium-key image in which the lights and darks are relatively balanced, the bars will be more uniformly distributed across the graph; and for a very light, high-key image that contains few or no shadow areas, the bars will be clustered primarily on the right side.

If an image has a wide tonal range, the bars will be more uniformly distributed in all the tonal zones, and will stretch fully from one end of the graph to the other. Also, the graph will be mostly solid and will have a relatively smooth contour instead of a spiky one.**A** If an image lacks detail in a particular tonal range, the graph will contain gaps and spikes, like teeth on a comb.

The following are some typical graph profiles:

➤ For an average-key but underexposed image that lacks details in the highlights, pixels will be clustered primarily on the left side of the histogram.**B**

➤ For an overexposed image that lacks details in the shadows, pixels will be clustered mostly on the right side of the histogram.**C**

➤ For an image in which pixels were clipped (details discarded) from the extreme shadow or highlight areas, a line or cluster of pixels will rise sharply at the left or right edge, respectively, of the histogram.**D**

➤ If an image has lost detail as a result of editing (such as from Photoshop filters or adjustments), the histogram will contain gaps and spikes.**E** The gaps indicate a loss of specific tonal or color levels, whereas the spikes indicate that pixels from different levels have been averaged together and been given the same value (the bar will be taller at that level). A few gaps and spikes are an acceptable result of editing, whereas large gaps signify that posterization has occurred and too many continuous tonal values have been discarded. On the other hand, an imperfect histogram doesn't always signify failure; the graph can be thrown off by a simple edit, such as adding a white border to the image. If you like the way the image looks, go with that!

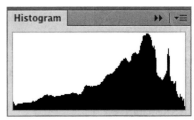

A *The tonal ranges in this image are well balanced.*

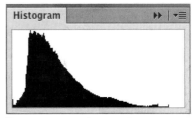

B *This image is underexposed.*

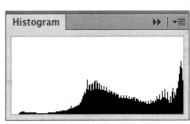

C *This image is overexposed.*

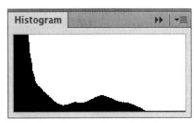

D *Shadow pixels are clipped in this image.*

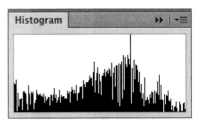

E *This image has lost some detail.*

Applying a Levels adjustment

Levels is a workhorse feature of Photoshop that you should learn well and use often. A bonus feature of this command is that it displays a histogram of the tonal values of your image. You can use Levels when you first bring a photo into Photoshop, and then use it again, if needed, during the course of editing. (Levels is also used on pages 214–215 and on page 238.)

To correct tonal values using Levels:

1. Click an image layer that needs tonal correction. **A**

2. On the Adjustments panel, 🌗 click the **Levels** button. 📊 ★ The Levels controls display on the Properties panel.

3. Do either of the following:

   To intensify the contrast, brighten the highlights by moving the white input highlights slider to the left and darken the shadows by moving the black input shadows slider to the right. **B** Any pixels located to the left of the black slider will become black; any pixels located to the right of the white slider will become white. (This shifting of tonal values to black or white is called "clipping.")

   To control when clipping starts to occur in a temporary high-contrast display called Threshold mode, hold down Alt/Option and drag the highlights slider, then release when only a few areas of color or white display (**A**, next page); those pixels will be given the lightest tonal value. Next, hold down Alt/Option and drag the shadows slider, then release when only a few areas of color or black appear (**B**, next page); those pixels will be given the darkest tonal value.

4. With the shadows and highlights sliders now in their proper positions, move the middle (midtones) **Input Levels** slider to lighten or darken just the midtones.

5. To compare the original and adjusted images, press and hold \, then release (**C–D**, next page).

➤ If the "Calculate More Accurate Histogram" alert button 📊A appears on the Properties panel as you're applying a Levels adjustment, you can click the button to refresh the histogram in the panel.

➤ To apply the current Levels settings to other images — such as to a group of images that were taken under similar lighting conditions and need the same adjustments — save and apply them as a preset (see page 206). There are also some ready-made presets that you can use.

A This image lacks contrast (looks flat and dull).

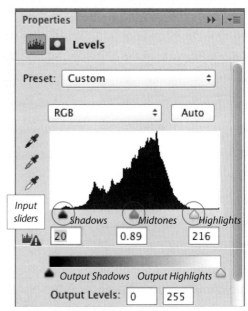

B The histogram in this Levels panel doesn't extend all the way to the edges, an indication that the tonal range of the photo is narrow. To expand the range, we moved the Shadows and Highlights input sliders inward to align with the outer edges of the histogram, and moved the middle slider to the right to darken the midtones.

A *We held down Alt/Option and dragged the white highlights slider.*

B *Next, we held down Alt/Option and dragged the black shadows slider.*

C *Our Levels adjustments improved the contrast (the shadows are darker and the highlights are brighter).*

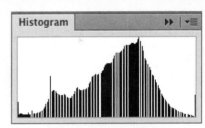

D *We can tell that the Levels adjustments expanded the tonal range of the image, because now the bars extend all the way from one end of the graph to the other.*

Applying a Brightness/Contrast adjustment

The Brightness and Contrast controls are ultra simple to use, but have a big impact.

To apply Brightness/Contrast adjustments:

1. Click a layer or the Background. **A**

2. On the Adjustments panel, 🌑 click the **Brightness/Contrast** button. 🔆 ★ The Brightness/Contrast controls display on the Properties panel.

3. Do either of the following:

   Move the **Brightness** and/or **Contrast** sliders. **B**

   Click **Auto** to let Photoshop set the sliders; you can tweak the settings afterward. ★

➤ The Use Legacy option for Brightness/Contrast causes tonal levels to be eliminated from the shadows or highlights (after adjustment, the histogram will show clipped areas on the left or right edge of the graph). Keep this option off to preserve pixel data (in which case, after moving the sliders, the histogram will show only a minor redistribution of tonal values).

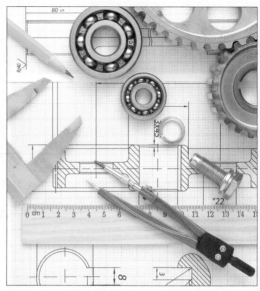

A *The original image is too light and lacks contrast.*

B *We reduced the Brightness to darken the image and increased the Contrast to intensify the shadows and highlights (settings shown at left).*

Applying a Photo Filter adjustment

To change the color temperature of a scene (make it look warmer or cooler) during a shoot, photographers use colored lens filters. In Photoshop, you can simulate the effect of these filters via a Photo Filter adjustment layer, either to neutralize an unwanted color cast or to apply a tint (as a special effect). You select one of the 20 preset tints that are offered or choose a custom color.

When using this feature, we recommend aiming for subtle (sophisticated) or extreme (so it looks deliberate), but not in between. If you go for in between, it can look like the image has an ugly color cast.

To apply a Photo Filter adjustment:

1. Click a layer or the Background. **A**

2. On the Adjustments panel, ⬛ click the **Photo Filter** button. 📷 ★ The Photo Filter controls display on the Properties panel.

3. Do either of the following:

   Click **Filter**, then from the menu, choose a preset warming or cooling filter, or a filter color. The current filter color displays in the swatch.

   Click the **Color** swatch, choose a color for the filter via the Color Picker, noting the change in the image, then click OK.

   ➤ For a subtle change, pick a color that is similar to colors in the image. Or for a more striking change, pick a color that is complementary to the predominant colors in the image (one that is on the opposite side of the color wheel — red/green, blue/orange, purple/yellow).

4. Using the **Density** slider or scrubby slider, choose an opacity percentage for the tint. Try a modest value between 10% and 25% first. **B–C**

   ➤ You can also lessen the Photo Filter effect after using the Properties panel by lowering the opacity of the adjustment layer.

5. Check **Preserve Luminosity** to preserve the overall brightness and contrast values of the image. With this option unchecked, the highlights may be softened, but the resulting colorization effect may be too pronounced.

6. To compare the original and adjusted images, press and hold \, then release.

A *This is the original image.*

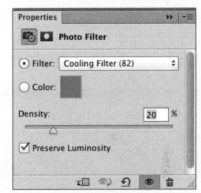

B *For our Photo Filter adjustment layer, we chose Cooling Filter (82) from the Filter menu and a Density value of 20%.*

C *The Photo Filter adjustment made the image look cooler.*

Applying an auto correction

The Auto Color Correction Options dialog offers preset algorithms (formulas) for automatic color and tonal corrections, two of which we cover in this section.

The Find Dark & Light Colors algorithm, used in the task below, analyzes the darkest and lightest colors in an image, then repositions the shadow and high-light settings in each channel based on those colors. You will also use controls in the dialog to adjust the brightness and color temperature of the midtones.

To apply the Find Dark & Light Colors algorithm:

1. Open an RGB image. A

2. On the Adjustments panel, 🌑 click the Levels 📊 or **Curves** button. 📈 ★

3. Hold down Alt/Option and click **Auto** on the Properties panel. 🖥️ The Auto Color Correction Options dialog opens. Move it out of the way if it's blocking the image, then click **Find Dark & Light Colors**.

4. Check **Snap Neutral Midtones**. Any colors in the image that are close to neutral will be adjusted to match the current values of the Midtones target color.

5. To choose a color value for the midtones, click the **Midtones** color swatch. In the Color Picker, click the H button in the HSB group, then drag the circle in the large square slightly to the right (keep the S value around 10–30). Next, on the vertical Hue bar, click a warm or cool hue. To adjust the brightness of the midtones, drag the circle in the big square slightly upward or downward. B

Note: Midtones is the only swatch you need to change; Photoshop will adjust the other two swatches automatically based on the printer color profile that is used when you output the file.

6. Click OK to exit the Color Picker, then once again to exit the Auto Color Correction Options dialog (A, next page).

7. When the alert dialog appears, offering you the option to save the new target colors as defaults, click No (thank you!) if you would rather choose settings on a case-by-case basis (as we do).

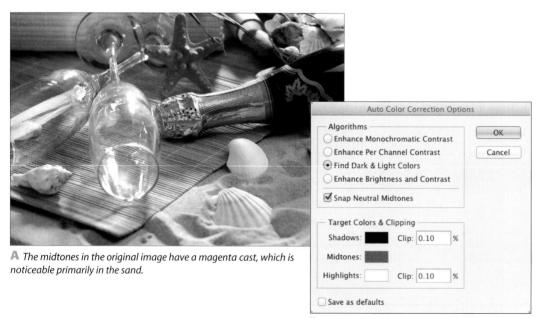

A *The midtones in the original image have a magenta cast, which is noticeable primarily in the sand.*

B *To neutralize the color cast, in the Auto Color Correction Options dialog, we clicked Find Dark & Light Colors, checked Snap Neutral Midtones, clicked the Midtones swatch, then chose a medium brown via the Color Picker (the new color appeared in the swatch).*

A *The adjustments made via the Auto Color Correction Options dialog successfully removed the magenta cast.*

The Enhance Brightness and Contrast algorithm is a good option for an image that needs substantial tonal correction (e.g., one that is very underexposed). This algorithm uses content-aware technology to evaluate data in the entire image, then via either the sliders or the curve, it corrects the tonal values for the composite RGB channel (instead of for each channel).

To apply the Enhance Brightness and Contrast algorithm: ★

1. Open an RGB image.B

2. On the Adjustments panel,⊘ click the **Levels** 📊 or **Curves** button.📈★ In the dialog, hold down Alt/Option and click **Auto**.

3. The Auto Color Correction Options dialog opens. Click **Enhance Brightness and Contrast**, then click OK.C

4. Hopefully, the auto algorithm took care of most of the heavy lifting. If further refinement is needed, click the Levels or Curves adjustment layer, and modify the controls on the Properties panel.

BEGIN WITH AN ALGORITHM

When applying a Levels, Curves, or Brightness/Contrast adjustment, you can use one of the auto correction algorithms as a starting point, then tweak the correction further using the sliders or curves.

B *The original image is very underexposed.*

C *The Enhance Brightness and Contrast algorithm did a quick but effective job of brightening the image. Not bad.*

Applying a Color Balance adjustment

You can use a Color Balance adjustment layer to apply a warm or cool cast to an image or, conversely, to neutralize an unwanted cast. You choose a tonal range to adjust first (Shadows, Midtones, and Highlights), then move any of the sliders toward a warmer or cooler hue. Note: If you need to restrict color adjustments to an even smaller tonal range, use Curves or Hue/Saturation.

To apply a Color Balance adjustment:

1. Click a layer or the Background.**A**

2. On the Adjustments panel,◉ click the **Color Balance** button.⚖★

3. The Color Balance settings display on the Properties panel. From the **Tone** menu,★ choose the range you want to adjust: **Shadows**, **Midtones**, or **Highlights**.

   Optional: Keep Preserve Luminosity checked to preserve the tonal values of the layer as you make color corrections, or uncheck this option to allow the adjustment to change only the color values.

4. Each slider pairs a cool hue with a warm one. Move a slider toward any color you want to add more of or away from any color you want to reduce somewhat **B–C** (and **A–B**, next page). For instance, you could move a slider toward green to reduce magenta, or toward yellow to reduce blue.

   ➤ Try moving two or more sliders toward similar hues. For example, to add a cool cast, you could move the first slider toward Cyan and the third one toward Blue. Or to make an image warmer, move the first slider toward Red and the third one toward Yellow.

5. Choose any other range from the Tone menu, then adjust the color sliders for that range. To compare the original and adjusted images, press and hold \, then release.

B *For a Color Balance adjustment layer, we chose Tone: Shadows, then moved the sliders toward Red, Green, and Yellow to neutralize the colors in that tonal range.*

A *This image has a blue cast.*

C *The shadow areas look more neutral than they did before, but further corrections are needed.*

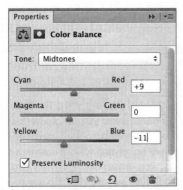

A *To neutralize the blue cast in the midtones, we chose Tone: Midtones, then moved the sliders toward Red and Yellow. Only the highlight adjustment remains.*

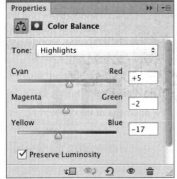

B *To warm the highlights and neutralize the remaining traces of the blue color cast, we chose Tone: Highlights, then moved the sliders toward Red and Yellow (and very slightly toward Magenta). Now the food and the plate look warmer (and more appetizing!) and the shadows look neutral.*

Applying a Hue/Saturation adjustment

Using Hue/Saturation, you can apply very targeted hue, saturation, and lightness adjustments (no selection is needed). In the example shown below, we use it to correct a color cast and to recolor a garment. This is a very useful command.

To apply a Hue/Saturation adjustment:

1. Click a layer. **A**

2. On the Adjustments panel, ◑ click the **Hue/Saturation** button. ▦ ★ The Hue/Saturation settings display on the Properties panel.

3. Do any of the following:

    To correct all the colors in the image, keep **Master** as the choice on the second menu; **B** to adjust a specific color range, choose that color on the

menu. Move the **Hue** slider to adjust the hue(s), **C** the **Saturation** slider to adjust the color intensity, or the **Lightness** slider to lighten or darken. If you adjust the Lightness, you may need to increase the Saturation to revive any colors that were lightened or darkened.

To change a hue, click the **Targeted Adjustment** tool 👆 on the panel, then Ctrl-drag/Cmd-drag horizontally over the color area in the image that you want to adjust. The color range you dragged over is now listed on the menu, and the **Hue** slider shifts to that color on the panel. Or to change the **Saturation** of a color range, drag horizontally with the same tool over a color area in the image without holding down Ctrl/Cmd.

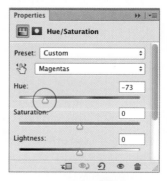

A The original image has a reddish color cast.

B To fix the color cast, we chose Master from the menu, then moved the Hue slider slightly toward the right.

C To recolor her top, we chose Magentas from the menu, then moved the Hue slider to –73 (blue).

SPREADING A HUE/SATURATION RANGE

When a color range (e.g., Yellows or Greens) is chosen on the second menu for a Hue/Saturation layer on the Properties panel, you can spread an adjustment of a color range more gradually into an adjacent one by dragging one of the little squares outward.

For instance, to spread an adjustment of the Greens range into the Yellows range, you would drag the little square to the left, into the yellow-orange area. Try it and see how it affects the image. (To change which hue is adjusted, use the Targeted Adjustment tool, as described in step 3 on the preceding page.)

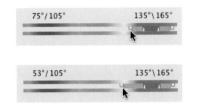

Applying a Vibrance adjustment

Here you will use the Vibrance controls to adjust the saturation of a color layer. On the next two pages, Vibrance is used as a desaturation method.

To guard against oversaturation and clipping, the Vibrance slider boosts the intensity of less saturated colors more than that of highly saturated colors, making this slider particularly useful for adjusting skin tones. The Saturation slider, by comparison, applies the same change to all colors regardless of their original saturation levels.

To adjust the vibrance of skin tones:

1. Click a layer or the Background. A

2. On the Adjustments panel, click the **Vibrance** button. ▽ ★ The Vibrance settings display on the Properties panel.

3. Increase the Vibrance value, then reduce the Saturation value slightly. B

A *The color in this portrait is oversaturated.*

B *For the Vibrance adjustment layer, we set the Vibrance value to +42 and the Saturation value to −15. Now the skin tones look more natural.*

In this task, you will use a Vibrance adjustment layer to either strip the color completely from a layer or desaturate a layer partially, and then use the Vibrance slider to adjust the intensity of the remaining color.

To desaturate a layer using a Vibrance adjustment:

1. Click a layer or the Background. **A**

2. On the Adjustments panel, ⊘ click the **Vibrance** button. ▽ ★ The Vibrance settings display on the Properties panel.

3. Do either of the following:

   For a simple, full desaturation, reduce the **Saturation** to its lowest value of –100.

   To adjust the color vibrance as you desaturate the layer, reduce the **Saturation** to between –60 and –80, then to control the color intensity in the now desaturated layer, increase or reduce the **Vibrance** value. **B–D** Remember, the Vibrance option boosts the intensity of the least saturated colors the most.

A *This is the original image.*

B *To desaturate the color partially, we lowered the Saturation value on a Vibrance adjustment layer to –60 and set the Vibrance value to –50.*

C *This is the image after we applied the Vibrance adjustment layer settings shown in the preceding figure.*

D *For this version, we kept the Saturation value of –60 but raised the Vibrance to the maximum value of +100.*

To desaturate a color layer using Vibrance, then restore color selectively:

1. Click a layer or the Background. **A**

2. On the Adjustments panel, ✪ click the **Vibrance** button. ▽ ★ The Vibrance settings display on the Properties panel.

3. Reduce the **Saturation** to the lowest value of −100.

4. Choose the **Brush** tool, ✎ and on the Options bar, choose a Soft Round brush, Normal mode, and an Opacity of 50% or less. Choose black as the Foreground color.

5. Adjust the brush diameter, make sure the mask thumbnail is still selected on the adjustment layer, then apply strokes where you want to restore the original colors. **B–C** You can change the brush opacity and diameter between strokes. To restore desaturated areas, set the brush Opacity to 100%, and paint with white (press X to swap the colors).

A *This is the original image.*

B *To strip the color from the image, we created a Vibrance adjustment layer, then lowered the Saturation value to −100. To reveal some color, we applied brush strokes to the adjustment layer mask.*

C *The pasta commands most of the attention now, because it is the only area in color.*

Applying a Curves adjustment

By using a Curves adjustment layer, you can limit tonal and color adjustments to a narrow range (such as to the highlights, quarter tones, midtones, three-quarter tones, or shadows). These corrections can be applied to the composite image (all the channels) or to individual color channels. In these steps, you will apply tonal corrections first, then apply color corrections. Note: These instructions pertain to RGB images (the Curves controls work in the opposite way for a CMYK image).

To apply tonal and color corrections using a Curves adjustment layer:

Part 1: Apply tonal adjustments

1. Open an image that needs color and/or tonal adjustments.**A**

2. On the Adjustments panel, ◑ click the **Curves** button. ▦ ★

3. On the Properties panel menu, choose Curves Display Options. In the dialog,**B** keep the Show Amount Of value on the default setting of Light, check all four of the Show options, then click OK.

4. If you need to increase the contrast in the image, do either of the following:

   The **Input** sliders set the white and black tonal values in the image. To darken the shadows and brighten the highlights, drag the black shadow Input slider and white highlight Input slider inward so they align with the ends of the

gray areas in the histogram (**A**, next page) — or until you see that the contrast in the image is improved. The steeper the curve (which is, for the moment, still a straight line), the stronger the contrast.

To establish the white and black values via a high-contrast display of clipping (called Threshold mode), Alt-drag/Option-drag the black slider until a few areas of color or black appear, and do the same for the white slider until a mere smidgen of white appears.

5. For more targeted adjustments, do either of the following:

   Drag part of the curve; a (selected) point appears on it. For example, to lighten the midtones, drag the middle of the curve upward, or to darken the midtones, drag the middle of the curve downward.

   ➤ When a tonal value is lightened, its Output value is increased above its Input value (the original brightness value). When a tonal value is darkened, its Output value is reduced below its Input value.

   Click the **Targeted Adjustment** tool ⟳ in the panel, then move the pointer over an area of the image that contains the tonal level you want to darken or lighten; a small circle appears on the curve. Drag upward to lighten that level

Curves display for each adjusted color channel

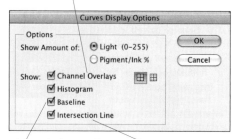

A straight diagonal line that represents no adjustments (for comparison) *Axis guides that appear as you move a point on the curve*

B For this task, check all the Show options in the Curves Display Options dialog. (The grid buttons control the size of the grid squares.)

A *This image is underexposed (too dark) and has a bluish cast.*

or downward to darken it. A point corresponding to that level appears on the curve. **B**

6. Keep the Curves controls showing on the panel. If the color also needs correcting, see the next page.

➤ If the "Calculate More Accurate Histogram" alert button ![icon]**A** appears on the Properties panel as you're applying a Curves adjustment, click the button to refresh the histogram in the panel.

➤ To cycle through and select the points on the curve, press the + (plus) key. To nudge a selected point, press an arrow key. To remove a selected point, press Backspace/Delete.

➤ To enlarge the graph and curve, drag an edge of the Properties panel. ★

Continued on the following page

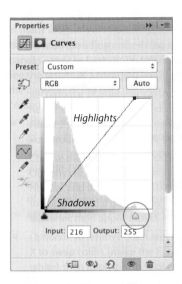

A To lighten the highlights, we created a Curves adjustment layer, then moved the white slider to the left.

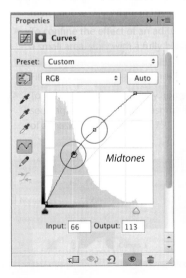

B To lighten the midtones, we clicked the Targeted Adjustment tool, dragged upward slightly on the left side of the basket, then did the same on the right side of the basket (points appeared on the curve). Although our Curves adjustments improved the tonal balance, the colors look a bit washed out. We'll correct that next.

Part 2: Correct the color

1. With the Curves adjustment layer still selected, from the second menu, choose **Red** to adjust that channel separately, then do any of the following:

   Add or subtract red in the shadows by dragging the lower part of the curve or the black slider, or in the highlights by dragging the upper part of the curve or the white slider.**A**

   Drag the middle of the curve upward to add red to the midtones or downward to subtract red **B** (to a lesser extent, this adjustment will also affect the reds in the shadows and highlights). Often, this midtone adjustment is all that's required.

   Click the Targeted Adjustment tool ⟲ in the panel, then drag upward in the image to add red to that tonal level or downward to subtract red (the part of the curve that corresponds to that level adjusts accordingly).

2. Choose the **Green** channel, then the **Blue** channel, adding or subtracting that color from the image, as in the preceding step. You can switch back and forth between the color channels, and readjust them if needed (**A–D**, next page).

3. *Optional:* To lessen the impact of the Curves adjustment layer, lower the layer opacity; or click the adjustment layer mask, then with the Brush tool and the Foreground color set to black, apply brush strokes to the image.

➤ To save your adjustment settings as a preset for future use, see page 206.

➤ As an alternative to adjusting the curves individually for each color channel, you could, theoretically, correct the overall color by clicking a neutral gray area in the image with the gray point (middle) eyedropper on the Properties panel for Curves. However, this method is less reliable than the method described in the steps on this page, because locating a neutral gray is harder than it sounds (in fact, the image may not even contain a neutral gray).

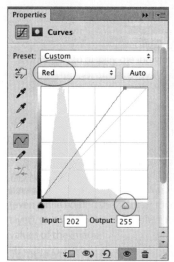

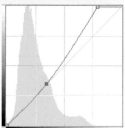

A To add red to the highlights (such as on the basket), with the Red channel selected, we moved the white slider slightly inward (to the left).

B We dragged slightly downward on the lower part of the curve (where most of the red pixels are clustered on the histogram). This produced a point on the curve (shown at right) and removed some red from the midtones.

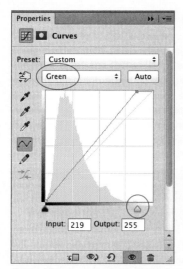

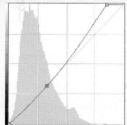

A *To add green to (and remove red and blue from) the highlights, with the Green channel selected, we dragged the white slider slightly inward.*

B *To reduce the amount of green in the midtones, we clicked the Targeted Adjustment tool, then dragged downward slightly in the image, starting from the center of the basket. A point appeared on the curve for the Green channel.*

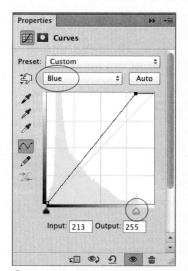

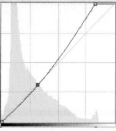

C *Finally, to add blue to (and remove green from) the highlights, with the Blue channel selected, we dragged the white slider slightly inward.*

D *To reduce the amount of blue in the midtones, we dragged downward slightly on the lower part of the curve on the panel (where most of blue pixels are clustered); a point appeared on the curve. Although we made only minor adjustments to the curve for each channel, in the final image, you can see that overall, the colors are now better balanced.*

Applying a Black & White adjustment

Our preferred way to strip color from a layer is via a Black & White adjustment. With this awesome command, you can control how the individual R, G, B and C, M, Y color channels are converted to grayscale values. As an added option, you can apply a tint. Note: A Black & White adjustment has no effect on the document color mode.

To convert a layer to grayscale via a Black & White adjustment:

1. Click a layer or the Background. **A**

2. On the Adjustments panel, ⬤ click the **Black & White** button. ■ ★ The Black & White controls appear on the Properties panel.

3. Do any of the following:

    Click **Auto** to let Photoshop choose the settings (**A–B**, next page) or choose a preset from the **Preset** menu. You can also customize the settings, as described below.

    Adjust any of the sliders. A lower value produces a darker gray equivalent for a color; a higher value produces a lighter gray equivalent (**C–D**, next page). For example, you could use the Yellows slider to lighten or darken the skin tones in a portrait or move the Cyans and Blues sliders to adjust the sky in a landscape.

    Click the **Targeted Adjustment** tool 🖐 in the panel, then drag to the right in an area of the image to lighten that shade, or to the left to darken it. The slider corresponding to the predominant color in that area will shift accordingly.

4. *Optional:* To apply a tint to the image, check Tint, click the color swatch, choose a color in the Color Picker, then click OK (**A**, page 228).

5. *Optional:* To restore some of the original color to the whole layer uniformly, lower the opacity of the adjustment layer. To restore color to specific areas, click the adjustment layer mask thumbnail, choose black as the Foreground color, then with the Brush tool, apply strokes to the image (for a more subtle effect, lower the opacity for the tool first).

AUTO-SELECTING THE TARGETED ADJUSTMENT TOOL

To have Photoshop select the Targeted Adjustment tool (🖐 or 🖐) automatically on the Properties panel when you create a Curves, Hue/Saturation, or Black & White adjustment layer, display the controls for one of those three adjustment types, then choose Auto-Select Targeted Adjustment Tool from the panel menu.

ORCHESTRATING A SCENE

In our environment, as in fine art and photography, colors help to define shapes and spatial relationships and draw our attention to some elements in a scene more than others. When converting an image to grayscale, you will need to reinterpret the composition and orchestrate visual movement using lights and darks instead of color. For example, say there's a bright red shape in the center of the original color layer. When the layer is reduced to grayscale, you would lighten or darken that shape via the Black & White controls, to distinguish it from surrounding grays.

A *This image layer is a good candidate for a conversion to grayscale, because it has clearly defined shapes.*

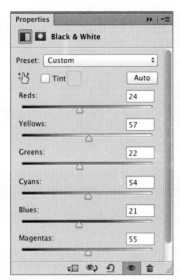

A *These are the slider values that Photoshop chose when we clicked the Auto button.*

B *This is the image after we created a Black & White adjustment layer and clicked Auto on the Properties panel.*

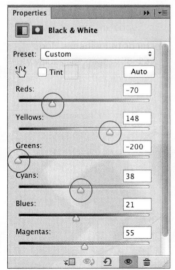

C *To darken the cabin on the boat, we reduced the Reds value; to lighten the upper midtones on the boat deck, we increased the Yellows value; to darken the water in the foreground, we reduced the Greens value; and to darken the sky slightly, we reduced the Cyans value.*

D *This final version of the image has better contrast than the Auto version shown above.*

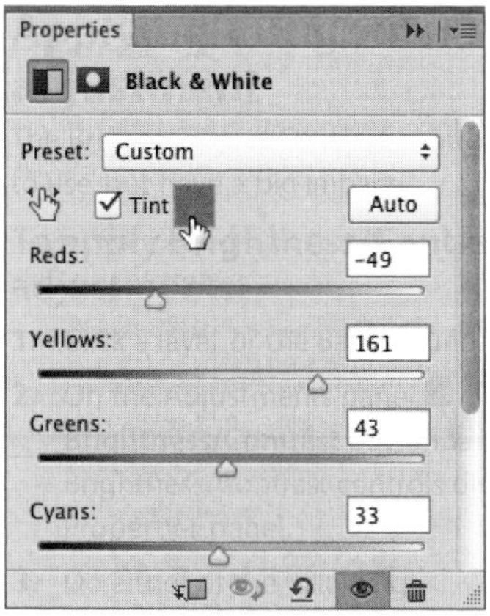

A *For a Black & White adjustment, we checked Tint on the Properties panel, clicked the Tint swatch, chose a color in the Color Picker, then used the sliders to intensify the color in some areas, such as on the boat cabin and upper sky. The results are shown at right.*

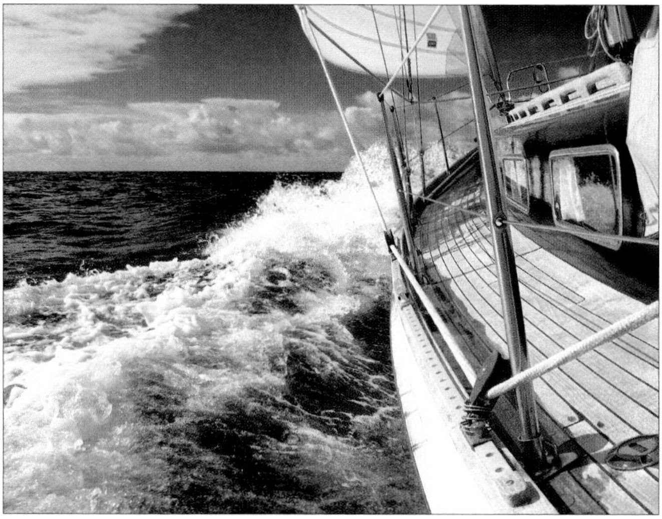

Tinting an image via a Gradient Map adjustment

A Gradient Map adjustment matches luminosity values of colors in a gradient to luminosity values in an image, replacing one with the other. It produces beautiful effects with little effort (you can look like a Photoshop pro even if you're not one—yet!). This is a fun feature to experiment with.

Note: A recommended prerequisite is familiarity with the Gradient Editor, which is covered on pages 196–197.

To tint an image via a Gradient Map adjustment:

1. Click a layer or the Background. **B**
2. On the Adjustments panel, click the **Gradient Map** button.
3. On the Properties panel, click the Gradient picker arrowhead, then via the picker menu, load a couple of preset libraries, including the new Photographic Toning library. Click a preset on the picker ★ (**A**, next page). To minimize visible banding on print output, check Dither.
4. *Optional:* Click the Gradient thumbnail to open the Gradient Editor, then edit the gradient (e.g., add or change some color stops, or reposition some stops or midpoint diamonds) (**B**, next page).
5. *Optional:* Check Reverse to apply the lightest colors in the gradient to the darkest values in the image, and the darkest colors to the lightest values in the image (the opposite of the default behavior). If the gradient contains dark colors, this option may produce a "film negative" effect.

Another optional step is to change the blending mode of the Gradient Map layer (**C**, next page).

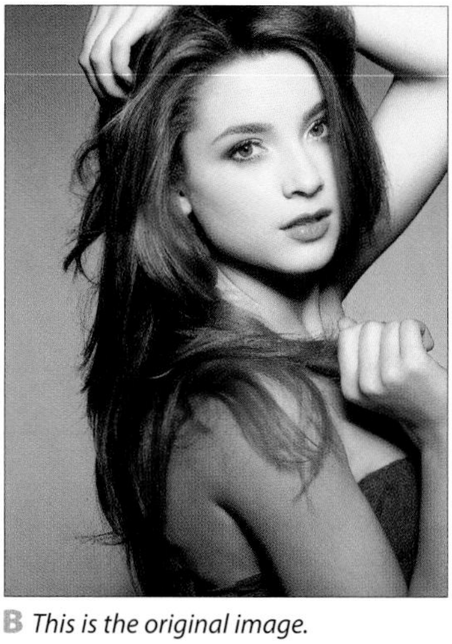

B *This is the original image.*

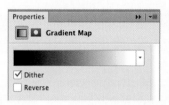

A *Via a Gradient Map adjustment, we applied the Sepia 2 gradient (Photographic Toning library); we kept the default settings for the gradient.*

B *This is another variation of a Gradient Map adjustment we made to the original image. We chose the Sepia-Selenium 2 gradient (Photographic Toning library). In the Gradient Editor, we deleted the second color stop, and also dragged the third color stop slightly to the left and lightened that color.*

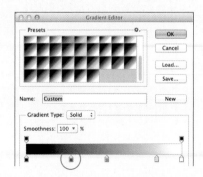

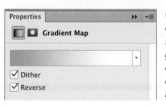

C *One more variation of a Gradient Map adjustment we made to the original image: Light Cyan gradient (Simple library), Reverse checked on the Properties panel, and Pin Light chosen as the blending mode for the adjustment layer.*

Applying the Shadows/Highlights command

Using the Shadows/Highlights command, you can apply separate corrections to the darkest and lightest areas of an image. It does an especially good job of recovering some or most of the details in overexposed highlight areas and underexposed shadow areas (such as subjects that are in shadow due to strong side or back lighting). As the command adjusts the tonal value of each individual pixel, it factors in the values of neighboring pixels. In fact, it preserves more pixels in each tonal range than Levels and Curves. This can be confirmed by studying the Histogram panel before and after applying the command.**A**

To apply the Shadows/Highlights command:

1. Click a layer or the Background **B** and display the Histogram panel, so you can monitor the tonal adjustments.

   The Shadows/Highlights command can't be applied via an adjustment layer. To keep the settings you choose for the command accessible, convert a copy of the image layer to a Smart Object (see page 248).

2. Choose Image > Adjustments > **Shadows/ Highlights**. The Shadows/Highlights dialog opens and the image is adjusted automatically. Check **Show More Options** to display the full assortment of sliders; they will give you added control over which image areas are affected by the adjustment.

3. For the **Shadows**:

   To lighten the shadows (and to recover details), increase the **Amount** value (**A–B**, next page); for a strong correction, increase this value to 60–80%.

   Use the **Tonal Width** slider to control the range of midtones that are affected by the adjustment. For example, if you need to limit the adjustment to just the darkest shadows, keep this value low (**C–D**, next page). Note: If you notice that halos have appeared along dark or light edges, lower the Tonal Width value.

   Raise or lower the **Radius** value to allow more or fewer neighboring pixels to be compared to each pixel in the shadow areas. Note: If you increase this value too much, Photoshop will compare too

Instructions continue on page 232

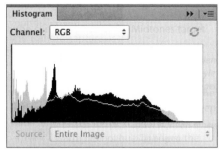

A *No gaps or spikes are created on the Histogram panel when you apply Shadows/Highlights, because the command preserves an adequate number of pixels in each tonal range.*

A *The shadow areas in this image lack detail.*

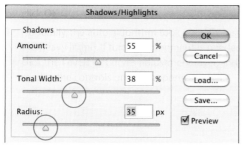

A *In the Shadows/Highlights dialog, we checked Show More Options, then under Shadows, we chose an Amount setting of 55.*

C *We reduced the Shadows: Tonal Width setting to restrict the adjustment to just the lower midtones and then, with that tonal restriction in place, we increased the Shadows: Radius setting to 35 to create slightly more contrast in the midtones.*

B *The first adjustment successfully lightened the shadows, but also lightened too many of the midtones.*

D *The adjustments so far successfully restored details to the shadows and midtones. For the highlights adjustment, see the next page.*

many pixels, which can reduce the contrast and negate the desired adjustment.

Note: After adjusting the Tonal Width or Radius value, you may need to readjust the Amount value.

4. For the **Highlights**:

Adjust the **Amount** value. You can increase this value to darken and recover details in overexposed highlight areas.

Use the **Tonal Width** and/or **Radius** sliders to control the range of midtones that Photoshop includes in the Highlights adjustment. 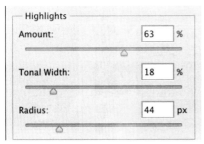 If needed, readjust the Highlights: Amount setting.

5. To compare the original and adjusted images, press P, then release.

6. Under **Adjustments**, use the **Color Correction** slider to adjust the saturation, which may have been thrown off by the other adjustments.

7. Use the **Midtone Contrast** slider to increase or decrease the contrast in the midtones.

8. *Optional:* To save your Shadows/Highlights settings as a preset for use with any image, click Save, enter a descriptive name (keep the .shh extension), choose a location for the preset file, then click Save again. (To load a saved preset in the dialog, click Load.)

9. Click OK.

Because you smartly applied the command to a Smart Object (see step 1 on page 230), you can access and edit the adjustment settings at any time by double-clicking the Shadows/Highlights listing on the Layers panel.

➤ To restore the default settings to the dialog, hold down Alt/Option and click Reset (Cancel becomes Reset).

A *Next, we increased the Highlights: Amount setting to recover details in the sky, which had an unintended result of making the lower part of the sky too dark. To lighten the upper midtones and thereby correct this problem, we lowered the Highlights: Tonal Width setting and increased the Radius setting slightly.*

B *As shown in this final image, using the Shadows/Highlights command, we were able to lighten the shadows and midtones and improve the overall balance among the tonal ranges.*

Dodging and burning with paint

When we need to lighten or darken small areas of an image by hand, we apply strokes with the Brush tool on a separate, editable layer, as in the steps below. (Although the Dodge and Burn tools might seem to be a logical choice for this job, we avoid them because they alter layer pixels permanently.)

To dodge or burn areas with the Brush tool:

1. On the Layers panel, click an image layer or the Background, A click the **New Layer** button, 🔲 then choose **Overlay** as the blending mode for the new layer.

2. Choose the **Brush** tool 🖌 (B or Shift-B). On the Options bar, choose a Soft Round brush and an Opacity of 15–20%. Press [or] to set the brush diameter.

3. Press D to make the Foreground color black, then apply brush strokes to areas you want to darken.

4. Press X to make the Foreground color white, then apply brush strokes to areas you want to lighten.

5. To further darken or lighten an area, apply additional brush strokes on top of existing ones (to build up the color). B

6. *Optional:* To lessen the effect, lower the Opacity of the paint layer. C Another option is to choose Soft Light as the layer blending mode.

➤ To remove any unwanted "dodge" or "burn" strokes from the paint layer, drag across them with the Eraser tool set to 100% Opacity.

A *We want to draw attention to the central figure in this image, but that area lacks contrast.*

B *This is a view of our paint strokes on the new layer, with the image layer hidden.*

We applied black strokes to darken (burn) the shadows on the sides of the buildings,...

... and applied white strokes to lighten (dodge) the cobblestones around the figure.

C *To convey the impression of reflected light on the cobblestones, we applied paint strokes on a blank layer, then we lowered the layer Opacity to 80% to soften the effect.*

Applying the Merge to HDR Pro command

To produce an HDR (High Dynamic Range) image, you combine multiple exposures of the same scene into one image. The composite image contains a wider range of tonalities than could be captured in a single shot.

To shoot photos for an HDR composite:

➤ Use a tripod to ensure that the shots align uniformly.

➤ Capture the photos as raw files.

➤ To keep the aperture constant, set the camera to Aperture Priority mode (A mode for a Nikon; AV mode for a Canon).

➤ Set the auto bracket feature to capture either 3 or 5 shots using different exposures (shutter speeds) automatically. For a Nikon, use the Auto Bracketing Set < AE option; for a Canon, use the Exposure Comp/AEB Setting option. For 3-shot bracketing, set exposures of 2 stops underexposed, 1 normal exposure, and 2 stops overexposed. For 5-shot bracketing, set exposure differences of 1 and 2 stops underexposed, 1 normal exposure, and 1 and 2 stops overexposed.

➤ *Optional:* To let your camera capture all the bracketed shots with one press of the shutter, set it to continuous-shooting mode.

To apply the Merge to HDR Pro command: ★

1. Do either of the following:

   In Bridge, select the 3 or 5 bracketed photos you captured for the HDR image, **A** then choose Tools > Photoshop > **Merge to HDR Pro**.

   In Mini Bridge, select the 3 or 5 bracketed photos you captured for the HDR image, then right-click a selected photo and choose Photoshop > **Merge to HDR Pro**.

2. Sit tight while Photoshop merges your photos. When the Merge to HDR Pro dialog opens, choose Mode: **16 Bit**, and choose **Local Adaptation** from the menu as the conversion method. (Avoid the 32-bit option, because 32-bit images are very large and can't be displayed or printed.)

3. Under Tone and Detail, increase the **Detail** value to boost the image sharpness and contrast, and to provide more pixel variation for the other sliders to work with.

4. Under Edge Glow, increase the **Strength** value to increase edge contrast and create a white edge glow. Increase or reduce the **Radius** value to adjust the size of the glow (**A**, next page).

   Optional: To preserve the edge quality, especially if you increased the Detail value, check Edge Smoothness.

5. Under Tone and Detail, use the **Gamma** slider to increase or reduce the contrast.

   Use the **Exposure** slider to adjust overall lighting (**B**, next page).

6. In the Advanced tab, use the **Shadow** slider to adjust the lightness of the shadow areas. Lower the **Highlight** value if you need to recover details in the highlights (**C**, next page). If you plan to refine the HDR image in Camera Raw, as we recommend, use these sliders to apply only minor adjustments.

   Readjust the Detail value to tweak the image sharpness.

A *This scene was shot using three different exposures: One for the exterior light, one for the interior light, and one in between.*

7. Check **Remove Ghosts**, then click an exposure thumbnail (at the bottom of the dialog) to remove any discrepancies between shots that resulted from the movement of the subject (**A–B**, next page). The normal (EV.0) or dark (EV.1) exposure thumbnail may work best.

8. To tweak the shadows, midtones, or highlights, click the Curve tab and gently drag that part of the curve, just as you would for a Curves adjustment (**C**, next page).

9. Click OK. The HDR file will open as a new document in Photoshop. Save it in the Photoshop PSD format, then follow the steps on page 237 to refine it in Camera Raw.

A In the Merge to HDR Pro dialog, we raised the Detail, Strength, and Radius values first to increase detail and edge definition in the image.

B We lowered the Radius value to reduce the edge glow, increased the Gamma value to decrease the contrast, and increased the Exposure value to lighten the overall image.

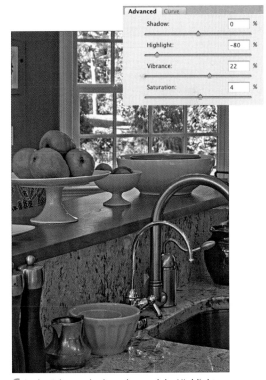

C In the Advanced tab, we lowered the Highlight value substantially to recover highlight details, reduced the Saturation value, and increased the Vibrance value to boost the color saturation.

A *The leaves outside the window moved as we were shooting our three exposures, which produced "ghosts" in the composite image.*

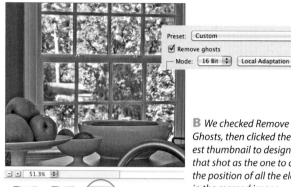

B *We checked Remove Ghosts, then clicked the darkest thumbnail to designate that shot as the one to control the position of all the elements in the merged image.*

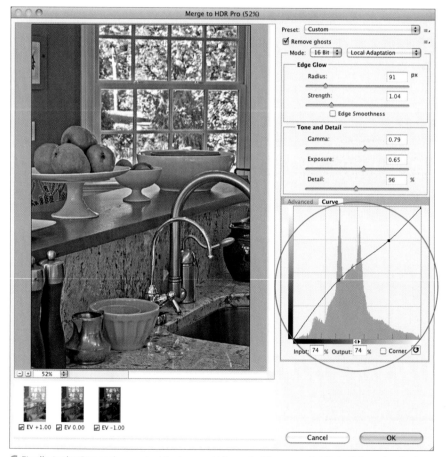

C *Finally, in the Curve tab, we raised the lower middle part of the curve slightly to lighten the shadows and lowered the upper part of the curve to darken the highlights and upper midtones. As you can see in the preview, these HDR Pro settings improved the image considerably.*

MAKING AN IMAGE LOOK SURREAL

In the HDR Pro dialog, the Detail, Radius, and Strength controls produce the most marked results. High values for these sliders will produce a stylized, surrealistic image, like the version shown below, whereas lower values will produce a more naturalistic image.

USING THE HDR TONING COMMAND ★

The Image > Adjustments > HDR Toning command offers the same edge, tone, color, and curve controls as the Merge to HDR Pro command, except you apply it to a single RGB photo. You could apply HDR Toning to an underexposed photo to correct the color and recover details or, for a very stylized result, choose settings that accentuate the edges and heighten the contrast. Note: HDR Toning will flatten all the layers in your document automatically, so be sure to save a copy of the file first!

After using the Merge to HDR Pro command, we like to tweak the exposure, color, and tonal values in the composite file via Camera Raw.

To process an HDR file in Camera Raw:

1. After following the steps on pages 234–236, use File > Save As to save another version of the file in the TIFF format.

2. From Bridge, open the TIFF file into Camera Raw.*

3. Use the Basic (or any other) tab sliders to further improve the image (see pages 61–65).

4. Click Open Image. In Photoshop, save the revised document in the Photoshop format, then sit back and admire your work.A

A *This is the final HDR image after we applied some adjustments via the Basic tab in Camera Raw.*

If the TIFF file won't open into Camera Raw, choose Edit/Adobe Bridge CS6 > Camera Raw Preferences, then from the TIFF Handling menu, choose Automatically Open All Supported TIFFs.

Screening back a layer using Levels

When printing dark text or a logo on top of a photo, you need to make sure the picture is light enough for the text or logo to be readable, but not so light that the image content is lost. Here, a Levels adjustment is used to screen back (lighten) an image layer.

To screen back a layer using Levels:

1. Open an image.**A**

2. *Optional:* To limit the adjustment to a specific area of the image, create a selection.

3. On the Adjustments panel,◉ click the **Levels** button.◼◼ ★ Levels controls display on the Properties panel.

4. To reduce contrast in the image, move the **Output Levels** shadows (black) slider to the right.

5. To lighten the midtone values in the image, move the **Input Levels** midtones (gray) slider to the left.**B**

6. To compare the original layer and the adjusted version, press and hold \, then release.**C**

A *This document contains an editable type layer above an image layer.*

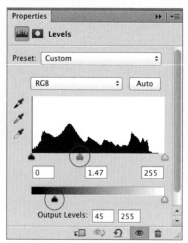

B *To lighten the selected image layer, we created a Levels adjustment layer and chose these settings.*

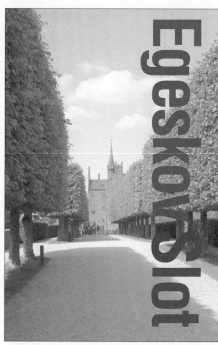

C *With the image screened back, the type is more eye-catching and easier to read.*

If we had to pick one topic that represents the heart and soul of Photoshop, it would be combining images. In this chapter, you will learn various ways to copy selections and layers within the same document and between documents; create, edit, and replace Smart Objects; combine multiple exposures; and soften the edge of a layer with a layer mask. You will also learn how to use the Clone Stamp tool to clone imagery, the Photomerge and Auto-Align Layers commands to merge multiple images, and Smart Guides and other Photoshop features to position and align layers. You'll be amazed at how easy (and how much fun) it is to create composite images!

Using the Clipboard

One way to transfer a selection of imagery from one layer or document to another is by using the Clipboard commands (on the Edit menu). You choose the Cut, Copy, or Copy Merged command first to put the current selection into a temporary storage area in memory, called the Clipboard. Then you choose a paste command, such as Paste or Paste in Place, to paste the Clipboard contents as a new layer in the same document or in another document. If there is an active selection in the target document, another method is to use the Paste Into or Paste Outside command to paste the Clipboard contents inside or outside of the selection.

If you cut (remove) a selection from the Background via the Cut command, the exposed area fills automatically with the current Background color. **A** If you cut a selection from a layer, the area left behind is replaced with transparent pixels (the same results that you get when you move pixels on a layer). **B**

The same Clipboard contents can be pasted as many times as needed. Only one selection can be stored on the Clipboard at a time, however, and it is replaced by new contents each time you use the Cut, Copy, or Copy Merged command. If Export Clipboard is checked

Continued on the following page

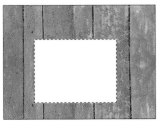

A *This selection was cut from the Background.*

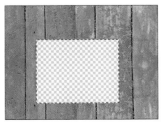

B *This selection was cut from a layer.*

13 (COMBINING IMAGES)

IN THIS CHAPTER

in Edit/Photoshop > Preferences > General, the Clipboard contents will stay in temporary system memory when you exit/quit Photoshop — but only until you shut down your computer.

▶ To empty the Clipboard at any time so as to reclaim system memory, choose Edit > Purge > Clipboard, then click OK if an alert appears. (To prevent the alert from reappearing, check Don't Show Again. ★)

When you use a paste command, the contents of the Clipboard appear automatically on a new layer.

To copy and paste a selection:

1. Read the sidebar on this page, and change the resolution of a copy of the source file, if needed.

2. Click a layer in the source document, then create a selection. *Optional:* Refine the selection edge via the Refine Edge dialog (see page 165).

3. Choose one of the following commands:

   Edit > **Copy** A (Ctrl-C/Cmd-C) to copy pixels from the current layer within the selection area.

   Edit > **Copy Merged** (Ctrl-Shift-C/Cmd-Shift-C) to copy all the pixels from all visible layers within the selection area.

   Edit > **Cut** (Ctrl-X/Cmd-X) to cut the selection out of the current layer.

4. Click in the same document or in another document.

5. Do either of the following:

   To have the Clipboard contents land in the center of the document window (or if the dimensions of the copied content are larger than those of the target document, to the top and left edges of the canvas area), choose Edit > **Paste** (Ctrl-V/Cmd-V).

   To have the Clipboard contents land in the same *x/y* location as in the source layer or document, choose Edit > Paste Special > **Paste in Place** (Ctrl-Shift-V/Cmd-Shift-V).

6. If the source file has a different color profile than the target file, the Paste Profile Mismatch alert dialog will appear. We recommend that you click Convert (Preserve Color Appearance) to preserve the colors of the source image, then click OK.

7. The pasted pixels will appear on a new layer. B You can restack the layer or reposition it in the image with the Move tool (see the next page).

A *We created a selection, then pressed Ctrl-C/Cmd-C to copy its contents.*

B *In another document, we pressed Ctrl-V/Cmd-V to paste the Clipboard contents; they arrived on a new layer.*

HEY! MY PICTURE SHRANK!

When you paste or drag and drop a selection between documents, the copied imagery adopts the resolution of the target document. If the resolution of the target file is higher than that of the source one, the copy will look smaller than imagery on other layers; if the resolution of the target file is lower than that of the source document, the copy will look larger. If you want to prevent a size discrepancy when copying imagery between files, before creating the copy, change the resolution of a copy of the source file via Image > Image Size to match that of the target document (resharpen the image, too).

▶ To compare the relative sizes of the source and target documents, use the Window > Arrange submenu to arrange them side by side, and choose the same zoom level for both (see page 125).

Working with pixels outside the canvas area

If the dimensions of the Clipboard contents that you paste are larger than those of the target document, some of the pasted pixels will be hidden from view outside the canvas area (they will save with the document). This will also occur if you use the Crop tool with the Delete Cropped Pixels option off. When you apply an image-editing command (such as a filter), it alters the entire layer, including any pixels outside the canvas area. Here are some ways to work with those pixels:

➤ To bring hidden pixels into view, click the layer, then hold down V (Move tool) and drag in the image. A

➤ To select all the nontransparent pixels on a layer, including any pixels outside the live canvas area (or that are hidden by a layer mask), Ctrl-click/ Cmd-click the layer thumbnail on the Layers panel. (Select > All, in comparison, selects only the rectangular boundary of the canvas area.)

➤ To enlarge the canvas area to include all hidden pixels on all layers, choose Image > Reveal All.

➤ To remove pixels that are outside the canvas area from all layers, choose Select > All, then choose Image > Crop. This can help reduce the file size.

➤ If a layer contains pixels outside the canvas area and you merge it with the Background (not with another layer), the hidden pixels will be discarded.

➤ To shrink the contents of the current layer, choose the Move tool, ⊕ check Show Transform Controls on the Options bar, Shift-drag a corner handle on the bounding box inward, then press Enter/Return.

ADJUSTING THE SELECTION EDGE

To shrink the edges of a selection before you move, copy, or drag-copy it, click Refine Edge on the Options bar, then lower the Shift Edge value. To soften the edges of the selection, use the Feather slider (see the sidebar on page 243). If you store a selection as a mask, you can use the mask controls on the Properties panel at any time to change the density or feather value of the mask.

COPYING THE LAYER SETTINGS, TOO

To copy layer settings (e.g., blending mode, opacity, and layer effects) along with imagery when creating composite documents, instead of using the Clipboard, use the method described on page 244 (copy the whole layer) or on pages 246–247.

COPYING IMAGERY TO A NEW LAYER

To copy imagery to a new layer within the same file without using the Clipboard, click a layer or the Background, create a selection, then press Ctrl-J/ Cmd-J, or right-click in the image and choose Layer via Copy. If you need to remove the selected pixels from the original layer and put them on a new layer, press Ctrl-Shift-J/Cmd-Shift-J or right-click in the image and choose Layer via Cut.

A *We're dragging a layer from left to right to reveal hidden pixels.*

When you use the Paste Into command to paste the contents of the Clipboard into a selection, Photoshop creates a new layer and converts the selection to a layer mask. You can reposition the pasted imagery within the mask, edit the mask to reveal more or less of the imagery that it is hiding, or adjust the mask density or feather value via the Properties panel.

To paste into a selection:

1. Select an area of a layer or the Background in the image from which you want to copy pixels. **A**

2. Choose Edit > **Copy** (Ctrl-C/Cmd-C) to copy pixels from only the currently selected layer, or choose Edit > **Copy Merged** (Ctrl-Shift-C/Cmd-Shift-C) to copy pixels within the selection area from all visible layers.

3. Click a layer in the same document or in another document.

4. Select the area (or areas) into which you want to paste the Clipboard contents. **B** *Optional:* Click Refine Edge and use the controls to refine the selection edge.

5. Choose Edit > Paste Special > **Paste Into** or press Ctrl-Alt-Shift-V/Cmd-Option-Shift-V. **C** A new layer and layer mask will appear.

6. *Optional:* Although the entire contents of the Clipboard were pasted, the layer mask may be hiding some of the imagery. To move the layer contents within the mask, hold down V (Move tool), click the layer thumbnail, then drag in the document. Or to move the layer mask, click the mask thumbnail before dragging. To move the layer and layer mask as a unit, make sure there is a Link icon 🔗 between the layer and mask thumbnails (if not, click there to make the icon appear), then hold down V and drag in the image.

7. *Optional:* To reshape the mask, click the mask thumbnail. With the Brush tool ✎ (B or Shift-B), a Soft Round brush, and white chosen as the Foreground color, paint in the document to expose more of the pasted image. To hide more of the image, press X to paint with black.

➤ The File > New dialog automatically displays the dimensions of the smallest rectangle that can surround the current contents of the Clipboard (if any).

➤ Unlike the Cut and Copy commands, the Edit > Clear command empties a selection area without putting anything onto the Clipboard.

A *We used the Rectangular Marquee tool to select an area of this image layer, then chose the Copy command.*

B *Next, we used the Quick Selection tool to select the sky area in this document.*

C *Finally, we pasted the Clipboard contents into the selection via the Paste Into command, for a more Baroque sky.*

Drag-copying a selection on the same layer

To drag-copy a selection on the same layer:

1. Select an area of a layer or the Background.

2. Do either of the following:

   Choose the **Move** tool ⊕ (V), then Alt-drag/Option-drag the selection.**A** The duplicate pixels will remain selected.**B**

   With a tool other than the Move tool chosen, Ctrl-Alt-drag/Cmd-Option-drag the selection.

3. Deselect (Ctrl-D/Cmd-D).

➤ Include Shift with either shortcut listed above to constrain the movement to increments of 45°.

A With the Rectangular Marquee tool, we selected the window area in this document, then held down Alt/Option and started dragging it to the right.

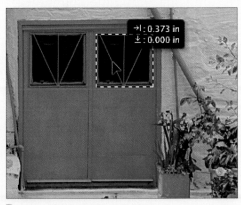

B A copy of the selection is made.

FEATHERING THE EDGES OF A SELECTION

With a selection active and a selection tool chosen, click Refine Edge on the Options bar (Ctrl-Alt-R/Cmd-Option-R). Choose View: On White (W), raise the Feather value, choose Output To: Selection, then click OK. The feather will become evident in the image when you move, drag-copy, copy and paste, or edit (e.g., apply brush strokes or filters to) the selection.

We created a selection.

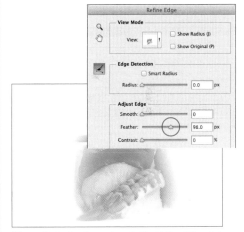

We applied a Feather value via the Refine Edge dialog.

We drag-copied the selection.

Drag-copying a selection or layer between files with the Move tool

When you drag and drop (drag-copy, for short) a selection of pixels from one document to another, presto, a duplicate of those pixels appears on a new layer in the target document. Pixels that land outside the canvas area can be moved into view at any time. An advantage of this method, as opposed to using the Clipboard, is that layer style settings (blending mode, opacity, and effects) in the layer that you drag and drop, along with any masks, are also copied. You can also drag-copy a shape, type, or Smart Object layer.

To drag-copy a selection or layer between documents with the Move tool:

1. Open the source and target documents. Change the resolution in a copy of the source file, if needed (see the sidebar on page 240).

   ➤ The target file could contain a white or solid-color Background, a photograph of a texture (as in our example), or a screened-back image.

2. Click in the source document, then on the Layers panel, click a layer or the Background. *Optional:* Select part of the layer or Background.

3. Choose the **Move** tool ⊹ (or hold down V).

4. Drag from inside the selection or layer in the source document to the tab of the target document, **A** pause until the target document displays, then release the mouse where you want the selection or layer to appear. **B**

   ➤ To drop the copied selection or layer in the center of the source document, hold down Shift as you release the mouse.

5. If the source file has a different color profile than the target file, the Paste Profile Mismatch alert dialog will appear. We recommend that you click Convert (Preserve Color Appearance) to preserve the colors of the source image, then click OK.

   An alert will also appear if the source and target files have a different bits-per-channel setting. Click Yes to accept the change in image quality (or click No to cancel).

6. The duplicate content will appear on a new layer. **C** You can reposition or scale it with the Move tool.

➤ You can also drag and drop multiple selected layers. To copy a layer group, after step 3, above, check Auto-Select on the Options bar and choose Group on the menu, then continue with steps 4–6.

A *Drag a selection from inside a tabbed window to the tab of another document.*

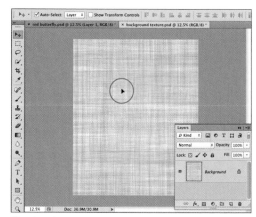

B *When the target image displays, drag the selection into the image, then release.*

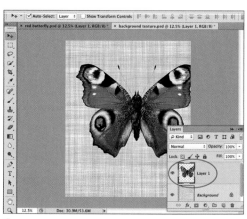

C *The selection appears as a new layer in the target image.*

REFINING THE EDGE OF A LAYER AFTER USING DRAG-COPY OR PASTE

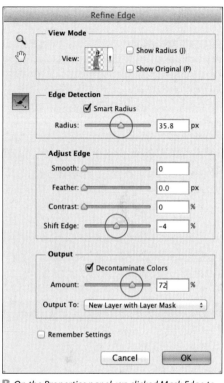

A *We drag-copied a layer containing a photo of a ukulele player from a source file into a beach image. We didn't like the white fringe around the edges of the figure, especially on the skirt (wrong kind of fringe!). To eliminate the fringe, our first step was to choose Layer > Layer Mask > From Transparency. The command converted the transparent areas of the layer into black areas in a layer mask.*

B *On the Properties panel, we clicked Mask Edge to open this dialog, then used the settings shown above to mask the fringe. We chose Output To: New Layer with Layer Mask, then clicked OK.*

C *Our adjusted layer content appeared on a new layer with the refined mask.*

Drag-copying layers between files via the Layers panel

In this exercise, you will drag-copy one or more layers from the Layers panel of a source document into a target document. An advantage of this method is that you can control specifically which layers are copied. Here, as with the Move tool method, any pixels that lie outside the live canvas area are also included.

To drag-copy a layer between files via the Layers panel:

1. Open the source and target documents. Change the resolution in a copy of the source file, if needed (see the sidebar on page 240).

2. From the Window > Arrange submenu, choose **2-Up Horizontal** or **2-Up Vertical**. ★

3. Click in the source document window, then on the Layers panel, click a layer, a layer group, or the Background, or Ctrl-click/Cmd-click multiple layers.

4. Drag from the Layers panel of the source document into the target document, or Shift-drag to make the new imagery appear in the center of the target document) (**A**, next page). The new layer (or layers) will be stacked above the previously selected one (**B**, next page).

5. If the source document has a different color profile than the target document, the Paste Profile Mismatch alert dialog will appear. We recommend that you click Convert (Preserve Color Appearance) to preserve the colors of the source image, then click OK.

   An alert will also appear if the source and target documents have a different bits-per-channel setting. Click Yes to accept the change in image quality (or click No to cancel).

6. Either close the source document or right-click a document tab and choose Consolidate All to Here from the context menu. ★

7. *Optional:* With the Move tool ⮥ (V), reposition the new layer or layers.

8. *Optional:* To scale a new layer, choose the Move tool and check Show Transform Controls on the Options bar. If you don't see all the handles on the bounding box, press Ctrl-0/Cmd-0 (Fit on Screen view). Shift-drag a corner handle on the bounding box, then press Enter/Return to accept the new size.

SELECTING A LAYER OR GROUP IN THE DOCUMENT WINDOW

You can select a layer or group in the document window without using the Layers panel: Hold down V (temporary Move tool), check Auto-Select on the Options bar, choose Group or Layer from the menu, then click a pixel area, type, or a shape in the document.

CREATING A NEW DOCUMENT FROM A LAYER

To quickly create a new document from a layer, click the layer, then from the Layers panel menu, choose Duplicate Layer. The Duplicate Layer dialog opens. From the Document menu, choose New, enter a name for the new document in the Name field, then click OK. Save the new file.

A *After clicking in the source document window, we are Shift-dragging a layer group from the Layers panel of that document into the target document window.*

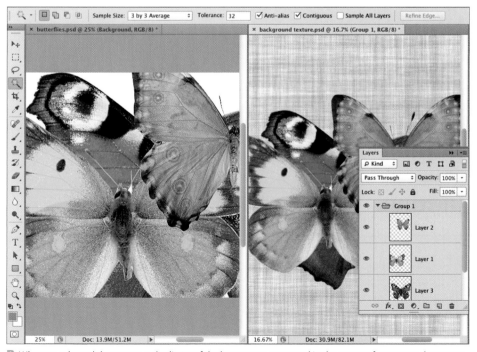

B *When we released the mouse, a duplicate of the layer group appeared in the center of our target document.*

Creating a layered document from file thumbnails

The Load Files into Photoshop Layers command imports multiple files as layers into a new Photoshop document. Photoshop does all the work for you. Love it.

To create a document from file thumbnails:

1. Do either of the following:

   In Bridge, select one or more image thumbnails, then choose Tools > Photoshop > **Load Files into Photoshop Layers.A**

   In Mini Bridge, select one or more image thumbnails, then right-click one of the thumbnails and choose Photoshop > **Load Files into Photoshop Layers.B ★**

2. Stand by as the files are imported as standard (non-Smart Object) layers in a new Photoshop document.**C**

3. Save the new file. If you want to convert one of the layers to the Background, see page 138.

A In Bridge, we selected six image thumbnails, and are choosing the Load Files into Photoshop Layers command.

B Another route to the same command is via the context menu in Mini Bridge.

Creating Smart Objects

A Smart Object is a copy of pixel or vector art that is embedded into a Photoshop file. Unlike an ordinary layer, you can scale a Smart Object, apply filters to it (and edit the filter settings), or edit its contents in the application in which it was created (such as Adobe Illustrator) without altering the original file.

To create a Smart Object, you either convert one or more existing layers in a Photoshop document, or you open or place an AI (Adobe Illustrator), PDF, PSD, TIFF, or Camera Raw file into Photoshop. On this page through page 251, we describe various methods for creating a Smart Object, then on pages 252–255, we describe how to duplicate, edit, and replace it.

To convert one or more layers in a Photoshop file to a Smart Object:

1. Open a Photoshop document, then select one or more layers on the Layers panel.

2. Right-click one of the selected layers and choose **Convert to Smart Object** (**A–B**, next page). (This command is also available on the Layers panel menu.)

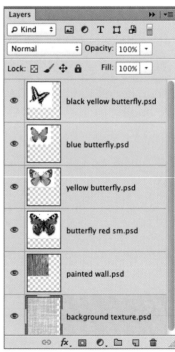

C The command imported the selected thumbnails as multiple layers into a new Photoshop document.

A *We selected three layers in a Photoshop document, then right-clicked and chose Convert to Smart Object from the context menu.*

B *The command combined the layers into one Smart Object. Note the icon in the corner of the layer thumbnail.*

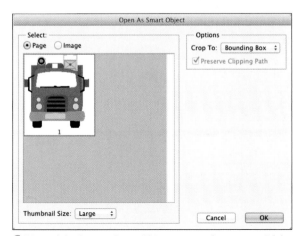

C *We used the Open as Smart Object command to open an Adobe Illustrator (AI) file into Photoshop.*

To open a file as a Smart Object in a new Photoshop document:

1. In Photoshop, choose File > **Open as Smart Object**. Locate and click a PSD, AI, PDF, JPEG, or TIFF file, then click Open.

2. For an AI or PDF file, the Open as Smart Object dialog opens. C For a multipage or multi-image PDF file or an AI file that contains multiple artboards, choose the Small or Medium Thumbnail Size option, and click the desired thumbnail. Also choose a Crop To option (to exclude blank areas from outside the artwork, choose Bounding Box).

3. The file opens as a Smart Object in a new Photoshop document. D Save the new file.

To open a file from Camera Raw into Photoshop as a Smart Object in a new document:

1. From Bridge or Mini Bridge, open a photo into Camera Raw.

2. Apply any needed corrections, then hold down Shift and click **Open Object** (Open Image becomes Open Object). (Note: If Open in Photoshop as Smart Objects is checked in the Workflow Options dialog, the button will be labeled Open Object; click it without holding down Shift. See also the tip on page 58.)

3. The photo appears as a Smart Object in a new Photoshop document. Save the new file.

D *The Illustrator file arrived as a Smart Object in a new Photoshop document.*

To paste Adobe Illustrator art into a Photoshop document as a Smart Object:

1. In Adobe Illustrator, go to Edit/Illustrator > Preferences > File Handling & Clipboard, check Copy As: **PDF** and **AICB**, click **Preserve Appearance and Overprints**, then click OK.

2. Continuing in Illustrator, open a file, then copy some artwork or type (Ctrl-C/Cmd-C).

3. Click in a Photoshop document, then paste (Ctrl-V/Cmd-V). The Paste dialog opens.**A**

4. Click Paste As: **Smart Object**, then click OK.

5. To accept the new Smart Object, double-click inside it, or click the Commit Transform button ✔ on the Options bar, or press Enter/Return. (Or to cancel it, press Esc.)

Another method is to drag or place a whole file (such as an AI, JPEG, PDF, PSD, TIFF, or Camera Raw file) into an existing Photoshop document as a Smart Object.

To drag or place a file into a Photoshop document as a Smart Object:

1. Open a Photoshop document.

2. Go to Edit/Photoshop > Preferences > General, check **Resize Image During Place** (to let Photoshop scale placed images automatically), and, more importantly, check **Place or Drag**

Raster Images as Smart Objects, to have Photoshop convert placed or drag-copied files to Smart Objects.

3. Do either of the following:

   From Bridge, Mini Bridge, or the Desktop, drag a file thumbnail into the Photoshop document.**B**

   In Bridge or Mini Bridge, right-click an image thumbnail and choose Place > **In Photoshop**. ★

4. For an Illustrator AI or PDF file, the Place PDF dialog opens. Choose a Thumbnail Size to preview the file. If there are multiple thumbnails, click one. Also choose a Crop To option (to exclude blank areas outside the artwork, choose Bounding Box).

   For a raw file or a file that was previously edited in Camera Raw, the Camera Raw dialog opens. Make any adjustments to the photo, if desired.

5. Click OK to exit any open dialog. The image will appear within a transform box in the Photoshop document (**A**, next page).

6. *Optional:* To scale the object proportionally, Shift-drag a handle on the transform box. To rotate it, position the pointer outside the transform box (two-headed arrow), then drag.

7. To accept the new Smart Object, double-click inside it (**B**, next page), or click the Commit

A *This cute little dialog opens if you paste a file into Photoshop.*

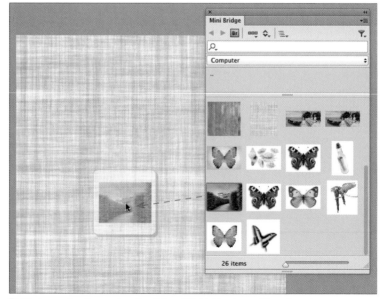

B *We dragged an image thumbnail from Mini Bridge into a Photoshop document.*

Transform button ✔ on the Options bar, or press Enter/Return. (Or to cancel it, press Esc.)

➤ When you place vector art into a Photoshop document as a Smart Object, it stays as vector content (and when output, it is rendered at the resolution of the printer).

➤ If you want to drag or place a raster file into Photoshop as an ordinary layer (non-Smart Object), uncheck Place or Drag Raster Images as Smart Objects in Preferences > General first.

➤ You can also access the Place command in Photoshop via File > Place.

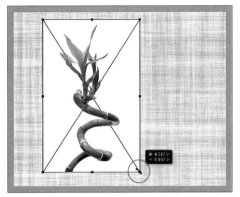

We opened a photo from Camera Raw into Photoshop, scaled it down via a transform handle, then accepted it.

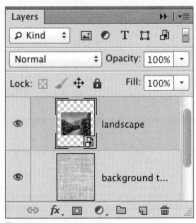

A *The image appeared in the target document.*

Later, we enlarged the Smart Object: The image quality remained high (the details are still crisp).

B *We double-clicked in the transform box to accept the placed file as a Smart Object.*

SMART OBJECTS SCALE BETTER

To compare, we opened the same Camera Raw photo as an ordinary pixel layer, shrank the layer, then enlarged it: The image quality was diminished.

Duplicating Smart Objects

When you create a linked duplicate of a Smart Object, any pixel edits (e.g., painting, adding layers) that you apply to the content of the embedded file will also appear in the duplicate one, and vice versa (see the next two pages). Edits that don't change the content of the embedded file, on the other hand, such as Smart Filters, layer styles, and transformations, will appear only in the currently selected Smart Object.

Note: The figures and captions on this page and the next three pages illustrate how to duplicate, edit, and replace a Smart Object. If you want to simply edit a Smart Object without duplicating it first (a more standard, everyday approach), skip the task on this page and follow just the steps on page 254. Smart Objects are created and edited in other chapters in this book. For examples, see pages 230–232 and pages 336–337.

To create a linked duplicate of a Smart Object:

Click a Smart Object, then press Ctrl-J/Cmd-J. A new Smart Object appears in the Layers panel, bearing the same name as the original (the word "copy" is added).**A–B**

➤ To create a duplicate of a Smart Object that isn't linked to the original, right-click the Smart Object and choose New Smart Object via Copy. Edits made to either layer won't affect the other. (This technique is used in the task on pages 256–257.)

A *In order to create an editable "template" using duplicate Smart Objects, our first step was to convert our "pasta" layer to a Smart Object.*

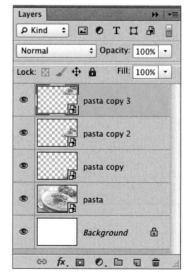

B *We copied the Smart Object, scaled down and repositioned the duplicate layer, then copied and repositioned that layer twice more. All the duplicate layers remain "linked" to the original one (although no link icon appears on the panel).*

Editing Smart Objects

To apply some kinds of edits to a Smart Object, such as Smart Filters (see pages 344–348), layer effects, transformations (scaling), and blending mode and opacity changes, you simply click the layer first.**A–B** Edits that change pixel data, however, such as those made with a painting, healing, sharpening, or cloning tool, can't be made directly to a Smart Object

(try it, and you'll get an alert regarding rasterizing the layer; click Cancel). To make those types of edits, you double-click the Smart Object thumbnail to open the embedded file in a separate (temporary) window. After you edit, save, and close that window, your changes will appear in the Photoshop document, as described on the following page.

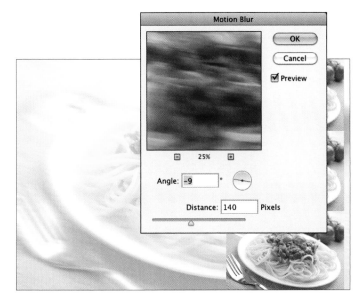

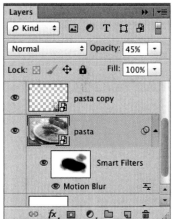

A We selected the original Smart Object (the large photo on the left), applied Motion Blur as a Smart Filter, and reduced the layer Opacity.

B Our edits didn't alter pixels in the embedded file, so they didn't appear in the linked copies of the original Smart Object.

To edit a Smart Object:

1. Double-click a Smart Object thumbnail. If an alert regarding saving your changes appears, click OK.

2. If the Smart Object contains one or more Photoshop layers, a separate document will open, containing those layers. Apply edits to the temporary document, press Ctrl-S/Cmd-S to save it, close it, then click the tab of the original Photoshop document.

   if the Smart Object contains imported content, that content will open in the creator application (e.g., Adobe Illustrator). If a PDF Modification Detected alert dialog appears, click "Discard Changes, Preserving Illustrator Editing Capabilities." Edit the temporary document, save it, close it, then click the tab of the original Photoshop document.

   If the Smart Object contains a Camera Raw photo, it will open in Camera Raw. Adjust the settings, then click OK.

   Note: Your edits will appear in the Smart Object in Photoshop. **A–B** The file from which the original Smart Object was created isn't altered.

A *We double-clicked the thumbnail for the original Smart Object (the Layers panel displayed only the embedded layer, as shown above), then darkened the layer via a Levels adjustment. Because we applied the adjustment to the Smart Object content, that edit also appeared automatically in all the linked copies.*

B *Finally, we created a Hue/Saturation adjustment layer for the middle duplicate Smart Object and a Black & White adjustment layer for the bottom one. To restrict each adjustment effect to just the underlying Smart Object, we clicked the Clip to Layer button on the Properties panel.*

Replacing Smart Objects

Optionally, the Replace Contents command can be used to swap existing Smart Object content with a different file. You must use this command if you edit the original file (from which a Smart Object was created) directly in the creator application — not by double-clicking the Smart Object thumbnail — and you want the embedded file to be updated in Photoshop. In either case, any transformations, filters, or layer style settings that were applied to the original Smart Object will apply automatically to the replacement or edited content.

To replace a Smart Object with a new or edited file:

1. Right-click a Smart Object (not the thumbnail) and choose **Replace Contents**. The Place dialog opens.

2. Locate a replacement file or the original (newly edited) file, then click Place.

3. Respond to any dialogs that open (e.g., the Camera Raw dialog or the Place PDF dialog). The new or updated image will appear in the original Smart Object and in any linked duplicates of that object.**A**

TURNING A COPY OF A SMART OBJECT INTO A NORMAL LAYER

Photoshop image layers that you convert to a Smart Object are embedded in the document, and are accessible for editing only when you double-click the layer thumbnail. If needed, you can bring a copy of an embedded layer back into your document. In Photoshop, double-click a Smart Object thumbnail, then click OK if an alert appears. The embedded file opens in a separate document tab. Via a command on the Window > Arrange submenu, display both documents. Click in the window for the embedded file, drag a layer (or multiple selected layers) from the Layers panel into the original document window, then close the window for the embedded file.

RASTERIZING A SMART OBJECT

To rasterize a Smart Object (convert it to a standard image layer), right-click it and choose Rasterize Layer. If the Smart Object contained any Smart Filters, they will be applied permanently to the rasterized layer, whereas the layer style settings (blending mode, effects, and opacity) will remain editable.

A *We right-clicked the large Smart Object listing and chose Replace Contents, then chose a new food photo to replace the original one. We used the command just once, and the new image appeared in that Smart Object and in all the "linked" copies. That's efficient work!*

Combining multiple "exposures"

You may have had the common experience of trying to shoot a subject against a bright sky or in front of a window. If you set the exposure properly for the figure or object in the foreground, the brighter areas are overexposed. One way to produce an image that captures the "best of both worlds" is to shoot dual exposures, one set for the foreground and one for the background, and then combine them into one image. If you didn't bracket your photos during the shoot, an alternative method (described here) is to produce two exposure variations of a single raw photo via Camera Raw, then blend the best of the two files in Photoshop via a layer mask.

To combine dual "exposures" into one photo:

1. Open a raw photo into Camera Raw.**A** (Note: Avoid using a JPEG photo, which is unlikely to contain enough pixel data for this technique to work successfully.)

2. *Optional:* Use sliders in the **Basic** tab 🔘 to adjust the exposure properly for the shadows and lower midtones.

3. Hold down Shift (Open Image becomes Open Object) and click **Open Object**. Note: If Open in Photoshop as Smart Objects is checked in the Workflow Options dialog, the button will be labeled Open Object; click it without holding down Shift.

A *Because the wide range of light conditions in this scene couldn't be captured in one shot, the interior was correctly exposed in the resulting photo but the exterior was overexposed.*

4. The photo opens as a Smart Object in a new Photoshop document. Save the file.

5. Right-click near the layer name and choose **New Smart Object via Copy** from the context menu (don't use Ctrl-J/Cmd-J, the Duplicate Layer command).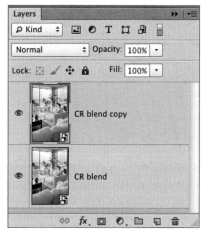

6. Double-click the thumbnail on the copy of the Smart Object to open the photo into Camera Raw. Use sliders in the **Basic** tab to set the proper exposure — this time for the upper midtones and highlights **B** — then click OK. Because the duplicate Smart Object was created via the New Smart Object Via Copy command, it isn't linked to the original one, and your Camera Raw edits affected just the copy.

7. Save the file again. To blend the best areas of the two layers, follow the steps on the next page.

A *The New Smart Object via Copy command created an unlinked copy of the Smart Object.*

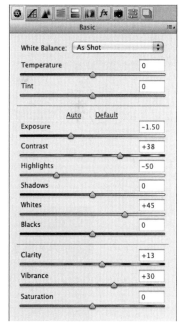

B *We opened the copy of the Smart Object into Camera Raw, used sliders in the Basic tab to recover highlight details (particularly in the exterior areas), then clicked OK to return to our Photoshop file.*

To blend two exposure versions via a layer mask:

1. Continuing in Photoshop, click the upper of the two Smart Objects. If more of the properly exposed areas are on the topmost layer, click the Add Layer Mask button ☐ on the Layers panel to create a white mask; if more of the properly exposed areas are in the lower layer, Alt-click/Option-click the button to create a black mask.

2. Choose the Brush tool ✐ (B or Shift-B), a Soft Round tip, Normal mode, and an Opacity setting of 80–100%.

3. If you created a white mask, keep the current Foreground color as black; if you created a black mask, press X to swap the two colors.

4. Press [or] to set the brush diameter, then apply strokes to hide areas of the current layer and expose the underlying layer, or to reveal areas of the current layer and hide the underlying layer. **A–C** If you need to remask any areas, press X and paint with the reverse color.

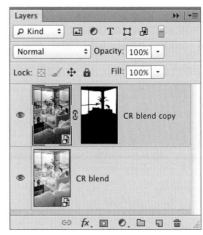

A We added a black mask to a copy of the Smart Object, then with the Brush tool (100% Opacity) and white as the Foreground color, we applied brush strokes in the window areas to reveal the corrected background and sky on that layer.

B In the original image (shown for comparison), only the interior of the room has the correct exposure.

C In the final image, the exposure data from the two Smart Objects is combined. The sky colors are stronger and you can see more details in the landscape.

Fading the edge of a layer via a gradient in a layer mask

Once you have gathered multiple image layers into one document (regardless of the method used), you can soften the edges of any layer to make it look as if it's blending with the underlying layers. To do this, you will apply a gradient to a layer mask.

To fade the edge of a layer via a gradient in a layer mask:

1. Gather image layers into a target document by following the steps on pages 244–245, pages 246–247, or page 248. Position and scale the new image layers with the Move tool, as necessary. **A**

2. In the target image, click one of the new image layers, then click the **Add Layer Mask** button ⬜ on the Layers panel. Keep the mask thumbnail selected.

3. Choose the **Gradient** tool ▤ (G or Shift-G). Click the Gradient picker arrowhead on the Options bar, then click the "Black, White" gradient. (If you don't see this preset, choose Reset Gradients on the picker menu, then click OK in the alert dialog; it's the third gradient in the default library.)

   Also click the Linear Gradient button ▤ on the Options bar, choose Mode: Normal, and choose an Opacity setting of 100%.

4. In the image, start dragging horizontally or diagonally from where you want the complete fadeout to be, and stop dragging where you want the layer to be fully visible. **B** Hold down Shift while dragging to constrain the angle to an increment of 45°.

   The gradient will appear in the layer mask, and the imagery on that layer will be partially hidden **C** (see also **A–B**, next page).

➤ To redo the mask effect, click the layer mask thumbnail, then with the Gradient tool at 100% Opacity, drag in the document again in a new direction, or start dragging from a new location.

A We dragged layers from other documents onto our target image (a photo of burlap), scaled and repositioned the new layers, and rotated a couple of them.

B We added a mask to the "BLUE" layer, chose the Gradient tool and the "Black, White" preset, then dragged to the left, as shown by the arrow.

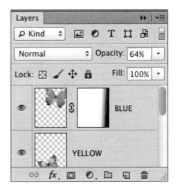

C The gradient in the mask is hiding the right side of the "BLUE" layer.

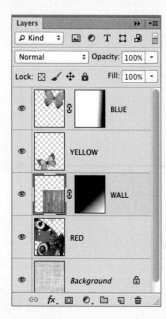

A *Next, we added a layer mask to the "WALL" layer, and dragged diagonally with the Gradient tool (note the gradient in each mask).*

B *This is the final image.*

HIDING A SEAM WITH A BRUSH

You can also edit a layer mask with the Brush tool, a basic Photoshop technique that is described fully on page 173.

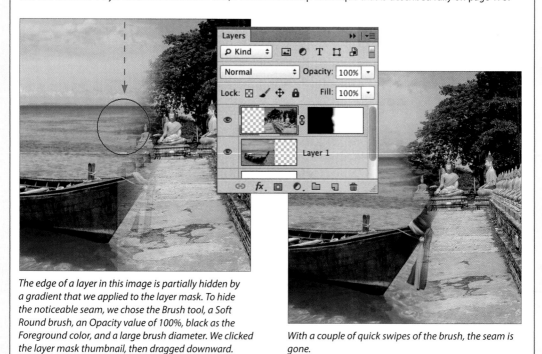

The edge of a layer in this image is partially hidden by a gradient that we applied to the layer mask. To hide the noticeable seam, we chose the Brush tool, a Soft Round brush, an Opacity value of 100%, black as the Foreground color, and a large brush diameter. We clicked the layer mask thumbnail, then dragged downward.

With a couple of quick swipes of the brush, the seam is gone.

Aligning and distributing layers

Similar to the way you might align objects in a drawing program, via buttons on the Options bar in Photoshop, you can align the visible parts of two or more layers to one another.

To align layers to one another:

1. Choose the **Move** tool ⊹ (V), then check **Auto-Select** and choose **Layer** on the Options bar.

2. In the document window, click one image, type, or shape layer, then Shift-click one or more additional layers.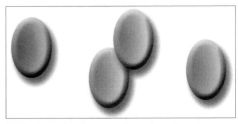

3. Click a vertical and/or horizontal **Align** button on the Options bar.**B**

➤ To align layers to the edge of a selection, create the selection before following the steps above.

The distribute buttons equalize the spacing among three or more selected or linked layers.

To equalize the spacing among layers:

1. Choose the **Move** tool ⊹ (V), then check **Auto-Select** and choose **Layer** on the Options bar.

2. In the document window, click one image, type, or shape layer, then Shift-click two or more additional layers.

3. Click a vertical and/or horizontal **Distribute** button on the Options bar.**C**

➤ Oops! Clicked the wrong button? Choose the Undo command before you try a different one.

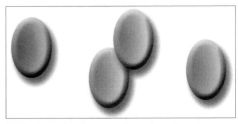

A *We chose the Move tool, then selected four layers.*

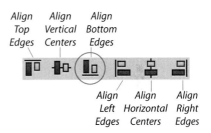

Align Top Edges Align Vertical Centers Align Bottom Edges

Align Left Edges Align Horizontal Centers Align Right Edges

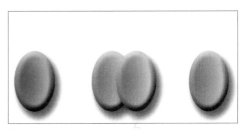

B *We clicked Align Bottom Edges.*

Distribute Top Edges Distribute Vertical Centers Distribute Bottom Edges Auto-Align Layers

Distribute Left Edges Distribute Horizontal Centers Distribute Right Edges

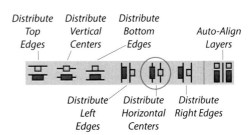

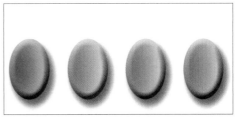

C *We clicked Distribute Horizontal Centers.*

Using the Clone Stamp tool and the Clone Source panel

By applying strokes with the Clone Stamp tool, you can clone all or part of an image from one layer to another in the same document or between documents. This tool is useful for creative montaging, commercial retouching, and video editing. Using the Clone Source panel, you can assign and keep track of up to five different source documents (represented by a row of buttons at the top of the panel), and transform the source pixels before or as you clone them.

To use the Clone Stamp tool and the Clone Source panel:

1. Open one or more RGB documents to be used as source imagery, and create or open a target document.

2. Choose the **Clone Stamp** tool (S or Shift-S). On the Options bar, choose a Soft Round brush, a Mode, an Opacity percentage, and a Flow percentage, and check Aligned.

   Optional: If you have a stylus and tablet, you can activate the Pressure for Opacity button and/or the Pressure for Size button on the Options bar.

   Optional: If the source file contains any adjustment layers and you want the Clone Stamp tool to ignore their effects when sampling, activate the Ignore Adjustment Layers When Cloning button.

3. Show the Clone Source panel. **A** By default, the first source button is selected. Check **Show Overlay** and **Auto Hide**, then set the **Opacity** to around 35–50% so you'll be able to preview the source as an overlay (a faint version of the source layer). If you want the overlay to display only within the brush cursor instead of across the whole document, check **Clipped**.

4. In the target document, create a new blank layer.

5. Click the source document tab. From the **Sample** menu on the Options bar, choose the part of the document from which you want to clone: **Current Layer**, **Current & Below**, or **All Layers**. For either of the first two options, also click a layer.

6. Alt-click/Option-click an area in the image to set the source point. **B** The source file and layer will be assigned to, and will be listed below, the first source button on the Clone Source panel.

7. Click the target document tab.

8. To position the clone, move the pointer over the image without clicking. Adjust the tool diameter by pressing [or], then start dragging to make the cloned pixels appear (**A**, next page). The overlay will disappear temporarily (because you checked Auto Hide), then will reappear when you release the mouse. (For other ways to transform the overlay, see the next page.)

9. To clone from another open document, click the second source button at the top of the Clone Source panel, then repeat steps 4–8. At any time, you can switch between clone sources by clicking a different button.

   Beware! The Clone Source panel keeps the links active only while the source documents are open. If you close a source document, its link to the Clone Source panel is broken. We warned ya.

➤ To use the Clone Stamp tool to retouch imagery within the same document, see pages 302–303.

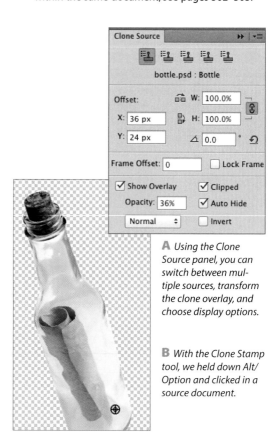

A *Using the Clone Source panel, you can switch between multiple sources, transform the clone overlay, and choose display options.*

B *With the Clone Stamp tool, we held down Alt/Option and clicked in a source document.*

A *We're dragging with the Clone Stamp tool on a new blank layer in our target document to "brush in" part of a bottle image layer from a source document.*

B *This time, before we began cloning the bottle, we clicked the Flip Horizontal button on the Clone Source panel and changed the Offset values (as shown in the panel at right).*

When you use the Clone Stamp tool, the position and orientation values of the source overlay stick unless you change them. Between strokes with the tool, you can reposition, scale, flip, or rotate the overlay via the Clone Source panel or via keyboard shortcuts. New settings will apply only to the currently selected clone source.

To reposition, scale, flip, or rotate the clone source overlay:

Do any of the following:

With the Clone Stamp tool ![icon] selected and an overlay displaying in your document, do any of the following (in the Clone Source panel, you can use the scrubby sliders):

To reposition the source overlay, change the **Offset X** and/or **Y** values on the panel or Alt-Shift-drag/Option-Shift-drag the overlay.

To scale the source overlay, change the **W** or **H** values on the panel or hold down Alt-Shift/Option-Shift and press (and keep pressing) [or]. To preserve the current aspect ratio of the source image layer, activate the Maintain Aspect Ratio button ![icon] before changing the W or H value. To preserve the image quality, avoid scaling the source more than 120 or –120%.

To flip the source, click the **Flip Horizontal** ![icon] and/or **Flip Vertical** ![icon] button.**B**

To rotate the overlay, change the **Rotate** value,![icon] or hold down Alt-Shift/Option-Shift and press (and keep pressing) < or >.

➤ To restore the default flip, scale, and rotation values to the current clone source, click the Reset Transform button.![icon]

➤ To show the Clone Source panel when the Clone Stamp tool is selected, click the Toggle Clone Source panel button ![icon] on the Options bar.

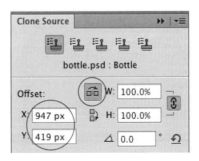

Using the Photomerge command

The Photomerge command combines two or more photos of the same scene into a single panoramic image. To accomplish this, it produces a layer from each photo, then blends the seams using a mask on each layer. It does all the work for you!

To merge photos into one document via the Photomerge command:

1. In Bridge or in Mini Bridge, arrange the photos in the correct sequence for the panorama (this will help Photomerge work faster), then select them all. PSD files process more quickly than raw files.

2. In Bridge, choose Tools > Photoshop > **Photomerge**, or in Mini Bridge, right-click one of the thumbnails and choose Photoshop > **Photomerge**. ★ The Photomerge dialog opens. **A**

3. Click a Layout option: **Auto** (Photoshop picks the best layout), **Perspective**, **Cylindrical**, **Spherical** (best for a 360° panorama), **Collage** (photos are combined by stretching and rotating), or **Reposition** (no stretching or rotating occurs). Unfortunately, the layout options can't be previewed.

4. Check any of these correction options, if available for your Layout choice:

Blend Images Together uses color matching and layer masks to produce seamless transitions between the photos. By default, this option is checked for all the Layout options.

Vignette Removal lightens any dark areas that the camera lens produced around the perimeter of the photos.

Geometric Distortion Correction corrects lens distortion, such as pincushioning (pinching), barreling (bulging), or extreme wide angles.

5. Click OK, then sit back while Photoshop opens the source files, aligns and blends them into a panorama, and opens a new document onscreen.

6. To eliminate any transparent areas that resulted around the edges, use the Crop tool ⊞ (**A–C**, next page).

7. Save the new document.

➤ The Tools > Photoshop > Process Collections in Photoshop command (in Bridge) locates a series of photos within the current folder that contain similar exposure settings and capture times, creates a panorama, saves the new file in the PSD format to the current folder, then closes it.

SHOOTING PHOTOS FOR A PANORAMA

To get good results from the Photomerge command, follow these guidelines from Adobe:

➤ For better alignment and to help prevent distortion, use a tripod and shoot all the photos from the exact same spot, in the sequence needed for the panorama.

➤ Choose the same focal length (zoom) setting for all the photos.

➤ Overlap the viewing area from one shot to the next by approximately 40%.

➤ Choose the same exposure or aperture setting for all the shots. As long as your basic settings are okay, Photomerge will be able to even out minor exposure discrepancies.

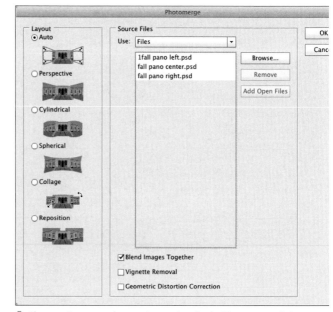

A *Choose a Layout and correction options in the Photomerge dialog.*

A *We chose these three source photos for our panorama.*

B *The Auto option in Photomerge used masks to produce this seamless composite image.*

C *We squared off the image with the Crop tool.*

Using the Auto-Align Layers command

It can be a challenge to get a whole group of people to smile simultaneously for a portrait (unless there happens to be a comedian in the crowd!) and to keep everyone from blinking. If you take multiple shots of the same scene, you can blend the choice areas of two of the best shots in Photoshop via the Auto-Align Layers command and a layer mask.

To blend two shots of the same scene:

1. Open two RGB photos from the same shoot that contain figures or areas that you want to combine. A–B (We used a portrait as an example, but other subject matter can be used.)

2. On the Window > Arrange submenu, choose a 2-Up option. Shift-drag the Background from the Layers panel of one photo onto the window of the other (Shift centers the copy in the document). Right-click the tab of the target document and choose Consolidate All to Here. Save the file.

3. On the Layers panel, Shift-click to select both layers, then choose Edit > **Auto-Align Layers**.

4. In the Auto-Align Layers dialog, click a Projection option. We recommend clicking **Reposition** if you used a tripod, or **Auto** for all other shooting situations to let Photoshop determine the best alignment option. C Click OK. The Background will be converted to a layer.

5. Click the top layer, Alt-click/Option-click the **Add Layer Mask** button 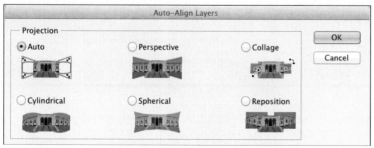 at the bottom of the

A We decided to combine the mother and child on the left from this photo...

B ... with the father and child on the right from this photo. To begin, we dragged the image layer from one document into the window of the other.

C In the Auto-Align Layers dialog, we clicked the Projection option of Auto.

A *The Auto-Align Layers command converted the Background to a layer and aligned the two layers. We added a black layer mask, which is fully blocking the top layer.*

Layers panel, and keep the mask thumbnail selected. For the moment, the mask is hiding the top layer entirely.**A**

6. Choose the **Brush** tool ✎ (B or Shift-B), a Soft Round tip, Normal mode, and 100% Opacity. Zoom in, then paint strokes with white as the Foreground color to reveal the more desirable parts of the top layer.**B–C**

7. To touch up the mask, decrease the brush diameter and zoom in further. Apply brush strokes along the edges of shapes, where necessary, to reveal more of the top layer, or press X and apply strokes with black to reveal more areas of the underlying layer.**D**

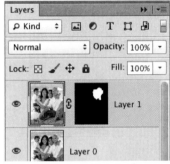

B *With the Brush tool, we applied white strokes to the black layer mask to expose the faces of the father and child from the top layer.*

C *In the process, we also revealed some of the light background along the edge of the child's face. We zoomed in, reduced the brush diameter, then painted with black to remask that area.*

D *The final image is a seamless composite of the two photos.*

Using Smart Guides, ruler guides, and the grid

Sometimes a great composite image comes together in a serendipitous way without much forethought or careful alignment. At other times, say, if your Photoshop image must fit perfectly within the confines of a specific Web or print page layout, you will need to plan ahead or position objects more precisely. To accomplish this, you can use one of the Photoshop layout features, such as grids, rulers, or guides.

Our favorite alignment feature is Smart Guides. If you turn this feature on in a multilayer document, then drag a layer, temporary magnetic guide lines will appear where that layer nears the top, middle, or bottom edge of a shape, type, or imagery on another layer.

To use Smart Guides while moving a layer:

1. Click a layer in a multilayer document.

2. Verify that both the View > **Extras** and View > Show > **Smart Guides** commands have a check mark.

3. With the **Move** tool ▶⊕ (V), drag the layer. Magenta (default color) lines will appear if the edge of the layer you're dragging nears the top, middle, or bottom of content on another layer. Let the layer snap to a horizontal or vertical guide, or to a pair of intersecting guides.**A–B**

➤ In Edit/Photoshop > Preferences > Guides, Grid & Slices, you can change the color and other characteristics of guides, Smart Guides, and the grid. Your preference settings will apply to all Photoshop documents. See page 442.

SHOWING EXTRAS

The View > Extras command (Ctrl-H/Cmd-H) shows or hides whichever features are currently enabled on the View > Show submenu, such as Layer Edges, Selection Edges, the Grid, (ruler) Guides, Smart Guides, and the Pixel Grid. These choices affect the current document and any documents that you subsequently open.

Mac OS users: A dialog may open when you choose the Extras command for the first time after installing Photoshop. See the Note on page 162.

A With the help of a Smart Guide, we are aligning the top edge of the blue butterfly layer to the top edge of the bottle layer.

B Here, we are aligning the bottom edge of the blue butterfly layer to the vertical center of the yellow butterfly layer.

When you enable the Rulers command in Photoshop, rulers display along the top and left sides of the document window. From the rulers, you can create magnetic, moveable horizontal and vertical guides.

To show or hide the rulers:

Choose View > **Rulers** or press Ctrl-R/Cmd-R.

Move the pointer in the image (mouse button up), and you'll notice that its current location is indicated by a dotted marker on each ruler. **A**

▶ To change the units for both rulers quickly, right-click in either ruler and choose a unit from the context menu. Or to get to the Units & Rulers panel in the Preferences dialog quickly, where you can change the units and other settings, double-click either ruler. Changing the units in one location also changes it in the other.

▶ To change the ruler origin (so as to measure distances from a specific location), starting from the upper-left corner where the two rulers meet, drag diagonally into the image. To restore the default origin, double-click in the upper-left corner.

Guides that you create from the horizontal or vertical ruler can be repositioned or removed at any time. Like Smart Guides, they have magnetism, but unlike Smart Guides, they linger onscreen and save with your document. (To use ruler guides, see the next page.)

To create ruler guides:

Show the rulers, then drag from the horizontal or vertical ruler into the image, releasing the mouse where you want the guide to appear.

If View > Snap is checked as you create a guide, you can snap it to a selection, to the edge of content on the currently selected layer, **B–C** or to the grid, if displayed (see the next page).

▶ You can reposition an existing guide with the Move tool (double arrow pointer), provided guides aren't locked (see the next page). As you move a guide, its current x or y position displays in a read-out onscreen. ★

▶ Alt-drag/Option-drag as you create a guide to switch its orientation from vertical to horizontal, or vice versa.

▶ To show the guides if they are hidden, choose View > Show > Guides.

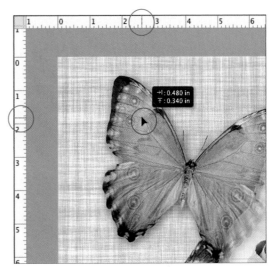

A As we move a layer, the current location of the pointer is indicated by a dotted line on each ruler.

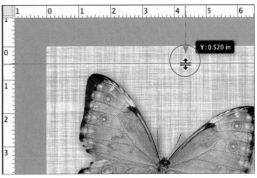

B To create a guide, we are dragging downward into the image from the horizontal ruler.

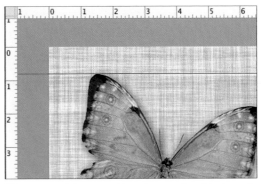

C We snapped the new guide to the top edge of the butterfly layer (which was selected).

When the View > Snap command is on — and depending on which options are checked on the View > Snap To submenu — as you move a selection or layer near a ruler guide, a grid line, the edge of layer imagery, or the edge of the canvas area, it will snap to the guide or edge with a little magnetic tug.

To turn on the Snap To feature:

1. Choose View > Snap To > **Guides**, **Grid**, **Layers**, **Slices**, **Document Bounds**, or **All** (of the above). Note: For the Snap To > Guides, Grid, or Slices option to be available, that option must have a check mark on the View > Show submenu.

2. Make sure View > **Snap** has a check mark (Ctrl-Shift-;/Cmd-Shift-;), and turn off View > Show > **Pixel Grid**. This command enables whichever options are currently checked on the Snap To submenu.

To reposition ruler guides (Move tool), they must be unlocked first. Conversely, to prevent guides from being moved, lock 'em up.

To lock or unlock all ruler guides:

Choose View > **Lock Guides** or press Ctrl-Alt-;/ Cmd-Option-;.

➤ If guides are unlocked and you change your document size via the Image Size command, Photoshop will maintain the relative position of the guides in the document.

To create a ruler guide at a specific location:

1. Choose View > **New Guide**.

2. In the New Guide dialog, click Orientation: **Horizontal** or **Vertical**, enter a **Position** value relative to the 0 (zero) point on the *x* or *y* axis in any measurement unit that is used in Photoshop, then click OK. A guide appears in the document.

To remove one or all ruler guides:

Do either of the following:

To remove one guide, make sure guides aren't locked, hold down V (Move tool), then drag the guide off the edge of the document window. (Don't press Backspace/Delete, which would delete the current layer!)

To remove all guides from the document, choose View > **Clear Guides**.

The grid is a nonprinting framework to which you can snap a layer or selection. It can be displayed or hidden as needed for each individual Photoshop document.

To show or hide the document grid:

To show or hide the grid, choose View > Show > **Grid** or press Ctrl-'/Cmd-'.**A**

(See also "To turn on the Snap To feature" at left.)

On page 133, you used the Ruler tool to straighten a crooked image. Here you will use it as a measuring device.

To measure the distance and angle between two points:

1. Choose the **Ruler** tool ![ruler icon] (I or Shift-I).

2. Drag in the document window. The angle (A) and length (L) of the ruler line will be listed on the Options bar and the Info panel. Shift-drag to constrain the angle to an increment of 45°.

3. *Optional:* With the Ruler tool, you can drag the measure line to a new location. To change the angle or length of the line, drag either one of its endpoints.

4. To hide the ruler line, choose another tool.

➤ To redisplay the measure line, hold down I (temporary Ruler tool). To remove the line, click Clear on the Options bar (not Backspace/Delete). A document can contain only one measure line at a time.

A *The grid is showing in this document.*

Brush settings apply to many Photoshop tools, such as the Brush, Pencil, Mixer Brush, Clone Stamp, History Brush, Sharpen, Dodge, Burn, and Eraser. In this chapter, you will paint with the Brush tool, choose basic brush settings, choose and customize brushes using a wide assortment of controls, and manage brush presets. You will also create bristle brushes for the Mixer Brush tool and use it to transform a photo into a painting, and use the History Brush tool to restore areas of an image.

Note: Although we recommend using a stylus and tablet for the instructions in this chapter, it's not a requirement.

Using the Brush tool

Before delving into the complexities of the Brush panel, take a few minutes to familiarize yourself with the Brush tool. To do this, you will choose a brush preset for the tool and choose Options bar settings to control its behavior.

To use the Brush tool:

1. Click an image layer or create a new, blank layer. *Optional:* To confine your brush strokes to a specific area of the layer, create a selection.

2. Choose the **Brush** tool ![brush icon] (B or Shift-B).

3. Choose a Foreground color.

4. On the Options bar, do the following:

   Click the **Brush Preset** picker arrowhead or thumbnail, **A** then click a preset.

   Choose a blending **Mode.**

   Choose an **Opacity** percentage. At 100%, the stroke will completely cover underlying pixels.

   Choose a **Flow** percentage for the rate at which "pigment" is applied (for thick or thin coverage).

Continued on the following page

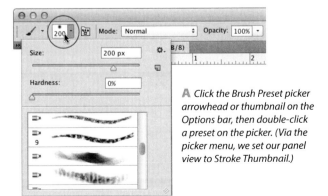

A *Click the Brush Preset picker arrowhead or thumbnail on the Options bar, then double-click a preset on the picker. (Via the picker menu, we set our panel view to Stroke Thumbnail.)*

14

USE YOUR GRAPHICS PROCESSOR

In order to access on-image hardness and opacity controls for brushes (see the next page), and to enhance painting performance (particularly for large brushes), go to Preferences > Performance and make sure Use Graphics Processor is checked (if it's not, check it, click OK, then relaunch Photoshop).

5. *Optional:* If you're using a stylus and tablet, you can activate the Pressure for Opacity button ✺ and/or the Pressure for Size button ✺ on the Options bar.

6. Draw strokes in the image. Feel free to change Options bar settings between strokes.

➤ On the Layers panel, click the Lock Transparent Pixels button ▦ for the current layer to allow the tool to edit only nontransparent pixels.

➤ To draw a straight stroke with a painting tool (e.g., the Brush tool), hold down Shift while dragging.

➤ To sample a color with a temporary Eyedropper, Alt-click/Option-click in the document.

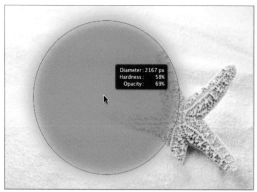

A *With Alt-right-click/Control-Option held down, we're dragging vertically in the image to change the brush hardness.*

SHORTCUTS FOR CHANGING TOOL SETTINGS

One or both of the shortcuts listed below apply to image-editing tools, such as the Healing Brush, Brush, Pencil, Clone Stamp, History Brush, Sharpen, Dodge, and Burn tools.

Cycle through blending modes for the tool	Shift- + (plus) or Shift - - (minus)
Change the opacity, exposure, or strength percentage (or Shift-press a number to change the Flow level)*	Press a digit between 0 and 9 (e.g., 2 = 20%) or quickly type a percentage (e.g., "38"); 0 = 100%

If the Airbrush button is activated on the Options bar, press a number to change the Flow percentage or Shift-press a number to change the Opacity.

Choosing temporary brush settings

There are a gazillion ways to customize a brush preset; we'll begin with size, hardness, and opacity. The settings will remain in effect until you choose a different preset.

To change the size or hardness of a brush via a slider:

1. Choose a tool that uses brush presets, such as the Brush, Pencil, or Mixer Brush, and click a preset on the Brush Preset picker or Brush Presets panel.

2. Do either of the following:

    Open the Brush Preset picker via the Options bar or by right-clicking in the image, then change the **Size** and, if available, the **Hardness** value (you can use the scrubby sliders), then press Enter/Return.

    On the Brush panel 🖌 or the Brush Presets panel, ⇥ adjust the **Size** value.

To change the brush size interactively:

1. Follow step 1, above.

2. Press [or] or hold down Alt-right-click/Control-Option and drag horizontally in the image.

➤ To have Photoshop display a readout of the current Size, Hardness, and Opacity values as you adjust a brush interactively, go to Preferences > Interface, then choose a location option on the Show Transformation Values menu. ★

To change the brush hardness or opacity interactively: ★

1. In Preferences > General, check **Vary Round Brush Hardness Based on HUD Vertical Movement** to set the shortcut to change the tool hardness, or uncheck this option to have it change the tool opacity. Also, to display the hardness or opacity value within the cursor as a tint, show the Performance panel and make sure Use Graphics Processor is checked (if it's not, check it, click OK, then relaunch Photoshop).

2. Choose the Brush tool, ✏ then hold down Alt-right-click/Control-Option and drag vertically in the image. **A** You can also use this method to change the hardness or opacity for the Pencil, Color Replacement, Clone and Pattern Stamp, History and Art History Brush, Background Eraser, Blur, Sharpen, Smudge, Dodge, and Burn tools. For the Eraser tool, you can change only the hardness.

Customizing a brush

Via a wide array of features on the Brush panel, you can customize the characteristics of any brush for use with the Brush, Mixer Brush, Eraser, or History Brush tool (all of which are featured in this chapter), and for the Pencil, Clone Stamp, Pattern Stamp, Art History Brush, Blur, Sharpen, Smudge, Dodge, or Burn tool.

On the Brush panel, most of the settings for customizing brushes are organized into option sets; a few lone options simply are switched on or off. Many of the options add randomness or variation to a stroke, such as to its shape, texture, or color.

The availability of options varies depending on the currently chosen tool and tip, and some options apply only to a graphics tablet and stylus (when an option set is unavailable, the set name is dimmed). The choices are vast, so we'll just focus on a few of our favorites here. With practice, you'll learn which options and settings suit your painting style.

To customize a brush via the Brush panel:

1. Choose one of the tools that we listed at the top of this page. To see the greatest differences among the settings, choose the **Brush** tool or **Mixer Brush** tool (B or Shift-B).

2. To show the Brush panel, click the panel tab or icon, or click the Toggle Brush Panel button on the Options bar or Brush Presets panel. Click **Brush Tip Shape** in the top left corner of the panel, and for this task, click a round or static tip (a tip that doesn't look like a brush, pencil, or airbrush).**A**

3. As you adjust settings for the tip, also keep an eye on the stroke preview at the bottom of the panel:

   To change the brush **Size** (diameter), use the slider or scrubby slider. For a static tip, the brush Size can be increased up to 5000 px. ★

   ➤ To restore the original size to a static tip, click the Restore Original Size button.

   To change the **Angle** (slant) of an elliptical tip, use the scrubby slider, or drag the arrowhead around the circle, or enter a specific angle.

   To change the **Roundness** of the tip (make it more oval or more circular),**B** use the scrubby slider or drag either of the two small dark circles on the ellipse inward or outward.

   To change the **Hardness** of the tip (feather or sharpen its edge),**C** use the scrubby slider.

Continued on the following page

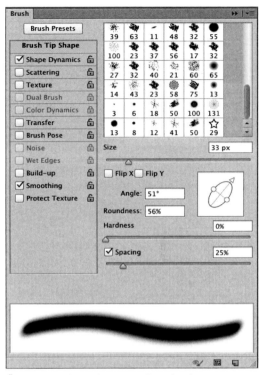

A *Via the Brush panel, you can select a brush tip, customize it via an assortment of options, and save it as a preset. The preview at the bottom of the Brush panel updates dynamically as you change the settings.*

B *100% Roundness*   *20% Roundness*

C *100% Hardness*   *4% Hardness*

SHOPPING FOR BRUSH TIPS

When you load a library of brush tips onto the Brush Presets panel (see page 117 or page 119), those presets also display in the scrolling window on the Brush panel. Not seeing them on the Brush panel? Click Brush Tip Shape at the top of the panel.

To control the distance between marks within the stroke, check **Spacing**, then move the slider **A–B** or turn this option off to let the speed of your brush stroke control the spacing.

4. Next, you'll customize the behavior variations for the brush using five of the option sets on the panel. Checking the box for an option set activates the current settings for that set; clicking the set name both activates the current settings and displays the set options.

To control the amount of allowable variation in the brush tip shape, click **Shape Dynamics**, then do any of the following:

Choose **Size Jitter,** **C** **Angle Jitter,** and **Roundness Jitter** values to establish an allowable amount of random variation for those attributes. The variations are more noticeable when the Spacing value (in the Brush Tip Shape option set) is greater than 10%.

Check **Brush Projection** to enable round and static tips to respond to stylus movement, or to Tilt and Rotation settings in the Brush Pose option set. ★

If you're using a stylus, from each of the **Control** menus, choose which stylus feature is to control the variation for that option. Note that variations will occur even when this setting is Off.

Choose **Minimum Diameter** and **Minimum Roundness** percentages.

5. To control the placement of pigment in the stroke, click **Scattering**, then do any of the following:

Check **Both Axes** to scatter pigment along and perpendicular to the stroke you draw, or uncheck this option to scatter pigment only perpendicular to the stroke. **D** Choose a Control option, if desired.

Choose a **Scatter** percentage to control how far the pigment can stray from the stroke. The lower the Scatter percentage, the more solid the stroke.

Choose a **Count** value to control the number of marks in the stroke (you may need to increase the Spacing value to see any effect).

Choose a **Count Jitter** percentage to control the amount of variation in the Count. **E**

6. Use settings in the **Color Dynamics** option set to control the amount of hue, saturation, and brightness variation. Check **Apply per Tip** ★ to allow jitter settings to display randomly in each tip mark in a stroke, for a multicolor effect.

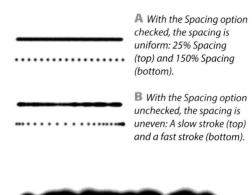

A With the Spacing option checked, the spacing is uniform: 25% Spacing (top) and 150% Spacing (bottom).

B With the Spacing option unchecked, the spacing is uneven: A slow stroke (top) and a fast stroke (bottom).

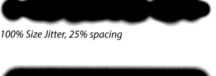

100% Size Jitter, 25% spacing

C *0% Size Jitter*

0% Scatter, 100% Spacing

500% Scatter, the Both Axes option checked

D *500% Scatter, the Both Axes option unchecked*

0% Count Jitter, 100% Spacing

E *100% Count Jitter: The Count varies randomly from 1% to 100% of the Count value.*

7. To display a subtle texture in the stroke, click **Texture**, then do all of the following:

Click the **Pattern** picker thumbnail, then click a pattern swatch.

Choose a **Scale** value for the pattern.

Choose values for **Brightness** and **Contrast**. ★ For a more prominent texture, choose a low Brightness value and a high Contrast value.

Choose a **Depth** value to simulate the depth of a fibrous drawing surface. High values produce more ridges and therefore a more noticeable texture.

8. To control how randomly the overall stroke opacity can vary as you use the tool, and to make the Texture option more pronounced,  click **Transfer**, then do any of the following:

Choose an **Opacity Jitter** percentage for the amount the opacity can vary.  Choose a Control option to control the fading.

Choose a **Flow Jitter** percentage to control the rate at which paint is applied. A high Flow Jitter will make the stroke dry and blotchy, but that may be the look you're after. Choose a Control option.

9. *Beware!* The custom settings that you have chosen are only temporary. To save them as a preset for future use, click the **Create New Brush** button 🗐 at the bottom of the Brush panel. Enter a descriptive name in the Brush Name dialog, check Capture Brush Size in Preset (if desired), then click OK. Your saved preset will appear at the bottom of the Brush Presets panel and in the Brush Preset picker.

10. You're ready to paint with your customized brush!

➤ Click the open 🔓 or closed 🔒 lock icon for an option set to prevent or allow the settings in that set from being edited, regardless of the current preset.

An Erodible Point tip behaves like a soft pencil: The beginning of the stroke is sharp and then it gradually wears down (widening and becoming more blunt) toward the end of the stroke.

To use an Erodible Point tip: ★

1. Choose the **Brush** tool ✎ or **Mixer Brush** tool. ✎

2. On the left side of the Brush panel, click Brush Tip Shape, then click an Erodible Point tip in the scrolling window (look for the blunt-tipped pencil icons).

3. Activate the **Live Tip Brush Preview** button ✎ (see the sidebar at right).

Continued on the following page

A Canvas pattern, 200% Scale, –90 Brightness, 80 Contrast

B The same Texture settings as above with Transfer: 60% Opacity Jitter, 60% Flow Jitter

C 10% Opacity Jitter, 10% Flow Jitter

D 80% Opacity Jitter, 80% Flow Jitter

USING THE LIVE TIP BRUSH PREVIEW ★

To display a schematic of the current brush tip that updates dynamically as you change the settings, activate the Live Tip Brush Preview button ✎ on the Brush or Brush Presets panel. For this feature to work, Use Graphics Processor must be checked in Edit/Photoshop > Preferences > Performance upon launch. Note: The Live Tip Brush Preview displays only for some tip varieties.

➤ To reposition the preview, move the pointer over the top left corner, then drag the black bar.

➤ To view the current tip at different angles, keep clicking in the preview.

4. Choose a **Size** value to set the width of the end of the stroke (where the tip is worn down), and choose a **Softness** value to control how quickly the tip erodes. Lower values keep the tip more sharp. **A**

5. On the **Shape** menu, choose a preset shape.

6. *Optional:* To display some texture in the stroke, click the Texture option set and choose a burlap or canvas texture in the Pattern picker.

▶ To mimic a tilted pencil or pastel stick when drawing with a mouse, increase the Tilt Y value in the Brush Pose option set.

▶ Once you start painting with an Erodible tip (Shape: Point or Round; increased Softness setting), you can resharpen the tip by clicking Sharpen Tip.

▶ To produce long strokes when using an Erodible Point tip with the Mixer Brush tool, choose the Dry, Heavy Load preset from the Useful Mixer Brush Combinations menu on the Options bar. **B**

The Airbrush tips simulate the look of paint that is sprayed from an airbrush device. Via panel options, you can control the degree of graininess and feathering.

To use an Airbrush tip: ★

1. Choose the **Brush** tool or **Mixer Brush** tool.

2. On the left side of the Brush panel, click **B rush Tip Shape**, then click one of the Airbrush tips in the scrolling window (look for the airbrush icons).

3. Activate the **Live Tip Brush Preview** button.

4. Change any of the following settings:

   Choose a **Size** value to set the size of the stroke.

   Choose a **Hardness** value to control the amount of feathering at the edges of the stroke.

   Increase the **Granularity** value to make the stroke look more speckly, and set a **Spatter Size** and **Spatter Amount** to control the size and number of droplets in the stroke. **C**

▶ If you're going to paint with a mouse, display the Brush Pose option set. To spray a conical stroke from the point where you click, change one or both Tilt values; for a wider stroke, lower the Pressure value. To further elongate a conical shape, in the Brush Tip Shape option set, choose a high Distortion value. (See also the sidebar on page 278.)

▶ When using an airbrush tip with the Mixer Brush tool, choose the Dry, Heavy Load preset (Useful … Combinations menu) to produce long strokes.

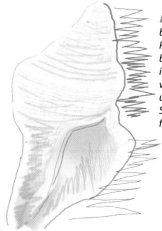

A *We used the Pencil brush preset (an Erodible Point tip) to create the blue lines in this drawing. A high Softness value was used for the upper stroke; a very low Softness value was used for the lower one.*

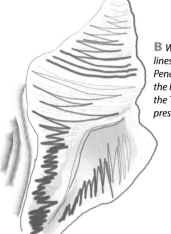

B *We drew the green lines with the Charcoal Pencil brush preset and the brown strokes with the Triangle Pastel brush preset.*

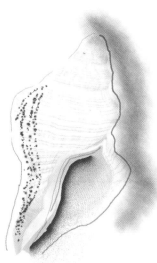

C *We used the Watercolor Spatter Big Drops preset (which has a high Granularity value) to draw the dotted stroke on the left, the Airbrush Soft High Density Grainy preset to draw the blue line in the center, and the Watercolor Wash brush preset to draw the wide blue stroke on the right.*

▶ *All of the presets used here are in the default library. To identify them by name, choose either of the List views on the Brush Presets panel.*

Managing brush presets

The Brush Presets panel stores and displays presets, like the Brush Preset picker, plus it offers several additional features. You can use this panel to save and choose brush presets, resize the current preset, save and load brush preset libraries, and access the Preset Manager.A Unlike the Brush Preset picker, the Brush Presets panel can be left open.

To use the Brush Presets panel:

1. Choose a tool that uses brushes, such as the Brush, Mixer Brush, or Pencil.

2. To show the Brush Presets panel, click the panel tab or icon 🖌 (Window > Brush Presets), or click Brush Presets in the upper-left corner of the Brush panel.

3. On the panel, do any of the following:

   Click a preset **brush** to be used with the current tool.

   Change the brush **Size** (diameter). Note: You can restore the original size of some kinds of brush tips by clicking the Restore Original Size button.🔄

   To **load** different presets onto the panel, choose a library name from the panel menu, then click

Append or OK (see also page 117). (Via the panel menu, you can also choose a different thumbnail or list option for the panel.)

To save the current brush and its settings as a preset, click the **Create New Brush** button,🔖 add to or change the name in the Brush Name dialog (be descriptive), then click OK.

To save all the presets that are currently on the panel as a new library, choose **Save Brushes** from the panel menu, type a name for the library, then click Save (see also page 117 or page 119).

To access the Preset Manager dialog, from which you can append, replace, and reset which items load onto the Brush and Brush Presets panels and the Brush Preset picker at startup, click the **Open Preset Manager** button,🖼 then see "Using the Preset Manager" on page 119. (This button is also available on the Brush panel.)

To delete the currently selected preset from the panel (but not from its library), click the **Delete Brush** button, then click OK.🗑

Activate the **Live Tip Brush Preview** button,🖌 (if available), to display a schematic of the tip.

A Use the Brush Presets panel to select a preset from the current library, change the brush size, load a different library, create a new library, or access the Preset Manager dialog.

QUICK ACCESS TO THE BRUSH PANELS

▶ From the Brush panel, you can open the Brush Presets panel by clicking this button: `Brush Presets`

▶ From the Brush Presets panel, you can open the Brush panel by clicking the Toggle Brush panel button: 🖌

RESETTING THE PRESETS

To restore the original settings to an individual brush preset (including settings in the option sets, and including the size, if the preset includes a size value), simply click the preset again. To restore the whole library of default presets to the Brush Presets panel, see page 118.

TOOL PRESETS HOLD EVEN MORE SETTINGS

The brush presets contain only settings from the Brush panel, not those on the Options bar. When you save settings as a tool preset via the Tool Presets panel or picker (e.g., for the Brush or Mixer Brush tool), that preset will contain the Brush and Options bar settings and, optionally for some tools, the current Foreground color (see page 120). The Airbrushes, Artists' Brushes, Dry Media, Pencil Brushes, and Pencils Mixer Brush preset libraries are new.★

Using the Mixer Brush tool

By choosing brush characteristics for the Mixer Brush tool, you can mimic different types of natural bristle brushes, such as oil paint or gouache. You can also control the wetness of the paint, the paint flow, and the degree to which existing colors mix with new strokes. Photoshop "paint" lacks the viscosity of traditional oils, but you can achieve some nice effects with it nevertheless.

To build a bristle brush:

1. Choose the **Mixer Brush** tool (B or Shift-B).

2. Display the Brush panel. If the bristle tips (which look like a drawing of a brush) aren't showing on the panel, as in figure **A**, click Brush Presets. From the Brush Presets panel menu, choose Reset Brushes. Click OK in the alert dialog, then click the Toggle Brush Panel button to return to the Brush panel.

3. Click **Brush Tip Shape**, then click a bristle tip in the scrolling window. The shape name is listed on the Shape menu.

4. Activate the **Live Tip Brush Preview** button.

5. To pare down the number of options that will affect your brush, either uncheck all the options on the left side of the panel except Smoothing or choose **Clear Brush Controls** from the panel menu.

6. Use the **Bristle Qualities** sliders to choose these physical characteristics for the tip, while noting the changes in the preview:

   Bristles controls the number (density) of bristles.

   Length controls the length of the bristles.

   Thickness controls the width of the bristles (and therefore affects the overall density of the stroke).

   Stiffness controls how easily the bristles bend. Choose a low value for smooth, fluid strokes or a high value for scratchy, dry bristle marks.

   Angle controls the brush angle if you're using a mouse. Angle variations are most noticeable when one of the "Flat" shapes is chosen for the tip.

7. Choose Options bar settings for the Mixer Brush tool by following the steps on the next page.

➤ You can record the creation of a painting or drawing via an action, and then replay the process again at any time. The artwork will reappear onscreen, stroke by stroke. See Chapter 22.

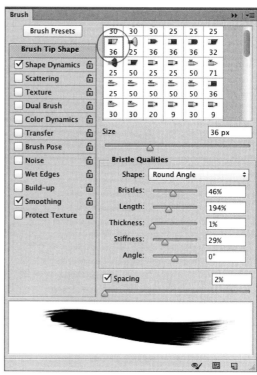

A When the Mixer Brush tool and a bristle tip are selected, Bristle Qualities options display on the Brush panel.

USING THE BRUSH POSE OPTION SET ★

When painting with a mouse, click the Brush Pose option set (Brush panel) to access brush handling options, such as the following:

➤ Use Tilt X or Tilt Y to tilt the entire brush as you apply brush strokes, and thereby apply more paint to the surface.

➤ Use a high Pressure value to bend the brush bristles more, mimicking the way a brush presses into the surface of the paper or canvas, for a darker stroke (akin to decreasing the Stiffness), or lower the Pressure value for a lighter stroke.

➤ Uncheck the Override boxes, which are for use with a stylus.

Before using the bristle brush that you have just chosen qualities for, you also need to choose settings to control how the brush will apply pigment.

To choose paint options for a bristle brush:

1. After following the instructions on the preceding page, and with the **Mixer Brush** tool still selected, on the Options bar, do both of the following:

   Activate the **Load Brush After Each Stroke** button to have the current Foreground color reload onto the brush after each stroke (the Mix value must be below 100% for this option to work).

   Activate the **Clean Brush After Each Use** button to have a clean Foreground color reload after each stroke, or deactivate this option to allow the last colors in the brush to mix with the current Foreground color.

2. From the **Useful Mixer Brush Combinations** menu, choose a preset combination of settings. The Dry presets are good for defining object details and edges, the Moist presets allow for moderate paint mixing, and the Wet and Very Wet presets work well for blending new strokes with existing ones.

   If you prefer to choose custom options (or to refine the settings from a preset), do any of the following:

   Choose a **Wet** value to control the dryness (or gloppiness) of the existing paint and the extent to which your brush can pick it up in the stroke. **A–B**

   Choose a **Load** value to control how much paint is supplied to the brush (how quickly the brush runs out of paint), most noticeable with a low Mix value.

   Choose a **Mix** value to control the degree to which existing strokes (including any white from the Background) mix or smear with new strokes. **C–D**

   Choose a **Flow** value to control the rate at which paint is applied (the amount of coverage).

   Check **Sample All Layers** to allow the brush to mix with and pick up paint from all layers.

3. Time to paint! Create a new, blank layer (it can be above an image layer), then stroke, stroke, stroke.

PICKING UP COLORS FROM AN IMAGE

Check Sample All Layers, then with the Mixer Brush tool, Alt-click/Option-click an area of an image layer. Pixel data from the sampled area will appear in the Current Brush Load thumbnail on the Options bar.

Use this method if you want to wipe a brush clean manually before applying more color — that is, override an activated Load Brush After Each Stroke or Clean Brush After Each Stroke button.

To wipe a bristle brush clean:

With the Mixer Brush tool selected, click the **Current Brush Load** menu on the Options bar, click **Clean Brush**, then click **Load Brush**.

A *Options bar settings of Wet 10 and Mix 10: The stroke barely blended with the existing color.*

B *Wet 90 and Mix 10: The stroke blended somewhat with the existing color.*

C *Wet 10 and Mix 90: The stroke blended and smeared more with the existing color.*

D *Wet 90 and Mix 90: The stroke blended and smeared almost entirely with the existing color.*

In this exercise, you will reinterpret shapes in a photo with the Mixer Brush tool, to produce a digital painting.

To turn a photo into a painting:

1. Open a photo A and duplicate the Background.

2. Hide the duplicate layer, click in the original Background, then use Edit > **Fill** to fill it with White. To add a texture, use Edit > Fill again, except this time choose Use: Pattern, choose the Canvas pattern (Artist Surfaces library) from the Pattern picker menu, set the Opacity to 75%, and click OK.

3. Click the Background copy, and make it visible again. Create several blank layers, and keep one of them selected. B

4. Choose the **Mixer Brush** tool 🖌 (B or Shift-B).

5. On the Brush Presets panel, 🖌 click a preset, such as a flat, blunt preset to fill in broad areas or a point preset to draw fine lines. ★

6. On the Options bar, do all of the following:

   From the **Useful Mixer Brush Combinations** menu, choose a preset to control the character of the paint. The Wet and Very Wet presets are good for painting broad areas, such as backgrounds, and for picking up colors from a photo; the Moist and Dry presets are better for defining details.

   Check **Sample All Layers** to allow the brush to pick up and mix colors from all the underlying layers (strokes will appear only on the selected layer).

If you're using a stylus and tablet, activate the **Pressure Controls Size** button. 🖌

7. To transform your photo into a painting, do either of the following:

   To reinterpret the photo with a "clean" brush, deactivate the **Load Brush After Each Stroke** button 🖌 on the Options bar and activate the **Clean Brush After Each Stroke** button ✗ (now the current Load button setting will have no effect). Start each new brush stroke over the desired color (because "Clean Brush After Each Stroke" is activated) (A, next page).

   To sample a color from the photo, activate the **Load Brush After Each Stroke** button on the Options bar, then Alt-click/Option-click in the photo. Lower the opacity of the photo layer, click a paint layer, then paint with the sampled color (B–C, next page and A–B, page 282).

   ➤ Paint the picture in sections, each one on one of the blank layers you created. To erase any unwanted strokes, use the Eraser tool (see page 282).

➤ As you apply brush strokes, mimic the direction of the original shapes in the photo. To add variety to your strokes, switch bristle tips.

A *This is the original photo — a quintessential New England landscape.*

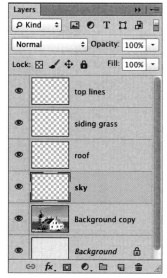

B *This is how the Layers panel looked by the end of step 3 on this page.*

A *We deactivated the Load Brush After Each Stroke option so we could pick up colors from the photo layer, chose "Wet, Heavy Mix" from the Useful MIxer Brush Combinations menu, then applied brush strokes on a few blank layers.*

B *We activated Load Brush After Each Stroke, sampled a color in the photo, lowered the opacity of the photo layer, clicked another blank layer, then painted with a couple of the Moist preset combinations and a couple of the Wet ones.*

➤ *When sampling a color, make sure the photo layer is at 90% to 100% Opacity. You can lower the opacity of the photo layer before painting.*

C *Next, we painted the sky with the Round Fan Stiff Thin Bristles and Flat Point Medium Stiff presets, painted the water with the Round Blunt Medium Stiff and Round Point Stiff presets, and painted the siding on the building with the Round Point Stiff preset and the Dry, Heavy Load combination.*

➤ *All the presets mentioned above are in the default brush library. To view the preset names, choose Small or Large List from the Brush Presets panel menu.*

Continued on the following page

A *Finally, on the topmost layer, Peter painted with the Round Point Stiff preset and used the Dry combination to prevent the final line work from blending with the other paint layers. Now the image looks like an artist's painting. Note that he didn't slavishly replicate every tiny detail in the photo — that's what artistic license is all about!*

B *Peter transformed this photo in a similar way to the one shown above, using the Mixer Brush tool, a bristle tip, and a few different Useful Combination presets.*

Using the Eraser tool

The Eraser tool removes image pixels permanently, so it should be used only to delete areas from a duplicate layer or from a layer that contains just retouching or painting edits that were made via the Sample All Layers option. Don't use it on the original Background!

To use the Eraser tool:

1. Choose the **Eraser** tool ✐ (E or Shift-E).

2. On the Options bar, do the following:

   Click a Soft Round brush on the **Brush Preset** picker.

   Choose a Mode (shape) of **Brush**, **Pencil**, or **Block**.

   For Brush or Pencil mode, choose an **Opacity** percentage; for Brush mode, deactivate the **Airbrush** button and keep the **Flow** setting at 100%.

3. Click a layer, make sure the Lock Transparent Pixels button ⊠ is deactivated, then drag to erase pixels. To adjust the brush diameter, press [or].

➤ Instead of erasing image pixels permanently, hide them via an editable layer mask (see pages 172–173).

Using the History Brush tool

When you apply strokes to a document with the History Brush tool, pixels below the pointer are restored from whichever state or snapshot you have designated as the history source.

Note: Photoshop prevents the use of the History Brush tool if you apply specific kinds of edits after opening your document, such as changing the document color mode or canvas size or cropping. Also, the tool can't be used to recover pixels from a layer that you have deleted, and it works only on 8-bit images.

To use the History Brush tool:

1. Click an image layer (or duplicate the Background), and apply some edits, such as a filter or brush strokes (but none of the edits listed in the Note above). **A–C**

2. Choose the **History Brush** tool 🖌 (Y or Shift-Y).

3. On the Options bar:

   Click the Brush Preset picker arrowhead, then click a brush on the picker.

Continued on the following page

A *This is the original image.*

B *We duplicated the image layer via Ctrl-J/ Cmd-J, then applied the Gaussian Blur filter to the duplicate.*

C *We used a Hue/Saturation adjustment layer (Colorize option) to apply a blue-green tint, then merged that layer into the duplicate image layer.*

Choose a blending Mode, Opacity percentage, and Flow percentage.

4. On the Layers panel, click the layer you edited, and make sure the Lock Transparent Pixels button ⊠ is deactivated.

5. On the History panel, click in the leftmost column for a state, to designate it as the source for the History Brush tool. The history source icon 🖌 appears in that slot.**A** Note: If you added a layer during the course of editing (step 1), set the history source to the New Layer or Layer Via Copy state.

6. Apply strokes to the image. Pixel data from the source state will replace the current data where you apply strokes.**B–C**

➤ We recommend using the History Brush immediately after applying edits that you want to remove selectively. This way, it will be easier for you to identify which state you want to use as a source.

➤ If you add a layer to your document that you want to remove edits from via the History Brush tool, set the source icon to the New Layer state.

A To set the history source icon, we clicked in the leftmost column for the state in which we duplicated the image layer.

B We set the opacity for the History Brush to 70% and chose the Round Blunt Medium Stiff bristle preset. We applied strokes to selectively restore the original, unedited image in scratchy strokes.

C Finally, with a Soft Round tip and the History Brush Opacity set to 50%, we partially restored some areas of the model's face and neck from the original Background image.

Photoshop provides tools for correcting many kinds of imperfections, from smoothing pores and wrinkles to removing unsightly power lines. There are also commands for changing colors, from whitening teeth to matching or replacing colors.

In this chapter, you will change colors by using the Match Color command, the Replace Color command, and the Color Replacement tool; whiten teeth or eyes; correct red-eye; smooth wrinkles with the Healing Brush and Patch tools; remove blemishes with the Spot Healing Brush tool; soften skin and other textures with the Surface Blur and Gaussian Blur filters; replace pixels with the Clone Stamp tool; eliminate elements with the Spot Healing Brush and Patch tools; apply a Content-Aware fill; and move or extend areas with the Content-Aware Move tool.

The following are some guidelines we recommend following when applying retouching edits:

➤ Do the small stuff first. For instance, if you need to remove blemishes or other small imperfections from a portrait as well as smooth the skin, start by healing the blemishes. Next, either merge the healing layer into the image layer or select both the healing and image layers, then copy and merge (stamp) them onto a new layer (see page 149). Finally, apply skin smoothing to the newly merged layer.

➤ Preserve the original pixels and keep your edits flexible. One way to accomplish this is by duplicating the image layer and editing the duplicate. For some tools, an even better option is to check Sample: All Layers on the Options bar, then apply edits to a new, blank layer. The tool will sample pixels from all the visible layers, and send the results to the new layer; you can easily erase your editing strokes at any time.

➤ Restore some realism. After applying edits to a duplicate or blank layer, you can lower the opacity of that healing or retouching layer slightly to reveal a bit of the original, imperfect (but more natural-looking) image.

RETOUCHING

15

IN THIS CHAPTER

Using the Match Color command

Using the Match Color command, you can match the color saturation and brightness of one layer or document to those of another layer or document, and also remove a color cast. For the best results, use this command to unify photos that were shot with only slightly different camera settings or in similar lighting conditions, such as indoor fashion or product shots of the same or closely related subject matter.

To correct color via the Match Color command:

1. Open an RGB document to be used as the source for color and tonal values, and a second RGB document to become the target of the color match.**A–B**

2. With the target document active, on the Layers panel, click the Background, press Ctrl-J/Cmd-J to duplicate it (in order to preserve the original pixels), and keep the duplicate layer selected.

3. Choose Image > Adjustments > **Match Color**. In the dialog, check Preview (**A**, next page).

4. From the **Source** menu, choose the name of the source document that you opened in step 1. The target document will instantly adopt color values from the source document. Note: If the source document contains multiple layers, choose a source layer (or Merged) from the Layer menu.

5. Under Image Options, do any of the following:

   Move the **Luminance** slider to adjust the overall brightness of the image (the default value is 100).

   Move the **Color Intensity** slider to adjust the color saturation (the default value is 100).

   Move the **Fade** slider to restore some of the original color to the image, if you want to blend the old with the new.

   Check **Neutralize** to remove any color casts from the target document. If this causes too great a color shift, lessen the effect via the Fade slider.

6. *Optional:* To save your settings for use in other documents, click Save Statistics, choose a location for the data file, then click Save.

7. Press P, then release, to toggle the Preview on and off. Readjust any sliders, if needed, then click OK (**B**, next page).

➤ To load your saved settings into the Match Color dialog, click Load Statistics.

A *We will correct the orange cast in this photo…*

B *…by matching its color and tonal values to the more balanced values in this photo.*

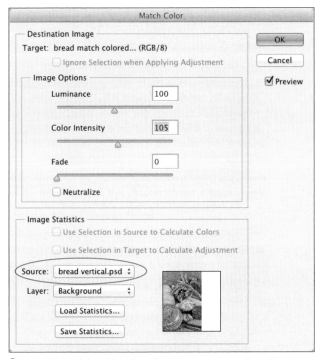

A *In the Match Color dialog, from the Source menu, we chose the image that contains the desired color values.*

➤ To limit the range of colors to be used as source data (and to help prevent odd color shifts), create a selection in the source document before opening the Match Color dialog, then in the dialog, check Use Selection in Source to Calculate Colors.

➤ To correct the color in a document without using another document as source data, choose None as the Source image in the Match Color dialog and check Neutralize. Use the Luminance, Color Intensity, and Fade sliders as needed. This method doesn't always work, but when it does, it's a decent quick fix.

B *Now the color and tonal values in this image are similar to those in figure* B *on the preceding page. If we were to import both images into the same layout document, they would make a harmonious pair.*

Using the Replace Color command

Using the Replace Color command, not only can you apply hue, saturation, and lightness adjustments, but via selection controls in the dialog, you can limit those edits to specific color areas of the image. This command works best for recoloring discrete areas that are easy to isolate.

To use the Replace Color command:

1. *Optional:* In an RGB document that you're going to send to a commercial printer, choose View > Proof Setup > Working CMYK to view a soft proof of the image in simulated CMYK color.

   Once you've made a choice from the Proof Setup submenu, you can toggle the proof on and off while the Replace Color dialog is open by pressing Ctrl-Y/Cmd-Y. Regardless of whether the Proof Colors command is on or off, the Color and Result swatches in the Replace Color dialog are going to display in RGB.

2. Click a layer (not a Smart Object) or the Background, press Ctrl-J/Cmd-J to duplicate it, and keep the duplicate layer selected.

3. *Optional:* To confine the color selection and replacement to an area of the image, create a selection.**A**

4. Choose Image > Adjustments > **Replace Color**. The Replace Color dialog opens.

5. In the document, click the color to be replaced. The color you click will appear in the Color swatch at the top of the dialog.

6. Do any of the following:

   To add more color areas to the selection, click the **Eyedropper** tool 🖉 in the dialog, then Shift-click or drag either in the preview or in the document.

   Increase the **Fuzziness** value to add similar colors to the selection, or reduce it to narrow the range of selected colors.**B**

   Check **Localized Color Clusters** to limit the selection to similar, contiguous colors. (We sometimes get similar or better results by lowering the Fuzziness value instead.)

7. If you need to subtract any areas from the selection, with the Eyedropper tool, 🖉 hold down Alt/Option and click or drag in the preview or document window (this is a temporary Subtract from Sample Eyedropper tool).

A *We want to recolor the purple eyeshadow in this image. We loosely selected that area first.*

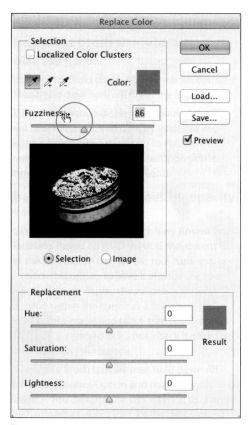

B *We opened the Replace Color dialog, then clicked the pot of eyeshadow. Areas matching that color displayed as a selection in the preview window. Next, we chose a Fuzziness value of 86.*

8. To replace the colors you have selected, do either of the following:

In the **Replacement** area, choose replacement **Hue**, **Saturation**, and **Lightness** values (you can use the scrubby sliders).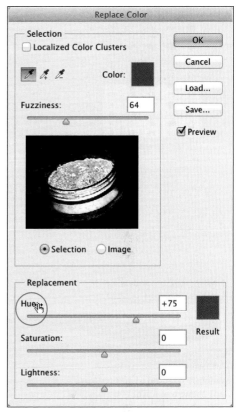 The Result swatch will update as you do this. Note: A Saturation value greater than +25 may produce a nonprintable color.

Click the **Result** swatch, choose a replacement color in the Color Picker, then click OK. The sliders will shift to reflect the values of the new color.

Note: The Replacement sliders will stay put if you click a different area of the image or add to or subtract from the selection.

➤ To toggle the selection and image in the preview, press and release Ctrl/Cmd (or click Selection or Image below the preview).

9. *Optional:* To save your settings for use in a series of similar photos, click Save, choose a location for the data file, then click Save.

10. Click OK.**B**

➤ In a CMYK document, the Replacement sliders don't affect the value of the Black (K) component. That value is established by the CMYK Working Space, which you chose in Edit > Color Settings.

➤ You can restore the original dialog settings by holding down Alt/Option and clicking Reset (Cancel becomes Reset), but be aware that your selection will be discarded.

A *Next, we lowered the Fuzziness value to 64, Shift-clicked more areas in the eyeshadow pot to add them to the selection, then changed the Hue.*

B *The original purple eyeshadow is now reddish brown.*

Using the Color Replacement tool

The Color Replacement tool lets you change color values in areas of an image, but instead of using a dialog, as you do with Replace Color, you apply changes manually with a brush. Unlike the Brush tool, the Color Replacement tool attempts to preserve the original texture (luminosity values) of an area as it replaces colors. This tool, like the Replace Color and Match Color commands, will be of particular interest to advertising and catalog designers.

To use the Color Replacement tool:

1. Duplicate the Background in an RGB image to preserve the original pixels, and keep the duplicate layer selected.

2. Choose the **Color Replacement** tool ![icon] (B or Shift-B).

3. As the replacement color, choose a **Foreground** color via the Color or Swatches panel, or sample a color by Alt/Option clicking in the document.

4. If the color you chose isn't on the Swatches panel, ![icon] add it to the panel by clicking the **New Swatch of Foreground Color** button. ![icon]

5. On the Options bar, choose parameters for the tool: **A**

   On the Brush Preset picker, choose a high **Hardness** value and a low **Spacing** value.

   To control which color characteristics the tool applies to the image, choose a **Mode** of Hue, Saturation, Color, or Luminosity. (We've gotten good results with Color mode.)

   Click a **Sampling** button: **Continuous** ![icon] to apply the current Foreground color to all pixels the brush touches (we prefer this option because it lets us replace both light and dark colors); or **Once** to sample the first pixel the brush clicks and apply the Foreground color only to pixels

that match that initial sampled color (because this option confines the sampling to just one color, if you need to replace, say, different shades of a particular color, you would have to sample each one separately); or **Background Swatch** ![icon] to replace only colors that match or are similar to the current Background color (for this last option, choose a Background color).

From the **Limits** menu, choose **Discontiguous** to recolor only pixels under the pointer; or **Contiguous** to recolor pixels under the pointer plus adjacent pixels; or **Find Edges** (our favorite option) to recolor pixels under the pointer while keeping the color replacement within discrete shapes.

Choose a **Tolerance** value (1–100%) for the range of colors to be replaced. A high Tolerance value permits a wide range of colors to be recolored; a low value allows only pixels that closely match the sampled color to be recolored.

Optional: Check Anti-alias for smoother transitions between the original and replacement colors.

If you're using a stylus and tablet, click the **Pressure Controls Size** ![icon] button, and from the Size menu on the Brush Preset picker, choose **Pen Pressure** or **Stylus Wheel**.

6. Adjust the brush diameter by pressing [or], then drag across the areas to be recolored (**A–D**, next page). Only pixels that fall within the chosen Sampling, Limits, and Tolerance parameters will be recolored.

▶ When using the Color Replacement tool, you can change Options bar settings or the brush diameter between strokes. To change the brush hardness or opacity interactively, see page 272.

![icon] ⋅ | 29 ▾ | Mode: Color ⬍ | ![icon] ![icon] ![icon] | Limits: Find Edges ⬍ | Tolerance: 20% ▾ | ☑ Anti-alias | ![icon]

A *Choose settings for the Color Replacement tool from the Options bar.*

A *We want to change the color of the light green stripes on this woman's sweater to aqua blue.*

B *With the Color Replacement tool and the settings shown in the figure on the preceding page, we're "painting" over the light green on the woman's sweater, to replace it with aqua blue (the current Foreground color).*

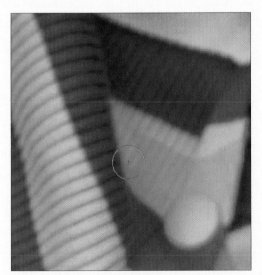

C *Next, we zoomed in to recolor some smaller areas. Using a Tolerance setting of 40%, we were able to replace the color in both the highlight and shadow areas within a stripe. When replacing the colors along the edges of the stripe, we used a lower Tolerance setting of 15%.*

D *We unintentionally recolored some dark stripes, which was possible even though the Limits setting for the tool was Find Edges. To repair this error, we Alt/Option clicked to sample the original color in the darker stripe (as shown above). Our next step will be to apply strokes with the sampled color.*

Whitening teeth or eyes

Another use for a Hue/Saturation adjustment layer, which you learned about in Chapter 12, is to whiten the teeth or whites of the eyes in a portrait. The first step is to select the problem area(s).

To whiten teeth or eyes in a portrait photo:

1. Open a portrait photo, zoom in on the area to be corrected, then do either of the following:

   Choose the **Quick Selection** tool, then drag to create a tight selection of the teeth A or of the white areas of both eyes.

   Paint a **Quick Mask** on the teeth (follow the steps on page 171). When you're done, restore the document to Standard mode (Q). Photoshop will convert the mask to a selection.

2. On the Adjustments panel, click the **Hue/Saturation** button. ★

3. On the Properties panel, choose **Yellows** from the second menu. Reduce the Saturation value and increase the Lightness value. ★ B

   ➤ Try not to overdo the whitening, or the teeth will look unnatural.

4. Also on the Properties panel, click the Masks button, then increase the **Feather** value to soften the edge of the mask and make the transition to the adjusted area less abrupt (try a value between 5 and 8 px). C–D

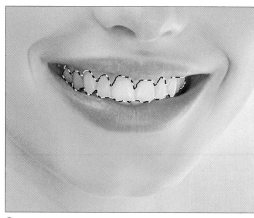

A *We used the Quick Selection tool to select the teeth in this photo.*

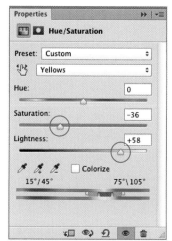

B *On the Properties panel for a Hue/Saturation layer, we lowered the Saturation and increased the Lightness.*

C *Then we adjusted the Feather value for the mask.*

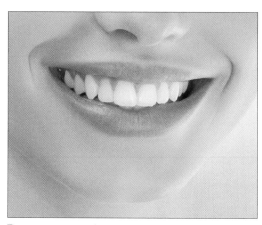

D *Brighter, whiter teeth!*

Using the Red Eye tool

Red-eye (red in the pupil areas) in a portrait photo results when a person situated in a relatively dark room looks straight into the camera lens, and light emitted by an electronic flash reflects off his or her retinas. This is less likely to occur if you use a flash bracket and an off-camera flash — and if the subject looks away from the camera. To remove red-eye from a photo that was taken without such preventive measures, you can use the Red Eye tool in Photoshop.

To remove red-eye from a portrait:

1. Open a portrait photo, and zoom way in on the eye area.

2. Choose the **Red Eye** tool (J or Shift-J).

3. On the Options bar, do both of the following:

   Choose a **Pupil Size** for the size of the correction. You can start with the default setting of 50%, and see if you like the results. You don't want the tool to enlarge (dilate) the pupil.

   Choose a **Darken Amount** to control how much the tool darkens the pupil in order to remove the red. A lower setting tends to work better for light eye colors than for dark ones. Try a value of 40%.

4. Click once on the red area in each pupil. The tool should remove all traces of red, replacing it with black**A–B** If not, see the next task.

   Note: If the tool enlarged the pupil too much, undo the results, lower the Pupil Size value, then click again. Similarly, if the red removal was incomplete or the pupil became too dark, undo the results, then try again with a different Darken Amount value.

➤ You don't need to drag across the eye with the Red Eye tool; the tool is clever enough to find the pupil area automatically with a simple click.

➤ The Red Eye Removal tool in Camera Raw is equivalent to the Red Eye tool in Photoshop, except with the former, you drag across the entire eye. The Camera Raw sliders work the same as the ones in Photoshop.

➤ Some photographers prefer to keep the red-eye feature of their camera off, because it delays the shutter action and they can miss the "moment." Also, the subject can mistake the click of the red-eye feature for the shutter, which comes afterward.

To remove any remaining traces of red from the iris of the eyes (the area around the pupils), follow these steps.

To remove the remaining traces of red:

1. Zoom in on one eye.

2. Choose the **Color Replacement** tool (B or Shift-B).

3. On the Options bar, choose Mode: Color, Sampling: Once, Limits: Contiguous, and Tolerance: 30%.

4. Make the brush tip very small, Alt-click/Option-click a color in the iris of the eye, then apply short strokes over the remaining traces of red to recolor them with the sampled color.

5. Repeat with the other eye.

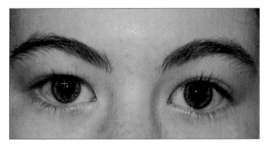

A With the Red Eye tool, we clicked once on each eye.

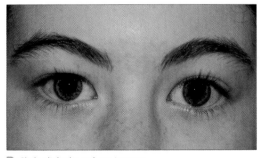

B Click, click, the red-eye is gone.

Unlike the Clone Stamp tool, which merely copies a source color without blending it into the target area (see pages 302–303), the three tools discussed next will sample a texture, apply it to the target area, and blend the texture into the existing color and brightness values. With these tools, it's easy to fix imperfections such as facial blemishes or paper creases in a vintage photo, and the results are usually seamless.

With the Healing Brush tool, you Alt-click/Option-click to sample from an unblemished or smooth area, then apply strokes in the area to be retouched. **A** The blemish pixels are replaced with sampled pixels.

With the Patch tool, you select the blemish area first, then drag the selection over an unblemished area for sampling. Here again, the blemish pixels are replaced with the sampled ones.

And with the Spot Healing Brush tool, you simply click a blemish without sampling. Pixels are replaced (almost magically!) based on data gathered from neighboring pixels.

Using the Healing Brush tool

To use the Healing Brush tool:

1. Choose the **Healing Brush** tool ![icon] (J or Shift-J).

2. Create a new, blank layer in a portrait photo. (The healing strokes will be applied to this layer.)

3. On the Options bar, do all of the following: **B**

   Right-click in the image and choose a high **Hardness** value (or use the interactive cursor, as described on page 272). Also, in Edit/Photoshop > Preferences > Cursors, click Full Size Brush Tip (so you will be able to preview the diameter of the brush cursor).

   Choose Mode: **Normal** to preserve the grain, texture, and noise of the area surrounding the target; or if you don't need to preserve those characteristics, choose a different mode, such as Lighten (for subtle retouching or to correct wrinkles or creases that are very close together, to prevent them from cloning onto one another).

   Click Source: **Sampled**.

   Check **Aligned** to maintain the same distance between the source point and the areas that

you drag across, even if you release the mouse between strokes, or uncheck this option to resample from the original source point each time you release the mouse.

From the Sample menu, choose **All Layers**. This will allow the tool to sample pixels from all the layers below the pointer (they are going to appear on the selected, blank layer).

Optional: If the document contains adjustment layers, the effects of which you want the Healing Brush tool to ignore when sampling (so the effect of the adjustments isn't doubled), activate the Ignore Adjustment Layers When Healing button. ![icon]

If you're using a stylus and tablet, click the **Pressure Controls Size** ![icon] button.

Click the **Toggle Clone Source** panel button, ![icon] then check **Show Overlay** and **Clipped** on the Clone Source panel so you will be able to preview the cloned pixels within the brush cursor.

A *We're going use the Healing Brush tool to soften the wrinkles around the woman's eyes in this photo.*

![Options bar: brush 25, Mode: Normal, Source: Sampled, Pattern, Aligned Sample: All Layers]

B *We chose these Options bar settings for the Healing Brush tool.*

4. Press [or] to scale the brush to suit the area to be healed.

5. Alt-click/Option-click a smooth or unblemished area to sample it as the source texture.**A** The sampled area displays within the brush cursor.

6. With the new, blank layer still selected, drag a short stroke across the area to be repaired.**B** When you release the mouse, the source texture will be applied to the target area and will be blended into neighboring pixels. It will render in two stages, so be patient.**C**

7. *Optional:* To establish a new source point for further repairs, Alt-click/Option-click a different area, then apply more strokes.

8. To soften the results, lower the Opacity of the healing layer slightly to blend it with the original layer.**D**

➤ Because you applied the healing strokes to a separate layer, you can easily erase any mistakes. Hide the image layers below the healing layer temporarily, then with the Eraser tool, drag across any unwanted strokes.

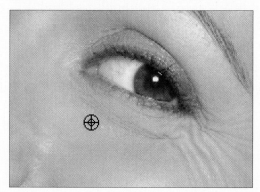

A *With the Healing Brush tool, we held down Alt/Option and clicked the area to be used as replacement pixels…*

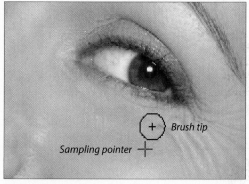

B *…then dragged across the area to be repaired. Note that the brush tip is separate from the sampling pointer.*

C *The wrinkles around her eyes are softened.*

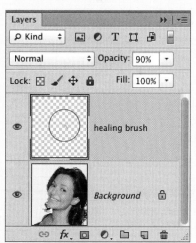

D *Our retouching brush strokes are on a separate layer (labeled "healing brush"). We lowered the Opacity of that layer to 90% to make the portrait look more natural.*

REMOVING FACIAL HOT SPOTS

The Healing Brush tool is also handy for removing shiny hot spots from a portrait, which are caused by harsh, uneven lighting. Choose Mode: Darken on the Options bar for the tool, then Alt-click/Option-click to sample a medium-tone area of skin.

Size the brush, create a new, blank layer, then drag once or twice over a hot spot, letting your stroke(s) follow the natural contours of the face.

With Darken mode chosen for the tool, it repaired only the lightest area. We repeated this process on the model's forehead and nose. (If you want to soften the results, lower the Opacity of the healing layer.)

Using the Spot Healing Brush tool

The Spot Healing Brush tool heals imperfections without your having to sample a source area. With one click or a very short drag, you can zap blemishes or wrinkles, or repair a tear or crease in a vintage or damaged photo.

To use the Spot Healing Brush tool:

1. Create a new, blank layer to contain your healing strokes, and keep it selected.

2. Choose the **Spot Healing Brush** tool (J or Shift-J), and zoom the document to 100%.

3. In Edit/Photoshop > Preferences > Cursors, under Painting Cursors, click Full Size Brush Tip (so you will be able to preview the diameter of the brush cursor) and check Show Crosshair in Brush Tip (to help you position the cursor).

4. On the Options bar, do all of the following:

   Choose a **Mode**. To preserve skin tones, try Normal or Lighten mode. (When used in Replace mode, the tool may pick up unwanted facial details in the stroke, such as hair or eyelashes.)

   To help preserve existing tonal values in the image, such as in skin tones, click Type: **Content-Aware** (for more about this option, see page 304).

   Check **Sample All Layers** to allow the brush to sample pixels from all the layers below the pointer.

5. Position the pointer above the area to be repaired, press [or] to make the brush just slightly wider than that area, then drag once across it in a short stroke. **A–B** Repeat to repair other problem areas.

6. *Optional:* For a more subtle result, lower the Opacity of the healing layer slightly.

7. Because you applied Spot Healing strokes to a separate layer, you can show and hide those edits (or erase any unwanted strokes with the Eraser tool) at any time.

A *With the Spot Healing Brush tool, we clicked a blemish.*

B *The blemish disappeared.*

RETOUCHING WITH LIQUIFY OR PUPPET WARP

To reshape an area of an image (e.g., to slim down a chin or waistline in a portrait), try using the Liquify filter (see pages 338–339) or the Puppet Warp command (see pages 336–337).

Healing areas with the Patch tool

The Patch tool is also a good choice for retouching bags or wrinkles below the eyes in a portrait and for repairing rips, stains, or dust marks in a scanned image (such as in a vintage photo).

To retouch an area using the Patch tool:

1. Press Ctrl-J/Cmd-J to duplicate the Background, and keep the duplicate layer selected.

2. Choose the **Patch** tool ⬚ (J or Shift-J).

3. On the Options bar, click **Patch: Normal** and **Source**.

4. Drag a selection around the entire area to be repaired.**A** You can Shift-drag to add to the selection or Alt-drag/Option-drag to subtract from it.

   ➤ If you're retouching an under-eye area, avoid selecting any of the lower eyelid.

5. Drag from inside the selection to the area to be sampled.**B** When you release the mouse, imagery from the sampled area will appear within the original selection, and will be blended with the luminosity and texture of original pixels. Deselect (Ctrl-D/Cmd-D).**C**

➤ See also the tip on page 308.

➤ If you use the Patch tool to remove wrinkles and the results look too smooth or slick, lower the Opacity of the duplicate layer (try 70 or 80%) to reveal some of the original skin folds and texture.**D**

A *With the Patch tool (Normal setting), we selected the area to be repaired.*

B *We dragged from the selected area to a nearby area for Photoshop to sample.*

C *Photoshop blended pixels from the sample area into the original selection area.*

D *We repeated the same steps for the left eye, then lowered the layer Opacity to 70% to soften the effect.*

Smoothing skin and other surfaces

Using the Surface Blur filter, you can easily smooth out skin pores, mottled surfaces on objects, or the paper texture in a scanned print.

To smooth surfaces with the Surface Blur filter:

1. Press Ctrl-J/Cmd-J to duplicate the Background in an image that needs some surface smoothing.A

2. Choose Filter > Blur > **Surface Blur**. The Surface Blur dialog opens. Check Preview.

3. Choose a low **Threshold** value (try 3–6) to blur only low-contrast areas, such as the cheeks and forehead in a portrait, while preserving the contrast in key details, such as the facial features.

4. To soften skin (e.g., cheeks, forehead), choose a **Radius** of around 6–12, or just to the point that the desired degree of smoothing is reached (so the skin doesn't become too smooth).

5. Readjust the **Threshold** to increase or decrease the amount of blurring in the low-contrast areas. Bear in mind that too much smoothing can make a face look artificial — but then again, this whole task is a lesson in artifice!

6. Click OK.B

7. *Optional:* To restore details from the original image, lower the Opacity of the duplicate layer slightly and/or follow the steps in the next task.

To selectively restore details that were blurred by the Surface Blur filter, apply strokes to a layer mask.

To restore details selectively after using the Surface Blur filter:

1. With the duplicate layer selected, click the **Add Layer Mask** button on the Layers panel.

2. Choose the **Brush** tool (B or Shift-B).

3. On the Options bar, choose a small Soft Round brush and an Opacity of 80–90%.

4. With black as the Foreground color, draw strokes on any areas that you want to restore sharpness to, such as the lips, eyes, eyebrows, or hair in a portrait.C To restore the blur effect to areas that you mask unintentionally, paint with white.

A *The pores on this woman's skin look too prominent.*

B *The Surface Blur filter successfully smoothed the skin texture while keeping the facial features crisp (we chose a Radius setting of 9 pixels and a Threshold setting of 6 levels for our 300 ppi file). Compare the cheeks and under-eye areas in this image with those in the preceding one.*

C *Finally, we lowered the Opacity of the blur layer and painted with black on the layer mask to reveal some facial details from the underlying layer.*

Here we show you how to soften a skin texture with an extra degree of control. You will apply the Gaussian Blur filter twice, in each case using a mask and a layer blending mode to control the visibility of the smoothing effect, first in the light areas, then in the dark areas.

To smooth skin with the Gaussian Blur filter:

1. Open an RGB photo of a face. **A** Press Ctrl-Alt-J/ Cmd-Option-J, rename the duplicate layer "blur darken," then click OK.

2. Choose Filter > Blur > **Gaussian Blur**. In the dialog, move the cheek or forehead area into view, then move the Radius slider until the skin starts to look smooth and blurry. Press, then release, on the preview to judge the blur effect. **B** Click OK. Don't be concerned that the face now looks too blurry.

3. Choose **Darken** as the blending mode for the "blur darken" layer (to smooth only lighter areas), then lower the layer Opacity until a hint of texture marks reappear in the skin.

4. Alt-click/Option-click the **Add Layer Mask** button ▣ on the Layers panel to add a black mask, and keep the mask thumbnail selected.

5. Choose the **Brush** tool ✎ (B or Shift-B), a Soft Round tip, Normal mode, and 100% Opacity, and press X to make the Foreground color white. Apply strokes to areas where you want to reveal

the smoothing effect, such as on the cheeks and forehead (**A–B**, next page).

If you unintentionally paint over any key features, such as the eyes or eyebrows, press X to make the Foreground color black, and paint over your strokes.

➤ Press [to reduce the brush diameter to paint over small areas, such as between the eyes and brows or between the nose and lips, then press] to enlarge it again.

6. Press Ctrl-Alt-J/Cmd-Option-J to duplicate the "blur darken" layer, rename the duplicate layer "blur lighten," then click OK.

7. Change the blending mode of the "blur lighten" layer to **Lighten** (to smooth only darker areas), then increase or reduce the layer Opacity setting until any dark texture marks on the skin look softer. The skin should now look smoother.

8. To group the top new layers, Shift-click the "blur darken" layer, then press Ctrl-G/Cmd-G (**C–D**, next page).

9. To make the smoothing effect look more realistic and less "plastic" looking, click the group listing, then lower the Opacity of the group until the desired amount of skin texture is revealed.

➤ To hide or show the layer group, click the group listing, then click its visibility icon.

A *In the original image, the pores of the woman's skin look too pronounced.*

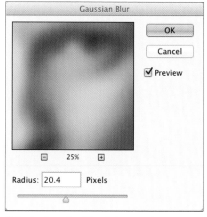

B *In the Gaussian Blur dialog, we chose a Radius value of 20.4 pixels.*

B *The smoothing effect is visible only where we added white areas to the layer mask, and is hidden by the black areas that still cover the rest of the face.*

A *We chose Darken as the blending mode for the "blur darken" layer, lowered the layer Opacity to 70%, clicked the layer mask thumbnail, then applied brush strokes to reveal the smoothing effect on the cheeks, chin, and nose. Because the layer blending mode is Darken, the effect can be seen only in the lighter areas.*

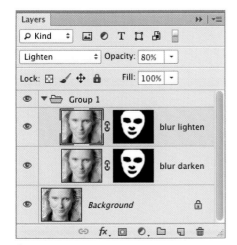

C *We duplicated the "blur darken" layer, renamed the duplicate "blur lighten," chose Lighten as the blending mode, and changed the layer Opacity to 80%. Finally, we put the two blur layers in a group.*

D *Now the skin on the woman's forehead, cheeks, and nose looks smoother, while the key areas (eyes, lips, and hair) are still sharp.*

Retouching by cloning

The Clone Stamp tool clones pixels either within the same document or between documents. Use it to remove distracting elements from an image, such as the metal pipe shown in our example, or to duplicate an element, such as leaves or a texture.

To retouch a photo by cloning imagery:

1. Open an RGB document, **A** and if desired, open a second RGB document from which to clone.

   ➤ If you have two documents open, you can choose a tiling option on the Window > Arrange submenu.

2. Choose the **Clone Stamp** tool 🖰 (S or Shift-S).

3. On the Options bar, do the following: **B**

   On the **Brush Preset** picker, choose a Soft Round brush.

   Choose **Normal** as the blending Mode.

   Choose an **Opacity** percentage.

   Choose a **Flow** percentage to control the rate of application.

   Check **Aligned** to maintain the same distance between the source point and the area that you

click or drag across, even if you release the mouse between strokes (to clone a large area seamlessly); or uncheck Aligned to resample from the original source point each time you release the mouse (to produce repetitive clones of a smaller area).

From the Sample menu, choose **All Layers** to sample pixels from all the visible layers that are directly below the pointer (and send them to the new layer).

Optional: If the source document contains adjustment layers, the effects of which you want the Clone Stamp tool to ignore when sampling (so the effect of the adjustments isn't doubled), activate the Ignore Adjustment Layers When Cloning button. 🖰

Optional: If you have a stylus and tablet, you can activate the Pressure Controls Opacity button 🖰 and/or the Pressure Controls Size button. 🖰

4. Click in the source document (it can be the same document or a second one), then Alt-click/Option-click a source point for Photoshop to sample as replacement pixels. **C** It should look very similar to the area you want to repair.

A *In this image, we want to remove the metal pipes from the side of the building and add more leaves to fill in the front of the trellis.*

C *We Alt/Option clicked with the Clone Stamp tool to sample a blank area of the wall.*

🖰 · | 15 | 🖰 🖰 | Mode: Normal ⬍ | Opacity: 100% ▾ | 🖰 | Flow: 100% ▾ | 🖰 | ☑ Aligned Sample: All Layers

B *We chose these Options bar settings for the Clone Stamp tool.*

5. Click in the target document (it can be the same document as the source or a different one). Create a new, blank layer, and keep it selected.

6. Press [or] to scale the brush, then click or drag in very short strokes to make the cloned pixels appear. A–B Imagery from the source point will display within the brush cursor. Note: If the whole layer displays in the overlay as you clone, show the Clone Source panel, ▦ then check Clipped.

7. *Optional:* To establish a new source point for further cloning, Alt-click/Option-click a different area in the source document. C–D You can also change settings for the Clone Stamp tool between strokes.

➤ To create a "double-exposure" effect, with the original pixels partially remaining, lower the Opacity percentage for the Clone Stamp tool.

➤ To keep track of multiple source documents while using the Clone Stamp tool, use the Clone Source panel (see page 262).

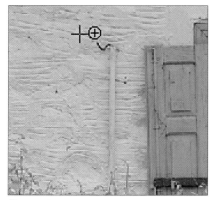

A *We're dragging with the Clone Stamp tool to replace the wire and pipe with pixels from the blank wall.*

➤ *To prevent noticeable (tacky!) seams from appearing in a cloned texture, either apply short strokes or just click, and sample multiple times.*

B *We're continuing to sample the wall and clone away the pipe.*

C *We're sampling the vine leaves because we want to add more leaves to the front of the trellis.*

D *Compare this new, improved image with the original one on the preceding page.*

USING THE CONTENT-AWARE OPTION OF THE SPOT HEALING BRUSH TOOL

For a quick, easy, and powerful way to remove an "object" from a photo, try using the Spot Healing Brush tool, ✎ with its Content-Aware option (Options bar). This tool works better if the object being removed is surrounded by many small random shapes (such as foliage, water, or clouds in a landscape) **A–B** than if the surrounding area contains isolated, distinct objects. This tool and option also work well for repairing tears or scratches in a vintage photo.

A *Our aim is to remove the fire hydrant from this image. For the Spot Healing Brush tool, we chose a brush Hardness of 100% (to let Content-Aware healing blend the edges, not the brush) and Normal mode, and clicked Content-Aware. With a medium-sized brush and one continuous stroke, we covered the hydrant and its shadow.*

B *We sat back while the Spot Healing Brush tool analyzed and sampled pixels from neighboring areas to use as replacement pixels for the hydrant… Poof! This is as easy as retouching gets.*

SAME FEATURE, DIFFERENT RESULTS

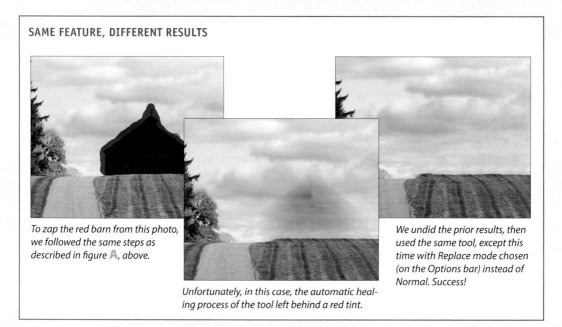

*To zap the red barn from this photo, we followed the same steps as described in figure **A**, above.*

Unfortunately, in this case, the automatic healing process of the tool left behind a red tint.

We undid the prior results, then used the same tool, except this time with Replace mode chosen (on the Options bar) instead of Normal. Success!

Applying a Content-Aware fill

A Content-Aware fill may do a seamless job of removing a distinct shape from a nondistinct background — but then again, it may not. You can touch up the results with the Clone Stamp, Healing Brush, or Patch tool (or undo and use one of those tools instead).

To replace an image element with a Content-Aware fill:

1. Duplicate the Background in an image (Ctrl-J/ Cmd-J), then hide the Background. Keep the duplicate layer selected.

2. *Optional:* Add a layer mask to the layer, and with the Brush tool and Black as the Foreground color, stroke over any areas in the background that you want to prevent Photoshop from sampling as replacement pixels. Click the layer thumbnail.**A**

3. Loosely select the element in the image to be removed, then choose Edit > **Fill**.

4. Choose Use: Content-Aware, Mode: Normal, and Opacity: 100%, then click OK.**B–C**

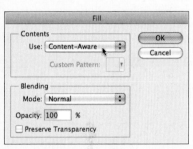

A *Our goal was to eliminate the red shed from this image. To prevent Photoshop from sampling the bushes and rocks on the right side, we hid those areas via a layer mask. Next, we selected the shed loosely with the Lasso tool.*

B *We chose these options in the Fill dialog.*

C *The command removed the shed and filled the selection area with random grass and stone textures — it even replaced a small section of the fence!*

NOT SURE WHICH AREAS TO MASK?

Do a "dry run" through the steps on this page, minus the mask (step 2), and note if there are any unwanted elements that Photoshop included in its calculations. Undo the Fill command, mask any areas that you want the program to ignore, then follow steps 3–4.

Using the Content-Aware Move tool

The Content-Aware Move tool can be used to reposition, or create an extension of, an element in an image. Photoshop will use Content-Aware calculations either to fill in the exposed areas or to camouflage the seams, blending pixels into the texture and colors of the destination area.

To move or reshape an image element with the Content-Aware Move tool: ★

1. Create a new, blank layer and keep it selected.

2. Choose the **Content-Aware Move** tool ⚏ (J or Shift-J). On the Options bar, check **Sample All Layers**.

3. Drag loosely around the object to be moved or extended.**A** To add areas to the selection, hold down Shift while dragging; to subtract areas, hold down Alt/Option while dragging.

4. Do either of the following:

   To move the selected area, choose **Move** from the Mode menu, then drag the selection, preferably to an area that looks like the original setting.**B**

   To extend the object, choose **Extend** from the Mode menu, then drag the selection in the direction in which you want it to be enlarged (**B–C**, next page).

5. The tool sends the selected pixels (and any areas that it filled in) to the new, blank layer. To control how the repositioned and replacement pixels are blended with their surroundings, on the Options bar, choose **Adaptation:** Very Strict, Strict, Medium, Loose, or Very Loose (**A** and **D**, next page). Note: You can change the Adaptation setting only while the selection is still active.

6. Deselect (Ctrl-D/Cmd-D).

➤ To hide (then show) the Content-Aware Move selection border, press Ctrl-H/Cmd-H.

IT'S NOT YOU!

We have made the Content-Aware Fill, Content-Aware Move, and Patch features look almost fail-safe by displaying only our successes. The truth is, we frittered away an afternoon trying these features on many images, with mixed results. Our only successful results were in images that had fairly simple backgrounds.

A *We dragged with the Content-Aware Move tool to loosely select the jogger and his shadow…*

B *… then we dragged the selection content to the right. With Adaptation set to Very Strict, there are obvious patches in the filled-in areas — sand, sea spray, water, and horizon (here, the selection edges are hidden).*

A *With Adaptation set to Medium, the replacement pixels look more seamless. (Admittedly, we got a duplicate mountain in the bargain, but we can clone that out with the Clone Stamp tool.)*

B *With the Content-Aware Move tool, we selected the pastry (more tightly than we selected the dude on the beach, who was on a simpler background).*

C *We set the tool Mode to Extend, dragged upward to create another tier of pastry, then chose Medium as the Adaptation setting. The added crust and filling look slightly distorted.*

D *Here the Adaptation setting of Very Loose blended the new pastry and filling more convincingly, with less distortion. Who doesn't like extra dessert?*

Removing an image element with the Patch tool

Another way to replace an image element is by using the Patch tool with its Content-Aware option. You draw a selection, then drag it to an area for Photoshop to analyze as replacement pixels. To vary the results before deselecting, change the Adaptation setting.

To eliminate an image element with the Patch tool: ★

1. Create a new, blank layer, and keep it selected.

2. Choose the **Patch** tool ⊞ (J or Shift-J).

3. On the Options bar, choose **Patch: Content-Aware** and check **Sample All Layers**.

4. Drag a selection around the area to be removed.**A** You can Shift-drag to add to the selection or Alt-drag/Option-drag to subtract from it.

5. Drag the selection to an area that looks most like the original background behind the object.**B** When you release the mouse, Photoshop will fill in the exposed area based on those sampled pixels.

6. To control how replacement pixels are blended into the image, on the Options bar, choose **Adaptation:** Very Strict, Strict, Medium, Loose, or Very Loose.**C–D** You can change Adaptation options only while the selection is still active.

7. Deselect (Ctrl-D/Cmd-D).

➤ To hide the selection border temporarily (and then to redisplay it), press Ctrl-H/Cmd-H. If you don't like the Patch results, press Ctrl-Z/Cmd-Z, then drag the selection to a different sample area.

A *With the Patch tool set to Content-Aware, we selected the elements to be removed.*

B *Next, we dragged the selection to an area that looked similar to the one around the elements being removed.*

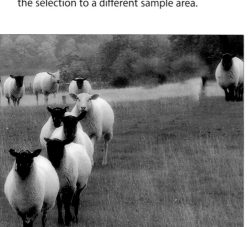

C *With Adaptation set to Very Strict, remnants were left of the original elements (not ruminants, heh-heh…).*

D *With Adaptation set to Very Loose, the replacement pixels make a cleaner, more believable match.*

Photographers use focusing techniques to enhance a scene, such as a shallow depth of field to differentiate a subject from its background or blurriness to convey a sense of motion. In Photoshop, you can imitate these camera techniques, as well as correct distortion problems that arise from the inherent limitations of a camera lens.

In this chapter, you'll blur areas with the Lens Blur filter and the new Iris Blur, Field Blur, and Tilt-Shift filters; correct distortion via the Lens Correction filter; simulate movement via the Motion Blur filter; and apply sharpening via the Sharpen tool and the Smart Sharpen and Unsharp Mask filters.

Applying the Lens Blur filter

In most photos, the foreground is naturally more in focus than the background. If your camera lets you adjust the depth of field via the aperture, or f-stop setting (in other words, it's not a mobile device or "point-and-shoot" type of camera), you can control the degree to which your subject matter stays in focus. Objects that are outside the depth of field — either in front of it or beyond it — will be blurred. Other factors affecting the focus are the zoom setting and the type of camera lens used. With the Lens Blur filter in Photoshop, you can simulate the depth of field that is created by a camera. You will use a mask to control which areas are kept in focus and use dialog options to control the level of blurriness.

To apply the Lens Blur filter:

1. Click an image layer (or duplicate the Background via Ctrl-J/Cmd-J), then click the **Add Layer Mask** button  on the Layers panel.

2. Keep the layer mask thumbnail selected. Choose the **Gradient** tool (G or Shift-G). On the Options bar, click the Linear Gradient button; also click the Gradient picker arrowhead, then click the "Black, White" preset (it's in the default library).

3. To apply the gradient to the mask, drag across the entire document window (e.g., from bottom to top, or diagonally); Shift-drag to constrain the angle.

4. Shift-click the layer mask thumbnail to disable the layer mask. It will be used by the Lens Blur filter, but you need to hide it so it doesn't mask the layer imagery.

Continued on the following page

REFOCUSING

16

5. Click the layer thumbnail, then choose Filter > Blur > **Lens Blur**.

6. The Lens Blur dialog opens.**A** Check Preview, and choose a processing speed for the preview: For a large file, say, larger than 100 MB, click **Faster** (previewing may be slow in a large image), or for a smaller file, you can click **More Accurate** for a higher-quality preview.

7. In the **Depth Map** area, do both of the following:

   From the **Source** menu, choose **Layer Mask** as the source for the depth map. The grayscale values in the source will control which areas remain in focus. (A setting of None would blur the whole image uniformly.)

To set the **Blur Focal Distance**, in the preview, click the area that you want to keep in focus. You can also use the slider to specify which grayscale value (from 0, black, to 255, white) in the depth map will remain in full focus. In either case, you are choosing a grayscale value from the gradient in the layer mask. Shades lighter or darker than this value will become progressively more blurry. You'll see the effect of this after setting the Radius in the next step.

Optional: Check Invert to swap the location where full blurriness occurs with the location where the image is in full focus.

8. In the **Iris** area, use the **Radius** value to control the intensity of the blur. This produces the most

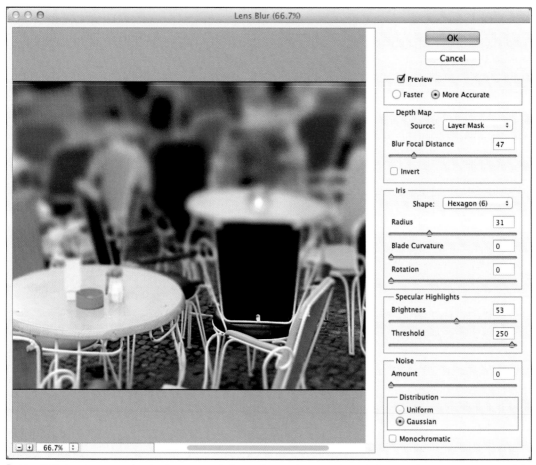

A After Shift-dragging upward in the document with the Gradient tool (starting from the bottom of the image), we opened the Lens Blur dialog.

pronounced effect of all the controls in the dialog. (The other Iris sliders produce photographic-type highlights.) Keep the Shape setting on the default setting of Hexagon (6).

➤ At any time while choosing settings, you can uncheck, then recheck Preview to compare the original and blurred images.

9. Blurring averages the values of neighboring pixels and tends to gray out white specular highlights. In the **Specular Highlights** area, you can use the **Brightness** slider to brighten highlight areas that have become blurred and lower the **Threshold** slider slightly to control the tonal range that the Brightness setting affects. At 255, only pure white pixels will be brightened; at a low setting, most of the blurred areas will be affected.

10. *Optional:* If the original photo contained some noise (texture) that the filter smoothed too much, you can reintroduce it via the Noise: Amount slider; start with a low value. Click Distribution: Uniform (flat noise distribution) or Gaussian, and optionally check Monochromatic to add only grayscale (not color) pixels.

11. Click OK. **A–B**

A *In the original photo, both the foreground and background areas are in focus.*

Light grayscale values are allowing full blurring in this area of the photo.

Intermediate grayscale values are allowing partial blurring in this area of the photo.

Because we chose a dark grayscale value (47) as the Blur Focal Distance, no blurring is occurring in this area of the photo.

B *Using the grayscale values in our mask, the Lens Blur filter is blurring the background of the photo. Our dialog settings are shown on the preceding page; a detail of the mask is shown at right.*

Applying the Field Blur, Iris Blur, and Tilt-Shift filters

The Field Blur, Iris Blur, and Tilt-Shift filters (collectively called the Blur Gallery) provide powerful and flexible on-image and slider controls for blurring targeted areas of an image. Note: Make sure Use Graphics Processor is checked in Preferences > Performance.

To apply the Field Blur, Iris Blur, or Tilt-Shift filter: ★

1. Duplicate the Background or image layer, preferably in an image that is all or mostly in focus.

2. Choose Filter > Blur > **Field Blur** to produce multiple blur areas, **Iris Blur** to blur areas around a focus ellipse, or **Tilt-Shift** to apply blurring in straight bands across portions of the image. (These filters can't be applied to a Smart Object.)

3. A default pin with controls appears in the image, and a Blur Tools panel appears in a dock on the right. On the Options bar, check Preview.

   To control the degree of blurring, either adjust the **Blur** slider in the dock or, in the image, drag around the blur ring that surrounds the pin (add more black to the ring to reduce the blur, or add more white to the ring to increase the blur).

4. For a **Field Blur**, add another pin by clicking in the image, then set the Blur value to 0% (full focus) for one pin and to a higher value for the other pin (blurring). To use the full potential of this filter, add more pins, some with a Blur value of 0 and some with a Blur value greater than 0 (see the example on the next page).

   For an **Iris Blur**, do any of the following: To adjust the diameter of the focus ellipse, drag one of the small outer round handles; to rotate the ellipse, drag outside it (double-arrow pointer); to reposition where the blurring begins, drag one of the feather handles (to move one feather handle separately, drag it while holding down Alt/Option); to change the ellipse to a rounded rectangle, drag the square Roundness knob outward (see the example on page 314).

   For a **Tilt-Shift Blur**, do any of the following: To adjust where the blurring begins, drag either or both of the solid focus lines; to adjust the transition between the in-focus and blurred areas, drag either or both of the dashed feather lines; to rotate the focus area, drag a rotation handle to the left or right (see the example on page 315).

5. You can also do any of the following:

   To **add** a pin, click in the image.

   To **reposition** a pin, drag its center point. You can move a pin outside the canvas area.

   To **delete** a pin, click its center point, then press Backspace/Delete.

   To control the amount of focus within a selected ellipse for Iris Blur, or between the two feather lines for a Tilt-Shift blur, adjust the **Focus** setting on the Options bar.

6. To hide the on-image controls to judge the blurring effect, press and hold down H (then release).

7. *Optional:* To brighten the blur highlights to the point that they become abstract, colored orbs, click a pin, check the box for **Bokeh**, then make any of these adjustments (**A–C**, page 316):

   To control the amount of highlight areas in the bokeh, adjust the **Light Bokeh** slider.

   To control the amount of color variation in the bokeh, adjust the **Bokeh Color** slider.

   To control the brightness values in which the bokeh can appear, drag the **Light Range** sliders. For smaller bokeh spots, position the sliders near each other at one end of the bar or the other.

   For higher-quality bokeh (but slower rendering), check **High Quality** on the Options bar.

8. *Optional:* To save the blur mask that Photoshop created for the filter to an alpha channel, check Save Mask to Channels on the Options bar (see the example on page 317). To preview the mask, press and hold down M.

9. To accept your blur filter edits, press Enter/Return or click OK on the Options bar.

➤ To remove all the pins from the image, click the Remove All Pins button ⟳ on the Options bar.

➤ To switch to a different filter in the Blur Tools panel, uncheck the box for the current filter, then expand the category for the desired one.

➤ Although you could apply more than one of the Blur Gallery filters simultaneously to the same photo, we don't recommend doing so, because it is likely to blur the whole photo. One exception might be to add a small Field Blur ring to an area that's in sharp focus.

A *This is the original image.*

THE FIELD BLUR FILTER ★

Use the Field Blur filter when you need the most flexibility and control in blurring specific areas of an image (such as the hair, arms, and background in the photo on this page), while keeping other (more important) areas in sharp focus.

Use as many pins as you like, but be sure place a few pins with a Blur value of 0% in areas that you want to keep in focus and place other pins with a Blur value between 5% and 100% in areas that you want to blur (the blurring occurs between the high and low values). **A–C** You can reposition any pin individually by dragging it in the image.

LOVE LOVE LOVE ♥

The Field Blur filter is our favorite new feature of Photoshop CS6!

USING A SELECTION WITH A BLUR FILTER

If you create a selection before choosing the Field Blur, Iris Blur, or Tilt-Shift filter, you can use the Selection Bleed slider on the Options bar to control the extent to which the blur settings in the selected areas will bleed (blend) into the unselected areas.

B *We applied the Field Blur filter using a Blur value of 0% for the pins on the woman's face and hands to keep those areas in focus, and Blur values above 10% for the other pins.*

C *This is the result.*

THE IRIS BLUR FILTER ★

The Iris Blur filter applies blurring around a focus ellipse. You can use just a single pin or click in the image to create additional ones.**A–D**

A *This is the original image.*

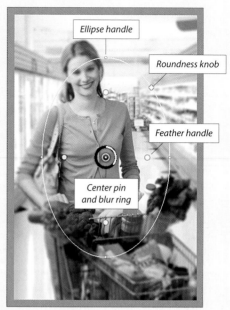

B *We chose the Iris Blur filter. This is the default widget.*

C *We moved the ellipse slightly to the left by dragging the pin, elongated the ellipse, rotated it slightly to match the angle of the figure, then held down Alt/Option and dragged just the top feather handle upward to keep the woman's face in full focus.*

D *In the final image, the figure and part of the shopping cart are in focus, while the background is blurred.*

THE TILT-SHIFT FILTER ★

The Tilt-Shift filter applies blurring in two straight bands across the image, while keeping a band in the center in focus. You can control the width of the blurred area by dragging either or both of the focus lines, adjust the amount of feathering by dragging either or both of the feather lines, or shift the whole widget to a new angle by dragging a rotation handle slightly. **A–C** You can also choose a negative Distortion value to distort a blurred area along imaginary lines that curve around the pin, or a positive value to distort a blurred area along lines that radiate outward from the pin. Additionally, you can check Symmetric Distortion to apply the distortion to both blur areas.

A *This is the original image.*

B *We chose the Tilt-Shift filter settings shown at right, then rotated and dragged the feather and focus lines.*

C *This is the result of our applying the Tilt-Shift filter.*

TILT-SHIFT IN PHOTOGRAPHY

When a small- or medium-format camera is outfitted with a special tilt-shift lens, that lens can be tilted slightly toward a landscape so as to capture the whole scene in focus. This tilt feature can also be used with selective focusing to make the foreground and background blurrier than the midground (an intentional change from what is expected), with the result that the landscape looks miniaturized.

The shift feature of a lens sets the image plane so it is parallel to the subject, thereby preventing buildings or other objects that have parallel planes from converging. This feature can also be used to heighten the convergence deliberately.

BOKEH ★

A *This is the original image.*

B *We created multiple pins for the Field Blur filter, checked Bokeh, increased the Light Bokeh value to brighten the bokeh, increased the Bokeh Color to intensify the color saturation, and moved the Light Range sliders near each other at the right end of the bar to limit the effect to the image highlights.*

Blur Effects	
Bokeh	☑
Light Bokeh:	66%
Bokeh Color:	62%
Light Range:	
179	221

C *This is the final image.*

USING THE MASK FROM A FIELD, IRIS, OR TILT-SHIFT BLUR ★

As stated in step 8 on page 312, you can save the blur mask that Photoshop creates for the Field Blur, Iris Blur, or Tilt-Shift filter to an alpha channel by clicking Save Mask to Channels on the Options bar. After accepting the filter, save your document.

To use the mask, before applying an image edit (such as an adjustment layer, artistic filter, or brush strokes), hold down Ctrl/Cmd and click the alpha channel thumbnail on the Channels panel 🔘 to load the mask as a selection. The selection will protect the nonblurred areas of the layer.A–D

B *We held down Ctrl/Cmd and clicked the alpha channel thumbnail to load the Blur Mask as a selection.*

A *When we applied the Iris Blur filter to this image, we checked Save Mask to Channel.*

C *We created a Color Balance adjustment layer, then moved the Yellow slider to the left to make the image slightly warmer.*

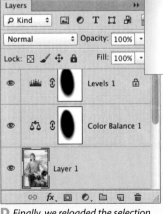

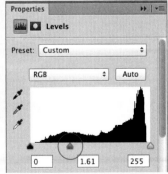

D *Finally, we reloaded the selection, then used a Levels adjustment to lighten the image. The mask on each adjustment layer is hiding the adjustment from the center of the image.*

Applying the Lens Correction filter

The Lens Correction filter lets you correct a photo that shows signs of lens distortion, such as a building or column that tilts away from the camera (called "keystoning"), color fringes along high-contrast edges (chromatic aberration), and under- or overexposure at the edges of a photo (vignetting).

To correct lens distortion:

1. Open an RGB photo. **A** On the Layers panel, click an image layer or duplicate the Background.

2. Right-click the layer to be corrected, and choose **Convert to Smart Object**. (The filter will be applied as a Smart Filter, so as to keep the settings editable.)

3. Choose Filter > **Lens Correction** (Ctrl-Shift-R/Cmd-Shift-R). At the bottom of the dialog, check Preview and uncheck Show Grid.

4. To try an automatic correction first, in the **Auto Correction** tab, from the menus under Search Criteria, choose your **Camera Make** and **Camera Model** (if your model isn't listed, choose All); from the **Lens Model** menu, choose your lens or the closest match to it. On the list of **Lens Profiles**, click the nearest match to your lens. **B**

   Right-click the Lens Profile that you have chosen. If the lens setting was recorded in the camera metadata, that setting (e.g., "28mm, f/4.5, 1 m.") will be chosen automatically. If the correct setting isn't listed, pick a setting that is the closest match to the one that was used to capture the photo.

5. Under Correction, check the problem in the photo that needs correction: **Geometric Distortion**, **Chromatic Aberration**, or **Vignette**.

   Check **Auto Scale Image**, and from the **Edge** menu, choose **Transparency**.

6. If the auto correction wasn't fully successful, uncheck Auto Scale Image, click the **Custom** tab, then do any of the following:

   Under Geometric Distortion, reduce the **Remove Distortion** value to spread the image out (to fix pincushion distortion), or increase this value to pinch the image inward (to fix barrel distortion).

   Use the **Chromatic Aberration** sliders to correct any color fringes along high-contrast edges.

   Use the **Vignette** sliders to correct under- or overexposure at the edges of the image.

7. To evaluate a correction for geometric distortion relative to grid lines, check **Show Grid** (below the preview window). You can change the grid size via the Size slider or change the grid color via the Color swatch.

8. To correct geometric distortion further, under **Transform**, do any of the following:

   Reduce the **Vertical Perspective** value to widen the top of the image (**A**, next page), or increase it to widen the bottom. After doing this, you may need to readjust the Remove Distortion value.

A Lens distortion from the camera caused the columns on the temple to appear as if they're leaning inward.

B Our selection of these settings in the Auto Correction tab of the Lens Correction dialog produced only a minor improvement.

Reduce the **Horizontal Perspective** value to widen the left edge of the image, or increase this value to widen the right edge of the image.

To rotate the image, change the **Angle** via the scrubby slider (it's easier to control than the dial).

➤ Press P to toggle the preview off, then on.

9. *Optional:* In the Custom tab, change the Scale value to scale the layer imagery. Note: You can also crop the image after exiting the dialog.

10. *Optional:* To save your current settings as a preset, from the Manage Settings menu ▼☰ in the Custom tab, choose Save Settings, type a name (keep the .lcs extension and default location),

then click Save; the preset can now be chosen from the Settings menu for any image. If your specific camera lens was detected and selected in step 4, you can save all the settings except the Transform settings as a preset by choosing Set Lens Default from the Manage Settings menu. ▼☰

11. Click OK. **B** To change the Lens Correction settings at any time, double-click the filter listing for the Smart Object on the Layers panel.

➤ From the Settings menu in the Custom tab, you can choose Previous Correction to apply the last-used settings or Default Correction to restore the default values to all the options.

A *To widen the top of the photo, in the Custom tab, we reduced the Remove Distortion value slightly and reduced the Vertical Perspective value.*

FILLING IN THE BLANKS

When you choose Transparency from the Edge menu in the Lens Correction dialog, as we recommend (see step 5), the filter may produce a transparent area on the layer. To fill it with an extension of the image, rasterize a copy of the Smart Object (Layer > Rasterize > Smart Object), hide the Smart Object, loosely select the transparent area, then apply Edit > Fill (Use: Content-Aware option).

B *Now the columns look more vertical. (To fill in the transparent areas that resulted, we followed the method described in the sidebar at left.)*

Applying the Motion Blur filter

One way photographers capture the blur of motion (e.g., when shooting athletes or wildlife) is by panning the camera in the direction the subject is moving. In Photoshop, you can create an illusion of motion in an existing photo via the Motion Blur filter. In this task, you will blur the whole image by applying the filter to a Smart Object, then partially reveal the original layer by editing the filter mask.

To apply the Motion Blur filter to an area of an image:

1. Click an image layer, then duplicate it by pressing Ctrl-J/Cmd-J.

2. Right-click the duplicate layer and choose **Convert to Smart Object.** (The filter will be applied as a Smart Filter, so as to keep the settings editable.)

3. Choose Filter > Blur > **Motion Blur.** The Motion Blur dialog opens.

4. Lower the zoom level for the preview. Choose a **Distance** value for the amount of blurring, choose an **Angle** value to apply the blur in the direction in which you think the subject was moving, then click OK.**B–C**

5. On the Layers panel, click the filter mask thumbnail for the Smart Filters listing.

6. Choose the **Brush** tool ✏ (B or Shift-B). On the Options bar, choose a Soft Round brush and an Opacity value between 50% and 80%. Choose black as the Foreground color.

7. Set the brush diameter by pressing [or], then paint over the area of the image from which you want to hide the Motion Blur effect and to which you want to restore the original focus (**A–B**, next page).

   Because the brush isn't at full opacity, you can apply more strokes to the same area to hide more of the motion blur.

   If you mask too much of the Motion Blur effect, paint with white (press X) to reveal it again.

➤ To change the Motion Blur filter settings, double-click the Smart Filter listing on the Layers panel.

➤ Don't remove the blur effect from the wheels of a moving vehicle in a photo. You want the wheels to look as if they're in motion.

A *This is the original photo.*

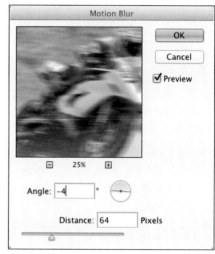

B *In the Motion Blur dialog, we chose a Distance value of 64 px and set the Angle dial to match the angle of the motorcycle.*

C *The Motion Blur filter is applied to the whole image.*

B *The final results convey fast motion.*

A *We clicked the filter mask thumbnail on the Layers panel, then applied strokes with black to hide the Motion Blur effect from the top part of the motorcyclist.*

Using the Sharpen tool

When used with the Protect Detail option checked on the Options bar, the Sharpen tool enhances details without introducing noticeable artifacts. With this tool, you can sharpen areas selectively without having to use a mask. Note: To sharpen an entire image, see the remaining pages in this chapter.

To use the Sharpen tool:

1. Create a new, blank layer to contain the sharpened pixels, and keep it selected.**C**
2. Choose the **Sharpen** tool △ (it's on the same fly-out menu as the Blur tool).
3. On the Options bar, choose a **Strength** value, and check **Sample All Layers** and **Protect Detail**.
4. Press [or] to adjust the brush diameter, then drag across the areas that need sharpening.**D** For stronger sharpening, drag again in the same area.
5. *Optional:* To reduce the overall effect of the sharpening, lower the opacity of the new layer.

C *The focus in this photo is soft.*

D *With the Sharpen tool, we quickly sharpened just her eyes.*

Applying the Smart Sharpen filter

Most digital photos need to be sharpened, and the need increases if you change a file's dimensions or resolution with the Resample Image option checked, convert a file to CMYK Color mode, or apply a transformation command.

To sharpen an image, you can use either the Smart Sharpen filter or the Unsharp Mask filter (the latter, despite its name, has a sharpening effect; see pages 325–326). Be aware that these filters can introduce noise to an image and therefore should be applied when you've finished making all your crop, transform, and Image Size changes, and image-editing, adjustment, and color correction work.

High-resolution commercial printing also causes some minor blurring due to dot gain. You can anticipate and compensate for this by sharpening the image again as you prepare it for output. With practice, you will learn how much sharpening is needed.

The Smart Sharpen filter has several unique features that you won't find in the Unsharp Mask dialog (see the sidebar below), but both are powerful and indispensable commands. We typically use the Smart Sharpen filter for targeted sharpening and the Unsharp Mask filter for output sharpening. The main point is to remember to sharpen, period!

To apply the Smart Sharpen filter:

1. Open a photo that needs sharpening. A To protect the original layer, on the Layers panel, click an image layer or the Background, then press Ctrl-J/Cmd-J to duplicate it. Right-click the duplicate layer and choose **Convert to Smart Object**.

2. Choose Filter > Sharpen > **Smart Sharpen**. The Smart Sharpen dialog opens. Move it out of the way if it's blocking your document.

   ➤ Set the zoom level for the preview to 67% or 100%. To bring a different area of the image into view, either drag in the preview or click in the document.

3. Check **More Accurate** to allow the filter to process the image in multiple passes, for high-quality sharpening with less distortion. This will take longer but is worth the wait.

4. From the **Remove** menu, choose an algorithm for the correction: Gaussian Blur is an adequate, all-purpose choice; Lens Blur sharpens details with fewer resulting halos (we prefer this option); Motion Blur is useful for correcting blurring due to slight movement of the camera or

---

SMART FEATURES OF THE SMART SHARPEN FILTER

➤ With Smart Sharpen, you can sharpen (then fade the sharpening) separately in the shadow and highlight areas of an image.

➤ With its More Accurate option checked, Smart Sharpen applies sharpening in multiple passes, for better results.

➤ Smart Sharpen detects edges, and therefore produces fewer color halos than Unsharp Mask.

➤ Smart Sharpen lets you choose from three algorithms (to correct Gaussian blur, lens blur, or motion blur), whereas Unsharp Mask corrects only Gaussian blur.

➤ Smart Sharpen lets you save and reuse your settings, for greater speed and consistency in your workflow.

A *We'll use the Smart Sharpen filter to sharpen specific tonal areas in this blurry portrait (the resolution of this image is 300 ppi).*

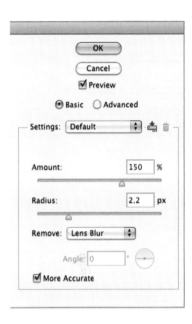

A *The settings we chose in the Basic panel of the Smart Sharpen dialog (shown above) successfully sharpened key details in the photo, such as the eyes and lips, but in the process, also oversharpened the skin (now the pores look too pronounced).*

subject, but to use this option effectively, you need to enter the correct angle of movement.

5. Try an **Amount** value of 60–150% for the degree to which contrast will be increased, and a **Radius** value between 1 and 2.2 pixels (for a high-resolution image). The image should now look slightly oversharpened. **A** You'll fade the effect next.

6. To control the amount of sharpening specifically in the shadow and highlight areas, click **Advanced**, then click the **Shadow** tab. **B** Drag in the preview to display an area of the image that contains both shadows and midtones, then make these adjustments:

Choose a **Radius** value (between 5 and 10) to control how many neighboring pixels will be compared to each adjusted pixel. The higher the Radius, the larger the area that Photoshop compares.

Choose a **Tonal Width** value to control the range of midtones that are affected by the Fade Amount. In other words, the higher the Tonal Width, the wider the range of midtones that are affected and the more gradually the sharpening fades into the shadows.

Continued on the following page

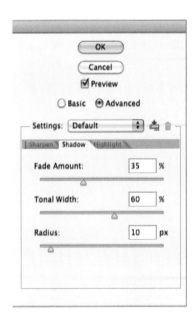

B *In the Shadow tab (Advanced panel), we chose a moderate Fade Amount to soften the sharpening in the shadows (such as on the right side of her face) and a moderate Tonal Width value to fully sharpen the shadows but only partially sharpen the midtones.*

Move the **Fade Amount** slider until you see the desired reduction of oversharpening in the shadows. Note: If the Tonal Width value is too low, the effectiveness of this slider will be limited.

7. Click the **Highlight** tab.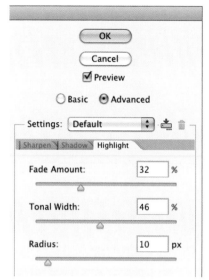 Drag the image in the preview to display an area that contains both highlights and midtones. Adjust the **Radius**, **Tonal Width**, and **Fade Amount** values, as you did in the preceding step.

8. To compare the unsharpened and sharpened versions of the image, press on the dialog preview, then release. Hopefully, just the key details or features of the image are now sharp. If the whole image now looks too sharp, click the **Sharpen** tab and reduce the **Amount** value slightly.

9. Click OK.**B–C**

➤ To save the current settings as a preset, click the Save a Copy button 🖫 in the dialog, enter a name, then click OK. Saved presets are available on the Settings menu for any image.

➤ To modify the Smart Sharpen results, double-click the Smart Sharpen listing for the Smart Object.

A *Finally, in the Highlight tab of the Smart Sharpen dialog, we chose a moderate Fade Amount to soften the sharpening in the broad, flat highlight areas of skin, and we chose a moderate Tonal Width value to fully sharpen the highlights and partially sharpen the light midtones.*

B *Compare this original image to the final image shown at right.*

C *The Smart Sharpen filter improved the clarity of the facial features without applying unflattering sharpening to the cheeks and forehead.*

Applying the Unsharp Mask filter

In order to do its job of sharpening, the Unsharp Mask filter increases the contrast between adjacent pixels. To control the level of contrast, you will choose settings for three variables: Amount, Radius, and Threshold.

To apply the Unsharp Mask filter:

1. Choose a zoom level of 50–100% for your image.

2. Duplicate an image layer (Ctrl-J/Cmd-J),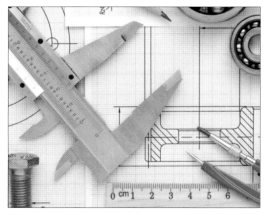 then right-click the duplicate layer and choose **Convert to Smart Object**.

3. With the Smart Object layer selected, choose Filter > Sharpen > **Unsharp Mask**.

4. In the dialog, choose an **Amount** percentage to control how much the contrast will be increased.**B** For some recommended settings, see the sidebar on this page.

   ➤ Press P to toggle the Preview off, then on, to compare the original and sharpened images. To bring a different area of the image into view, drag in the preview or click in the document.

5. The **Radius** controls how many neighboring pixels around high-contrast edges the filter affects. When choosing a Radius value, you need to consider the pixel count of the image and its subject matter. The higher the pixel count, the higher the Radius value needed.**C** For a low-contrast image that contains large, simple objects and smooth transitions, try a high Radius of 2; for an intricate, high-contrast image that contains many sharp transitions, try a lower Radius of around 1.

Continued on the following page

SUGGESTED SETTINGS FOR UNSHARP MASK

For an image that is 2000 x 3000 pixels or larger, try using these values:

Soft-edged subjects, such as landscapes	Amount 100–150, Radius 1–1.5, Threshold 6–10
Portraits	Amount 100–120, Radius 1–2, Threshold 4–6, or to the point that skin areas begin to look smoother
Buildings, objects, etc. for which contrast is a priority	Amount 150–200 or more, Radius 1.5–3, Threshold 0–3

A This original 300 ppi image is slightly blurry.

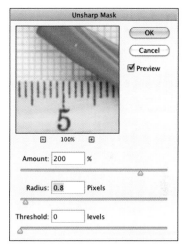

B A high Amount value and a low Radius value for the Unsharp Mask filter barely sharpened the image.

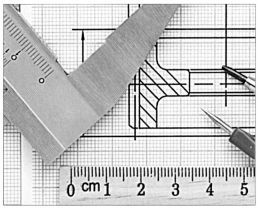

C A high Radius value of 4.0, on the other hand, produced ugly halos around the numerals on the ruler and on the blue lines of the graph paper.

Note: The Amount and Radius settings are interdependent, meaning if you raise the Radius, you'll need to lower the Amount, and vice versa.

6. Choose a **Threshold** value to establish how different in value an area of pixels must be from an adjacent area for the filter to affect it.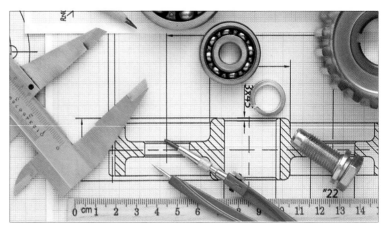 Start with a Threshold value of 0 (to sharpen the entire image), then increase it gradually. At a Threshold of 5–10, high-contrast areas will be sharpened and areas of lesser contrast will be sharpened much less. When increasing the Threshold, you can also increase the Amount and Radius to sharpen the edges. A proper Threshold setting will prevent the filter from oversharpening low-contrast areas.

7. Click OK.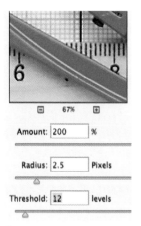 To adjust the filter settings at any time, double-click the Unsharp Mask listing on the Layers panel.

➤ If the sharpening produced color halos along the edges of some of the objects, choose Luminosity as the blending mode for the Smart Object. This mode will limit the sharpening to luminosity (light and dark) values and remove it from hue and saturation (color) values.

A At a high Threshold value of 12, the Unsharp Mask filter sharpened only the high-contrast edges, and the lines on the graph paper are still slightly blurry.

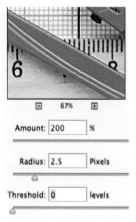
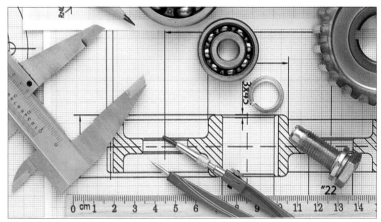

B A Threshold value of 0–1 properly sharpened all the edges. A low Threshold value was necessary for this image, because it contains a lot of flat surfaces, hard edges, and fine linear details.

Now that you're familiar with many of the basic controls in Photoshop, it's time to explore some fun commands that can be applied to layers. In this chapter, you will learn how to clip (hide the visibility of) multiple layers using a mask, blend pixels between layers using advanced controls, apply transformation commands to a layer (including normal and Content-Aware scaling), apply the Puppet Warp and Warp commands, and apply the Liquify filter.

Note: To speed the preview of edits of the transform, Puppet Warp, Liquify, and Warp commands, check Use Graphics Processor in Preferences > Performance. ★

Using clipping masks

When layers are put into a clipping mask, the content of the bottommost layer, called the "base" layer, clips (limits which areas are visible on) the layers above it. The mode and opacity of the base layer are also applied to the clipped layers. You can edit or reposition individual layers in a clipping mask at any time, including the base layer. If you use type as the base layer, you can warp it via the Warp Text command (it will remain fully editable).

To create a clipping mask:

1. On the Layers panel, make sure the layers to be clipped are listed consecutively. The base layer can be a type, image, or shape layer or a Smart Object; stack it below the layers to be clipped.**A**

2. Do either of the following:

   Click a layer to be clipped, or Shift-click multiple layers to be clipped (not the base layer) (**A**, next page), then press Ctrl-Alt-G/Cmd-Option-G (**B–C**, next page).

Continued on the following page

17

IN THIS CHAPTER

YUM YUM

To create the image shown above, we used a type layer to clip an image layer (see this page and next), warped the type (see page 340) and applied the Emboss, Stroke, and Outer Glow effects (see Chapter 20). We duplicated the type and image layers, moved the duplicate type layer downward, then added a Pattern Fill layer just above the Background. To see a picture of the Layers panel for this image and a few related tips, see our blog at elaineandpeter.com.

A *This document contains five layers (including an editable type layer that is currently hidden behind the image layers).*

To clip one layer at a time, Alt-click/Option-click the line between two layers (the pointer becomes a square next to a downward pointing arrow), or right-click one of the layers to be clipped (not the base layer) and choose Create Clipping Mask.

3. *Optional:* To include more layers in the mask, either restack them between existing layers in the mask or repeat the preceding step.

➤ To use grouped layers in a clipping mask, all the layers (including the base layer) must be in the group.

➤ To reposition two or more clipped layers, Ctrl-click/Cmd-click their listings, then hold down the V key to spring-load the Move tool and drag in the document.D

When you release a layer from a clipping mask, any and all of the masked layers above it are also released.

To release one or more layers from a clipping mask:

Do either of the following:

Alt-click/Option-click the line below the layer to be released.

Click a layer to be released (not the base layer), then press Ctrl-Alt-G/Cmd-Option-G.

To release an entire clipping mask:

Alt-click/Option-click the line above the base layer.

Click the layer directly above the base layer, then press Ctrl-Alt-G/Cmd-Option-G.

➤ To merge clipped layers, see pages 148–149.

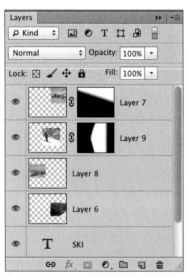

A *We Shift-clicked four layers …*

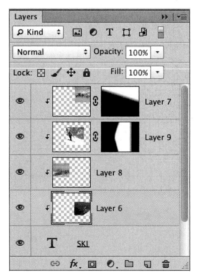

B *… then pressed Ctrl-Alt-G/ Cmd-Option-G to put them in a clipping group. The base layer name has an underline, whereas the clipped layers are indented.*

C *The type (base) layer is clipping the four image layers (it's a "ski mask," ha-ha).*

D *We selected and moved the clipped image layers to the left with the Move tool, while the base layer stayed put.*

Blending layers

In these steps, you'll edit a duplicate image layer, then blend the original and duplicate layers via the Opacity and blending mode controls on the Layers panel. You can use this method to soften the effect of a filter or other image edits or simply to see how various blending modes or Opacity settings affect your document.

To blend a modified layer with the original one:

1. On the Layers panel, click an image layer, then press Ctrl-J/Cmd-J to duplicate it.

2. *Optional:* If you want to apply a filter as an editable Smart Filter (next step), right-click the duplicate image layer and choose Convert to Smart Object (see page 344).

3. Apply some creative edits to the duplicate layer, such as brush strokes or a filter. A (To learn about the Filter Gallery, see pages 342–343.)

4. Keep the duplicate layer selected, then on the Layers panel, do either or both of the following:

   Choose a different **blending mode**. You can press Shift - – or Shift- + to cycle through the blending modes.

   Adjust the **Opacity** for the desired level of transparency. B–C

A *We duplicated the Background in this image, converted the duplicate layer to a Smart Object, then applied the Ocean Ripple filter.*

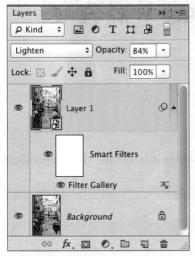

B *We chose Lighten mode for Layer 1 and lowered the layer Opacity to 84%.*

C *The final image combines characteristics of the original Background and the filtered Smart Object.*

330 | Chapter 17

The Advanced Blending options in the Layer Style dialog let you control how a layer blends with underlying layers. Here, we'll focus on the Blend If sliders.

To choose blending options for a layer:

1. Double-click next to the name of a layer or layer group on the Layers panel, **A–B** or right-click a layer or group and choose **Blending Options** from the context menu.

2. The Layer Style dialog opens (Blending Options should be selected in the upper left). Check Preview.

   The first three controls — Blend Mode, Opacity, and Fill Opacity — are the same as on the Layers panel. (The Fill Opacity changes the layer opacity without altering the opacity of any layer effects. To learn about layer effects, see Chapter 20.)

3. Use the **Blend If** sliders to control which pixels in the current layer stay visible and which pixels from the underlying layer show through the current layer:

A *We opened a photo of a surface texture, then created some editable type in a dark color.*

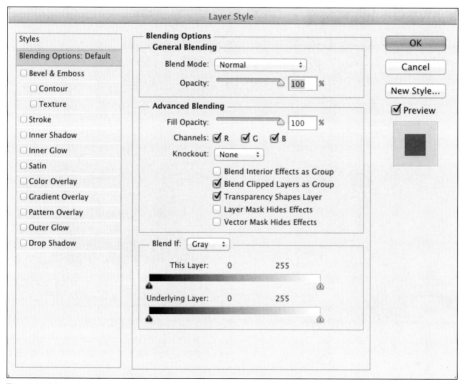

B *We double-clicked the type layer name to open the Layer Style dialog.*

Move the black **This Layer** slider to the right to drop out shadow areas from the current layer.

Move the white **This Layer** slider to the left to drop out highlight areas from the current layer.

Move the black **Underlying Layer** slider to the right to reveal shadow areas from the underlying layer.**A**

Move the white **Underlying Layer** slider to the left to reveal highlight areas from the underlying layer.

To adjust midtone colors separately from the lightest and darkest colors, Alt-drag/Option-drag a slider (it will divide in two).**B**

4. Click OK. On the Layers panel, the layer will have this badge, 🔲 indicating that the Advanced Blending options currently have nondefault settings. ★

➤ To display only layers that contain nondefault Advanced Blending settings, choose Attribute from the Filter Type menu on the Layers panel, and Advanced Blending from the second menu. ★

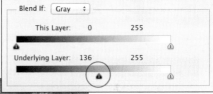

A In the Blend If area of the Layer Style dialog, we dragged the black Underlying Layer slider to the right. Dark colors from the texture layer now show through the type layer.

B Next, we held down Alt/Option and dragged the Underlying Layer sliders to enable midtone colors from the underlying texture layer to show through the type layer. Now the type looks as if it's been worn away by the elements.

Applying transformations

You can apply scale, rotate, skew, distort, and perspective transformations to a layer or layer group, among other things (see the sidebar at right). We'll show you how to apply multiple transformations via the Free Transform command and the Move tool — the methods we find to be the most intuitive.

Note: To help preserve the image quality, if you need to apply multiple transformations, do them consecutively and accept the edits only after the last one; Photoshop will resample the image data just once.

To apply transformations using the Free Transform command or the Move tool:

1. On the Layers panel, click a layer, a Smart Object, a layer group, or the Background, or Shift-select multiple layers.**A** Any layers that are linked to the one(s) you have selected will also be transformed.

   To transform the Background, you *must* create a selection, you must use the Free Transform command in step 3 (not the Move tool), and you need to choose a Background color (Photoshop will fill any exposed areas with that color).

2. *Optional:* If you clicked a single image layer, you can create a selection to limit which area is transformed.

3. Do either of the following:

   Choose Edit > **Free Transform**, or for a shape layer, choose Edit > **Free Transform Path** (Ctrl-T/Cmd-T).

   Choose the **Move** tool (V), check **Show Transform Controls** on the Options bar, then click any handle on the transform box to display transform features on the Options bar.

4. If you chose the Free Transform command, you can select a resampling method from the **Interpolation** menu (Options bar) (not available for a shape layer or Smart Object). Choose Bicubic Automatic to let Photoshop use the most suitable method. ★

5. A transform box with handles now surrounds either the whole selection or just the opaque part of the layer. Do one or more of the following:

   To **scale** the item horizontally and vertically, drag a corner handle; to scale it just horizontally or vertically, drag a side handle; to scale it proportionally, Shift-drag a corner handle; or to scale it from the current reference point (represented by crosshairs in the transform box), Alt-drag/Option-drag a handle (add Shift to scale it proportionally from the reference point).**B**

WHAT CAN I TRANSFORM?

You can transform any of the following: an image, type, or shape layer; a layer group; a Smart Object; a selection of pixels on an image layer or on the Background; or the white area in an alpha channel. Note that you can scale, rotate, or skew an editable type layer, but in order to apply a distortion or perspective transformation to type, you must rasterize it first (see page 368). To transform a selection border (not the contents), choose Select > Transform Selection. Read about the Snap Vector Tools and Transforms to Pixel Grid preference on page 434. ★

USING SMART GUIDES

Check View > Extras and View > Show > Smart Guides. As you apply a transformation, you can snap the edge of the transform box to a Smart Guide, which will display as your pointer nears the edge or middle of the contents of another layer.

A *This is the original image.*

B *We selected the car, then copied it to a new layer. Here, we're scaling the new layer.*

To **rotate** it, position the pointer outside the transform box (the pointer becomes a curved, two-headed arrow), then drag. Shift-drag to constrain the rotation to a multiple of 15°.

To **skew** it, Ctrl-drag/Cmd-drag a side handle. Include Shift to constrain the movement.

To **distort** it, Ctrl-drag/Cmd-drag a corner handle.**A–B**

To apply **perspective**, Ctrl-Alt-Shift-drag/Cmd-Option-Shift-drag a corner handle along the horizontal or vertical axis (the pointer becomes an arrowhead, and an adjacent corner also moves).**C**

➤ As you perform a transformation, a dynamic readout that lists the dimensions or angle of your edits displays next to the pointer. ★ To undo the last handle edit, choose Edit > Undo.

6. To resume normal editing, you must either accept or cancel the transformation:

To accept the edit(s), double-click inside the bounding box, press Enter/Return, or click the Commit Transform button ✔ on the Options bar.

To cancel the edit(s), press Esc or click the Cancel Transform button.🚫

➤ Before dragging a handle, you can drag the reference point, from which the layer or selection is transformed, to a new location.

MORE TRANSFORM SHORTCUTS

EDIT	METHOD
Transform a duplicate of a selected layer*	Hold down Alt/Option and choose Edit > Free Transform (or Edit > Free Transform Path)
Repeat the last transformation (the repeat transformation is added to the last one)	Choose Edit > Transform (or Edit > Transform Path) > Again or press Ctrl-Shift-T/Cmd-Shift-T
Repeat the last transformation and duplicate the current layer*	Press Control-Alt-Shift-T/Cmd-Option-Shift-T

If applied to a vector shape layer, Photoshop combines the transformed duplicate with the existing shape.

B *We're applying a distort transformation.*

A *This is the original shape layer.*

C *We're applying a perspective transformation.*

APPLYING TRANSFORMATIONS VIA THE OPTIONS BAR

When you choose the Edit > Free Transform command (Ctrl-T/Cmd-T), transform controls become available on the Options bar (you can enter specific values or use the scrubby sliders). If you want to change the reference point from which a transformation occurs, click a square on the Reference Point locator.

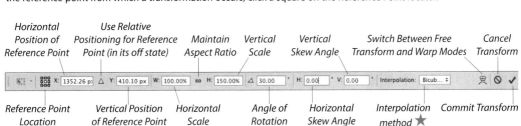

Horizontal Position of Reference Point   *Use Relative Positioning for Reference Point (in its off state)*   *Maintain Aspect Ratio*   *Vertical Scale*   *Vertical Skew Angle*   *Switch Between Free Transform and Warp Modes*   *Cancel Transform*

Reference Point Location   *Vertical Position of Reference Point*   *Horizontal Scale*   *Angle of Rotation*   *Horizontal Skew Angle*   *Interpolation method* ★   *Commit Transform*

Applying Content-Aware scaling

The standard transform features in Photoshop scale an entire layer uniformly, regardless of the layer content. The Content-Aware Scale command is fairly smart in that it tries to scale background areas without distorting shapes that have clearly defined borders, such as figures or objects. You can help protect areas from distortion by creating and using an alpha channel.

To apply Content-Aware scaling:

1. Duplicate an image layer to be scaled, then hide the original layer (**A**, next page).

2. *Optional:* To minimize distortion in an area of the layer, select that area, then on the Channels panel, click the Save Selection as Channel button. Deselect.

3. Choose Edit > **Content-Aware Scale** (Ctrl-Alt-Shift-C/Cmd-Option-Shift-C).

4. On the Options bar, do either of the following:

   If you created an alpha channel (step 2, above), select the channel name from the **Protect** menu.

   If the image contains figures, check the **Protect Skin Tones** button 🏃 to help prevent distortion. Note that this feature does a better job of recognizing skin than clothing.

5. Slowly drag a handle on the bounding box (**B**, next page), or Shift-drag a corner handle for proportional scaling.

6. *Optional:* To permit some normal (non Content-Aware) scaling, lower the Amount below 100%. The lower the Amount, the greater the distortion and the less protective the effect of the alpha channel.

7. To accept the transformation, press Enter/Return or click the Commit Transform button ✔ on the Options bar (**C–D**, next page). To cancel the edits, press Esc or click the Cancel Transform button. ⊘

➤ You can't apply the Content-Aware Scale command to an adjustment, type, shape, or video layer, or to a layer mask, multiple selected layers, a layer group, or a Smart Object.

➤ To specify the stationary point from which the layer is scaled, click a square on the reference point locator.

➤ To scale the layer based on a percentage of its original size, enter a W (width) or H (height) percentage. Activate the Maintain Aspect Ratio button 🔗 first to scale proportionally.

PROTECTING AREAS FROM SCALING

We selected the buildings in this image, then saved the selection as an alpha channel.

We chose the Content-Aware Scale command, selected the channel name from the Protect menu, then dragged the middle right handle of the bounding box to the left.

The channel protected the buildings while allowing the rest of the image to be scaled.

A *This is the original image.*

B *We chose Edit > Content-Aware, then dragged a side handle to the left.*

C *The figures scaled less than the surrounding landscape.*

D *For comparison, we scaled the original image with the Move tool instead of the Content-Aware Scale command. The whole picture looks squashed, including the figures.*

Applying the Puppet Warp command

With the Puppet Warp command, you stretch or bend areas of a layer by dragging pins on a mesh, as you might pull the strings of a puppet.

To apply the Puppet Warp command:

1. Duplicate an image layer or the Background. To warp an object or figure without its background, duplicate a layer that contains imagery and transparency. To keep the warp results editable, convert the duplicate layer to a Smart Object.

2. Choose Edit > **Puppet Warp**.

3. On the Options bar, choose these settings:

   A **Mode** option to control the elasticity of the mesh: Rigid for limited 2-dimensional distortion, Normal for 2-dimensional distortion across a larger area, or Distort for 3-dimensional distortion and scaling.

   A **Density** option to control the spacing of points in the mesh: Fewer Points for a faster but less precise warp; Normal for an average number of points; or More Points for a warp that takes longer to process but is more precise.

   An **Expansion** value to expand or contract the mesh, and therefore the total area that is warped.

   Optional: Uncheck Show Mesh.

4. In the document, click to set pins in both the areas to be warped and the areas that you want to anchor in place.**A**

5. Drag any individual pin,**B** or to move multiple pins, Shift-click them first (selected pins have a white dot in the center) (see also **A–D**, next page).

6. To apply rotation, do either of the following:

   Click one pin, choose **Auto** from the **Rotate** menu on the Options bar, then drag the pin. The angle of rotation changes as you drag.

   To rotate imagery around a pin, click the pin, position the cursor near (but not over) it, hold down Alt/Option, and when a circle with handles appears, drag in a circular direction. The Rotate menu for that pin will now be set to **Fixed** and the angle of rotation won't change, even if you drag that pin or a different one. To unfix the rotation angle of a pin at any time, click it, then choose Auto from the Rotate menu.

7. *Optional:* To remove a pin and its warp effect, Alt-click/Option-click it (scissors pointer). To remove all the pins, click the Remove All Pins button on the Options bar, or right-click in the image and choose Remove All Pins.

8. To hide the mesh, if showing, press Ctrl-H/Cmd-H. To hide all the pins temporarily, press and hold H.

9. Make any further adjustments, then press Enter/Return or click the Commit Puppet Warp button ✔ (Options bar). (To cancel the warp, press Esc.)

   Note: Because you applied the Puppet Warp command to a Smart Object, you can double-click the Puppet Warp listing on the Layers panel at any time to edit the warp.

➤ To move a shape (e.g., an extremity on a figure) in front of or behind another extremity, click its pin, then click the Pin Depth: Set Pin Forward or Set Pin Backward button on the Options bar.

A *To reshape the feather in this photo, we duplicated the image layer, chose the Puppet Warp command, then clicked to set pins on and around the feather.*

B *We Shift-clicked four pins, then dragged one of the selected pins upward to elongate the feather.*

APPLYING THE PUPPET WARP COMMAND

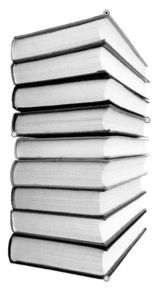

A *To add some character to this boring stack of books (not the books, mind you, the photo!), we copied a selection of just the books to a separate layer, chose the Puppet Warp command, then clicked to set four pins.*

B *To accentuate the perspective, we dragged the top and bottom pins away from each other (one at a time), with the pins on the sides serving as anchors.*

C *We deleted the pin from the middle right side and added a pin to the upper-left corner.*

We pivoted the stack of books around the two unselected stationary pins on the right side.

D *Finally, to bend and rotate the books, we simultaneously dragged two pins (shown in the highlight circles) toward the right.*

Using the Liquify filter

Using the tools in the Liquify dialog (preferably with restraint), you can slim or reshape a waistline, chin, or oddly shaped clothing — instant liposuction! If only dieting were this easy …

To use the distortion tools in Liquify:

1. Open an RGB image. **A** Duplicate the Background, and keep the duplicate layer selected. Note: If you copy a selection of pixels to a separate layer, you won't have to worry about protecting background areas.

2. Choose Filter > **Liquify** (Ctrl-Shift-X/Cmd-Shift-X). In the dialog, check Advanced Mode ★ and zoom in on the area to be reshaped.

3. Click the **Twirl Clockwise** tool 🌀 (C), **Pucker** tool 🗇 (S), **Bloat** tool 🔵 (B), or **Push Left** tool ⋙ (O).

4. Under **Tool Options** on the right side of the dialog, do all of the following:

   To control the amount of feathering and soften the distortion that occurs at the edge of the brush, set the **Brush Density**.

   To control the strength of the distortion, set the **Brush Pressure**.

   To control the speed at which the distortion occurs, choose a **Brush Rate**.

   If you're using a stylus (recommended), check **Stylus Pressure** and lower the Brush Pressure value.

5. Press [or] to size the brush cursor so that it covers the width of the area to be edited. ★ (The maximum diameter for brushes is larger in CS6. ★)

6. To use the Push Left tool to push areas to the right (e.g., to slim down the left edge of a waistline), drag downward; **B** or to push areas to the left, drag upward. **C–D** Repeat, if necessary. To push pixels in the opposite direction from the default behavior, hold down Alt/Option while dragging.

   If you're using the Twirl Clockwise, Pucker, or Bloat tool, click and hold on an area. Repeat for a stronger effect (**A**, next page).

7. To compare the Liquify layer with the original Background, check **Show Backdrop** and choose All Layers from the Use menu.

8. Click OK (**B**, next page). If you want to intensify the results, reapply the last Liquify filter edits by pressing Ctrl-F/Cmd-F immediately. ★

A *The shirt and pants on this fellow are billowing out in a rather unflattering way.*

B *With the Push Left tool, we dragged downward along the left side of the shirt a few times (here the Show Backdrop option is on).*

C *Next, we dragged upward with the same tool (smaller brush size) on the right side of the shirt…*

D *…and the hip area (here the Show Backdrop option is off).*

There are several ways to restore layer pixels to their original, pre-Liquify state.

To remove individual Liquify edits:

Do either of the following:

Under Reconstruct Options, click **Reconstruct**. In the Revert Reconstruction dialog, set the Amount slider to 100% to undo the edits fully or a lesser value to undo the edits partially.★

Choose the **Reconstruct** tool ![tool icon] (R), then press and hold on the areas to be restored.

To remove all of your Liquify edits:

Click **Restore All** (or Cancel out of the dialog).

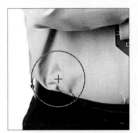 

A *With the Pucker tool, we clicked and held the mouse down on the billowy shirt to contract it inward.*

B *This image contains all of our Liquify edits.*

PROTECTING AREAS OF AN IMAGE FROM LIQUIFY EDITS

► To paint a mask to protect areas of an image from distortion (or to add to an existing mask), choose the Freeze Mask tool ![icon] (F), choose settings under Tool Options (e.g., a maximum Brush Pressure setting), then draw strokes over areas in the preview. You can show or hide the mask via the Show Mask check box.

► To remove areas of the mask, choose the Thaw Mask tool ![icon] (D), then draw strokes on areas in the preview.

► To apply a mask based on a selection, layer transparency, a layer mask, or an alpha channel (and thereby prevent those areas from being edited), choose that option from the first menu under Mask Options.

► To reload the last-used mesh, click Load Last Mesh.★

► To reverse the masked and unmasked areas, click Invert All.

► To unmask the entire image at any time (make all the pixels editable again), click None.

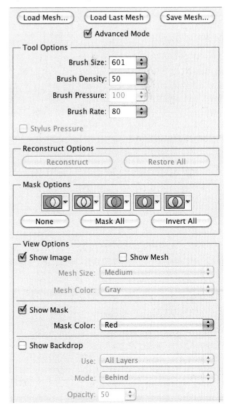

Applying the Warp command

To apply warp edits to a layer:

1. Click a type or image layer or a Smart Object, then choose Edit > Transform > **Warp**; or click a shape layer, then choose Edit > Transform Path > Warp.

2. Do either or both of the following:

   On the Options bar, choose a preset style from the **Warp** menu.**A–C** You can also click the **Warp Orientation** button to toggle horizontal and vertical distortion (not available for all presets), or reshape the grid by using the scrubby sliders for **Bend**, **H** (horizontal distortion), or **V** (vertical distortion).

   Choose **Warp: Custom** on the Options bar (not available for editable type), then drag any of the interior squares, square corner points, grid lines, or direction line handles in the grid.**D** Note: If you don't see the grid, turn on View > Extras.

3. To accept the warp edits, press Enter/Return or click the Commit Transform button ✔ on the Options bar (to cancel the edits, click the Cancel Transform button ⊘ or press Esc).**E**

➤ The Type > Warp Text dialog has the same controls as the Warp command, except it's just for type.

➤ While warp or transform controls are showing in your document, you can click the Switch Between Free Transform and Warp Modes button 🐀 on the Options bar to toggle the two modes. In fact, to minimize resampling and preserve the image quality, when you need to apply multiple transform and/or warp edits, it's best to toggle between the two commands, then accept them all at once.

➤ To access and edit the warp settings for a type or shape layer or a Smart Object, repeat step 1 at left. (If you want to remove the warp, choose None from the Warp menu on the Options bar.)

➤ To remove warp edits from an image layer, click the state prior to the "Warp" one on the History panel.

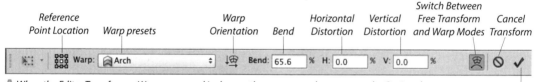

| Reference Point Location | Warp presets | Warp Orientation | Bend | Horizontal Distortion | Vertical Distortion | Switch Between Free Transform and Warp Modes | Cancel Transform |

A When the Edit > Transform > Warp command is chosen, these commands appear on the Options bar.   Commit Transform

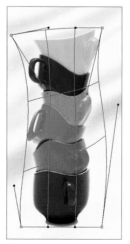

B We copied a selection of cups to a layer above a yellow Background.

C We applied the Warp command to the cups layer (Twist preset).

D We chose the Custom option, then dragged a few control handles on the grid.

E This is the result (it reminds us of the Mad Hatter tea party!).

You may have already used a filter or two in Photoshop (perhaps as a step in an earlier chapter). In this chapter, filters are the star players. Depending on which filters you apply and which settings you choose, the results can range from a subtle change to a total morph.**A–B** You can make an image look (almost) as if it's hand painted, silk-screened, or sketched; apply distortion; add a pattern, texture, or noise; create a mosaic or a patchwork of tiles — the creative possibilities are infinite. Once you start using the Filter Gallery, you'll see … time will fly by.

Using this chapter, you will learn techniques for applying filters, including using the Filter Gallery and Smart Filters, and use filters to make a photo look like an oil painting or tinted drawing. (To locate tasks in which we use individual filters, see "Filter menu" in the index.)

FILTERS

18

Applying filters

You can apply filters to a whole layer or just to a selection on a layer. Most of the Photoshop filters are applied either via the Filter Gallery or via an individual dialog. A small handful of them, such as Clouds and Blur, are applied in one step simply by choosing the filter name from a submenu on the Filter menu. If you apply a filter to a Smart Object, it becomes an editable, removable Smart Filter (see pages 344–345).

If you try to select a filter and discover that it's not available, the likely cause is that it's incompatible with the current document color mode or bit depth. All the Photoshop filters are available for RGB files, most of the filters are available for Grayscale files, fewer are available for CMYK Color, Lab Color, and 16-bits-per-channel files, still fewer are available for 32-bits-per-channel files, and none are available for Bitmap and Indexed Color files.

A *This is the original image.*

B *We applied the Charcoal filter.*

Most of the Photoshop filters are housed conveniently under one roof in the Filter Gallery dialog. There you can preview dozens of filters and filter settings, show and hide each filter effect that you've already previewed, and change the sequence in which Photoshop applies them to your document.

To use the Filter Gallery:

1. Click an image layer; or for more flexibility, click a duplicate image layer or a Smart Object (see "To apply a Smart Filter" on page 344).

2. *Optional:* To limit the filter to a specific area of the image, create a selection.

3. The Foreground and/or Background colors are used by many filters (see the sidebar on this page), and you must choose those colors now, before opening the Filter Gallery.

4. Choose Filter > **Filter Gallery**. The resizable gallery opens (**A**, next page).

5. To change the zoom level for the preview, click the Zoom Out button ⊟ or Zoom In button ⊞ in the lower-left corner of the dialog, or choose a preset zoom level from the menu. (If the preview is magnified, you can drag it in the window.)

6. Do either of the following:

   In the middle pane of the dialog, click an arrowhead to expand any of the six filter categories, then click a filter thumbnail.

   Choose a filter name from the menu below the Cancel button.

7. On the right side of the dialog, choose settings for the filter.

8. To edit the list of effects (bottom right portion of the dialog), do any of these optional steps:

   To apply an additional filter effect, click the **New Effect Layer** button, 🗔 click a filter thumbnail in any category, then choose settings. The effect may take a moment or two to process.

   To **replace** one filter effect with another, click a filter effect name on the scroll list (don't click the New Effect Layer button), then choose a replacement filter and settings.

   To **hide** a filter effect, click the visibility icon 👁 next to the effect name (click again to redisplay).

   To change the **stacking** position of a filter effect to produce a different result in the image, drag the effect name upward or downward on the list.

   To remove a filter effect from the list, click it, then click the **Delete Effect Layer** button. 🗑

9. Click OK.

▶ To hide or show the previews in the Filter Gallery for all but one filter effect, Alt-click/Option-click the visibility icon for that effect.

▶ To remove a non-Smart Filter, click a prior document state or snapshot on the History panel.

▶ In Edit/Photoshop > Preferences > Plug-Ins, uncheck Show All Filter Gallery Groups and Names to list, on the submenus on the Filter menu, only filters that are not in the Filter Gallery, or check this option to list all Photoshop filters on the submenus, including those that are available in the Filter Gallery (the gallery opens when you choose a filter name). ★

FILTERS THAT USE THE FOREGROUND AND BACKGROUND COLORS

The filters listed below use the current Foreground and/or Background colors. Some filters, such as Charcoal, Graphic Pen, and Photocopy (in the Sketch category), look good in the default Photoshop colors of black and white, whereas others look better in color. But don't just take our word for it— experiment and see for yourself.

▶ Artistic > Colored Pencil (Background color), Neon Glow (Foreground and Background colors)

▶ Distort > Diffuse Glow (Background color)

▶ Pixelate > Pointillize (Background color)

▶ Render > Clouds, Difference Clouds, Fibers (Foreground and Background colors)

▶ Sketch > Bas Relief, Chalk & Charcoal, Charcoal, Conté Crayon, Graphic Pen, Halftone Pattern, Note Paper, Photocopy, Plaster, Reticulation, Stamp, Torn Edges (Foreground and Background colors)

▶ Stylize > Tiles (Foreground or Background color)

▶ Texture > Stained Glass (Foreground color)

REAPPLYING THE LAST FILTER QUICKLY

▶ To reapply the last-used filter(s) using the same settings, choose Filter > [last filter name or Filter Gallery] (Ctrl-F/Cmd-F).

▶ To reopen either the last-used filter dialog or the Filter Gallery showing the last-used settings, press Ctrl-Alt-F/Cmd-Option-F.

Click this button to hide or show the thumbnails and expand or shrink the preview area.

To preview a filter effect, click a thumbnail or choose a filter name from the menu.

Zoom controls

Hide or show a filter effect preview

New Effect Layer

A *The Filter Gallery dialog includes a preview area, filter categories (with thumbnails), settings for the currently selected filter effect, and a listing of the currently applied effects.*

USING THE PREVIEW IN AN INDIVIDUAL FILTER DIALOG

Some Photoshop filters are applied via an individual dialog (not via the Filter Gallery). Of those individual dialogs, some have a preview window and some do not.

► For individual filter dialogs that contain a preview window, you can click the + button to zoom in or the – button to zoom out (we usually do the latter). Most of the individual dialogs also have a Preview check box.

► In some filter dialogs (such as Blur > Gaussian Blur and Motion Blur), if you click in the document window (square pointer), that area of the image will appear in the preview window. You can drag the image inside the preview window.

► To compare the image with and without the current filter effect, click and hold on the preview, then release.

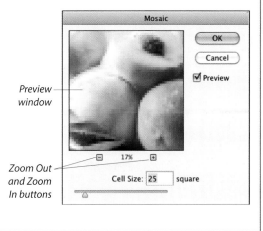

Preview window

Zoom Out and Zoom In buttons

Creating and editing Smart Filters

When you apply a filter to a Smart Object, it becomes what is called a Smart Filter. You can edit or remove a Smart Filter at any time, apply multiple filters to the same Smart Object, hide individual filters while keeping others visible, and move or copy filters from one Smart Object to another. You can also edit the filter mask (which is created automatically), change the stacking order of the filters, and edit the Smart Object itself. To learn about Smart Objects, see pages 248–255.

The file formats that support Photoshop layers — such as PSD, PDF, and TIFF — also support Smart Filters. Some third-party (non-Adobe) filters can also be applied as Smart Filters.

To apply a Smart Filter:

1. On the Layers panel, ☰ do either of the following:

   Click an existing Smart Object.

   Click an image layer, then choose Filter > **Convert for Smart Filters** (or right-click the layer and choose Convert to Smart Object). If an alert appears, click OK.

2. *Optional:* Create a selection to control which area of the image the filter affects. (The selection shape will appear in the filter mask once you apply a filter.)

3. Apply a filter. A Smart Filters listing, mask thumbnail, and filter listing will appear on the Layers panel. **A** (Note: Filter > Liquify and Filter > Vanishing Point can't be applied as Smart Filters.)

The most significant advantage to using Smart Filters is that you can edit the filter settings at any time.

To edit the settings for a Smart Filter:

1. Do either of the following:

   Double-click on or next to the Smart Filter name on the Layers panel.

   Right-click the Smart Filter name and choose **Edit Smart Filter** from the context menu.

2. If any Smart Filters are listed above the one you're editing, an alert will appear, indicating that those filter effects will be hidden until you exit the Filter Gallery or filter dialog. **B** Check Don't Show Again to prevent the warning from appearing again (if desired), then click OK.

3. Make the desired changes in the filter dialog, then click OK.

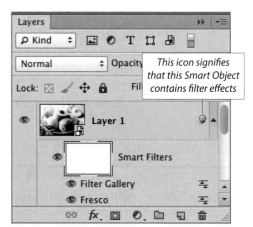

A *If you apply a Smart Filter by choosing Filter > Filter Gallery, the filter will be listed as "Filter Gallery," whereas if you apply a Smart Filter by choosing its individual name, it will be listed by its name.*

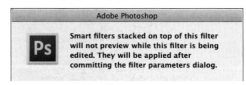

B *If you edit a Smart Filter and other filters are listed above it on the same layer, this alert dialog appears.*

CHANGING THE COLOR MODE OR BIT DEPTH

When changing the document color mode or bit depth, if the image contains Smart Filters that aren't supported by the new mode or depth, an alert will appear (shown below). If you click Don't Rasterize and then click Don't Flatten or Don't Merge, this symbol **A** will display next to the filter names on the Layers panel, signifying that the filter effect is inaccessible. If you then convert the file to a mode or depth that does support the filter (and respond to the alerts the same way), the icon will disappear and the filter settings will be editable again.

Not only can you change the blending mode and opacity of a Smart Object, you can also change the blending mode and Opacity setting of each Smart Filter that is applied to that object. Granted, this can be a lot to keep track of. And unfortunately, there is no indicator on the Layers panel to let you know if those settings have been changed from the defaults.

To edit the blending options for a Smart Filter:

1. Double-click the **Blending Options** icon ![icon] next to a filter name on the Layers panel,**A–B** then click OK if an alert dialog appears.

2. The Blending Options dialog opens.**C** Check Preview and, if desired, lower the zoom level. Change the blending **Mode** and/or **Opacity** (use the latter to fade the filter effect), then click OK.**D**

Hiding, copying, and deleting Smart Filters

To hide (or show) Smart Filter effects:

Do either of the following:

Click the visibility icon ![icon] for the Smart Filters listing to hide all the Smart Filters on that layer.

Click the visibility icon ![icon] for any individual Smart Filter. This may take longer to process than clicking the visibility icon for all the filters.

Click where the icon formerly was to redisplay the hidden filter effects.

To copy Smart Filters from one Smart Object to another:

1. Expand the list of Smart Filters for a Smart Object.

2. Alt-drag/Option-drag either the Smart Filters listing or an individual filter listing to another Smart Object.

➤ You can restack any Smart Filter within a Smart Object list (pause for the edit to process).

➤ If you drag a filter or the Smart Filters listing from one Smart Object to another without holding down Alt/Option, the filters will be removed from the source layer and added to the target layer. Any preexisting filters on the target layer will be preserved. Pause for the edit to process.

A *We applied the Fresco and Dry Brush filters to this image.*

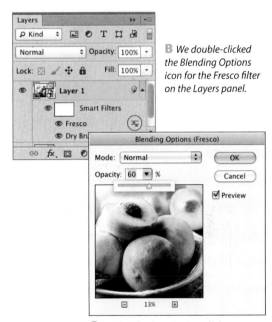

B *We double-clicked the Blending Options icon for the Fresco filter on the Layers panel.*

C *Via the Blending Options dialog, we lowered the opacity of the Fresco filter.*

D *Now more of the Dry Brush filter is showing through.*

If you delete a Smart Filter from a Smart Object that contains multiple filters, it may take a moment or two for Photoshop to update the display.

To delete a Smart Filter:

Do either of the following:

Right-click a Smart Filter listing and choose **Delete Smart Filter**.

Drag a Smart Filter listing to the **Delete Layer** button.🗑

Working with the Smart Filter mask

When you apply a filter to a Smart Object, a filter mask appears on the layer automatically. If you create a selection before applying the first filter to a Smart Object, the selection will appear as the white area in the mask. A filter mask can also be edited using the same methods as for a layer mask. For an illustration of how this works, see the next two pages.

To edit a filter mask:

1. Click the filter mask thumbnail.
2. Do either of the following:

   Click the **Brush** tool,🖌 then apply strokes with black to hide the filter effect, or with white to reveal areas you've hidden. For a partial mask, use black and lower the tool opacity (**A–E**, next page).

   To hide the filter effect gradually from one side of the image to the other, click the **Gradient** tool,▭ then drag across the image (**A–C**, page 348).

➤ To display the filter mask by itself in the document, Alt-click/Option-click the mask; repeat to redisplay the full Smart Object.

➤ To soften the transition between black and white areas in a filter mask, click the filter mask thumbnail, then on the Properties panel,🔲 adjust the Feather value. To control the overall opacity of the mask, use the Density slider.

If for some reason a filter mask was deleted and you want to restore it, do as follows.

To create a filter mask:

1. *Optional:* Create a selection.
2. Right-click the Smart Filters listing on the Layers panel and choose **Add Filter Mask**.

To deactivate a filter mask temporarily:

Shift-click the mask thumbnail (a red X appears over the thumbnail). Repeat to reactivate the mask.

To delete a filter mask:

Do either of the following:

Drag the filter mask thumbnail to the Delete Layer button 🗑 on the Layers panel.

Click the filter mask thumbnail, then on the Properties panel, click the Delete Mask button.🗑

DIMINISHING A FILTER EFFECT

To reduce the effect of a Smart Filter, lower its opacity via the Blending Options dialog. Or if you applied the filter to a duplicate image layer (not to a Smart Object), lower the opacity of the upper layer.

SOLVING MEMORY PROBLEMS

If you encounter memory problems when applying filters (Photoshop memory, that is, not your own forgetfulness!), try choosing Edit > Purge > All to free up memory, or exit/quit other open applications. Also bear in mind that the processing time may vary for any given filter slider or option. For instance, a higher setting that produces many small shapes may take longer to process than a setting that produces just a few large shapes.

WORKING WITH SMART FILTERS: AN EXAMPLE

A *This is the original image.*

C *We reduced the Opacity of the Smart Object to 62%.*

B *We duplicated the Background, converted the copy to a Smart Object, pressed D to reset the default Foreground and Background colors, then applied Filter Gallery > Sketch > Charcoal (values at left).*

E *This is the Layers panel for the image shown at left.*

D *We clicked the filter mask, then with the Brush tool at 50% Opacity and black as the Foreground color, applied strokes to partially restore the tiger's face to its virgin state.*

Continued on the following page

A *Next, to wipe the filter mask clean so we could try a different approach, we clicked the mask thumbnail, pressed Ctrl-A/Cmd-A to select the whole mask, pressed Backspace/Delete, then pressed Ctrl-D/Cmd-D to deselect.*

B *With the Gradient tool (100% Opacity, "Black, White" preset, radial type), we dragged from the center of the image outward. The filter effect is at full strength where the mask is white, and it fades to nil where the mask is black.*

C *The gradient in the filter mask is diminishing the impact of the filter in the center of the image — the tiger's face — right where we want the focal point to be.*

FILTERS AND AN ADJUSTMENT LAYER

A *We duplicated the Background in this image, then converted the duplicate layer to a Smart Object.*

More filter techniques

If you apply filters to a Smart Object, you can easily change the settings — and will feel more free to experiment. If you come up with a filter formula that you like, record your steps in an action. Here are a few more suggestions:

➤ Filters tend to make an image more abstract, reducing recognizable elements to line work, or to fewer or flatter areas of color. Start with an image that has a strong composition. Look for shapes that contrast in scale and have interesting contours, which will carry more weight once you apply filters.

➤ Use an adjustment layer above the filtered layer to fine-tune the resulting luminosity levels or colors. **A–D**

➤ Apply filters separately to a Smart Object one by one, then via the Blending Options dialog, lower the opacity of the topmost filter and/or change its blending mode. You can also apply filters to separate layers, then change the layer opacity or blending mode of any layer (**A–E**, next page).

➤ For less predictable and "machine made" results, apply two or more filters that have contrasting or complementary effects. For instance, you could apply one filter that reduces shapes to line work (such as Poster Edges) and another filter that changes the color or applies an overall texture, such as Grain > Texturizer.

➤ For a personal touch, apply some paint strokes (**A–C**, page 351).

B *We applied Filter > Filter Gallery > Diffuse Glow.*

C *We created a Black & White adjustment, then lowered the opacity of the adjustment layer to 52%.*

D *This is the final image.*

FILTERS, AN ADJUSTMENT LAYER, AND BLENDING MODES

C *We changed the blending mode of the Smart Object to Linear Burn.*

A *We converted a duplicate of the Background to a Smart Object.*

B *We applied Filter > Other > Minimum (Radius 1), then Filter > Stylize > Find Edges.*

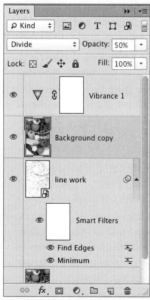

D *We created a second duplicate of the Background, moved the duplicate to the top of the Layers panel, changed the blending mode of that layer to Divide, and lowered its Opacity to 50%. Finally, we used a Vibrance adjustment to boost the colors slightly.*

E *This is the final image.*

A TEXTURE FILTER AND PAINT STROKES

B *This is the Layers panel for the final image.*

A *This is the original image.*

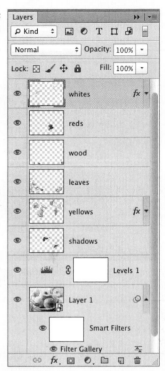

C *This is the image after we converted a duplicate image layer to a Smart Object, applied the Texturizer filter (Burlap texture) via the Filter Gallery, and used the Mixer Brush tool (Sample All Layers checked) to apply paint strokes to six new layers. We also applied the Drop Shadow effect to a couple of the paint layers for added depth, and a Levels adjustment to heighten the contrast in the underlying image.*

Turning a photo into a painting or a drawing

The Oil Paint filter turns a photo into a quasi oil painting. You can't vary the size or direction of the brush strokes in different parts of the image, but it does produce some rich textural effects — and it's a fun filter to play with. Note: For this filter to work, Use Graphics Processor must be checked in Preferences > Performance.

To turn a photo into an oil painting: ★

1. Duplicate an image layer in an RGB image, then right-click the duplicate and choose **Convert to Smart Object.** Keep the Smart Object selected.**A**

2. Choose Filter > **Oil Paint.** In the Oil Paint dialog, zoom in on the preview so you'll be able to examine the shape of the brush strokes.**B**

3. Under Brush and Lighting, adjust the sliders:

   Stylization controls the smoothness of the strokes.

   Cleanliness controls the purity of (amount of color variegation in) the colors.

   Scale controls the width of the strokes.

   Bristle Detail controls the visibility of bristle marks in the paint strokes.

   Angular Direction controls the position of the highlights on the paint surface.

   Shine controls the intensity of highlight reflections on the paint surface. This slider has a strong impact.

4. Click OK **C** (and **A–D**, next page).

A *This is the original photo.*

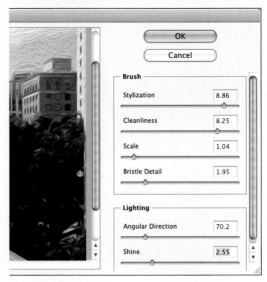

B *We chose these values in the Oil Paint dialog.*

C *This is the final "oil painting."*

THE OIL PAINT FILTER PLUS THE PALETTE KNIFE FILTER AND ADJUSTMENTS

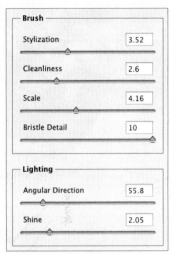

A *In this image, we converted a duplicate of the Background to a Smart Object.*

B *To the Smart Object, we applied the Palette Knife filter (Filter Gallery), then the Oil Paint filter (settings shown above).*

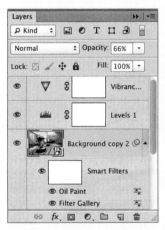

C *We lowered the Opacity of the Smart Object to 66%, then used a Levels adjustment layer to boost the contrast and a Vibrance adjustment layer to boost the color intensity slightly.*

D *The Palette Knife filter contributes an irregular texture to the Oil Paint effect.*

In these steps, you'll turn a photo into a watercolor by applying a series of filters. Try devising some of your own formulas, too!

To turn a photo into a tinted drawing:

1. Duplicate an image layer in a high-resolution photo.**A**

2. Choose Filter > Stylize > **Find Edges**.**B**

3. Choose the **Brush** tool. Choose a large, Soft Round brush, Normal mode, and an Opacity below 50% on the Options bar. Also make the Foreground color black.

4. Click the **Add Layer Mask** button on the Layers panel, then with the layer mask thumbnail selected, apply strokes to the image to reveal areas of the underlying layer.

5. Do any of the following optional steps:

   Lower the Opacity of the duplicate layer.

   Change the blending mode of the duplicate layer (try Lighter Color, Color Dodge, Hard Light, Pin Light, or Luminosity).**C–D**

   Intensify the contrast via a Levels adjustment layer.

A *We duplicated the Background in this original image.*

B *We applied the Find Edges filter to the duplicate layer.*

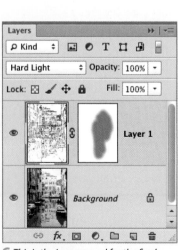

C *This is the Layers panel for the final image, which is shown at right.*

D *We applied brush strokes to the layer mask to reveal some of the underlying image, and chose Hard Light as the blending mode for the duplicate layer.*

We've never heard the phrase "A word is worth a thousand pictures," but in Photoshop, where you can do such artful things with type, the line between pictures and words is blurred (sometimes literally!).

In this chapter, you'll learn how to create editable type, then style and format it using a wide assortment of character and paragraph controls. You will also learn special techniques, such as how to transform type, screen it back (as in the image shown at right), rasterize it, and make it look like cut paper. Finally, you will learn how to put type shapes into a spot color channel.

When you use the Horizontal Type tool or Vertical Type tool, editable type appears in your document and a new layer appears on the Layers panel. You can easily change the attributes of editable type, such as the font family, style, and size; kerning, tracking, leading, alignment, and baseline shift values; and color. Moreover, you can transform, warp, or apply layer effects to editable type; change its blending mode; and change its opacity and fill values. To style type, we'll show you how to use the Character panel **A** **A**, the Paragraph panel, ¶ the Paragraph Styles panel, the Character Styles panel, and the Options bar.

Note: Many type controls that were on the Layer menu > Type submenu in Photoshop CS5 are located on a new Type menu in CS6. ★

TYPE

19

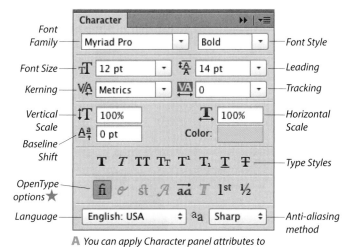

Font Family — Myriad Pro / Bold — Font Style

Font Size — T 12 pt / A 14 pt — Leading

Kerning — VA Metrics / VA 0 — Tracking

Vertical Scale — T 100% / T 100% — Horizontal Scale

Baseline Shift — A 0 pt / Color:

T T TT Tr T¹ T₁ T T — Type Styles

OpenType options ★ — fi ℰ st A aa T 1ˢᵗ ½

Language — English: USA / aa Sharp — Anti-aliasing method

A You can apply Character panel attributes to all the type on a layer or to selected characters or words.

Creating editable type

You can be casual about where you position editable type initially and about which typographic attributes you choose for it, because you can easily edit those attributes or move, transform, or restack the layer.

To create an editable type layer:

1. Choose the **Horizontal Type** tool T or **Vertical Type** tool ↓T (T or Shift-T).

2. On the Options bar, 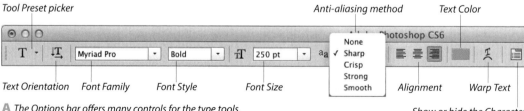 do all of the following:

   Choose a **font family**, and from the adjacent menu, choose a **font style**. A sample of each font displays on the menu.

   Choose or enter a **font size** (you can use the scrubby slider).

   Choose an **anti-aliasing** method for the way in which Photoshop introduces partially transparent pixels along the edges of the characters, to make them look smoother: Sharp (sharpest), Crisp (somewhat sharp), Strong (heavier), or Smooth (smoothest). With anti-aliasing off (None), the edges of the type will be jagged; choose None for Web output. **B–C**

   Click an **alignment** button to align point type relative to your original insertion point or to align paragraph type to the left edge, right edge, or center of the bounding box (see also page 364).

   Click the **Text Color** swatch, then choose a color via the Color Picker or Swatches panel, or click a color in the document, then click OK.

3. Do either of the following:

   To create **point** type (suitable for a small amount of text), click in the document to establish an insertion point, then type the desired text. You can press Enter/Return to create line breaks, where necessary, to prevent the type from disappearing off the edge of the canvas. (You can also move the type later with the Move tool.)

   To create **paragraph** type (suitable for a larger block of text), drag to define a bounding box for the type to fit into, then type the desired text. Let the words wrap naturally to the edges of the bounding box, pressing Enter/Return only when you need to start a new paragraph. Note: If you prefer to specify dimensions for the bounding box first, Alt/Option click in the document, then enter dimensions in the Paragraph Text Size dialog.

4. To accept the new text, press Enter on the keypad (not on the main keyboard) or click the Commit button ✔ on the right end of the Options bar. (To cancel the type, press Esc or click the Cancel button ⊘ on the Options bar.) Each time you create new type with the Horizontal or Vertical Type tool, it appears on a new layer (**A–B**, next page).

   Note: If you prefer not to establish new default Options bar settings for your type tool, click or

---

Tool Preset picker   Anti-aliasing method   Text Color

Text Orientation   Font Family   Font Style   Font Size   Alignment   Warp Text

A The Options bar offers many controls for the type tools.

Show or hide the Character and Paragraph panel group

B With Anti-aliasing off, type edges look jagged.

C With Anti-aliasing on, type edges look smoother.

drag with the tool in the document before choosing settings.

➤ Photoshop uses vector outlines for specific font families and styles when you resize editable type, save a file to the PDF format, or output a file to a PostScript printer. Like vector graphics, editable type outputs at the resolution of the printer, not at the resolution of the file.

➤ If you need to typeset a sizable quantity of text for a particular project, you may find it easier to create just the imagery in Photoshop and then add the type in a layout or Web page creation program.

➤ You can right-click an editable type listing on the Layers panel and choose an anti-aliasing method from the context menu. The new setting will display on the Anti-Aliasing menu on the Character panel.

➤ To display either East Asian Features or Middle Eastern Features on the Character and Paragraph panels and panel menus, see "Choose Text Engine Options" on page 443. ★

➤ To fill a type bounding box with "dummy" text quickly, choose Type > Paste Lorem Ipsum. ★ For overflow text, see page 366.

➤ If you place phrases, words, or characters on separate layers, you'll be able to move and apply effects to them individually. To organize multiple type layers, gather them into layer groups. To display only type layers, choose Kind from the Filter Type menu at the top of the Layers panel, then click the Filter for Type Layers button. **T** ★

A *After typing "EcoStorage," we pressed Enter/Return, so we could type the next word on a second line.*

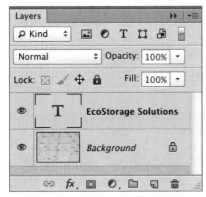

B *Editable type layers have a* **T** *icon in the thumbnail and are given the name of the first word or few words of type in the layer.*

REMEMBER TO USE SMART QUOTES!

To specify that Photoshop use curly quotation and apostrophe marks (a rule in typesetting that is too often ignored), in Preferences > Type, check Use Smart Quotes. Straight quotes should be used solely as abbreviations for foot and inch measurements.

IMPORTING TYPE AS A SMART OBJECT

For quick round-trip editing between Adobe Illustrator and Photoshop, put type on its own layer in Illustrator, save the file in the Illustrator Document (.ai) format, and import it into Photoshop via the Place or Paste command (see pages 250–251). If you use the Place command, the layer will be labeled by the Illustrator file name; if you use the Paste command, the layer will be labeled "Vector Smart Object."

To edit the embedded type file in Illustrator, double-click the Smart Object or Vector Smart Object thumbnail. When you're done editing the file, save and close it, then return to Photoshop; the type will update in Photoshop automatically (see page 254).

Selecting type

Before you can change the character or paragraph attributes or content of type, you have to select a type layer or a specific string of characters or phrases.

Note: To apply some kinds of edits to type, such as filters or brush strokes, you must rasterize it first (see page 368). Note that once type is rasterized, its character or paragraph attributes (such as the font and leading) can't be edited.

To select type for editing or style changes:

Do one of the following:

Click a type layer, choose the **Horizontal Type** tool T or **Vertical Type** tool ↓T (T or Shift-T), then drag across some characters or words to select them, A or double-, triple-, or quadruple-click, as described in the sidebar on this page.

With any tool selected, double-click the T icon on the Layers panel. All the type on the layer becomes selected. To reduce the selection, drag or double- or triple-click.

To change the attributes of all the type on a layer via the Character or Paragraph panel, such as the font size, leading, or alignment, simply click the layer (you don't need to select a type tool).

➤ To delete type that you have selected, press Backspace/Delete. Or to delete one character at a time, click with a type tool to the right of a character to be deleted (or in the case of vertical type, click below the character), then press Backspace/Delete.

To exit type-editing mode:

When you're done editing your type, do one of the following:

Click the Commit button ✔ on the Options bar.

Press Enter on the keypad (not on the main keyboard).

Click a different tool.

Click a different layer.

(To cancel your edits before confirming them, either click the Cancel button ⊘ on the Options bar or press Esc.)

A To select type characters for editing, drag across them with a type tool.

SELECTING TYPE CHARACTERS

To select type for copy editing or restyling, choose the Horizontal Type or Vertical Type tool, then do any of the following:

Select consecutive characters or words	Drag across them. Or click at the beginning of a series of words, then Shift-click the end.
Select a word	Double-click a word.
Select consecutive words	Double-click a word, then drag (without releasing the mouse).
Select a line	Triple-click a line.
Select a paragraph	Quadruple-click in the paragraph.
Select all the characters in the type object	Double-click the T icon on the Layers panel; or click in the text, then press Ctrl-A/Cmd-A.

Recoloring type

To recolor type:

1. On the Layers panel, click a type layer.

2. Do either of the following:

    Choose the **Horizontal Type** tool $\top$ or **Vertical Type** tool,$\downarrow\top$ then click the **Text Color** swatch on the Options bar.

    On the Character panel, 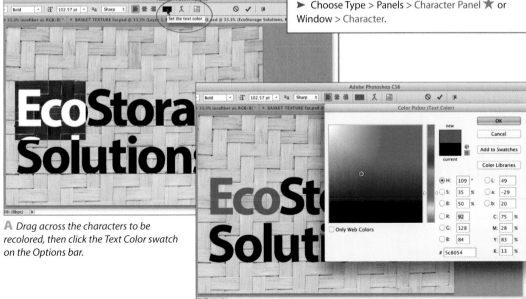 click the **Color** swatch.

3. Choose a color via the Color Picker or Swatches panel, or click a color in the image, then click OK to exit the Color Picker.

➤ You can also apply a color, gradient, or pattern to a type layer via an editable overlay layer effect (see pages 378–379).

To recolor selected characters or words:

1. With the **Horizontal Type** tool $\top$ or **Vertical Type** tool,$\downarrow\top$ select the characters or words to be recolored.

2. On the Options bar, click the **Text Color** swatch.

3. Choose a color via the Color Picker B or Swatches panel, or click a color in the image, then click OK to exit the Color Picker.

Changing the font family and font style

To change the font family and font style:

1. Select the type to be restyled (use any method in step 1 on the preceding page).

2. On the Options bar or the Character panel, choose from the **Font Family** menu, then choose from the adjacent **Font Style** menu.

➤ To deal with missing fonts in a file, see page 35.

➤ When the Type > Font Preview Size submenu has a setting other than None, ★ a sample of each font family displays next to the font listings in the Font menu on the Options bar and the Character panel. From the Font Preview Size menu, you can select a size for the previews (e.g., Small, Medium, or Large). Note: If the samples are previewing too slowly, either choose a smaller preview size or choose None to turn the feature off.

SHOWING THE CHARACTER PANEL

➤ If the Character panel is open but collapsed to an icon, click the A icon.

➤ Select the Horizontal Type tool or Vertical Type tool, then click the Toggle the Character and Paragraph Panels button on the Options bar.

➤ Choose Type > Panels > Character Panel ★ or Window > Character.

A Drag across the characters to be recolored, then click the Text Color swatch on the Options bar.

B Choose a replacement color from the Color Picker.

Converting type

To convert paragraph type to point type:

On the Layers panel, right-click the name of a paragraph type layer and choose **Convert to Point Text**. A paragraph return will be inserted at the end of every line of type except the last one. If the type object contains hidden (overflow) text, an alert dialog may appear, warning you that the hidden text will be deleted if you proceed; click OK.

To convert point type to paragraph type:

On the Layers panel, right-click the name of a point type layer and choose **Convert to Paragraph Text**. To reshape the resulting bounding box, follow the steps on page 366. Be sure to delete any unwanted hyphens that may have been inserted.

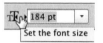

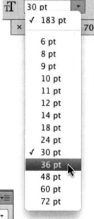

A *To change the font size of selected type via the Options bar, use the scrubby slider, enter a value, or choose a preset size from the menu.*

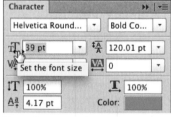

B *Another way to change the type size is via the Font Size scrubby slider, field, or menu on the Character panel.*

C *To scale type proportionally with the Move tool, Shift-drag a corner handle on the transform box.*

Changing the font size

To assign a specific font (point) size to all the characters you select, use either the Options bar or the Character panel.

To change the font size:

Method 1 (Options bar)

1. Choose the **Horizontal Type** or **Vertical Type** tool, then click a type layer or select the type characters to be resized.

2. On the Options bar, use the **Font Size** icon as a scrubby slider (Alt-drag/Option-drag for smaller increments), or enter a value, or choose a preset size from the menu.**A**

Method 2 (Character panel)

On the Layers panel, click a type layer, then choose a Font Size on the Character panel.**B**

➤ To choose a measurement unit for the Character and Paragraph panels, see page 441.

You can also resize type interactively with the Move tool. This is especially useful if your type selection contains different point sizes and you want to preserve those relative differences while resizing.

To scale type with the Move tool:

1. On the Layers panel, click a type layer.

2. Click the **Move** tool and check **Show Transform Controls** on the Options bar. On the bounding box for the type, click any handle.

3. Do either of the following:

   To scale both the height and the width of the type, drag a corner handle. To preserve the original proportions of the characters while scaling them (better!), Shift-drag a corner handle.**C**

   To scale just the height or width of the type, drag a side handle.

4. To accept the scale transformation, click the Commit ✔ button on the Options bar or double-click in the text block. (To cancel the edit before accepting it, click the Cancel Transform ⊘ button on the Options bar or press Esc.)

➤ To typeset narrow or wide characters, we recommend using a condensed or extended font, in which the proportions are balanced, instead of the Vertical Scale or Horizontal Scale control on the Character panel, which produce distortion.

Applying kerning and tracking

Kerning changes the spacing between a pair of text characters, whereas tracking changes the spacing between multiple characters.

To apply kerning:

1. On the Layers panel, double-click a **T** icon, then click to create an insertion point between two characters.

2. Do either of the following:

   On the Character panel, choose Metrics from the Kerning menu to apply the kerning value built into the current font or choose Optical to let Photoshop control the kerning; or use the Kerning icon **VA** as a scrubby slider (for finer increments, hold down Alt/Option); **A** or enter or choose a positive or negative value.**B**

   Press Alt/Option plus the left or right arrow key on the keyboard (to kern in a larger increment, hold down Ctrl-Alt/Cmd-Option while pressing).

   ➤ To restore the spacing between two characters to the kerning setting of Optical, select both characters, then choose Optical from the Kerning menu.

To apply tracking:

1. Do either of the following:

   To apply tracking to a whole layer, click the layer.

   To apply tracking to part of a layer, double-click a **T** icon, then select some characters or words.

2. Do either of the following:

   On the Character panel, use the **Tracking** icon **VA** as a scrubby slider (hold down Alt/Option for finer increments) or enter or choose a positive or negative value.**C**

   If type is selected, you can press Alt/Option and the left or right arrow key (to track in a larger increment, hold down Ctrl-Alt/Cmd-Option).

   ➤ To reset the tracking value of selected characters to 0, press Ctrl-Shift-Q/Cmd-Control-Shift-Q.

   ➤ If Fractional Widths is checked on the Character panel menu, Photoshop uses fractions of pixels to control the spacing of type (on the entire layer), to optimize its appearance. Keep this option checked unless you're setting small type for Web output.

   ➤ To reset the Character panel and any selected type to the default settings, choose Reset Character from the Character panel menu.

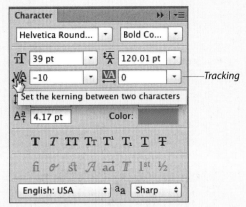

A *The Kerning and Tracking controls are available only on the Character panel (not on the Options bar).*

B *Use a negative kerning value to tighten the gap between a pair of characters (we chose a value of –100).*

T R A C K I N G   I T   O U T
Tracking can make type more or less readable, depending on the tracking value used. Try not to overdo it!

C *On occasion, we might spread out a few words, as in the header in this figure, but never a whole paragraph (that's a typesetting no-no!).*

Adjusting the leading

The Leading value controls the spacing between each line of paragraph type and the line above it. In a block of text that has a uniform font size, uniform leading looks best. Note: Leading has no effect on the spacing above the first line in a paragraph. To reposition a whole layer, drag it with the Move tool (simple, yet easy to forget!).

To adjust leading in horizontal paragraph type:

1. On the Layers panel, do either of the following:

   Click a type layer.

   Double-click the **T** icon for a type layer, then select the paragraphs for which you want to change the leading value.

2. Show the Character panel. 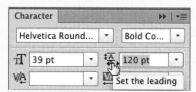 Use the **Leading** icon as a scrubby slider **A–C** (Alt-drag/Option-drag for finer increments), or enter a value in the field, or choose a preset value from the menu. The leading will change from Auto to a numerical value. If you're not sure what value to use, start with a number that's a couple of points larger than the current font size, then readjust it if needed.

   Note: The character with the highest leading value in a line controls the spacing of that line.

➤ The Auto setting for leading is calculated as a percentage of the current font size, and is set in the Justification dialog (choose Justification from the Paragraph panel menu). For instance, with Auto Leading set to the default percentage of 120%, the leading for 30-point type will be 36 points. To restore the Auto setting to selected type, press Ctrl-Alt-Shift-A/Cmd-Option-Shift-A.

➤ To adjust the vertical spacing between characters in vertical type, click the type layer, then change the Tracking value (not the leading value) on the Character panel.

➤ To change the orientation of type, right-click a type layer name on the Layers panel and choose Horizontal or Vertical. Or double-click a type layer thumbnail, then on the Options bar, click the Toggle Text Orientation button. After changing the orientation, you may need to move the type or adjust the tracking. To rotate each character of vertical type 90° clockwise, select the type, then uncheck Standard Roman Vertical Alignment on the Character panel menu.

A This is the Leading area on the Character panel.

B This type has a leading value of 154 pt.

C A leading value of 120 pt. brought the bottom line of type closer to the top one.

FADING PART OF A TYPE LAYER

To fade the editable type shown below, we added a layer mask to the type layer, then dragged with the Gradient tool from right to left.

Shifting type from the baseline

Use the Baseline Shift feature to raise or lower type characters from the normal baseline (1 point at a time).

To shift characters from the baseline:

1. On the Layers panel, double-click a **T** icon, then select the characters or words to be shifted.

2. On the Character panel, **A** use the **Baseline Shift** icon as a scrubby slider (Alt-drag/Option-drag for finer increments), or enter a value. **A** A positive value raises characters upward; a negative value moves them downward. **B–D**

Inserting special characters

The OpenType buttons on the Character panel substitute alternate glyphs for standard characters, if available in the current OpenType font. For instance, a fraction glyph would be substituted when you type the characters for a fraction, such as ½ for 1/2 or ¾ for 3/4. Among the other OpenType options are ligature glyphs for specific letter pairs (such as ff, ffl, and st) and swash and titling characters. The OpenType "Pro" fonts contain the most glyph options.

To insert or specify alternate glyphs for OpenType characters: ★

1. Do either of the following:

   To change all applicable occurrences in existing text, either click a type layer on the Layers panel or highlight characters with a type tool, and if you haven't already done so, choose an OpenType font family and font style.

   To specify alternate glyph options for text to be entered in a specific OpenType font, choose a type tool and that font family and style.

2. On the Character panel, **A** click the desired — and available (not dimmed) — OpenType button(s). **E**

USING THE STYLE BUTTONS

If you click a style button on the Character panel and the current font doesn't include that style or glyph, Photoshop will produce a simulated version of it.

$$T \quad T \quad TT \quad T_T \quad T^1 \quad T_1 \quad \underline{T} \quad \overline{T}$$

The buttons are Faux Bold, Faux Italic, All Caps, Small Caps, Superscript, Subscript, Underline, and Strikethrough.

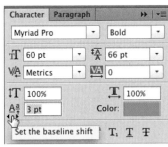

A Use the Baseline Shift feature to shift characters or words upward or downward by a few points.

B These characters have a Baseline Shift value of 0.

C Here the characters have an assortment of different Baseline Shift values, some positive and some negative.

D To emphasize the curve more, we applied Edit > Transform > Warp (Flag preset); see page 340.

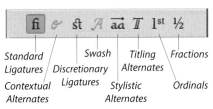

Standard Ligatures / Contextual Alternates / Discretionary Ligatures / Swash / Stylistic Alternates / Titling Alternates / Ordinals / Fractions

E These are the OpenType buttons on the Character panel.

Applying paragraph settings

Using the Paragraph panel, you will find options for justification, alignment, indents, and paragraph spacing, similar to those found in a page layout program. The controls on this panel apply primarily to paragraph type; the first three alignment buttons are the only controls that apply to point type.

To choose a paragraph alignment or justification option for horizontal type:

1. Do either of the following:

   On the Layers panel, double-click a **T** icon, then click in a paragraph or select a series of paragraphs.

   To apply settings to all the type in a layer, click the layer, but don't select anything.

2. Show the Paragraph panel.¶

   ➤ If the Paragraph panel is closed, choose Type > Panels > Paragraph Panel. ★ Or if a type tool is selected, you can click the Toggle Character and Paragraph Panels 📋 button on the Options bar, then click the Paragraph tab.

3. Click an alignment and/or justification button at the top of the panel: **A**

   The buttons in the first group — **Left Align Text**, **Center Text**, and **Right Align Text** — align type to the center or an edge of the bounding box that surrounds the type. These options can also be used on point or paragraph type.

   The buttons in the second group — **Justify Last Left**, **Justify Last Centered**, and **Justify Last Right** — justify the type, forcing all but the last line to span the full width of the bounding box.

The last button, **Justify All**, forces all lines of type, including the last one, to span the full width of the bounding box.

4. Check **Hyphenate** at the bottom of the panel to enable automatic hyphenation. If you chose a justify alignment option, we recommend that you also turn on hyphenation, to help minimize the gaps between words.

➤ To change the alignment and/or justification values for vertical type, the procedure is the same as described above, except the buttons have different labels.

➤ To reset all currently selected type and the Paragraph panel to the default settings, choose Reset Paragraph from the panel menu.

➤ To specify parameters for hyphenation, choose Hyphenation from the Paragraph panel menu.

PICKING YOUR FAVORITE COMPOSER

The Single-Line Composer and Every-Line Composer algorithms on the Paragraph panel menu control the way in which lines of type wrap within the bounding box, in an effort to make the paragraph look aesthetically pleasing. We prefer Every-Line Composer, because it automatically adjusts word breaks at the beginning of a paragraph, when necessary, to improve the line breaks and appearance of the paragraph toward the end. Both composers abide by the current Word Spacing and Letter Spacing values in the Justification dialog, which also opens from the Paragraph panel menu.

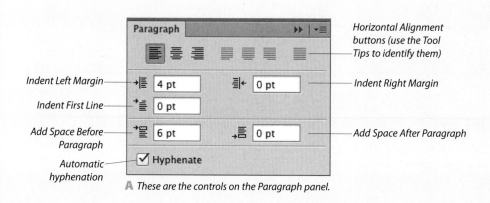

A These are the controls on the Paragraph panel.

Formatting type with paragraph and character styles

Using paragraph and character styles, you can format and style type quickly and ensure that it looks consistent throughout your document. When you edit a type style, all the type to which it is linked updates instantly.

To create a paragraph style: ★

1. Apply the desired character and paragraph settings to some type in your document, then click in the text.

2. On the Paragraph Styles panel, ⬛ click the **New Paragraph Style** button.⬛

➤ To rename a style, double-click the style name, enter the desired name in the dialog, then click OK.

To apply a paragraph style: ★

1. Click a type layer, or click in a paragraph, or drag through a string of paragraphs.

2. On the Paragraph Styles panel, click a style.**A**

➤ If a style doesn't apply correctly, click the Clear Overrides button ⬛ (overrides are attributes in the text that are unrelated to the style, as indicated by a plus sign next to the style name).

To create a character style: ★

1. Apply the desired character settings to a character or word, and keep the type selected.

2. On the Character Styles panel, ⬛ click the **New Character Style** button.⬛

To apply a character style: ★

1. Select the characters or words to be styled.

2. On the Character Styles panel, click a style.**B**

To edit a paragraph or character style: ★

Do either of the following:

Select and restyle a paragraph (or characters) that contain the style you want to edit, so it has the desired new attributes. From the menu on the Paragraph Styles (or Character Styles) panel, choose **Redefine Style**.

Choose Select > Deselect Layers, then on the Paragraph Styles or Character Styles panel, double-click a style. The Paragraph Style Sheet or Character Style Sheet dialog opens. Change the settings in any of the panels, then click OK.**C**

A *We applied a paragraph style to this type.*

B *Next, we applied a character style to the numerals.*

C *We edited the color and font in the character style: The changes appeared instantly in the whole document.*

Transforming the bounding box for paragraph type

If you change the shape of the bounding box that surrounds paragraph type (e.g., make the box narrower or wider), the type will reflow to fit the new dimensions without the characters becoming distorted. Enlarging the bounding box is a necessity when you want to reveal overflow type (indicated by a tiny plus sign in the lower-right corner handle). Instructions are also given here for rotating the bounding box.

To transform paragraph type via its bounding box:

1. On the Layers panel, double-click the **T** icon for a paragraph type layer, then click anywhere in the text. A dashed bounding box surrounds the type.

2. Do one of the following:

   To **reshape** the bounding box, drag a control handle.**A** To preserve the proportions of the bounding box while scaling it, start dragging a corner handle, then hold down Shift and continue to drag. The type will reflow into the new shape.**B**

   To **rotate** the bounding box, position the pointer just outside one of the corners (it will become a curved, double-arrow pointer), then drag in a circular direction.

3. To accept the transformation, press Enter on the keypad or click the Commit button ✔ on the Options bar. (To cancel the edits, press Esc or click the Cancel button ⊘ on the Options bar.)

➤ To align or distribute multiple layers, such as type layers, see page 261.

➤ To access the Move tool temporarily while you're working with type (perhaps to move the type), hold down Ctrl/Cmd. Note: If you press V to access the Move tool instead, make sure your type cursor isn't inserted in type, or you will either replace the selected type with that letter or insert the letter into your text.

A Drag a control handle to transform the bounding box.

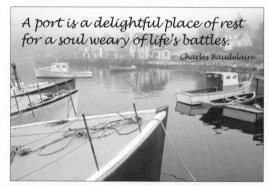

B When we widened the bounding box, the type reflowed into the new shape.

TRANSFORMING TYPE

➤ You can apply any transform command, such as Free Transform, to paragraph or point type (see pages 332–333). Both the bounding box and the characters within it will be affected by the transformation.

➤ You can move, scale, rotate, or skew editable or rasterized type; you can apply a distortion or perspective transformation command only to rasterized type.

➤ If you want to transform characters individually, create each one on a separate layer.

WAYS TO EMBELLISH TYPE

➤ Apply layer effects or styles to an editable or rasterized type layer (see the next chapter).

➤ "Fill" editable type with imagery by using it as the base layer in a clipping mask (see pages 327–328).

Screening back type

In these steps, you'll use a Levels adjustment layer to screen back type. A lightened version of the image will be visible only within the type shapes. This is a very "Photoshoppy" way to combine type with imagery.

To screen back type:

1. Create a document that contains a medium to dark image layer and an editable type layer (the type color doesn't matter), preferably in a large font size and a bold or black font style. **A**

2. On the Layers panel, Ctrl-click/Cmd-click the **T** icon to load the type as a selection. Hide the type layer, then click the underlying image layer or Background.

3. On the Adjustments panel, click the **Levels** button. ★ The Levels controls display on the Properties panel, and the selection disappears from view temporarily.

4. Move the middle Input Levels slider to the left to lighten the midtones in the type (you can also move the highlights slider). Move the Output Levels shadows slider to the right to reduce the contrast in the type. **B–C**

➤ To screen back the imagery instead of the type, after following the steps above, click the adjustment layer mask thumbnail, then on the Properties panel, click Invert.

➤ To reposition the type in the image, click the adjustment layer, then Ctrl/Cmd drag in the document.

➤ You can apply layer effects to the adjustment layer. For some great results, try Drop Shadow, Inner Shadow, or Bevel & Emboss.

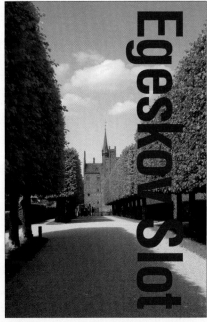

A *The original document contains an image layer and an editable type layer.*

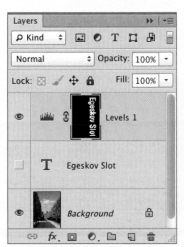

B *The mask on the Levels adjustment layer is hiding the adjustment everywhere but within the type shapes.*

C *In this screened-back version, the Levels adjustment is visible only within the type shapes.*

Rasterizing a type layer

If you want to edit type by applying a filter or the Transform > Distort or Perspective command, or draw strokes on it directly with a tool such as the Brush, you have to convert it to pixels first via the Rasterize Type command. Although you can't change the typographic attributes of rasterized type, there are countless creative things you can do with it.

To rasterize type into pixels:

1. *Optional:* To preserve the editable type layer, duplicate it (Ctrl-J/Cmd-J), then hide the original. Keep the duplicate layer selected.

2. Right-click the editable type layer name and choose **Rasterize Type** (or choose Type > Rasterize Type Layer ⭐). In the layer thumbnail, you will see the type shapes surrounded by transparent pixels (checkerboard pattern).

CREATING A CUT PAPER EFFECT

In this example, we'll "attack" the type characters with knives (well, actually, a lasso tool)!

1. Create an editable type layer, duplicate it, then right-click the duplicate layer and choose **Rasterize Type.** Hide the editable type layer.

2. To select a portion of a type "character," drag with the **Lasso** tool 𝒫 (L or Shift-L) or click with the **Polygonal Lasso** tool.▽ A

3. Choose the **Move** tool ▶✛ or hold down Ctrl/Cmd, then drag the selection in the document window or press any of the arrow keys.B

4. Repeat steps 2–3 for other "characters" to create an aesthetically pleasing design (A–F, next page).

A *We created editable type in an extra bold font, duplicated and hid the type layer, and rasterized the duplicate. With the Polygonal Lasso tool, we created a straight-edged selection of the stem on the letter P.*

B *We repositioned the selection with the Move tool.*

A With the Lasso tool, we created an irregular-shaped selection of the top of the letter A.

B We moved the selection.

C This is the final "cut paper" image after we moved more straight-edged and irregular selections of the rasterized type layer.

PUTTING SECTIONS OF RASTERIZED TYPE ONTO SEPARATE LAYERS

D With the Magic Wand tool (Tolerance 0, Contiguous checked), we clicked each piece of "cut paper" separately, then used the Layer > New > Layer Via Cut command (Ctrl-Shift-J/Cmd-Shift-J) to put it on a new layer. Note: If you follow these steps, remember to reselect the original rasterized layer each time before clicking with the Magic Wand.

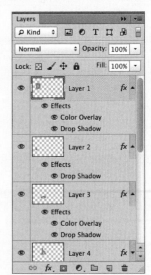

E With the sections on different layers, we were able to apply the Color Overlay and Drop Shadow layer effects to each separate layer, and also move the layers individually. Fun!

F These are some of the Layers panel listings for the image shown at left.

Putting type in a spot color channel

Note: Show the Layers and Channels panels, both of which you will be using in this exercise.

To put type in a spot color channel:

1. Make sure your document has a suitable resolution for commercial printing (typically, 300 ppi).

2. If you haven't already done so, create some editable type. When you're done, choose the Move tool.

3. Display the Channels panel, then from the panel menu, choose **New Spot Channel**.

4. In the New Spot Channel dialog, click the **Color** swatch, and if necessary, click **Color Libraries** to get to the Color Libraries dialog.

5. From the **Book** menu, choose a spot color matching system, such as a PANTONE + (nonprocess) system, click the desired color or type a number that you have gotten from a fan book, then click OK twice to exit both dialogs.

6. Ctrl-click/Cmd-click the **T** icon on the Layers panel to select the type shapes, 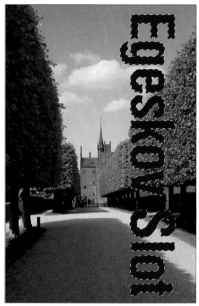 then hide the type layer.

7. On the Channels panel, make sure the new spot color channel is still selected, then choose Edit > **Fill** (Shift-Backspace/Shift-Delete). In the dialog, choose Use: Black; Mode: Normal; and an Opacity value that matches the tint, or density, value of the spot color ink to be used on press. Click OK. The selection will fill with the spot color.

8. Deselect (Ctrl-D/Cmd-D). On the Channels panel, the type shapes should display in only the spot channel thumbnail. 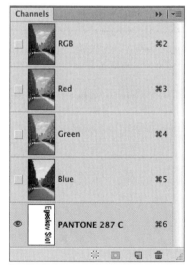 Click the RGB channel.

9. To preserve the spot color channel, save the file in the Photoshop or Photoshop PDF format.

➤ To reposition the type shapes, click the spot channel listing on the Channels panel, drag in the document with the Move tool, then click the RGB channel listing.

➤ You can't edit the type characters in a spot color channel, since technically they're just areas of color, not type. If you don't like the results, you will need to redo it from scratch. Fill the channel with White, 100% Opacity, redisplay and edit the original type layer, then repeat steps 6–8, above.

A *The type is converted to a selection.*

B *Because our type shapes are now in a spot color channel, our commercial printer will be able to create a special printing plate for them.*

As a Photoshop user, you're in the business of creating illusions. With layer effects, you can accomplish this in a few easy steps. The Photoshop effects that you can apply to a layer, either alone or in combination, include Bevel & Emboss, Stroke, Inner Shadow, Inner Glow, Satin, Color Overlay, Gradient Overlay, Pattern Overlay, Outer Glow, and Drop Shadow. Once applied, layer effects can be edited, hidden, or removed at any time. And best of all, when you modify type or pixels on a layer, any effects on that layer will update automatically (they should be called "Smart Effects"!). Once you develop a combination of effects that you like, you can save it collectively (along with other Layers panel settings) as a style, for use in any document.

In this chapter, we include generic instructions for applying, copying, moving, and removing layer effects; provide specific steps for some individual effects; teach you how to create and apply layer styles; and finally, show you a couple of fun exercises that involve type and layer styles.

Layer effect essentials

Layer effects can be applied to any type, image, Smart Object, or shape layer (or a group thereof ★), but not to the Background. They are applied and edited via the Layer Style dialog and are listed on the Layers panel below the layer they belong to. Layer effects appear either on or along the edges of layer pixels or vector shapes (including type), and will update instantly if you add, modify, or delete areas (or type characters) from the layer. You can edit the settings for a layer effect at any time, and turn its visibility on or off.

Before exploring any of the individual effects, familiarize yourself with these generic instructions.

To apply layer effects (generic steps):

1. Do any of the following:

   Double-click to the right of a layer or layer group name; or for an image layer (not a type or shape layer or a Smart Object), you can double-click the layer thumbnail instead.

   Click a layer or layer group, ★ then choose an effect from the **Add Layer Style** menu *fx* from the bottom of the Layers panel.

   The Layer Style dialog opens (**A**, next page). Check Preview.

Continued on the following page

STYLES USED FOR THE ARROW

The arrow, above, was styled with the Bevel effect (under Bevel & Emboss, Style: Inner) and the Gradient Overlay effect.

2. Click an effect name on the left side of the dialog, then choose settings on the right side.

3. *Optional:* Click other effect names to apply additional effects to the same layer.

4. Click OK.

5. Edit the layer (e.g., transform or move a shape, edit the type in a type layer, add pixels to an image layer). Watch as the "smart" effect(s) update instantly.

   On the Layers panel, any layer that contains effects will have this icon: *fx*. Click the arrowhead next to the icon to collapse or expand that list of effects (**B**, next page).

6. To change the settings for an effect or to add more effects to a layer, double-click the layer or

the Effects listing or double-click an individual effect name (nested below the layer name).

7. To hide or show one layer effect, expand the effects list for the layer, then click the visibility icon 👁 for the effect.

   To hide or show all the effects on a layer, click the visibility icon for the Effects listing.

➤ Some effects have an Angle setting (e.g., Inner Shadow, Satin, and Drop Shadow). If you change the Angle for an individual effect while Use Global Light is checked, the angle will update on any other effects in which the Global Light option is being used. Use this feature to keep the lighting uniform among multiple effects.

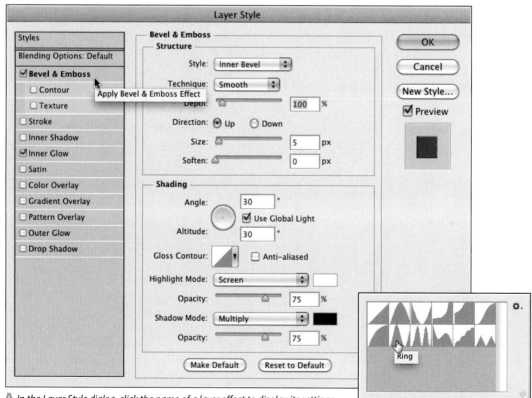

A *In the Layer Style dialog, click the name of a layer effect to display its settings (the box becomes checked automatically).*

The Contour presets define the effect profile. Gray areas in the thumbnail represent opaque pixels, white areas represent transparency. To close the preset picker, either double-click a contour or click anywhere outside the picker.

Choosing imagery for layer effects

➤ We usually apply layer effects that work inward or outward from edges — Bevel, Emboss, Stroke, Inner Shadow, Inner Glow, Outer Glow, and Drop Shadow — to a type or shape layer, or to an image layer that contains some transparent areas. **A** To produce such a layer, create a selection, then press Ctrl-J/Cmd-J (the Layer via Copy command).

➤ The Satin, Color Overlay, Gradient Overlay, and Pattern Overlay effects look fine on any kind of layer, whether the layer contains transparency or not.

➤ When applying effects that spread outward (e.g., Outer Glow, Drop Shadow) to type, allow some breathing room between the characters. You can use the Tracking and/or Kerning controls on the Character panel to adjust the horizontal spacing (see page 361).

DEFAULT LAYER STYLE SETTINGS

➤ To establish new default settings for a particular layer effect, choose the desired settings in the Layer Style dialog, then click Make Default.

➤ To restore the default settings to a layer effect that you established by clicking Make Default (or to restore the factory default settings, if you didn't establish your own default settings), click Reset to Default.

➤ To restore all settings (in all panels) that were in place when you opened the Layer Style dialog, Alt-click/Option-click Reset (Cancel becomes Reset).

➤ To restore the factory default settings to all layer effects, you have to reset all the Photoshop settings files (do this only if it's a necessity): Hold down Ctrl-Alt-Shift/Cmd-Option-Shift while relaunching Photoshop, and click Yes in the alert.

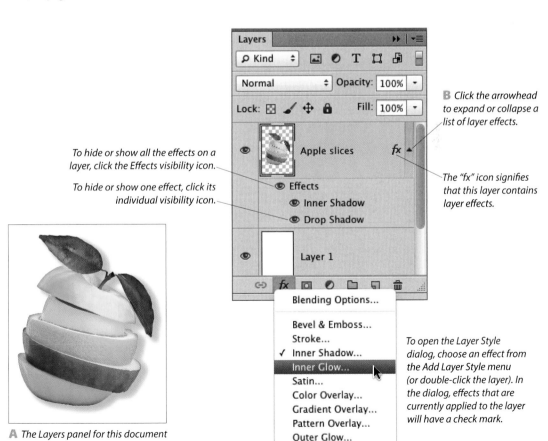

B *Click the arrowhead to expand or collapse a list of layer effects.*

To hide or show all the effects on a layer, click the Effects visibility icon.

To hide or show one effect, click its individual visibility icon.

The "fx" icon signifies that this layer contains layer effects.

To open the Layer Style dialog, choose an effect from the Add Layer Style menu (or double-click the layer). In the dialog, effects that are currently applied to the layer will have a check mark.

A *The Layers panel for this document is shown at right. Note that the image layer contains transparent areas.*

Applying a bevel or emboss effect

The Bevel and Emboss effects create an illusion of volume by adding a highlight and shading. The results can range from a chiseled bevel to a pillowy emboss that looks as if it's been stamped onto porous paper. For variety, experiment with the Contour options.

To apply the Bevel or Emboss effect:

1. On the Layers panel, double-click a layer **A** to open the Layer Style dialog.

2. Click **Bevel & Emboss**.

3. Under Structure, choose a **Size** for the depth of the bevel or emboss effect. **B**

4. Choose other **Structure** settings:

   Choose a **Style** option: **Outer Bevel, Inner Bevel, Emboss, Pillow Emboss,** or **Stroke Emboss C–D** (and **A–B**, next page). (Note: Before applying the Stroke Emboss style, we recommend applying the Stroke effect, at an increased Size setting.)

   From the **Technique** menu, choose **Smooth, Chisel Hard,** or **Chisel Soft**.

   Choose a **Depth** for the intensity of the highlight and the shadow.

   Click the **Up** or **Down** button to swap the positions of the highlight and shadow (try this on the Pillow Emboss style).

   Raise the **Soften** value if you want to blur the effect. The softening is most noticeable when a Chisel option is chosen as the Technique.

Steps 5–7 are optional.

5. Under **Shading**, do any of the following:

   Choose an **Angle** and an **Altitude** (height) to change the location of the light source, and therefore the position of the highlight and shadow. Check **Use Global Light** to apply the same Angle and Altitude settings to all effects in which the Global Light option is being used, for uniform lighting, or uncheck it to apply a unique setting for just this effect. Note: If you change the Angle or Altitude for an effect while Use Global Light is checked, all other effects that are using the Global Light option will adopt those values.

   Click the **Gloss Contour** arrowhead, then choose a profile in the Contour Preset picker.

   ➤ For a reverse bevel, try the Rolling Slope – Descending contour.

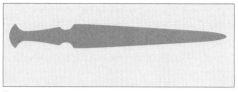

A *The original image contains two layers.*

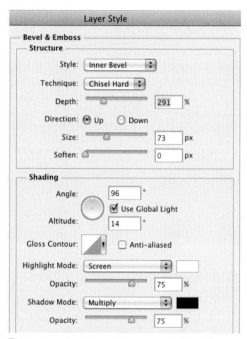

B *We chose these Layer Style options for figure* **C***.*

C *The Inner Bevel effect is applied (and also the Drop Shadow effect).*

D *Here we applied the Outer Bevel effect (plus a Drop Shadow).*

Choose a **Highlight Mode** and **Opacity** for the highlight and a **Shadow Mode** and **Opacity** for the shadow.

To change the highlight or shadow **color**, click the corresponding color swatch, then choose a color via the Color Picker (or, while the picker is open, click a color in the Swatches panel or the document). Click OK.

6. To add a Contour to the edges of the bevel or emboss, do the following:

On the left side of the dialog, under Bevel & Emboss, click **Contour**. Click the Contour arrowhead, then click a contour preset in the picker. This option can alter the appearance of the effect dramatically.

Check **Anti-aliased** to soften the transition between the dark and light areas in the contour.

For the Style option of Outer Bevel or Inner Bevel, adjust the **Range** (the position of the bevel on the chosen contour) to minimize or maximize the prominence of the bevel.

7. To add a texture to the effect, click **Texture** on the left side of the dialog, click the Pattern arrowhead, click a pattern in the picker, then do any of the following:

Adjust the **Scale** of the pattern.

Change the **Depth** to increase or reduce the contrast between the highlights and shadows in the pattern.

Check **Invert** to swap the highlights and shadows. This has the same effect as changing the Depth percentage from negative to positive, and vice versa.

Check **Link with Layer** to link the texture and layer so they will move as a unit when dragged in the document.

Drag in the document to reposition the texture within the effect; click **Snap to Origin** to realign the pattern to its default location.

8. Click OK.

➤ For another use of the Emboss effect, see page 386.

SAVE YOUR SETTINGS!

If you produce a layer effect or combination of effects and Layers panel settings that you want to preserve for future use, save that collection of settings as a style on the Styles panel, then save it in a library (see page 383).

A *We imported these original Illustrator objects into Photoshop as a Smart Object.*

B *We applied the Pillow Emboss effect (Technique: Smooth).*

C *We added the Texture option of the Emboss effect.*

Applying a shadow effect

You can create an inner shadow or drop shadow with just a few clicks of the mouse.

To apply the Inner Shadow or Drop Shadow effect:

1. On the Layers panel, double-click next to a layer name to open the Layer Style dialog. A

2. Click **Inner Shadow** or **Drop Shadow.** B–D

3. Choose a **Distance** value (in pixels) by which you want the shadow to be offset from the edge of the layer shapes.

   ➤ You can reposition a drop shadow by dragging in the document while the dialog is open, but be aware that this will also reposition any other effects that are using the Global Light option.

   Choose a **Choke** percentage for an Inner Shadow or a **Spread** percentage for a Drop Shadow to control where the shadow begins to fade.

   Choose an overall **Size** for the shadow (in pixels).

4. Do any of the following (optional):

   Choose a **Blend Mode** from the menu. (For a drop shadow, we usually keep this on the default setting of Multiply.)

   To choose a different shadow **color**, click the color swatch, choose a color via the Color Picker or click a color in the document with the eyedropper (the color previews in the document), then click OK.

   Choose an **Opacity** percentage for the transparency level of the shadow. For a drop shadow, we usually lower the Opacity below the default value of 75%.

   Choose an **Angle** for the position of the shadow relative to the original layer shapes.

   In the Quality area, click the **Contour** arrowhead and choose a preset in the picker for the edge profile of the shadow (we're usually content with the shape of the default Contour).

   Check **Anti-aliased** to soften any jagged edges between the shadow and the layer imagery.

   Adjust the **Noise** level. The addition of noise (speckling) can help prevent banding on print output, but a very low value is best.

   For the Drop Shadow effect, if the Fill value of the layer is below 100% or the blending mode of the layer isn't set to Normal, check **Layer Knocks Out**

A This original image consists of an image layer (hammer and nail and transparent pixels) above a solid-color background.

B We applied the Drop Shadow effect to the image layer.

C This image consists of an image layer (popsicle and transparent pixels) above a solid white Background.

D We applied the Inner Shadow effect to the popsicle layer. Slurp.

Drop Shadow to prevent the shadow from showing through.

5. Click OK. If you want to reshape the shadow, follow the steps below.

Depending on the time of day and the angle of the sun or other light source, cast shadows tend to be either short or elongated. You can reshape a drop shadow via the Distort command to mimic this natural effect.

To transform a Drop Shadow effect:

1. Apply the Drop Shadow effect to a layer (see the preceding instructions) and no other effects. Keep the layer selected.

2. To transfer the shadow effect to its own layer, right-click the Effects listing on the Layers panel, then choose **Create Layer** from the context menu. If an alert dialog appears, click OK.

3. Click the new Drop Shadow layer. **A**

4. Choose Edit > Transform > **Distort**, drag the handles of the transform box to slant the shape, or for a symmetrical perspective distortion, hold down Ctrl-Alt-Shift/Cmd-Option-Shift while dragging a corner handle. Press Enter/Return. **B** Note: If you don't see all the handles, press Ctrl-0/Cmd-0 (zero) to fit the image in the document window.

➤ To link the image and shadow layers so they will move and transform as a unit, Shift-click them, then click the Link Layers button 🔗 at the bottom of the panel.

➤ To limit any painting or fill edits that you apply to the Drop Shadow layer to just the pixels on the shadow layer, activate the Lock Transparent Pixels button on the Layers panel first.

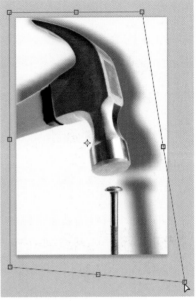

A Starting with the image shown in figure **B** on the preceding page, we applied the Create Layer command to transfer the drop shadow to its own layer and then, as shown above, we applied a Distort transformation.

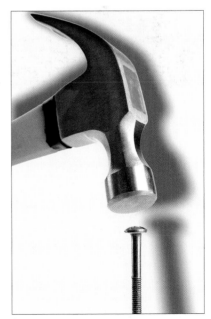

B This is the final image, the Layers panel for which is shown at left. Note: We lowered the Fill setting for the Drop Shadow to 68%.

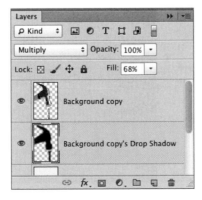

Applying the Stroke effect

The Stroke effect works particularly well on type.

To apply the Stroke effect:

1. Double-click a layer on the Layers panel to open the Layer Style dialog.

2. Click **Stroke**.

3. Do any of the following:

   Choose a **Size** (width) for the stroke.

   From the **Position** menu, choose a location for the stroke relative to the layer content: Outside, Inside, or Center.

   Choose a **Blend Mode**.

   Choose an **Opacity** percentage.

   For the **Fill Type**, choose **Color**, **Gradient** (see steps 3–5 below), or **Pattern** (see steps 3–4 on the next page) and choose settings for the options that become available.

4. Click OK.

Applying the Gradient and Pattern Overlay effects

You can apply the Gradient Overlay and Pattern Overlay effects to an image, shape, or type layer. On an image layer, the overlays work effectively whether the layer contains transparency or not. (Color Overlay, not covered here, works the same way.)

To apply the Gradient Overlay effect:

1. Double-click a layer on the Layers panel to open the Layer Style dialog.**B**

2. Click **Gradient Overlay**.**C–D**

3. Click the **Gradient** arrowhead, then click a gradient on the picker. (To load gradients from another library, choose a library name from the lower part of the picker menu; see page 119.) You could also click the gradient thumbnail and edit the gradient.

4. From the **Style** menu, choose Linear, Radial, Angle, Reflected, or Diamond.

5. Do any of the following:

   Choose a **Blend Mode**.

   Check **Dither** to help prevent noticeable color bands in the gradient on print output. ★

   Adjust the **Opacity** of the overlay.

   Check **Reverse** to swap the position of the colors in the gradient.

A We applied the Stroke effect to a type layer, selecting Gradient as the Fill Type.

B We applied a Bevel effect (Inner Bevel style) to this type.

Layer Style

Gradient Overlay
  Gradient

Blend Mode:	Normal	☑ Dither
Opacity:	100 %
Gradient:	☐ Reverse
Style:	Reflected	☑ Align with Layer
Angle:	23 °
Scale:	77 %

C We chose these options for the Gradient Overlay layer effect.

D We added the Gradient Overlay effect.

Check **Align with Layer** to fit the gradient within just the nontransparent pixels, type, or shape on the layer, or uncheck this option to center the gradient on the full layer.

Set the **Angle** of the gradient.

Choose a **Scale** percentage to control how gradually the gradient colors transition across the layer.

Drag in the document to reposition the gradient within the layer shapes.

6. Click OK.

➤ If you apply two overlay effects to the same layer, such as Gradient Overlay and Pattern Overlay, lower the Opacity of the one that's listed first in the dialog; otherwise the bottom one won't be visible.

The patterns that you apply via the Pattern Overlay effect can range from those that have an obvious repeat, such as polka dots or stripes, to overall textures resembling surfaces, such as gritty sandpaper, handmade paper, woven fabric, or variegated stone.

To apply the Pattern Overlay effect:

1. Double-click a layer on the Layers panel to open the Layer Style dialog.

2. Click **Pattern Overlay**.

3. Click the **Pattern** arrowhead, then click a pattern preset in the picker. To load patterns from another library, choose a library name from the lower part of the picker menu (see page 119). To create a custom pattern, see page 199.

4. Do any of the following:

   Change the **Blend Mode**.

   Adjust the **Opacity** of the overlay.

   Drag in the document to reposition the pattern; click **Snap to Origin** to realign the pattern with the upper left corner of the document.

   Choose a **Scale** percentage for the pattern size.

   Check **Link with Layer** to link the pattern to the layer so they'll move as a unit if you drag the layer.

5. Click OK. **A–B**

SCALING LAYER EFFECTS

To scale the effects on a layer without scaling other layer content, right-click the Effects listing and choose Scale Effects from the context menu, then specify the desired Scale percentage in the dialog.

A *To produce these metallic letters, we created a pattern from a photograph of rusted metal, then applied it as a Pattern Overlay layer effect. (We also applied the Drop Shadow and Emboss effects.)*

B *To learn how to create the grommets shown above, visit our blog at elaineandpeter.com.*

APPLYING THE SATIN EFFECT

To make the surfaces of objects, type, or brush strokes look reflective or metallic, use the Satin effect.

➤ If you don't see enough of the Satin effect, try increasing the Distance and/or Size values.

➤ Before adding this effect to type, try applying a medium or light type color and a strong Inner Glow or Bevel effect.

To the type shown in figure **B** *on the preceding page (which has an Inner Bevel), we added the Satin effect.*

Copying, moving, and removing layer effects

If you like how an effect looks on one layer, you can copy it to another one.

To copy an individual effect from one layer to another:

Alt-drag/Option-drag an individual effect name from one layer to another.

You can also move an individual effect from one layer to another. No existing effects will be deleted from the target layer. However, if an existing effect bears the same name as the incoming effect, the new settings will override the existing ones.

To move an effect to another layer without replacing any existing effects:

Drag an individual effect name from one layer to another. The effect will be removed from the source layer and placed on the target layer.

And finally, you can also move all the effects from one layer to another (that is, replace any existing effects on the target layer and remove them from the source layer).

To move all the effects from one layer to another, replacing existing effects:

Drag the Effects listing from one layer to another.

Clicking to remove the visibility icon for a layer effect or unchecking the box for an effect in the Layer Style dialog doesn't remove the effect—it merely hides it from view. If you want to permanently delete one or all effects from a layer, do as follows.

To remove layer effects:

Do either of the following:

Drag a single effect name to the Delete Layer button 🗑 at the bottom of the Layers panel.

To remove all the effects from a layer, drag the Effects listing over the Delete Layer button. 🗑

➤ If you turn off an effect via the check box in the Layer Style dialog and then check it to turn it back on again, the last-used options for that effect will redisplay.

LAYER EFFECTS ARE LIVE

Layer effects reshape automatically when you edit the object(s) they're applied to, as illustrated below.

We applied the Emboss, Gradient Overlay, Outer Glow, and Drop Shadow effects to the type layer, and the Inner Glow and Drop Shadow effects to the image layer.

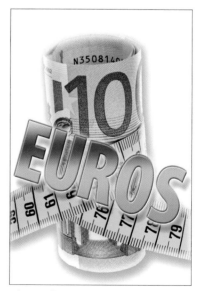

When we shrank the image layer and added a type character, the effects updated automatically.

Changing the layer fill percentage

The Fill setting on the Layers panel controls the opacity of a layer, excluding any layer effects (as shown below), whereas the Opacity setting controls the opacity of a layer, including any layer effects (see page 144).

To change the layer fill percentage:

1. Click any kind of layer (not the Background) or select multiple layers.**A**

2. On the Layers panel, choose a **Fill** percentage (you can use the scrubby slider).**B** The lower the Fill value, the more pixels from the underlying layer(s) will be revealed.

RASTERIZING LAYER STYLES AND EFFECTS

► To rasterize all the layer style settings on the current layer, including layer effect, blending mode, and opacity and fill settings, click a layer that contains layer styles (or select multiple layers), then choose Layer > Rasterize > Layer Style. ★ *Beware!* If you apply this command to a type, shape, or Smart Object layer, that layer will also be rasterized.

► To flatten all the layer effects in a document— on all layers—choose File > Scripts > Flatten All Layer Effects. Like the Rasterize > Layer Style command, this script rasterizes type, shape, and Smart Object layers that contain effects.

A *This image contains three image layers and an editable type layer. The Drop Shadow effect is applied to all the layers.*

B *When we lowered the Fill percentage of the type layer to 60%, the Drop Shadow effect remained at full opacity. When we lowered the Opacity of the basil and bay leaf image layers to 70%, the drop shadows on those layers became lighter, too.*

Applying layer styles

You can conveniently store multiple layer settings collectively as a style on the Styles panel. The style will include layer effects (e.g., Drop Shadow, Outer Glow) and/or blending options (blending mode and layer Opacity and Fill settings). Once stored, styles can be quickly applied to a type, image, or shape layer. To acquaint yourself with this panel, apply one of the predefined styles to a type layer or to a layer that contains some transparency.

To apply a style to a layer:

1. Show the Styles panel. 🎨 You can load additional style libraries onto the panel via the panel menu.

2. Do one of the following:

   Click a layer (not the Background) on the Layers panel, then click a style on the Styles panel. **A–D**

   Double-click a layer to open the Layer Style dialog, click Styles at the top left, click a style thumbnail, then click OK. **E**

➤ Normally, when you apply a style, it replaces any and all existing effects on the current layer. If you want to add the effects from a style to the existing effects on a layer, Shift-click as you apply the style. Note: Whether or not you hold down Shift, if two effects have the same name, the settings in the incoming style will replace the old.

To remove styling from a layer:

Click a (hidden or visible) layer that contains layer style edits, then click the **Clear Style** button ⊘ on the Styles panel (or right-click the layer listing and choose Clear Layer Style from the context menu). All layer effects are removed, the layer Opacity is reset to 100%, and the blending mode is reset to Normal.

A Click a layer, then click a style thumbnail on the Styles panel.

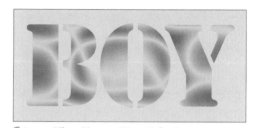

B Web Styles library > Blue Paper Clip

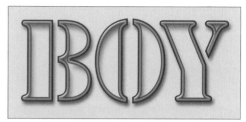

C Image Effects library > Water Reflection

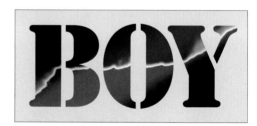

D KS Styles library > Lightning

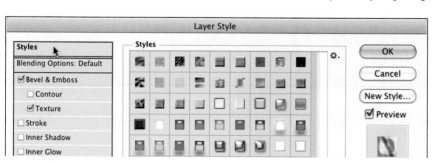

E Styles can also be applied to a layer via the Layer Style dialog. Click Styles at the top left side of the dialog, then click a thumbnail.

Creating layer styles

In addition to using the layer style presets, you can create and save custom layer styles. You can use an applied preset as a starting point or begin from scratch with your own settings. An option is provided via a dialog for the style to include the layer effects and/or the blending option settings that are applied to the currently selected layer.

To save a style to the Styles panel:

1. To any layer, apply the effects settings and/or blending option settings that you want to save collectively as a style.

2. Do either of the following:

    On the Layers panel, click the layer that contains the desired settings, **A** then on the Styles panel, click either the blank area or the **New Style** button. **B**

    On the Layers panel, double-click the layer that contains the desired settings, then on the right side of the Layer Style dialog, click **New Style**.

3. In the New Style dialog, enter a name for the new style, check whether you want to **Include Layer Effects** and/or **Include Layer Blending Options** (e.g., layer opacity, blending mode, and fill opacity settings) in the style, then click OK. If the Layer Style dialog is open, click OK to exit.

    The new style appears as the last listing or thumbnail on the Styles panel, and can be used in any document. **C–D**

4. Your custom styles will be deleted from the Styles panel if you allow them to be replaced by another library or if the Photoshop Preferences file is deleted or damaged. To save the styles on the panel as a permanent library, click Save, enter a name, keep the default location, then click Save again. (See also page 117 or 119.)

➤ To copy a style between layers, right-click the layer that contains the desired effects and settings and choose Copy Layer Style. Click the target layer, then right-click it and choose Paste Layer Style. The incoming style will replace any existing style settings on the target layer.

➤ You can't edit an existing style on the Styles panel, but you can apply a style, edit the settings, and save the new settings as a separate custom style.

A *On the Layers panel, we clicked a layer that contains the effects and/or other settings to be saved as a style.*

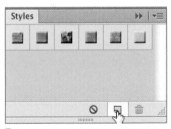

B *On the Styles panel, we clicked the New Style button.*

C *Our new custom style appeared at the bottom of the panel.*

D *We applied the new style to a shape layer in another document.*

Making type look like rusted metal

With the exception of Drop Shadow and Overlay, layer effects tend to produce a more convincing visual illusion when applied in combination, as in the example shown here. **A–B** (and **A–C**, next page). After applying a series of effects, remember to preserve your settings as a layer style — and in a custom library!

A We created editable type (Bauhaus 93 Regular font, 223 pt.) above a photo of rusted metal.

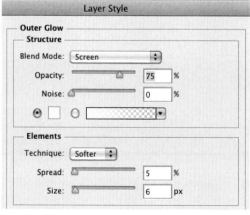

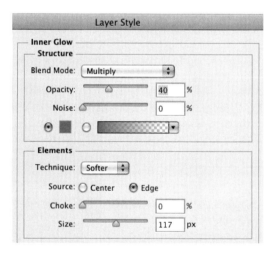

B We applied the Inner Shadow, Inner Glow, Outer Glow, and Drop Shadow effects, using the settings shown above.

A *To reveal some of the underlying layer within the type, we lowered the Fill percentage of the type layer.*

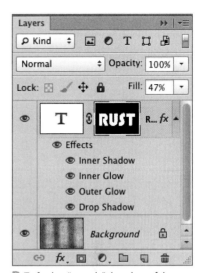

B *To further "corrode" the edges of the letters, we Ctrl/Cmd clicked the type layer thumbnail to create a selection from the characters, clicked the Add Layer Mask button, then applied Filter > Brush Strokes > Spatter. The filter roughed up the edges of the mask. This is the Layers panel for the final image, which is shown below.*

C *The Spatter filter added just the finishing touch we were after. (You can use the Distort > Glass filter instead of Spatter.)*

Embossing leather

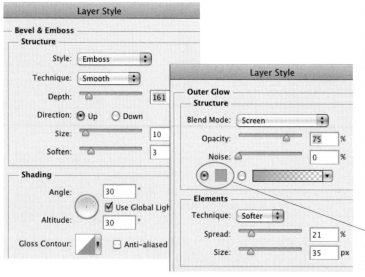

A *Note: For the Outer Glow effect, we clicked the color swatch, then clicked to sample a color in the image.*

B *To create these embossed letters, we opened a photo of leather and created some type (Trajan Pro font, Bold, 112 pt.). We chose the Move tool, clicked the Color swatch on the Character panel, chose a color for the type by clicking in the image (eyedropper pointer), then exited the Color Picker. We chose the Emboss and Outer Glow settings shown above, chose Multiply mode for the type layer, and lowered the layer Opacity and Fill settings.*

C *We saved the settings shown above as a layer style, then applied it to a type layer above a Background photo of a leather-covered book. We changed the color of the Outer Glow effect by sampling a light area in the image, and also lowered the Fill value to 10%.*

We added the fleur-de-lis at the top of this image by using the Custom Shape tool (stroke of None) and the Fleur-De-Lis shape preset (see pages 387–388). Finally, to apply the same style to the shape as we did to the type, we right-clicked the type layer listing and chose Copy Layer Style, then right-clicked the shape layer and chose Paste Layer Style.

In this chapter, you will learn how use the shape tools to create vector paths, which have clean and precise edges, like the vector paths in a drawing program. You will also learn how to create vector masks, which hide areas of a layer as pixel masks do, except that they're made from paths, not pixels.

Creating vector shapes

Like the vector objects in Adobe Illustrator, the underlying structure of a vector shape in Photoshop is an editable path, complete with anchor points and direction lines. In Photoshop CS6, the layer listing for a vector shape doesn't have a mask, unlike the way Photoshop created shapes as a fill layer (with vector mask) in previous versions. At any time, you can transform a vector shape, change its contour by manipulating its anchor points and direction lines, change the fill color, and change the stroke color and style (see pages 389–390).

The easiest way to create a vector shape is by using one of the ready-made presets, as in the steps below.

To create a vector shape: ★

1. On the Layers panel, click the layer above which you want the new shape layer to appear.

2. On the Tools panel, choose one of the shape tools (U or Shift-U).**A**

3. On the Options bar, do the following:

   From the **Tool Mode** menu, choose **Shape**.

   (Ignore the Fill and Stroke controls for the moment; they are covered fully on pages 389–390.)

   Open the **Tool Options** menu, ⚙. then click **Unconstrained** (the default setting).

   If you're using the Custom Shape tool,🐾 click a shape on the **Custom Shape** picker (or right-click in the image and choose from the preset picker on the context menu).**B**

Continued on the following page

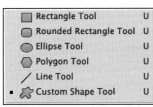

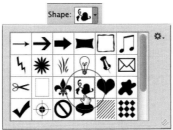

A We chose the Custom Shape tool on the Tools panel.

B We clicked a preset on the Custom Shape picker.

VECTOR SHAPES & MASKS

21

A VECTOR BY ANOTHER NAME

Throughout this book, we use the term "shape layer" to describe a layer that contains vector shapes, or what others may refer to as a "vector layer."

THE VECTOR ADVANTAGE

Shapes are resolution independent, meaning they print at the resolution of the output device, not at the resolution of the file. Transformations don't affect the sharpness of vector layers, as they do pixel layers.

4. To produce the shape, do either of the following:

Drag in the document. To constrain the pro-portions of the shape, hold down Shift while dragging.**A–B**

Click in the document, enter values and choose settings in the dialog, then click OK.**C**

A new vector shape layer appears on the Layers panel. All the Layers panel settings are available for it (e.g., blending mode, opacity, layer effects).

➤ To load other libraries onto the Custom Shape picker, see page 117 or 119.

➤ To reposition a shape, click the shape layer, click the Path Selection tool ◥ or Move tool, ✛ then drag the shape in the image.

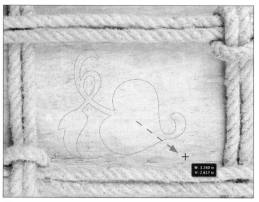

A *We chose the Custom Shape tool, the Shape option from the Tool Mode menu, and a preset on the Custom Shape picker, then Shift-dragged to produce the shape.*

B *The last-used Fill and Stroke attributes appeared in the shape. (To reveal the underlying wood texture within it, we chose Color Burn as the blending mode for the shape layer.)*

Aligning shapes for Web output ★

➤ Before creating, transforming, or editing paths for Web output, make sure **Snap Vector Tools and Transforms to Pixel Grid** is checked in General Preferences. Photoshop will snap Pen tool anchor points or the bounding box of a shape to the pixel grid, for sharper onscreen rendering. This option doesn't affect anti-aliasing.

➤ To have Photoshop minimize or remove anti-aliasing from the edges of a vector shape, check **Align Edges** on the Options bar for your shape tool. Horizontal and vertical edges of the shape (including any subpaths) that touch the bound-ing box will be aligned to the pixel grid. Note that this feature may cause the stroke on a shape to be offset from its path.

DRAWING AND EDITING CUSTOM SHAPES ★

➤ If you're adept at drawing with the Pen tool in Adobe Illustrator, you have the skills to create cus-tom shapes in Photoshop. Choose the Pen tool, ✎ choose Shape from the Tool Mode menu on the Options bar, then draw a path. To reshape the path contour, click the edge with the Direct Selection tool, ◤ then manipulate the points and direction lines.

➤ To save a customized shape for future use, on the Layers panel, click the shape layer, choose Edit > Define Custom Shape, enter a name in the Shape Name dialog, then click OK. The new shape appears last on the Custom Shape picker, and is available for use in any document. To save the shapes on the picker as a permanent library, see page 117.

DRAWING STRAIGHT LINES

To draw a line, we recommend using the Pen tool (click, click), which creates a solid line, instead of the Line tool, which creates a very thin hollow rectangle.

C *You can also create a shape by clicking in the document with the tool, then enter-ing values.*

Changing the fill and stroke on a vector shape

In the world of vector shapes, the fill color is applied to the interior of a shape, and the stroke color is applied along the edge of the shape. You can change the fill and stroke colors (or remove them) at any time. (To choose width and style options, see the next page.)

To recolor a vector shape: ★

1. Choose the **Path Selection** tool � (A or Shift-A).

2. Do either of the following:

   Click a shape layer listing on the Layers panel.

   If the shape already has a fill or stroke color, click the shape in the document.

3. On the Options bar, click the **Fill** or **Stroke** swatch to open a picker, then do one of the following:

   Click the **No Color** button ☐ to apply a Fill or Stroke of None.

   Click the **Solid Color** button, then click a color swatch;**A** or click the Color Picker button,☐ choose a color, then click OK. You can add the current Foreground color by clicking the gray area below the swatches. Colors that you try out are added as temporary swatches below Recently Used Colors.

Click the **Gradient** button to display a gradient editor, then click a gradient swatch.**B** To add another color stop, click below the bar. To recolor a stop, double-click the stop to open the Color Picker, choose a color, then click OK. To use the other controls on the picker (e.g., add opacity stops, change the gradient style or angle), see pages 196–197.

Click the **Pattern** button, click a pattern swatch, and adjust the Scale percentage, if desired.**C**

4. Click outside the Fill or Stroke picker to close it (or click Esc to cancel your edits).

➤ To load another library onto the Solid Color, Gradient, or Pattern preset picker, see page 119.

➤ Only one set of fill and stroke settings can be applied to multiple shapes on the same layer.

➤ To copy a Fill or Stroke color, gradient, or pattern between shapes, click a shape layer, choose the Path Selection tool, choose Copy [Fill or Stroke] from the Fill or Stroke picker menu, click another shape layer, then choose Paste [Fill or Stroke] from the same picker menu.

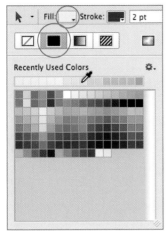

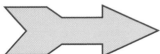

A *We clicked the Fill swatch to open the picker, clicked the Solid Color button, clicked a few colors, then clicked a swatch under Recently Used Colors. (We also applied a stroke color.)*

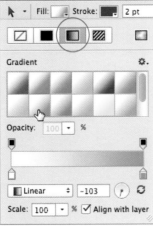

B *We clicked the Gradient button, then clicked a gradient.*

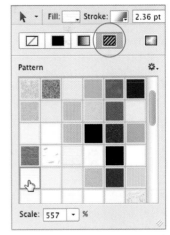

C *We clicked the Pattern button, then clicked a pattern (we also applied a gradient to the stroke).*

In addition to the stroke color, you can change the stroke width, style (solid, dotted, or dashed), alignment, cap style, and corner style.

To change the stroke styling on a vector shape: ★

1. Click a shape layer listing on the Layers panel; or choose the **Path Selection** tool ▶ (A or Shift-A), then click a shape in the document.

2. On the Options bar, change the **Stroke Width.**A

3. Click the **Stroke Type** picker, then do any of the following:

   Click a stroke preset in the scrolling window.**B**

   Choose an **Align** option to change the position of the stroke on the path.**C**

   Choose a **Caps** option to change the shape of the stroke at the endpoints, if the path is open.

   Choose a **Corners** option to change the shape of any angles (corners) in the path.

   To learn how to create and save a custom dashed or dotted stroke, see our blog at elaineandpeter.com.

4. *Optional:* To save the current stroke settings as a preset, choose **Save Stroke** from the picker menu.

5. Click anywhere outside the picker to close it (or click Esc to cancel your edits).

➤ To copy Stroke Options settings (not colors) between shapes, click a shape layer, choose Copy Stroke Details from the Stroke Type picker menu, click another shape layer, then choose Paste Stroke Details from the same menu.

➤ To copy all the stroke and fill settings from one shape to another, including the colors and stroke styling, right-click a shape layer and choose Copy Shape Attributes from the context menu. Click another shape layer, then choose Paste Shape Attributes from the context menu.

➤ To align multiple shape layers, see page 261.

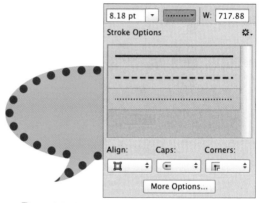

A *We're changing the Stroke Width (the scrubby slider changes the value in 1-point increments).*

B *We clicked a preset in the scroll window.*

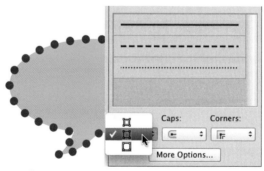

C *We're choosing the Align: Center option.*

PASTING SHAPES FROM ILLUSTRATOR

To paste a path from Adobe Illustrator to Photoshop as a shape layer, in Illustrator, copy a vector object. In Photoshop, choose Edit > Paste. In the Paste dialog, click Paste As: Shape Layer, then click OK. The current Fill color will appear within the shape, and the shape will have a stroke of None.

CONVERTING SHAPES TO PIXELS

To convert a vector layer to a standard pixel layer, right-click the shape layer and choose Rasterize Layer from the context menu. If you want to restrict image edits to the former shape areas, activate the Lock Transparent Pixels button ▣ on the Layers panel.

Combining multiple vector shapes

You can combine multiple shapes onto one layer in different ways: combine, subtract, intersect, or exclude.

To combine multiple shapes on a layer: ★

1. Click an existing shape layer.**A**

2. Choose any shape tool.

3. On the Options bar, choose **Shape** from the Tool Mode menu and choose an option from the **Path Operations** menu, then draw a shape:

   To add a shape to the existing one, choose **Combine Shapes,** or to cut out an area from a shape, choose **Subtract Front Shape.** Draw a new shape.**B**

   ➤ To add a shape to a layer without having to use the Path Operations menu, hold down Shift and drag, release Shift, then keep dragging. To subtract from the existing shape, hold down Alt/Option while dragging.**C**

To preserve only the intersection of the existing shape and a new one, choose **Intersect Shape Areas** ; or to add a new shape while subtracting overlapping areas, choose **Exclude Overlapping Shapes.** Draw a new shape that overlaps the existing one.**D**

4. *Optional:* To reposition a shape, select and move it with the Path Selection tool **E–F**; to copy it, hold down Alt/Option while dragging it. (To discard a selected shape, press Backspace/Delete.)

➤ To combine shapes from different layers, select the layers, then choose Layer > Combine Shapes.

➤ To align shapes on a layer, Shift-click them with the Path Selection tool, then choose one or more options from the Path Alignment menu.

➤ The current choice displays as the icon for the Path Operations menu.

A *We created this shape with the Rectangle tool.*

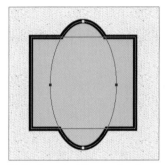

B *We chose the Ellipse tool and the Combine Shapes option, then dragged to add an oval. The resulting shape contains two paths.*

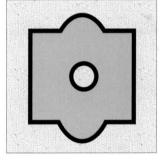

C *Next, we held down Alt/Option and dragged a small circle to subtract (cut through) the other two shapes.*

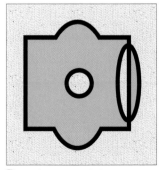

D *We chose the Exclude Overlapping Shapes option, then drew an ellipse on the right side.*

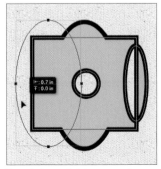

E *With the Path Selection tool, we dragged the large ellipse to the left.*

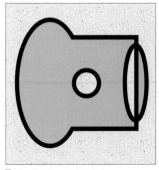

F *The final combined shape contains four paths.*

Creating vector masks

One advantage of vector masks is that they occupy less storage space than pixel masks or alpha channels. Like a pixel mask, each vector mask belongs to only one layer and displays as a thumbnail on the Layers panel. You can reposition the path within the mask, or discard the mask, at any time. Here we will show you how to create a vector mask from a new shape layer, from an existing shape layer, and from a type layer.

To create a vector mask from a custom shape: ★

1. On the Layers panel, ☙ click the image layer or layer group to which you want to add a vector mask.

2. Choose a shape tool (U or Shift-U).

3. On the Options bar, choose **Path** from the Tool Mode menu. If you're using the Custom Shape tool, click a shape on the Custom Shape picker.

4. Drag in the document, or Shift-drag to preserve the original proportions of the shape.**A** To move the path while drawing it, add the Spacebar to the mix.

   ➤ To move the finished path, press and hold A (for a temporary Path Selection tool), then drag inside the path.

5. On the Options bar, click Make: **Mask** to produce the vector mask.**B**

6. *Optional:* To reshape a vector mask, click the layer it is attached to, then use the Free Transform command (see pages 332–333) or manipulate the points or direction lines.

➤ If you're a vector drawing pro and want to draw the path for a vector mask with the Pen tool (it takes dexterity and practice!), substitute drawing the path for steps 2–4 in the instructions above.

To create a vector mask from an existing shape layer: ★

1. On the Layers panel, ☙ click a shape layer.

2. Hold down Ctrl-Alt/Cmd-Option and drag from the shape layer to an image layer.

To create a vector mask from type: ★

1. Have an image layer available (not the Background), and create a type layer (**A**, next page).

2. Right-click the type layer listing and choose **Create Work Path**. Hide the type layer.

A *We created a path with the Custom Shape tool (Diamond Card preset, Shapes library).*

B *We clicked the Mask option to convert the shape to a mask on the current image layer.*

3. On the Layers panel, ❧ click an image layer, then Ctrl-click/Cmd-click the **Add Vector Mask** button. ⬚ **B–C** (If the image layer has a layer mask, you can click the Add Vector Mask button without holding down Ctrl/Cmd.)

Working with vector masks

If you want to hide or reveal a different part of a layer, move the vector mask separately from the layer pixels.

To reposition a vector mask:

1. On the Layers panel, ❧ click a vector mask thumbnail.

2. Choose the **Path Selection** tool ▸ (A or Shift-A).

3. If the mask contains multiple subpaths (such as type shapes), drag a marquee around the ones you want to reposition.

4. Drag in the document. **D–E**

To deactivate a vector mask: ★

Do either of the following:

On the Layers panel, Shift-click a vector mask thumbnail.

On the Layers panel, click the vector mask thumbnail, then on the Properties panel, ▦ click the **Disable/Enable Mask** button. ⬚

A red X appears in the thumbnail, and the entire layer is visible (**A**, next page). To reactivate the mask at any time, repeat either method above (the X disappears).

A *We created an editable type layer above an image layer.*

B *We produced a work path from the type, then added a vector mask to the image layer. (The Background contains a texture.)*

C *The image is visible only within the white areas of the mask.*

D *We're moving a vector mask.*

E *Now a different part of the image is visible within the mask shape.*

To copy a vector mask to another layer:

Alt-drag/Option-drag a vector mask thumbnail from one layer to another (not the Background). A copy of the mask appears in the destination layer.

To move a vector mask from one layer to another:

Drag a vector mask thumbnail from one layer to another (not the Background). The mask is removed from the original layer, and is placed on the destination layer.

You can switch the function of a vector mask so that it hides areas of the layer instead of reveals them.

To switch the function of a vector mask: ★

1. Choose the **Path Selection** tool ▶ (A or Shift-A).
2. In the document, click a vector mask shape to select its path (or double-click it, if necessary).
3. If the mask contains subpaths (e.g., shapes created from type), drag a marquee around them. All the anchor points and segments will be selected.**B**
4. Choose **Subtract Front Shape** ⬚ from the Path Operations menu on the Options bar, or press – (minus key).**C**

➤ To restore the default reveal and hide functions to a vector mask, choose Combine Shapes ⬚ from the Path Operations menu on the Options bar, or press + (plus key).

➤ To apply the effect of a vector mask to a layer permanently, click the mask thumbnail, then click the Apply Mask button ◈ on the Properties panel.

You can delete any vector masks that you no longer need (although you won't recoup much in the way of file storage space by doing so).

To discard a vector mask:

Do one of the following:

On the Layers panel, click the thumbnail for the vector mask to be removed, click the **Delete Layer** button, 🗑 then if an alert dialog appears, click OK (or Alt-click/Option-click the button to bypass the prompt).

On the Layers panel, right-click the vector mask thumbnail and choose **Delete Vector Mask**.

On the Layers panel, click the vector mask thumbnail, then on the Properties panel, 🗁 click the **Delete Mask** button. 🗑

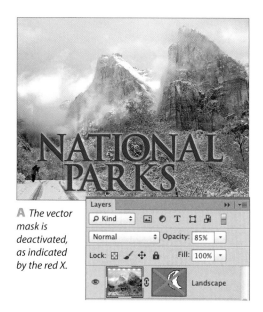

A *The vector mask is deactivated, as indicated by the red X.*

B *We selected the leaf-shaped vector mask in this document.*

C *We switched the function of the mask by pressing – (minus key). Now the vector shape is hiding an area of the layer instead of revealing it.*

To automate repetitive (and boring) editing tasks, you can record a sequence of
commands in an action and then replay the
action on one image or on a batch of images.

Actions can be used to execute anything from a simple
edit, such as converting files to a different format or
color mode, to a complex sequence of commands,
such as applying a series of adjustments or filters or a
sequence of preflight steps to ready your files for output.
With actions, you can boost your productivity, relieve
your life of (some) drudgery, and standardize your editing steps. Photoshop ships with dozens of ready-made
actions, some of which you may find useful. In this
chapter, you'll learn how to record, play, and edit custom
actions, and how to save and load action sets.

Recording an action

Using the Actions panel,  you can record, store, edit,
play, delete, save, and load actions. The panel has two
modes: List (edit) **A** and Button (**A**, page 397). When the
panel is in List mode, you can expand or collapse the list
of commands in an action; toggle a dialog control on or
off; add, exclude, delete, rerecord, or change the order of
commands; or save actions and action sets to an actions
file. To put the panel into List mode, uncheck Button
Mode on the panel menu.

Continued on the following page

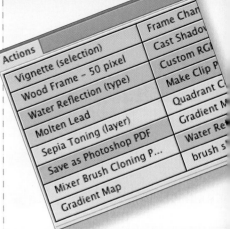

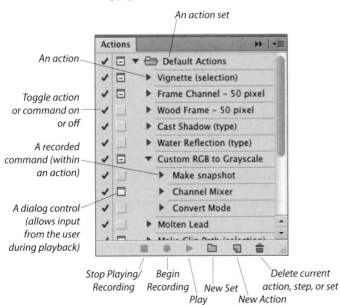

An action set

An action

*Toggle action
or command on
or off*

*A recorded
command (within
an action)*

*A dialog control
(allows input
from the user
during playback)*

*Stop Playing/
Recording* *Begin
Recording* *New Set* *Delete current
action, step, or set*

Play *New Action*

A *This Actions panel is in List mode.*

Each command that is recorded in an action is nested below the action name on the Actions panel. Actions, in turn, are stored in sets. Note: To learn how to include edits in an action that aren't directly recordable, see pages 401–402.

To record an action:

1. The action you're about to record has to be stored in a set. To create a set, click the New Set button  at the bottom of the Actions panel, type a descriptive Name, then click OK.

2. Open a document or create a new one. We recommend copying the document using File > Save As.

3. Click the **New Action** button at the bottom of the Actions panel.

4. In the New Action dialog, enter a **Name** for the action, and from the **Set** menu, choose a set (either the one you created in step 1 or a different one).**A**

5. *Optional:* Choose a shortcut from the Function Key menu, and check Shift and/or Command to prevent conflicts with the function keys that are assigned to system commands. Choose a color to display when the panel is in Button mode.

6. Click **Record**.

7. We recommend as a first step that you create a snapshot of the current state of the document on the History panel. Next, execute the commands that you want to record, as you would normally apply them to any image. Any time you enter values in a dialog and click OK, your settings will be recorded (unless you click Cancel).

8. When you're done recording edits for the action, click the **Stop Playing/Recording** button.

9. The new action will appear on the panel.

➤ If you create layers or alpha channels while recording an action, assign them descriptive, nongeneric names to prevent the wrong layer or channel from being edited when the action is played.

➤ When recording the Save As command in an action, be especially careful not to enter a specific file name, or that file will be overwritten when the action is played. Either avoid entering a name or add a modal control to have the action pause at the Save As command (see page 403).

➤ To reopen the Action Options dialog, in which you can change an assigned shortcut or color, double-click the action listing.

RULER UNITS MATTER IN ACTIONS

Photoshop records edits that involve the use of a tool in a specific location in the image, such as the Brush or Gradient tool or a selection or shape tool, based on the current ruler units. The units can be actual (e.g., inches or picas) or relative (Percent). An action that is recorded when the default unit is actual can be played on a file that is the same size as the file in which it was recorded. An action that is recorded when the default unit is Percent will work on a file of any dimensions. To establish the units setting, go to Preferences > Units & Rulers, and from the Units: Rulers menu, choose either a specific unit or Percent.

RECORDING BRUSH STROKES ★

You can record the strokes for painting tools (Brush, Pencil, Mixer Brush). Set the desired ruler units (see "Ruler Units Matter In Actions" above), and check Allow Tool Recording on the Actions panel menu. While recording an action, select the desired tool. For the Brush tool, choose a Foreground color and Brush panel settings. Apply strokes in the image. You can change settings between strokes. Note that if a desired setting is already chosen, you will need to choose a different one, then the desired one.

For the Mixer Brush tool, before you begin recording, you need to create a tool preset (via the Tool Presets panel) that contains the desired color and Options bar settings. Choose your preset while recording the action. For added variety, you can create multiple tool presets, then switch among them while recording.

A *Use the New Action dialog to assign a name and set to your action, as well as an optional function key and/or color, and begin recording.*

Playing an action

An action can be triggered in various ways: via the Play button on the Actions panel; via a keyboard shortcut that was assigned to it; by dragging a file or folder full of files onto a droplet icon that was made from the action; or by using the Batch feature. We'll begin with the Play button and shortcuts.

To play an action on one image:

1. Open an image and click an image layer.

2. *Optional:* If the action to be played doesn't include creation of a snapshot as an initial step, use the History panel to do so now, to preserve the option to restore the document to its pre-action state.

3. Do one of the following:

   If the Actions panel is in **List** mode, click an action name, then click the **Play** button.

   If the panel is in **Button** mode, click the button for the action to be played.**A**

   Execute the keyboard **shortcut**, if one has been assigned to the desired action.

▶ To play an action starting from a specific command in the action, put the panel in List mode, click the command name, then click the Play button. Or to play just one command in an action, click the command name, then Ctrl-click/Cmd-click the Play button; or simply Ctrl-double-click/Cmd-double-click the command.

▶ If the Actions panel is in List mode, you can click the arrowhead next to an action name to expand or collapse its list of commands.

▶ To load other action set libraries onto the panel, see page 404.

To exclude a command from playback:

1. Put the Actions panel in List mode (actions can't be edited in Button mode).

2. Expand the list for the action to be edited.

3. Click in the leftmost column for the command that you want to exclude from playback, to remove the check mark.**B** The check mark for the main action listing turns red. (To reinclude the command, click in the same column again.)

   Note: If you click the check mark for an entire action or action set, as an alert will inform you, Photoshop will recheck any commands that you had unchecked individually.

A *When the Actions panel is in Button mode, each action is listed as a colored button. Assigned shortcuts, if any, are also listed.*

CHOOSING PLAYBACK OPTIONS

To choose an option for playback, put the Actions panel in List mode, choose Playback Options from the panel menu, then click one of these options in the dialog:

▶ Accelerated: The fastest playback option.

▶ Step by Step: The list for the action expands on the panel, and the name of each command or edit becomes highlighted as it's executed.

▶ Pause for [ ] seconds: This option works like Step by Step, except that a pause for the designated duration occurs after each step.

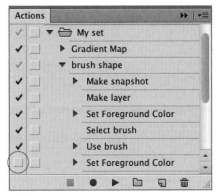

B *To exclude a color change in our "brush shape" action from playback temporarily, we unchecked that step.*

The ability to play an action on multiple files is a great timesaver. This can be done quickly by dragging a folder of files onto a droplet (see "To create a droplet for an action" on page 400). Or if you need to choose a destination, a file-naming scheme, and other options for the files to be processed by the action, use the Batch command instead, as described on this page.

To play an action on a batch of images:

1. Do either of the following:

   In Bridge, put all the files to be processed into one folder and display the folder contents (or to limit which images are to be processed, select those thumbnails), then choose Tools > Photoshop > **Batch**.

   In Mini Bridge, click a folder listing to display its contents (or to limit which images are to be processed, select specific thumbnails). Right-click a thumbnail, then choose Photoshop > **Batch**. ★

2. The Batch dialog opens (**A**, next page). Under Play, choose an action set from the **Set** menu and an action from the **Action** menu.

3. For the **Source**, choose **Bridge**.

4. *Optional:* If the action contains an Open command, check Override Action "Open" Commands to have the batch command ignore the specific file name that was chosen when the Open step was recorded.

5. Check **Suppress File Open Options Dialogs** and/or **Suppress Color Profile Warnings** to prevent those dialogs or alerts from appearing onscreen as source files are opened.

6. From the **Destination** menu, choose one of the following options:

   None to keep all the files open after processing.

   Save and Close to have the files save after processing and then close.

   Folder to have the files save to a new folder and to make the File Naming options for naming the resulting files accessible (the naming options prevent the new files from replacing the original

ones). Click Browse/Choose, choose a destination folder, then click Browse/Choose again.

   Optional: If the action contains a Save As command, you should check Override Action "Save As" Commands to have the save process in the batch command ignore the name and location that was recorded in the action.

7. If you chose Folder as the Destination, you can do the following:

   Choose options from the menus in the **File Naming** area, or type text to be included in the name. Note the Example to verify your naming convention choice.

   If you chose a naming option that uses sequential (serial) numbers, enter a one- to four-digit starting number in the **Starting Serial #** field.

   Check any or all of the file name **Compatibility** options for the platforms you need the files to be compatible with.

8. *Optional:* By default, Photoshop will stop the Batch process if it encounters an error. To have it play the whole action and keep track of error messages in a text file instead, from the Errors menu, choose Log Errors to File, then click Save As. In the Save dialog, type a name for the text file (keep the extension), choose a location for it, then click Save. If errors are encountered, you will be alerted via a prompt that errors were logged into the designated error log file.

9. Click OK to start the batch processing.

➤ You can also play an action on a batch of images via the Image Processor command (File > Scripts submenu in Photoshop, or Tools > Photoshop submenu in Bridge). In the dialog, check Run Action, then choose an action set and an action from the menus.

➤ When you play an action on an image, the action steps are listed as states on the History panel.

➤ To stop the batch command while it's processing, press Esc.

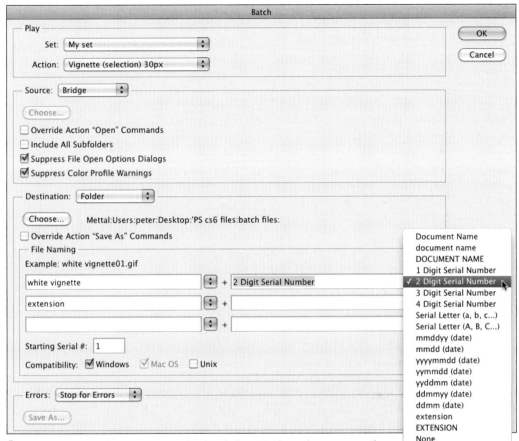

A *In the Batch dialog, choose an Action to be played, choose Bridge as the source, specify a Destination for the processed files, and choose optional File Naming settings.*

PUTTING IDEAS INTO ACTIONS

Can't think of a use for actions? Observe your typical Photoshop edits over the course of a week or two. Are there repetitive commands or tasks that you execute frequently? Did you devise a great image-editing effect that requires many time-consuming steps? (Remember, you can apply an action to one image or to a whole batch of them.)

Here are a few suggestions:

➤ Record the use of the Crop tool, set to a specific size and resolution.

➤ Use the Image Size dialog to size a document to a specific resolution or pixel dimensions.

➤ Record the steps needed to prepare a file for commercial printing: Flatten the file, convert the document color mode to CMYK Color, apply sharpening, and save a copy of the file.

➤ Create a new document from the currently selected layer (Duplicate Layer command, choose New in the dialog).

➤ Create a few adjustment layers that you typically use for tonal or color correction. (The adjustment settings can be changed after the action is played.)

➤ Copy a layer, convert the copy to a Smart Object, then apply one or more of your favorite filters via the Filter Gallery.

➤ Record an action that applies a vignette (see page 405). Add an Insert Stop command (see page 401) to let the user size and position the selection for the vignette.

An action can be turned into its own little mini-app, called a droplet, that sits on the Desktop or in a folder, waiting to be triggered.**A** If you drag a file or a folder full of files onto a droplet icon, Photoshop will launch (if it's not yet running), and the action that the droplet represents will be played on those files. Droplets can be shared among Photoshop users.

To create a droplet for an action:

1. Choose File > Automate > **Create Droplet**. The Create Droplet dialog opens.**B**

2. Click **Choose**. The Save dialog opens. Enter a name in the Save As field (keep the extension), choose a convenient location for the droplet, then click Save.

A This is a droplet icon for an action.

3. In the Create Droplet dialog, choose an action set from the **Set** menu, then an **Action** to be saved as a droplet.

4. Check any **Play** options to be included in the droplet, and choose **Destination** and **Errors** options for the processed files (see steps 4–8 on page 398).

5. Click OK. The droplet will appear in the designated location.

6. To use the droplet, drag a file or a folder full of files onto it. The action plays on the files.

MAKING A DROPLET PLATFORM-COMPATIBLE

► To make a droplet that was created in Windows usable in Macintosh, drag it onto the Macintosh Photoshop CS6 application icon.

► To make a droplet that was created in Macintosh usable in Windows, save it with an ".exe" extension.

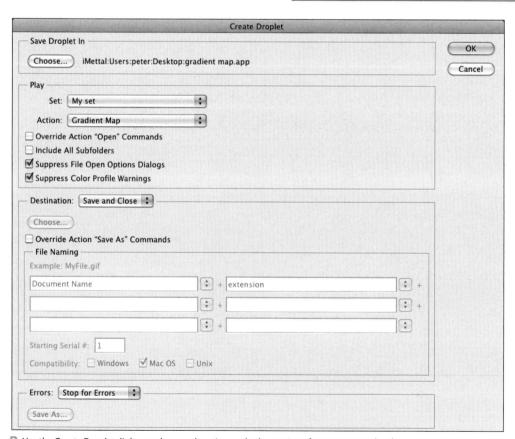

B Use the Create Droplet dialog to choose a location and other options for your action droplet.

Editing an action

If you want to experiment with an action or add to it without messing around with the original, duplicate it, then edit the duplicate. (Also remember to save your action sets to a file, as described on page 404.)

To duplicate an action:

Do either of the following:

Click an action, then choose **Duplicate** from the Actions panel menu.

Drag an action over the **New Action** button  on the Actions panel.

➤ To rename an action, double-click the name.

When you insert a Stop in an action, the playback will pause at that point so the user can perform a manual or nonrecordable edit (e.g., choose a source point for a cloning tool or create a selection at a specific size and location). You can also include an instructional message for the user, which will appear in an alert dialog when the pause occurs, such as a directive to use a tool in a specific way or to choose specific panel settings. After completing the manual edit, the user resumes the playback by clicking the Play button.

To insert a Stop in an action:

1. Do either of the following:

   While recording an action, pause at the point at which you want the Stop to appear.

   To add a Stop to an existing action, on the Actions panel, click the command name after which you want it to appear.

2. Choose **Insert Stop** from the Actions panel menu.

3. In the Record Stop dialog, type an instructional or alert message.**A** We recommend also spelling out in the message that after clicking Stop and performing the desired edit, the user should click the Play button to continue the playback.

4. *Optional:* Check Allow Continue to include a Continue button in the alert dialog (in addition to a Stop button). If the user opts not to perform the requested manual edits, he or she can click Continue to resume the playback (instead of having to click Stop, then click the Play button on the panel). Don't check Allow Continue if the requested manual edit is essential to the

user's execution of the remaining steps in the action (e.g., the creation and positioning of a selection).

5. Click OK. The Stop listing will appear below the command you paused after or clicked in step 1.**B–C**

A *In the Record Stop dialog, we typed an instructional message for the user. We also checked Allow Continue to add a Continue button to the alert dialog, which will appear when the action is played.*

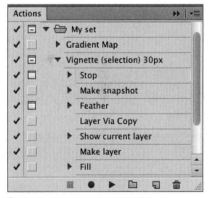

B *The Stop command appeared as a step within the action.*

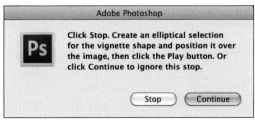

C *When we played the action on an image, our instructional message and a Continue button appeared in this alert.*

Perhaps you neglected to include a particular menu command when you initially recorded an action. The Insert Menu Item command gives you a second chance. Also, some menu commands (e.g., on the View or Window menu) can't be included when an action is initially recorded. Using this feature, you can insert those commands afterward.

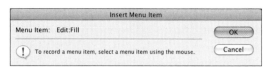

A *When we chose the Fill command from the Edit menu, the command name appeared automatically in the Insert Menu Item dialog.*

To insert a menu item in an action:

1. Expand the listing for an existing action, then click the command after which you want the new menu command to be inserted.

2. From the Actions panel menu, choose **Insert Menu Item**. The Insert Menu Item dialog opens.

3. From the Photoshop menu bar, choose the command to be added to the action. The command name appears in the Insert Menu Item dialog.A

4. Click OK.B

5. If the menu command that you inserted requires user input in a dialog, you will need to add a modal control to the action for that command. See the first task on the next page.

If you forgot to include a particular command or editing step in an action, or you want to improve an action by adding a command, here's your second opportunity.

To add a command or edit to an action:

1. On the Actions panel, expand the list that you want to add an edit to, then click the command name after which you want the new edit to appear.

2. Click the **Begin Recording** button.

3. Execute the desired command(s). Note: You can't add a command that's available only under certain conditions (e.g., the Feather command, which requires an active selection) unless the creation of those conditions is also included as steps in the action.

4. Click the **Stop Playing/Recording** button.

► To expand or collapse all the steps that are nested within an action, Alt-click/Option-click the arrowhead next to the action name.

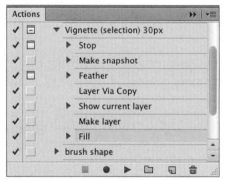

B *The menu item that we inserted appeared as a listing within the action on the Actions panel.*

DUPLICATING COMMANDS WITHIN OR BETWEEN ACTIONS

► To copy a command from one action to another, expand the listings for both actions, then Alt-drag/Option-drag the command to be copied from one list to the other (if you don't hold down Alt/Option, you'll move the command out of the original action). Note: Use caution when copying a Save command, as it may contain information that pertains only to the original action.

► To duplicate a command within an action, either drag the command over the New Action button or Alt-drag/Option-drag it to the desired position within the listings.

You can enable a modal control, or pause, for any step in an action that enables user input, such as a dialog in which they choose settings or an edit that requires pressing Enter/Return in order to be executed (such as a transform command).

To add a modal control to a command in an action:

1. Put the Actions panel in List mode, and expand the list for an action.

2. For any individual listing within the action, click in the second column; the **Dialog** icon ⬜ appears.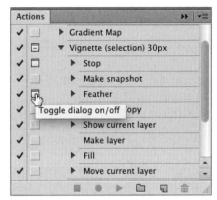

When the action is played, it will pause when it encounters a command that has a modal control, and the dialog or on-image controls will appear onscreen. In the case of a dialog, the user can enter new values, accept the original recorded settings by clicking OK, or click Cancel. When the user exits the dialog or commits to the edit, the playback continues automatically.

➤ To toggle a modal control off or on, click the Dialog icon.

To enable or disable all modal controls for an action:

Click in the Dialog column for an action name. Depending on their current state, all the modal controls in the action will be turned on or off.

Note: A short horizontal line in the Dialog icon ⬛ ★ for an action listing indicates that the modal controls in the action are in a mixed state (some off and some on). To reset the modal controls to their original state, click the Dialog icon; if an alert prompt appears, click OK.

To rerecord an action using different dialog settings:

1. Click the name of the action that contains the settings to be edited.

2. From the Actions panel menu, choose **Record Again**.

3. The action will play back, stopping at each command that uses a dialog. Enter new settings where needed, then click OK. Each time you close a dialog, the rerecording continues.

4. To stop the rerecording, either click Cancel in a dialog or click the Stop Playing/Recording button ⬛ on the panel.

A Via the Dialog icon, you give the user an opportunity to enter different settings in a dialog when it opens during playback.

To change the settings for a command in an action:

1. On the Actions panel, expand the listing for an action, then double-click a command that uses a dialog (or alert dialog) for which you want to change the settings.

2. Enter new settings.

3. Click OK. (Click Cancel to cancel your revisions.)

This may seem obvious, but remember that if you change the order of edits in an action, the revised action may produce different results than the original.

To change the order of edits in an action:

1. On the Actions panel, expand the list for an action, if it's not already expanded.

2. Drag a command upward or downward on the list.

Deleting commands and actions

You can delete a whole action, or just delete individual commands.

To delete an action or delete a command from an action:

1. If you created (or edited) any custom action sets that you want to preserve for future use, follow the steps in "To save an action set to a file," at right.

2. On the Actions panel, do either of the following:

   Click the action to be deleted.

   Click the individual command to be deleted. Ctrl-click/Cmd-click to highlight additional commands, if desired.

3. Click the **Delete** button, 🗑 then click OK (or to bypass the prompt, Alt-click/Option-click the Delete button).

Saving and loading action sets

Be sure to save any custom or edited action sets that you want to preserve for future use — and potentially share with other Photoshop users.

To save an action set to a file:

1. On the Actions panel, click the action set to be saved.

2. Choose **Save Actions** from the panel menu.

3. In the **Save** dialog, type a name for the action set file, keep the extension and default location, then click Save. Each file is regarded as one set, regardless of how many actions it contains.

4. When you relaunch Photoshop, your newly saved set will appear on the Actions panel menu. Note: If you edit any actions in the set, you will need to resave the set by following the steps above.

Photoshop includes many useful actions beyond those in the default set. To load them on the panel, or to load any user-created set, follow the instructions below.

To load a set onto the Actions panel:

1. On the Actions panel, click the set name that you want the loaded set to appear below.

2. From the Actions panel menu, choose a predefined action set (Commands, Frames, Image Effects, LAB–Black & White Technique, Production, Stars Trails, Text Effects, Textures, or Video Actions), or a user-saved set.

To reload the default action set:

From the Actions panel menu, choose **Reset Actions**. In the alert dialog, click Append to add the default set to the existing sets on the panel, or click OK to replace the existing sets with the default one.

In this chapter, you'll learn various ways to frame your photos, and ways to showcase them for clients. You will spotlight your subject matter as a vignette; add an artistic border; embed a watermark for copyright protection; create a Web gallery, contact sheet, or PDF presentation of multiple images; create and present layer comps (layer variations within a single document); and create a video.★

Creating a vignette

We'll show you several ways to create a vignette (lighten or darken the outer part of an image).

To create a white-bordered vignette: ★

1. Duplicate the Background in an image (Ctrl-J/Cmd-J).

2. Click the Background, then press Shift-Backspace/ Shift-Delete. In the Fill dialog, choose Use: White, Mode: Normal, and Opacity: 100%, then click OK.

3. Click the image layer. Choose the **Elliptical Marquee** tool 🔘 (M or Shift-M). To select the area of the image you want to keep visible, drag with Alt/Option held down (to draw the selection from the center).

4. On the Layers panel, click the **Add Layer Mask** button. 🔲

5. On the Properties panel, adjust the **Feather** value to soften the edge of the mask. **A**

6. *Optional:* To reposition the mask to reveal a different part of the image, on the Layers panel, click between the layer and mask thumbnails to unlink them, click the mask thumbnail, then hold down V (temporary Move tool) and drag in the document.

PRESENTATION

23

IN THIS CHAPTER

A *An oval, feathered mask gives this garden photo a vintage look.*

Another way to create a vignette is by manipulating light and dark values. Here you will use the layer mask on a Brightness/Contrast adjustment layer to control where the vignette is located in the image. It's like shining a spotlight.

To create a vignette via a tonal adjustment and mask:

1. Choose the **Elliptical Marquee** tool ⬭ (M or Shift-M), then drag with Alt/Option held down to select the area of the image you want to feature (Alt/Option draws the selection from the center).

2. On the **Adjustments** panel, ◐ click the **Brightness/Contrast** button. ☀ ★ Press Ctrl-I/ Cmd-I to invert the adjustment layer mask, then on the Properties panel, lower the Brightness value to darken the unmasked areas of the image.

3. To soften the edge of the mask nondestructively, click the **Masks** icon ◙ on the Properties panel, then increase the **Feather** value. **B**

4. If you need to reposition the "spotlight," on the Layers panel, click the mask thumbnail on the adjustment layer, click the **Link** icon 🔗 to unlink the mask, then hold down V (temporary Move tool) and drag the mask in the image. **C–D** When you're done, click between the thumbnails to restore the link icon.

A We created an elliptical selection, then rotated it via the Select > Transform Selection command.

B Next, we applied a Brightness/Contrast adjustment, inverted the mask, then softened the edge of the mask via the Feather slider.

C We clicked between the adjustment layer and mask thumbnails to remove the Link icon, then with the Move tool, we dragged the layer mask slightly to the left.

D Now the mask is positioned fully on the bottle.

A third way to create a vignette is by using the Vignette controls in the Lens Correction filter dialog. With this method, you can't control where the vignette is positioned, but it's quick and easy and you can readjust the settings at any time.

To create a vignette via the Lens Correction filter:

1. Duplicate the Background in an RGB image.

2. Right-click the duplicate layer and choose **Convert to Smart Object**.

3. Choose Filter > **Lens Correction** (Ctrl-Shift-R/Cmd-Shift-R). At the bottom of the dialog, check Preview and uncheck Show Grid.

4. Click the Custom tab, then under Vignette, do the following: **B**

   Choose a negative **Amount** value for the amount of darkening.

   Adjust the **Midpoint** value to control where the darkening effect begins in the image (you may need to readjust the Amount value as you do this).

5. Click OK.**C** To edit the Lens Corrections settings at any time, double-click the Lens Correction listing on the Layers panel.

➤ To create a vignette in Camera Raw, see page 77.

A *This is the original image.*

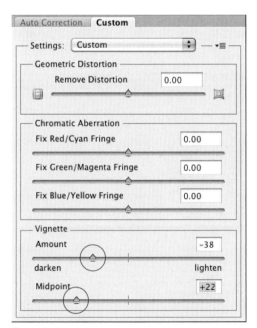

B *We chose these values in the Custom tab of the Lens Correction dialog.*

C *This is the result.*

Adding an artistic border

Using options in the Refine Edge dialog, it's super easy to add an artistic border to an image.

To add an artistic border to an image:

1. Click the Background on the Layers panel.

2. Choose the **Rectangular Marquee** tool  (M or Shift-M), then draw a selection within the image where you want the border to begin.**A** You can reposition the selection border with the same tool.

3. On the Options bar, click **Refine Edge**.

4. In the Refine Edge dialog, choose View: **On White** (W), then adjust the **Radius**, **Smooth**, **Contrast**, and **Shift Edge** values to create rough edges.**B**

5. From the Output To menu, choose **New Layer with Layer Mask**, then click OK.**C**

6. Click the Background, make it visible, then press Shift-Backspace/Shift-Delete. In the Fill dialog, choose Use: White, Mode: Normal, and Opacity: 100%, then click OK.

➤ The actions in the Frames library apply various kinds of frames (apply to a one-layer document).

A *We created a rectangular selection.*

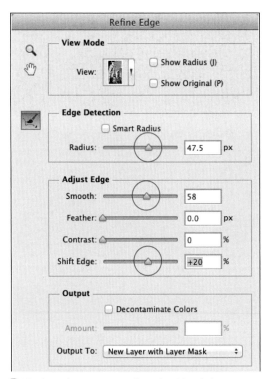

B *We chose these settings in the Refine Edge dialog.*

C *So easy!*

USING ARTISTIC BORDERS IN A MONTAGE

To create this Paris montage, we added a border to each image separately in its own file, using the technique described on the preceding page. We dragged each image layer into a larger document, which contains a photo of burlap as the Background image. To complete the composition, we scaled and moved — and rotated two of — the layers.

Adding a watermark to an image

If you're planning to display any of your images online, you should help protect them from unauthorized use by embedding a copyright or custom watermark into them (akin to traditional watermarking on paper). In these steps, you'll create a custom watermark using the Type tool, then save the type as a custom shape preset, for use in any document.

To create a watermark shape from text:

1. Open an RGB image.

2. Choose the **Horizontal Type** tool, T create the desired text for the watermark, then scale and style it as desired. To create the copyright symbol, type Alt + 0169/Option-G.

3. Choose Type > **Convert to Shape.** A ★

4. Choose Edit > **Define Custom Shape**, enter a name (we entered the same name as in our watermark), then click OK.

5. Delete the shape layer.

To add your watermark to an image: ★

1. Choose the **Custom Shape** tool 🐾 (U or Shift-U).

2. On the Options bar, do the following:

    From the Tool Mode menu, choose **Shape.**

    Click the **Shape** picker thumbnail, then click your new custom shape (you'll find it at the bottom of the picker).**B**

    Click the **Fill Color** swatch, then click a gray swatch in the picker.

    Click the **Stroke Color** swatch, then click the No Color button ⬜ in the picker.

3. Shift-drag in the document to produce the watermark. A shape layer appears on the Layers panel.**C**

A To create a custom watermark, we converted this text to a shape.

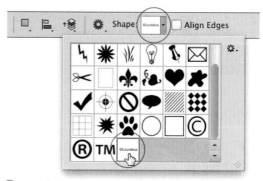

B We clicked our new custom shape on the Shape picker.

C After we dragged with the Custom Shape tool, a new shape layer appeared on the Layers panel.

4. On the Layers panel, change the **Fill** value for the shape layer to 0%.

5. Double-click next to the shape layer name to open the Layer Style dialog, then click **Bevel & Emboss** (but not Contour). Choose Style: Inner Bevel, Technique: Smooth, Depth between 80 and 130%, Size 6–15, and Soften 7–10, then click OK.

6. You can use the Move tool to reposition the shape on the image. For a better view of the watermark, click another layer.**A**

7. To save your layer settings and layer effects as a preset in the Styles panel for future use, click the shape layer for the watermark. On the Styles panel, ▧ click the **New Style** button.⬜ Type a name in the dialog, then click OK.

8. *Optional:* To soften the edges of the watermark to make it look as if it's embedded into the image, click the shape layer on the Layers panel, then on the Properties panel, increase the Feather value.**B**

A *This is our watermark shape with a Fill of 0 and the layer style applied.*

B *We softened the edges of the shape via the Feather control.*

RESPECT YOUR FELLOW ARTISTS — AND THE LAW!

It's easy and tempting for any of us to help ourselves to imagery that we see on the Web, and to repurpose it for our own needs. But consider that for every image you view and enjoy, a fellow artist took the trouble to shoot it, correct it, put their personal stamp on it, and optimize it. They have the rights to it, and we don't. Just as we urge you to take steps to protect your own work (however difficult the law is to enforce), if you don't have rights to a photo or it's not in the public domain, don't download it or use it. (Okay … end of lecture.)

FOR BETTER PROTECTION, USE DIGIMARC

For a more thorough method of protecting your images from copyright infringement, explore the services and features offered by the Digimarc company (digimarc.com). When you install their plug-in in your system, it becomes accessible in Photoshop (Filter > Digimarc submenu). When you use the command, it embeds an imperceptible watermark into an image that can survive substantial image editing (e.g., copying, scaling, cropping, and compression).

By enrolling in one of their annual subscription packages, Digimarc lets you manage and monitor the use of your images on the Internet. The Basic service embeds a watermark. If someone downloads your image, they will be notified of your ownership and contact information. The Professional service includes the basic service plus a way for you track the use of your images on the Internet.

For a free trial of the watermark feature, check out the demo version on the Filter > Digimarc submenu in Photoshop.

Creating a Web gallery

When displayed as a Web Gallery, your photos can be viewed either as static thumbnails that the viewer can click, or as a slideshow with viewer controls for the playback. You will create the gallery (periodically previewing the current settings in your browser), then save it and upload it to the Web.

To create a Web Gallery: ★

1. In Adobe Bridge, put all the files for the gallery in the same folder, in the order in which you want them to be viewed.

2. Display the **Output** workspace, then click **Web Gallery** at the top of the Output panel. A large Preview panel and an Output panel display. Note: If the Output workspace isn't listed, go to Edit/Adobe Bridge CS6 > Preferences > Startup Scripts, check Adobe Output Module, then relaunch Bridge.

3. In the **Folders** panel on the left side, click the folder that you set up in step 1. The images will display as thumbnails in the Content panel.

Ctrl-click/Cmd-click approximately 10 thumbnails (limiting the number enables previewing to run more quickly).

4. Double-click the vertical bar between the left and center panes to hide the Favorites and Folders panels.

5. From the **Template** menu at the top of the Output panel, choose a layout option. Note: Images in the HTML Gallery, Airtight PostcardViewer, and Airtight SimpleViewer templates can't be viewed as a slideshow.

The **Standard** template displays the thumbnails in rows to the left of a large preview.

The **Left Filmstrip** and **Filmstrip** templates display the thumbnails either to the left of or below the large preview.

The **Journal with Filmstrip** and **Journal with Slideshow** templates list metadata information for the currently selected thumbnail.

A *In the Output panel in Bridge, we clicked Web Gallery, then chose the Standard gallery template and Style: Medium Thumbnail. (We hid the left pane of the Bridge window.)*

The **Slideshow** template displays just a large preview (no thumbnails).

The **Airtight PostcardViewer** template displays small tilted thumbnails that enlarge when clicked; the **Airtight AutoViewer** template displays a sequence of large thumbnails with left and right navigation arrows; the **Airtight SimpleViewer** template displays multiple small thumbnails and one large preview.

6. For the Standard, Left Filmstrip, or Lightroom Flash Gallery template, choose a preset thumbnail or style option from the **Style** menu.

7. Click **Preview in Browser** to preview your selected thumbnails, template, and style in your default browser.**A–D** You can click a thumbnail in the gallery to view it as a large preview.

Note: All the features discussed in steps 8–10 are available for the Standard, Left Filmstrip, Filmstrip, and Slideshow templates. Other options are available for other templates.

8. Click the **Site Info** bar to expand that category, then enter text for the **Gallery Title** and **Gallery Caption** (**A**, next page).

Continued on the following page

A *The Standard template (Medium Thumbnail style) was used for this Web Gallery.*

B *The Left Filmstrip template (Medium Thumbnail style) was used for this Web Gallery.*

C *The Lightroom Flash Gallery template (Classic style) was used for this Web Gallery.*

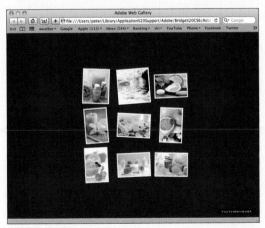

D *The Airtight PostcardViewer template was used for this Web Gallery. Note that there are no title or menu bars at the top.*

9. Click the Site Info bar to collapse that category, then click the **Color Palette** bar. To change the color for any of the components of the gallery — Background, Title, Menu (below the title), or frame around the Thumbnail — click the color swatch, choose a color from the system color picker, then click OK/Close button. **B** Click **Preview in Browser** again to preview your new choices.

10. Click the Color Palette bar to collapse it, then click the **Appearance** bar. Check **Show File Names** if you want file names to display in the gallery (to help the viewer identify specific photos). Choose a **Slideshow Size**, **Gallery Image Size**, and **Thumbnail Size** (these settings will overwrite

the current Style menu choice, if any). Choose a **Quality** setting for JPEG compression (the higher the value, the better quality, but the larger the file size), enter a **Slide Duration** value, and choose a **Transition Effect** option. Once more, click (you guessed it!) **Preview in Browser**.

The Airtight templates offer different Appearance settings, and two different categories — Image Info and Output Settings — which you can use to control the size, position, and quality of the gallery thumbnails and previews.

11. Follow the first set of instructions on the next page to save your settings as a preset, and then the second set to view the gallery as a slideshow.

A Next, we clicked the bar for Site Info and entered text in some fields for display on the Menu and Title bars of the gallery.

B In the Color Palette category, we chose new colors for the title bar and text and the menu text. In the Appearance category, we increased the Gallery Image Size and Thumbnail Size values, and chose a Slide Duration setting of 4 seconds.

You can save all the custom settings you have chosen for your Web Gallery as a custom style preset, for future use.

To save the current Web Gallery settings as a preset: ★

1. After choosing a template and entering custom text and settings in the Output panel categories, click the **Save Style** button 🔲 (next to the Style menu).

2. In the New Style dialog, enter a name, then click Create. Your custom style will be listed at the top of the Style menu.

➤ To save newly changed settings to an existing custom style preset, choose the preset from the Style menu, click the Save Style button, enter the same name as the existing style, click Create, then click Yes in the alert dialog.

To play a slideshow in your default browser: ★

1. With the Output panel still displaying, select up to 20 image thumbnails, then click **Preview in Browser**. Note: Images in the HTML Gallery and the Airtight PostcardViewer and SimpleViewer templates can't be viewed as a slideshow.

2. Click the **View Slideshow** button 🔲 below the large preview image to hide the thumbnails.

3. Click the **Play Slideshow** button 🔲 to start the slideshow and preview your settings. A To stop the show, click the Pause Slideshow button. To redisplay the thumbnails, click the **View Gallery** button.🔲

4. When you're done watching the gallery, exit/quit your browser, then click in the Bridge window.

   To save and upload the gallery, follow the steps on the next page. Note: Although only up to 20 thumbnails can be previewed in the browser, you can upload as many thumbnails as you like.

A As you preview the gallery in your default browser, you can click any thumbnail or use the navigation or slideshow buttons. (To create this gallery, we chose some custom Site Info and Color Palette settings for the Left Filmstrip template.)

Once you've finalized your gallery, be sure to save it!

To save a Web Gallery: ★

1. Arrange the image thumbnails in the order in which you want them to appear in the Web Gallery, then select them.

2. Click **Create Gallery** to expand that category, then enter a Gallery Name for a folder to be created. For the **Save Location**, click Browse and locate a destination folder, then click OK/Open.

3. Click **Save** at the bottom of the Output panel, then pause for processing. All the necessary files for the gallery will be saved to the chosen folder on your hard disk.

To upload a Web Gallery via Bridge: ★

1. Obtain the necessary data from your Web administrator.

2. Expand the Create Gallery category, then enter the data in the **FTP Server, User Name, Password,** and **Folder** fields.**A** (The folder is the location on the server to which the gallery files will be uploaded.)

3. *Optional:* To save the data as a preset that can be accessed from the Custom menu, click the Save Preset Name button, ⬛ enter a name, then click Create.

4. At the bottom of the Output panel, click **Upload**. Your gallery files will be sent to the server.

5. Give your viewers the Web address so they can view your beautiful gallery!

A *In the Create Gallery category, enter Save and Upload Location information.*

Creating a contact sheet

A contact sheet is an arrangement of image thumbnails that you either output to a printing device or view onscreen. It's a useful way to catalog images (such as the photos that you back up onto DVDs or need to present to clients). We'll show you two ways to create a contact sheet, one via the Contact Sheet II command (it's baaack!) and the other via the Output workspace in Bridge (see pages 418–419).

To use the Contact Sheet II command: ★

1. In Bridge, click a folder to display its contents or Ctrl-click/Cmd-click multiple image thumbnails.

2. Choose Tools > File > Photoshop > **Contact Sheet II.** (Note: This command is also accessible in Photoshop via File > Automate > Contact Sheet II.)

3. In the dialog, under **Source Images,** choose Use: Bridge (**A**, next page).

4. Under **Document,** choose Width, Height, and Resolution values for the contact sheet file, and also choose Mode, Bit Depth, and Color Profile settings.

   Optional: Check Flatten All Layers to have all the images (and optional captions) appear on a single layer, or uncheck this option to have the command create a separate image layer (with a mask) for each image, plus a separate layer for each text caption.

5. Under **Thumbnails,** choose a Place option for the order of thumbnails, and the desired number of Columns and Rows. Check Use Auto-Spacing to let Photoshop calculate the spacing between images, or uncheck this option and enter specific Vertical and Horizontal spacing values. Uncheck Rotate for Best Fit to have the images keep their original orientation, or check this option to let Photoshop rotate horizontal images vertically, and vice versa.

6. *Optional:* Check Font to have a caption containing the file name appear below each image, then choose a font, font style, and font size.

7. Click OK. Grab a snack while Photoshop opens each image and creates the contact sheet(s). Save the new document(s) (**B**, next page).

➤ To save your Contact Sheet II settings, click Save. To load your settings, use the Load button.

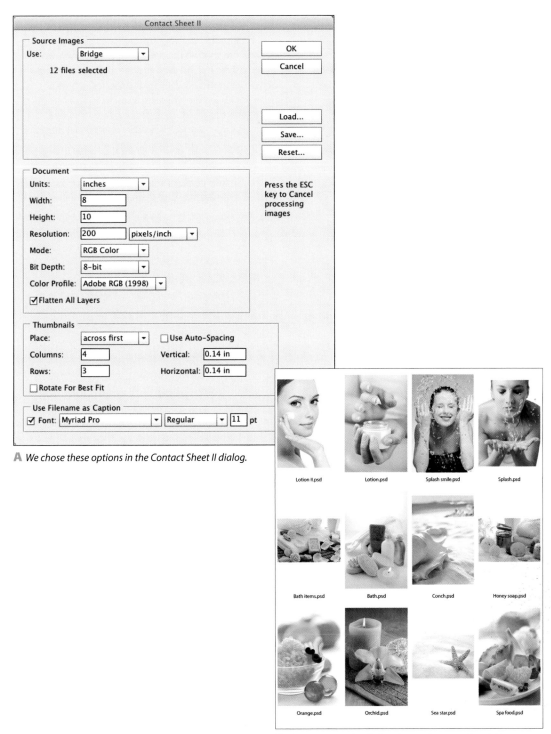

A We chose these options in the Contact Sheet II dialog.

B The settings in the dialog shown above produced this contact sheet.

To create a PDF contact sheet via Bridge:

1. In Bridge, put all the files to be displayed on the contact sheet in the same folder, in the order in which you want them to appear on the sheet (they can be grouped in a stack), then display the contents of the folder.

2. Choose the **Output** workspace (or from the Output menu ▮▶▮ on the toolbar, choose Output to Web or PDF).**A** Note: If this work-space isn't listed, go to Edit/Adobe Bridge CS6 > Preferences > Startup Scripts, check Adobe Output Module, then relaunch Bridge.

3. At the top of the Output panel, click **PDF**, then from the **Template** menu, choose **4*5 Contact Sheet** or **5*8 Contact Sheet** (the numerals indi-cate the number of columns and rows).

   If you're content with the default settings for the chosen template, skip ahead to step 10 or 11; or if you prefer to customize the template, follow the remaining steps.

4. In the **Document** category, do all of the following:

   Choose a **Page Preset**.

   Choose a preset **Size**, or to produce a custom-size sheet, enter Width and Height values. Click the Portrait or Landscape orientation icon.

   Choose image **Quality** settings. As an example, for onscreen output, choose 72 ppi and move the Quality slider to 60–70. These settings will affect the storage size of the resulting file.

   From the **Background** menu, choose a back-ground color for the contact sheet. For print output, we recommend choosing White.

   For the Password options, see the optional steps in step 4 on page 420.

5. Select approximately 10–15 thumbnails (this restricted number will minimize the preview time), then click **Refresh Preview**. The contact sheet displays in a new Output Preview panel.

6. In the **Layout** category, change any of the following settings:

   Choose an **Image Placement** option for the order in which the images are arranged.

   Enter the desired number of **Columns** and **Rows** for the contact sheet, depending on how many images you want it to contain.

Check **Use Auto-Spacing** to let Bridge calculate the spacing between thumbnails; or uncheck this option, then enter specific Vertical and Horizontal values for the desired spacing between thumbnails, and enter Top, Bottom, Left, and Right values for the outer margins.

Optional: Uncheck Rotate for Best Fit to keep the original orientation of the images, or check this option to let Photoshop rotate horizontal images vertically, and vice versa.

Keep **Repeat One Photo per Page** unchecked.

7. *Optional:* In the Overlays category, check Filename and Extension to have that data appear below each image, and choose Font, Size, and Color settings for that text.

8. *Optional:* To display a header at the top of the sheet, in the Header category, check Add Header, choose an alignment option, enter text, and choose text attributes; and if desired, choose a width and color for a Divider (rule below the header). Repeat, if desired, to add Footer text.

9. In the Playback category, uncheck all options (the sheet is going to be viewed manually).

10. *Optional:* In the Watermark category, check Add Watermark, then click Insert Text and enter copyright info to appear in the center of each image (choose Font, Size, Color, and Offset options, and a low Opacity). Or click Insert Image, click the Path button, ▮▮▮ locate a water-mark image file, then click Open.

11. Select all the thumbnails (or a thumbnail stack) for the contact sheet, then click **Refresh Preview** (**A**, next page). If needed, adjust any settings or rearrange any thumbnails, then click Refresh Preview once more.

A *In Bridge, display a folder of image thumbnails and the Output workspace.*

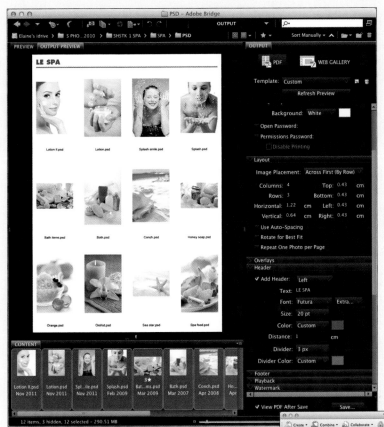

A *In the Output panel in Bridge, we chose these settings for our PDF contact sheet, then clicked Refresh Preview to preview them.*

12. At the bottom of the panel, check **View PDF After Save**, then click Save. In the Save As dialog, enter a file name, choose a location, then click Save.

13. A PDF file will be created, and will display in Adobe Reader, Acrobat Standard, or Acrobat Pro. **B** If the document contains multiple pages, you can click the Next Page and Previous Page buttons to cycle through them.

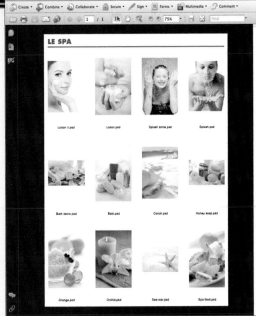

B *Our contact sheet opened in Adobe Acrobat Pro.*

Creating a PDF presentation of images

Another way to package and send files to a client or friend is via a PDF presentation, in which images play sequentially onscreen. To view the presentation in Adobe Reader, Acrobat Standard, or Acrobat Pro, all the viewer has to do is double-click the PDF file icon.

To create a PDF presentation:

1. In Bridge, put all the image files you want to display in the presentation in the same folder, in the order in which you want them to appear (they can be grouped in a stack). Display the contents of the folder, and click one of the thumbnails.

2. Click the **Output** workspace (or from the Output menu ▐▶ on the toolbar, choose Output to Web or PDF).**A** (If this workspace isn't listed, go to Preferences > Start Scripts, check Adobe Output Module, then relaunch Bridge.)

3. At the top of the Output panel, click **PDF**, then from the **Template** menu, choose Maximize Size.

4. In the **Document** category, do the following:

   From the **Page Preset** menu, choose Web, and from the **Size** menu, choose 800 x 600 or 1024 x 728.

   Choose **Quality** settings. For Web or other onscreen output, choose 72 ppi and set the Quality to 60–70. These settings affect the file size and the speed of transmission.

   From the **Background** menu, choose a color to be displayed behind the images (or click the color swatch then choose a color via the Color Picker).

   Optional: Check Open Password and enter a password. Your viewers will need to enter this password in order to open the PDF file.

   Optional: Check Permissions Password and enter a password to restrict how the PDF file can be used. Your viewers will need to enter this password in order to print or edit the PDF file. You can also disable printing separately by checking Disable Printing.

5. In the **Layout** category, uncheck the options at the bottom, including Rotate for Best Fit, to prevent any images from being rotated.

6. *Optional:* In the Overlays category, check Filename and Extension to have that data appear below each image, choose a Font and Size, and choose a color that will stand out well against the Background color (or click the swatch and use the Color Picker).

7. *Optional:* To display a header at the top of the presentation, in the Header category, check Add Header, choose an alignment option, enter text, and choose text attributes. If desired, also choose a width and color for a Divider (rule below the header). Ditto for a Footer.

8. Under **Playback**, check these slideshow options:

   To display the presentation images at full-screen size in Acrobat, check **Open in Full Screen Mode**.

   To have the frames advance automatically, check **Automatic Advance to the Next Page**, then enter the Duration (Seconds) for each frame to display.

   To have the slide show loop continuously, check **Loop After Last Page** (after the last frame displays, the show replays from the first frame).

   Optional: To display a transition effect between frames, choose a Transition option (e.g., Dissolve or Fade). Also choose a Direction option (if available) and a Speed option.

9. *Optional:* In the Watermark category, check Add Watermark, then click Insert Text and enter copyright info to appear in the center of each image (choose Font, Size, Color, and Offset options, and a low Opacity). Or click Insert Image, click the Path button, ▐▀▐ locate a watermark image file, then click Open.

10. Select all the thumbnails for the presentation, then click **Refresh Preview** to preview the first frame (**A**, next page).

11. Check **View PDF After Save** to have the presentation play automatically when you click Save.

12. Click Save. In the Save As dialog, enter a file name, choose a location, then click Save. A PDF file will be created, and Adobe Reader or Acrobat will launch. If an alert pertaining to Acrobat appears, click Yes. The PDF file will open onscreen, then the slideshow will play (**B**, next page). To halt the show at any time, press Esc.

A *In Bridge, display a folder of image thumbnails and the Output workspace.*

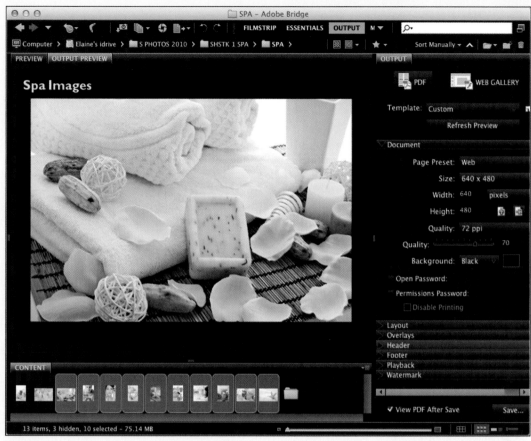

A *In Bridge, the first frame of our PDF presentation displayed in the Output Preview panel. (We double-clicked the vertical bar between the center and left panes to hide the left pane.)*

B *Adobe Acrobat launched, and the presentation played on the full screen. The image at left shows a Glitter transition.*

Creating and using layer comps

A layer comp (short for "composition") is a set of layer characteristics, which can include visibility, position, and layer effect settings. Via the Layer Comps panel, you can store multiple comps in one document. By displaying different comps, you can quickly present multiple design variations to coworkers or clients.

To create a layer comp:

1. Create design variations within your document using multiple image, type, fill, or adjustment layers. The layers can have different colors, type-faces, masks, layer styles, Smart Filter settings, adjustment settings, imagery, etc.

2. To create the first comp, for each layer in the document, do any of the following: Choose a visibility setting, a position (location), and layer style settings (blending mode, Opacity setting, etc.).

3. Show the Layer Comps panel, 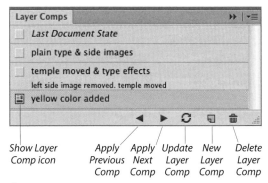 **A** then click the **New Layer Comp** button at the bottom of the panel. The New Layer Comp dialog opens. **B**

4. Enter a **Name** for the comp, then check the layer settings you want it to contain: **Visibility**, **Position**, and/or **Appearance (Layer Style)**.

5. *Optional:* Enter text in the Comment field, such as an explanatory note, to appear on the panel.

6. Click OK. **C** To create more comps from different design variations, repeat steps 2–6 (e.g., hide or show different layers, move the content of a layer, change the layer style or adjustment settings).

► To change which layer settings a comp is storing (and therefore displaying), or to add or edit the Comment data, double-click to the right of the comp name; the Layer Comp Options dialog opens.

► To bypass the Layer Comp Options dialog when creating a comp, Alt-click/Option-click the New Layer Comp button. The options you chose for the last comp will apply to the new one.

► To rename a comp quickly, double-click its name on the panel.

To display a layer comp:

Do either of the following:

On the Layer Comps panel, click in the left column. The Layer Comp icon moves to that slot.

Show Layer Comp icon — Apply Previous Comp — Apply Next Comp — Update Layer Comp — New Layer Comp — Delete Layer Comp

A *Use the Layer Comps panel to create, store, apply, edit, update, and delete layer comps.*

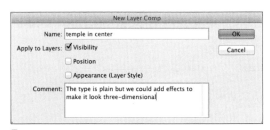

B *In the New Layer Comp dialog, we typed a Name, decided to save only the layer visibility settings in the comp, and entered a comment for the viewer.*

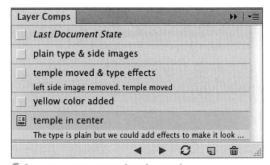

C *Our new comp appeared on the panel.*

CREATING A LAYER COMP FROM A DUPLICATE

If you don't want to create a new layer comp from scratch, start from a duplicate instead: right-click a layer comp name and choose Duplicate Layer Comp. To edit and update the duplicate, see "To update a layer comp" on the next page.

To cycle through the layer comps, click the **Apply Next Selected Layer Comp** button ▶ or **Apply Previous Selected Layer Comp** ◀ button.**A**

Let's say you edit your document, then display a layer comp. If you want to restore the document to its state before you displayed the comp, do as follows.

To restore the last document state:

On the Layer Comps panel, do either of the following:

Click in the left column next to the **Last Document State** listing.

Right-click a layer comp and choose **Restore Last Document State**.

You can update any existing layer comp to incorporate new edits that you have made to your document.

To update a layer comp:

1. On the Layer Comps panel, click the layer comp you want to edit.

   ➤ If you need to remind yourself which Apply to Layers settings are turned on for the comp (or to change them), double-click the comp. The Layer Comp Options dialog opens.

2. Add, edit, or delete layers; change their visibility settings or position; or change the layer style settings.

3. Click the **Update Layer Comp** button ↻ at the bottom of the panel.

If you change the layer count (e.g., delete or merge layers) in a document that contains layer comps, an alert icon, **△** indicating that the "Layer Comp Cannot Be Fully Restored," will appear next to the name of the comps that are missing data.

To clear an alert icon:

When you do either of the following, the alert icon disappears and the comp is synced with the current status of the Layers panel (this just gets rid of the alert; the deleted layers aren't retrieved):

Click a layer comp that has an alert icon, then click the icon. In the alert dialog, click **Clear**.

Right-click the alert icon and choose **Clear Layer Comp Warning** (or to clear all alert icons, choose Clear All Layer Comp Warnings instead).

A *The variations shown above are layer comps within a single image.*

CREATING A PERMANENT "SNAPSHOT"

To preserve the original state of a document, when you first open your unedited image, duplicate the Background, then create a layer comp (check Visibility and Position). Yes, snapshots on the History panel serve a similar purpose, but they disappear when you close your document, whereas layer comps save with the file and remain accessible.

When you delete a layer comp, no layers are deleted, and the appearance of the document is preserved.

To delete a layer comp:

1. On the Layer Comps panel, click the layer comp to be deleted.

2. Click the **Delete Layer Comp** button 🗑 at the bottom of the panel.

Creating a PDF presentation of layer comps

You can use the Layer Comps to PDF script to produce a PDF presentation from the layer comps in your document, which any viewer will be able to watch as a slideshow.

To create a PDF presentation of layer comps: ★

1. Open a Photoshop file that contains layer comps.

   ➤ To create the PDF presentation from select layer comps in your document (instead of all of them), Ctrl-click/Cmd-click those comps.

2. Choose File > Scripts > **Layer Comps to PDF**. The Layer Comps to PDF dialog opens.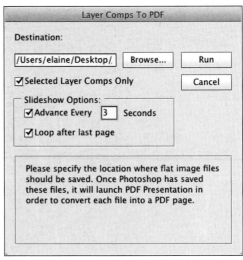

3. Click **Browse.** In the Save As dialog, enter a file name and choose a location for the PDF file, then click Save.

4. If you selected some layer comps in step 1, check **Selected Layer Comps Only.**

5. Under Slideshow Options, check **Advance Every [ ] Seconds** to let the comps advance automatically (and enter a time value).

   Optional: Check Loop After Last Page to allow the slideshow to replay continuously (after the last frame displays, the show replays from the first frame).

6. Click Run. Pause while the script produces a PDF file from your document. When it's done processing, an alert dialog will appear, indicating that the script was successful. Click OK.

7. In Bridge, locate and double-click the PDF file. Adobe Reader, Acrobat Standard, or Acrobat Pro will launch. If an alert pertaining to Acrobat appears, click Yes.

8. The PDF file will open onscreen, then the slideshow will play. To end the show at any time, press Esc.

A *In the Layer Comps to PDF dialog, choose a destination folder and options for the PDF slideshow.*

Importing video clips into Photoshop

The quality of video that current digital SLR cameras produce rivals that of stand-alone video cameras, but until the inclusion of the Timeline panel in Photoshop, users had to edit their videos in other programs. Although the video editing tools in Photoshop won't replace stand-alone video applications, they offer all the features that a photographer who shoots occasional video will ever need. If you fall into that category, you will enjoy the added bonus of being able to use many of the Photoshop features that you're already familiar with for video editing.

To edit video in Photoshop, you will use the Timeline panel.**A** The first step is to set up your Photoshop workspace.

To set up the Photoshop workspace for video editing: ★

1. Choose Window > Workspace > **Motion**. By default, the Timeline panel is nested at the bottom of the Application frame.

2. On the Timeline panel menu, check **Enable Timeline Shortcut Keys**.

3. From the Timeline panel menu, choose **Panel Options**. In the Animation Panel Options dialog, click Timeline Units: **Timecode**, then click OK.

➤ To reopen the Timeline panel if it's hidden, choose Window > Timeline. You can dock it at the bottom of the Application frame.

➤ To enlarge the Timeline panel if it's docked, drag the top of the panel (the dark line) upward. If the panel isn't docked, drag the side, bottom, or corner.

LEARNING THE VIDEO LINGO

➤ The work area for editing a video project in Photoshop is called the timeline.

➤ Each video file that you open into Photoshop is called a video clip. Each video clip displays as a blue bar on the Timeline panel.

➤ Each horizontal row (labeled Video Group) on the timeline is called a track. A track can contain one or more video clips and/or title clips (type). Audio clips are on separate tracks, and display as green bars.

➤ Each split-second image within a video clip is called a frame. The first frame of each clip is shown in a thumbnail on the Timeline panel.

➤ The Playhead (blue marker at the top of the red vertical line) designates the frame at which a video will begin to play.

➤ Effects that are used to blend the end of one clip to the beginning of the next are called transitions.

➤ The markers that designate where changes in a frame sequence start and end are called keyframes.

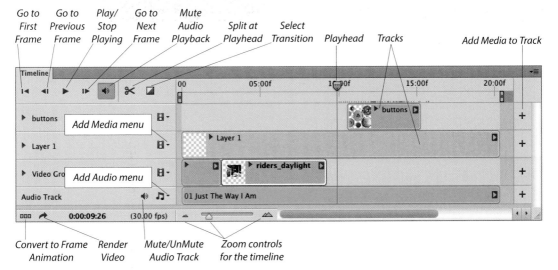

Go to First Frame · Go to Previous Frame · Play/Stop Playing · Go to Next Frame · Mute Audio Playback · Split at Playhead · Select Transition · Playhead · Tracks · Add Media to Track

Add Media menu · Add Audio menu

Convert to Frame Animation · Render Video · Mute/UnMute Audio Track · Zoom controls for the timeline

A The Timeline panel is used for video editing in Photoshop.

Both standard and high definition video files can be imported into Photoshop, in many popular formats. When you import a video, your edits are stored in a Photoshop document; the original video file isn't altered. In order to play your final video, you will need to render it (see page 432).

To import a video file into a new Photoshop document: ★

1. Close all open Photoshop documents, then do one of the following:

    From Bridge, drag a video file thumbnail into the Application frame in Photoshop.

    From Mini Bridge, drag a video file thumbnail into the Application frame.

    On the Timeline panel, choose Add Media from the **Add Media** menu or, at the right end of the timeline, click the **Add Media to Track** button. In the Add Clips dialog, select one or more clip files, then click Open.

2. Respond to any Profile Mismatch or Pixel Aspect Ratio alerts that appear. A new document appears in Photoshop. The video clip appears on the Layers panel within a Video Group listing,**A** and on the Timeline panel as a blue bar.**B** The first frame of the clip displays as a thumbnail within the bar.

3. *Optional:* Add more clips via the Add Media menu (not via dragging). They will appear from left to right on the timeline in the sequence in which you import them.

    Note: Once you have imported a video into a Photoshop file, don't move the original video file, or the link to that file will be broken.

4. Save your file in the Photoshop format—and remember to save it periodically while editing it.

➤   As your video gets more complex, you will need to scroll the window horizontally in order to view the clips.

Adding video tracks to a timeline

By default, clips that you add to a timeline appear within the currently selected Video Group (track), and are also listed on the Layers panel. The first clip in a track corresponds to the bottommost layer on the Layers panel, and plays back first. If you want clips to play simultaneously, such as a title clip on top of video footage, you need to put them on separate tracks.

To add a track to the timeline: ★

1. From the **Add Media** menu on the Timeline panel, choose **New Video Group**. A new Video Group appears on both the Timeline and Layers panels.

2. Drag a video clip from another track (Video Group) into the new track, or import it via the Add Media menu or the Add Media to Track button.

FREE VIDEO FILES

You can download video clips of national parks and historic sites from nps.gov/pub_aff/video/index.html. The clips are in the public domain.

A *The three clips that we added to a Video Group are listed on the Layers panel.*

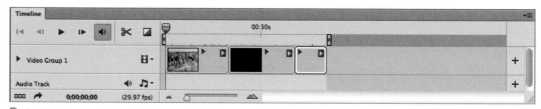

B *This Timeline panel is showing the same Video Group as on the Layers panel. The three layers display as clips on one track.*

Changing the length, order, or speed of a clip

One of the first edits you should make to a video is to trim off any excess footage.

To trim a clip by dragging: ★

Position the pointer over either end of a clip (the Trim cursor appears ✥), then drag inward to shorten the clip.**A**

As you trim the clip, the frame at which the clip will begin or end displays temporarily in what is called a trim window. The window also lists the current position of the Trim cursor on the timeline (the left value, which is labeled Start or End) and the current Duration (length) of the clip.

➤ Trimmed frames aren't deleted. To retrieve trimmed frames at any time, drag the start or end of the clip outward.

To specify the length or speed of a clip via a panel: ★

1. To display the Video panel, right-click a clip or click the arrowhead at the end of the clip.**B**

2. Do either or both of the following:

   To adjust the length of the clip, click the **Duration** arrowhead, then adjust the slider; or enter a value in the field.

   To adjust the speed at which the clip plays, click the **Speed** arrowhead, then adjust the slider; or enter a value in the field. Any audio in the clip will be muted, as the change in speed will cause audio distortion.

There are two ways to change the order of clips in a track.

To change the order of clips: ★

Do either of the following:

On the Timeline panel, ⊞ drag a clip to the left or right, either between two other clips or to the beginning or end of its track, and release when the vertical black bar or rectangle displays. The other clips will rearrange automatically.

On the Layers panel, ⬙ drag a clip layer upward or downward. The clip that is listed at the bottom of a Video Group plays first.

To delete a clip or track: ★

Do one of the following:

On the Timeline panel, click a Video Group listing or a clip (colored bar), then press Backspace/ Delete.

On the Layers panel, expand a Video Group listing, click a clip layer, then press Backspace/ Delete.

PLAYING AND REVIEWING YOUR VIDEO

➤ To play your video at normal playback speed, press the Play button on the Timeline panel. ▶ Had enough? To stop the playback, press the button again ■ (same button, different icon).

➤ If you want to review just a section of your video (a process called scrubbing), simply drag the Playhead along that section of the timeline.

➤ To mute the audio in all video clips, click the Mute Audio Playback button at the top of the Timeline panel. ◀♪ To mute the audio in one video clip, right-click the clip, click the Audio icon, ♫ then check Mute Audio on the temporary panel.

A As we dragged the end of a clip to shorten it, the frame at which the clip would end displayed temporarily in a trim window.

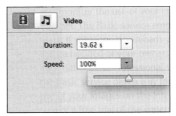

B We right-clicked a clip to display this Video panel, then chose new Duration and Speed settings.

Splitting a clip

When you split a clip into sections, an insertion point is created, into which you can add other clips. You also have the option to move or delete any of the sections that result from the split.

To split a clip: ★

1. On the Timeline panel, drag the Playhead (the blue marker at the top of the red line) over the frame where you want a clip to be split.

2. Click the **Split at Playhead** button.✂A

3. *Optional:* To split the clip further, reposition the Playhead at the end of the section to be split, then click the Split at Playhead button again.**B**

   You can click any section that results from a split, then drag it to a new location within the same track or into another track, or press Backspace/Delete to remove it. Any resulting gap in the track will close automatically.

➤ When you split a clip, no frames are deleted. If you want to restore "cut" frames, position the pointer over either end of the split clip (the Trim cursor appears), then drag to lengthen the clip. Each section of a split clip contains all the video footage of that clip; you can control how much of the video file is played for each clip.

Adding transitions to video clips

Although a video editor might sometimes use a "jump cut" (abrupt transition) between scenes to convey a sense of action and energy, a smoother transition, such as a fade, creates a more gentle segue between clips, and can be used to convey the passage of time.

To add a transition to a clip: ★

1. On the Timeline panel, click the **Transition** button, ◼ then drag a transition from the panel to the start or end of any clip (**A**, next page), or between two clips to have the transition apply to the end of one clip and the beginning of the next one.

2. To change the transition style, right-click the transition ramp in the lower-left or lower-right corner of the clip and choose a different option from the menu on the temporary Transition panel.

To adjust the duration of a transition: ★

Do either of the following:

Position the cursor over the transition ramp on the clip, then drag inward to shorten the effect or back outward to lengthen it (Trim cursor) (**B**, next page).

Right-click the transition ramp on the clip to display the **Transition** panel, then change the **Duration** value via the slider or field.

A To split a clip, we moved the Playhead to the desired position, then clicked the Split at Playhead button.

B To split the clip once more, we moved the blue Playhead further along the timeline. Because we split the clip, we now have the option to delete any unwanted sections or move a section to a different track.

Adding still images to a video

You can also add still images to a timeline, then make them "come to life" by choosing a pan, zoom, or rotate option. You can have a still image play on top of a video track, or import a series of still image clips into one track, to be played in succession, like a slideshow.

To add a still image to a video: ★

1. Create a copy of a photo, then use the Image Size dialog to change its resolution to 72 ppi.
2. Click a Video Group, then from the **Add Media** menu, choose **Add Media**.
3. The Add Clips dialog opens. Select a still image, then click Open. The still image will appear as a new purple bar on the timeline.
4. *Optional:* Drag the Playhead over the image clip. Press Ctrl-T/Cmd-T, then press Ctrl-0/Ctrl-0 to zoom out. Shift-drag a corner handle to scale the clip, then double-click in the transform box to accept the edit.
5. *Optional:* Each still image is assigned a default play interval of 5 seconds. You can adjust that interval by dragging its edge.

➤ For the most flexibility in trimming and positioning a still image clip, move it to a separate track.

To apply a motion effect to a still image: ★

Right-click a still image clip or click its arrowhead, then on the **Motion** panel, choose an option from the first menu.◖ For a "Ken Burns" type effect, choose Pan & Zoom.

Adding title clips to a video

The addition of titles to a video adds a professional touch, and sometimes necessary information. Just make sure your titles are concise, carefully kerned, and easy to read. Avoid using serif fonts, which can become fuzzy on a low-resolution monitor, and the color red, which can smear or bleed onscreen.

To add a title clip to a video: ★

1. On the Timeline panel, position the Playhead where you want the title to appear.
2. With the Horizontal Type tool, create an editable type layer. The type layer will appear within the currently selected Video Group on the Layers panel and as a purple clip on the Timeline panel.

To have a title clip play on top of a video clip: ★

1. Do either of the following:

   Create a new Video Group above the other tracks, then drag the title clip into that group.

   On the Layers panel, drag the type layer to the top of the layer stack.

2. *Optional:* To extend the duration that the title clip plays, drag its right edge. (The maximum duration is the current length of the timeline.)

You can apply a motion effect to a title clip to make it less static, just as you can to a still image.

To apply motion to a title clip: ★

See the second task, at left. If you want the title to fill the entire screen when the video plays, check **Resize to Fill Canvas** on the Motion panel.

A We clicked the Transition button on the Timeline panel to open this temporary panel. Next, we will drag an option from the panel to a clip on our timeline.

B We're dragging a transition ramp to change its duration.

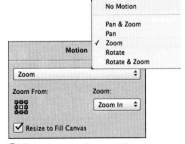

C We're choosing Zoom as the motion option from the first menu on the Motion panel.

Applying adjustment layers and filters to a video

You can apply any Photoshop adjustment command to a clip, to a track, or to the whole timeline. As expected, you can edit the adjustment layer settings at any time. By default, each adjustment layer is clipped to, and only affects, the clip directly below it. You have the option to expand the adjustment effect to all the clips in the Video Group or to all the tracks on the timeline.

To apply an adjustment layer to one clip: ★

1. On the Layers panel or the Timeline panel, click the clip to be adjusted, then on the Timeline panel, drag the Playhead over that clip.

2. Create an adjustment layer. Try applying a Color Lookup adjustment, ⊞ ★ which adds Hollywood movie-like effects.

To apply an adjustment layer to all the clips in a Video Group: ★

1. On the Layers panel or Timeline panel, click a Video Group.

2. Create an adjustment layer.

3. To unclip the adjustment layer, on the Layers panel, Alt-click/Option-click the line between the clip layer and the adjustment layer, then drag the adjustment layer upward to the top of its Video Group.

   Note: The adjustment clip won't display as a clip on the timeline (except if you follow the steps in the next task).

To apply an adjustment layer to all the tracks in a timeline: ★

1. On the Layers panel, click the topmost Video Group.

2 If you haven't already done so, create an adjustment layer.

3. Drag the adjustment layer above (and outside of) its original Video Group. A it will appear in a new track.

4. On the Timeline panel, drag the end of the adjustment clip to adjust its duration. B

➤ When an adjustment layer is in its own track, you can apply keyframing edits (such as opacity changes) to have the effect appear gradually over time (see the next page).

A On the Layers panel, we dragged an adjustment layer out of a Video Group.

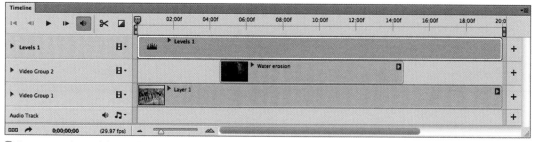

B Because we dragged the Levels adjustment layer clip to its own track, the adjustment will apply to all the tracks in the timeline. We lengthened the adjustment clip to have it apply to the entire duration of the video.

You can apply any Photoshop filter to a clip. By default, a filter will affect only one frame in a video clip (where the Playhead is located). To have a filter affect an entire clip, you must convert the clip to a Smart Object first.

To apply a filter to a clip: ★

1. On the Timeline panel, click a clip.

2. Choose Filter > Convert for Smart Filters; the clip color changes to purple. Apply one or more filters (Filter menu). If an alert appears, click OK.

➤ To apply a filter to just a section of a clip, split the clip, click a section, then follow step 2, above.

➤ To make a filter effect fade in and then out over time, duplicate a clip, put the duplicate clip in a track directly above the original one, apply the filter to the duplicate, then use keyframing to lower the opacity of the effect (see "To create a manual fade" on this page).

Keyframing

By using keyframe markers, you can apply an edit to a video that occurs over a specified span, such as a transformation (e.g., scale change), opacity change, or layer style change (blending mode or layer effect).

To create a picture-in-a-picture: ★

1. Make sure your timeline contains at least two video clips that are on separate tracks. Drag the upper clip to the right (so the video begins with the lower clip).

2. Click the clip on the upper track, then to enable it to be transformed, if it's not already a Smart Object, choose Layer > Smart Objects > Convert to Smart Object. If you need to edit the original

clip (e.g., change its Speed setting), double-click the Smart Object thumbnail on the Layers panel.

3. Move the Playhead to align with the left edge of the upper clip, expand that Video Group, then click the **Enable Keyframe Animation** button ⏱ for **Transform**. A yellow diamond-shaped marker appears on the timeline.

4. Move the Playhead to the right to designate the amount of time the clip is to play at full size.

5. Click the **Add Keyframe** button ◈ to mark the location where the clip begins to scale.

6. Move the Playhead to the point on the timeline where the scaling is to end.

7. Press Ctrl-T/Cmd-T for the Transform command, Shift-drag a corner handle in the document window to shrink the clip (while preserving its aspect ratio), then press Enter/Return to accept the transformation. A second keyframe marker appears on the timeline.

8. Drag the scaled clip to the desired location in the timeline. As you play the video, the still image will shrink and move between the keyframes. **A**

To create a manual fade: ★

1. On the timeline, click a clip (not in the bottom-most Video Group), then position the Playhead several seconds inward from the end of the clip.

2. Expand the Video Group and click the **Enable Keyframe** button ⏱ for **Opacity**.

3. Move the Playhead to the end of the clip.

4. On the Layers panel, lower the Opacity value to 0%. A second keyframe marker appears on the timeline.

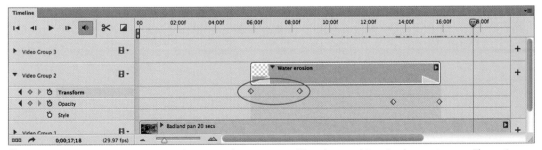

A *We added keyframes to a video clip to designate where we wanted Transform and Opacity changes to occur. The section between each pair of diamonds (within a row) marks the area of transition.*

Adding audio clips

By default, one audio track (for narration or music) is included in each timeline. You can add more audio clips or tracks as needed, plus you can fade, mute, or adjust the volume for any existing audio clip.

To adjust the settings of an audio clip: ★

1. To display the Audio panel, right-click a video clip, then click the **Audio** icon 🎵 **A**; or right-click an audio clip.**B**

2. Adjust the **Volume**, **Fade In**, and **Fade Out** sliders. If you want to mute the clip, check **Mute Audio**.

➤ If the audio doesn't play as you play the video, click the Enable Audio Playback button.◀

To add an audio clip or track to a timeline: ★

1. *Optional:* To add an audio clip to a new track, from the Add Audio menu 🎵▾ on an audio track, choose New Audio Track.

2. From the **Add Audio** menu 🎵▾ on an audio track, choose **Add Audio**; or click the **Add Audio to Track** button ➕ at the right end of the timeline.

3. The Add Audio Clips dialog opens. Locate an audio file, then click Open.

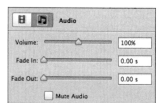

A We're adjusting the audio settings for a video clip via the Audio panel.

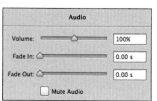

B We right-clicked an audio clip to display these Audio panel settings.

DON'T STEAL THE MUSIC

Although it may be tempting to grab a favorite song from the Internet to add to your video, make absolutely certain you are not violating a copyright if you post it in a public forum.

Rendering clips into a movie

Rendering is the essential final step of combining edited clips into a playable movie file.

To render a timeline into a final video: ★

1. Save your file. On the Timeline panel, click the **Render Video** button.✏

2. The Render Video dialog opens.**C** Do all of the following:

   Enter a **Name** for your video file (keep the default extension).

   Click **Select Folder**, choose a location for the file, then click OK/Choose.

   Choose a **Format** and **Size** for the video. (The Preset menu for the H.264 format offers presets for many common tablets, devices, and video services.) Leave the other menus alone.

   Under Range, click **All Frames**, or click **Start Frame** and enter a specific range of frames.

   Click **Render**. The rendering process may take a while, depending on the speed of your computer and length of the video.

➤ To enable your Photoshop video to be played on a home DVD player, use Windows Live Movie or Apple iMovie to convert it to the proprietary file format for DVD players.

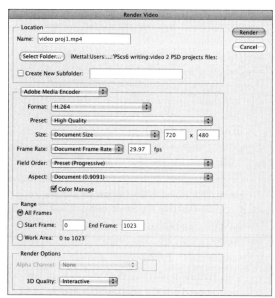

C The Render Video dialog offers a number of output options.

Preferences are settings that you specify for various Photoshop application features, such as the gray shades for the Photoshop interface and measurement units for the rulers. Most preference changes take effect immediately (and are saved to the Preferences file) when you exit/quit Photoshop, but a handful of preference changes don't take effect until you relaunch Photoshop or Bridge; we note such exceptions.

Opening the Preferences dialogs

To open the Preferences dialog for **Photoshop**, press Ctrl-K/Cmd-K, or choose Edit/Photoshop > Preferences > General or another option from the submenu. In the dialog, click one of the 11 panel names on the left side, A or click Prev or Next, or press a shortcut between Ctrl-1/Cmd-1 and Ctrl-0/Cmd-0 (zero).

To open the Preferences dialog for **Bridge**, in Bridge, press Ctrl-K/Cmd-K or choose Edit/Adobe Bridge CS6 > Preferences.

PREFERENCES

24

General	Guides	
Interface		
File Handling	Color: ☐ Cyan	
Performance	Style: Lines	
Cursors		
Transparency & Gamut	Smart Guides	
Units & Rulers		
Guides, Grid & Slices	Color: ☐ Magenta	
Plug–Ins		
Type		
3D	Grid	
	Color: Custom...	

A *The Preferences dialog in Photoshop contains 11 panels.*

RESETTING ALL THE PREFERENCES

► To reset all the Photoshop preferences to their default settings, hold down Ctrl-Alt-Shift/Cmd-Option-Shift as you launch the program. When the alert dialog appears, click Yes to delete (and reset) the Adobe Photoshop Settings file.

► To reset the Bridge preferences, hold down Ctrl/Option as you launch Bridge. When the Reset Settings dialog appears, check Reset Preferences, then click OK.

General Preferences (A, next page)

For the default **Color Picker**, choose either Adobe (the default setting) or your system color picker.

For the onscreen **HUD** (Heads-Up Display) **Color Picker**, choose a strip or wheel style and size. The two options labeled "(Small)" are new. ★ See page 186.

Choose a default **Image Interpolation** option for Photoshop edits that involve resampling or transforming, such as the Image Size dialog and the Crop tool: Nearest Neighbor (Preserve Hard Edges), the fastest and the best for hard-edged graphics but the least precise; Bilinear, for medium quality; Bicubic (Best for Smooth Gradients), higher quality but slower; Bicubic Smoother (Best for Enlargement); Bicubic Sharper (Best for Reduction); or the new default setting of Bicubic Automatic ★ (Photoshop determines the best method).

Options

Check **Auto-Update Open Documents** to have open Photoshop documents that you edit in other applications update automatically when you return to Photoshop, such as when you assign metadata to a file in Bridge.

Check **Beep When Done** to have a beep sound when a command is done processing. This can be handy for commands that take a while to process (so you can grab a snack!).

Check **Dynamic Color Sliders** to have the colors above the sliders on the Color panel update as you move the sliders.

Check **Export Clipboard** to retain the current Clipboard contents on the system Clipboard when you switch between Photoshop and other programs.

With **Use Shift Key for Tool Switch** checked, in order to access tools from a fly-out menu, you must press Shift plus the assigned letter (e.g., press Shift-B to cycle through the Brush, Pencil, Color Replacement, and Mixer Brush tools). If you uncheck this option (as we do), you can cycle through related tools simply by pressing their assigned letter. To learn the tool shortcuts, see pages 102–104 or use Tool Tips.

Check **Resize Image During Place** to have pixel images from other Photoshop files or other applications scale to fit the current canvas area automatically when imported via the File > Place command.

Check **Animated Zoom** for smooth, continuous zooming as you drag or hold down the Zoom tool

(Use Graphics Processor must be checked in the Performance panel of this dialog; see page 439).

With **Zoom Resizes Windows** checked, a floating document window will resize when you change the zoom level via the Ctrl/Cmd- + (plus) or Ctrl/Cmd- – (minus) shortcut or the Zoom tool. You can also control this behavior for the Zoom tool via the Resize Windows to Fit check box on the Options bar. Note: As you change the zoom level, the document is positioned over — but not docked into — the document window area of the Application frame.

If your mouse has a scroll wheel and you check **Zoom with Scroll Wheel**, you can change the zoom level by scrolling the wheel horizontally or vertically.

Check **Zoom Clicked Point to Center** to have Photoshop center the image at the location you click when zooming.

Check **Enable Flick Panning** to enable a magnified image to quickly float across the screen when you drag it with the Hand tool a short distance, then release the mouse (Use Graphics Processor must be checked in the Performance panel of this dialog upon launch; see page 439).

With **Vary Round Brush Hardness Based on HUD Vertical Movement** checked, you can Alt-right-click/ Control-Option and drag vertically to change the brush hardness; with this option unchecked, the shortcut changes the brush opacity instead. ★ This option affects the Brush, Pencil, Color Replacement, Clone Stamp, History Brush, Sharpen, and other tools (see page 272). HUD stands for "Heads Up Display," and it refers to the ability of the user to choose settings via on-image controls. Note: To display the hardness or opacity value as a tint within the cursor, check Use Graphics Processor in the Performance panel of this dialog.

Check **Place or Drag Raster Images as Smart Objects** to have raster images that are drag-copied into Photoshop, or placed via the Place command, arrive automatically as Smart Objects (see pages 250–251).

Check **Snap Vector Tools and Transforms to Pixel Grid** to have future vector paths that you create, and existing shapes that you transform, snap to the pixel grid, for sharper rendering onscreen (see page 388). This option is designed for online output. ★

History Log

Check **History Log** to have Photoshop generate a log of your editing activity from each work session. The log can be useful if you need to preserve an exact record of your editing steps or need to tally your billable hours for clients.

For **Save Log Items To**, choose where the log is to be saved: to the Metadata of a file, to a separate Text File, or to Both of the above. For either of the latter two options, choose a location for the text file in the dialog that opens automatically, then click Save.

From the **Edit Log Items** menu, choose what data is to be saved in the log: Sessions Only to log just the date and time when you launch or exit/quit Photoshop and which files were opened; Concise to log Sessions information plus a list of edits (states on the History panel); or Detailed to include all of the above data plus any actions used and the options and parameters used in each editing step.

Reset Warning Dialogs

Click **Reset All Warning Dialogs** to reactivate all alert dialogs in which you have clicked Don't Show Again.

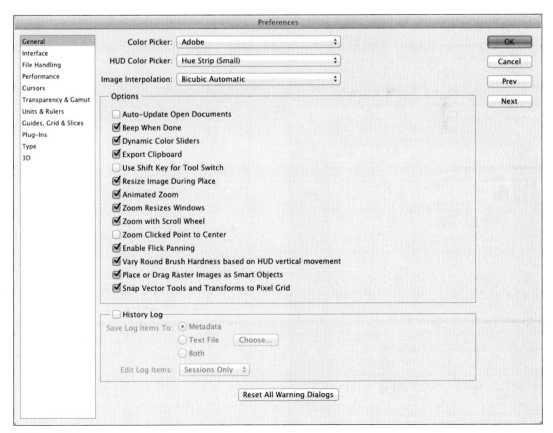

A *General Preferences*

Interface Preferences (A, next page)

Appearance

Click a **Color Theme** for the Photoshop interface, including the background and text color in the panels and Options bar, the Application frame, and the blank background behind the canvas area. ★

Via the Color menus next to **Standard Screen Mode**, **Full Screen with Menus**, and **Full Screen**, choose a shade or color for the background behind the canvas area for each screen mode: Default (the shade associated with the current Color Theme); Black or a Gray option; ★ or Select Custom Color. For the latter option, choose a color from the Color Picker; thereafter, that color will appear if you choose the Custom option. For the Border around the canvas area, choose Line, Drop Shadow, or None. Note: For the Line and Drop Shadow options, you must also check Use Graphics Processor in Performance preferences. For the screen modes, see page 92.

Options

If **Auto-Collapse Iconic Panels** is checked and you open a collapsed panel, it will collapse back to an icon when you click anywhere outside it. With this option unchecked, the panel will remain expanded. See page 94.

Check **Auto-Show Hidden Panels** to allow panel docks that you have hidden to redisplay temporarily. In Standard Screen mode, hide the docks via the Tab or Shift-Tab shortcut, then redisplay them temporarily by letting the pointer pause on the dark gray vertical bar at the right edge of the Application frame (or the left edge of the frame, for the Tools panel). Move the pointer away from the docks, and they will disappear again. In either of the Full Screen modes, let the pointer pause at the edge of your monitor to make the dark bar appear.

Check **Open Documents as Tabs** to have documents dock automatically as tabs when opened instead of as floating windows (we recommend checking this option). Note: In the Mac OS, if you check this option but hide the Application frame, images will dock as tabs within one document window automatically.

Check **Enable Floating Document Window Docking** to allow a floating document window to be docked as a tab when you drag its title bar just below the Options bar in the Application frame or next to an existing document tab in a floating window. (We recommend keeping this option checked.)

Check **Show Channels in Color** to display RGB or CMYK channels in color thumbnails on the Channels panel and in the document window when clicked individually. Uncheck this option (as we do) to display the channels in grayscale, which is useful for judging luminosity values.

Check **Show Menu Colors** to activate the display of background colors that have been assigned to menu commands via Edit > Menus and to workspaces in which they were saved (e.g., the "New in CS6" workspace).

Check **Show Tool Tips** to allow a label to appear briefly onscreen showing the name or function of whichever Photoshop feature the pointer is currently hovering over (mouse button up). This is a good way to identify panel and dialog options, as well as tools and tool shortcuts.

Mac OS users: Check **Enable Gestures** if you have a laptop with a multi-touch trackpad (or are using a Magic Mouse or Magic Trackpad with any Macintosh computer) and you want to enable the capability of the trackpad to zoom, rotate, or flick images. Uncheck this option if you find that the gestures are causing unwanted changes.

Check **Enable Text Drop Shadow** to display a very subtle drop shadow behind text labels in panels. ★

From the **Show Transformation Values** menu, choose a location (e.g., Top Left or Bottom Right) for the label that appears and updates dynamically as you transform objects, indicating the current rotation, scaling, or other values. ★ Choose Never from the menu if you prefer to turn this feature off.

Click **Restore Default Workspaces** to restore, to the Workspace menu, any predefined Adobe workspaces that were deleted via the Window > Workspaces > Delete Workspace dialog.

Text

As noted in the dialog, to implement these Text options, you must relaunch Photoshop.

If you are using a multilingual version of Photoshop, from the **UI Language** menu, choose a language for the interface.

From the **UI Font Size** menu, choose Small, Medium, or Large as the font size for features in the Photoshop user interface (panels, Options bar, etc.). We set this option to Medium.

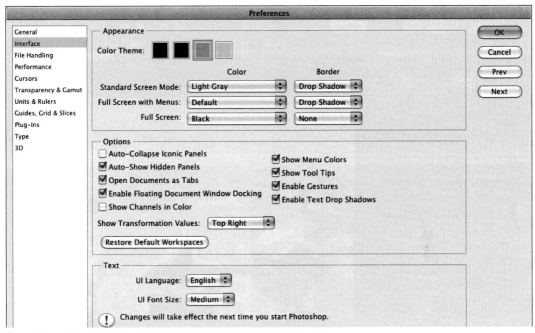

A *Interface Preferences*

File Handling Preferences (A, next page)

File Saving Options

Choose **Image Previews:** Never Save to save files without a thumbnail preview for the Desktop, or Always Save (our preference) to have an updated preview save with files each time they're saved, or Ask When Saving to decide which previews to include via Image Previews check boxes when saving files via the Save or Save As dialog. See pages 18–20.

In the Mac OS, check **Icon** to have the thumbnails of files display as their icons on the Desktop and in the File > Open dialog. Check **Windows Thumbnail** to have the thumbnail for a file display when the file is selected in File > Open.

In the Mac OS, choose **Append File Extension:** Always (our preference) to include a three-letter abbreviation of the file format (e.g., .tif, .psd) automatically when a file is saved; or Ask When Saving to be given the option to decide in each case whether to include the extension via File Extension check boxes in the Save As dialog. Extensions are helpful when converting files for Windows, and are necessary when saving files for the Web. Keep Use Lower

Case checked to have file extensions appear in lowercase characters instead of in uppercase.

In Windows, choose **File Extension:** Use Lower Case or Use Upper Case.

Check **Save As to Original Folder** (as we do) to have the location in the Save As dialog always default to the existing location of the current file.

Check **Save in Background** to permit image-editing to occur while Photoshop is saving a file. ★

Check **Automatically Save Recovery Information Every,** and choose a time interval from the menu, to let Photoshop save a temporary copy of the current document to your hard disk. If Photoshop exits/quits unexpectedly, the temp file will open by default upon relaunch. ★

File Compatibility

Click **Camera Raw Preferences** to open that dialog.

Check **Prefer Adobe Camera Raw for Supported Raw Files** to have raw files that you open via File >

Continued on the following page

Open open into Camera Raw, as opposed to other conversion software. We keep this option checked.

Ignore EXIF Profile Tag enables Photoshop to read a camera's EXIF metadata color space data when opening files. This option is necessary only for files from early digital cameras, so we keep it unchecked.

Check **Ignore Rotation Metadata** to have Photoshop ignore any rotation settings that are applied to image thumbnails in Bridge. ★

Check **Ask Before Saving Layered TIFF Files** to have an "Including layers will increase file size" alert dialog appear when saving a layered file in the TIFF format. You can use this alert as a reminder to uncheck the Layers option in the Save As dialog.

Check **Disable Compression of PSD and PSB Files** to prevent Photoshop from compressing files when saving them in the PSD or PSB format. Documents will save more quickly, but in a larger file size. ★

Check **Maximize PSD and PSB File Compatibility** to have Photoshop save a composite preview with your layered files (for much older versions of Photoshop and for applications that don't support layers), and also save a rasterized copy of any vector art in the document (for applications that don't support vector data). Although this option produces larger files that take longer to save, in many cases it's a requirement for the needed compatibility. Choose Ask to have Photoshop offer compatibility as an option via an alert when files are saved, or choose Always to have Photoshop produce compatible files automatically without an alert. See pages 18–20.

Note: Upon saving a layered file, if Ask is the current Maximize PSD and PSB File Compatibility preference and you check Maximize Compatibility and Don't Show Again in the Photoshop Format Options dialog, Photoshop will switch the preference setting to Always. If you uncheck Maximize Compatibility but do check Don't Show Again in the alert, the preference setting will switch to Never.

Adobe Drive

For information on Adobe Drive, search for "adobe drive" at Adobe.com.

File list

In the **Recent File List Contains [ ] files** field, enter the maximum number of files (up to 30) that can be listed at a time on the File > Open Recent submenu in Photoshop.

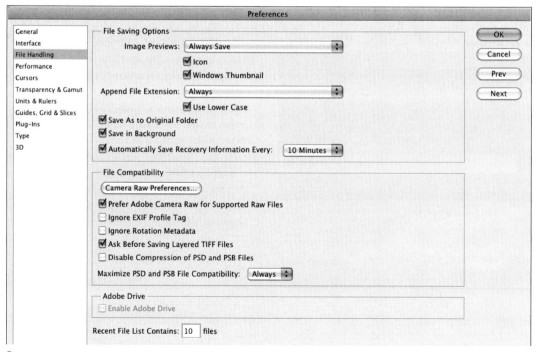

A *File Handling Preferences*

Performance Preferences A

Note: To implement changes made in this panel, you must relaunch Photoshop.

In the **Description** window at the bottom of the dialog, you can read about the feature your pointer is currently hovering over.

Memory Usage
The **Let Photoshop Use** field and slider control the maximum percentage of your computer's RAM that can be used by Photoshop. We recommend keeping this value on the default setting.

History & Cache
Low-resolution versions of the current file are saved in cache buffers to help the image and histograms redraw more quickly onscreen. To optimize the cache levels and tile size for Photoshop, click a generic document type (not your body type!): **Tall and Thin** (for smaller documents that contain many layers), **Default** (best for general use), or **Big and Flat** (best for larger documents that contain few layers).

Enter the maximum number of **History States** the History panel can list at a time. When this number is reached, older states are deleted.

Choose a higher **Cache Levels** value for large files that contain few layers and a lower Cache Levels value for smaller files that contain many layers.

The **Cache Tile Size** value controls how much data Photoshop processes at a given time. For faster processing of large images, choose a higher value.

Scratch Disks
Check which hard drives Photoshop may use as **Scratch Disks** when available RAM is insufficient for processing or storing image data. To change the sequence of drives, click the up or down arrow.

➤ Hold down Ctrl-Alt/Cmd-Option while launching Photoshop to open the Scratch Disk Preferences dialog.

➤ From the Info panel ⓘ menu in Photoshop, choose Panel Options, then check Efficiency under Status Information. When Photoshop is using the scratch disk, the Efficiency readout value is below 100%.

Graphics Processor Settings
The **Detected Graphics Processor** ★ area lists the graphics card that is currently installed in your system.

Check **Use Graphics Processor** ★ if your system has OpenGL capability and you want to use the OpenGL features of Photoshop, such as Animated Zoom, Scrubby Zoom, Flick Panning, Pixel Grid, HUD Color Picker, the Sampling Ring for the Eyedropper tool, a tint in the brush cursor for hardness and/or opacity, the Live Tip Brush Preview, and the Rotate View tool. (For a complete list, see the Description area.)

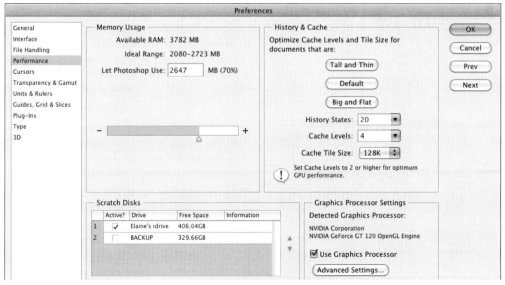

A Performance Preferences

Cursors Preferences A

Painting Cursors

For the **Painting Cursors** (the Art History Brush, Background Eraser, Blur, Brush, Burn, Clone Stamp, Color Replacement, Dodge, Eraser, Healing Brush, History Brush, Mixer Brush, Pattern Stamp, Pencil, Quick Selection, Sharpen, Smudge, Sponge, and Spot Healing Brush tools), click the preferred cursor to be displayed onscreen: **Standard** for the tool icon; **Precise** for crosshairs; **Normal Brush Tip** for a circle that is half the size of the current brush; or **Full Size Brush Tip** for a circle that is the full size of the current brush. For either of the latter two options, you can also check **Show Crosshair in Brush Tip** to have crosshairs appear in the center of the circle and/or **Show Only Crosshair While Painting** to have only crosshairs display when the mouse is dragged, for faster performance when using large brushes.

Other Cursors

For the **Other Cursors** (all those not listed in the preceding paragraph, such as the Eyedropper and Crop tools), click **Standard** to have the tool icon display onscreen as you use the tool or click **Precise** to display crosshairs instead.

➤ Press Caps Lock to turn a Standard cursor into a Precise cursor (crosshairs) or, if Precise is the current Painting Cursors setting, to turn any Painting cursor into a Full Size Brush Tip (circle).

Brush Preview

Click the **Color** swatch and choose a color via the Color Picker to represent the current brush hardness or opacity as a tint in the brush cursor as you Alt-right-click/Control-Option drag vertically (Use Graphics Processor must be checked in the Performance panel).

Transparency & Gamut Preferences B

Transparency Settings

Choose a **Grid Size** for the checkerboard that Photoshop uses to represent layer transparency on the Layers panel and in the document window.

For the transparency checkerboard, choose one of the **Grid Colors** options from the menu, or click each color swatch and choose a color via the Color Picker.

Gamut Warning

To change the color that Photoshop uses to mark out-of-gamut colors when the View > **Gamut Warning** feature is on, click the Color swatch. You can also change the Opacity of the Gamut Warning color.

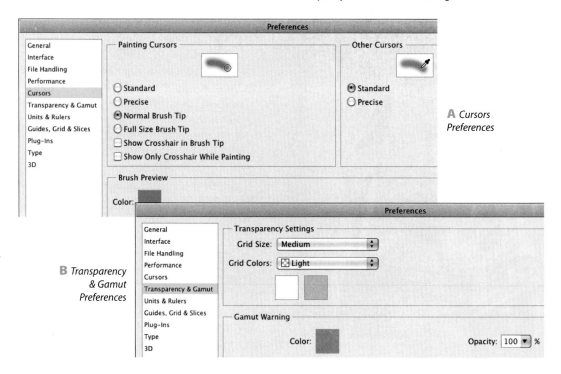

A Cursors Preferences

B Transparency & Gamut Preferences

Units & Rulers Preferences A

▶ To get directly to the Units & Rulers panel of the Preferences dialog, double-click either ruler.

Units

From the **Rulers** menu, choose a unit of measure to display on the horizontal and vertical rulers; in dialogs, such as Image > Canvas Size; and on panels, such as the Info panel. To learn about the rulers in Photoshop, see pages 268–270.

▶ To change the ruler units without opening the Preferences dialog, right-click either one of the rulers in the document window and choose a unit from the context menu. When changed this way or via the Info Panel Options dialog, the ruler units also change here in the Preferences dialog, and vice versa.

From the **Type** menu, choose Pixels, Points, or Millimeters as the unit of measure for the Character panel and Paragraph panels, and for the Options bar when a type tool is selected.

Column Size

If you need to fit your Photoshop images into a specific column width in a page layout program, enter values in the **Width** and **Gutter** fields here. Thereafter, when you open the New, Image Size, or Canvas Size dialog and then choose Columns from the units menu next to the Width field, Photoshop will use your Width and Gutter preference values to calculate the Width.

New Document Preset Resolutions

Enter a **Print Resolution** value in either one of the available units to display as the Resolution setting in the New dialog when you choose a print preset (the default value is 300 ppi). For the **Screen Resolution,** enter a value to display as the Resolution when you choose the Web, Mobile & Devices, or Film & Video preset (the default value is 72 ppi). See pages 15–16.

Point/Pica Size

Click **PostScript** (the default, and recommended, setting) to have Photoshop use the standard PostScript value as the points-to-inch ratio.

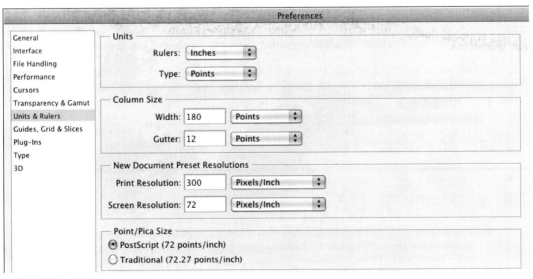

A *Units & Rulers Preferences*

Guides, Grid & Slices Preferences A

Note: Changes made in this dialog will preview immediately in your document.

Guides

For ruler guides, choose a **Color** from the menu (or click the swatch and use the Color Picker), and choose a **Style**. See pages 268–270.

Smart Guides

For Smart Guides, temporary lines that display as you move a layer or selection, choose a **Color** from the menu (or click the swatch and use the Color Picker). See page 268.

Grid

For the nonprinting grid, choose a **Color** and **Style**.

➤ To show or hide the grid, press Ctrl-'/Cmd-'.

To display grid lines onscreen at specific intervals, choose a unit from the menu, then enter a **Gridline Every** value. If you choose Percent from the menu and enter a value, grid lines will appear at those percentage intervals of the document width, starting from the left edge of the canvas. To control the spacing between the thinner grid lines that fall within the main grid lines, enter a **Subdivisions** value.

Slices

Choose a **Line Color** for the slice boundaries. Check **Show Slice Numbers** to have Photoshop display a slice number in the upper-left corner of each slice. (To learn about the slice tools, see Photoshop Help.)

Plug-ins Preferences (A, next page)

Note: To implement changes made in this panel, you must relaunch Photoshop.

Plug-ins

In order to use third-party plug-ins that aren't currently residing in the Adobe Photoshop CS6 > Plug-ins folder, you must check **Additional Plug-ins Folder**, find the folder in which they are installed via the dialog that opens automatically, then click Choose in that dialog.

➤ To deactivate all your installed third-party plug-ins just for the current work session, hold down Shift while launching Photoshop, then click Yes in the alert dialog. ★

Filters

Check **Show All Filter Gallery Groups and Names** to list all Photoshop filters in the submenus on the Filter menu, including those that are available in the Filter Gallery. With this option off, the submenus will list only filters that are not in the Filter Gallery. ★

Extension Panels

Check **Allow Extensions to Connect to the Internet** to enable Photoshop extension panels to connect to the Internet in order to access updated content. These panels include Window > Extensions > Kuler (see page 111) and Mini Bridge (see pages 48–49). Panels from third-party suppliers are also accessed from this submenu.

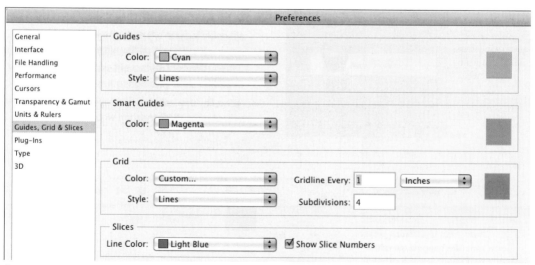

A *Guides, Grid & Slices Preferences*

Check **Load Extension Panels** to have the extension panels that are currently residing in the Plug-ins folder (within the Adobe Photoshop CS6 application folder) load automatically when you launch Photoshop.

A *Plug-ins Preferences*

Type Preferences B

Type Options

Be sure to check **Use Smart Quotes** to have Photoshop insert typographically correct (curly) apostrophes and quotation marks automatically when you input type, instead of the incorrect foot and inch marks.

Check **Enable Missing Glyph Protection** to permit Photoshop to substitute Roman characters for missing glyphs, such as Japanese or Chinese characters.

Check **Show Font Names in English** to have non-Roman font names display in English on the Font menus (e.g., "Adobe Ming Std" instead of the equivalent Chinese characters).

Choose Text Engine Options ★

To display special language features on the Character and Paragraph panels and panel menus, click **East Asian** or **Middle Eastern** here (relaunch Photoshop if you make a switch), then on the Type > Language Options submenu in Photoshop, check East Asian Features or Middle Eastern Features. (One of those two options will be listed in addition to the standard setting, which is Default Feature.)

Note: The Font Preview Size options that were formerly located in this dialog are now more conveniently located on the Font Preview Size submenu on the main Type menu in Photoshop.

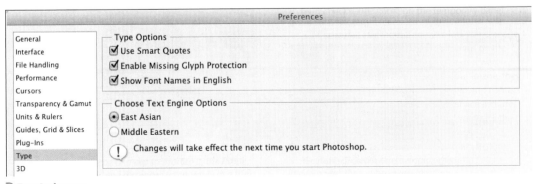

B *Type Preferences*

Preferences for Adobe Bridge
General Preferences A

Appearance

Click a **Color Theme** for the Bridge interface. ★

Choose a gray value as the overall **User Interface Brightness**, which appears in the side panes.

Choose a gray value for the **Image Backdrop**, the area behind the Content and Preview panels. This value also displays as the background behind images when displayed in Full Preview View or in Slideshow or Review mode.

Choose an **Accent Color** for the highlight border around selected folders, thumbnails, and stacks, and for text that is selected in the panels.

Behavior

Check **When a Camera Is Connected, Launch Adobe Photo Downloader** to make the Downloader the default system utility for acquiring photos (this option is for Mac OS users only).

Check **Double-Click Edits Camera Raw Settings in Bridge** to have raw files open into Camera Raw, hosted by Bridge, when double-clicked. See page 54.

If **Ctrl-Click/Cmd-Click Opens the Loupe When Previewing or Reviewing** is checked, you have to hold down Ctrl/Cmd while clicking an image preview to make the loupe display. With this option unchecked, you can make the loupe appear simply by clicking the preview (see page 32).

For **Number of Recent Items to Display**, enter the maximum number of files (0–30) that can be listed at a time on the Open Recent File menu ▆ and on the Reveal Recent File or Go to Recent Folder menu ▆ on the Path bar.

Favorite Items

Check the items and system-generated folders you want Bridge to list in the **Favorites** panel.

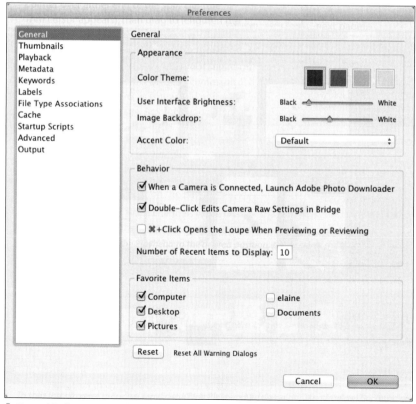

A General Preferences, in Bridge

Thumbnails Preferences A

Performance and File Handling
Note: To implement a change to the Performance and File Handling setting, you must purge the folder cache (Tools > Cache submenu).

For **Do Not Process Files Larger Than**, enter the maximum file size for which you will permit Bridge to display a thumbnail (the default value is 1000 MB). Bear in mind that large files preview slowly.

Details
For **Additional Lines of Thumbnail Metadata**, check Show and choose the category of file information you want Bridge to list next to the image thumbnails in the Content panel (see page 37).

Check **Show Tooltips** to allow Tool Tips to display when you rest the pointer on Bridge features, such as image thumbnails.

Playback Preferences
The **Stack Playback Frame Rate** controls the speed at which a stack of thumbnails plays back via the Play button.

Under Audio and Video, choose options to control whether audio and video files will play automatically when previewed and/or loop automatically when viewed in the Preview panel.

Metadata Preferences
Check the categories of metadata you want Bridge to display in the **Metadata** panel.

Check **Hide Empty Fields** to hide any fields on the Metadata panel that are empty.

Check **Show Metadata Placard** to display camera data in a separate area at the top of the Metadata panel (see page 30).

Continued on the following page

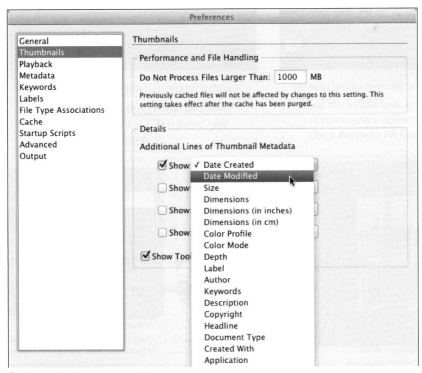

A *Thumbnails Preferences, in Bridge*

Keywords Preferences

Check **Automatically Apply Parent Keywords** to have the parent keyword also apply automatically when a subkeyword box is checked in the Keywords panel. If this option is on and you want to apply just a subkeyword, Shift-click the check box in the Keywords panel. See pages 38–39.

For **Write Hierarchical Keywords,** click an Output Delimiter character to be used to separate keywords in files that are exported from Bridge; and for **Read Hierarchical Keywords,** click an Input Delimiter character to be used to separate keywords in files that are imported into Bridge.

Labels Preferences

Check whether to **Require the Control/Command Key** [to be pressed in the shortcut] **to Apply Labels and Ratings** to selected file thumbnails (see page 40). You can also change the label names here, but not the colors.

File Type Associations Preferences

These settings tell Bridge the applications into which it may open files of different types. Don't monkey around with these settings unless you know what you're doing!

Cache Preferences

Options

Check **Keep 100% Previews in Cache** to save large JPEG previews of image thumbnails to disk for faster previewing when using the loupe and when previewing images in Slideshow mode at 100% or in Full Screen Preview view. We keep this option unchecked, because it uses a lot of disk space.

Check **Automatically Export Caches to Folders When Possible** to have Bridge export all cache files (in which metadata and thumbnail information is stored) to the same folders in which the images are located or that they are copied to. See page 50.

Location

To specify a different location for the Bridge cache, click **Choose,** choose a folder, click Open, then relaunch Bridge. We recommend leaving this setting alone.

Manage

If you have a very large hard disk, you can use the **Cache Size** slider to increase the maximum number of items that can be stored in the cache.

Click **Compact Cache** to allow previously cached items that are no longer available to be removed from the cache, for improved performance.

Click **Purge Cache** to purge all cached thumbnails and previews from the central database, in order to free up space on your hard disk or as a remedy if Bridge is having trouble displaying your image thumbnails. Do this only when absolutely necessary.

Startup Scripts Preferences

All **Startup Scripts** that are checked in this dialog will be activated at startup. We recommend checking all of them, unless you have a specific reason to uncheck any. Changes to these settings take effect when you relaunch Bridge.

Advanced Preferences

Miscellaneous

If (and only if) you encounter display problems in Bridge, check **Use Software Rendering,** then relaunch Bridge. This option turns off hardware acceleration for the Preview panel and Slideshow mode.

Check **Generate Monitor-Size Previews** to have Bridge generate previews for your display size. In a dual-monitor setup, the previews are sized according to the resolution of the larger of the two monitors.

Check **Start Bridge at Login** to have Bridge launch automatically upon startup.

International

Choose a **Language** for the Bridge interface, and for the **Keyboard,** then relaunch Bridge.

Output Preferences

Check **Use Solo Mode for Output Panel Behavior** to display only one expanded category at a time in the side panel of the Output workspace.

Check **Convert Multi-Byte Filenames to Full ASCII** to remove multi-byte characters from Chinese and Japanese file names, to help prevent problems when outputting PDF or Web Gallery files.

Check **Preserve Embedded Color Profile** to preserve any embedded profiles in files that are output as PDF or Web Gallery files.

Click **Reset Panel to Defaults** to restore all the default settings to the Output panel.

When you're done editing your Photoshop image, you can output it to a desktop inkjet printer, prepare it for commercial printing, export it to another application (such as Adobe InDesign), or optimize for the Web.

In the first task in this chapter, you will view a simulation of your document onscreen as if it were output from Photoshop to an inkjet device, to a commercial printer, or to the Web. This simulation is called a soft proof, and it provides a useful "first glance." After that, we show you how to output a file to an inkjet printer, and how to convert it to CMYK Color mode for commercial printing. We offer guidelines for exporting files to Adobe InDesign and Adobe Illustrator, give instructions for saving files in the TIFF and PDF formats, and finally, show you how to optimize your document for output to the Web.

Important note: If you intend to output your document to a desktop inkjet printer, keep it in RGB Color mode. Although desktop printers print using six or more process ink colors, their drivers are designed to receive RGB data, and they perform the conversion to printer ink colors internally.

PRINT & EXPORT

25

IN THIS CHAPTER

Proofing document colors onscreen

In this phase of color management, you'll create a custom proof setting for your specific inkjet printer and paper, and use it to view a soft proof (onscreen simulation) of your print output. Although this proof won't be perfectly accurate, it will give you a rough idea of how your colors will look (without costing you a cent).

To proof a document as an inkjet print onscreen:

1. Open an RGB image. From the View > **Proof Setup** submenu, choose **Custom**. The Customize Proof Condition dialog opens. In the next steps, you will choose custom proofing settings for your output device.

2. Check Preview, then from the **Device to Simulate** menu, choose the correct color profile for your inkjet printer and paper (the profile you either downloaded from the manufacturer's website or installed with your printer driver file). **A** See page 11.

3. Uncheck **Preserve RGB Numbers**, if available, to allow Photoshop to simulate how the colors will look when converted to the output profile.

4. Choose a **Rendering Intent** to control how colors will change as the image is shifted from one profile to another (see the sidebar on the next page). We recommend choosing either Perceptual or Relative Colorimetric. Note: You can evaluate a couple of options via the preview and by outputting some test prints.

   Check **Black Point Compensation** to allow adjustments to be made for differences in the black point among different color spaces. With this option chosen, the full dynamic range of the image color space is mapped to the full dynamic range of the color space for the output device (the printer). With this option off, black areas in the image may display or print as grays. We recommend checking this option for an inkjet proof.

5. *Optional:* For Display Options (On-Screen), check Simulate Paper Color to preview the white of the printing paper as defined in the chosen printer profile, or if you're going to print the file on uncoated paper, check Simulate Black Ink to preview the full range of black values that the printer profile can produce.

6. To save your custom proof setup, click **Save**, enter a name, keep the .psf extension, keep the location as the default Proofing folder, then click Save.

7. Your saved proof setup appears on the Custom Proof Condition menu. Click OK. The new setup is also available on the View > Proof Setup submenu for future use, and View > **Proof Colors** is checked automatically so you can examine the soft proof (also for the moment, the Device to Simulate profile is listed in the document tab).

   Remember, the Proof Setup options control only how Photoshop simulates colors onscreen. Colors in the actual file won't be converted to the chosen profile until you output the document to an inkjet printer or convert it to a different color mode (such as from RGB to CMYK).

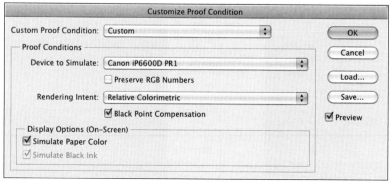

A *To generate a soft proof of our document, from the Device to Simulate menu in the Customize Proof Condition dialog, we've chosen the profile for our Canon Pixma inkjet printer.*

CHOOSING A RENDERING INTENT

➤ Perceptual changes colors in a way that seems natural to the human eye, while attempting to preserve the appearance of the overall image. It's a good choice for continuous-tone images.

➤ Saturation changes colors with the intent of preserving vivid colors, but in so doing compromises color fidelity. Nevertheless, it is a good choice for charts and graphics, which normally contain fewer colors than continuous-tone images.

➤ Absolute Colorimetric maintains the color accuracy only of colors that fall within the destination color gamut (i.e., the color range of your printer) but in so doing sacrifices the accuracy of colors that are outside that gamut.

➤ Relative Colorimetric, the default intent for all the Adobe predefined settings in the Color Settings dialog, compares the white, or highlight, of your document's color space to the white of the destination color space (the white of the paper, in the case of print output), shifting colors where needed. This is the best rendering intent choice for documents in which most of the colors fall within the color range of the destination gamut, because it preserves most of the original colors.

Note: Consult your printer manual before choosing a rendering intent. For example, for some inkjet printers, Perceptual is recommended over Relative Colorimetric.

DO THE RESEARCH

➤ When preparing files for commercial printing, don't be shy about asking your output service provider which settings and formats you should select in Photoshop.

➤ For more specialized technical information that is beyond the scope of this chapter, refer to the documentation for your specific printer model, and to Photoshop Help.

➤ Regardless of your output medium, you can gain valuable feedback and knowledge from trial and error (output the file, study it, make adjustments, output it again …). The experts become expert by learning from both their successes and failures.

In this task, you will choose a Proof Setup preset, then turn on the soft-proof feature so you can preview onscreen how the colors in your file will look when printed using CMYK inks or viewed online on a Windows or older Macintosh display.

To proof colors onscreen for commercial printing or online output:

1. From the View > **Proof Setup** submenu, choose the preset for the output display type that you want Photoshop to simulate:

   Working CMYK to simulate colors for the type of commercial press that is currently selected on the CMYK menu under Working Spaces in the Edit > Color Settings dialog in Photoshop.

   ➤ If your file will be sent to a commercial print shop, ask them for a .csf or .icc profile. After you install the profile, it will be available in the Color Settings dialog (see page 11). If you're not given a profile, ask your print shop to suggest which predefined CMYK profile you should choose instead.

   Legacy Macintosh RGB (Gamma 1.8) or **Internet Standard RGB (sRGB)** to simulate colors for online output using the legacy Mac gamma (1.8) or the more common Windows gamma (2.2) as the proofing space.

   Monitor RGB to simulate colors using the current display profile that is assigned to your monitor.

2. View > **Proof Colors** will be checked automatically. When you're ready to turn soft proofing off, uncheck it on the menu or press Ctrl-Y/Cmd-Y.

Outputting a file to an inkjet printer

In this section, we'll show you how to output your file to an inkjet printer and have the results match, as closely as possible, the document you have been viewing onscreen. We have divided the steps for using this dialog into three parts: Choose settings for your printer driver, choose settings for printing (including color management), and finally, verify that color management has been turned off for the printer and print the file in either Windows or the Mac OS.

Phase 1

In Phase 1, you will tell Photoshop what type of printer you're going to use via the Print Settings dialog, then use the print dialog for your operating system to specify the paper size, paper type, and other options for your printer.

Choose settings for your printer driver ★

1. Open the RGB file to be printed, then choose File > **Print** (Ctrl-P/Cmd-P). The Print dialog opens.**A** (You can enlarge the dialog to increase the preview size.)

2. From the **Printer** menu, choose your target inkjet device.

3. Click **Print Settings** to open the [**Printer Name**] **Properties/Print** dialog for your operating system.

4. The menu names vary with the chosen printer model and your operating system, so we refer to them generically:

   In Windows, in the Main (or other) tab, choose the best-quality option for photo printing. For the paper options, choose the source for your paper, the specific type of paper to be used, and the paper size (**A**, next page).

   In the Mac OS, if necessary, click Show Details to display the full dialog. The inkjet printer you chose in step 2 will be listed on the Printer menu. Choose the desired paper size for the print (for a borderless print, pick a size that includes the word "borderless"). From the fourth menu, choose the category that offers print quality and paper options (e.g., Quality & Media or Print

A In the Print dialog for Photoshop, choose your inkjet device from the Printer menu, then click Print Settings.

Settings). From the media or paper type menu, choose the type of paper you will be using, **B** and from another menu, choose a print quality option.**C**

➤ In Windows and Mac OS, the printer and paper type should match the printer profile you have downloaded and installed (see page 11).

5. Click Save to close the print dialog for your operating system and return to the Print dialog for Photoshop. Follow the steps on the next page to choose print settings for Photoshop.

➤ The gray background in the preview matches the current background in the Photoshop document window. If you want to change that shade, right-click the gray area in the preview.

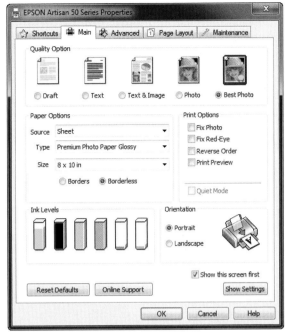

A *This is the Print Settings > [Print Name] Properties dialog for an Epson printer in Windows 7. We chose a Quality Option and Paper Options.*

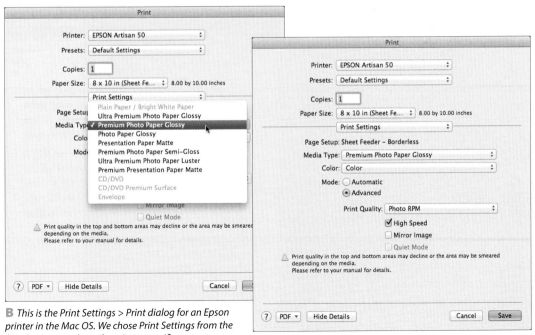

B *This is the Print Settings > Print dialog for an Epson printer in the Mac OS. We chose Print Settings from the fourth menu, and are choosing a specific paper type from the Media Type menu.*

C *Next, in the same dialog, we clicked Mode: Advanced and chose a Print Quality option.*

Phase 2

After choosing print settings as described on the preceding two pages, the next step is to choose color management, position, scale, and output options in the Print dialog for Photoshop.

Choose settings in the Print dialog ★

1. In the Print dialog for Photoshop (**A**, next page), click the portrait 📖 or landscape 📖 **Layout** button.

2. Expand the **Color Management** category. The current document profile is listed at the top.

   From the **Color Handling** menu, choose **Photoshop Manages Colors** to let Photoshop handle the color conversion, for optimal color management (see the sidebar on the next page).

3. From the **Printer Profile** menu, choose the custom printer/ink/paper profile that you downloaded from the printer or paper manufacturer's website and installed in your system (see page 11). This is the last phase of the color management workflow that you began in Chapter 1. Note: All installed profiles for the currently selected printer are listed on the top part of the menu.

4. In the Mac OS, if the chosen device has the capacity to output a 16-bit file (and your document is 16-bit), you can check **Send 16-Bit Data** to produce a print with finer details and smoother color gradations.

5. From the next menu, choose **Normal Printing**.

   From the **Rendering Intent** menu, choose the same intent that you used when you created the soft-proof setting for your inkjet printer, which most likely was either Perceptual or Relative Colorimetric (see the sidebar on page 449).

   ➤ You can run one test print for the Perceptual intent and one for the Relative Colorimetric intent, and see which yields better results.

6. Check **Black Point Compensation**. This option maps the full color range of the document profile to the full range of the printer profile so as to preserve shadow details and the darkest blacks.

7. Expand the **Position and Size** category.

   Under Position, check **Center** to print the image in the center of the paper; or to reposition the image on the paper, uncheck Center Image and enter new Top and Left values (as shown in the preview). If the image size is smaller than the paper size, you can drag the image in the preview.

8. *Optional:* To scale the print output slightly, under Scaled Print Size, do either of the following:

   Check **Scale to Fit Media** to fit the image automatically on the paper size you chose in step 4 on page 450.

   Uncheck Scale to Fit Media, then change the **Scale** percentage or enter specific **Height** and **Width** values (you can change the unit via the Units menu). These three values are interdependent; changing one causes the other two to change.

   Note: Use these features to scale the print by only a small amount (i.e., a fraction of an inch or 5–10 percentage points). If a greater scale change is needed, cancel out of the dialog, use Image > Image Size to scale the image (see pages 122–123), then resharpen it.

9. Uncheck **Print Selected Area** to reset the margins to the chosen paper size, or check it to adjust the margins for the current printout. If you check this option, drag a margin control ▼ to adjust the top, bottom, left, or right margin for the printout; or Alt/Option-drag a margin control to move the top and bottom, or left and right, margins as a pair; or Ctrl/Cmd-drag a margin control to move all four margins simultaneously.

10. Below the preview, do the following:

    Check **Match Print Colors** to display a color-managed soft proof of the image in the preview, based on the current printing device and printer profile settings.

    Uncheck **Gamut Warning**. Monitoring out-of-gamut colors (shown as gray in the preview) is beneficial only when printing to a commercial CMYK printer.

    Check **Show Paper White** to have Photoshop simulate the paper color in any white areas in the preview, based on the current printer profile.

11. Before printing the image, you need to verify that color management has been turned off for your printer by following the steps on page 455 for Windows or on page 456 for the Mac OS. (You're almost done!)

    ➤ If you want to save all of your settings for the current document and close the dialog without printing the document, click Done in the Print dialog, then save your file.

A *Choose settings in the various categories in the Print dialog in Photoshop.*

BENEFITS TO LETTING PHOTOSHOP MANAGE YOUR DOCUMENT COLORS

Via the Color Handling menu of the Print dialog, you can opt to have Photoshop or your printing device manage colors. What's the difference?

► If you choose Photoshop Manages Colors (the option we recommend), you will be able to select a profile that matches the paper type you selected in the Print Settings dialog. Choose either the printer and paper profile that you downloaded from a paper or print manufacturer's website or a profile that was installed for your printing device. Photoshop will adjust colors to fit that profile, then send the data to the printer. By using the profile, your color-managed workflow is preserved, and Photoshop produces the best color possible.

► If you choose Printer Manages Colors, the printer driver will handle the color conversion instead of Photoshop. This may limit the print quality, for two reasons. First, the printer won't be aware of your custom paper choice and custom printer profile. And second, the color conversion will be subject to the printer's ability to convert colors rather than the color management settings you have established. If you're still not convinced to avoid this setting, at least resist the temptation to adjust the amount of individual ink colors used by the printer (in the Print Settings dialog), which would override the printer settings.

454 | Chapter 25

CHOOSING OUTPUT OPTIONS ★

Options for commercial printing on a PostScript printer are found in the Printing Marks and PostScript Options categories in the Print dialog. Some of the Printing Marks options are listed (and illustrated) below; for other options, see Photoshop Help.

In the Printing Marks category, check any of the following options:

➤ Corner Crop Marks and Center Crop Marks print short little lines that a print shop uses as guide lines when trimming the final print.

➤ Registration Marks prints marks that a print shop uses to align color separations.

➤ Description prints user data below the image. Click Edit in this category to enter or edit a description (you can also enter data in the Description field of the Description tab in the File > File Info dialog).

➤ Labels prints the file name on each page (outside the image area).

The following two options in the PostScript Options category are just for PostScript printing:

➤ Calibration Bars prints a grayscale and/or color calibration strip outside the image area.

➤ Include Vector Data prints vector objects (such as type or shapes) at the printer resolution, not at the document resolution. This option is checked automatically (and should be kept checked) if the file contains type or shape layers.

To specify a bleed width for your document:

Click Bleed in the Functions category, then enter a distance (0–3 inches). Crop marks will be placed within the image area at that specified distance from the outer edge of the image.

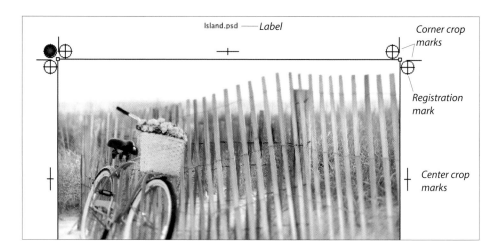

Island.psd —— *Label*

Corner crop marks

Registration mark

Center crop marks

OUTPUTTING A QUASI HARD PROOF ★

To output a quasi "hard" proof (simulation of output from your target device) to a desktop printer, expand the Color Management category and choose Hard Proofing from the menu. From the Proof Setup menu, choose the soft-proof setup that you created by following the steps on page 449. Check Simulate Paper Color to preview the white of the paper as defined in the chosen printer profile, or uncheck this option and check Simulate Black Ink to preview the full range of black values as defined by the printer profile.

Phase 3

The final step before outputting a file to an inkjet printer is to verify that color management was turned off for your printer, to enable Photoshop to manage the color conversion from RGB color to actual inks. (Remember, you chose Photoshop Manages Colors in Phase 2 of this print workflow.) Note: Mac OS users, see the next page.

The color management controls in the Print dialog vary depending on the printer driver for the chosen output device, and also differ for each operating system. In the following steps, we describe how to verify that color management is turned off for an Epson device. If your device is a different brand or you see different options in the dialog, do some research on how to access print quality and color management settings for your printer, and use these steps as general guidelines.

Windows: Verify that color management is turned off for your printer, then print the file

1. In the Print dialog for Photoshop, click **Print Settings** to get to the [Printer Name] Properties dialog for your Windows system.

2. Click the **Advanced** tab.**A** The set of options includes controls for color management.

3. In the Color Management area, if it's not already selected, click **ICM** to switch control of color management from the Epson driver to the color management system that's built into Windows.

4. Below the ICM button, make sure **Off** (**No Color Adjustment**) is checked.**B**

5. Click OK to close the Properties dialog and return to the Print dialog for Photoshop.

6. Click **Print**. Phew! You made it.

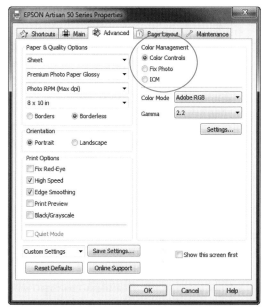

A In the Print Settings > Properties dialog for an Epson printer in Windows, we clicked the Advanced tab to display these Color Management options.

B We verified that ICM was selected, and that Off (No Color Adjustment) was checked.

The final step before outputting a file to an inkjet printer is to turn off color management for your printer, to enable Photoshop to manage the color conversion from RGB color to actual inks. (Remember, you chose Photoshop Manages Colors in Phase 2 of this print setup workflow.)

The color management controls in the Print dialog vary depending on the printer driver for the chosen output device, and also differ for each operating system. In the following steps, we describe how to verify that color management is turned off for an Epson device. If your device is a different brand or you see different options in the dialog, do some research on how to access print quality and color management settings for your printer, and use these steps as general guidelines.

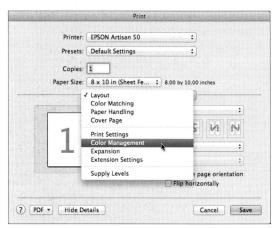

A *In the Print dialog (which we accessed by clicking Print Settings) for an Epson printer in the Mac OS, we chose Color Management from the fourth menu.*

Mac OS: Verify that color management is turned off for your printer, then print the file ★

1. In the Photoshop Print dialog, click **Print Settings** to open the Print dialog for your Mac operating system.

2. From the fourth menu, choose **Color Management.**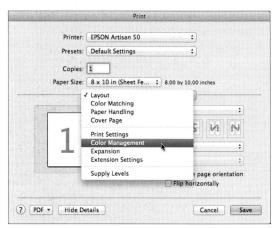

3. Verify that **Off (No Color Adjustment)** is selected. **B** Note that with color management turned off for the printer, depending on the printer model, the color controls and the Advanced Settings sliders either won't display at all or will be dimmed.

4. Click **Save** to return to the Print dialog for Photoshop.

5. Click **Print.** Congratulations!

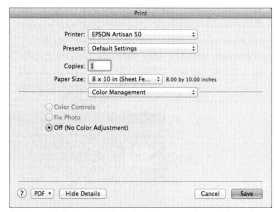

B *We verified that Off (No Color Adjustment) was selected.*

Preparing a file for commercial printing

Computer monitors display additive colors by projecting red, green, and blue (RGB) light, whereas commercial presses print subtractive colors using CMYK (cyan, magenta, yellow, and black) and/or spot color (mixed) inks. Obtaining high-quality CMYK color reproduction from a commercial press is an art that takes experience and a lot of know-how.

When preparing a file to be sent to a print shop for output to a commercial press, you need to establish the correct CMYK working space in Photoshop. Ask your print shop to give you the necessary color settings file, then be sure to save it in the correct folder (see page 11) so it's available in the Color Settings dialog for the CMYK conversion.

A WORKFLOW FOR COMMERCIAL, FOUR-COLOR PRINTING

The steps needed to prepare a file for commercial printing are too complex for us to cover fully in this QuickStart Guide, but we offer this summary:

1. Make sure your display is properly calibrated, and that you have established all the necessary color settings (see Chapter 1).

2. Ask your commercial print shop what type of press and lines-per-inch setting will be used to print your document and what settings they recommend you choose in Photoshop, such as the resolution, file format, and color mode. Save the file according to their specs.

3. Ask your commercial printer to supply you with a printer profile for their press, ink, and paper, then load it into the Color Settings dialog (see page 11).

4. Use the printer profile to create a custom proof condition, and view a soft (onscreen) proof of the image for that specific press (see pages 448–449).

5. Save a copy of the file in the requested format.

6. Convert your RGB files to CMYK, using the printer profile from your print shop.

7. Make any final tonal adjustments (e.g., to the midtones, contrast) and any final color adjustments.

8. Sharpen the image (see pages 322–326).

9. Have your print shop output a CMYK color proof for you to analyze. If it looks good, it's good to go. If not, tweak the image based on problems you see in the proof, then print and analyze another proof.

To convert your file from RGB to CMYK Color mode:

1. Use the File > Save As dialog to save a flattened copy of your file (uncheck Layers).

2. Choose Edit > **Color Settings** (Ctrl-Shift-K/ Cmd-Shift-K).

3. To specify which profile will be used to control the conversion of your image to CMYK color mode, do either of the following:

   From the **Settings** menu, choose the .csf profile your commercial printer has given you and that you have installed.

   In the Working Spaces area, from the **CMYK** menu, choose either the .icc prepress profile that your print shop has given you or the predefined Adobe profile your print shop says is the best match for their press and paper.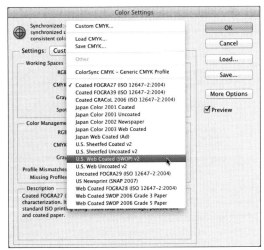

4. Click OK. To convert the file to CMYK color mode, choose Image > Mode > **CMYK Color**.

5. Save the file.

A In the Color Settings dialog, from the CMYK menu in the Workspace Spaces area, choose the correct CMYK profile.

Getting Photoshop files into Adobe InDesign and Illustrator

Photoshop to Adobe InDesign

Files in the Photoshop PSD and Photoshop PDF formats can be imported directly into Adobe InDesign using the File > **Place** command.

InDesign can color-separate RGB and CMYK files, and can read embedded ICC color profiles. And because InDesign is in the Adobe Creative Suite, you can continue to use Bridge for your file and color management. Photoshop layers (and layer comps) are preserved, and you can turn their visibility on or off in InDesign; alpha channels, layer masks, and transparency are also preserved. If you want to import just an area of a Photoshop image into InDesign, see our easy steps on the next page.

Photoshop to Adobe Illustrator

Photoshop and Illustrator files are compatible in many (although not all) respects. Here are some ways to get Photoshop content into Illustrator:

Method 1

With the Move tool ▶+ in Photoshop, **drag and drop** a selection or layer from a document window into an open document in Illustrator. In Windows, the imagery will appear on the Layers panel as an image layer; in the Mac OS, it will appear as an image layer within a layer group. The opacity settings are reset to 100% (but are preserved visually), nondefault blending modes are ignored, the effects of any layer or vector masks are applied, and transparent areas are filled with white. Type and vector shapes are rasterized.

Method 2

Copy and **paste** an image layer from Photoshop into Illustrator. The effects of any layer or vector masks, nondefault blending modes, and nondefault opacity settings are discarded.

Method 3

Use File > **Place** in Illustrator to import either a whole Photoshop image or one layer comp. If you place a Photoshop image with the Link option checked, the image will appear on the Layers panel on a single image layer, and any masks will be applied. If you embed the Photoshop image as you place it (uncheck the Link option), you will be given the option via the Photoshop Import Options dialog to **Convert**

Layers to Objects (Make Text Editable Where Possible) or **Flatten Layers to a Single Image (Preserves Text Appearance)**.

If you click Convert Layers to Objects, each layer will appear on a separate nested layer within a group, and the Background (if any) will become a separate layer. Opacity values are preserved, whereas only the blending modes that match those on the blending mode menu (Transparency panel) in Illustrator are preserved. Both transparency and modes are listed as editable appearances. Layer masks become opacity masks. Layer effects are applied to the layer and their visual effects are preserved.

If you click Flatten Layers to a Single Image, the effect of all opacity settings, blending modes, and layer masks will be preserved visually, but those features won't be editable in Illustrator.

Check **Import Hidden Layers** if you want Illustrator to include hidden image layers when it imports your Photoshop file.

Method 4

Use File > **Open** in Illustrator to open a Photoshop image as a new Illustrator document. See also the information regarding the Link and Convert to Layers/Flatten Layers options in Method 3, above.

➤ Either of these two conditions will prevent layers in a Photoshop document from becoming individual layers in Illustrator: Visible adjustment layers or a layer that has both a layer effect and a nondefault blending mode. Before importing the file, hide (or merge down) the adjustment layers to prevent them from being imported, and reset the blending mode to Normal.

➤ Any shape layers that contain layer effects will be rasterized.

➤ Via the Effect menu in Illustrator, some Photoshop (raster) effects and some Illustrator (vector) effects can be applied to an imported Photoshop image.

➤ When you open or place a TIFF, EPS, or PSD file into Illustrator, it adopts the color mode of the Illustrator file.

To place just a portion of a Photoshop PSD image into InDesign or Illustrator, you need to isolate that area via a layer mask or onto a separate layer, then save a copy of the file.

To isolate part of an image layer in Photoshop:

1. Do either of the following:

   Select an area of a layer, then create a layer mask.**A**

   Select the area to be isolated, and put it on its own layer by pressing Ctrl-J/Cmd-J.**B**

2. Using File > Save As, save a copy of the file in the Photoshop format. In the dialog, check As a Copy (keep Layers checked).

3. Follow the steps for InDesign or Illustrator, at right.

To place a Photoshop layer into InDesign:

1. In InDesign, open or create a document, then import the Photoshop file via File > **Place** (in the Place dialog, uncheck Show Import Options).

2. Choose Object > **Object Layer Options**.

3. In the dialog, check Preview, show the layer that contains transparency or a mask, hide all other layers (click their visibility icons), then click OK.

To open or place a Photoshop layer into Illustrator:

1. In Illustrator, open the file via File > **Open**, or import it via File > **Place** with the Link option unchecked.

2. In the Photoshop Import Options dialog, click **Convert Layers to Objects**, then click OK. On the Layers panel, the image components will be listed on nested layers within a group.**C–D**

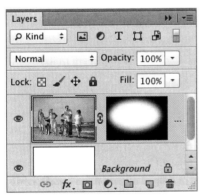

A In Photoshop, we hid part of an image layer via a layer mask.

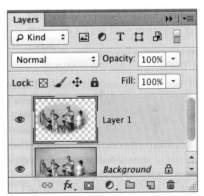

B Alternatively, we could have copied a selected area to a new layer.

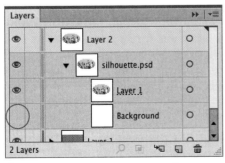

C We imported the Photoshop file into Illustrator. On the Layers panel in Illustrator, we clicked the visibility icon to hide the Background.

D This is how the imported Photoshop file looks in Illustrator (you have to take our word for it!).

Saving a file in the PDF format

PDF (Portable Document Format) files can be opened in many Windows and Macintosh applications and in all of the Acrobat programs (Adobe Reader, Acrobat Standard, and Acrobat Pro). This format saves 8-bit and 16-bit files (but not 32-bit files) in any color mode except Multichannel.

Options chosen in the Save Adobe PDF dialog determine which of two kinds of PDF files Photoshop will create. The Photoshop PDF format preserves image, font, layer, and vector data, and saves just one image per file. To create this kind of file, check Preserve Photoshop Editing Capabilities in the Save Adobe PDF dialog. Note: If you need to save multiple images within one PDF file, see "Creating a PDF presentation of images" on pages 420–421.

The second option is to have Photoshop produce a generic PDF file, similar to the PDFs that are created by a drawing or page layout application. The image will be flattened and rasterized, so your ability to re-edit it in Photoshop will be very limited. If you decide to go this route, uncheck the aforementioned Preserve Photoshop Editing Capabilities option.

To save a file in the PDF format:

1. Choose File > **Save As**, enter a file name or keep the current name in the File Name/Save As field, choose a location for the file, choose Format: **Photoshop PDF**, then click Save. If an alert dialog appears, click OK.

2. From the **Adobe PDF Preset** menu in the Save Adobe PDF dialog, A choose a preset that's best suited to your target output medium. The High

Quality Print and Press Quality presets produce a large Photoshop PDF file, compress the file using the JPEG setting of Maximum image quality, embed all fonts automatically, and preserve transparency. The Preserve Photoshop Editing Capabilities option is checked. Note: For commercial printing, ask your shop which settings to use.

High Quality Print (the default preset) creates PDF files for desktop printers and color proofing devices. The color conversion is handled by the printer driver. The file won't be PDF/X-compliant (see PDF/X… below).

Press Quality is designed for high-quality prepress output. Colors are converted to CMYK.

Preserve Photoshop Editing Capabilities isn't available for the PDF/X presets and is unchecked for the Smallest File Size preset, so these presets produce generic PDF files:

PDF/X-1a:2001, PDF/X-3:2002, and **PDF/X-4: 2008** create PDF files that will be checked for compliance with specific printing standards, to help prevent printing errors.

Smallest File Size uses high levels of JPEG compression to produce very compact PDF files for output to the Web, transmission via e-mail, and the like. All colors are converted to sRGB.

3. Click Save PDF, then click Yes if an alert dialog appears.

➤ To learn more about the PDF format, see Photoshop Help.

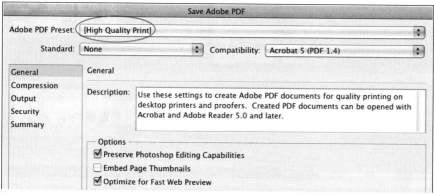

A *In the Save Adobe PDF dialog, choose a preset from the Adobe PDF Preset menu.*

Saving a file in the TIFF format

TIFF files are versatile in that they can be imported into most applications and are usable in many color management scenarios. If your target application can't read a Photoshop PSD or Photoshop PDF file, this is the next best option. Both InDesign and QuarkXPress can color-separate a CMYK color TIFF.

Note: Although Photoshop files as large as 4 GB can be saved in the TIFF format, other applications aren't likely to be able to read a TIFF file that is larger than 2 GB.

To save a file in the TIFF format:

1. If you have arranged for your file to be printed on a four-color press and your commercial printer requests that you convert the color mode of your document to CMYK, choose Image > Mode > CMYK Color (see page 457).

2. Choose File > **Save As**, enter a name or keep the current one, choose Format: **TIFF**, and choose a location for the file.

3. In the Save area:

   Check **Save a Copy** to keep the existing file open onscreen and save a copy of it to disk.

   Uncheck **Layers** to flatten the file (or check this option if you must preserve layers). Note that few other image or layout programs can work with layered TIFFs, and those that don't are going to flatten the layers without your choice or ignore the layer data.

   If you need to save **Alpha Channels**, **Notes**, or **Spot Colors** in the file, check any of those options.

4. Check ICC Profile/Embed Color Profile to include the embedded color profile (if any) with the file. For more about color management, see Chapter 1.

5. Click Save. The TIFF Options dialog opens.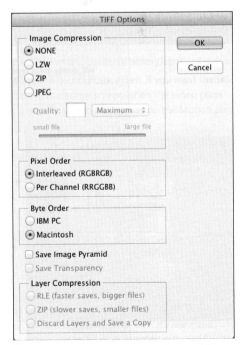

6. If the file is going to be color-separated (e.g., from InDesign), under **Image Compression**, click None (output service providers prefer uncompressed files). If you need to reduce the storage size of the file, click LZW or ZIP; these methods are non-lossy (they don't discard image data). Note that some programs can't read a ZIP-compressed TIFF, so that's something to look into. Avoid the JPEG compression option, which is lossy.

   Leave the **Pixel Order** on the default setting of **Interleaved (RGBRGB)**.

Click **Byte Order: IBM PC** or **Macintosh**, for the platform on which the file will be used.

Optional: Check Save Image Pyramid to save multiple resolutions of the image in one file. Photoshop doesn't offer options for opening image pyramids, whereas Adobe InDesign does.

If the bottommost layer in the file is a layer (not a Background), and the layer opacity setting is below 100%, you can check **Save Transparency** to preserve that transparency. If an alert dialog appears, click Yes.

If the file contains layers, click a **Layer Compression** method.

7. Click OK.

A *This is the TIFF Options dialog in the Mac OS.*

Saving multiple files in the JPEG, PSD, or TIFF format

If you have multiple files that you need to save in a different format (or formats), you can get the job done quickly via the Image Processor command. While you're at it, you can also run an action.

To save multiple files in the JPEG, PSD, or TIFF format:

1. Do either of the following:

   In Bridge, open a folder that contains multiple PSD or JPEG files and/or raw photos. (If desired, you can Ctrl-click/Cmd-click to select specific thumbnails.) Choose Tools > Photoshop > **Image Processor**.

   In Mini Bridge, Ctrl-click/Cmd-click the thumbnails for multiple PSD or JPEG files and/or raw photos, then right-click one of the thumbnails and choose Photoshop > **Image Processor**.

   The Image Processor dialog opens.**A**

2. *Optional:* If you selected a series of raw photos, check Open First Image to Apply Settings to have the Camera Raw dialog open for the first selected raw photo, giving you the opportunity to choose settings. Check this option only if you're certain all the other raw photos you have selected need the same adjustments.

3. To choose a location for the new files, do either of the following:

   Click **Save in Same Location**.

   Click the button for Select Folder, click **Select Folder**, navigate to the desired folder, then click Open.

4. Click the desired **File Type** (or types) and the needed applicable settings.

5. Under Preferences, do the following:

   Optional: Check Run Action, then choose an action set and action to be played on all the files.

   Optional: Enter Copyright Info (such as your name), to be added to the files' metadata.

   Check **Include ICC Profile** to include each file's color profile so its display and output can be color-managed.

6. Click Run. If any files open into Camera Raw, choose settings, then click **Open Image**. After Photoshop finishes opening, processing, and

closing the new files, they will appear within one or more new folders (bearing the name of the chosen file format), in the designated location.

➤ Via the Save button, you can save the current Image Processor settings as a preset. To apply a preset to other images, use the Load button.

CREATING A COMPRESSED ZIP FILE

To reduce the storage size of a file without discarding any of its data, you can create a compressed version of it using the ZIP compression command that's built into your system.

➤ To create a ZIP file in Windows, right-click a file and choose Send To > Compressed (Zipped) Folder from the context menu. A compressed version of the file will appear in a new folder within the current folder.

➤ To create a ZIP file in the Mac OS, right-click a file name in the Finder and choose Compress [file name] from the context menu.

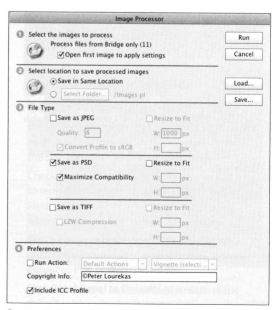

A *Using the Image Processor command, you can quickly save multiple files in the JPEG, PSD, or TIFF format.*

Saving files for the Web

Optimization is the process by which a file is prepared for online viewing. You choose a format first, then control the file size by choosing various settings, such as the degree of compression and the number of colors. Your goal is to compress a file to the point that it downloads quickly, while keeping its quality as high as possible. Although the compression applied by the GIF and JPEG formats cause a small reduction in image quality, it's a necessary trade-off for faster speed.

File formats

GIF and JPEG, the two file formats most commonly used for Web graphics, are suited to different types of Photoshop images. Below, we outline a few of their advantages and drawbacks.

GIF

▶ GIF preserves flat colors and sharp edges (such as type and shapes) better than JPEG.

▶ GIF is an 8-bit format, meaning it can save no more than 256 colors. This color restriction makes it a better choice for graphics that contain a limited number of solid colors than for continuous-tone images (such as photographs or images containing gradients), which contain countless colors and tonal values.

▶ GIF is the only optimization format that preserves transparency. If preserving areas of transparency in your Photoshop document is a necessity, the decision is made.

▶ If you use the GIF format, you don't have to use all of the allotted 256 colors. Lowering the color depth may cause color areas to look dithered (grainy looking) and a bit dull, but it further reduces the file size. Note: The collection of specific colors in a GIF file is called the "color table."

JPEG

▶ The JPEG format preserves the color fidelity of continuous-tone images better than GIF because it retains a file's full 24-bit color depth.

▶ The JPEG format can shrink an image significantly. When saving an image in this format, you choose a quality setting. The higher the quality, the larger the file.

▶ The JPEG format doesn't preserve transparency.

▶ Each time an image is optimized in the JPEG format, some image data is lost. The higher the level of compression, the greater the loss.

File size

In the Save for Web dialog, in addition to previewing and comparing various optimization settings, you can specify dimensions for your optimized file. The browser window width for the majority of Web viewers is approximately 1000 pixels, so you should keep your file to a width between 800 and 1000 pixels.

When optimizing a file that contains 16 bits per channel (regardless of which format you choose), the file is automatically converted to 8 bits per channel. Also, all the optimization formats will convert your file to 72 ppi (pixels per inch), the standard resolution value for onscreen display.

Web browsers universally display images at a magnification of 100%. With all the decisions you have to make about image quality, at least you don't have to worry about your graphics looking unexpectedly smaller or larger!

Finally, bear in mind that some types of images are more compressible than others. A small document that contains, say, a solid background color and a few solid-color shapes can be compressed more than a large document that contains numerous color areas, gradients, textures, or patterns.

On the next page, you'll learn how to preview a file using various optimization settings — steps that apply to both GIF and JPEG. After that, we provide detailed steps for optimizing a file in the GIF format, then finally the steps for optimizing a file in the JPEG format.

Previewing an optimized file

In the Save for Web dialog, you'll find everything you need to optimize your graphics for the Web, including multiple previews that let you test and compare the effects of different optimization settings.

To preview a file with optimization settings:

1. Choose File > **Save for Web** (Ctrl-Alt-Shift-S/Cmd-Opt-Shift-S). The dialog opens.**A**

2. Click the **4-Up** tab to display the original image and three previews. Photoshop will use the current optimization settings to generate the first preview (to the right of the original), then automatically generate two other preview variations on those settings. You can click any preview and change just its own settings (via the panel on the right), or choose a different Size/Download

Time for any preview from its **Download Speed** menu. ⚐☰

3. From the **Preview** menu on the right side of the dialog, choose a gamma value for Photoshop to simulate onscreen (see the sidebar on page 468).

4. After choosing settings for a GIF (see the next two pages) or for a JPEG (see pages 467–468), click which image preview you want to test in your browser, then click the **Preview** button or the browser icon at the bottom of the dialog. The image appears in the default Web browser for your system. (If you want to choose a different browser that is installed on your system, from the menu next to the browser icon, choose that browser name, or choose Other and then locate the desired browser.)

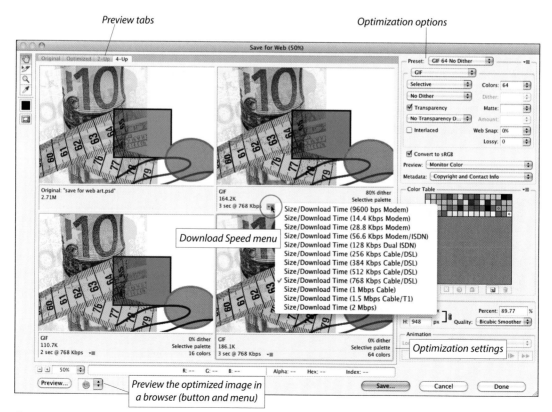

Preview tabs

Optimization options

Download Speed menu

Preview the optimized image in a browser (button and menu)

Optimization settings

A *Using the Save for Web dialog, you can choose, and preview the effect of, various optimization settings on your document.*

Optimizing a file in the GIF format

The GIF format preserves flat colors and sharp edges (e.g., type, shapes), but the resulting files can contain only a maximum of 256 colors. Use this format if you need to preserve transparency in the image.

To optimize a file in the GIF format:

1. Choose File > **Save for Web** (Ctrl-Alt-Shift-S/ Cmd-Opt-Shift-S).

2. Click the **2-Up** tab at the top of the Save for Web dialog so you can compare the original and optimized previews of the image. To change the zoom level for the previews, press Ctrl/Cmd + or –.

3. Do either of the following:

   To optimize the file using a preset, from the **Preset** menu, choose one of the **GIF** options. Leave the preset settings as they are, then click Save. In the Save Optimized As dialog, keep the .gif extension, choose a location, then click Save.

   To choose custom optimization settings, follow the remaining steps.

4. From the **Optimized File Format** (second) menu, choose **GIF.A**

5. From the **Color Reduction Algorithm** menu, choose a method to reduce the number of colors in the image (see the sidebar on this page and **A**, next page).

6. Choose a maximum number of **Colors** for the color table by choosing a preset value from the menu or by entering an exact number in the field. The fewer the number of colors, the smaller the file size.

7. Choose a method from the **Dither Algorithm** menu. Dithering is a process by which Photoshop mixes dots of different colors to simulate more colors. Although the Diffusion option produces a larger file, it tends to yield the best compromise between quality and file size. With the No Dither option chosen, gradients may display visible bands (instead of smooth gradations).

   Also choose a **Dither** percentage. The higher the dither value, the larger the file size (**B**, next page).

8. Check **Transparency** to preserve any fully transparent pixels in the image and allow the image area to be nonrectangular, or uncheck this option to allow transparent pixels to be filled with the color that's currently listed on the Matte menu. Regardless

Continued on the following page

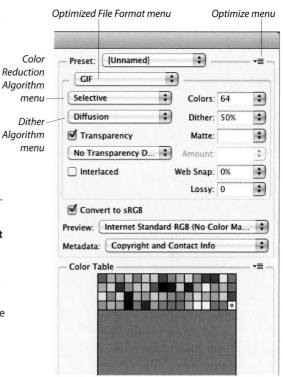

Optimized File Format menu   *Optimize menu*

Color Reduction Algorithm menu

Dither Algorithm menu

A *These options are available for the GIF format in the Save for Web dialog.*

THE COLOR REDUCTION ALGORITHMS

▶ Perceptual generates a color table based on the colors in the document, with a bias toward how colors are actually perceived.

▶ Selective, the default option, generates a color table based on the colors in the document, in an effort to preserve flat colors, Web-safe colors, and overall color integrity.

▶ Adaptive generates a color table from the span of the color spectrum in which the predominant colors in the document fall.

▶ Restrictive (Web) generates a color table by shifting image colors to colors in the standard Web-safe palette (the 216 colors that Windows and Macintosh browsers have in common). This choice produces the fewest colors and the smallest file size but not necessarily the best-looking image. With today's improved display technology, you can avoid this option.

of the Transparency setting, partially transparent pixels will be filled with the current Matte color.

Leave the **Interlaced** option unchecked.

9. If the image contains partially transparent pixels (e.g., a Drop Shadow effect) on top of transparent areas and you choose a **Matte** color that is the same as the background color on the Web page, those pixels will look as if they're blended in with that background.  If you set the Matte color to None, pixels with an opacity greater than 50% will become opaque, and pixels with an opacity less than 50% are made permanently transparent.

To blend partially transparent pixels so the image looks the same on any background, choose **Matte: None**, then check Transparency and choose an option from the **Transparency Dither Algorithm** menu. Diffusion applies a random pattern to partially transparent pixels (this method usually produces the most subtle results and allows you to set the dithering Amount); Pattern applies a halftone pattern to the partially transparent pixels; Noise applies a pattern similar to Diffusion without affecting adjacent pixels.

10. *Optional:* You can adjust the **Lossy** value to further reduce the file size. As the name "Lossy" implies, this option discards some image data, but the savings in file size may justify the slight reduction in image quality.

11. Check **Convert to sRGB** to convert the color to sRGB, the standard color profile for Web browsers.

12. From the **Preview** menu, choose a display gamma value to be simulated when you preview the optimized image (see the sidebar on page 468).

13. From the **Metadata** menu, choose which metadata is to be saved with the file, such as Copyright and Contact Info. This data was assigned to the file by your camera, or by you in Bridge via the Metadata panel or the File Info dialog.

14. Under Image Size, enter the desired **W** and **H** values in pixels for the dimensions of the GIF file, or enter a scale percentage in the **Percent** field.

15. Follow steps 2–4 on page 464 to preview your optimization settings. Make any necessary adjustments, then click Save. The Save Optimized As dialog opens. Change the name, if desired (don't enter any spaces); keep the .gif extension; choose a location; then click Save.

A *This image was optimized as a GIF with 32 colors using the Selective algorithm, and no Dither.*

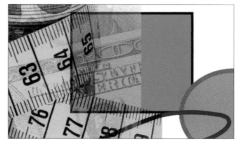

B *This the same image optimized with 100% Dither.*

C *This image was optimized as a GIF with Transparency checked and Matte set to a color (aqua): Partially transparent pixels blend in with the Matte color.*

D *This image was optimized as a GIF with Transparency checked and Matte set to None: Partially transparent pixels became (permanently) transparent.*

Optimizing a file in the JPEG format

JPEG is the best format for optimizing continuous-tone images. Although this format doesn't preserve transparency and its compression methods discard image data, it does save 24-bit color, so your image colors will look good on any computer that can display millions of colors.

To optimize a file in the JPEG format:

1. Choose File > **Save for Web** (Ctrl-Alt-Shift-S/ Cmd-Opt-Shift-S). The Save for Web dialog opens.

2. Click the **2-Up** tab at the top of the dialog so you can compare the original and optimized previews of the image. To change the zoom level for the previews, press Ctrl/Cmd + or –.

3. Do either of the following:

   To optimize the file using a preset, from the **Preset** menu, 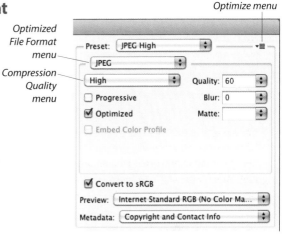 choose one of the **JPEG** options. Leave the preset settings as they are, then click Save. In the Save Optimized As dialog, keep the .jpg extension, choose a location, then click Save.

   To choose custom optimization settings, follow the remaining steps.

4. From the **Optimized File Format** (second) menu, choose **JPEG**.

5. Do either of the following:

   From the **Compression Quality** menu, choose a quality level for the optimized image.  **B–D**

   Choose a **Quality** value for the exact amount of compression needed. The higher the

Continued on the following page

Optimize menu

Optimized File Format menu

Compression Quality menu

A *These options are available for the JPEG format in the Save for Web dialog.*

B *This image was optimized as a JPEG, High quality.*

C *Here, it was optimized as a JPEG, Medium quality.*

D *And here, it was optimized as a JPEG, Low quality.*

compression quality, the better the image quality — but the larger the file size.

6. Increase the **Blur** value to lessen the visibility of artifacts due to the JPEG compression method, and to reduce the file size. Be careful not to overblur the image, though, or the details will be softened too much.

7. Choose a **Matte** color to be substituted for areas of transparency in the original image. If you choose None, transparent areas will be filled with white in the optimized image.

   ➤ Although the JPEG format doesn't support transparency, you can simulate it by choosing a Matte color that is the same as the solid background color on the Web page (if known). Click the Matte color swatch, and enter values in the Color Picker dialog.

8. Leave **Progressive** unchecked.

9. *Optional:* Check Optimized to produce a smaller file size. Note that some older browsers don't support this option.

10. Check **Embed Color Profile**. The browser will use a file's embedded color profile to display a color-managed image.

11. Check **Convert to sRGB** to convert the optimized color to sRGB, the standard profile for Web browsers. Note: Even with this option checked, the conversion of image colors will be more accurate if the embedded color profile is included, as advised in the preceding step.

12. From the **Preview** menu, choose a display gamma value to be simulated when you preview the optimized image (see the sidebar on this page).

13. From the **Metadata** menu, choose which metadata you want saved with the optimized file, such as Copyright and Contact Info. This data was assigned to the file by your camera, or by you in the File Info dialog or via the Metadata panel in Bridge.

14. In the Image Size area, enter the desired **W** and **H** size dimensions in pixels for the JPEG file, or enter a scale percentage in the **Percent** field.

15. Follow steps 2–4 on page 464 to preview your optimization settings. Make any necessary adjustments, then click Save. The Save Optimized As dialog opens. Change the name (if desired) but don't enter any spaces, keep the .jpg extension, choose a location, then click Save.

CHOOSING A PREVIEW OPTION FOR GIF AND JPEG OPTIMIZATION

Monitor Color	Current display gamma
Legacy Macintosh (No Color Management)	Mac 1.8 gamma
Internet Standard RGB (No Color Management)	Windows 2.2 gamma, the most common gamma
Use Document Profile	Adjusts the gamma to match the document color profile, if the file has one

CREATING AN OPTIMIZATION PRESET

To preserve the current optimization settings in the Save for Web dialog, choose Save Settings from the Optimize menu. ▼≡ In the Save Optimization Settings dialog, enter a name (keep the .irs extension), keep the location as the Optimized Settings folder, then click Save. Your saved set is now available on the Preset menu in the Save for Web dialog for any file.

Unless noted otherwise, the listings in this index pertain to Photoshop.

Photography credits

Shutterstock.com
Photographs on the following pages
are © ShutterStock.com: 1, 33, 40, 42,
45, 49, 57, 61, 66, 72, 76, 77, 80, 85, 88,
91, 92, 121, 123, 125, 126, 127, 128,
129, 131, 134, 136, 137, 139, 146, 151,
152, 153, 154, 155, 156, 158, 159, 160,
161, 162, 163, 166, 170, 171, 177, 182,
183, 184, 186, 192, 193, 201, 202, 204,
207, 210, 212, 213, 214, 216, 218, 219,
220, 221, 222, 228, 230, 240, 242, 243,
245, 250, 251, 252, 255, 256, 260, 262,
266, 272, 280, 283, 285, 286, 288, 294,
296, 297, 298, 299, 300, 302, 305, 306,
307, 308, 309, 311, 313, 314, 315, 318,
321, 322, 325, 327, 335, 336, 337, 338,
340, 341, 345, 349, 350, 351, 352, 353,
357, 362, 373, 375, 376, 380, 381, 383,
386, 388, 392, 393, 394, 405, 406, 407,
408, 409, 412, 413, 415, 416, 433, 447,
450, 454

Gettyimages.com
Pages 14, 291, 332, 341, 366

Other photographs
Page 25 Wayne Palmer © Palmer
Multimedia
Page 467 © Victor Gavenda

All other photographs © Elaine
Weinmann and Peter Lourekas